Henk Barendregt Tobias Nipkow (Eds.)

Types for Proofs and Programs

International Workshop TYPES '93
Nijmegen, The Netherlands, May 24-28, 1993
Selected Papers

Springer-Verlag
Berlin Heidelberg New York
London Paris Tokyo
Hong Kong Barcelona
Budapest

Series Editors

Gerhard Goos
Universität Karlsruhe
Postfach 69 80
Vincenz-Priessnitz-Straße 1
D-76131 Karlsruhe, Germany

Juris Hartmanis
Cornell University
Department of Computer Science
4130 Upson Hall
Ithaca, NY 14853, USA

Volume Editors

Henk Barendregt
Faculty of Mathematics and Computer Science, University of Nijmegen
Toernooiveld 1, 6525 ED Nijmegen, The Netherlands

Tobias Nipkow
Institut für Informatik, Technische Universität München
Arcisstraße 21, D-80290 München

CR Subject Classification (1991):F.4.1, F.3.1, D.3.3, I.2.3

ISBN 3-540-58085-9 Springer-Verlag Berlin Heidelberg New York
ISBN 0-387-58085-9 Springer-Verlag New York Berlin Heidelberg

CIP data applied for

Printed in Germany

Typesetting: Camera-ready by author
SPIN: 10131138 45/3140-543210 - Printed on acid-free paper

Lecture Notes in Comp[uter Science] 806

Edited by G. Goos and J. Hartmanis

Preface

This book is a selection of papers presented at the first annual workshop held under the auspicies of the ESPRIT Basic Research Action 6453, *Types for Proofs and Programs*. It took place in Nijmegen, The Netherlands, from the 24th to the 28th of May, 1993 and was organized by the first editor. Seventy people attended the Workshop.

We thank the European Community for the funding which made the workshop possible. We also thank Mariëlle van der Zandt who took care of the local arrangements, and Herman Geuvers who edited the preliminary proceedings as an electronic document. Finally, we thank the following researchers who acted as referees: P. Aczel, S. Berardi, T. Coquand, R. Crole, J. Despeyroux, G. Dowek, D.J.N. van Eijck, H. Geuvers, S. Hayashi, L. Helmink, M. Hofmann, F. Honsell, R. Jones, B. Jacobs, J. McKinna, M. Parigot, C. Paulin-Mohring, L. Paulson, F. Pfenning, R. Pollack, R. van der Sandt, A. Sellink, K. Slind, T. Streicher, A. Tasistro and F. Vaandrager.

This volume is a follow-up to the books *Logical Frameworks* and *Logical Environments*, which document the work of the ESPRIT Basic Research Action *Logical Frameworks*. Both volumes were edited by G. Huet and G. Plotkin and published by Cambridge University Press

March 1994

Henk Barendregt
Tobias Nipkow

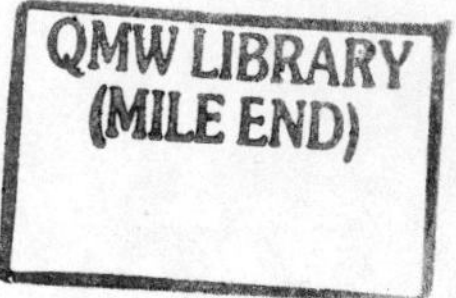

Preface

[illegible]

[illegible]

[illegible]

[illegible]

[illegible]

Contents

Introduction

Every new technology has three aspects: foundations, design, and applications. The foundations explain why certain engines are possible. The design is directed to the actual construction of these. The applications can be performed using the constructed engines.

For example, take the steam engine. The foundations are formed by the laws of physics, in particular that of Boyle. James Watt became known not because he invented steam engines (he did not), but because he improved their design: he added automated speed regulators and was able to convert a pumping motion into a turning one. In this case, the applications are well known (steam engine driven manufacturing, transportation by steam locomotives and sea steamers) and have caused the industrial revolution of the nineteenth century. From this example, it is clear that the three aspects are related. This is true in general.

In the Basic Research Action "Types for proofs and programs", we also have a new technology. There has not yet emerged a standard name for this. One can call it "Systems for theory development". By systems we mean modern workstations, with their rich toolkits of ergonomic interfaces. By theory development we mean the human-machine interaction leading towards exact representation of concepts and reasoning. The systems help in

1. designing mathematical axiomatisations;
2. performing computer-aided logical reasoning;
3. managing data-bases of mathematical facts.

Other possible names are "proof assistants" or "proof checkers". (The latter name was coined by N.G. de Bruijn in his project AUTOMATH that started the new technology.) But then one forgets to emphasize the important phase of setting up a theory using primitive notions, axioms and definitions.

A related technology is that of systems for symbolic computation (also called systems for "computer algebra", although many of these computations are analytical). This technology has now reached an industrial standard with systems like Axiom, Maple and Mathematica. This technology has as its foundation a large collection of algorithms. The applications are genuinely useful for mathematicians and scientists. In these systems the numbers $\sqrt{2}$ or π can be represented exactly and integrals can be computed symbolically.

The technology of systems for theory development is less advanced than that of symbolic computing. But the potential of theory development goes further. For example it is possible to represent exactly a reasoning like "$\forall\epsilon{>}0\exists\delta{>}0 \ldots$, hence ..." or a Hilbert space (both the abstract notion and concrete examples of such spaces) on such a system.

The foundations are concerned with formal systems that can be used to represent definitions, statements, and proofs. Type theory is particularly adequate for this goal. Properties of the various type systems are important for the intended use.

The design of systems for theory development based on type theory has two interesting aspects: the implementation of type theory and the human-machine interface. Several prototypes of systems for theory development based on type theory have been built or are under construction. In the mentioned BRA the following are used: Alf, Coq, Lego, and Isabelle.

The theory development systems have the following applications. The development of proofs and their verification; the extraction of executable algorithms from formal proofs; and possibly the use in mathematical education.

In this volume the papers by Altenkirch, van Benthem Jutting and McKinna and Pollack, Coquand, Geuvers, Hayashi, Hofmann, Pollack, Raffalli, and Wolfram are related to foundations. The papers by Magnusson and Nordström, Parent, Pollack, and Ranta are related to the design of the interface. Finally the papers of Helmink and Sellink and Vaandrager, Leclerc and Paulin-Mohring, Maharaj, Miculan, Parent, and Raffalli are directed towards applications ranging from program extraction to proof verification and theory development.

Proving Strong Normalization of CC by Modifying Realizability Semantics

Thorsten Altenkirch

Department of Computer Science, Chalmers University of Technology
412 64 Gothenburg, Sweden

1 Introduction

We will outline a strong normalization argument for the Calculus of Constructions (CC) which is obtained by modifying a realizability interpretation (the D-set or ω-set model [1]). By doing so we pursue two goals:

- We want to illustrate how *semantics can be used to prove properties of syntax.*
- We present a simple and extensible SN proof for CC. An example of such an extension is a system with inductive types and *large eliminations.*

This presentation corresponds to a part of the author's PhD thesis [Alt93a], a preliminary version has been presented in [Alt93b]. In my thesis I present a more general soundness result for a class of models for CC — CC-structures — from which the strong normalization argument can be derived as an instance. Here we shall restrict ourselves to the reasoning needed for the strong normalization proof.

The proof that every term typable in the calculus of constructions is strongly normalizing is known to be notoriously difficult. The original proof in Coquand's PhD thesis [Coq85] contained a bug which was fixed in [CG90] by using a Kripke-style interpretation of contexts. Although this solves the original problem the proof remains quite intricate due to the use of typed terms and contexts. Another construction is due to Geuvers and Nederhof (see [Geu93], p. 168), who define a forgetful, reduction-preserving map from CC to F^ω. Thereby, they reduce the problem to strong normalization for F^ω, which can be shown using the usual Girard-Tait method. The main problem with this construction is that it is not all clear, how this argument can be extended to a system with large eliminations (e.g. see [Wer92]), this is a system which allows the definition of a dependent type by primitive recursion. As an example consider the recursive definition of

[1] See [Ehr89, Str89, Str91].

a type $T : \mathrm{Nat} \to \mathrm{Set}$:

$$\begin{aligned} T(0) &= A \\ T(n+1) &= Tn \to Tn \end{aligned}$$

where $A : \mathrm{Set}$ is arbitrary. The problem is to find a non-dependent type which approximates T. The obvious choice seems to be a recursive type which solves the equation $A = A \to A$ but such a calculus would not be strongly normalizing.

Our construction avoids the use of Kripke-structures and can be understood as a generalization of the concept of saturated sets to dependent types. Moreover it is straightforward to extend it to inductive types with large eliminations and allows to interpret types like T. We shall not treat this here but refer to [Alt93a], pp. 76.

The paper is organized as follows: We start by introducing a judgement presentation of CC and define some basic notations. The presentation of the model construction is divided in two parts: First we present Λ-sets and note that these do not give rise to a sound interpretation. Then we solve this problem by introducing saturated Λ-sets and show soundness. As a corollary we obtain strong normalization for the stripped terms. We then show how strong normalization for typed terms and decidability of equality can be derived by simple syntactic reasoning.

2 The judgement presentation of CC

CC is often presented in the equality-as-conversion style [CH88, Bar92], i.e. the equality is just the untyped β-conversion between preterms. When we are interested in a semantical analysis of the system it seems easier to use the equality-as-judgement presentation, as it is usual for Martin-Löf's Type Theory. The reason is that it is not clear how untyped conversion can be interpreted semantically. Not surprisingly this presentation is used in [Str91] who studies the categorical semantics of CC.

We will also follow [Str91] in that we use a very explicit notation: we differentiate between operations on Set (often called Prop) and types; we annotate applications and λ-abstractions with types and in one place we go even further and also annotate the codomain of a λ-abstraction. Essentially our terms are a linear notation for derivations where the applications of the conversion rule are omitted. The more implicit notation can be justified (e.g. see [Str91, Alt93a]), but semantically it seems to be more appropriate to consider the explicit presentation as the fundamental one.

We introduce precontexts Cn, pretypes Ty, preterms Tm and constructions Co [2] by the following grammar - the set of natural numbers ($i, j, k \in \omega$) is used for variables, since we use de-Bruijn-indices.

$$\mathrm{Cn}(\Gamma) \ ::= \ \bullet \mid \Gamma.\sigma$$

[2]In the following definition we introduce the sets together with a naming convention.

$$\begin{array}{rcl}\mathrm{Ty}(\sigma,\tau) & ::= & \Pi\sigma.\tau \mid \mathrm{Set} \mid \mathrm{El}(M) \\ \mathrm{Tm}(M,N) & ::= & i \mid \lambda\sigma(M)^{\tau} \mid \mathrm{app}^{\sigma.\tau}(M,N) \mid \forall\sigma.M \\ \mathrm{Co}(C,D) & ::= & \mathrm{Ty} \mid \mathrm{Tm}\end{array}$$

In our use of de-Bruijn-indices [3] we follow [Bar84], pp.577 with the minor difference that we start counting with 0. We denote substitution for the free variable with index i by $M[N]^i, \sigma[N]^i$ and all the variables with a greater index are decreased by one. We also require the operation of weakening M^{+i}, σ^{+i} which increases the indices of all free variables greater or equal i by one. If $i = 0$ we omit it. The precise definition of these operations can be found in [Alt93a],p. 24.

Given a sequence of terms $\vec{N} = N_{n-1}, N_{n-2}\ldots, N_0$ [4] we can define a notion of parallel substitution as a derived notion:

$$M[\vec{N}] = M[N_0^{\overbrace{+\cdots+}^{n-1 \text{ times}}}][N_1^{\overbrace{+\cdots+}^{n-2 \text{ times}}}]\ldots[N_{n-1}]$$

and analogously for $\sigma[\vec{N}]$. If the indices of all free variables in M are less than n then

$$M[n-1, n-2, \ldots, 0] = M.$$

We define the following judgements: $\vdash \Gamma$ (context validity), $\Gamma \vdash \sigma$ (type validity), $\Gamma \vdash M : \sigma$ (typing), $\Gamma \vdash \sigma \simeq \tau$ (type equality) and $\Gamma \vdash M \simeq N : \sigma$ (equality). The derivable judgements are given as the least relations closed under the following rules — we have omitted the obvious congruence rules to save space.

$$\vdash \bullet \qquad \text{(Empty)}$$

$$\frac{\vdash \Gamma \qquad \Gamma \vdash \sigma}{\vdash \Gamma.\sigma} \qquad \text{(Compr)}$$

$$\frac{\Gamma.\sigma \vdash \tau}{\Gamma \vdash \Pi\sigma.\tau} \qquad \text{(Pi)}$$

$$\frac{\vdash \Gamma}{\Gamma \vdash \mathrm{Set}} \qquad \text{(Set)}$$

$$\frac{\Gamma \vdash A : \mathrm{Set}}{\Gamma \vdash \mathrm{El}(A)} \qquad \text{(El)}$$

$$\frac{\Gamma.\sigma \vdash A : \mathrm{Set}}{\Gamma \vdash \mathrm{El}(\forall\sigma.A) \simeq \Pi\sigma.\mathrm{El}(A)} \qquad \text{(All-Elim)}$$

---

[3] We believe that de-Bruijn-indices are the best way to make the notion of bound variables precise. We can often omit side conditions and reason about λ-terms in a purely algebraic fashion. Moreover, this notation reflects our semantic intuition that variables denote projections out of a context. However, when presenting syntax we may used named variables, meaning the obvious translation into a de-Bruijn-term.

[4] We write these sequences backwards since contexts are also written backwards.

$$\frac{\Gamma \vdash M : \sigma \qquad \Gamma \vdash \sigma \simeq \tau}{\Gamma \vdash M : \tau} \quad \text{(CONV)}$$

$$\frac{\Gamma \vdash \sigma}{\Gamma.\sigma \vdash 0 : \sigma^+} \quad \text{(VAR-0)}$$

$$\frac{\Gamma \vdash i : \sigma \qquad \Gamma \vdash \tau}{\Gamma.\tau \vdash i+1 : \sigma^+} \quad \text{(VAR-S)}$$

$$\frac{\Gamma.\sigma \vdash M : \tau}{\Gamma \vdash \lambda\sigma(M)^\tau : \Pi\sigma.\tau} \quad \text{(LAM)}$$

$$\frac{\Gamma \vdash M : \Pi\sigma.\tau \qquad \Gamma \vdash N : \sigma}{\Gamma \vdash \mathrm{app}^{\sigma.\tau}(M, N) : \tau[N]} \quad \text{(APP)}$$

$$\frac{\Gamma.\sigma \vdash A : \mathrm{Set}}{\Gamma \vdash \forall\sigma.A : \mathrm{Set}} \quad \text{(ALL)}$$

$$\frac{\Gamma.\sigma \vdash M : \tau \qquad \Gamma \vdash N : \sigma}{\Gamma \vdash \mathrm{app}^{\sigma.\tau}(\lambda\sigma(M)^\tau, N) \simeq M[N] : \tau[N]} \quad \text{(BETA-EQ)}$$

We can easily establish a number of rather trivial properties of this presentation such that all judgements are consistent with weakening and substitution - see [Alt93a] for details.

3 Saturated Λ-sets and strong normalization

3.1 Λ-sets

In the following section we define an interpretation of CC which resembles the ω-set semantics. The main difference is that we use λ-terms instead of ω (i.e. indices of recursive functions). Another novelty is that we present this interpretation in elementary terms avoiding the use of categories - although the construction is clearly motivated by the categorical semantics of CC.

Definition 1 *Assuming some encoding of pairing (x, y) and projections π_1, π_2 we have the usual set-theoretic counterparts of the basic type-theoretic operations (assume A is a set and $\{B_a\}_{a\in A}$ a family of sets indexed by A):*

$$\begin{aligned} \Sigma a \in A.B_a &= \{(a, b) \mid a \in A, b \in B_a\} \\ \Pi a \in A.B_a &= \{f \subseteq \Sigma a \in A.B_a \mid \forall_{a\in A}\exists!_{b\in B_a}(a, b) \in f\} \end{aligned}$$

We consider application $f(x)$ as a partial operation which is defined if there is an $(x, y) \in f$ and then $f(x) = y$. We denote set-theoretic λ-abstraction by $\mapsto$, i.e.

$$x \in A \mapsto E[x] \equiv \{(x, E[x]) \mid x \in A\}.$$

Given a set X we denote the set of finite sequences over X by X^*. The empty sequence is denoted by ϵ and given a sequence $\vec{x} \in X^*$ and $y \in X$ we denote the extended sequence by $\vec{x}y \in X^*$.

Definition 2 *We use Λ to denote the set of untyped λ terms enriched by a special binder $\forall M$. To every preterm M we assign a stripping $|M| \in \Lambda$ by deleting all types.*

$\rhd \subseteq \Lambda \times \Lambda$ is the usual one-step β-reduction extended by a ξ-rule for $\forall$. $\mathrm{SN} \subseteq \Lambda$ is the set of strongly normalizing (w.r.t. $\rhd$) λ-terms.

We are ready to define Λ-sets which are used to interpret types and Λ^*-sets for interpreting contexts.

Definition 3 (Λ-sets)
A Λ-set X is a pair $(\overline{X}, \Vdash_X)$ with X is a set and $\Vdash_X \subseteq \Lambda \times \overline{X}$ s.t.

$$\forall_{x \in \overline{X}} \exists_{i \in \Lambda} i \Vdash_X x.$$

We denote the class of Λ-sets by $\mathfrak{L}$ and for any Λ-set $X \in \mathfrak{L}$ we use $\overline{X}$ and $\Vdash_X$ to denote its components.

$\mathfrak{L}^*$ is defined analogously by replacing Λ by Λ^*, i.e. sequences of λ-terms.

We introduce operations on Λ- and Λ^*-sets corresponding to the context and type forming operations. Additionally we define sections which given $\Gamma \vdash \sigma$ correspond to $\{M \mid \Gamma \vdash M : \sigma\}$ in the syntax.

Definition 4 *Assume $G \in \mathfrak{L}^*$, $\{Y_\gamma \in \mathfrak{L}\}_{\gamma \in \overline{G}}$, $X \in \mathfrak{L}$, $\{Z_x \in \mathfrak{L}\}_{x \in \overline{X}}$ and let:*

$$\begin{aligned}
\mathbf{1}_\Lambda &= (\{\epsilon\}, \Lambda \times \{\epsilon\}) \\
&\in \mathfrak{L}^* \\
\Sigma_\Lambda(G, \{Y_\gamma\}_{\gamma \in \overline{G}}) &= (\Sigma_{\gamma \in \overline{G}} \overline{Y_\gamma}, \{(\vec{M}N, (\gamma, y)) \mid \vec{M} \Vdash_G \gamma \wedge N \Vdash_{Y_\gamma} y\}) \\
&\in \mathfrak{L}^* \\
\mathrm{Sect}(G, \{Y_\gamma\}_{\gamma \in \overline{G}}) &= \{f \in \Pi_{\gamma \in \overline{G}} \overline{Y_\gamma} \mid \exists_{M \in \Lambda} M \Vdash_{\mathrm{Sect}(G,\{Y_\gamma\}_\gamma)} f\} \\
&\in \mathfrak{L} \\
\textit{where } \Vdash_{\mathrm{Sect}(G,\{Y_\gamma\}_\gamma)} &= \{(M, f) \mid \forall_{\gamma \in \overline{G}} \forall_{\vec{N} \in \Lambda^*} \vec{N} \Vdash_G \gamma \to M[\vec{N}] \Vdash_{Y_\gamma} f(\gamma)\} \\
\Pi_\Lambda(X, \{Z_x\}_{x \in \overline{X}}) &= (\{f \in \Pi_{x \in \overline{X}} \overline{Z_x} \mid \exists_{M \in \Lambda} M \Vdash_{\Pi_\Lambda(X,\{Z_x\}_x)} f\}, \Vdash_{\Pi_\Lambda(X,\{Z_x\}_x)}) \\
&\in \mathfrak{L} \\
\textit{where } \Vdash_{\Pi_\Lambda(X,\{Z_x\}_x)} &= \{(M, f) \mid \forall_{x \in \overline{X}} \forall_{N \in \Lambda} M \Vdash_X x \to MN \Vdash_{Z_x} f(x)\}
\end{aligned}$$

Note that the only difference between Sect and Π_Λ is that the first one uses substitution and the second application. Indeed they are identified in the ω-set semantics.

We have not yet given an interpretation for Set and El, which is the main problem in finding an interpretation for CC. As in the usual ω-set semantics we will use the set of partial equivalence relations which is *equivalent* [5] to the subclass of modest Λ sets.

[5] The properties we show can be used to establish an equivalence of categories. We do not make this precise because we do not introduce PERs and Λ-sets as categories.

Definition 5 *We call $X \in \mathfrak{L}$ modest, iff*

$$\forall_{x,y \in \overline{X}} \forall_{M \in \Lambda} M \Vdash_X x \land M \Vdash_X y \to x = y,$$

We write $\mathfrak{M}$ for the subclass of modest Λ-sets.

A straightforward but important property of modest Λ-sets is that they are closed under Π_Λ:

Lemma 1 *Assume $X \in \mathfrak{L}$ and $\{Y_x \in \mathfrak{M}\}_x \in \overline{X}$ then*

$$\Pi_\Lambda(X, \{Y_x\}_x) \in \mathfrak{M}$$

Proof: Simple. ∎

We define the set of PERs together with translation operators to and from modest Λ-sets:

Definition 6

$$\mathrm{PER}(\Lambda) = \{R \subset \Lambda \times \Lambda \mid R \textit{ is symmetric and transitive}\}$$

For any $R \in \mathrm{PER}(\Lambda)$ we define the set of equivalence classes $\Lambda/R \in \mathcal{P}(\Lambda)$ in the usual way.

Assume $R \in \mathrm{PER}(\Lambda)$ and $X \in \mathfrak{M}$:

$$\begin{aligned} \mathrm{EL}(R) &= (\Lambda/R, \in) \\ &\in \mathfrak{M} \\ \mathrm{EL}^{-1}(X) &= \{(M, N) \mid \exists_{x \in \overline{X}} M \Vdash_X x \ \land N \Vdash_X x\} \\ &\in \mathrm{PER}(\Lambda) \end{aligned}$$

It is easy to see that we have $\mathrm{EL}^{-1}(\mathrm{EL}(R)) = R$ but the converse fails. Indeed the operation

$$\Theta(X) = \mathrm{EL}(\mathrm{EL}^{-1}(X))$$

assigns to any modest Λ-set X a canonical representation where $x \in \overline{X}$ is replaced by the set of its realizers. This is reflected by the fact that we have:

$$\begin{aligned} \vartheta_X(x \in \overline{X}) &= \{M \mid M \Vdash_X x\} \\ &\in \Theta(X) \end{aligned}$$

with the following properties:

Lemma 2 *Let X be a modest Λ-set*

1. *ϑ_X is a bijection.*
2. *$M \Vdash_X x$ iff $M \Vdash_{\Theta(X)} \vartheta_X(x)$*

Proof: The preservation of realizers is quite easy to check and implies the first property since X is modest. ∎

We will use Θ to *normalize* modest sets and hence reflect type equality by equality of sets. To simplify notation we introduce $\tilde{\Theta}$ and $\tilde{\vartheta}$ as an extension of Θ and ϑ which are just identities on non-modest sets.

The following defines a partial interpretation of the syntax in terms of Λ-sets. We use $\cong$ for Kleene-equality and $\underset{\sim}{\in}$ to denote a partial version of $\in$: if both sides are defined then the relation $\in$ holds.

Definition 7
We define partial interpretation functions $[\![\vdash \Gamma]\!] \underset{\sim}{\in} \mathfrak{L}^*$, $\{[\![\Gamma \vdash \sigma]\!]\gamma \underset{\sim}{\in} \mathfrak{L}\}_{\gamma \underset{\sim}{\in} \overline{[\![\vdash\Gamma]\!]}}$ *and* $\{[\![\Gamma \vdash M]\!]\gamma\}_{\gamma \underset{\sim}{\in} \overline{[\![\vdash\Gamma]\!]}}$ *by induction over the structure of the syntax:*

$$\begin{array}{rcl}
[\![\vdash \bullet]\!] & \cong & \mathbf{1}^\Lambda \\
[\![\vdash \Gamma.\sigma]\!] & \cong & \Sigma^\Lambda([\![\vdash \Gamma]\!], [\![\Gamma \vdash \sigma]\!]) \\
[\![\Gamma \vdash \Pi\sigma.\tau]\!]\gamma & \cong & \tilde{\Theta}(\Pi^\Lambda([\![\Gamma \vdash \sigma]\!]\gamma, \{[\![\Gamma.\sigma \vdash \tau]\!](\gamma, x)\}_x)) \\
[\![\Gamma \vdash \mathrm{Set}]\!]\gamma & \cong & (\mathrm{PER}(\Lambda), \Lambda \times \mathrm{PER}(\Lambda)) \\
[\![\Gamma \vdash \mathrm{El}(A)]\!]\gamma & \cong & \mathrm{EL}([\![\Gamma \vdash A]\!]\gamma) \\
[\![\Gamma \vdash i]\!]\gamma & \cong & \pi_2(\pi_1^i(\gamma)) \\
[\![\Gamma \vdash \lambda\sigma(M)^\tau]\!]\gamma & \cong & \tilde{\vartheta}_{[\![\Gamma\vdash\Pi\sigma.\tau]\!]\gamma}(x \in \overline{[\![\Gamma \vdash \sigma]\!]} \mapsto [\![\Gamma.\sigma \vdash M]\!](\gamma, x)) \\
[\![\Gamma \vdash \mathrm{app}^{\sigma.\tau}(M, N)]\!]\gamma & \cong & \tilde{\vartheta}^{-1}_{[\![\Gamma\vdash\Pi\sigma.\tau]\!]\gamma}([\![\Gamma \vdash M]\!]_\gamma)([\![\Gamma \vdash N]\!]\gamma) \\
[\![\Gamma \vdash \forall^\sigma.A]\!]\gamma & \cong & \mathrm{EL}^{-1}(\Pi^\Lambda([\![\Gamma \vdash \sigma]\!]\gamma, \{\mathrm{EL}([\![\Gamma.\sigma \vdash A]\!](\gamma, x))\}_x))
\end{array}$$

This interpretation is *not sound*, where by soundness we mean the following properties:

1. $\dfrac{\vdash \Gamma}{[\![\vdash \Gamma]\!] \text{ is defined.}}$

2. $\dfrac{\Gamma \vdash \sigma \qquad \gamma \in \overline{[\![\vdash \Gamma]\!]}}{[\![\Gamma \vdash \sigma]\!]\gamma \text{ is defined.}}$

3. $\dfrac{\Gamma \vdash M : \sigma}{[\![\Gamma \vdash M]\!] \in \mathrm{Sect}([\![\vdash \Gamma]\!], [\![\Gamma \vdash \sigma]\!])}$

4. $\dfrac{\Gamma \vdash \sigma \simeq \tau \qquad \gamma \in \overline{[\![\vdash \Gamma]\!]}}{[\![\Gamma \vdash \sigma]\!]\gamma = [\![\Gamma \vdash \tau]\!]\gamma}$

5. $\dfrac{\Gamma \vdash M \simeq N : \sigma \qquad \gamma \in \overline{[\![\vdash \Gamma]\!]}}{[\![\Gamma \vdash M]\!]\gamma = [\![\Gamma \vdash N]\!]\gamma}$

We will see in the next section how we can obtain soundness by a small modification. To motivate this it is instructive to see where soundness for the interpretation above fails. Indeed, the above interpretation is not closed under (LAM).

For simplicity assume we have $\sigma \vdash M : \tau$ from which we can derive $\bullet \vdash \lambda\sigma(M)^{\tau} : \Pi\sigma.\tau$. Now as a hypothesis we assume

$$[\![\sigma \vdash M]\!] \in \mathrm{Sect}([\![\vdash \sigma]\!], [\![\sigma \vdash \tau]\!]).$$

From the definition of Sect it follows that there is an $M' \in \Lambda$ s.t. for all $N \Vdash_{[\vdash\sigma]} x$ we have that $M'[N] \Vdash_{[\sigma\vdash\tau]x} [\![\sigma \vdash M]\!]x$.

Can we conclude that

$$[\![\bullet \vdash \lambda\sigma(M)^{\tau} : \Pi\sigma.\tau]\!] \in \mathrm{Sect}([\![\vdash \bullet]\!], [\![\Pi\sigma.\tau]\!])?$$

By expanding the definition of the interpretation this goal can be reduced to showing:

$$[\![\sigma \vdash M]\!] \in \Pi^{\Lambda}([\![\vdash \sigma]\!], [\![\sigma \vdash \tau]\!])$$

I.e. we have to find a realizer M'' s.t. for any $N \Vdash_{[\vdash\sigma]} x$ we have that

$$M''N \Vdash_{[\sigma\vdash\tau]} [\![\sigma \vdash M]\!](x).$$

An obvious guess would be $M'' = \lambda M'$. However, since we have not identified β-equal terms we cannot reason that $M''N = M'[N]$ and indeed there is no reason to assume that an appropriate realizer exists at all.

This failure also suggests an obvious way to repair the problem: identify β-equal terms, i.e. use $\Lambda/=_{\beta}$ instead of Λ. Actually, it is not even necessary to identify all β-equal terms, it is sufficient to use weak β-equality, the equality generated by combinatory logic. This construction brings us very close to ω-sets or its generalization to arbitrary *Partially Combinatory Algebras* D-sets. [6]

However, we would hope to obtain a system which only contains strongly normalizing realizers and even weak β-equality is not closed under strong normalization. Hyland and Ong [HO93] propose to overcome this problem by using a generalization of PCAs (conditional PCAs) which can be used to define a partial congruence which identifies only strongly normalizing terms. Here we will go another way and generalize the notion of *saturated sets*, which are used in the strong normalization arguments of simply typed λ-calculus or System F.

3.2 Saturated Λ-sets

In this section we identify the subclass of saturated Λ-sets which has the following properties:

- All realizers are strongly normalizing.
- Π-types are closed under saturated Λ-sets.

[6] The D-set semantics differs only in two ways from the one proposed above: one uses a partial combinatory algebra which is a slight generalization of a combinatory algebra and the substitution machinery which we just imported from the untyped λ calculus is encoded by combinators.

- The set of realizers for a certain element are closed under certain β-expansions, s.t. (LAM) is sound.

By modifying the interpretation of Set we can obtain an interpretation which interprets every type by a saturated Λ-set. By establishing also that every interpretation of a term is realized by its stripping we obtain strong normalization as a simple corollary.

We introduce the notion of weak head-reduction, which means that only a head-redex not inside a λ-abstraction is reduced. This can be defined inductively by the following rules:

$$(\lambda M)N \rhd_{\mathsf{whd}} M[N] \qquad \frac{M \rhd_{\mathsf{whd}} M'}{MN \rhd_{\mathsf{whd}} M'N}$$

Certainly we have that $\rhd_{\mathsf{whd}} \subseteq \rhd$.

Void $\subseteq$ SN is the set of strongly normalizing weak-head normal forms which are not λ-abstractions. This set can be inductively defined as: [7]

1. $i \in \mathrm{Void}$.
2. $\dfrac{M \in \mathrm{Void} \qquad N \in \mathrm{SN}}{MN \in \mathrm{Void}}$
3. $\dfrac{M \in \mathrm{SN}}{\forall M \in \mathrm{Void}}$

We need the following properties of SN:

Lemma 3

1. $\dfrac{M, N, M[N] \in \mathrm{SN}}{(\lambda M)N \in \mathrm{SN}}$

2. $\dfrac{M' \rhd_{\mathsf{whd}} M \qquad MN \in \mathrm{SN}}{M'N \in \mathrm{SN}}$

Proof: See [Alt93a], pp.69. ∎

These properties can be shown by noetherian induction, i.e. induction over the longest reduction of a strongly normalizing term. For the second proposition it is useful to establish as a lemma that weak-head reductions can be always postponed.

It is interesting to note that these are precisely the same properties which are needed to show strong normalization in the simply typed case.

---

[7] Yet another alternative is to say that void terms have the form $iM_1 \ldots M_n$ with $M_i \in \mathrm{SN}$. However, our presentation has the advantage that it is easier to generalize to inductive types (see [Alt93a], p. 87).

Definition 8 *We call a Λ-set X saturated — $X \in \mathfrak{S}$ — iff the following conditions hold:*

SAT1 *Every realizer is strongly normalizing.*

$$\forall_{M \Vdash_X x} M \in \mathrm{SN}$$

SAT2 *There is a $\bot_X \in \overline{X}$ which is realized by every void term.*

SAT3 *The set of realizers for a certain element x is closed under weak head expansion inside* SN*:*

$$\forall_{M \Vdash_X x} \forall_{M' \in \mathrm{SN}} (M' \rhd_{\mathrm{whd}} M) \rightarrow (M' \Vdash_X x)$$

This can be extended to $\mathfrak{L}^*$-sets by the following inductive definition:

1. $\mathbf{1}_\Lambda \in \mathfrak{S}^*$.
2. $$\frac{G \in \mathfrak{S}^* \qquad \{X_\gamma \in \mathfrak{S}\}_{\gamma \in \overline{G}}}{\Sigma_\Lambda(G, \{X_\gamma\}_{\gamma \in \overline{G}}) \in \mathfrak{S}^*}$$

Note that for any saturated Λ-set $(\overline{X}, \Vdash_X)$ the set of realizers $\{M \mid \exists_{x \in \overline{X}} M \Vdash_X x\}$ is saturated in the conventional sense [8]

$\mathbf{1}_\Lambda$ and Σ_Λ restrict to operations on saturated Λ-sets by definition but it remains to show that this is also true for Π_Λ:

Lemma 4 *Assume $X \in \mathfrak{S}$, $\{Y_x \in \mathfrak{S}\}_{x \in \overline{X}}$ then $\Pi_\Lambda(X, \{Y_x\}_x) \in \mathfrak{S}$.*

Proof:

SAT1 Assume $M \Vdash_{\Pi_\Lambda(X,\{Y_x\}_x)} f$, certainly $0 \Vdash_X \bot_X$ (**SAT2** for X). Now we know that $M0 \Vdash_{Y_{\bot_X}} f(\bot_X)$, therefore $M0 \in \mathrm{SN}$ (**SAT1** for Y_x), which implies $M \in \mathrm{SN}$.

SAT2 Assume $M \in$ Void, now for every $N \Vdash_X x$ we have that $MN \in$ Void (**SAT1** for X and definition of Void) and therefore $MN \Vdash_{Y_x} \bot_{Y_x}$. This implies $M \Vdash_{\Pi_\Lambda(X,\{Y_x\}_x)} x \mapsto \bot_{Y_x}$, so we just set $\bot_{\Pi_\Lambda(X,\{Y_x\}_x)} = x \mapsto \bot_{Y_x}$.

SAT3 Assume $M \Vdash_{\Pi_\Lambda(X,\{Y_x\}_x)} f$, $M' \in \mathrm{SN}$ and $M' \rhd_{\mathrm{whd}} M$. For any $N \Vdash_X x$ we have that $MN \Vdash_{Y_x} f(x)$. By (App-L) $M'N \rhd_{\mathrm{whd}} MN$ and by lemma 3 (2.) $M'N \in \mathrm{SN}$. Using **SAT3** for Y_x we have that $M'N \Vdash_{Y_x} f(x)$. Therefore we have established that $M' \Vdash_{\Pi_\Lambda(X,\{Y_x\}_x)} f$.

∎

The essential idea of saturated Λ-sets is that we can prove closure under the λ-introduction rule.

---

[8] E.g. see [Bar92].

Lemma 5 *Let* $G \in \mathfrak{S}^*, \{X_\gamma \in \mathfrak{S}\}_{\gamma \in \overline{G}}, \{Z_\delta \in \mathfrak{S}\}_{\delta \in \overline{\Sigma_\Lambda(G,\{X_\gamma\}_\gamma)}}$ *then*

$$\frac{M \Vdash_{\mathrm{Sect}(\Sigma_\Lambda(G,\{X_\gamma\}_\gamma),\{Z_\delta\}_\delta)} f}{\lambda M \Vdash_{\mathrm{Sect}(G,\{\Pi_\Lambda(X_\gamma,\{Z_{(\gamma,x)}\}_x)\}_\gamma)} \gamma \in G \mapsto (x \in \overline{X_\gamma} \mapsto f(\gamma, x))}$$

Proof: Assume any $\gamma \in \overline{G}, \vec{N} \Vdash_G \gamma, x \in X_\gamma, N \Vdash_{X_\gamma} x$. We would like to show that

$$(\lambda M)[\vec{N}]N \Vdash_{Z_{(\gamma,x)}} f(\gamma, x).$$

Now $(\lambda M)[\vec{N}]N = (\lambda M[\vec{N}0])N \rhd_{\mathrm{whd}} M[\vec{N}N]$ and

$$M[\vec{N}N] \Vdash_{Z_{(\gamma,x)}} f(\gamma, x)$$

follows from the premise.

To apply (SAT3) we have to verify that $N, M[\vec{N}N], M[\vec{N}0] \in \mathrm{SN}$. The first two are immediate by (SAT1) and for the last one we need that $0 \Vdash_{X_\gamma} \perp$ (SAT2) and by premise

$$M[\vec{N}0] \Vdash_{Z_{\gamma,\perp}} f(\gamma, \perp)$$

and therefore $M[\vec{N}0] \in \mathrm{SN}$ (SAT1). ∎

We will now modify the interpretation simply by changing the interpretation of Set.

Definition 9 *We define a new interpretation* $[\![\vdash \Gamma]\!]'$, $\{[\![\Gamma \vdash \sigma]\!]'\gamma\}_{\gamma \underset{\sim}{\in} \overline{[\![\vdash\Gamma]\!]'}}$, $\{[\![\Gamma \vdash M]\!]'\gamma\}_{\gamma \underset{\sim}{\in} \overline{[\![\vdash\Gamma]\!]'}}$ *by the same rules as before but modifying* $[\![\Gamma \vdash \mathrm{Set}]\!]$:

$$[\![\Gamma \vdash \mathrm{Set}]\!]\gamma \;\; \cong \;\; (\mathrm{PER}'(\Lambda), \mathrm{SN} \times \mathrm{PER}'(\Lambda))$$

where

$$\mathrm{PER}'(\Lambda) = \{R \in \mathrm{PER}(\Lambda) \mid \mathrm{EL}(R) \in \mathfrak{S}\}.$$

Before we can prove the general soundness theorem, we need a technical result, i.e. that weakening and substitution are interpreted properly.

Lemma 6 (Soundness of weakening and substitution) *For any* $\gamma \in \overline{[\![\vdash \Gamma]\!]'}$ *and* $x \in \overline{[\![\Gamma \vdash \tau]\!]'\gamma}$ *we have*

$$\begin{aligned}
[\![\Gamma \vdash \sigma]\!]'\gamma &\cong [\![\Gamma.\tau \vdash \sigma^+]\!]'\gamma x \\
[\![\Gamma \vdash M]\!]'\gamma &\cong [\![\Gamma.\tau \vdash M^+]\!]'\gamma x \\
[\![\Gamma.\tau \vdash \sigma]\!]'\gamma([\![\Gamma \vdash N]\!]'\gamma) &\cong [\![\Gamma \vdash \sigma[N]]\!]'\gamma \\
[\![\Gamma.\tau \vdash M]\!]'\gamma([\![\Gamma \vdash N]\!]'\gamma) &\cong [\![\Gamma \vdash M[N]]\!]'\gamma
\end{aligned}$$

Proof: See [Alt93a], section 3.2. ∎

It should be noted that only a generalization of the proposition to arbitrary weakenings and substitutions can be shown by induction over the syntax.

Theorem 1 (Soundness)

1. $$\frac{\vdash \Gamma}{[\![\vdash \Gamma]\!]' \in \mathfrak{S}^*}$$

2. $$\frac{\Gamma \vdash \sigma \qquad \gamma \in \overline{[\![\vdash \Gamma]\!]'}}{[\![\Gamma \vdash \sigma]\!]'\gamma \in \mathfrak{S}}$$

3. (a) $$\frac{\Gamma \vdash M : \sigma}{[\![\Gamma \vdash M]\!]' \in \mathrm{Sect}([\![\vdash \Gamma]\!]', [\![\Gamma \vdash \sigma]\!]')}$$

   (b) $$\frac{\Gamma \vdash M : \sigma}{|M| \Vdash_{\mathrm{Sect}([\![\Gamma]\!]', [\![\Gamma \vdash \sigma]\!]')} [\![\Gamma \vdash M]\!]'}$$

4. $$\frac{\Gamma \vdash \sigma \simeq \tau \qquad \gamma \in \overline{[\![\vdash \Gamma]\!]'}}{[\![\Gamma \vdash \sigma]\!]'\gamma = [\![\Gamma \vdash \tau]\!]'\gamma}$$

5. $$\frac{\Gamma \vdash M \simeq N : \sigma \qquad \gamma \in \overline{[\![\vdash \Gamma]\!]'}}{[\![\Gamma \vdash M]\!]'\gamma = [\![\Gamma \vdash N]\!]'\gamma}$$

Proof: (Sketch) The result can be obtained by a straightforward induction over the structure of derivations. All the congruence rules and (CONV) follow directly from the fact that we interpret syntactic equality by semantic (i.e. set-theoretic) equality.

1. Immediate from the definition of $\mathfrak{S}^*$.

2. For (PI) we need Lemma 4 and observe that Θ preserves saturatedness. (EL) follows from the definition of $\mathrm{PER}'(\Lambda)$ and (SET) is straightforward as well.

3. (VAR-0),(VAR-S) require soundness of weakening, (APP) is straightforward but uses soundness of substitution. (LAM) follows directly from Lemma 5.

4. The only interesting case is (ALL-ELIM):

$$\begin{aligned} & [\![\Gamma \vdash \mathrm{El}(\forall\sigma.A)]\!]'\gamma \\ = \quad & \mathrm{EL}(\mathrm{EL}^{-1}(\Pi_\Lambda([\![\Gamma \vdash \sigma]\!]'\gamma, \{\mathrm{EL}([\![\Gamma.\sigma \vdash A]\!]'(\gamma, x))\}_x))) \\ = \quad & \Theta(\Pi_\Lambda([\![\Gamma \vdash \sigma]\!]'\gamma, \{\mathrm{EL}([\![\Gamma.\sigma \vdash A]\!]'(\gamma, x))\}_x)) \\ = \quad & [\![\Pi_\Lambda \sigma.\mathrm{El}(A)]\!]'\gamma \end{aligned}$$

   Note that we implicitly use Lemma 1

5. (BETA-EQ) requires soundness of substitution.

∎

The theorem has strong normalization as a corollary:

Corollary 1 (Strong normalization) *If* $\Gamma \vdash M : \sigma$ *then* $|M| \in \mathrm{SN}$.

Proof: Let n by the length of Γ.Using (SAT2) we know that

$$n-1, n-2, \ldots 0 \Vdash_{[\Gamma]'} \bot, \bot \ldots \bot = \vec{\bot}$$

by Theorem 1, (3b) we know

$$|M| = |M|[n-1, n-2, \ldots 0] \Vdash_{[\Gamma \vdash \sigma]' \vec{\bot}} [\![\Gamma \vdash M]\!]' \vec{\bot}$$

and therefore $M \in \mathrm{SN}$ by SAT1. ∎

4 Decidability

We have only established strong normalization for the stripped terms. It is not immediate that this implies strong normalization for typed terms and decidability of equality. The main problem with typed terms is that we have to allow reductions inside the type annotations to reflect the congruence rules.

It would be possible to redo the model construction using typed terms instead. However, it seems that the presentation of the interpretation would get quite overloaded with a lot of trivial syntactic reasoning. Here we go another way and show how this result can be derived from strong normalization for the stripped terms by a simple syntactic argument.

In the following text we assume a notion of reduction on types and terms $\rhd_l \subseteq \mathrm{Cn} \times \mathrm{Cn}$ which is just the natural extension of untyped β reduction to constructions. We also use SN_l to denote the set of strongly normalizing constructions wrt. $\rhd_l$. The l stands for *loose* in contrast it to tight reduction $\rhd_t$ where only redexes with agreeing types can be reduced (see below).

We define a type-preserving map blow which blows up terms such that every reduction in a typed term can be mirrored by a reduction in a stripped term:

Definition 10 *Let*

$$\begin{aligned} \bot &= \forall x : \mathrm{Set}.x \\ M(\sigma, N) &= \mathrm{app}^{x:\mathrm{Set}.\sigma^+}(\lambda x : \mathrm{Set}(M^{+x})^{\sigma^{+x}}, N) \end{aligned}$$

We now define $\mathrm{blow} \in \mathrm{Cn} \to \mathrm{Cn}$*:*

$$\begin{aligned} \mathrm{blow}(\Pi\sigma.\tau) &= \mathrm{blow}(\sigma)(\mathrm{Set}, \mathrm{blow}(\tau)) \\ \mathrm{blow}(\mathrm{Set}) &= \bot \\ \mathrm{blow}(\mathrm{El}(A)) &= \mathrm{blow}(A) \\ \mathrm{blow}(i) &= i \\ \mathrm{blow}(\mathrm{app}^{\sigma.\tau}(M,N)) &= \mathrm{app}^{\sigma.\tau}(\mathrm{blow}(M), \mathrm{blow}(N))(\tau[N], \mathrm{blow}(\sigma))(\tau[N], \mathrm{blow}(\tau)) \\ \mathrm{blow}(\lambda\sigma(M)^\tau) &= \lambda\sigma(\mathrm{blow}(M))^\tau(\Pi\sigma.\tau, \mathrm{blow}(\sigma))(\Pi\sigma.\tau, \mathrm{blow}(\tau)) \\ \mathrm{blow}(\forall\sigma.A) &= \forall\sigma.\mathrm{blow}(A)(\mathrm{Set}, \mathrm{blow}(\sigma)) \end{aligned}$$

We have the following properties:

Lemma 7

1. $$\frac{\Gamma \vdash \sigma}{\Gamma \vdash \mathrm{blow}(\sigma) : \mathrm{Set}}$$

2. $$\frac{\Gamma \vdash M : \sigma}{\Gamma \vdash \mathrm{blow}(M) : \sigma}$$

3. *If* $C \rhd_1 D$ *then* $|\mathrm{blow}(C)| \rhd_1^+ |\mathrm{blow}(D)|$.

From this it should be obvious how to derive the following (using Corollary 1):

Lemma 8

1. $$\frac{\Gamma \vdash \sigma}{\sigma \in \mathrm{SN}_l}$$

2. $$\frac{\Gamma \vdash M : \sigma}{M \in \mathrm{SN}_l}$$

In the conversion presentation the previous result would suffice to establish decidability because conversion is just defined as the transitive symmetric closure of $\rhd_1$. In our presentation the reasoning is a bit more intricate, because we would have to establish a *subject reduction property*, which is a non-trivial property of the system.

To avoid this we define another notion of reduction — tight reduction:

$$\mathrm{app}^{\sigma.\tau}(\lambda\sigma(M)^{\tau}, N) \rhd_{\mathrm{t}} M[N] \qquad (\text{BETA-RED})$$

For $\rhd_{\mathrm{t}}$ the subject reduction property can be easily established. We can also show the weak Church Rosser property and it is easy to see that $\rhd_{\mathrm{t}}$ is strongly normalizing for derivable terms and types because $\rhd_{\mathrm{t}} \subseteq \rhd_1$.

5 Discussion

It should be noted that our strong normalization argument (i.e. Corollary 1) can be extended to η-reduction without any problems — this relies on the fact that Lemma 3 also holds for η-reduction. Alas, this does not entail decidability for CC $\beta\eta$-equality — this is the CC extended by the rule:

$$\frac{\Gamma \vdash M : \Pi\sigma.\tau}{\Gamma \vdash \lambda\sigma(\mathrm{app}^{\sigma^+.\tau^{+1}}(M^+, 0))^{\tau} \simeq M : \Pi\sigma.\tau} \qquad (\text{ETA-EQ})$$

The problem is that we need *strengthening*:

$$\frac{\Gamma.\sigma \vdash M^+ : \tau^+}{\Gamma \vdash M : \tau}$$

to derive subject reduction for tight reduction. However, it is not clear to me how to prove strengthening (I conjecture that this is not derivable by simple syntactic reasoning). [9]

The essential problem in extending our strong normalization argument to a system with inductive types which allows the definition of Sets by recursion is to extend the usual realizability interpretation since the extension to saturated Λ-sets follows the same lines. This corresponds to showing that initial T-algebras exist in D-set for a general class of functors on modest sets. Although this proposition seems to be folklore we could not find a satisfying presentation. In [Alt93a] we show how the D-set and the saturated Λ-set semantics can be extended to a non-algebraic inductive type with large eliminations. We claim that the same argument works for a general class of inductive definitions.

Acknowledgements

I would like to thank Stefano Berardi, Rod Burstall, Thierry Coquand, Peter Dybjer, Herman Geuvers, Healfdene Goguen, Martin Hofmann, Zhaohui Luo, Eike Ritter, Thomas Streicher and Benjamin Werner for interesting discussions related to the subject. I learnt a lot about ω-sets from Wesley Phoa's lectures [Pho92] and about the D-set semantics of CC from Thomas Streicher's book [Str91]. I would also like to thank the referees for their helpful and detailed comments on the preliminary version of the paper.

References

[Alt93a] Thorsten Altenkirch. *Constructions, Inductive Types and Strong Normalization.* PhD thesis, University of Edinburgh, November 1993.

[Alt93b] Thorsten Altenkirch. Yet another strong normalization proof for the Calculus of Constructions. In *Proceedings of El Vintermöte*, number 73 in Programming Methodology Group Reports. Chalmers University, Göteborg, 1993.

[Bar84] H.P. Barendregt. *The Lambda Calculus - Its Syntax and Semantics (Revised Edition).* Studies in Logic and the Foundations of Mathematics. North Holland, 1984.

[Bar92] H.P. Barendregt. Lambda calculi with types. In *Handbook of Logic in Computer Science, Vol. 2*, pages 118 – 310. Oxford University Press, 1992.

[9] In Nijmegen I proposed to use a modified η-rule instead:

$$\frac{\Gamma.\sigma \vdash M : \Pi\sigma^{+}.\tau^{+1}}{\Gamma \vdash \lambda\sigma(\mathrm{app}^{\sigma^{+}.\tau^{+1}}(M^{+},0))^{\tau} \simeq M : \Pi\sigma.\tau} \quad (\text{ETA-EQ}')$$

For this rule subject reduction is derivable. However, as Thomas Streicher showed me, this rule is highly problematic, since it forbids models with empty types.

[CG90] Thierry Coquand and Jean Gallier. A proof of strong normalization for the theory of constructions using a Kripke-like interpretation. Informal Proceedings of the First Annual Workshop on Logical Frameworks, Antibes, 1990.

[CH88] Thierry Coquand and Gerard Huet. The calculus of constructions. *Information and Computation*, 76:95 – 120, 1988.

[Coq85] Thierry Coquand. *Une théorie des constructions.* PhD thesis, Université Paris VII, 1985.

[Ehr89] Thomas Ehrhard. Dictoses. In D.H. Pitt et al., editors, *Category Theory and Computer Science*, pages 213–223. Springer, 1989. LNCS 389.

[Geu93] Herman Geuvers. *Logics and Type Systems.* PhD thesis, Katholieke Universiteit Nijmegen, 1993.

[HO93] J.M.E. Hyland and C.-H. L. Ong. Modified realizability toposes and strong normalization proofs. In J.F. Groote M. Bezem, editor, *Typed Lambda Calculi and Applications*, LNCS 664, 1993.

[Pho92] Wesley Phoa. An introduction to fibrations, topos theory, the effective topos and modest sets. LFCS report ECS-LFCS-92-208, University of Edinburgh, 1992.

[Str89] Thomas Streicher. *Correctness and Completeness of a Categorical Semantics of the Calculus of Constructions.* PhD thesis, Universität Passau, Passau, West Germany, June 1989.

[Str91] Thomas Streicher. *Semantics of Type Theory.* Birkhäuser, 1991.

[Wer92] Benjamin Werner. A normalization proof for an impredicative type system with large eliminations over integers. In *Workshop on Logical Frameworks.* BRA Types, 1992. Preliminary Proceedings.

Checking Algorithms for Pure Type Systems*

L.S. van Benthem Jutting[1], J. McKinna[2] and R. Pollack[2]

[1] Faculty of Mathematics and Computer Science, University of Nijmegen, Toernooiveld 1, 6525 ED Nijmegen, The Netherlands
[2] Laboratory for Foundations of Computer Science, University of Edinburgh, The King's Buildings, Edinburgh, EH9 3JZ, Scotland
jhm@dcs.ed.ac.uk, rap@dcs.ed.ac.uk

1 Introduction

This work is motivated by the problem of finding reasonable algorithms for typechecking Pure Type Systems [Bar91] (PTS). There are several implementations of formal systems that are either PTS or closely related to PTS. For example, LEGO [LP92] implements the Pure Calculus of Constructions (PCC) [CH88], the Extended Calculus of Constructions [Luo90] and the Edinburgh Logical Framework (LF) [HHP87]. ELF [Pfe89] implements LF; CONSTRUCTOR [Hel91] implements arbitrary PTS with finite set of sorts. Are these implementations actually correct? Of course, we may enumerate all derivations of a given PTS, and Jutting [vBJ93] has shown that a large class of normalizing PTS have decidable typechecking by computing the normal forms of types, but such techniques are obviously not usable in practice. Algorithms in the literature for particular type systems, such as Huet's Constructive Engine [Hue89], do not obviously extend even to such tame classes as the normalizing and functional PTS.

In the rest of this section we briefly review the definition and well-known theory of PTS, outline the basic approach to checking algorithms, and analyse the difficulty in using this approach for checking PTS. In section 1.5, we outline the plan for the rest of this paper.

1.1 Pure Type Systems

A *Pure Type System* is a quadruple $\mathfrak{S} = \{\mathcal{S}, \mathcal{V}, \mathcal{A}, \mathcal{R}\}$, where

- $\mathcal{S}$ is the set of *sorts*; elements of $\mathcal{S}$ will be denoted by $s, s_0, s_1, \ldots$,
- $\mathcal{V}$ is the set of *variables*; elements of $\mathcal{V}$ will be denoted by x, y, z,
- $\mathcal{S} \cap \mathcal{V} = \emptyset$,
- $\mathcal{A} \subseteq \mathcal{S} \times \mathcal{S}$ is the set of *axioms* which we assume to be nonempty,
- $\mathcal{R} \subseteq \mathcal{S} \times \mathcal{S} \times \mathcal{S}$ is the set of *Π-rules.*

We usually assume we are discussing some specific PTS, $\mathfrak{S} = \{\mathcal{S}, \mathcal{V}, \mathcal{A}, \mathcal{R}\}$, which may be assumed to have special properties in later sections. Let us also assume $\mathcal{S}$ is denumerable, and $\mathcal{A}$ and $\mathcal{R}$ are decidable relations, although these assumptions are only used in discussing algorithmic properties of inductive presentations of relations, not the relationships between different presentations.

---

* This work was supported by the ESPRIT Basic Research Actions on Logical Frameworks and Types for Proofs and Programs, and by grants from the British Science and Engineering Research Council.

Definition 1 Pseudoterms. The set T of *pseudoterms* of $\mathfrak{S}$ is the smallest set satisfying

$\mathcal{S} \cup \mathcal{V} \subseteq \mathsf{T}$,
If $a \in \mathsf{T}$ and $b \in \mathsf{T}$ then $a\, b \in \mathsf{T}$,
If $A \in \mathsf{T}$, $B \in \mathsf{T}$ and $x \in \mathcal{V}$ then $(\Pi x{:}A.B) \in \mathsf{T}$,
If $A \in \mathsf{T}$, $b \in \mathsf{T}$ and $x \in \mathcal{V}$ then $(\lambda x{:}A.b) \in \mathsf{T}$.

Elements of T will be denoted by a, b, c, ..., A, B, C, ... The notions of free and bound variables are defined as usual, with $\mathsf{FV}(a)$ denoting the set of free variables of a. We consider equality between terms to be equivalence modulo α-conversion and this equivalence will be denoted by $=$.

Convention 2 Variables. In this presentation we are informal about variables, and omit side conditions such as "x is a fresh variable". Much of this paper has been formalized in the LEGO system in a presentation with explicit variable names [MP93], but thinking in terms of de Bruijn nameless variables will clarify many questions that might arise about variables in the following.

Reduction and conversion We denote the substitution of a for x in b by $b[x := a]$, and write $\rightarrow$ for one step β-reduction, $\twoheadrightarrow$ for β-reduction and $\simeq$ for β-convertibility.

From section 4 onward we extend our concept of reduction by allowing for contractions of the form

$$(\Pi x{:}A.B)\, a \rightarrow_\pi B[x := a]$$

i.e. for application of a product to an argument. Intuitively a π-redex $(\Pi x{:}A.B)\, a$ denotes a coordinate axis in the product $\Pi x{:}A.B$. Such considerations first appear in the pioneering work of the AUTOMATH group [vD80], and allows a presentation of the basic typing relation free of any direct appeal to substitution, which in contemporary presentations of type theory such as [Bar92] appears explicitly in the rule for typing an application (rule App below). We then have the new notion of *$\beta\pi$-reduction*, $\twoheadrightarrow_\pi$, and *$\beta\pi$-conversion*, $\simeq_\pi$, generated by the elementary β- and π- contractions. The well known properties of substitution and reduction, e.g. the Church-Rosser property, extend to $\twoheadrightarrow_\pi$ and $\simeq_\pi$. These properties will be used freely in the sequel.

Contexts A *context*, Γ, is a sequence of assignments $x{:}A$. If

$$\Gamma = x_1{:}A_1, x_2{:}A_2, \ldots, x_n{:}A_n \qquad (n \geq 0)$$

we write $x_i{:}A_i \sqsubseteq \Gamma$ for $1 \leq i \leq n$, and $\mathsf{dom}(\Gamma)$ for the set $\{x_1, x_2, \ldots, x_n\}$. The free variables of Γ are defined by $\mathsf{FV}(\Gamma) = \bigcup_i \mathsf{FV}(A_i)$. The empty context is written $\oslash$, and the set of all contexts is C.

Inclusion between contexts is defined by

$$\Gamma_1 \sqsubseteq \Gamma_2 \quad \stackrel{\Delta}{=} \quad \forall x, A\ [x{:}A \sqsubseteq \Gamma_1 \Rightarrow x{:}A \sqsubseteq \Gamma_2]$$

The notion of (one step) β-reduction is easily extended to contexts:

$$A \rightarrow B \Rightarrow \Gamma_1, x{:}A, \Gamma_2 \rightarrow \Gamma_1, x{:}B, \Gamma_2 .$$

1.2 Correctness

We define a relation, $\vdash$, called *correctness* as follows.

Definition 3 Correctness. The relation $\vdash \subseteq \mathsf{C} \times \mathsf{T} \times \mathsf{T}$ is the smallest relation satisfying the following rules.

Srt $\quad \oslash \vdash s_1 : s_2 \qquad \langle s_1, s_2 \rangle \in \mathcal{A}$

Var $\quad \dfrac{\Gamma \vdash A : s}{\Gamma, x{:}A \vdash x : A}$

Wk $\quad \dfrac{\Gamma \vdash b : B \qquad \Gamma \vdash A : s}{\Gamma, x{:}A \vdash b : B} \qquad b \in \mathcal{S} \cup \mathcal{V}$

Pi $\quad \dfrac{\Gamma \vdash A : s_1 \qquad \Gamma, x{:}A \vdash B : s_2}{\Gamma \vdash \Pi x{:}A.B : s_3} \qquad \langle s_1, s_2, s_3 \rangle \in \mathcal{R}$

Lda $\quad \dfrac{\Gamma \vdash A : s_1 \qquad \Gamma, x{:}A \vdash b : B \qquad \Gamma, x{:}A \vdash B : s_2}{\Gamma \vdash \lambda x{:}A.b : \Pi x{:}A.B} \qquad \langle s_1, s_2, s_3 \rangle \in \mathcal{R}$

App $\quad \dfrac{\Gamma \vdash a : \Pi x{:}B.A \qquad \Gamma \vdash b : B}{\Gamma \vdash a\, b : A[x := b]}$

Cnv $\quad \dfrac{\Gamma \vdash a : A \qquad \Gamma \vdash B : s}{\Gamma \vdash a : B} \qquad A \simeq B$

The cognoscenti will notice that the rule Wk in the definition above is not the usual one, as b is restricted to variables and sorts. It is easy to see from the lemmas below that the relation defined above is equivalent to the usual PTS system. In fact the presentation above gives a better development of the basic metatheory, because the generation lemma does not depend on weakening. The following properties of PTS can be proved along the lines of [GN91] or [Bar92]. Most proofs are by induction on the structure of $\vdash$ derivations.

Lemma 4 Free Variables.

If $\quad \Gamma \vdash a : A$
then $\quad \mathit{FV}(a) \cup \mathit{FV}(A) \subseteq \mathit{dom}(\Gamma)$.

Lemma 5 Start. *Suppose* $\Gamma \vdash a : A$.

i $\quad \langle s_1, s_2 \rangle \in \mathcal{A} \quad \Leftrightarrow \quad \Gamma \vdash s_1 : s_2$
ii $\quad$ *If* $\; x{:}B \sqsubseteq \Gamma \;$ *then* $\; \Gamma \vdash x : B$

Lemma 6 Generation.

i $\quad$ *If* $\quad \Gamma \vdash s : A$
$\quad$ *then* $\quad \exists s_0\ [A \simeq s_0$ *and* $\langle s, s_0 \rangle \in \mathcal{A}]$.
ii $\quad$ *If* $\quad \Gamma \vdash x : A$
$\quad$ *then* $\quad \exists A_0\ [A \simeq A_0$ *and* $x{:}A_0 \sqsubseteq \Gamma]$.

iii *If* $\Gamma \vdash \Pi x{:}C.D : A$
then $\exists s_1, s_2, s_3\ [A \simeq s_3,\ \langle s_1, s_2, s_3\rangle \in \mathcal{R},\ \Gamma \vdash C : s_1$ *and* $\Gamma, x{:}C \vdash D : s_2]$.

iv *If* $\Gamma \vdash \lambda x{:}C.d : A$
then $\exists s_1, s_2, s_3, D\ [A \simeq \Pi x{:}C.D,\ \langle s_1, s_2, s_3\rangle \in \mathcal{R},$
$\Gamma \vdash C : s_1,\ \Gamma, x{:}C \vdash d : D$ *and* $\Gamma, x{:}C \vdash D : s_2]$.

v *If* $\Gamma \vdash c\,d : A$
then $\exists x, C, D\ [A \simeq C[x := d],\ \Gamma \vdash c : \Pi x{:}D.C$ *and* $\Gamma \vdash d : D]$.

Lemma 7 ***Weakening.***

If $\Gamma_1 \sqsubseteq \Gamma_2,\ \Gamma_1 \vdash a : A$ *and* $\Gamma_2 \vdash b : B$
then $\Gamma_2 \vdash a : A$.

Lemma 8 ***Substitution.***

If $\Gamma_1, x{:}A, \Gamma_2 \vdash b : B$ *and* $\Gamma_1 \vdash a : A$
then $\Gamma_1, \Gamma_2[x := a] \vdash b[x := a] : B[x := a]$.

Lemma 9 ***Correctness of Types.***

If $\Gamma \vdash a : A$
then *either* $A \in \mathcal{S}$ *or* $\exists s \in \mathcal{S}\ [\Gamma \vdash A : s]$.

Lemma 10 ***Closure under β-reduction, Subject Reduction.***

If $\Gamma \vdash a : A,\ \Gamma \twoheadrightarrow \Gamma_0,\ a \twoheadrightarrow a_0$ *and* $A \twoheadrightarrow A_0$
then $\Gamma_0 \vdash a_0 : A_0$.

1.3 Syntax Directed Systems

It is our purpose to describe algorithms, which for given Γ, a and A construct a derivation for $\Gamma \vdash a : A$. It is known that this problem is undecidable for some PTS, e.g. $\lambda\star$, so a semi-algorithm is all we can hope for. There is a trivial such semi-algorithm by enumerating all possible derivations in turn. However we want an *efficient* semi-algorithm, and we want to know something about when the problem is decidable. In [vBJ93] it is shown that if a PTS is normalizing (i.e. all well-typed terms have a normal form) and has a finite set of sorts, $\mathcal{S}$, then it is decidable, but the given algorithm computes the normal form of types, so while much better than the trivial semi-algorithm above, it is still infeasible.

Consider the rules for correctness, definition 3. There is one rule for deriving the type of a sort, Srt; one rule for the type of a variable, Var; etc. for Pi, Lda and App. Thus it is natural to construct a derivation of $\Gamma \vdash a : A$ by looking at the shape of a: if a is a sort, use Srt, etc. This is not quite right, because Srt and Var also specify the shape of the context in their conclusion; e.g. Srt only works on the empty context. But this is what rule Wk is for; it is applicable exactly when we want to use Srt or Var, but cannot because the context is of the wrong shape. (This is one reason we prefer our restricted weakening rule to the general one in [Bar92].) This improved plan, to build a derivation $\Gamma \vdash a : A$ guided by the shape of Γ and a (which we call the *subject* of the judgement) still has one flaw: the rule Cnv may be used at any point in a derivation without changing the shape of the subject. Putting it the other way around, you cannot decide when to use Cnv in a derivation by looking at the shape of the subject. A system which does not suffer from such a drawback will be called *syntax directed*. The idea to use a syntax directed presentation for type checking is found in [Mar72] and [Hue89]. We define this notion somewhat informally.

Definition 11 syntax directed.

A set of rules for a relation $\vdash$ is called *nearly syntax directed* if for every Γ, a there is at most one rule with a conclusion $\Gamma \vdash a : A$.

A set of rules for a relation $\vdash$ is called *syntax directed* if for every Γ, a there is at most one rule with a conclusion $\Gamma \vdash a : A$ and this rule (if present) produces exactly one type A for a.

The relation defined by a syntax directed set of rules is necessarily the graph of a partial function $\Gamma, a \mapsto A$. Whether or not the rules allow us to decide this relation depends on the side conditions of the rules, that is, those "premisses" that are not the relation being defined. Similarly, how efficiently we can compute the partial function defined by the rules depends on how efficiently we can compute the side conditions.

Let us assume we have a syntax directed set of rules for a relation equivalent to the correctness relation, $\vdash$. Given an algorithm to compute the corresponding partial function $\Gamma, a \mapsto A$, which we may call a *type-synthesis* algorithm, how are we to solve our original problem of *typechecking*, that is, given Γ, a and A to construct a derivation of $\Gamma \vdash a : A$? We use our algorithm to compute some type A_0 for a, and some type B for A. Provided that B reduces to some sort s (otherwise A was not a possible type), it now suffices to test A and A_0 for convertibility, and then appeal to the Cnv rule.

In order to produce a syntax directed system that is equivalent to the correctness relation, $\vdash$, we consider how the rule Cnv is used in derivations, and are led to propose a nearly syntax directed system of rules defining a relation $\vdash_{nsd}$. In order to define it, we first introduce some notation.

Notation 12. We write $\Gamma \vdash_{nsd} a :\twoheadrightarrow A$ for $\Gamma \vdash_{nsd} a : A_0$ and $A_0 \twoheadrightarrow A$. Similar notations eliding the names of intermediate terms will be used in the rest of the paper.

Definition 13 $\vdash_{nsd}$. The relation $\vdash_{nsd} \subseteq \mathsf{C} \times \mathsf{T} \times \mathsf{T}$ is the smallest relation satisfying the following rules.

Srt-nsd $\quad \emptyset \vdash_{nsd} s_1 : s_2 \qquad \langle s_1, s_2 \rangle \in \mathcal{A}$

$$\text{Var-nsd} \quad \frac{\Gamma \vdash_{nsd} A :\twoheadrightarrow s}{\Gamma, x{:}A \vdash_{nsd} x : A}$$

$$\text{Wk-nsd} \quad \frac{\Gamma \vdash_{nsd} b : B \qquad \Gamma \vdash_{nsd} A :\twoheadrightarrow s}{\Gamma, x{:}A \vdash_{nsd} b : B} \qquad b \in \mathcal{S} \cup \mathcal{V}$$

$$\text{Pi-nsd} \quad \frac{\Gamma \vdash_{nsd} A :\twoheadrightarrow s_1 \qquad \Gamma, x{:}A \vdash_{nsd} B :\twoheadrightarrow s_2}{\Gamma \vdash_{nsd} \Pi x{:}A.B : s_3} \qquad \langle s_1, s_2, s_3 \rangle \in \mathcal{R}$$

$$\text{Lda-nsd} \quad \frac{\Gamma \vdash_{nsd} A :\twoheadrightarrow s_1 \quad \Gamma, x{:}A \vdash_{nsd} b :\twoheadrightarrow B \quad \Gamma, x{:}A \vdash_{nsd} B :\twoheadrightarrow s_2}{\Gamma \vdash_{nsd} \lambda x{:}A.b : \Pi x{:}A.B} \qquad \langle s_1, s_2, s_3 \rangle \in \mathcal{R}$$

$$\text{App-nsd} \quad \frac{\Gamma \vdash_{nsd} a :\twoheadrightarrow \Pi x{:}B.A \qquad \Gamma \vdash_{nsd} b :\twoheadrightarrow B}{\Gamma \vdash_{nsd} a\, b : A[x := b]}$$

For this system we can prove soundness.

Lemma 14 Soundness of $\vdash_{nsd}$.

If $\Gamma \vdash_{nsd} a : A$ *then* $\Gamma \vdash a : A$.

Proof. By induction on $\Gamma \vdash_{nsd} a : A$, using correctness of types (lemma 9) and closure (lemma 10) for $\vdash$. □

Conversely we would like to have

Completeness of $\vdash_{nsd}$: If $\Gamma \vdash a : A$ then $\exists A_0 \in \mathsf{T}\ [A \simeq A_0$ and $\Gamma \vdash_{nsd} a : A_0]$.

However we have not been able to prove this. In fact the rule Lda-nsd turns out to be an obstacle, both in proving this property directly and of proving some form of closure or correctness of types for $\vdash_{nsd}$.

1.4 Expansion Postponement

In order to analyse the situation, split Cnv into two rules, one for expansion and one for reduction, getting a new system with correctness relation $\vdash_{er}$.

Definition 15 $\vdash_{er}$**.** The relation $\vdash_{er} \subseteq \mathsf{C} \times \mathsf{T} \times \mathsf{T}$ is the smallest relation satisfying the ordinary PTS-rules, but having instead of Cnv the following two rules.

$$\text{Red-er} \quad \frac{\Gamma \vdash_{er} a : A}{\Gamma \vdash_{er} a : B} \quad A \twoheadrightarrow B$$

$$\text{Exp-er} \quad \frac{\Gamma \vdash_{er} a : A \qquad \Gamma \vdash_{er} B : s}{\Gamma \vdash_{er} a : B} \quad B \twoheadrightarrow A$$

Lemma 16 Equivalence of $\vdash$ and $\vdash_{er}$. $\Gamma \vdash a : A \quad \Leftrightarrow \quad \Gamma \vdash_{er} a : A$

Proof. We treat the two cases.

$\Rightarrow$ By induction on $\Gamma \vdash a : A$. The interesting case is the use of Cnv: $\Gamma \vdash a : B$ as a consequence of $\Gamma \vdash a : A$, $\Gamma \vdash B : s$ and $A \simeq B$. The induction hypothesis gives $\Gamma \vdash_{er} a : A$ and $\Gamma \vdash_{er} B : s$. By Church-Rosser A and B have a common reduct C, so $\Gamma \vdash_{er} a : C$ by Red-er and $\Gamma \vdash_{er} a : B$ by Exp-er.

$\Leftarrow$ By induction on $\Gamma \vdash_{er} a : A$ using closure for $\vdash$ in the case Red-er. □

In the spirit of our program to remove non-syntax-directed rules, we ask whether Exp-er has any use in derivations (the question was proposed in this form by Henk Barendregt), i.e. we consider a new system, $\vdash_r$, which does not have the expansion rule.

Definition 17 $\vdash_r$**.** The relation $\vdash_r \subseteq \mathsf{C} \times \mathsf{T} \times \mathsf{T}$ is the smallest relation satisfying the ordinary PTS-rules, but having instead of the rule Cnv the following rule.

$$\text{Red-r} \quad \frac{\Gamma \vdash_r a : A}{\Gamma \vdash_r a : B} \quad A \twoheadrightarrow B$$

Observe that $\vdash_r$ is equivalent to $\vdash_{nsd}$

Lemma 18 equivalence of $\vdash_r$ and $\vdash_{nsd}$.

i *If* $\Gamma \vdash_{nsd} a : A$ *then* $\Gamma \vdash_r a : A$

ii *If* $\Gamma \vdash_r a : A$ *then* $\exists A_0\ [A_0 \twoheadrightarrow A$ *and* $\Gamma \vdash_{nsd} a : A_0]$

The proof is straightforward; in fact we constructed $\vdash_{nsd}$ from $\vdash_r$ by moving uses of Red-r to the end of derivations, i.e by permuting Red-r downward wherever possible through the premisses of other rules.

Clearly $\vdash_r$ is contained in $\vdash$, i.e. $\vdash_r$ is sound for $\vdash$. We would also like to prove $\vdash_r$ is complete for $\vdash$ in the following sense

Expansion Postponement: If $\Gamma \vdash a : A$ then $\exists A_0\ [A \twoheadrightarrow A_0\ \textit{and}\ \Gamma \vdash_r a : A_0]$.

All attempts to prove this have failed to date. The reason is that no form of a closure lemma has been proved for $\vdash_r$ and this is due to the failure of inductive proofs on the third premiss of the rule Lda-r. (This is the crux of the difficulty in proving $\vdash_{nsd}$ complete for $\vdash$.) Informally we might say that the difficulty is that B moves from right of the colon in the second premiss, where it is an "output" of the subderivation $\Gamma, x{:}A \vdash_r b : B$, to left of the colon in the third premiss, where it is an "input" to the subderivation $\Gamma, x{:}A \vdash_r B : s_2$. We don't have enough structural information on outputs to reason about them as inputs. In proving closure for $\vdash$ we use (the expansion part of) Cnv to adjust the shape of outputs, but this is not available in $\vdash_r$. Closure is a very delicate property of PTS. At this moment the authors feel that they cannot honestly call expansion postponement for arbitrary PTS a conjecture.

Expansion postponement is an *intensional* concept. It concerns a set of derivation rules for some relation, rather then the relation itself. See remark 3.1 for a frustrating illustration of this point.

We now have, somewhat inexactly,

$$\vdash_{nsd} \;=\; \vdash_r \;\subseteq\; \vdash_{er} \;=\; \vdash$$

Expansion postponement is the property that $\vdash_r \supseteq \vdash_{er}$. Thus, if we assume that expansion postponement holds for some specific PTS, then $\vdash_{nsd}$ is a nearly syntax directed presentation of the $\vdash$ relation for that PTS.

Remark. Since we cannot now prove $\vdash_r$ has subject reduction or predicate reduction, it is interesting to define a relation $\vdash_R$, similar to $\vdash_r$, having the same rules as $\vdash$ except for Cnv, which is replaced by

$$\text{Red-R}\quad \frac{\Gamma \vdash_R a : A \qquad \Gamma \vdash_R B : s}{\Gamma \vdash_R a : B}\quad A \twoheadrightarrow B$$

There is an expansion postponement problem for $\vdash_R$, which we also cannot prove or disprove. Clearly $\vdash_R \subseteq \vdash_r$, so $\vdash_R$ is "even worse" than $\vdash_r$. However $\vdash_R$ is easily seen to have the correctness-of-types property, which we cannot prove for $\vdash_r$. In fact, we can show that correctness-of-types for $\vdash_r$ implies r-expansion-postponement for all *functional* PTS (functional PTS are defined in section 2.2), but this has not helped in the expansion postponement problem for $\vdash_R$.

1.5 Plan for this paper

There are two obstructions to deriving syntax directed presentations of arbitrary PTS, namely the possible non-determinism of the side conditions, and, more seriously, the third premiss of the Lda rule. The purpose of this premiss is to guarantee correctness of the type derived for a lambda term using the Lda rule, that is, to make Correctness of Types (lemma 9) true. In this paper we consider two different approaches for removing this troublesome premiss while preserving some form of equivalence with $\vdash$. We begin in section 2 with further introductory and motivating observations.

Our first approach, in section 3, is to consider a subclass of PTS, called *semi-full*, which have the property that the first two premisses of the Lda rule imply the third premiss. This allows a nearly syntax directed presentation for this class, that fails to be syntax directed only because of non-functionality of the relations $\mathcal{A}$ and $\mathcal{R}$. We introduce a technique of *schematization* to make this presentation syntax directed, and to use it as a typechecking algorithm. This section is a warm-up for the use of schematization in later sections.

Special subclasses of PTS such as semi-full are so redundant that the third premiss of the Lda rule is unnecessary. Even for the general PTS this premiss is more restrictive than necessary. In the rest of the paper our second, more general approach, looks more deeply at the presentation of $\vdash$ in order to take advantage of this redundancy. In section 4 we discuss two closely connected typing relations $\vdash_o, \vdash_{tp}$ which are more liberal than $\vdash$. Alone, the system $\vdash_{tp}$ is too weak to have any reasonable properties (for example, closure obviously fails), but corollaries 54 and 55 show that for terms already known to be well-typed, $\vdash_{tp}$ suffices for correct typechecking. As it stands, this last statement is somewhat inexact, but for now we postpone the precise account of the delicate interaction between $\vdash, \vdash_o$ and $\vdash_{tp}$.

These liberal relations are used in section 5 to give a nearly syntax directed presentation of the general PTS, in particular replacing the troublesome third premiss of the Lda rule with an appeal to $\vdash_{tp}$. This presentation allows arguments about PTS that we do not know how to carry out in the standard presentation of $\vdash$ given above; for example we prove strengthening for arbitrary PTS. Sections 4 and 5 are the core of the new ideas in this paper, and can be read on their own by a knowledgable reader.

For non-functional PTS, the Lda rule retains an essential non-determinism, as terms may acquire more types by reduction (see example 1 in section 2.2 below), but for functional PTS the nearly syntax directed presentation of section 5 can easily be made syntax directed, as explained in section 6, and can then be seen as an efficient semi-decision procedure for all functional PTS, and as an efficient decision procedure for the decidable ones.

In section 7 we give a syntax directed system that is related to the general PTS, and discuss how to make it into an efficient semi-decision procedure.

A machine-checked presentation From an early draft of this paper, the second and third authors worked to give a completely machine-checked presentation in the LEGO system of all the results of this paper. We have achieved this objective [MP94], except for considerations of schematic terms and judgments (see subsection 3.2 below). For example, the strengthening theorem (63) is formally checked. Further extensions of this work, for example to systems with cumulativity rules for the sorts, may be found in the the third author's forthcoming Ph.D. thesis [Pol94].

2 Preliminary Observations

This section is still introductory. We address several points that are used in future sections, but whose discussion there would be lost in the fray of other matters.

2.1 Making the Application Rule Syntax Directed

Remembering that, lacking a proof of Expansion Postponement, $\vdash_{nsd}$ is not necessarily complete for $\vdash$, we nonetheless examine the App-nsd rule in more detail, as motivation for following sections.

$$\text{App-nsd} \quad \frac{\Gamma \vdash_{nsd} a :\twoheadrightarrow \Pi x{:}B.A \qquad \Gamma \vdash_{nsd} b :\twoheadrightarrow B}{\Gamma \vdash_{nsd} a\, b : A[x := b]}$$

It fails to be syntax directed because we haven't specified when to stop reducing in the left premiss. In particular A, which appears to the right of the colon in the conclusion, is not determined. The intention is to check that a has some functional type (i.e. some Π-type), and that the type of b matches the domain of a's functional type. For this it is sufficient to do weak-head reduction (denoted by $\twoheadrightarrow^{wh}$) on the type of a, since every Π-type is a weak-head normal form. We are led to an alternative, syntax directed rule

$$\frac{\Gamma \vdash_{nsd} a :\twoheadrightarrow^{wh} \Pi x{:}B.A \qquad \Gamma \vdash_{nsd} b : B'}{\Gamma \vdash_{nsd} a\, b : A[x := b]} \quad B \simeq B'$$

in which the type of $a\,b$ is uniquely determined by the type of a. Rules of this shape will be used in several following sections.

2.2 Functional Pure Type Systems

We digress to define a well behaved class of PTS that occur commonly in practice.

Definition 19 Functional PTS. A PTS is called *functional* iff

- $\langle s_1, s\rangle \in \mathcal{A}$ and $\langle s_1, s'\rangle \in \mathcal{A}$ implies $s = s'$, and
- $\langle s_1, s_2, s\rangle \in \mathcal{R}$ and $\langle s_1, s_2, s'\rangle \in \mathcal{R}$ implies $s = s'$.

For a functional PTS $\mathcal{A}$ and $\mathcal{R}$ are the graphs of partial functions from $\mathcal{S}$ to $\mathcal{S}$ and from $\mathcal{S} \times \mathcal{S}$ to $\mathcal{S}$ respectively, but we do not necessarily have procedures to compute these functions. It is well known that for functional PTS we have uniqueness of types (cf. [GN91] or [Bar92]).

Lemma 20 Uniqueness of Types. *For functional PTS*

If $\quad \Gamma \vdash a : A_0$ *and* $\Gamma \vdash a : A_1$
then $\quad A_0 \simeq A_1$.

Subject Expansion By the Subject Reduction Lemma (lemma 10) we know that a term does not lose any types by reduction. Might a well-typed term *gain* types by reduction? For functional PTS this cannot happen.

Lemma 21 Subject Expansion. *For PTS with Uniqueness of Types*

If $\quad \Gamma \vdash a : A,\ b \twoheadrightarrow a,$ *and* $\Gamma \vdash b : B$
then $\quad \Gamma \vdash b : A$

The condition $\Gamma \vdash b : B$ in this lemma, that b has some type, is necessary to rule out untypable expansions.

Proof. By closure (lemma 10) $\Gamma \vdash a : B$. By uniqueness of types $A \simeq B$. By correctness of types (lemma 9) $A \in \mathcal{S}$ or $\Gamma \vdash A : s$ for some s. In the first case, $B \twoheadrightarrow A$, and we are done by closure. In the second case we are done by the rule Cnv. □

The general PTS does not have the subject expansion property:

Example 1. Consider the non-functional PTS

$$\mathcal{S} = \{\star,\ \triangle,\ \triangledown,\ \Box\}$$
$$\mathcal{A} = \{\langle\star,\triangle\rangle,\ \langle\star,\triangledown\rangle,\ \langle\triangle,\Box\rangle\}$$
$$\mathcal{R} = \{\langle\Box,\Box,\Box\rangle\}$$

Let $a = (\lambda x{:}\,\triangle\,.x)\,\star$. We have $a \twoheadrightarrow \star$, with $\oslash \vdash \star : \triangle$ and $\oslash \vdash \star : \triangledown$. Consider the types of a in the empty context. First notice that $\oslash \vdash a : \triangle$

$$\dfrac{\dfrac{\oslash \vdash \triangle : \Box \qquad \dfrac{\oslash \vdash \triangle : \Box}{x{:}\triangle \vdash x : \triangle} \qquad \dfrac{\oslash \vdash \triangle : \Box \quad \oslash \vdash \triangle : \Box}{x{:}\triangle \vdash \triangle : \Box}}{\oslash \vdash \lambda x{:}\,\triangle\,.x : \Pi x{:}\,\triangle\,.\triangle}\ \langle\Box,\Box,\Box\rangle \in \mathcal{R} \qquad \oslash \vdash \star : \triangle}{\oslash \vdash (\lambda x{:}\,\triangle\,.x)\,\star : \triangle}$$

Now we claim that $\oslash \vdash a : \triangledown$ is *not* derivable, so the well-typed term a gains types by reduction to $\star$. To prove this claim we use the generation lemma (lemma 6). In general, if $\oslash \vdash a : X$ for some X, then there exist Y, Z, with $\oslash \vdash \lambda x{:}\,\triangle\,.x : \Pi x{:}Y.Z$ and $X \simeq Z[x := \star]$. By the generation lemma again, $x{:}\triangle \vdash x : W, x{:}\triangle \vdash W : s$, and $Z \simeq W$. By the generation lemma again, $W \simeq \triangle$, hence $\oslash \not\vdash a : \triangledown$. Notice also that this argument never appeals to "there is no rule of a certain shape"; even if we expand $\mathcal{R}$ to $\mathcal{S} \times \mathcal{S} \times \mathcal{S}$, every type of a converts with $\triangle$.

Examining this example more closely, observe that a variable can have only one type (up to conversion), while a sort can have several types in non-functional PTS (see [vBJ93] for a deep analysis of this point). In the example, we use reduction to replace a variable by a sort, increasing the types derivable for a term. However, this is not the only way that subject expansion can fail: consider the term $b = (\lambda x{:}\,\triangle\,.\star)\,\star$. We leave it to the reader to check that again $b \twoheadrightarrow \star$, $\oslash \vdash b : \triangle$ but $\oslash \not\vdash b : \triangledown$. In this case the reason is that $\oslash \vdash \triangle : \Box$, but $\triangledown$ has no type at all.

Must this process of obtaining more types by reduction eventually stop or are there (non-functional) PTS with infinitely many sorts, and (non normalizing) terms in these PTS that keep acquiring more and more types by reduction?

As an aside, notice that this PTS is strongly normalizing. It can be mapped into three levels of a strongly normalizing predicative type hierarchy (for definiteness we mention ECC [Luo90], but much weaker systems will do) by the PTS-morphism ([Geu, Geu93])

$$\star \mapsto \mathit{Type}(0) \qquad \triangle \mapsto \mathit{Type}(1) \qquad \triangledown \mapsto \mathit{Type}(1) \qquad \Box \mapsto \mathit{Type}(2).$$

Since this mapping preserves sorts, axioms and rules, any well-typed term in the system above has a well-typed image, and therefore strongly normalizes. Further, since $\mathcal{S}$ is finite, this system has decidable typechecking [vBJ93]. □

It is quite difficult to think of a PTS of independent interest that is not functional!

2.3 Side Conditions and Decidability of Typechecking

Remember that we assumed $\mathcal{A}$ and $\mathcal{R}$ are decidable. Clearly, however, the set

$$\mathcal{A}_\bullet \triangleq \{s \in \mathcal{S} \mid \exists s_0 \in \mathcal{S}\ [\langle s, s_0\rangle \in \mathcal{A}]\}$$

may not be decidable[3]. (This is true even for functional PTS.) Furthermore, if $\mathcal{A}_\bullet$ is not decidable, then the PTS does not have decidable typechecking, because

$$x{:}s \vdash x : s \quad \Leftrightarrow \quad s \in \mathcal{A}_\bullet.$$

Similarly if the relation

$$\mathcal{R}_\bullet \triangleq \{\langle s_1, s_2\rangle \in \mathcal{S} \times \mathcal{S} \mid \exists s_3 \in \mathcal{S}\ [\langle s_1, s_2, s_3\rangle \in \mathcal{R}]\}$$

is not decidable, then the PTS may not have decidable typechecking, but since some Π-rules may not be usable the situation is not as clear.

In a functional PTS, $\mathcal{A}$ (respectively $\mathcal{R}$) is the graph of a partial function. If $\mathcal{A}_\bullet$ (respectively $\mathcal{R}_\bullet$) is decidable, then we can compute that function: use decidability of $\mathcal{A}_\bullet$ (respectively $\mathcal{R}_\bullet$) to decide if the function is defined on particular input, and if so use decidability of $\mathcal{A}$ (respectively $\mathcal{R}$) to search the denumerable set $\mathcal{S}$ for the function value.

As $\mathcal{A}$ and $\mathcal{R}$ are arbitrary given relations, there is not much interesting to say about these side conditions.

2.4 An Optimization: Valid Contexts

There is one easy optimization of the definition of PTS which will shorten derivations, and therefore also the checking algorithms which could produce such derivations. In the premisses of the rules Wk, Pi, Lda, App and Cnv the context Γ occurs more then once, and in order to construct a complete derivation its validity must be checked in each subderivation in which it appears. It is much more efficient to assume that we start with a valid context, and only check that when rules extend the context (i.e. the right premiss of Pi and the two right premisses of Lda) they maintain validity. This is also more in keeping with the implementations which are actually used, where we work in a "current context" of mathematical assumptions. (In practice, the context also contains definitions, but in this paper we will not discuss definitions.)

We formalize this optimization in the following definition. $\Gamma \vdash_{vtyp} a : A$ should be interpreted as "a has type A relative to the (possibly incorrect) context Γ" and $\Gamma \vdash_{vcxt}$ as "Γ is a valid (or correct) context".

---

[3] The set of *topsorts*, $\mathcal{A}^\bullet \triangleq \mathcal{S} \backslash \mathcal{A}_\bullet$, is interesting in its own right; see [Ber90] or [Pol94].

Definition 22 $\vdash_{vtyp}$ and $\vdash_{vcxt}$. The relation $\vdash_{vtyp} \subseteq \mathsf{C} \times \mathsf{T} \times \mathsf{T}$ is the smallest relation satisfying the following rules.

Srt-vtyp $\quad \Gamma \vdash_{vtyp} s_1 : s_2 \qquad \langle s_1, s_2 \rangle \in \mathcal{A}$

Var-vtyp $\quad \Gamma \vdash_{vtyp} x : A \qquad x{:}A \sqsubseteq \Gamma$

Pi-vtyp $\quad \dfrac{\Gamma \vdash_{vtyp} A : s_1 \qquad \Gamma, x{:}A \vdash_{vtyp} B : s_2}{\Gamma \vdash_{vtyp} \Pi x{:}A.B : s_3} \qquad \langle s_1, s_2, s_3 \rangle \in \mathcal{R}, \; x \notin \mathsf{dom}(\Gamma)$

Lda-vtyp $\quad \dfrac{\Gamma \vdash_{vtyp} A : s_1 \qquad \Gamma, x{:}A \vdash_{vtyp} b : B \qquad \Gamma, x{:}A \vdash_{vtyp} B : s_2}{\Gamma \vdash_{vtyp} \lambda x{:}A.b : \Pi x{:}A.B} \qquad \langle s_1, s_2, s_3 \rangle \in \mathcal{R}, \; x \notin \mathsf{dom}(\Gamma)$

App-vtyp $\quad \dfrac{\Gamma \vdash_{vtyp} a : \Pi x{:}B.A \qquad \Gamma \vdash_{vtyp} b : B}{\Gamma \vdash_{vtyp} a\, b : A[x := b]}$

Cnv-vtyp $\quad \dfrac{\Gamma \vdash_{vtyp} a : A \qquad \Gamma \vdash_{vtyp} B : s}{\Gamma \vdash_{vtyp} a : B} \qquad A \simeq B$

The predicate $\vdash_{vcxt}$ is the smallest predicate on C satisfying the following rules.

Nil-vcxt $\quad \oslash \vdash_{vcxt}$

Cons-vcxt $\quad \dfrac{\Gamma \vdash_{vcxt} \qquad \Gamma \vdash_{vtyp} A : s}{\Gamma, x{:}A \vdash_{vcxt}} \qquad x \notin \mathsf{dom}(\Gamma)$

Lemma 23 Equivalence of $\vdash$ and $\vdash_{vtyp}$.

$$\Gamma \vdash a : A \quad \Leftrightarrow \quad \Gamma \vdash_{vcxt} \text{ and } \Gamma \vdash_{vtyp} a : A$$

In order to prove this, first observe that weakening is trivial for $\vdash_{vtyp}$. Also it is easy to derive generation properties (compare lemma 6) for sorts and variables.

Lemma 24 Weakening and Generation for $\vdash_{vtyp}$.

i   *If* $\Gamma_1 \vdash_{vtyp} a : A$ *and* $\Gamma_1 \sqsubseteq \Gamma_2$
then $\Gamma_2 \vdash_{vtyp} a : A$

ii   *If* $\Gamma \vdash_{vtyp} x : A$
then $x{:}A_0 \sqsubseteq \Gamma$, *where either* $A = A_0$ *or* $[\Gamma \vdash_{vtyp} A : s$ *and* $A \simeq A_0]$

iii   *If* $\Gamma \vdash_{vtyp} s : A$
then $\langle s, s_0 \rangle \in \mathcal{A}$ *and either* $A = s_0$ *or* $[\Gamma \vdash_{vtyp} A : s_1$ *and* $A \simeq s_0]$

Proof of lemma 23.

$\Rightarrow$ By induction on $\Gamma \vdash a : A$, using 24 for the case of Wk.

$\Leftarrow$ By induction on the lexicographic order, first the sum of the lengths of the derivations of $\Gamma \vdash_{vcxt}$ and $\Gamma \vdash_{vtyp} a : A$, second the length of the derivation of $\Gamma \vdash_{vtyp} a : A$. □

In what follows we consider many different rule systems related to PTS. These systems could be based on the optimized presentation $\vdash_{vtyp}$, or could be optimized by this technique as they come up. In fact, for simplicity, we will start from the basic PTS, $\vdash$, and will not mention this optimization again, leaving its application to the reader.

3 Semi-full Pure Type Systems

A PTS is called *full* iff for all $s_1, s_2 \in \mathcal{S}$ there exists $s_3 \in \mathcal{S}$ with $\langle s_1, s_2, s_3\rangle \in \mathcal{R}$. In full PTS the troublesome third premiss of the Lda-rule can be omitted. Let us focus on the Lda-rule:

$$\text{Lda}\quad \frac{\Gamma \vdash A : s_1 \qquad \Gamma, x{:}A \vdash b : B \qquad \Gamma, x{:}A \vdash B : s_2}{\Gamma \vdash \lambda x{:}A.b : \Pi x{:}A.B} \quad \langle s_1, s_2, s_3\rangle \in \mathcal{R}$$

The purpose of premisses $\Gamma \vdash A : s_1$ and $\Gamma, x{:}A \vdash B : s_2$ is to guarantee that the type $\Pi x{:}A.B$ will be well-formed. But we know from the premiss $\Gamma, x{:}A \vdash b : B$ that $\Gamma \vdash A : s_A$ for some s_A, and by correctness of types we have either $B \in \mathcal{S}$ or $\Gamma, x{:}A \vdash B : s_B$ for some s_B. In this latter case, for full PTS, we conclude there exists s with $\langle s_A, s_B, s\rangle \in \mathcal{R}$, so $\Pi x{:}A.B$ is well formed, and it seems sound to replace the right premiss of the Lda-rule by the requirement that $B \notin \mathcal{A}^\bullet$ or rather, making a positive statement, that $B \in \mathcal{S}$ implies $\langle B, s_B\rangle \in \mathcal{A}$. We can generalize this idea somewhat beyond full PTS.

Definition 25 Semi-Full. A PTS is *semi-full* iff for all $s_1 \in \mathcal{S}$

$$\exists s_2, s_3\ [\langle s_1, s_2, s_3\rangle \in \mathcal{R}] \quad \Rightarrow \quad \forall s_2\ \exists s_3\ [\langle s_1, s_2, s_3\rangle \in \mathcal{R}].$$

While the Pure Calculus of Constructions, $\lambda P\omega$, and various extensions with type universes are full (e.g. ECC [Luo90]), the Edinburgh Logical Framework, λP, is semi-full. In [HHP92] it is shown that λP is decidable by giving an algorithm which computes the normal form of types; a very expensive computation in practice. We will show that the algorithm which is actually used in LEGO is both sound and complete. Notice that $\lambda P\omega$ and λP are the only semi-full systems in the λ-cube.

3.1 A Nearly Syntax Directed system for Semi-full PTS's

To begin, define a correctness relation $\vdash_{sf}$ which, for a semi-full PTS, is equivalent to the ordinary relation $\vdash$.

Definition 26 $\vdash_{sf}$. The relation $\vdash_{sf} \subseteq \mathsf{C} \times \mathsf{T} \times \mathsf{T}$ is the smallest relation satisfying the ordinary PTS-rules, but having instead of the rule Lda the following two rules

$$\text{Lda1-sf}\quad \frac{\Gamma \vdash_{sf} A : s_1 \qquad \Gamma, x{:}A \vdash_{sf} b : B}{\Gamma \vdash_{sf} \lambda x{:}A.b : \Pi x{:}A.B} \quad \begin{array}{r}\langle s_1, s_2, s_3\rangle \in \mathcal{R}\\ B \notin \mathcal{S}\end{array}$$

$$\text{Lda2-sf}\quad \frac{\Gamma \vdash_{sf} A : s_1 \qquad \Gamma, x{:}A \vdash_{sf} b : s_b}{\Gamma \vdash_{sf} \lambda x{:}A.b : \Pi x{:}A.s_b} \quad \begin{array}{r}\langle s_1, s_2, s_3\rangle \in \mathcal{R}\\ \langle s_b, s_4\rangle \in \mathcal{A}\end{array}$$

Lemma 27 Equivalence of $\vdash_{sf}$ and $\vdash$. *For semi-full PTS*

$$\Gamma \vdash a : A \quad \Leftrightarrow \quad \Gamma \vdash_{sf} a : A.$$

Proof. We do both cases.

$\Rightarrow$ Induction on $\Gamma \vdash a : A$. The interesting case is the Lda rule: $\Gamma \vdash \lambda x{:}A.b : \Pi x{:}A.B$ as a consequence of $\Gamma \vdash A : s_1$, $\Gamma, x{:}A \vdash b : B$ and $\Gamma, x{:}A \vdash B : s_2$, for some s_1, s_2, s_3 such that $\langle s_1, s_2, s_3\rangle \in \mathcal{R}$. By induction hypothesis $\Gamma \vdash_{sf} A : s_1$, $\Gamma, x{:}A \vdash_{sf} b : B$ and $\Gamma, x{:}A \vdash_{sf} B : s_2$. If $B \notin \mathcal{S}$ we are done by Lda1-sf. If $B \in \mathcal{S}$ it follows that $\langle B, s_2\rangle \in \mathcal{A}$ by the generation lemma for $\vdash_{sf}$, so use Lda2-sf.

$\Leftarrow$ Induction on the derivation of $\Gamma \vdash_{sf} a : A$. The interesting cases are Lda1-sf and Lda2-sf.

Lda1-sf $\Gamma \vdash_{sf} \lambda x{:}A.b : \Pi x{:}A.B$ because of $\Gamma \vdash_{sf} A : s_1$, $\Gamma, x{:}A \vdash_{sf} b : B$ and $\langle s_1, s_2, s_3\rangle \in \mathcal{R}$, while $B \notin \mathcal{S}$. By induction hypothesis$\Gamma \vdash A : s_1$ and $\Gamma, x{:}A \vdash b : B$. It follows by correctness of types that $B \in \mathcal{S}$ or $\Gamma, x{:}A \vdash B : s_B$. As the first case does not apply, and as our system is semi-full, we have $\langle s_1, s_B, s_0\rangle \in \mathcal{R}$. Hence $\Gamma \vdash \lambda x{:}A.b : \Pi x{:}A.B$ by Lda.

Lda2-sf
$\Gamma \vdash_{sf} \lambda x{:}A.b : \Pi x{:}A.B$ because $\Gamma \vdash_{sf} A : s_1$, $\Gamma, x{:}A \vdash_{sf} b : B$ and $\langle s_1, s_2, s_3\rangle \in \mathcal{R}$, while $B \in \mathcal{S}$ and $\langle B, s_4\rangle \in \mathcal{A}$. By induction hypothesis $\Gamma \vdash A : s_1$ and $\Gamma, x{:}A \vdash b : B$. Also $\oslash \vdash B : s_4$ by Srt, so $\Gamma, x{:}A \vdash B : s_4$ by weakening, and because our system is semi-full we have $\langle s_1, s_4, s_0\rangle \in \mathcal{R}$, hence again $\Gamma \vdash \lambda x{:}A.b : \Pi x{:}A.B$ by Lda. □

Remark on Expansion Postponement. Consider two variants of $\vdash_{sf}$ (see section 1.4 and remark 1.4), replacing Cnv-sf by either of the rules

Red-sf-r $\quad \dfrac{\Gamma \vdash_{sf-r} a : A}{\Gamma \vdash_{sf-r} a : B} \quad A \twoheadrightarrow B \qquad$ or

Red-sf-R $\quad \dfrac{\Gamma \vdash_{sf-R} a : A \quad \Gamma \vdash_{sf-R} B : s}{\Gamma \vdash_{sf-R} a : B} \quad A \twoheadrightarrow B$

We have, up to conversion, the following diagram (for semi-full PTS):

$$\begin{array}{ccccc} \vdash_R & \subseteq & \vdash_r & \subseteq & \vdash \\ \| & & \mid\!\cap & & \| \\ \vdash_{sf-R} & \subseteq & \vdash_{sf-r} & = & \vdash_{sf} \end{array}$$

The rightmost vertical equality is lemma 27, and, since $\vdash_R$ has correctness of types, the same proof gives the leftmost vertical equality. However $\vdash_r$ is not known to have correctness of types, so the middle of the three vertical relations remains an inequality. The rightmost equality on the bottom row is by straightforward induction: this is what we gain by removing the right premiss of the lambda rule. As you see, we cannot yet conclude that every $\vdash$-derivation can be mimicked up to conversion by a $\vdash_r$-derivation, or by a $\vdash_R$-derivation, even when restricted to semi-full PTS.

As Lda-sf does not have the troublesome third premiss, it is now straightforward to define a nearly syntax directed system, which is sound and complete for $\vdash_{sf}$.

Definition 28 $\vdash_{sfnsd}$**.** The relation $\vdash_{sfnsd} \subseteq \mathsf{C} \times \mathsf{T} \times \mathsf{T}$ is the smallest relation satisfying the following rules.

Srt-sfnsd $\quad \oslash \vdash_{sfnsd} s_1 : s_2 \qquad \langle s_1, s_2 \rangle \in \mathcal{A}$

Var-sfnsd $$\frac{\Gamma \vdash_{sfnsd} A :\twoheadrightarrow s}{\Gamma, x{:}A \vdash_{sfnsd} x : A}$$

Wk-sfnsd $$\frac{\Gamma \vdash_{sfnsd} b : B \qquad \Gamma \vdash_{sfnsd} A :\twoheadrightarrow s}{\Gamma, x{:}A \vdash_{sfnsd} b : B} \qquad b \in \mathcal{S} \cup \mathcal{V}$$

Pi-sfnsd $$\frac{\Gamma \vdash_{sfnsd} A :\twoheadrightarrow s_1 \qquad \Gamma, x{:}A \vdash_{sfnsd} B :\twoheadrightarrow s_2}{\Gamma \vdash_{sfnsd} \Pi x{:}A.B : s_3} \qquad \langle s_1, s_2, s_3 \rangle \in \mathcal{R}$$

Lda1-sfnsd $$\frac{\Gamma \vdash_{sfnsd} A :\twoheadrightarrow s_1 \qquad \Gamma, x{:}A \vdash_{sfnsd} b : B}{\Gamma \vdash_{sfnsd} \lambda x{:}A.b : \Pi x{:}A.B} \qquad \begin{array}{r}\langle s_1, s_2, s_3 \rangle \in \mathcal{R}\\ B \notin \mathcal{S}\end{array}$$

Lda2-sfnsd $$\frac{\Gamma \vdash_{sfnsd} A :\twoheadrightarrow s_1 \qquad \Gamma, x{:}A \vdash_{sfnsd} b : s_b}{\Gamma \vdash_{sfnsd} \lambda x{:}A.b : \Pi x{:}A.s_b} \qquad \begin{array}{r}\langle s_1, s_2, s_3 \rangle \in \mathcal{R}\\ \langle s_b, s_4 \rangle \in \mathcal{A}\end{array}$$

App-sfnsd $$\frac{\Gamma \vdash_{sfnsd} a :\twoheadrightarrow^{wh} \Pi x{:}B_0.A \qquad \Gamma \vdash_{sfnsd} b : B_1}{\Gamma \vdash_{sfnsd} a\, b : A[x := b]} \qquad B_0 \simeq B_1$$

Lemma 29 Equivalence of $\vdash_{sf}$ ***and*** $\vdash_{sfnsd}$***.*** *For semi-full PTS*

i *If* $\Gamma \vdash_{sfnsd} a : A$ *then* $\Gamma \vdash_{sf} a : A$
ii *If* $\Gamma \vdash_{sf} a : A$ *then* $\exists A_0\ [A \simeq A_0$ *and* $\Gamma \vdash_{sfnsd} a : A_0]$

Proof. We prove both parts.

i Induction on $\Gamma \vdash_{sfnsd} a : A$, using the fact that closure holds for $\vdash_{sf}$ by equivalence (lemma 27) and closure for $\vdash$ (lemma 10). We treat the case of App-sfnsd: $\Gamma \vdash_{sfnsd} a\, b : A[x := b]$ from $\Gamma \vdash_{sfnsd} a : A_0$, $A_0 \twoheadrightarrow^{wh} \Pi x{:}B_0.A$, $\Gamma \vdash_{sfnsd} b : B_1$ and $B_0 \simeq B_1$. By induction $\Gamma \vdash_{sf} a : A_0$ and $\Gamma \vdash_{sf} b : B_0$. Take a common reduct B of B_0 and B_1. It follows by closure for $\vdash_{sf}$ that $\Gamma \vdash_{sf} a : \Pi x{:}B.A$ and $\Gamma \vdash_{sf} b : B$, and therefore $\Gamma \vdash_{sfnsd} a\, b : A[x := b]$ by App-sf.

ii Induction on $\Gamma \vdash_{sf} a : A$, using correctness of types for $\vdash_{sf}$, which is again a consequence of equivalence (lemma 27) and correctness of types for $\vdash$ (lemma 9). Again we do only one case, Lda1-sf: $\Gamma \vdash_{sf} \lambda x{:}A.b : \Pi x{:}A.B$ from $\Gamma \vdash_{sf} A : s_1$, $\Gamma, x{:}A \vdash_{sf} b : B$ and $\langle s_1, s_2, s_3 \rangle \in \mathcal{R}$, while $B \notin \mathcal{S}$. By induction hypothesis $\Gamma \vdash_{sfnsd} A : A_0 \simeq s_1$ and $\Gamma, x{:}A \vdash_{sfnsd} b : B_0 \simeq B$. It remains to show that $B_0 \in \mathcal{S}$ implies $\langle B_0, s \rangle \in \mathcal{A}$ for some s. So suppose $B_0 \in \mathcal{S}$, hence $B \twoheadrightarrow B_0$. By correctness of types $\Gamma \vdash_{sf} B : s_B$, hence $\Gamma \vdash_{sf} B_0 : s_B$ by closure, so by generation $\langle B_0, s_B \rangle \in \mathcal{A}$ and we are done. □

3.2 A Syntax Directed system for Semi-full PTS's

The only failure of syntax-directedness in the rules of system $\vdash_{sfnsd}$ is due to possible non-functionality of the PTS. For example, if $\langle s_1, s_2 \rangle \in \mathcal{A}$ and $\langle s_1, s_2' \rangle \in \mathcal{A}$, the rule Srt-sfnsd can be used to derive the judgements $\oslash \vdash_{sfnsd} s_1 : s_2$ and $\oslash \vdash_{sfnsd} s_1 : s_2'$.

Similarly Pi-sfnsd, Lda1-sfnsd and Lda2-sfnsd may be non-syntax-directed due to non-functionality of $\mathcal{R}$. For functional PTS $\vdash_{sfnsd}$ is already syntax directed, and may be used directly for typechecking.

For non-functional semi-full PTS we will remove this non-determinism by a method suggested in [Hue87, HP91, Pol92], and for this purpose we first introduce some technical machinery.

Schematic Terms Introduce a new set Σ, disjoint from $\mathcal{V}$ and $\mathcal{S}$. Elements of Σ will be called *sort variables* and will be denoted by $\sigma, \sigma_0, \sigma_1, \ldots$. The symbols $\alpha, \beta, \gamma, \ldots$ will range over $\Sigma \cup \mathcal{S}$.

Definition 30 Schematic Terms. The set, T^Σ, of *schematic terms* is the smallest set satisfying:

$\Sigma \subseteq \mathsf{T}^\Sigma$,
If $X \in \mathsf{T}^\Sigma$ and $b \in \mathsf{T}$ then $X\,b \in \mathsf{T}^\Sigma$,
If $A \in \mathsf{T}$, $X \in \mathsf{T}^\Sigma$ and $x \in \mathcal{V}$ then $\Pi x{:}A.X \in \mathsf{T}^\Sigma$.

We use X, Y, Z to range over $\mathsf{T} \cup \mathsf{T}^\Sigma$.

In this section we will only need schematic terms of the form $\Pi x_1{:}A_1.\ldots\Pi x_n{:}A_n.\sigma$, but in section 7 the more general notion will be used.

If $X \in \mathsf{T} \cup \mathsf{T}^\Sigma$ we denote by $\mathsf{SV}(X)$ the sort variables of X. Substitution and β- and π-reduction are easily extended to T^Σ.

A *sort assignment* is a partial function from Σ to $\mathcal{S}$. If $X \in \mathsf{T}^\Sigma$ and $\mathsf{SV}(X) \in \mathsf{dom}(\phi)$ then $\phi X \in \mathsf{T}$ is defined in the obvious way. Substitution of pseudoterms and reduction are conserved by assignments, i.e. $X \twoheadrightarrow Y$ iff $\phi X \twoheadrightarrow \phi Y$ for any assignment ϕ.

A *constraint* is a finite set of formulas of the form $\langle\alpha,\beta\rangle \in \mathcal{A}$, $\langle\alpha,\beta,\gamma\rangle \in \mathcal{R}$ and $\alpha = \beta$. The set of all constraints is denoted by Cnstr. If $\mathcal{C}$ is a constraint then $\mathsf{SV}(\mathcal{C})$ denotes the set of sort variables occurring in $\mathcal{C}$. A sort assignment ϕ is said to *satisfy* a constraint $\mathcal{C}$, written $\phi \models \mathcal{C}$, iff $\mathsf{SV}(\mathcal{C}) \subseteq \mathsf{dom}(\phi)$ and each of the propositions in $\phi\mathcal{C}$ is true. A constraint, $\mathcal{C}$, is said to be *consistent* or *satisfiable*, written $\mathcal{C}\mathsf{con}$, if there is a sort assignment satisfying it.

We say that a PTS has *decidable constraints* if for every constraint, $\mathcal{C}$, it is decidable whether or not $\mathcal{C}$ is satisfiable. If $\mathcal{S}$ is finite then this condition is clearly fulfilled, but PTS with $\mathcal{S}$ infinite may also have this property, as the following example shows.

Example 2. Consider the PTS with infinitely many stratified universes

$$\mathcal{S} = \{\, Type_i \mid i \in \mathsf{N} \,\}$$
$$\mathcal{A} = \{\, \langle Type_i, Type_j\rangle \mid i < j \,\}$$
$$\mathcal{R} = \{\, \langle Type_i, Type_j, Type_k\rangle \mid i \leq k, j \leq k \,\}$$

The constraints of this theory only contain formulas of the form $\alpha < \beta$ and $\alpha \leq \beta$ ($\alpha = \beta$ being expressible by the pair $\alpha \leq \beta$ and $\beta \leq \alpha$). All such sets are decidable (in time polynomial in both the number of constraints and the number of variables and constants) by checking acyclicity of a directed graph whose nodes are variables and constants, and whose edges are the relations $<$ and $\leq$. This result is due to Chan [Cha77], and its application for solving constraints of typechecking was suggested by Huet [Hue87] and detailed in [HP91]. □

Our purpose will be to compute for any pair Γ, a a term $X \in \mathsf{T} \cup \mathsf{T}^{\Sigma}$ and a constraint $\mathcal{C}$, (we denote this by $\Gamma \vdash_{sfsd} a : X \,|\, \mathcal{C}$), such that

i If $\Gamma \vdash_{sfsd} a : X \,|\, \mathcal{C}$ and $\phi \models \mathcal{C}$ then $\Gamma \vdash a : \phi X$
ii If $\Gamma \vdash a : A$ then $\Gamma \vdash_{sfsd} a : X \,|\, \mathcal{C}$ and $\exists \phi [\phi \models \mathcal{C}$ and $\phi X \simeq A]$

The tools developed so far will enable us to make the rules Srt-sfnsd and Pi-sfnsd syntax directed. Let us turn our attention now to the rule App-sfnsd.

$$\text{App-sfnsd} \quad \frac{\Gamma \vdash_{sfnsd} a :\twoheadrightarrow^{wh} \Pi x{:}B_0.A \qquad \Gamma \vdash_{sfnsd} b : B_1}{\Gamma \vdash_{sfnsd} a\, b : A[x := b]} \quad B_0 \simeq B_1$$

We have already made the reduction of the type of a to $\Pi x{:}B_0.A$ deterministic by requiring weak head-reduction; now consider the convertibility of B_0 and B_1. B_1 could be a schematic term, so we must define the constraints under which two terms X, $Y \in \mathsf{T} \cup \mathsf{T}^{\Sigma}$ are convertible, in order to give the application rule of $\vdash_{sfsd}$.

Definition 31 Schematic Equality and Schematic Conversion. *schematic equality* is the smallest relation $\_ =_{\Sigma} \_ | \_ \subseteq (\mathsf{T} \cup \mathsf{T}^{\Sigma}) \times (\mathsf{T} \cup \mathsf{T}^{\Sigma}) \times \mathsf{Cnstr}$, satisfying

- $\alpha =_{\Sigma} \beta \,|\, \{\alpha = \beta\}$.
- If $X =_{\Sigma} Y \,|\, \mathcal{C}$ then $\Pi x{:}A.X =_{\Sigma} \Pi x{:}A.Y \,|\, \mathcal{C}$ and $X\,a =_{\Sigma} Y\,a \,|\, \mathcal{C}$.
- If $X = Y$ then $X =_{\Sigma} Y \,|\, \emptyset$.

*schematic β-conversion*is the relation $\_ \simeq \_ | \_ \subseteq (\mathsf{T} \cup \mathsf{T}^{\Sigma}) \times (\mathsf{T} \cup \mathsf{T}^{\Sigma}) \times \mathsf{Cnstr}$ defined by

$$X \simeq Y \,|\, \mathcal{C} \;\triangleq\; \exists X_0, Y_0\, [X \twoheadrightarrow X_0, Y \twoheadrightarrow Y_0 \text{ and } X_0 =_{\Sigma} Y_0 \,|\, \mathcal{C}]$$

Clearly for normalizing X and Y the relation $\exists \mathcal{C}\; [X \simeq Y \,|\, \mathcal{C}]$ is decidable, and for arbitrary X and Y this relation is semi-decidable.

Lemma 32 Properties of Schematic Conversion.

If $X \simeq Y \,|\, \mathcal{C}$ *and* $\phi \models \mathcal{C}$ *then* $\phi X \simeq \phi Y$
If $\phi X \simeq \phi Y$ *then* $\exists \mathcal{C}\; [X \simeq Y \,|\, \mathcal{C}$ *and* $\phi \models \mathcal{C}]$

The syntax directed system

Notation 33. We extend notation 12 and write

$$\Gamma \vdash_{sfsd} a :\twoheadrightarrow X \,|\, \mathcal{C} \quad \text{for} \quad \Gamma \vdash_{sfsd} a : X_0 \,|\, \mathcal{C} \text{ and } X_0 \twoheadrightarrow X.$$

Definition 34 $\vdash_{sfsd}$. The relation $\vdash_{sfsd} \subseteq \mathsf{C} \times \mathsf{T} \times (\mathsf{T} \cup \mathsf{T}^{\Sigma}) \times \mathsf{Cnstr}$ is the smallest relation satisfying the following rules.

Srt-sfsd $\quad \emptyset \vdash_{sfsd} s : \sigma \mid \{\langle s, \sigma\rangle \in \mathcal{A}\}$

Var-sfsd
$$\frac{\Gamma \vdash_{sfsd} A :\twoheadrightarrow \alpha \mid \mathcal{C}}{\Gamma, x{:}A \vdash_{sfsd} x : A \mid \mathcal{C}}$$

Wk-sfsd
$$\frac{\Gamma \vdash_{sfsd} b : X \mid \mathcal{C} \qquad \Gamma \vdash_{sfsd} A :\twoheadrightarrow \alpha \mid \mathcal{D}}{\Gamma, x{:}A \vdash_{sfsd} b : X \mid \mathcal{C} \cup \mathcal{D}} \qquad b \in \mathcal{S} \cup \mathcal{V}$$

Pi-sfsd
$$\frac{\Gamma \vdash_{sfsd} A :\twoheadrightarrow \alpha \mid \mathcal{C} \qquad \Gamma, x{:}A \vdash_{sfsd} B :\twoheadrightarrow \beta \mid \mathcal{D}}{\Gamma \vdash_{sfsd} \Pi x{:}A.B : \sigma \mid \mathcal{C} \cup \mathcal{D} \cup \{\langle \alpha, \beta, \sigma\rangle \in \mathcal{R}\}}$$

Lda1-sfsd
$$\frac{\Gamma \vdash_{sfsd} A :\twoheadrightarrow \alpha \mid \mathcal{C} \qquad \Gamma, x{:}A \vdash_{sfsd} b : X \mid \mathcal{D}}{\Gamma \vdash_{sfsd} \lambda x{:}A.b : \Pi x{:}A.X \mid \mathcal{C} \cup \mathcal{D} \cup \{\langle \alpha, \sigma_2, \sigma_3\rangle \in \mathcal{R}\}} \qquad X \notin \Sigma \cup \mathcal{S}$$

Lda2-sfsd
$$\frac{\Gamma \vdash_{sfsd} A :\twoheadrightarrow \alpha \mid \mathcal{C} \qquad \Gamma, x{:}A \vdash_{sfsd} b : \beta \mid \mathcal{D}}{\Gamma \vdash_{sfsd} \lambda x{:}A.b : \Pi x{:}A.\beta \mid \mathcal{C} \cup \mathcal{D} \cup \{\langle \alpha, \sigma_2, \sigma_3\rangle \in \mathcal{R}\} \cup \{\langle \beta, \sigma_4\rangle \in \mathcal{A}\}}$$

App-sfsd
$$\frac{\Gamma \vdash_{sfsd} a :\twoheadrightarrow^{wh} \Pi x{:}B.X \mid \mathcal{C} \qquad \Gamma \vdash_{sfsd} b : Y \mid \mathcal{D}}{\Gamma \vdash_{sfsd} a\, b : X[x := b] \mid \mathcal{C} \cup \mathcal{D} \cup \mathcal{E}} \qquad Y \simeq B \mid \mathcal{E}$$

In the definition we assume all the sort variables which are introduced to be fresh. For example in rule Pi-sfsd we assume σ to be a fresh variable, and also $\mathsf{SV}(\mathcal{C})$ and $\mathsf{SV}(\mathcal{D})$ should be disjoint. Similarly in rule App-sfsd $\mathsf{SV}(\mathcal{C})$ and $\mathsf{SV}(\mathcal{D})$ will be disjoint, but $\mathsf{SV}(\mathcal{D})$ and $\mathsf{SV}(\mathcal{E})$ might intersect.

Note that for any Γ and a there is (up to the names of sort variables) at most one derivable judgement $\Gamma \vdash_{sfsd} a : X \mid \mathcal{C}$, and at most one derivation of such a judgement. Further, derivations in $\vdash_{sfsd}$ depend on the language of the PTS, but are independent of the axioms, $\mathcal{A}$, and Π-rules, $\mathcal{R}$, of the PTS; it is in the satisfaction of constraints that a particular PTS is observed.

***Lemma 35 Equivalence of** $\vdash_{sfnsd}$ **and** $\vdash_{sfsd}$.*

i *If* $\Gamma \vdash_{sfsd} a : X \mid \mathcal{C}$ *and* $\phi \models \mathcal{C}$ *then* $\Gamma \vdash_{sfnsd} a : \phi X$
ii *If* $\Gamma \vdash_{sfnsd} a : A$ *then* $\exists X, \mathcal{C}, \phi\ [\phi \models \mathcal{C},\ A = \phi X$ *and* $\Gamma \vdash_{sfsd} a : X \mid \mathcal{C}]$

Proof.

i Induction on $\Gamma \vdash_{sfsd} a : X \mid \mathcal{C}$. We treat App-sfsd:

App-sfsd
$$\frac{\Gamma \vdash_{sfsd} a : X' \mid \mathcal{C} \quad X' \twoheadrightarrow^{wh} \Pi x{:}B.X \quad \Gamma \vdash_{sfsd} b : Y \mid \mathcal{D}}{\Gamma \vdash_{sfsd} a\, b : X[x := b] \mid \mathcal{C} \cup \mathcal{D} \cup \mathcal{E}} \qquad Y \simeq B \mid \mathcal{E}$$

Now suppose $\phi \models \mathcal{C} \cup \mathcal{D} \cup \mathcal{E}$. By induction

$$\Gamma \vdash_{sfnsd} a : \phi X' \twoheadrightarrow^{wh} \Pi x{:}B.\phi X \quad \text{and} \quad \Gamma \vdash_{sfnsd} b : \phi Y.$$

By lemma 32 $\phi Y \simeq B$, so $\Gamma \vdash_{sfnsd} a\, b : (\phi X)[x := b] = \phi\,(X[x := b])$.

ii Induction on $\Gamma \vdash_{sfnsd} a : A$. We consider Lda1-sfnsd:

$$\frac{\Gamma \vdash_{sfnsd} A : C \twoheadrightarrow s_1 \qquad \Gamma, x{:}A \vdash_{sfnsd} b : B}{\Gamma \vdash_{sfnsd} \lambda x{:}A.b : \Pi x{:}A.B} \quad \begin{array}{r}\langle s_1, s_2, s_3\rangle \in \mathcal{R}\\ B \notin \mathcal{S}\end{array}$$

By induction

$$\begin{array}{l}\exists X, \mathcal{C}, \phi_{\mathcal{C}}, \alpha\ [\phi_{\mathcal{C}} \models \mathcal{C},\ C = \phi_{\mathcal{C}} X \text{ and } \Gamma \vdash_{sfsd} A : X \,|\, \mathcal{C} \text{ where } X \twoheadrightarrow \alpha]\\ \exists Y, \mathcal{D}, \phi_{\mathcal{D}}\ [\phi_{\mathcal{D}} \models \mathcal{D},\ B = \phi_{\mathcal{D}} Y \text{ and } \Gamma \vdash_{sfsd} b : Y \,|\, \mathcal{D}]\end{array}$$

where we may assume $\mathsf{SV}(\mathcal{C})$ disjoint from $\mathsf{SV}(\mathcal{D})$ (change the names of sort variables if necessary). Since $\phi_{\mathcal{D}} Y = B \notin \mathcal{S}$, $Y \notin \Sigma \cup \mathcal{S}$, and by Lda1-sfsd

$$\Gamma \vdash_{sfsd} \lambda x{:}A.b : \Pi x{:}A.Y \,|\, \mathcal{C} \cup \mathcal{D} \cup \{\langle \alpha, \sigma_2, \sigma_3\rangle \in \mathcal{R}\}$$

We must have $\phi_{\mathcal{C}} \alpha = s_1$, so take

$$\phi = \phi_{\mathcal{C}} \cup \phi_{\mathcal{D}} \cup \{\sigma_2 \mapsto s_2,\ \sigma_3 \mapsto s_3\}$$

and $\phi \models \mathcal{C} \cup \mathcal{D} \cup \{\langle \alpha, \sigma_2, \sigma_3\rangle \in \mathcal{R}\}$ as required. □

An algorithm for typechecking normalizing semi-full PTS with decidable constraints We cannot use $\vdash_{sfsd}$ to decide $\vdash$ because $\vdash_{sfsd}$ does not incrementally check consistency of constraints, so we may try to normalize a schematic term that has no well-typed instance. We now fix this deficiency.

Definition 36 $\vdash_{sfa}$. The relation $\vdash_{sfa} \subseteq \mathsf{C} \times \mathsf{T} \times (\mathsf{T} \cup \mathsf{T}^{\Sigma}) \times \mathsf{Cnstr}$ is the smallest relation satisfying the following rules.

Srt-sfa $\quad \oslash \vdash_{sfa} s : \sigma \,|\, \{\langle s, \sigma\rangle \in \mathcal{A}\}$

Var-sfa $$\frac{\Gamma \vdash_{sfa} A : X \,|\, \mathcal{C} \quad \mathcal{C}\mathsf{con} \quad X \twoheadrightarrow \alpha}{\Gamma, x{:}A \vdash_{sfa} x : A \,|\, \mathcal{C}}$$

Wk-sfa $$\frac{\Gamma \vdash_{sfa} b : X \,|\, \mathcal{C} \quad \Gamma \vdash_{sfa} A : Y \,|\, \mathcal{D} \quad \mathcal{D}\mathsf{con} \quad Y \twoheadrightarrow \alpha}{\Gamma, x{:}A \vdash_{sfa} b : X \,|\, \mathcal{C} \cup \mathcal{D}} \quad b \in \mathcal{S} \cup \mathcal{V}$$

Pi-sfa $$\frac{\Gamma \vdash_{sfa} A : X \,|\, \mathcal{C} \quad \mathcal{C}\mathsf{con} \quad X \twoheadrightarrow \alpha \quad \Gamma, x{:}A \vdash_{sfa} B : Y \,|\, \mathcal{D} \quad \mathcal{D}\mathsf{con} \quad Y \twoheadrightarrow \beta}{\Gamma \vdash_{sfa} \Pi x{:}A.B : \sigma \,|\, \mathcal{C} \cup \mathcal{D} \cup \{\langle \alpha, \beta, \sigma\rangle \in \mathcal{R}\}}$$

Lda1-sfa $$\frac{\Gamma \vdash_{sfa} A : Y \,|\, \mathcal{C} \quad \mathcal{C}\mathsf{con} \quad Y \twoheadrightarrow \alpha \quad \Gamma, x{:}A \vdash_{sfa} b : X \,|\, \mathcal{D}}{\Gamma \vdash_{sfa} \lambda x{:}A.b : \Pi x{:}A.X \,|\, \mathcal{C} \cup \mathcal{D} \cup \{\langle \alpha, \sigma_2, \sigma_3\rangle \in \mathcal{R}\}} \quad X \notin \Sigma \cup \mathcal{S}$$

Lda2-sfa $$\frac{\Gamma \vdash_{sfa} A : Y \,|\, \mathcal{C} \quad \mathcal{C}\mathsf{con} \quad Y \twoheadrightarrow \alpha \quad \Gamma, x{:}A \vdash_{sfa} b : \beta \,|\, \mathcal{D}}{\Gamma \vdash_{sfa} \lambda x{:}A.b : \Pi x{:}A.\beta \,|\, \mathcal{C} \cup \mathcal{D} \cup \{\langle \alpha, \sigma_2, \sigma_3\rangle \in \mathcal{R}\} \cup \{\langle \beta, \sigma_4\rangle \in \mathcal{A}\}}$$

App-sfa $$\frac{\Gamma \vdash_{sfa} a : Z \,|\, \mathcal{C} \quad \mathcal{C}\mathsf{con} \quad Z \twoheadrightarrow^{wh} \Pi x{:}B.X \quad \Gamma \vdash_{sfa} b : Y \,|\, \mathcal{D} \quad \mathcal{D}\mathsf{con} \quad Y \simeq B \,|\, \mathcal{E}}{\Gamma \vdash_{sfa} a\, b : X[x := b] \,|\, \mathcal{C} \cup \mathcal{D} \cup \mathcal{E}}$$

4 The typing relations $\vdash_o$ and $\vdash_{tp}$

We now begin a deeper study of the general PTS. In section 1.3 we noticed that the third premiss of the Lda rule is a serious obstacle to a syntax directed characterization of $\vdash$. In section 3 we showed that for a special class of PTS that premiss could be replaced by innocuous side conditions, and proceeded to characterize that class by a syntax directed presentation, as advertised. Now we show that in general the troublesome third premiss asks for too much checking; that in the presence of the first two premisses of the Lda rule we can replace the third premiss by a more liberal judgement. For this purpose we introduce two liberal typing judgements, $\vdash_o$ and $\vdash_{tp}$, which are closely related to the typing operators in [vBJ93]. We remind the reader here of the extensions to the reduction and conversion relations arising from our π-contractions

$$(\Pi x{:}A.B)\,a \to_\pi B[x := a].$$

4.1 Well-formed Contexts

We start with a very weak notion of well-formedness for contexts.

Definition 37. $\vdash_{wfcxt}$ is the smallest predicate on C satisfying the following rules.

Empty-wfcxt $\quad \oslash \vdash_{wfcxt}$

Extend-wfcxt $\quad \dfrac{\Gamma \vdash_{wfcxt} \qquad \mathsf{FV}(A) \subseteq \mathsf{dom}(\Gamma)}{\Gamma, x{:}A \vdash_{wfcxt}}$

Recall convention 2. It is easily seen that $\Gamma \vdash a : A$ implies $\Gamma \vdash_{wfcxt}$.

4.2 A Nearly Syntax Directed Relation, $\vdash_o$

We define a relation, $\vdash_o$, closely connected with $\vdash$, which is nearly syntax directed. We will prove (lemma 39) that $\vdash_o$ is complete for $\vdash$. $\vdash_o$ is too liberal to be sound for $\vdash$, but if $\Gamma \vdash a : A$ for some A, and if also $\Gamma \vdash_o a : B$, then B is, in a sense, convertible to a type for a. This is expressed in our Key Theorem 46.

Definition 38 $\vdash_o$. The relation $\vdash_o \subseteq \mathsf{C} \times \mathsf{T} \times \mathsf{T}$ is the smallest relation satisfying the following rules.

Srt-o $\quad \dfrac{\Gamma \vdash_{wfcxt}}{\Gamma \vdash_o s_1 : s_2} \qquad \langle s_1, s_2\rangle \in \mathcal{A}$

Var-o $\quad \dfrac{\Gamma \vdash_{wfcxt}}{\Gamma \vdash_o x : A} \qquad x{:}A \in \Gamma$

Pi-o $\quad \dfrac{\Gamma \vdash_o A :\twoheadrightarrow_\pi s_1 \qquad \Gamma, x{:}A \vdash_o B :\twoheadrightarrow_\pi s_2}{\Gamma \vdash_o \Pi x{:}A.B : s_3} \qquad \langle s_1, s_2, s_3\rangle \in \mathcal{R}$

Lda-o $\quad \dfrac{\Gamma, x{:}A \vdash_o b : B}{\Gamma \vdash_o \lambda x{:}A.b : \Pi x{:}A.B}$

App-o $\quad \dfrac{\Gamma \vdash_o a : A \twoheadrightarrow_\pi \Pi x{:}B.A_0 \qquad \Gamma \vdash_o b :\twoheadrightarrow_\pi B}{\Gamma \vdash_o a\,b : A\,b}$

Notice that the rule App-o may cause Π-application, and therefore create π-redexes. Also, the rules for $\vdash_o$ are nearly syntax directed, and consequently it is easy to see that $\vdash_o$ has a strong generation lemma (compare with 6) which we will freely use without further comment.

Lemma 39 Completeness of $\vdash_o$.

If $\Gamma \vdash a : A$
then $\exists A_0\ [A_0 \simeq_\pi A$ *and* $\Gamma \vdash_o a : A_0]$.

Proof. By induction on $\Gamma \vdash a : A$. We consider App:

$$\Gamma \vdash a\,b : A[x := b] \quad \text{because} \quad \Gamma \vdash a : \Pi x{:}B.A \text{ and } \Gamma \vdash b : B.$$

By induction hypothesis we have $\Gamma \vdash_o a : A_0 \simeq_\pi \Pi x{:}B.A$ and $\Gamma \vdash_o b : B_0 \simeq_\pi B$. Let A_1, B_1 be such that $A_0 \twoheadrightarrow_\pi \Pi x{:}B_1.A_1$, and $B_0 \twoheadrightarrow_\pi B_1$. Then

$$\Gamma \vdash_o a\,b : A_0\,b \quad \text{where} \quad A_0\,b \simeq_\pi (\Pi x{:}B.A)\,b \rightarrow_\pi A[x := b]$$

as required. □

Now we derive properties of $\vdash_o$ leading to a weak closure (subject reduction) theorem.

Lemma 40 Free variables for $\vdash_o$.

If $\Gamma \vdash_o a : A$
then $\Gamma \vdash_{wfcxt}$ *and* $\mathsf{FV}(a) \cup \mathsf{FV}(A) \subseteq \mathsf{dom}(\Gamma)$

Lemma 41 Weakening for $\vdash_o$.

If $\Gamma_1 \vdash_o a : A$, $\Gamma_1 \sqsubseteq \Gamma_2$ *and* $\Gamma_2 \vdash_{wfcxt}$
then $\Gamma_2 \vdash_o a : A$

Lemma 42 Approximate substitution for $\vdash_o$.

If $\Gamma_1, x{:}A, \Gamma_2 \vdash_o b : B$, $\Gamma_1 \vdash_o a : A_0$ *and* $A_0 \simeq_\pi A$
then $\Gamma_1, \Gamma_2[x := a] \vdash_o b[x := a] : B_0[x := a]$ *where* $B_0 \simeq_\pi B$

Proof. Use induction on $\Gamma_1, x{:}A, \Gamma_2 \vdash_o b : B$, noticing that, since $\mathsf{FV}(a) \subseteq \mathsf{dom}(\Gamma_1)$, we have $\Gamma_1, \Gamma_2[x := a] \vdash_{wfcxt}$. We consider some cases.

Var-o $\Gamma_1, x{:}A, \Gamma_2 \vdash_o y : B$ because $y{:}B \in \Gamma_1, x{:}A, \Gamma_2$. We discern between cases $y = x$ and $y \neq x$.

For $y = x$, $\Gamma_1, \Gamma_2[x := a] \vdash_o a : A_0$ by weakening. Also $a = y[x := a]$, and $A_0 = A_0[x := a]$ because $x \notin \mathsf{FV}(A_0)$ by the free variables lemma.

For $y \neq x$ we have either $y{:}B \in \Gamma_1$ or $y{:}B \in \Gamma_2$. In the first case we use the well-formedness of contexts to show that $x \notin \mathsf{FV}(B)$, in the second case we are done immediately.

App-o. $\Gamma_1, x{:}A, \Gamma_2 \vdash_o c\,d : C\,d$ because

$$\Gamma_1, x{:}A, \Gamma_2 \vdash_o c : C \twoheadrightarrow_\pi \Pi y{:}D_0.C_0 \quad \text{and} \quad \Gamma_1, x{:}A, \Gamma_2 \vdash_o d : D \twoheadrightarrow_\pi D_0.$$

By induction hypothesis

$$\Gamma_1, \Gamma_2[x := a] \vdash_o c[x := a] : C_1[x := a] \quad \text{and} \quad \Gamma_1, \Gamma_2[x := a] \vdash_o d[x := a] : D_1[x := a]$$

where $C_1 \simeq_\pi C$ and $D_1 \simeq_\pi D$. Let C_2, D_2 be such that $C_1 \twoheadrightarrow_\pi \Pi y{:}D_2.C_2$ and $D_1 \twoheadrightarrow_\pi D_2$. Then

$$C_1[x := a] \twoheadrightarrow_\pi \Pi y{:}D_2[x := a].C_2[x := a] \quad \text{and} \quad D_1[x := a] \twoheadrightarrow_\pi D_2[x := a].$$

It follows that $\Gamma_1, \Gamma_2[x := a] \vdash_o (c\,d)[x := a] : (C_1\,d)[x := a]$, where $C_1\,d \simeq_\pi C\,d$. □

Lemma 43 Reduction of contexts.

If $\Gamma_1 \vdash_o a : A_1$ *and* $\Gamma_1 \twoheadrightarrow \Gamma_2$
then $\Gamma_2 \vdash_o a : A_2$ *where* $A_1 \twoheadrightarrow A_2$

Proof. Use induction on $\Gamma_1 \vdash_o a : A_1$, noticing that that since $\Gamma_1 \vdash_{wfcxt}$ we have $\Gamma_2 \vdash_{wfcxt}$. Consider the rule App-o: $\Gamma_1 \vdash_o a\,b : A\,b$ as a consequence of $\Gamma_1 \vdash_o a : A \twoheadrightarrow_\pi \Pi x{:}B_0.A_0$ and $\Gamma_1 \vdash_o b : B \twoheadrightarrow_\pi B_0$. By the induction hypothesis we have $\Gamma_2 \vdash_o a : A_1$ and $\Gamma_2 \vdash_o b : B_1$, where $A \twoheadrightarrow A_1$ and $B \twoheadrightarrow B_1$. Let A_2, B_2 be such that $A_1 \twoheadrightarrow_\pi \Pi x{:}B_2.A_2$ and $B_1 \twoheadrightarrow_\pi B_2$. Then $\Gamma_2 \vdash_o a\,b : A_0\,b$ where $A\,b \twoheadrightarrow A_1\,b$. □

Lemma 44 One step Closure.

If $\Gamma \vdash_o a : A$ *and* $a \rightarrow b$
then $\Gamma \vdash_o b : B$ *where* $B \simeq_\pi A$

Proof. Induction on $\Gamma \vdash_o a : A$. The interesting case is the rule App-o, where we have $\Gamma \vdash_o a\,b : A\,b$ as a consequence of $\Gamma \vdash_o a : A \twoheadrightarrow_\pi \Pi x{:}B_0.A_0$ and $\Gamma \vdash_o b : B \twoheadrightarrow_\pi B_0$. We discern cases.

$a = \lambda x{:}B_1.a_0$ and $a\,b \rightarrow a_0[x := b]$. As $\Gamma \vdash_o a : A$ we have $\Gamma, x{:}B_1 \vdash_o a_0 : A_1$ and $A = \Pi x{:}B_1.A_1$. ($\vdash_o$ has a stronger generation lemma than $\vdash$.) Hence $B \simeq_\pi B_1$, and by the approximate substitution lemma (42), $\Gamma \vdash_o a_0[x := b] : A_2[x := b]$ where $A_2 \simeq_\pi A_1$. It follows that

$$A\,b = (\Pi x{:}B_1.A_1)\,b \rightarrow_\pi A_1[x := b] \simeq_\pi A_2[x := b],$$

so we are done.

$a \rightarrow c$ so $a\,b \rightarrow c\,b$. We have by the induction hypothesis $\Gamma \vdash_o c : C$ where $C \simeq_\pi A$. It follows that $\Gamma \vdash_o c\,b : C\,b$ where $C\,b \simeq_\pi A\,b$.

$b \rightarrow c$ so $a\,b \rightarrow a\,c$. By the induction hypothesis $\Gamma \vdash_o c : C$ where $C \simeq_\pi B$. It follows that $\Gamma \vdash_o a\,c : A\,c$ where $A\,c \simeq_\pi A\,b$. □

Now we can easily prove the main result of the current subsection, analogous to lemma 10.

Lemma 45 Weak Closure for $\vdash_o$.

If $\Gamma \vdash_o a : A, \Gamma \twoheadrightarrow \Gamma_0$ *and* $a \twoheadrightarrow a_0$
then $\Gamma_0 \vdash_o a_0 : A_0$ *where* $A_0 \simeq_\pi A$

How is it possible to have proved a closure lemma for $\vdash_o$ without having a type correctness lemma such as lemma 9? (See [GN91, Bar92, MP93] for discussion of the proof of closure for $\vdash$.) The central point is that $\vdash_o$, having no conversion rule, has a stronger generation lemma than $\vdash$, as noted in the proof of 44 above. To take advantage of this, we use an approximate substitution lemma: compare 8 with 42. In the case of $\vdash_o$ it is also possible to separate context reduction from term reduction, while for $\vdash$ these must be proved by simultaneous induction; this latter point, however, is inessential.

4.3 The Key Theorem

In lemma 39 we proved completeness of $\vdash_o$ for $\vdash$. In this section we will show that $\vdash_o$ is sound, in the weak sense that, if a is some term already well-typed in $\vdash$, $\vdash_o$ gives it types "correct up to $\beta\pi$-conversion". The precise statement is as follows:

Theorem 46 Key Theorem for $\vdash_o$.

If $\Gamma \vdash a : A_0$ *and* $\Gamma \vdash_o a : A_1$
then either $A_1 \simeq_\pi A_0$
or $A_1 \twoheadrightarrow_\pi \Pi x_1{:}C_1.\dots \Pi x_n{:}C_n.s_0$,
$a \twoheadrightarrow \lambda x_1{:}C_1.\dots\lambda x_n{:}C_n.a_0$
and $\Gamma, x_1{:}C_1, \dots, x_n{:}C_n \vdash a_0 : s_0$

Notice that the second alternative is phrased to allow for the fact that the abstractions $\Pi x_1{:}C_1.\dots\Pi x_n{:}C_n.s_0$ and $\lambda x_1{:}C_1.\dots\lambda x_n{:}C_n.a_0$ may not be well-formed in the absence of sufficient rule instances in $\mathcal{R}$. The reader should compare the statement of this theorem with that of Theorem 5.5 of [vBJ93].

Proof. By induction on $\Gamma \vdash a : A_0$. We discuss some interesting cases.

Pi $\Gamma \vdash \Pi x{:}A.B : s_3$ from $\Gamma \vdash A : s_1$, $\Gamma, x{:}A \vdash B : s_2$ and $\langle s_1, s_2, s_3\rangle \in \mathcal{R}$. Suppose $\Gamma \vdash_o \Pi x{:}A.B : s$. Then $\Gamma \vdash_o A : A_1 \twoheadrightarrow_\pi s_A$ and $\Gamma, x{:}A \vdash_o B : B_1 \twoheadrightarrow_\pi s_B$, where $\langle s_A, s_B, s\rangle \in \mathcal{R}$. Define C such that $A \twoheadrightarrow C$ and $\Gamma \vdash C : s_A$ as follows:
- If $s_A = s_1$ we take $C = A$.
- Otherwise, by the induction hypothesis $A \twoheadrightarrow C_0$ such that $\Gamma \vdash C_0 : s_A$, and we take $C = C_0$.

Similarly define a reduct D of B such that $\Gamma, x{:}A \vdash D : s_B$. It follows by closure that $\Gamma, x{:}C \vdash D : s_B$, and hence $\Gamma \vdash \Pi x{:}C.D : s$.

Lda $\Gamma \vdash \lambda x{:}A.b : \Pi x{:}A.B$ from $\Gamma \vdash A : s_1$, $\Gamma, x{:}A \vdash b : B$, $\Gamma, x{:}A \vdash B : s_2$ and $\langle s_1, s_2, s_3\rangle \in \mathcal{R}$. Suppose $\Gamma \vdash_o \lambda x{:}A.b : C$. Then we have $\Gamma, x{:}A \vdash_o b : B_0$ and $C = \Pi x{:}A.B_0$. Now by induction

either $B \simeq_\pi B_0$
or $B_0 \twoheadrightarrow_\pi \Pi x_1{:}C_1.\dots\Pi x_n{:}C_n.s_0$,
$b \twoheadrightarrow \lambda x_1{:}C_1.\dots\lambda x_n{:}C_n.b_0$,
and $\Gamma, x{:}A, x_1{:}C_1, \dots, x_n{:}C_n \vdash b_0 : s_0$.

In both cases we are done.

App $\Gamma \vdash a\,b : A[x := b]$ from $\Gamma \vdash a : \Pi x{:}B.A$ and $\Gamma \vdash b : B$. Suppose $\Gamma \vdash_o a\,b : C$. Then

$$\Gamma \vdash_o a : A_1 \twoheadrightarrow_\pi \Pi x{:}B_0.A_0, \quad \Gamma \vdash_o b : B_1 \twoheadrightarrow_\pi B_0 \quad \text{and} \quad C = A_1\,b.$$

By the left induction hypothesis we have

$$\begin{array}{ll} \text{either} & A_1 \simeq_\pi \Pi x{:}B.A \\ \text{or} & A_1 \twoheadrightarrow_\pi \Pi x_0{:}C_0.\ldots\Pi x_n{:}C_n.s_0, \\ & a \twoheadrightarrow \lambda x_0{:}C_0.\ldots\lambda x_n{:}C_n.a_0, \\ & \text{and } \Gamma, x_0{:}C_0,\ldots,x_n{:}C_n \vdash a_0 : s_0. \end{array}$$

(Notice $n \geq 0$ because $A_1 \simeq_\pi \Pi x{:}B_0.A_0$ cannot reduce to a sort.) In the first case we have

$$C = A_1\, b \simeq_\pi (\Pi x{:}B.A)\, b \simeq_\pi A[x := B]$$

so we are done. In the second case we have by closure for $\vdash$ (lemma 10) that

$$\Gamma \vdash \lambda x_0{:}C_0.\ldots\lambda x_n{:}C_n.a_0 : \Pi x{:}B.A.$$

By generation for $\vdash$ (lemma 6) $C_0 \simeq_\pi B$ and $\Gamma \vdash C_0 : s$ for some $s \in \mathcal{S}$; hence $\Gamma \vdash b : C_0$ by Cnv. Therefore we have by substitution for $\vdash$ (lemma 8) that

$$\Gamma, x_1{:}C_1[x := b],\ldots,x_n{:}C_n[x := b] \vdash a_0[x := b] : s_0.$$

Also

$$C = A_1\, b \twoheadrightarrow_\pi (\Pi x_0{:}C_0.\ldots\Pi x_n{:}C_n.s_0)\, b \rightarrow_\pi \Pi x_1{:}C_1[x := b].\ldots\Pi x_n{:}C_n[x := b].s_0$$

and

$$a\, b \twoheadrightarrow (\lambda x_0{:}C_0.\ldots\lambda x_n{:}C_n.a_0)\, b \rightarrow \lambda x_1{:}C_1[x := b].\ldots\lambda x_n{:}C_n[x := b].a_0[x := b]$$

as required. □

Corollary 47.

If $\Gamma \vdash a : A$ *and* $\Gamma \vdash_o a :\twoheadrightarrow_\pi s$
then $a \twoheadrightarrow a_0$ *where* $\Gamma \vdash a_0 : s$

Proof. By the Key Theorem we have either $A \simeq_\pi s$ or $a \twoheadrightarrow a_0$ where $\Gamma \vdash a_0 : s$. In the first case notice that A, occurring in a $\vdash$-judgement, contains no π-redexes, so $A \twoheadrightarrow s$, and we are done by closure (lemma 10). □

The following example shows that in general we cannot expect more with respect to soundness; given $\Gamma \vdash a : A$ and $\Gamma \vdash_o a : s$, reduction of a may be necessary to obtain a term of type s.

Example 3. Recall example 1; we have $\oslash \vdash a : \triangle$, and $\oslash \vdash_o a : \nabla$ but $\oslash \not\vdash a : \nabla$. The best we can say is $a \twoheadrightarrow \star$ and $\oslash \vdash \star : \nabla$. □

Obviously this is due to our liberal Lda-o rule.

4.4 The relation $\vdash_{tp}$

We now introduce a relation $\vdash_{tp}$, similar to $\vdash_o$ but with no correctness check for application. $\vdash_{tp}$ is more efficient for type checking, but it lacks the beautiful properties of $\vdash_o$. In fact it is easy to see that weak closure does not hold for $\vdash_{tp}$. We will show that $\vdash_{tp}$-judgements "lift" to $\vdash_o$-judgements in a sense that is sufficient to prove the Key Theorem for $\vdash_{tp}$.

Definition 48 $\vdash_{tp}$. The relation $\vdash_{tp} \subseteq \mathsf{C} \times \mathsf{T} \times \mathsf{T}$ is the smallest relation satisfying the rules for $\vdash_o$, but having instead of the rule App-o:

$$\text{App-tp} \quad \frac{\Gamma \vdash_{tp} a : A}{\Gamma \vdash_{tp} a\, b : A\, b}$$

Clearly $\vdash_o$ is contained in $\vdash_{tp}$, hence, from lemma 39, we have:

Lemma 49 Completeness of $\vdash_{tp}$.

If $\Gamma \vdash a : A$
then $\exists A_0\, [A_0 \simeq_\pi A$ *and* $\Gamma \vdash_{tp} a : A_0]$

In order to prove the Key Theorem for $\vdash_{tp}$ we borrow a technical notion from [vD80]:

Definition 50 Similarity. The relation $\approx \subseteq \mathsf{T} \times \mathsf{T}$ is the smallest relation satisfying:

$a \approx a$
$s_1 \approx s_2$,
If $A_1 \approx A_2$ then $\Pi x{:}B.A_1 \approx \Pi x{:}B.A_2$,
If $A_1 \approx A_2$ then $A_1\, b \approx A_2\, b$.

Lemma 51 Properties of $\approx$. If $A \approx B$ then

i $A[x := c] \approx B[x := c]$.
ii *If* $A \to_\pi A_0$ *then* $B \to_\pi B_0$ *where* $A_0 \approx B_0$.
iii *If* $A \twoheadrightarrow_\pi A_0$ *then* $B \twoheadrightarrow_\pi B_0$ *where* $A_0 \approx B_0$.
iv *If* $A = \Pi x{:}C.A_0$ *then* $B = \Pi x{:}C.B_0$ *where* $A_0 \approx B_0$.

Proof. **i** is proved by induction on $A \approx B$. **ii** is proved similarly, using i. **iii** follows immediately from ii. **iv** is a simple generation property of $\approx$. □

Lemma 52 $\vdash_{tp}$ uniqueness of types.

If $\Gamma \vdash_{tp} a : A_0$ *and* $\Gamma \vdash_{tp} a : A_1$
then $A_0 \approx A_1$

In particular, if $\Gamma \vdash_o a : A_0$ *and* $\Gamma \vdash_o a : A_1$ *then* $A_0 \approx A_1$.

Proof. By induction on the structure of a, using the generation lemma for $\vdash_{tp}$. □

Lemma 53 Lifting $\vdash_{tp}$ to $\vdash_o$.

If $\Gamma \vdash_o a : A_0$ *and* $\Gamma \vdash_{tp} a : A_1$
then $\Gamma \vdash_o a : A_1$

Proof. Induction on $\Gamma \vdash_o a : A_0$. Obviously the only interesting case is App-o; $\Gamma \vdash_o a\, b : A\, b$ as a consequence of $\Gamma \vdash_o a : A \twoheadrightarrow_\pi \Pi x{:}B_2.A_2$ and $\Gamma \vdash_o b : B \twoheadrightarrow_\pi B_2$. As $\Gamma \vdash_{tp} a\, b : A_1$, it follows that $\Gamma \vdash_{tp} a : A_3$ where $A_1 = A_3\, b$. By induction we have $\Gamma \vdash_o a : A_3$. Hence $A_3 \approx A$ by lemma 52, and, by 51(iii), $A_3 \twoheadrightarrow_\pi C$ where $\Pi x{:}B_2.A_2 \approx C$. Now $C = \Pi x{:}B_2.C_2$ by 51(iv), and $\Gamma \vdash_o a\, b : A_3\, b = A_1$ as required. □

As a corollary we have

Theorem 54 Key Theorem for $\vdash_{tp}$.

If $\Gamma \vdash a : A_0$ *and* $\Gamma \vdash_{tp} a : A_1$
then either $A_1 \simeq_\pi A_0$
or $A_1 \twoheadrightarrow_\pi \Pi x_1{:}C_1 \ldots . \Pi x_n{:}C_n.s_0$,
$a \twoheadrightarrow \lambda x_1{:}C_1 \ldots . \lambda x_n{:}C_n.a_0$
and $\Gamma, x_1{:}C_1, \ldots, x_n{:}C_n \vdash a_0 : s_0$

Proof. By completeness for $\vdash_o$ (39) we have $\Gamma \vdash_o a : A_0$ and hence, by the previous lemma $\Gamma \vdash_o a : A_1$, so we can apply the Key Theorem for $\vdash_o$. □

Corollary 55.

If $\Gamma \vdash a : A$ *and* $\Gamma \vdash_{tp} a : \twoheadrightarrow_\pi s$
then $a \twoheadrightarrow a_0$ *where* $\Gamma \vdash a_0 : s$

4.5 A First Application of $\vdash_{tp}$

$\vdash_o$ is more liberal than $\vdash$, and $\vdash_{tp}$ is still more liberal. In the Introduction we hinted that $\vdash$ checks too much to be used in the third premiss of Lda, and in the next section we will be precise about using $\vdash_{tp}$ for this purpose. Another application where, intuitively, $\vdash$ does too much checking is computing the type of a subterm of a term already known to be well typed. In application, this problem arises when implementing a unification algorithm for a PTS, for the variables of unification carry types, and before instantiating a variable with some subterm we must check that subterm has the correct type. For this purpose, $\vdash_{tp}$ is more efficient than a correct typechecking algorithm, and this is so even for well behaved PTS such as the Calculus of Constructions, which is full, functional and normalizing.

Assume we have some judgement $\Gamma \vdash a : A$, and b is a "locally closed" subterm of a, i.e. $\mathsf{FV}(b) \subseteq \Gamma$. Then it is easy to see that $\Gamma \vdash b : B$ for some B, and our goal is to compute B. By completeness for $\vdash_{tp}$, $\Gamma \vdash_{tp} b : B_0 \simeq_\pi B$.

5 Application to Pure Type Systems

We present a nearly syntax directed system for arbitrary PTS which is, in a sense to be made precise, equivalent to the original system. We start by giving the definition, in which we replace the third premise of the Lda rule by an appeal to $\vdash_{tp}$, motivated by corollary 55 above.

Definition 56 $\vdash_{nsdtp}$. The relation $\vdash_{nsdtp} \subseteq \mathsf{C} \times \mathsf{T} \times \mathsf{T}$ is the smallest relation satisfying

Srt-nsdtp $\quad \oslash \vdash_{nsdtp} s_1 : s_2 \qquad \langle s_1, s_2 \rangle \in \mathcal{A}$

$$\text{Var-nsdtp}\quad \frac{\Gamma \vdash_{nsdtp} A :\twoheadrightarrow s}{\Gamma, x{:}A \vdash_{nsdtp} x : A}$$

$$\text{Wk-nsdtp}\quad \frac{\Gamma \vdash_{nsdtp} b : B \qquad \Gamma \vdash_{nsdtp} A :\twoheadrightarrow s}{\Gamma, x{:}A \vdash_{nsdtp} b : B} \qquad b \in \mathcal{S} \cup \mathcal{V}$$

$$\text{Pi-nsdtp}\quad \frac{\Gamma \vdash_{nsdtp} A :\twoheadrightarrow s_1 \qquad \Gamma, x{:}A \vdash_{nsdtp} B :\twoheadrightarrow s_2}{\Gamma \vdash_{nsdtp} \Pi x{:}A.B : s_3} \qquad \langle s_1, s_2, s_3 \rangle \in \mathcal{R}$$

$$\text{Lda-nsdtp}\quad \frac{\Gamma \vdash_{nsdtp} A :\twoheadrightarrow s_1 \qquad \Gamma, x{:}A \vdash_{nsdtp} b :\twoheadrightarrow B}{\Gamma \vdash_{nsdtp} \lambda x{:}A.b : \Pi x{:}A.B} \qquad \begin{array}{r}\Gamma, x{:}A \vdash_{tp} B :\twoheadrightarrow_\pi s_2 \\ \langle s_1, s_2, s_3 \rangle \in \mathcal{R}\end{array}$$

$$\text{App-nsdtp}\quad \frac{\Gamma \vdash_{nsdtp} a :\twoheadrightarrow^{wh} \Pi x{:}B_1.A \qquad \Gamma \vdash_{nsdtp} b : B_2}{\Gamma \vdash_{nsdtp} a\, b : A[x := b]} \qquad B_1 \simeq B_2$$

Informally notice that $\vdash_{nsdtp}$ is better than $\vdash_{nsd}$ from an algorithmic viewpoint, as the occurrence of $\vdash_{tp}$ in Lda-nsdtp is cheaper to compute than the corresponding occurrence of $\vdash_{nsd}$ in Lda-nsd. That is, our inability to prove Expansion Postponement may be costing us simplicity, but it is not costing efficiency.

Scanning the rules of $\vdash_{nsdtp}$ we see that they are not fully syntax directed. First there are the rules Srt-nsdtp and Pi-nsdtp, which may give various types to the a term. We have seen how to solve such difficulties by introducing schematic terms. This requires the extension of $\vdash_{tp}$ to schematic terms, which seems to pose no problems.

Second there is the rule Lda-nsdtp

$$\text{Lda-nsdtp}\quad \frac{\Gamma \vdash_{nsdtp} A :\twoheadrightarrow s_1 \qquad \Gamma, x{:}A \vdash_{nsdtp} b :\twoheadrightarrow B}{\Gamma \vdash_{nsdtp} \lambda x{:}A.b : \Pi x{:}A.B} \qquad \begin{array}{r}\Gamma, x{:}A \vdash_{tp} B :\twoheadrightarrow_\pi s_2 \\ \langle s_1, s_2, s_3 \rangle \in \mathcal{R}\end{array}$$

which fails to be syntax directed because the reduction strategy for the type of b is not fixed. In section 2.1 we repaired the non syntax directed aspect of rule App-nsd, replacing reduction by weak head reduction to *some* Π-type, as in App-nsdtp. But a Π-type is a weak head normal form, and if weak head reduction fails to terminate in the first premiss of App-nsdtp then the term in question has no type. When should we stop reducing in the second premiss of Lda-nsdtp? We do not in general know if the type of b has a normal form. In section 6 below, we see that, for functional PTS, no reduction is required in this premiss, but for general PTS this is not complete (example 4).

To begin the theory of $\vdash_{nsdtp}$, observe:

Lemma 57 Completeness of $\vdash_o$ for $\vdash_{nsdtp}$.

If $\quad \Gamma \vdash_{nsdtp} a : A$
then $\quad$ *i* $\quad \exists A_0 \quad A_0 \simeq_\pi A$ *and* $\Gamma \vdash_o a : A_0$
$\qquad$ *ii* $\quad A \in \mathcal{S}$ *or* $\Gamma \vdash_o A :\twoheadrightarrow_\pi s$

Proof. By induction on $\Gamma \vdash_{nsdtp} a : A$. The interesting case is Lda-nsdtp:

$$\text{Lda-nsdtp}\ \frac{\Gamma \vdash_{nsdtp} A :\twoheadrightarrow s_1 \qquad \Gamma, x{:}A \vdash_{nsdtp} b : B' \twoheadrightarrow B}{\Gamma \vdash_{nsdtp} \lambda x{:}A.b : \Pi x{:}A.B} \quad \begin{array}{r} \Gamma, x{:}A \vdash_{tp} B : D \twoheadrightarrow_{\pi} s_2 \\ \langle s_1, s_2, s_3 \rangle \in \mathcal{R} \end{array}$$

By induction we have $\Gamma \vdash_o A :\twoheadrightarrow_\pi s_1$ and $\Gamma, x{:}A \vdash_o b : B'_0 \simeq_\pi B'$ where $B' \in \mathcal{S}$ or $\Gamma, x{:}A \vdash_o B' :\twoheadrightarrow_\pi s_{B'}$. By Lda-o we have $\Gamma \vdash_o \lambda x{:}A.b : \Pi x{:}A.B'_0 \simeq_\pi \Pi x{:}A.B$. To finish, we claim $\Gamma \vdash_o \Pi x{:}A.B :\twoheadrightarrow_\pi s_3$. To show this claim using Pi-o and the left induction hypothesis, it remains to show $\Gamma, x{:}A \vdash_o B :\twoheadrightarrow_\pi s_2$. Consider the two cases $B' \in \mathcal{S}$ or $\Gamma, x{:}A \vdash_o B' :\twoheadrightarrow_\pi s_{B'}$. In the first case $B \in \mathcal{S}$ so it must be that $\langle B, D \rangle \in \mathcal{A}$ (a generation property of $\vdash_{tp}$); but then $\Gamma, x{:}A \vdash_o B : D$ and $D = s_2$. In the second case, B' has some type in $\vdash_o$, and by lemma 45 (weak closure for $\vdash_o$) B also has some type in $\vdash_o$. Now we are done by lemma 53 (lifting $\vdash_{tp}$ to $\vdash_o$) and the side condition of our original instance of Lda-nsdtp. □

Now we prove that $\vdash_{nsdtp}$ is complete and sound with respect to $\vdash$.

Lemma 58 Completeness of $\vdash_{nsdtp}$.

If $\quad \Gamma \vdash a : A$
then $\quad \exists A_0\ [A_0 \simeq A$ *and* $\Gamma \vdash_{nsdtp} a : A_0]$.

Proof. By induction on $\Gamma \vdash a : A$. We give two cases.

Lda

$$\frac{\Gamma \vdash A : s_1 \qquad \Gamma, x{:}A \vdash b : B \qquad \Gamma, x{:}A \vdash B : s_2}{\Gamma \vdash \lambda x{:}A.b : \Pi x{:}A.B} \quad \langle s_1, s_2, s_3 \rangle \in \mathcal{R}$$

By induction

$$\Gamma \vdash_{nsdtp} A :\twoheadrightarrow s_1 \text{ and } \Gamma, x{:}A \vdash_{nsdtp} b : B_0 \simeq B.$$

Also $\Gamma, x{:}A \vdash_o B :\twoheadrightarrow_\pi s_2$ by completeness for $\vdash_o$. Taking a common reduct B_1 of B and B_0 we have $\Gamma, x{:}A \vdash_o B_1 :\twoheadrightarrow_\pi s_2$ by closure for $\vdash_o$, so also $\Gamma, x{:}A \vdash_{tp} B_1 :\twoheadrightarrow_\pi s_2$. Moreover $\Gamma, x{:}A \vdash_{nsdtp} b :\twoheadrightarrow B_1$, and therefore by Lda-nsdtp $\Gamma \vdash_{nsdtp} \lambda x{:}A.b : \Pi x{:}A.B_1 \simeq \Pi x{:}A.B$.

App $\Gamma \vdash a\,b : A[x := b]$ as a consequence of $\Gamma \vdash a : \Pi x{:}B.A$ and $\Gamma \vdash b : B$. By the induction hypothesis $\Gamma \vdash_{nsdtp} a : A_0$ and $\Gamma \vdash_{nsdtp} b : B_0$ where $A_0 \simeq \Pi x{:}B.A$ and $B_0 \simeq B$. It follows that $A_0 \twoheadrightarrow^{wh} \Pi x{:}B_1.A_1$ where $A_1 \simeq A$ and $B_1 \simeq B$. Therefore $B_0 \simeq B_1$ so $\Gamma \vdash_{nsdtp} a\,b : A_1[x := b]$ where $A[x := b] \simeq A_1[x := b]$. □

Lemma 59 Soundness of $\vdash_{nsdtp}$.

If $\quad \Gamma \vdash_{nsdtp} a : A$
then $\quad \exists A_0\ [A \twoheadrightarrow A_0,\ \Gamma \vdash a : A_0,$ *and* $[A \in \mathcal{S}$ *or* $\exists s_0\ \Gamma \vdash A_0 : s_0]]$

Proof. By induction on $\Gamma \vdash_{nsdtp} a : A$. Again we treat the lambda rule and the application rule.

Lda-nsdtp

$$\frac{\Gamma \vdash_{nsdtp} A : A_0 \twoheadrightarrow s_1 \qquad \Gamma, x{:}A \vdash_{nsdtp} b : B_0 \twoheadrightarrow B}{\Gamma \vdash_{nsdtp} \lambda x{:}A.b : \Pi x{:}A.B} \quad \begin{array}{r} \Gamma, x{:}A \vdash_{tp} B :\twoheadrightarrow_\pi s_2 \\ \langle s_1, s_2, s_3 \rangle \in \mathcal{R} \end{array}$$

It follows by the induction hypothesis that $\Gamma \vdash A : A_1$ and $\Gamma, x{:}A \vdash b : B_1$, where $A_0 \twoheadrightarrow A_1$ and $B_0 \twoheadrightarrow B_1$. Therefore $A_1 \twoheadrightarrow s_1$ and hence $\Gamma \vdash A : s_1$ by closure. Also either $B_0 \in \mathcal{S}$ or $\Gamma, x{:}A \vdash_o B_0 : B_2 \twoheadrightarrow_\pi s$ by lemma 57(ii).

In the first case $B = B_0 = B_1$, hence $\langle B, s_2 \rangle \in \mathcal{A}$ and therefore $\Gamma, x{:}A \vdash B : s_2$. Hence we have $\Gamma \vdash \lambda x{:}A.b : \Pi x{:}A.B$ and $\Gamma \vdash \Pi x{:}A.B : s_3$.

In the second case we have by closure for $\vdash_o$ that $\Gamma, x{:}A \vdash_o B : B_3 \simeq_\pi B_2$. It follows by lemma 53 that $\Gamma, x{:}A \vdash_o B :\twoheadrightarrow_\pi s_2$. Taking a common β-reduct B_4 of B and B_1 we have by closure for $\vdash$ that $\Gamma, x{:}A \vdash b : B_4$ and by closure for $\vdash_o$ that $\Gamma, x{:}A \vdash_o B_4 :\twoheadrightarrow_\pi s_2$. By correctness of types for $\vdash$ either $B_4 \in \mathcal{S}$ or $\Gamma, x{:}A \vdash B_4 : s_0$ for some s_0. In the first case we have $\langle B_4, s_2 \rangle \in \mathcal{A}$ so $\Gamma, x{:}A \vdash B_4 : s_2$, hence $\Gamma \vdash \lambda x{:}A.b : \Pi x{:}A.B_4$ by Lda and $\Gamma \vdash \Pi x{:}A.B_4 : s_3$ by Pi, while $B \twoheadrightarrow B_4$. In the second case we have by the corollary to the Key Theorem for $\vdash_o$ (47) that $\Gamma, x{:}A \vdash B_5 : s_2$ for some reduct B_5 of B_4, and therefore as before $\Gamma \vdash \lambda x{:}A.b : \Pi x{:}A.B_5$ by Lda and $\Gamma \vdash \Pi x{:}A.B_5 : s_3$ by Pi, while $B \twoheadrightarrow B_5$.

App-nsdtp We have

$$\frac{\Gamma \vdash_{nsdtp} a : A_0 \twoheadrightarrow^{wh} \Pi x{:}B.A \qquad \Gamma \vdash_{nsdtp} b : B_0}{\Gamma \vdash_{nsdtp} a\, b : A[x := b]} \quad B_0 \simeq B$$

By induction hypothesis $\Gamma \vdash a : A_1$ and $\Gamma \vdash b : B_1$ where $A_0 \twoheadrightarrow A_1$ and $B_0 \twoheadrightarrow B_1$. Take a common reduct $\Pi x{:}B_2.A_2$ of A_1 and $\Pi x{:}B.A$ and note that $B_2 \simeq B_1$. Taking again a common reduct B_3 we have by closure $\Gamma \vdash a : \Pi x{:}B_3.A_2$ and $\Gamma \vdash b : B_3$, so $\Gamma \vdash a\, b : A_2[x := b]$ while $A \twoheadrightarrow A_2$. Moreover we have by correctness of types for $\vdash$ that $\Gamma \vdash \Pi x{:}B_3.A_2 : s$ for some s, hence $\Gamma, x{:}B_3 \vdash A_2 : s_0$ by generation and $\Gamma \vdash A_2[x := b] : s_0$ by the substitution lemma. □

As a consequence we can characterize $\vdash$ completely in terms of $\vdash_{nsdtp}$.

Corollary 60 $\vdash_{nsdtp}$ ***characterizes*** $\vdash$.

$$\Gamma \vdash a : A \quad \Leftrightarrow$$
$$\exists A_0\ [A_0 \simeq A \text{ and } \Gamma \vdash_{nsdtp} a : A_0] \quad \text{and} \quad [A \in \mathcal{S} \text{ or } \exists s_0\ \Gamma \vdash_{nsdtp} A :\twoheadrightarrow s_0]$$

Proof.

$\Rightarrow$ Suppose $\Gamma \vdash a : A$ then the first statement is completeness of $\vdash_{nsdtp}$. Also we have by correctness of types that either $A \in \mathcal{S}$ or $\Gamma \vdash A : s_0$. In the first case we are done and in the second case we apply once more completeness of $\vdash_{nsdtp}$.

$\Leftarrow$ Now suppose $\Gamma \vdash_{nsdtp} a : A_0 \simeq A$. Then we have by soundness of $\vdash_{nsdtp}$ that $\Gamma \vdash a : A_1$, where $A_0 \twoheadrightarrow A_1$. Now if $A \in \mathcal{S}$ we have $A_1 \twoheadrightarrow A$ so $\Gamma \vdash a : A$ by closure. And if $\Gamma \vdash_{nsdtp} A : A_2 \twoheadrightarrow s_0$, then again by soundness of $\vdash_{nsdtp}$ we see $\Gamma \vdash A : A_3$ where $A_3 \twoheadrightarrow s_0$, hence $\Gamma \vdash A : s_0$; and $\Gamma \vdash a : A$ follows by Cnv. □

As corollaries we have also:

Lemma 61 Weak Closure for $\vdash_{nsdtp}$.

If $\quad \Gamma \vdash_{nsdtp} a : A,\ \Gamma \twoheadrightarrow \Gamma_0$ *and* $a \twoheadrightarrow a_0$
then $\quad \Gamma_0 \vdash_{nsdtp} a_0 : A_0$ *where* $A \simeq A_0$

Lemma 62 Weak Correctness of Types for $\vdash_{nsdtp}$.

If $\quad \Gamma \vdash_{nsdtp} a : A$
then $\quad$ *either* $A \in \mathcal{S}$ *or* $\exists A_0, s_0\ [A \twoheadrightarrow A_0$ *and* $\Gamma \vdash_{nsdtp} A_0 :\twoheadrightarrow s_0]$.

5.1 Strengthening

Strengthening is the property that a type assignment to a variable which is never used may be dropped from the context. Formally it is the proposition

Theorem 63 Strengthening for $\vdash$.

If $\Gamma_1, x{:}A, \Gamma_2 \vdash b : B$ *and* $x \notin FV(\Gamma_2) \cup FV(b)$
then $\Gamma_1, \Gamma_2 \vdash b : B_0$ *where* $B \twoheadrightarrow B_0$.

This formulation was first stated and proved for Constructions-like calculi by Luo [Luo90]. A proof for functional PTS appears in [GN91]; strengthening for arbitrary PTS was proved in [vBJ93]. Our results above have strengthening for arbitrary PTS as an easy consequence.

Lemma 64 Strengthening for $\vdash_{tp}$.

If $\Gamma_1 \vdash_{tp} b : B,\ \Gamma_2 \vdash_{wfcxt},\ \Gamma_2 \sqsubseteq \Gamma_1$ *and* $FV(b) \subseteq dom(\Gamma_2)$
then $\Gamma_2 \vdash_{tp} b : B$.

As usual, we have

Lemma 65 Free Variables for $\vdash_{nsdtp}$.

If $\Gamma \vdash_{nsdtp} a : A$
then $FV(a) \cup FV(A) \subseteq dom(\Gamma)$.

More interestingly, because $\vdash_{nsdtp}$ has no conversion rule, we have:

Lemma 66.

If $\Gamma_1, x{:}A, \Gamma_2 \vdash_{nsdtp} b : B$ *and* $x \notin FV(\Gamma_2) \cup FV(b)$
then $x \notin FV(B)$.

Lemma 67 Strengthening for $\vdash_{nsdtp}$.

If $\Gamma_1, x{:}A,\ \Gamma_2 \vdash_{nsdtp} b : B$ *and* $x \notin FV(\Gamma_2) \cup FV(b)$
then $\Gamma_1, \Gamma_2 \vdash_{nsdtp} b : B$

The proofs of these lemmas are by easy induction. They give us strengthening for $\vdash$.

Proof of Theorem 63. Assume $\Gamma_1, x{:}A, \Gamma_2 \vdash b : B$. By completeness (58), strengthening for $\vdash_{nsdtp}$ (67), and soundness (59), $\Gamma_1, \Gamma_2 \vdash b : B_1$, where $B \simeq B_1$. Taking a common reduct B_0 of B and B_1 we have by closure $\Gamma_1, \Gamma_2 \vdash b : B_0$. □

6 Functional Pure Type Systems

We observed that $\vdash_{nsdtp}$ fails to be syntax directed only because of the axiom side condition of Srt-nsdtp, the Π-rule side condition of Lda-nsdtp and the non-deterministic reduction of the type of b in the second premiss of Lda-nsdtp. In the case of functional PTS the side conditions mentioned are in fact single valued, so the only remaining problem is the reduction in the second premiss of Lda-nsdtp. We have also seen that, although terms really can get more types by reduction (example 3), this does not happen for functional PTS (lemma 21). Thus for functional PTS we might hope to remove reduction in the right premiss of Lda-nsdtp, and in fact this is the case. For the most part this section parallels the development of section 5, but the following result shows what the difference is: for functional PTS, the relations $\vdash_{tp}$ and $\vdash_{o}$ are functions.

Lemma 68 Uniqueness of types for $\vdash_{tp}$. For functional PTS

If $\Gamma \vdash_{tp} a : A_0$ *and* $\Gamma \vdash_{tp} a : A_1$
then $A_0 = A_1$

In particular, if $\Gamma \vdash_o a : A_0$ *and* $\Gamma \vdash_{tp} a : A_1$ *then* $A_0 = A_1$.

Now we define a syntax directed system $\vdash_f$ for functional PTS's which is similar to $\vdash_{nsdtp}$ but has a syntax directed Lda rule. For the rest of this section we assume that the PTS under discussion is functional.

Definition 69 $\vdash_f$. The relation $\vdash_f \subseteq \mathsf{C} \times \mathsf{T} \times \mathsf{T}$ is the smallest relation satisfying the rules of the system $\vdash_{nsdtp}$, defined in definition 56, but having instead of Lda-nsdtp the rule

$$\text{Lda-f} \quad \frac{\Gamma \vdash_f A :\twoheadrightarrow s_1 \qquad \Gamma, x{:}A \vdash_f b : B}{\Gamma \vdash_f \lambda x{:}A.b : \Pi x{:}A.B} \quad \begin{array}{c} \Gamma, x{:}A \vdash_{tp} B :\twoheadrightarrow_\pi s_2 \\ \langle s_1, s_2, s_3 \rangle \in \mathcal{R} \end{array}$$

Trivially $\vdash_f \subseteq \vdash_{nsdtp}$, so from lemma 57 we have:

Lemma 70 Completeness of $\vdash_o$ for $\vdash_f$.

If $\Gamma \vdash_f a : A$
then *i* $\exists A_0\, [A_0 \simeq_\pi A$ *and* $\Gamma \vdash_o a : A_0]$
ii $A \in \mathcal{S}$ *or* $\Gamma \vdash_o A :\twoheadrightarrow_\pi s$

We prove that $\vdash_f$ is complete and sound with respect to $\vdash$; in fact we have even $\vdash_f \subseteq \vdash$.

Lemma 71 Completeness of $\vdash_f$.

If $\Gamma \vdash a : A$
then $\exists A_0\, [A_0 \simeq A$ *and* $\Gamma \vdash_f a : A_0]$.

Proof. By induction on $\Gamma \vdash a : A$. All cases are as in the proof of completeness for $\vdash_{nsdtp}$ (lemma 58) except Lda: we have $\Gamma \vdash \lambda x{:}A.b : \Pi x{:}A.B$ because $\Gamma \vdash A : s_1$, $\Gamma, x{:}A \vdash b : B$ and $\Gamma, x{:}A \vdash B : s_2$, where $\langle s_1, s_2, s_3 \rangle \in \mathcal{R}$. It follows by induction that $\Gamma \vdash_f A :\twoheadrightarrow s_1$ and $\Gamma, x{:}A \vdash_f b : B_0$ where $B_0 \simeq B$. Also $\Gamma, x{:}A \vdash_o B :\twoheadrightarrow_\pi s_2$ by completeness of $\vdash_o$ with respect to $\vdash$ (lemma 39). Either $B_0 \in \mathcal{S}$ or $\Gamma, x{:}A \vdash_o B_0 :\twoheadrightarrow_\pi s$ for some s by completeness of $\vdash_o$ with respect to $\vdash_f$ (lemma 70). If $B_0 \in \mathcal{S}$ then $B \twoheadrightarrow B_0$, hence $\Gamma, x{:}A \vdash_o B_0 :\twoheadrightarrow_\pi s_2$ by closure for $\vdash_o$. It follows that $\Gamma \vdash_f \lambda x{:}A.b : \Pi x{:}A.B_0$. Alternatively, assume $\Gamma, x{:}A \vdash_o B_0 :\twoheadrightarrow_\pi s$. Taking a common reduct B_2 of B and B_1 we have $\Gamma, x{:}A \vdash_o B_2 :\twoheadrightarrow_\pi s_2$ and $\Gamma, x{:}A \vdash_o B_2 :\twoheadrightarrow_\pi s$, both by closure for $\vdash_o$. It follows by functionality that $s = s_2$ and therefore again $\Gamma \vdash_f \lambda x{:}A.b : \Pi x{:}A.B_0$. □

Lemma 72 Soundness for $\vdash_f$.

If $\Gamma \vdash_f a : A$
then $\Gamma \vdash a : A$

Proof. By induction on $\Gamma \vdash_f a : A$. We treat the Lda-f rule: $\Gamma \vdash_f \lambda x{:}A.b : \Pi x{:}A.B$ as a consequence of $\Gamma \vdash_f A : A_0 \twoheadrightarrow s_1$ and $\Gamma, x{:}A \vdash b : B$, where $\Gamma, x{:}A \vdash_{tp} B :\twoheadrightarrow_\pi s_2$ and $\langle s_1, s_2, s_3 \rangle \in \mathcal{R}$. It follows by induction that $\Gamma \vdash A : A_0$ and $\Gamma, x{:}A \vdash b : B$. Hence $\Gamma \vdash A : s_1$ by closure. Also by correctness of types (lemma 9) either $B \in \mathcal{S}$ or $\Gamma, x{:}A \vdash B : s$ for some s. If $B \in \mathcal{S}$ then $\langle B, s_2 \rangle \in \mathcal{A}$ (because of $\Gamma, x{:}A \vdash_{tp} B :\twoheadrightarrow_\pi s_2$)

and therefore $\Gamma, x{:}A \vdash B : s_2$. It follows that $\Gamma \vdash \lambda x{:}A.b : \Pi x{:}A.B$ by Lda. Alternatively assume $\Gamma, x{:}A \vdash B : s$; we have by completeness for $\vdash_o$ (lemma 39) that $\Gamma, x{:}A \vdash_o B :\twoheadrightarrow_\pi s$. It follows by functionality (lemma 68) that $s = s_2$ and therefore again $\Gamma \vdash \lambda x{:}A.b : \Pi x{:}A.B$ by Lda. □

As corollaries we have:

Lemma 73 Weak Closure for $\vdash_f$.

If $\Gamma \vdash_f a : A$, $\Gamma \twoheadrightarrow \Gamma_0$ *and* $a \twoheadrightarrow a_0$
then $\Gamma_0 \vdash_f a_0 : A_0$ *where* $A \simeq A_0$

Lemma 74 Correctness of Types for $\vdash_f$.

If $\Gamma \vdash_f a : A$
then *either* $A \in \mathcal{S}$ *or* $\exists s\ \Gamma \vdash_f A :\twoheadrightarrow s$.

Proof. Assume $\Gamma \vdash_f a : A$ then by soundness for $\vdash_f$ we have $\Gamma \vdash a : A$, hence by correctness of types for $\vdash$ either $A \in \mathcal{S}$ or $\Gamma \vdash A : s$ for some s. In the latter case $\Gamma \vdash_f A :\twoheadrightarrow s$ by completeness for $\vdash_f$. □

An important consequence is the following theorem.

***Theorem 75 Decidability for normalizing functional* PTS.** *If a PTS is functional and normalizing, and* $\exists s \in \mathcal{S}\,[\langle s_1, s\rangle \in \mathcal{A}]$ *and* $\exists s \in \mathcal{S}\,[\langle s_1, s_2, s\rangle \in \mathcal{R}]$ *are decidable relations then the relation* $\vdash$ *is decidable.*

Proof. It follows from 72 that $\Gamma \vdash_f a : A$ implies that a and A are normalizing. Therefore all the side conditions in the rules for $\vdash_f$ are decidable. □

6.1 Incompleteness of $\vdash_f$

We promised to show that $\vdash_f$ is in fact incomplete for the general PTS, i.e. that Lda-nsdtp is essentially non-syntax-directed.

Example 4. Consider the following PTS, extending example 3:

$$\mathcal{S} = \{\star, \triangle, \triangledown, \square\}$$
$$\mathcal{A} = \{\langle \star, \triangle\rangle, \langle \star, \triangledown\rangle, \langle \triangle, \square\rangle\}$$
$$\mathcal{R} = \{\langle \square, \square, \square\rangle, \langle \triangle, \triangledown, \square\rangle\}$$

As before let $a = (\lambda x{:}\triangle.x)\star$. We know that $\oslash \vdash a : \triangle$, and now verify that in fact $\oslash \vdash_f a : \triangle$, hence also $\oslash \vdash_{nsdtp} a : \triangle$

$$\dfrac{\dfrac{\oslash \vdash_f \triangle : \square \qquad \dfrac{\oslash \vdash_f \triangle : \square}{x{:}\triangle \vdash_f x : \triangle} \qquad \dfrac{x{:}\triangle \vdash_{wfcxt}}{x{:}\triangle \vdash_{tp} \triangle : \square}}{\oslash \vdash_f \lambda x{:}\triangle.x : \Pi x{:}\triangle.\triangle}\ \langle \square,\square,\square\rangle \in \mathcal{R} \qquad \oslash \vdash_f \star : \triangle}{\oslash \vdash_f (\lambda x{:}\triangle.x)\star : \triangle}$$

Now we verify $y{:}a \vdash_{nsdtp} \lambda z{:}\star.y : \Pi z{:}\star.\star$

$$\dfrac{\dfrac{\vdots}{y{:}a \vdash_{nsdtp} \star : \triangle} \quad \dfrac{\vdots}{y{:}a, z{:}\star \vdash_{nsdtp} y : a \twoheadrightarrow \star} \quad \dfrac{y{:}a, z{:}\star \vdash_{wfcxt}}{y{:}a, z{:}\star \vdash_{tp} \star : \triangledown}}{y{:}a \vdash_{nsdtp} \lambda z{:}\star.y : \Pi z{:}\star.\star} \ \langle \triangle, \triangledown, \square \rangle \in \mathcal{R}$$

Obviously (because $\vdash_f$ is nearly syntax directed) the only possible derivation in $\vdash_f$ of a type for $\lambda z{:}\star.y$ in the context $y{:}a$ has shape

$$\dfrac{\dfrac{\vdots}{y{:}a \vdash_f \star : X \twoheadrightarrow \alpha} \quad \dfrac{\vdots}{y{:}a, z{:}\star \vdash_f y : a} \quad \dfrac{\dfrac{\dfrac{y{:}a, z{:}\star, x{:}\triangle \vdash_{tp} x : \triangle}{}}{y{:}a, z{:}\star \vdash_{tp} \lambda x{:}\triangle.x : \Pi x{:}\triangle.\triangle}}{y{:}a, z{:}\star \vdash_{tp} a : (\Pi x{:}\triangle.\triangle)\star \twoheadrightarrow_\pi \triangle}}{y{:}a \vdash_f \lambda z{:}\star.y : \Pi z{:}\star.a} \ \langle \alpha, \triangle, ? \rangle \in \mathcal{R}$$

As there is no rule $\langle \alpha, \triangle, ? \rangle \in \mathcal{R}$, $\vdash_f$ does not derive any type for $\lambda z{:}\star.y$ in the context $y{:}a$. We see that $\vdash_f$ is strictly weaker than $\vdash_{nsdtp}$, and is incomplete for non-functional PTS. □

7 A syntax directed system for arbitrary PTS's

Before defining a syntax directed system we must decide on the lambda rule; given the pseudoterm $\lambda x{:}A.b$ how far will we reduce B, the type of b, in order to find its sorts? To make the reduction path unique, we reduce B using complete developments.

Definition 76 complete development. The relation $\overset{1}{\Rightarrow} \subseteq \mathsf{T} \times \mathsf{T}$ is the smallest relation satisfying the following rules.

$a \overset{1}{\Rightarrow} a$ if $a \in \mathcal{V} \cup \mathcal{S}$.
If $A_1 \overset{1}{\Rightarrow} A_2$ and $B_1 \overset{1}{\Rightarrow} B_2$ then $\Pi x{:}A_1.B_1 \overset{1}{\Rightarrow} \Pi x{:}A_2.B_2$.
If $A \overset{1}{\Rightarrow} B$ and $a \overset{1}{\Rightarrow} b$ then $\lambda x{:}A.a \overset{1}{\Rightarrow} \lambda x{:}B.b$.
If $a \overset{1}{\Rightarrow} a_0$ and $b \overset{1}{\Rightarrow} b_0$ then $(\lambda x{:}A.a)b \overset{1}{\Rightarrow} a_0[x := b_0]$.
If $a \overset{1}{\Rightarrow} a_0$, $b \overset{1}{\Rightarrow} b_0$ and $a \neq \lambda x{:}A.a_1$ then $a\,b \overset{1}{\Rightarrow} a_0\,b_0$.

Clearly $\overset{1}{\Rightarrow}$ is a function, $\overset{1}{\Rightarrow} \subset \twoheadrightarrow$, and if $a \twoheadrightarrow b$, $a \overset{1}{\Rightarrow} a_1$ and $b \overset{1}{\Rightarrow} b_1$ then $a_1 \twoheadrightarrow b_1$. Note that $a \overset{1}{\Rightarrow} a$ iff a is normal. We will denote by $\overset{n}{\Rightarrow}$ the result of applying $\overset{1}{\Rightarrow}$ n times, and have by induction: if $a \twoheadrightarrow b$, $a \overset{n}{\Rightarrow} a_n$ and $b \overset{n}{\Rightarrow} b_n$ then $a_n \twoheadrightarrow b_n$.

The complete development strategy has the advantage of simplicity, and is moreover a *cofinal* reduction strategy, in the sense that if $a \twoheadrightarrow b$, then for some n and c, $a \overset{n}{\Rightarrow} c$, with $b \twoheadrightarrow c$. So by closure (lemma 10), we know that if *some* reduct of B has sort s, it suffices to consider complete developments of B in order to compute s. This behaviour should be contrasted with non-cofinal strategies, such as leftmost-outermost reduction; in the case of non-normalising systems such strategies may not capture all possible sorts for B.

Now for every $n \in \mathsf{N}$ we define a relation, $\vdash_{nsd-n}$, by a nearly syntax directed set of rules whose only non syntax directedness (in rules Srt-nsd-n and Pi-nsd-n) is a consequence of the non-functionality of the PTS. In general $\vdash_{nsd-n}$ is not equivalent to $\vdash$ for any particular n, but by using unbounded n we will derive a semi-algorithm for typechecking an arbitrary PTS.

Definition 77 $\vdash_{nsd-n}$. For each $n \in \mathsf{N}$ the relation $\vdash_{nsd-n} \subseteq \mathsf{C} \times \mathsf{T} \times \mathsf{T}$ is the smallest relation satisfying the rules of the relation $\vdash_{nsdtp}$ but for the Lda-rule which is replaced by:

$$\text{Lda-nsd-n} \quad \frac{\Gamma \vdash_{nsd-n} A :\twoheadrightarrow s_1 \qquad \Gamma, x{:}A \vdash_{nsd-n} b :\overset{n}{\Rightarrow} B}{\Gamma \vdash_{nsd-n} \lambda x{:}A.b : \Pi x{:}A.B} \quad \begin{array}{r}\Gamma, x{:}A \vdash_{tp} B :\twoheadrightarrow_\pi s_2 \\ \langle s_1, s_2, s_3 \rangle \in \mathcal{R}\end{array}$$

$\vdash_{nsd-n}$ is sound and complete with respect to $\vdash_{nsdtp}$.

Lemma 78 Soundness of $\vdash_{nsd-n}$ ***with respect to*** $\vdash_{nsdtp}$.

If $\quad \Gamma \vdash_{nsd-n} a : A$
then $\quad \Gamma \vdash_{nsdtp} a : A$.

For proving completeness we need some properties of $\vdash_{nsd-n}$.

Lemma 79 Completeness of $\vdash_o$ ***for*** $\vdash_{nsd-n}$.

If $\quad \Gamma \vdash_{nsd-n} a : A$
then $\quad$ *i* $\quad \exists A_0\, [A_0 \simeq_\pi A$ *and* $\Gamma \vdash_o a : A_0]$.
$\quad$ *ii* $\quad A \in \mathcal{S}$ *or* $\exists s\, [\Gamma \vdash_o A :\twoheadrightarrow_\pi s]$.

Lemma 80 Monotonicity of $\vdash_{nsd-n}$.

If $\quad \Gamma \vdash_{nsd-m} a : A$ *and* $n \geq m$
then $\quad \exists B\, [A \twoheadrightarrow B$ *and* $\Gamma \vdash_{nsd-n} a : B]$.

Proof. By induction on $\Gamma \vdash_{nsd-m} a : A$. We treat some cases.

Lda-nsd-m We have $\Gamma \vdash_{nsd-m} \lambda x{:}A.c : \Pi x{:}A.C$ as a consequence of

- $\Gamma \vdash_{nsd-m} A : A_0$, where $A_0 \twoheadrightarrow s_1$,
- $\Gamma, x{:}A \vdash_{nsd-m} c : C_0$, where $C_0 \overset{m}{\Rightarrow} C$, and
- $\Gamma, x{:}A \vdash_{tp} C :\twoheadrightarrow_\pi s_2$ where $\langle s_1, s_2, s_3 \rangle \in \mathcal{R}$.

The induction hypothesis gives us: first $\Gamma \vdash_{nsd-n} A : A_1$ with $A_0 \twoheadrightarrow A_1$ (and hence $A_1 \twoheadrightarrow s_1$); second $\Gamma, x{:}A \vdash_{nsd-n} c : C_1$, with $C_0 \twoheadrightarrow C_1$. Now define D by $C_1 \overset{n}{\Rightarrow} D$ then we have by the properties of $\overset{n}{\Rightarrow}$ that $C \twoheadrightarrow D$. As $\vdash_o \subseteq \vdash_{tp}$ it follows by the lemmas 79 and 45 that $\Gamma, x{:}A \vdash_{tp} D :\twoheadrightarrow_\pi s_2$. Therefore $\Gamma \vdash_{nsd-n} \lambda x{:}A.c : \Pi x{:}A.D$.

App-nsd-m We have $\Gamma \vdash_{nsd-m} a\, b : A[x := b]$ because of $\Gamma \vdash_{nsd-m} a : A_0$ where $A_0 \twoheadrightarrow^{wh} \Pi x{:}B_1.A$ and $\Gamma \vdash_{nsd-m} b : B_2$, while $B_1 \simeq B_2$. By induction, first $\Gamma \vdash_{nsd-n} a : A_1$ with $A_0 \twoheadrightarrow A_1$ (and hence $A_1 \twoheadrightarrow^{wh} \Pi x{:}B_3.B$ with $A \twoheadrightarrow B$ and $B_1 \twoheadrightarrow B_3$); secondly $\Gamma \vdash_{nsd-n} b : B_4$ with $B_2 \twoheadrightarrow B_4$. It follows that $B_3 \simeq B_4$ and hence $\Gamma \vdash_{nsd-n} a\, b : B[x := b]$. □

Now we can prove completeness.

Lemma 81 Completeness of $\vdash_{nsd-n}$ ***with respect to*** $\vdash_{nsdtp}$.

If $\quad \Gamma \vdash_{nsdtp} a : A$
then $\quad \exists n, A_0\, [A \twoheadrightarrow A_0$ *and* $\Gamma \vdash_{nsd-n} a : A_0]$.

Proof. Induction on $\Gamma \vdash_{nsdtp} a : A$. We select interesting cases.

Wk-nsdtp We have $\Gamma, x{:}A \vdash_{nsd} b : B$ as a consequence of $\Gamma \vdash_{nsd} b : B$, $\Gamma \vdash_{nsd} A : A_0$ where $A_0 \twoheadrightarrow s$ and $b \in \mathcal{S} \cup \mathcal{V}$. By induction hypothesis we have $\Gamma \vdash_{nsd-k} b : B_0$ where $B \twoheadrightarrow B_0$ and $\Gamma \vdash_{nsd-m} A : A_1$ where $A_0 \twoheadrightarrow A_1$. Take $n = \max(k, m)$ and, by 80, $\Gamma \vdash_{nsd-n} b : B_1$ where $B_0 \twoheadrightarrow B_1$ and $\Gamma \vdash_{nsd-n} A : A_2$ where $A_1 \twoheadrightarrow A_2$. It follows that $A_2 \twoheadrightarrow s$ and hence $\Gamma, x{:}A \vdash_{nsd-n} b : B_1$.

Lda-nsdtp We have $\Gamma \vdash_{nsdtp} \lambda x{:}A.b : \Pi x{:}A.B$ as a consequence of $\Gamma \vdash_{nsdtp} A : A_0$ where $A_0 \twoheadrightarrow s_1$ and $\Gamma, x{:}A \vdash_{nsdtp} b : B_0$ where $B_0 \twoheadrightarrow B$, in k steps, say. And also we know $\Gamma, x{:}A \vdash_{tp} B : D$ where $D \twoheadrightarrow_\pi s_2$ and $\langle s_1, s_2, s_3 \rangle \in \mathcal{R}$. By the induction hypothesis we have $\Gamma \vdash_{nsd-l} A : A_1$ where $A_0 \twoheadrightarrow A_1$ and $\Gamma, x{:}A \vdash_{nsd-m} b : B_1$ where $B_0 \twoheadrightarrow B_1$. Take $n = \max(k, l, m)$, getting, by lemma 80, $\Gamma \vdash_{nsd-n} A : A_2$ where $A_1 \twoheadrightarrow A_2$ and $\Gamma, x{:}A \vdash_{nsd-n} b : B_2$ where $B_1 \twoheadrightarrow B_2$. First observe that $A_1 \twoheadrightarrow s_1$. Next define C_0 and C_2 by $B_0 \overset{n}{\Rrightarrow} C_0$ and $B_2 \overset{n}{\Rrightarrow} C_2$. Then we have $B \twoheadrightarrow C_0 \twoheadrightarrow C_2$ by the properties of $\overset{n}{\Rrightarrow}$. Also, by 57(ii), either $B_0 \in \mathcal{S}$ or $\Gamma \vdash_o B_0 : D_0$ where $D_0 \twoheadrightarrow_\pi s \in \mathcal{S}$. If $B_0 \in \mathcal{S}$ then $B = B_0 = C_2$ and hence $\Gamma, x{:}A \vdash_{tp} C_2 :\twoheadrightarrow_\pi s_2$. And if $\Gamma \vdash_o B_0 : D_0$ then by 45 we have $\Gamma, x{:}A \vdash_o B : D_1$ and, it follows by 53 that $\Gamma, x{:}A \vdash_o B : D$ and hence again by 45 $\Gamma, x{:}A \vdash_o C_2 : D_2$ where $D_2 \twoheadrightarrow_\pi s_2$. Therefore $\Gamma \vdash_{nsd-n} \lambda x{:}A.b : \Pi x{:}A.C_2$.

App-nsdtp We have

$$\frac{\Gamma \vdash_{nsdtp} a : A_0 \twoheadrightarrow^{wh} \Pi x{:}B_1.A \qquad \Gamma \vdash_{nsdtp} b : B_2}{\Gamma \vdash_{nsdtp} a\, b : A[x := b]} \quad B_1 \simeq B_2$$

By induction hypothesis

$$\Gamma \vdash_{nsd-k} a : A_1, \quad A_0 \twoheadrightarrow A_1, \quad \Gamma \vdash_{nsd-m} b : B_3, \quad \text{and} \quad B_2 \twoheadrightarrow B_3.$$

Take $n = \max(k, m)$ and, by lemma 80, $\Gamma \vdash_{nsd-n} a : A_2$ where $A_1 \twoheadrightarrow A_2$, and $\Gamma \vdash_{nsd-n} b : B_4$ where $B_3 \twoheadrightarrow B_4$. It follows that $A_2 \twoheadrightarrow^{wh} \Pi x{:}B_0.A_3$ and $A \twoheadrightarrow A_3$. Hence $\Gamma \vdash_{nsd-n} a\, b : A_3[x := b]$ where $A[x := b] \twoheadrightarrow A_3[x := b]$. □

Now we prove that $\vdash$ and $\vdash_{nsd-n}$ are – in a sense – equivalent.

Lemma 82 Equivalence of $\vdash$ and $\vdash_{nsd-n}$.

$$\Gamma \vdash a : A \quad \Leftrightarrow \quad \begin{array}{ll} i & \exists n, A_0\ [A \simeq A_0 \textit{ and } \Gamma \vdash_{nsd-n} a : A_0] \\ ii & \textit{either } A \in \mathcal{S} \textit{ or } \exists n, s\ [\Gamma \vdash_{nsd-n} A :\twoheadrightarrow s]. \end{array}$$

Proof.

$\Rightarrow$ Suppose $\Gamma \vdash a : A$, then by 60 we have that $\Gamma \vdash_{nsdtp} a : A_0$] where $A_0 \simeq A$, and also that either $A \in \mathcal{S}$ or $\Gamma \vdash_{nsdtp} A :\twoheadrightarrow s$. It follows from 81 that for some $n \in \mathsf{N}$ there exists A_1 with $\Gamma \vdash_{nsd-n} a : A_1$ and $A \simeq A_1$. And also either $A \in \mathcal{S}$ or by the same argument $\Gamma \vdash_{nsd-n} A :\twoheadrightarrow s$.

$\Leftarrow$ Now suppose that $A \simeq A_0$ and $\Gamma \vdash_{nsd-n} a : A_0$, and that either $A \in \mathcal{S}$ or $\Gamma \vdash_{nsd-m} A :\twoheadrightarrow s$. Then we have by 78 that $\Gamma \vdash_{nsdtp} a : A_0$ and either $A \in \mathcal{S}$ or $\Gamma \vdash_{nsdtp} A :\twoheadrightarrow s$ and again by 60 $\Gamma \vdash a : A$. □

Monotonicity ensures that any strictly increasing sequence n_j in N gives rise to a nearly syntax directed search for possible types via the systems $\vdash_{nsd-n_j}$.

Applying the methods of section 3.2 we will define a syntax directed set of rules for arbitrary PTS. But as the types in this system will be schematic terms, we have to extend our relations $\vdash_o$ and $\vdash_{tp}$ to schematic terms. In order to do this we extend the notion of β-convertibility of schematic terms modulo a constraint as defined in 31 to $\pi\beta$-convertibility.

$$X \simeq_\pi Y \,|\, \mathcal{C} \;\triangleq\; \exists X_0, Y_0\, [X \twoheadrightarrow_\pi X_0, Y \twoheadrightarrow_\pi Y_0 \textit{ and } X_0 =_\Sigma Y_0 \,|\, \mathcal{C}]$$

Just as in the case of β-reduction we have

Lemma 83 Equivalence of schematic conversion and conversion.

i *If* $X \simeq_\pi Y \,|\, \mathcal{C}$ *and* $\phi \models \mathcal{C}$ *then* $\phi X \simeq_\pi \phi Y$
ii *If* $\phi X \simeq_\pi \phi Y$ *then* $\exists \mathcal{C}\, [X \simeq Y \,|\, \mathcal{C}$ *and* $\phi \models \mathcal{C}]$
iii *If* $\phi_1 X \simeq_\pi \phi_2 Y$ *then* $\exists \mathcal{C}\, [X \simeq_\pi Y \,|\, \mathcal{C}]$

Now we can define the schematized version of $\vdash_o$

Definition 84 $\vdash_{o+}$. The relation $\vdash_{o+} \subseteq \mathsf{C} \times (\mathsf{T} \cup \mathsf{T}^\Sigma) \times (\mathsf{T} \cup \mathsf{T}^\Sigma) \times \mathsf{Cnstr}$ is the smallest relation satisfying the following rules.

Srt-o+
$$\frac{\Gamma \vdash_{wfcxt}}{\Gamma \vdash_{o+} \alpha : \sigma \,|\, \{\langle \alpha, \sigma \rangle \in \mathcal{A}\}} \qquad \alpha \in \mathcal{S} \cup \Sigma$$

Var-o+
$$\frac{\Gamma \vdash_{wfcxt}}{\Gamma \vdash_{o+} x : A \,|\, \emptyset} \qquad x : A \in \Gamma$$

Pi-o+
$$\frac{\Gamma \vdash_{o+} A :\twoheadrightarrow_\pi \alpha \,|\, \mathcal{C} \qquad \Gamma, x{:}A \vdash_{o+} X :\twoheadrightarrow_\pi \beta \,|\, \mathcal{D}}{\Gamma \vdash_{o+} \Pi x{:}A.X : \sigma \,|\, \mathcal{C} \cup \mathcal{D} \cup \{\langle \alpha, \beta, \sigma \rangle \in \mathcal{R}\}}$$

Lda-o+
$$\frac{\Gamma, x{:}A \vdash_{o+} b : X \,|\, \mathcal{C}}{\Gamma \vdash_{o+} \lambda x{:}A.b : \Pi x{:}A.X \,|\, \mathcal{C}}$$

App-o+
$$\frac{\Gamma \vdash_{o+} X : Y \,|\, \mathcal{C} \qquad \Gamma \vdash_{o+} b : Z \,|\, \mathcal{D}}{\Gamma \vdash_{o+} X\, b : Y\, b \,|\, \mathcal{C} \cup \mathcal{D} \cup \mathcal{E}} \qquad \begin{array}{c} Y \twoheadrightarrow_\pi \Pi x{:}B.Y_0 \\ Z \simeq_\pi B \,|\, \mathcal{E} \end{array}$$

Lemma 85 Equivalence of $\vdash_o$ ***and*** $\vdash_{o+}$.

i *If* $\Gamma \vdash_{o+} X : Y \,|\, \mathcal{C}$ *and* $\phi \models \mathcal{C}$ *then* $\Gamma \vdash_o \phi X : \phi Y$
ii *If* $\Gamma \vdash_o \phi X : A$ *then* $\exists Y, \mathcal{C}, \phi_1\, [\phi_1 \supseteq \phi,\, \phi_1 \models \mathcal{C},\, A = \phi_1 Y$ *and* $\Gamma \vdash_{o+} X : Y \,|\, \mathcal{C}]$

Proof.
i Induction on $\Gamma \vdash_{o+} X : Y \,|\, \mathcal{C}$. We treat App-o+: $\Gamma \vdash_{o+} X\, b : Y\, b \,|\, \mathcal{C} \cup \mathcal{D} \cup \mathcal{E}$ because $\Gamma \vdash_{o+} X : Y \,|\, \mathcal{C}$ and $\Gamma \vdash_{o+} b : Z \,|\, \mathcal{D}$, where $Y \twoheadrightarrow_\pi \Pi x{:}B.Y_0$ and $Z \simeq_\pi B \,|\, \mathcal{E}$. Now suppose $\phi \models \mathcal{C} \cup \mathcal{D} \cup \mathcal{E}$. By induction $\Gamma \vdash_o \phi(X) : \phi(Y)$ and $\Gamma \vdash_o \phi(b) : \phi(Z)$. Moreover by 83(i), $\phi Z \simeq_\pi \phi B$ and hence $\phi Y \twoheadrightarrow_\pi \phi(\Pi x{:}B.Y_0) = \Pi x{:}\phi B.\phi Y_0 \simeq_\pi \Pi x{:}\phi Z.\phi Y_0$. Therefore $\Gamma \vdash_o \phi(X)\, \phi(b) : \phi(Y)\, \phi(b)$ while $\phi(X)\, \phi(b) = \phi(X\, b)$ and $\phi(Y)\, \phi(b) = \phi(Y\, b)$.
ii Induction on $\Gamma \vdash_o \phi X : A$. We consider some cases.
Srt-o $X \in \mathcal{S} \cup \Sigma$ and $A = s \in \mathcal{S}$, with $\langle \phi X, s \rangle \in \mathcal{A}$. It follows that $\Gamma \vdash_{o+} X : \sigma \,|\, \{\langle X, \sigma \rangle \in \mathcal{A}\}$ and defining $\phi_1 = \phi \cup \{\langle \sigma, s \rangle\}$ we are done.

Lda-o As there are no schematic λ-terms we have $\Gamma \vdash_o \lambda x{:}A.b : \Pi x{:}A.B$ as a consequence of $\Gamma, x{:}A \vdash_o b : B$. By induction hypothesis $\Gamma, x{:}A \vdash_{o+} b : X \,|\, \mathcal{C}$ and we have a sort assignment ϕ satisfying $\mathcal{C}$ such that $B = \phi X$. We conclude that $\Gamma \vdash_{o+} \lambda x{:}A.b : \Pi x{:}A.X \,|\, \mathcal{C}$ and also $\Pi x{:}A.B = \Pi x{:}A.\phi(X) = \phi(\Pi x{:}A.X)$.

App-o $\Gamma \vdash_o \phi(X)\, b : A\, b$ from $\Gamma \vdash_o \phi(X) : A$, $\Gamma \vdash_o b : B$ and $A \simeq_\pi \Pi x{:}B.A_0$. By induction hypothesis $\Gamma \vdash_{o+} X : Y \,|\, \mathcal{C}$ and $\Gamma \vdash_{o+} b : Z \,|\, \mathcal{D}$ where we may assume $\mathsf{SV}(\mathcal{C})$ and $\mathsf{SV}(\mathcal{D})$ to be disjoint. Also we have a sort assignments ϕ_1 and ϕ_2 respectively satisfying $\mathcal{C}$ and $\mathcal{D}$ such that $A = \phi_1 Y$ and $B = \phi_2 Z$. Taking $\phi_3 = \phi_1 \cup \phi_2$, we have $\phi_3 Y \simeq_\pi \Pi x{:}B\;\;{}_0$, hence $Y \twoheadrightarrow_\pi \Pi x{:}B_0.Y_0$ where $B_0 \simeq_\pi B = \phi_3 Z$. Now, as $\phi_3 B_0 = B_0$ it follows by 83(ii) that $B_0 \simeq_\pi Z \,|\, \mathcal{E}$ for some constraint $\mathcal{E}$ which is satisfied by ϕ_3. Hence $\Gamma \vdash_{o+} X\, b : Y\, b \,|\, \mathcal{C} \cup \mathcal{D} \cup \mathcal{E}$, $\phi_3 \models \mathcal{C} \cup \mathcal{D} \cup \mathcal{E}$ and $A\, b = \phi_3(Y)\, b = \phi_3(Y\, b)$. □

We want to show that the substitution lemma and the closure lemma of $\vdash_o$ carry over to $\vdash_{o+}$. In order to avoid reasoning about schematic derivations to prove these, we introduce a technical device. Define a new PTS, $\{\mathcal{S}_0, \mathcal{V}, \mathcal{A}_0, \mathcal{R}_0\}$, the *completely full* PTS derived as follows from the PTS $\{\mathcal{S}, \mathcal{V}, \mathcal{A}, \mathcal{R}\}$ under consideration:

$$\begin{aligned} \mathcal{S}_0 &= \mathcal{S} \\ \mathcal{A}_0 &= \{\, \langle s_1, s_2 \rangle \mid s_1, s_2 \in \mathcal{S} \,\} \\ \mathcal{R}_0 &= \{\, \langle s_1, s_2, s_3 \rangle \mid s_1, s_2, s_3 \in \mathcal{S} \,\} \end{aligned}$$

The possible constraints in the two systems are identical, but in our new PTS every formula of the form $\langle \alpha, \beta \rangle \in \mathcal{A}$ or $\langle \alpha, \beta, \gamma \rangle \in \mathcal{R}$ is satisfied by every sort assignment; only the equations in a constraint are important for satisfiability. Further, consider the assignment, ϕ_0, that maps every $\sigma \in \Sigma$ to some one, arbitrary, $s_0 \in \mathcal{S}$, and hence satisfies every constraint.

Lemma 86 Approximate substitution for $\vdash_{o+}$.

If $\quad \Gamma_1, x{:}A, \Gamma_2 \vdash_{o+} b : Y \,|\, \mathcal{D}, \quad \Gamma_1 \vdash_{o+} a : X \,|\, \mathcal{C}$ *and* $X \simeq_\pi A \,|\, \mathcal{E}$
then $\exists Y_0, \mathcal{D}_0, \mathcal{E}_0\, [\Gamma_1, \Gamma_2[x := a] \vdash_{o+} b[x := a] : Y_0 \,|\, \mathcal{D}_0$ *and* $Y_0 \simeq_\pi Y[x := a] \,|\, \mathcal{E}_0]$.

Proof. Suppose $\Gamma_1, x{:}A, \Gamma_2 \vdash_{o+} b : Y \,|\, \mathcal{D}$, $\Gamma_1 \vdash_{o+} a : X \,|\, \mathcal{C}$ and $X \simeq_\pi A \,|\, \mathcal{E}$. As in our new system $\phi_0 \models \mathcal{C} \cup \mathcal{D} \cup \mathcal{E}$, it follows from 85(i) that in this system $\Gamma_1, x{:}A, \Gamma_2 \vdash_o b : \phi_0 Y$, $\Gamma_1 \vdash_o a : \phi_0 X$ and $\phi_0 X \simeq_\pi A$. Hence we have by 42 that $\Gamma_1, \Gamma_2[x := a] \vdash_o b[x := a] : B_0[x := a]$ where $B_0 \simeq_\pi \phi_0 Y$, and by 85(ii) there is Y_0, $\mathcal{D}_0$ and ϕ such that $\Gamma_1, \Gamma_2[x := a] \vdash_{o+} b[x := a] : Y_0 \,|\, \mathcal{D}_0$ and $\phi Y_0 = B_0[x := a]$. But $\phi Y_0 = B_0[x := a] \simeq_\pi (\phi_0 Y)[x := a] = \phi_0(Y[x := a])$ and it follows from 83 that $Y_0 \simeq_\pi Y[x := a] \,|\, \mathcal{E}_0$ for some constraint $\mathcal{E}_0$. □

Lemma 87 Weak Closure for $\vdash_{o+}$.

If $\quad \Gamma \vdash_{o+} a : X \,|\, \mathcal{C}$, $\Gamma \twoheadrightarrow \Gamma_0$ *and* $a \twoheadrightarrow a_0$
then $\exists X_0, \mathcal{C}_0, \mathcal{D}_0\, [\Gamma_0 \vdash_{o+} a_0 : X_0 \,|\, \mathcal{C}_0$ *and* $X_0 \simeq_\pi X \,|\, \mathcal{D}_0]$.

Proof. Suppose $\Gamma \vdash_{o+} a : X \,|\, \mathcal{C}$, $\Gamma \twoheadrightarrow \Gamma_0$ and $a \twoheadrightarrow a_0$. As $\phi_0 \models \mathcal{C}$ in the new system we have by 85 that $\Gamma \vdash_o a : \phi_0 X$, and hence by closure for $\vdash_o$ (45) that $\Gamma_0 \vdash_o a_0 : A_0$ where $A_0 \simeq_\pi \phi_0 X$. Again by 85 there is X_0, $\mathcal{C}_0$ and ϕ such that $\Gamma_0 \vdash_{o+} a_0 : X_0 \,|\, \mathcal{C}_0$ where $\phi X_0 = A_0$. It follows from 83 that $\phi X_0 = A_0 \simeq_\pi \phi_0 X$ and hence $X_0 \simeq_\pi X \,|\, \mathcal{D}_0$ for some $\mathcal{D}_0$. □

Now we define the relation $\vdash_{tp+}$.

Definition 88 $\vdash_{tp+}$. The relation $\vdash_{tp+} \subseteq \mathsf{C} \times (\mathsf{T} \cup \mathsf{T}^{\Sigma}) \times (\mathsf{T} \cup \mathsf{T}^{\Sigma}) \times \mathsf{Cnstr}$ is the smallest relation satisfying the rules for $\vdash_{o+}$, but having instead of the rule App-o+ the following rule for application.

$$\text{App-tp+} \quad \frac{\Gamma \vdash_{tp+} a : X \,|\, \mathcal{C}}{\Gamma \vdash_{tp+} a\, b : X\, b \,|\, \mathcal{C}}$$

Clearly $\vdash_{o+} \subseteq \vdash_{tp+}$, or more precisely, if $\Gamma \vdash_{o+} a : X \,|\, \mathcal{C}$ then $\Gamma \vdash_{tp+} a : X \,|\, \mathcal{D}$ for some $\mathcal{D}$. As the systems are syntax directed we have also: if $\Gamma \vdash_{tp+} a : X \,|\, \mathcal{D}$ and $\Gamma \vdash_{o+} a : Y \,|\, \mathcal{C}$ then $X = Y$.

Lemma 89 Equivalence of $\vdash_{tp}$ *and* $\vdash_{tp+}$.

i *If* $\Gamma \vdash_{tp+} X : Y \,|\, \mathcal{C}$ *and* $\phi \models \mathcal{C}$ *then* $\Gamma \vdash_{tp} \phi X : \phi Y$

ii *If* $\Gamma \vdash_{tp} \phi X : A$ *then* $\exists Y, \mathcal{C}, \phi_1 [\phi_1 \supseteq \phi,\ \phi_1 \models \mathcal{C},\ A = \phi Y$ *and* $\Gamma \vdash_{tp+} X : Y \,|\, \mathcal{C}]$

The proof is similar to the proof of 85.

We are ready to define a syntax directed set of rules for arbitrary PTS.

Definition 90 $\vdash_{sd-n}$. For each $n \in \mathsf{N}$ the relation $\vdash_{sd-n} \subseteq \mathsf{C} \times \mathsf{T} \times (\mathsf{T} \cup \mathsf{T}^{\Sigma}) \times \mathsf{Cnstr}$ is the smallest relation satisfying the following rules

$$\text{Srt-sd-n} \quad \oslash \vdash_{sd-n} s : \sigma \,|\, \{\langle s, \sigma\rangle \in \mathcal{A}\}$$

$$\text{Var-sd-n} \quad \frac{\Gamma \vdash_{sd-n} A :\twoheadrightarrow \alpha \,|\, \mathcal{C}}{\Gamma, x{:}A \vdash_{sd-n} x : A \,|\, \mathcal{C}}$$

$$\text{Wk-sd-n} \quad \frac{\Gamma \vdash_{sd-n} b : X \,|\, \mathcal{C} \qquad \Gamma \vdash_{sd-n} A :\twoheadrightarrow \alpha \,|\, \mathcal{D}}{\Gamma, x{:}A \vdash_{sd-n} b : X \,|\, \mathcal{C} \cup \mathcal{D}} \qquad b \in \mathcal{S} \cup \mathcal{V}$$

$$\text{Pi-sd-n} \quad \frac{\Gamma \vdash_{sd-n} A :\twoheadrightarrow \alpha \,|\, \mathcal{C} \qquad \Gamma, x{:}A \vdash_{sd-n} B :\twoheadrightarrow \beta \,|\, \mathcal{D}}{\Gamma \vdash_{sd-n} \Pi x{:}A.B : \sigma \,|\, \mathcal{C} \cup \mathcal{D} \cup \{\langle \alpha, \beta, \sigma\rangle \in \mathcal{R}\}}$$

$$\text{Lda-sd-n} \quad \frac{\Gamma \vdash_{sd-n} A :\twoheadrightarrow \alpha \,|\, \mathcal{C} \qquad \Gamma, x{:}A \vdash_{sd-n} b :\overset{n}{\Rightarrow} X \,|\, \mathcal{D}}{\Gamma \vdash_{sd-n} \lambda x{:}A.b : \Pi x{:}A.X \,|\, \mathcal{C} \cup \mathcal{D} \cup \mathcal{E} \cup \{\langle \alpha, \beta, \sigma\rangle\} \in \mathcal{R}} \qquad \Gamma, x{:}A \vdash_{tp+} X :\twoheadrightarrow_{\pi} \beta \,|\, \mathcal{E}$$

$$\text{App-sd-n} \quad \frac{\Gamma \vdash_{sd-n} a :\twoheadrightarrow^{wh} \Pi x{:}B.X \,|\, \mathcal{C} \qquad \Gamma \vdash_{sd-n} b : Y \,|\, \mathcal{D}}{\Gamma \vdash_{sd-n} a\, b : X[x := b] \,|\, \mathcal{C} \cup \mathcal{D} \cup \mathcal{E}} \qquad Y \simeq B \,|\, \mathcal{E}$$

We prove soundness and completeness of $\vdash_{sd-n}$ with respect to $\vdash_{nsd-n}$.

Lemma 91 Soundness of $\vdash_{sd-n}$ *with respect to* $\vdash_{nsd-n}$.

If $\Gamma \vdash_{sd-n} a : X \,|\, \mathcal{C}$ *and* $\phi \models \mathcal{C}$
then $\Gamma \vdash_{nsd-n} a : \phi X$.

Proof. Induction on $\Gamma \vdash_{sd-n} a : A$.

Srt-sd-n $\oslash \vdash_{sd-n} s : \sigma \,|\, \{\langle s, \sigma\rangle\} \in \mathcal{A}$ If $\phi \models \{\langle s, \sigma\rangle \in \mathcal{A}\}$ then $\phi\sigma = s_0$ where $\langle s, s_0\rangle \in \mathcal{A}$. Hence $\oslash \vdash_{nsd-n} s : s_0$.

Var-sd-n $\Gamma, x{:}A \vdash_{sd-n} x : A \,|\, \mathcal{C}$ because $\Gamma \vdash_{sd-n} A :\twoheadrightarrow \alpha \,|\, \mathcal{C}$. Suppose $\phi \models \mathcal{C}$, then by induction hypothesis $\Gamma \vdash_{nsd-n} A :\twoheadrightarrow \phi\,\alpha$. As $\phi\,\alpha \in \mathcal{S}$ it follows that $\Gamma, x{:}A \vdash_{nsd-n} x : A$.

Wk-sd-n $\Gamma, x{:}A \vdash_{sd-n} b : X \,|\, \mathcal{C} \cup \mathcal{D}$ because $\Gamma \vdash_{sd-n} b : X \,|\, \mathcal{C}$, $\Gamma \vdash_{sd-n} A :\twoheadrightarrow \alpha \,|\, \mathcal{D}$ and $b \in \mathcal{S} \cup \mathcal{V}$. Suppose $\phi \models \mathcal{C} \cup \mathcal{D}$, then by induction hypothesis $\Gamma \vdash_{nsd-n} b : \phi\,X$ and $\Gamma \vdash_{nsd-n} A :\twoheadrightarrow \phi\,\alpha$. Again $\phi\,\alpha \in \mathcal{S}$, so $\Gamma, x{:}A \vdash_{nsd-n} b : \phi\,X$.

Pi-sd-n $\Gamma \vdash_{sd-n} \Pi x{:}A.B : \sigma \,|\, \mathcal{C} \cup \mathcal{D} \cup \{\langle\alpha,\beta,\sigma\rangle \in \mathcal{R}\}$ because

$$\Gamma \vdash_{sd-n} A :\twoheadrightarrow \alpha \,|\, \mathcal{C} \quad \text{and} \quad \Gamma, x{:}A \vdash_{sd-n} B :\twoheadrightarrow \beta \,|\, \mathcal{D}.$$

Suppose $\phi \models \mathcal{C} \cup \mathcal{D} \cup \{\langle\alpha,\beta,\sigma\rangle \in \mathcal{R}\}$, then by induction hypothesis $\Gamma \vdash_{nsd-n} A :\twoheadrightarrow \phi\,\alpha$ and $\Gamma, x{:}A \vdash_{nsd-n} B :\twoheadrightarrow \phi\,\beta$. As earlier we conclude $\Gamma \vdash_{nsd-n} \Pi x{:}A.B : \phi\,\sigma$ because $\langle\phi\alpha, \phi\beta, \phi\sigma\rangle \in \mathcal{R}$.

Lda-sd-n $\Gamma \vdash_{sd-n} \lambda x{:}A.b : \Pi x{:}A.X \,|\, \mathcal{C} \cup \mathcal{D} \cup \mathcal{E} \cup \{\langle\alpha,\beta,\sigma\rangle \in \mathcal{R}\}$ because

$$\Gamma \vdash_{sd-n} A :\twoheadrightarrow \alpha \,|\, \mathcal{C}, \quad \Gamma, x{:}A \vdash_{sd-n} b :\overset{n}{\Rightarrow} X \,|\, \mathcal{D} \quad \text{and} \quad \Gamma, x{:}A \vdash_{tp+} X :\twoheadrightarrow_{\pi} \beta \,|\, \mathcal{E}.$$

Suppose $\phi \models \mathcal{C} \cup \mathcal{D} \cup \mathcal{E} \cup \{\langle\alpha,\beta,\sigma\rangle \in \mathcal{R}\}$. By induction hypothesis $\Gamma \vdash_{nsd-n} A :\twoheadrightarrow \phi\alpha$ and $\Gamma, x{:}A \vdash_{nsd-n} b :\overset{n}{\Rightarrow} \phi X$. Also by 89 we have $\Gamma, x{:}A \vdash_{tp} \phi\,X :\twoheadrightarrow_{\pi} \phi\,\beta$ and it follows that

$$\Gamma \vdash_{nsd-n} \lambda x{:}A.b : \Pi x{:}A.\phi\,X$$

because $\langle\phi\,\alpha, \phi\,\beta, \phi\,\sigma\rangle \in \mathcal{R}$.

App-sd-n $\Gamma \vdash_{sd-n} a\,b : X[x := b] \,|\, \mathcal{C} \cup \mathcal{D} \cup \mathcal{E}$ because

$$\Gamma \vdash_{sd-n} a :\twoheadrightarrow^{wh} \Pi x{:}B.X \,|\, \mathcal{C}, \quad \Gamma \vdash_{sd-n} b : Y \,|\, \mathcal{D} \quad \text{and } quadY \simeq B \,|\, \mathcal{E}.$$

Suppose $\phi \models \mathcal{C} \cup \mathcal{D} \cup \mathcal{E}$, then by induction hypothesis

$$\Gamma \vdash_{nsd-n} a :\twoheadrightarrow^{wh} \Pi x{:}B.\phi\,X \quad \text{and} \quad \Gamma \vdash_{nsd-n} b : \phi\,Y.$$

Also we have $\phi\,Y \simeq_{\pi} B$ by 32. Hence

$$\Gamma \vdash_{nsd-n} a\,b : \phi\,(X[x := b])$$

because $(\phi\,X)[x := b] = \phi\,(X[x := b])$. □

Lemma 92 Completeness of $\vdash_{sd-n}$ with respect to $\vdash_{nsd-n}$.

If $\quad \Gamma \vdash_{nsd-n} a : A$
then $\exists X \in \mathcal{T} \cup \mathcal{T}^{\Sigma}\, \exists \mathcal{C} \in \mathit{Cnstr}\, \exists\phi \models \mathcal{C}\,[A = \phi\,X$ *and* $\Gamma \vdash_{sd-n} a : X \,|\, \mathcal{C}]$.

Proof. Induction on $\Gamma \vdash_{nsd-n} a : A$.

Srt-nsd-n We have $\oslash \vdash_{nsd-n} s_1 : s_2$ because $\langle s_1, s_2\rangle \in \mathcal{A}$. Hence $\oslash \vdash_{sd-n} s_1 : \sigma \,|\, \{\langle s_1, \sigma\rangle \in \mathcal{A}\}$ where σ is a fresh sort variable. Defining $\phi\,\sigma = s_2$ we have $\phi \models \{\langle s_1, \sigma\rangle \in \mathcal{A}\}$ and we are done.

Var-nsd-n We have $\Gamma, x{:}A \vdash_{nsd-n} x : A$ as a consequence of $\Gamma \vdash_{nsd-n} A : A_0$ where $A_0 \twoheadrightarrow s$. By the induction hypothesis $\Gamma \vdash_{sd-n} A : X_0 \,|\, \mathcal{C}$ and we have $\phi \models \mathcal{C}$ and $\phi\,X_0 = A_0$. Now as $A_0 \twoheadrightarrow s$, also $X_0 \twoheadrightarrow \alpha$ where $\phi\,\alpha = s$. It follows that $\Gamma, x{:}A \vdash_{sd-n} x : A \,|\, \mathcal{C}$.

Wk-nsd-n $\Gamma, x{:}A \vdash_{nsd-n} b : B$ because $\Gamma \vdash_{nsd-n} b : B$ and $\Gamma \vdash_{nsd-n} A : A_0$ where $A_0 \twoheadrightarrow s$, and $b \in \mathcal{S} \cup \mathcal{V}$. Induction gives $\Gamma \vdash_{sd-n} b : Y \,|\, \mathcal{C}$ and $\Gamma \vdash_{sd-n} A : X_0 \,|\, \mathcal{D}$, where we assume $\mathsf{SV}(\mathcal{C})$ and $\mathsf{SV}(\mathcal{D})$ to be disjoint. Also we have ϕ_1 satisfying $\mathcal{C}$ and ϕ_2 satisfying $\mathcal{D}$ with $\phi_1 Y = B$ and $\phi_2 X_0 = A_0$. As $A_0 \twoheadrightarrow s$ it follows that $X_0 \twoheadrightarrow \alpha$. So, taking $\phi = \phi_1 \cup \phi_2$ we have $\Gamma, x{:}A \vdash_{sd-n} b : Y \,|\, \mathcal{C} \cup \mathcal{D}$ where $\phi \models \mathcal{C} \cup \mathcal{D}$ and $\phi Y = B$.

Pi-nsd-n $\Gamma \vdash_{nsd-n} \Pi x{:}A.B : s_3$ as a consequence of $\Gamma \vdash_{nsd-n} A : A_0$ and $\Gamma, x{:}A \vdash_{nsd-n} B : B_0$ where $A_0 \twoheadrightarrow s_1$, $B_0 \twoheadrightarrow s_2$ and $\langle s_1, s_2, s_3 \rangle \in \mathcal{R}$. As before we have $\Gamma \vdash_{sd-n} A : X_0 \,|\, \mathcal{C}$ and $\Gamma, x{:}A \vdash_{sd-n} B : Y_0 \,|\, \mathcal{D}$ where we assume $\mathsf{SV}(\mathcal{C})$ and $\mathsf{SV}(\mathcal{D})$ disjoint, ϕ_1 and ϕ_2 satisfying $\mathcal{C}$ and $\mathcal{D}$ respectively, and $\phi_1 X_0 = A_0$, $\phi_2 Y_0 = B_0$. Hence again $X_0 \twoheadrightarrow \alpha$ and $Y_0 \twoheadrightarrow \beta$, where $\phi_1 \alpha = s_1$ and $\phi_2 \beta = s_2$. It follows that $\Gamma \vdash_{sd-n} \Pi x{:}A.B : \sigma \,|\, \mathcal{C} \cup \mathcal{D} \cup \{\langle \alpha, \beta, \sigma \rangle \in \mathcal{R}\}$. So taking $\phi = \phi_1 \cup \phi_2 \cup \{\langle \sigma, s_3 \rangle\}$ we have $\phi \models \mathcal{C} \cup \mathcal{D} \cup \{\langle \alpha, \beta, \sigma \rangle \in \mathcal{R}\}$ and $\phi\, \sigma = s_3$.

Lda-nsd-n $\Gamma \vdash_{nsd-n} \lambda x{:}A.b : \Pi x{:}A.B$ because $\Gamma \vdash_{nsd-n} A : A_0$ where $A_0 \twoheadrightarrow s_1$, $\Gamma, x{:}A \vdash_{nsd-n} b : B_0$ where $B_0 \overset{n}{\Rightarrow} B$, $\Gamma, x{:}A \vdash_{tp} B :\twoheadrightarrow_\pi s_2$ and $\langle s_1, s_2, s_3 \rangle \in \mathcal{R}$. By induction hypothesis we have $\Gamma \vdash_{sd-n} A : X_0 \,|\, \mathcal{C}$ and $\Gamma, x{:}A \vdash_{sd-n} b : Y_0 \,|\, \mathcal{D}$. We observe that $\mathsf{SV}(\mathcal{C})$ and $\mathsf{SV}(\mathcal{D})$ might be chosen to be disjoint. Also we have ϕ_1 and ϕ_2 satisfying $\mathcal{C}$ and $\mathcal{D}$ respectively, where $\phi_1 X_0 = A_0$ and $\phi_2 Y_0 = B_0$. We define $\phi_3 = \phi_1 \cup \phi_2$. Then we have $\phi_3\, \alpha = s_1$ and $\phi_3 Y_0 = B_0$. And because $B_0 \overset{n}{\Rightarrow} B$ we have also $Y_0 \overset{n}{\Rightarrow} Y$ with $\phi_3 Y = B$. Hence we have $\Gamma, x{:}A \vdash_{tp} \phi_3 Y :\twoheadrightarrow_\pi s_2$ and therefore by 89 $\Gamma \vdash_{tp+} Y :\twoheadrightarrow_\pi \beta \,|\, \mathcal{E}$ and there is an extension ϕ_4 of ϕ_3 with $\phi_4 \models \mathcal{E}$ and $\phi_4\, \beta = s_2$. It follows that

$$\Gamma \vdash_{sd-n} \lambda x{:}A.b : \Pi x{:}A.Y \,|\, \mathcal{C} \cup \mathcal{D} \cup \mathcal{E} \cup \{\langle \alpha, \beta, \sigma \rangle \in \mathcal{R}\}.$$

Also if we take $\phi = \phi_4 \cup \{\langle \sigma, s_3 \rangle\}$ we have $\phi Y = B$, so

$$\phi(\Pi x{:}A.Y) = \Pi x{:}A.B \quad \text{and} \quad \phi \models \mathcal{C} \cup \mathcal{D} \cup \mathcal{E} \cup \{\langle \alpha, \beta, \sigma \rangle \in \mathcal{R}\}.$$

App-nsd-n We have $\Gamma \vdash_{nsd-n} a\, b : A[x := b]$ because

$\Gamma \vdash_{nsd-n} a : A_0$, and $\Gamma \vdash_{nsd-n} b : B_2$ where $A_0 \twoheadrightarrow^{wh} \Pi x{:}B_1.A$ and $B_1 \simeq B_2$.

By induction hypothesis $\Gamma \vdash_{sd-n} a : X_0 \,|\, \mathcal{C}$ and $\Gamma \vdash_{sd-n} b : Y_2 \,|\, \mathcal{D}$ and as before we consider $\mathsf{SV}(\mathcal{C})$ and $\mathsf{SV}(\mathcal{C})$ to be disjoint, and we have also ϕ_1 and ϕ_2 satisfying $\mathcal{C}$ and $\mathcal{D}$ respectively, where $\phi_1 X_0 = A_0$ and $\phi_2 Y_2 = B_2$. It follows that $X_0 \twoheadrightarrow^{wh} \Pi x{:}B_1.X$ and as $\phi_2 Y_2 \simeq_\pi \phi_2 B_1$ we have also $Y_2 \simeq_\pi B_1 \,|\, \mathcal{E}$ where $\phi_2 \models \mathcal{E}$. Hence we have $\Gamma \vdash_{sd-n} a\, b : X[x := b] \,|\, \mathcal{C} \cup \mathcal{D} \cup \mathcal{E}$ and taking $\phi = \phi_1 \cup \phi_2$ we have also $\phi X = A$ and $\phi \models \mathcal{C} \cup \mathcal{D} \cup \mathcal{E}$. □

For proving our second completeness result we need the following property of $\vdash_{sd-n}$.

Lemma 93 Weak Completeness of $\vdash_{o+}$ ***for*** $\vdash_{sd-n}$.

If $\quad \Gamma \vdash_{sd-n} a : X \,|\, \mathcal{C}$
then *i* $\quad \exists Y, \mathcal{D} \quad Y \simeq_\pi X$ *and* $\Gamma \vdash_{o+} a : Y \,|\, \mathcal{D}$
ii $\quad \exists \alpha, \mathcal{D} \quad \Gamma \vdash_{o+} X :\twoheadrightarrow_\pi \alpha \,|\, \mathcal{D}$

Now we prove a second completeness lemma for $\vdash_{sd-n}$.

Lemma 94 Weak Completeness of $\vdash_{sd-n}$ ***with respect to*** $\vdash_{nsdtp}$.

If $\quad \Gamma \vdash_{nsdtp} a : A$
then $\quad \forall n\, \exists X, \mathcal{C}, \mathcal{D}\, [A \simeq X \,|\, \mathcal{C}$ *and* $\Gamma \vdash_{sd-n} a : X \,|\, \mathcal{D}]$.

Proof. Induction on $\Gamma \vdash_{nsdtp} a : A$. We select interesting cases.

Wk-nsdtp We have $\Gamma, x{:}A \vdash_{nsdtp} b : B$ as a consequence of $\Gamma \vdash_{nsdtp} b : B$, $\Gamma \vdash_{nsdtp} A : A_0$ where $A_0 \twoheadrightarrow s$ and $b \in \mathcal{S} \cup \mathcal{V}$. By induction hypothesis we have $\Gamma \vdash_{sd-n} b : X \,|\, \mathcal{D}_1$ where $B \simeq X \,|\, \mathcal{C}_1$ and $\Gamma \vdash_{sd-n} A : Y \,|\, \mathcal{D}_2$ where $A_0 \simeq Y \,|\, \mathcal{C}_2$. Now as $A_0 \twoheadrightarrow s$ it follows that $Y \twoheadrightarrow \alpha$ and hence $\Gamma, x{:}A \vdash_{sdtp-n} b : X \,|\, \mathcal{D}_1 \cup \mathcal{D}_2$.

Lda-nsdtp We have $\Gamma \vdash_{nsdtp} \lambda x{:}A.b : \Pi x{:}A.B$ as a consequence of $\Gamma \vdash_{nsdtp} A : A_0$ where $A_0 \twoheadrightarrow s_1$ and $\Gamma, x{:}A \vdash_{nsdtp} b : B_0$ where $B_0 \twoheadrightarrow B$. And also we know $\Gamma, x{:}A \vdash_{tp} B : C$ where $C \twoheadrightarrow_\pi s_2$ and $\langle s_1, s_2, s_3 \rangle \in \mathcal{R}$. By the induction hypothesis we have: $\Gamma \vdash_{sd-n} A : X \,|\, \mathcal{D}_1$ where $A_0 \simeq X \,|\, \mathcal{C}_1$, and $\Gamma, x{:}A \vdash_{sd-n} b : Y \,|\, \mathcal{D}_2$ where $B_0 \simeq Y \,|\, \mathcal{C}_2$. We observe that $X \twoheadrightarrow \alpha$. Also we have by 93 that $\Gamma, x{:}A \vdash_{o+} Y :\twoheadrightarrow_\pi \beta \,|\, \mathcal{E}$. Now we define Y_n by $Y \overset{n}{\Rightarrow} Y_n$. Then also $\Gamma, x{:}A \vdash_{o+} Y_n :\twoheadrightarrow_\pi \beta \,|\, \mathcal{E}_1$ by 87, and therefore also $\Gamma, x{:}A \vdash_{tp+} Y_n :\twoheadrightarrow_\pi \beta \,|\, \mathcal{E}_2$. It follows that

$$\Gamma \vdash_{sdtp-n} \lambda x{:}A.b : \Pi x{:}A.Y_n \,|\, \mathcal{D}_1 \cup \mathcal{D}_2 \cup \mathcal{E}2 \cup \{\langle \alpha, \beta, \sigma \rangle \in \mathcal{R}\}$$

by Lda-sd-n, and also $\Pi x{:}A.Y_n \simeq \Pi x{:}A.B \,|\, \mathcal{C}_2$, because $B_0 \simeq Y \,|\, \mathcal{C}_2$, $B \simeq B_0$ and $Y_n \simeq Y$.

App-nsdtp We have $\Gamma \vdash_{nsdtp} a\, b : A[x := b]$ as a consequence of $\Gamma \vdash_{nsdtp} a : A_0$ where $A_0 \twoheadrightarrow^{wh} \Pi x{:}B.A$ and $\Gamma \vdash_{nsdtp} b : B_0$ where $B_0 \simeq B$. By the induction hypothesis $\Gamma \vdash_{sd-n} a : X \,|\, \mathcal{D}_1$ where $A_0 \simeq X \,|\, \mathcal{C}_1$ and $\Gamma \vdash_{sd-n} b : Y \,|\, \mathcal{D}_2$ where $B_0 \simeq Y \,|\, \mathcal{C}_2$. It follows that $X \twoheadrightarrow^{wh} \Pi x{:}B_1.X_1$ where $B \simeq B_1$ and therefore also $Y \simeq B_0 \,|\, \mathcal{C}_2$. Hence $\Gamma \vdash_{sd-n} a\, b : X[x := b] \,|\, \mathcal{D}_1 \cup \mathcal{D}_2 \cup \mathcal{C}_2$ by App-sd-n. □

It is the place to collect results. We will characterize $\vdash$ in terms of the relations $\vdash_{sd-n}$. As the latter have syntax directed presentations there is an obvious way to construct checking algorithms for them, and hence we have an (efficient) algorithm for typechecking $\vdash$.

Lemma 95 Soundness of $\vdash_{sd-n}$ for $\vdash$.

If $\Gamma \vdash_{sd-n} a : X \,|\, \mathcal{C}$, $\Gamma \vdash_{sd-n} A :\twoheadrightarrow \alpha \,|\, \mathcal{D}$, $X \simeq A \,|\, \mathcal{E}$ *and* $\phi \models \mathcal{C} \cup \mathcal{D} \cup \mathcal{E}$
then $\Gamma \vdash a : A$

Proof. We have by 91 that $\Gamma \vdash_{nsd-n} a : \phi X$ and $\Gamma \vdash_{nsd-n} A :\twoheadrightarrow \phi\alpha$. Hence we have by 78 that $\Gamma \vdash_{nsdtp} a : \phi X$ and $\Gamma \vdash_{nsdtp} A :\twoheadrightarrow \phi\alpha$. And therefore by 14 $\Gamma \vdash a : \phi X$ and $\Gamma \vdash A : A_0$ where $A_0 \twoheadrightarrow \phi\alpha$. Now $\phi\alpha = s \in \mathcal{S}$ and it follows by closure that $\Gamma \vdash A : s$. And as $\phi \models \mathcal{E}$ we have $\phi X \simeq A$, so $\Gamma \vdash a : A$ by Cnv. □

The next lemma states that for all n, $\vdash_{sd-n}$ succeeds on every well typed subject; the rub is that, if n is not large enough, the constraints may not be satisfiable.

Lemma 96 Weak Completeness of $\vdash_{sd-n}$ for $\vdash$.

If $\Gamma \vdash a : A$
then $\forall n\, \exists X, \alpha, \mathcal{C}, \mathcal{D}, \mathcal{E}\ [\Gamma \vdash_{sd-n} a : X \,|\, \mathcal{C},\ A \simeq X \,|\, \mathcal{E}$ *and*
$[A \in \mathcal{S}$ *or* $\Gamma \vdash_{sd-n} A :\twoheadrightarrow \alpha \,|\, \mathcal{D}]]$.

Proof. If $\Gamma \vdash a : A$ then we have by 58 that $\Gamma \vdash_{nsdtp} a : A_0$ where $A_0 \simeq A$. It follows by lemma 94 that $\Gamma \vdash_{sd-n} a : X \,|\, \mathcal{C}$ where $A_0 \simeq X \,|\, \mathcal{E}$ and hence also $A \simeq X \,|\, \mathcal{E}$. And we have also either $A \in \mathcal{S}$ or $\Gamma \vdash A : s$. In the first case we are done. In the second case we repeat our argument, getting $\Gamma \vdash_{sd-n} A : Y \,|\, \mathcal{D}$ with $s \simeq Y \,|\, E_1$ and therefore $Y \twoheadrightarrow \alpha \in \mathcal{S} \cup \Sigma$. □

Lemma 97 Completeness of $\vdash_{sd-n}$ *for* $\vdash$.

If $\Gamma \vdash a : A$
then $\exists n, X, \alpha, \mathcal{C}, \mathcal{D}, \phi\ [\phi \models \mathcal{C} \cup \mathcal{D},\ \Gamma \vdash_{sd-n} a : X \mid \mathcal{C},\ A \simeq \phi X$ *and* $[A \in \mathcal{S}$ *or* $\Gamma \vdash_{sd-n} A :\twoheadrightarrow \alpha \mid \mathcal{D}]]$.

The proofs are similar to the proofs of the corresponding lemma's for $\vdash_{sd-n}$, and use the fact that all terms and all schematic terms considered will normalize, as they are β-convertible to terms of the underlying PTS.

8 Conclusion

We have presented efficient syntax directed presentations of two subclasses of PTS:

- the semi-full systems, via the $\vdash_{sdsf}$ relation
- the functional systems, via the $\vdash_f$ relation

The only remaining defect in these presentations lies in the possible failure of tests for conversion in the application rule. Thus for normalizing functional and semi-full systems, everything has been said.

For non-functional systems the situation is less clear. We know of no *a priori* bound on the amount of reduction necessary to correctly type λ-abstractions, so we must be content with the collective completeness of the family of syntax directed systems $\vdash_{sd-n}$.

We have made little impact on the Expansion Postponement problem, which we leave as future work. We can however bask in the relative peace of mind gained from the machine-checked presentation of most (i.e. those not concerning schematic judgments) of the above results.

References

[Bar91] Henk Barendregt. Introduction to generalised type systems. *J. Functional Programming*, 1(2):125–154, April 1991.

[Bar92] Henk Barendregt. Lambda calculi with types. In Gabbai Abramsky and Maibaum, editors, *Handbook of Logic in Computer Science*, volume II. Oxford University Press, 1992.

[Ber90] Stefano Berardi. *Type Dependence and Constructive Mathematics.* PhD thesis, Dipartimento di Informatica, Torino, Italy, 1990.

[CH88] Thierry Coquand and Gérard Huet. The calculus of constructions. *Information and Computation*, 76(2/3):95–120, February/March 1988.

[Cha77] Tat-Hung Chan. An algorithm for checking PL/CV arithmetical inferences. Technical Report 77–236, Computer Science Department, Cornell University, Ithaca, New York, 1977.

[Geu] Herman Geuvers. The calculus of constructions and higher order logic. In preparation.

[Geu93] Herman Geuvers. *Logics and Type Systems.* PhD thesis, Department of Mathematics and Computer Science, University of Nijmegen, 1993. To appear.

[GN91] Herman Geuvers and Mark-Jan Nederhof. A modular proof of strong normalization for the calculus of constructions. *Journal of Functional Programming*, 1(2):155–189, April 1991.

[Hel91] Leen Helmink. Goal directed proof construction in type theory. In *Logical Frameworks*. Cambridge University Press, 1991.

[HHP87] Robert Harper, Furio Honsell, and Gordon Plotkin. A framework for defining logics. In *Proceedings of the Symposium on Logic in Computer Science*, pages 194–204, Ithaca, New York, June 1987.

[HHP92] Robert Harper, Furio Honsell, and Gordon Plotkin. A framework for defining logics. *Journal of the ACM*, 40(1):143–184, 1992. Preliminary version in LICS'87.

[HP91] Robert Harper and Robert Pollack. Type checking with universes. *Theoretical Computer Science*, 89:107–136, 1991.

[Hue87] Gérard Huet. Extending the calculus of constructions with Type:Type. unpublished manuscript, April 1987.

[Hue89] Gérard Huet. The constructive engine. In R. Narasimhan, editor, *A Perspective in Theoretical Computer Science*. World Scientific Publishing, 1989. Commemorative Volume for Gift Siromoney.

[LP92] Zhaohui Luo and Robert Pollack. LEGO proof development system: User's manual. Technical Report ECS-LFCS-92-211, LFCS, Computer Science Dept., University of Edinburgh, The King's Buildings, Edinburgh EH9 3JZ, May 1992. Updated version.

[Luo90] Zhaohui Luo. *An Extended Calculus of Constructions*. PhD thesis, Department of Computer Science, University of Edinburgh, June 1990.

[Mar72] Per Martin-Löf. An intuitionistic theory of types. Technical report, University of Stockholm, 1972.

[MP93] James McKinna and Robert Pollack. Pure type systems formalized. In M.Bezem and J.F.Groote, editors, *Proceedings of the International Conference on Typed Lambda Calculi and Applications, TLCA'93*, pages 289–305. Springer-Verlag, LNCS 664, March 1993.

[MP94] James McKinna and Robert Pollack. Pure type systems formalized. Available by anonymous ftp from `ftp.dcs.ed.ac.uk`, directory `export/lego`, file `PTSproofs.tar.Z`, 1994.

[Pfe89] Frank Pfenning. Elf: A language for logic definition and verified metaprogramming. In *Proceedings of the Fourth Annual Symposium on Logic in Computer Science, Asilomar, California*, June 1989.

[Pol92] R. Pollack. Typechecking in pure type systems. In *Informal Proceedings of the 1992 Workshop on Types for Proofs and Programs, Båstad, Sweden*, pages 271–288, June 1992. available by ftp.

[Pol94] Robert Pollack. *The Theory of LEGO; A Proof Checker for the Extended Calculus of Constructions*. PhD thesis, University of Edinburgh, 1994. In preparation.

[vBJ93] L.S. van Benthem Jutting. Typing in pure type systems. *Information and Computation*, 105(1):30–41, July 1993.

[vD80] D. T. van Daalen. *The Language Theory of Automath*. PhD thesis, Technische Hogeschool Eindhoven, 1980.

Infinite Objects in Type Theory

Thierry Coquand

Programming Methodology Group. Department of Computer Sciences. Chalmers University of Technology and University of Göteborg. S-412 96 Göteborg, Sweden
e-mail coquand@cs.chalmers.se

Abstract. We show that infinite objects can be constructively understood without the consideration of partial elements, or greatest fixed-points, through the explicit consideration of proof objects. We present then a proof system based on these explanations. According to this analysis, the proof expressions should have the same structure as the program expressions of a pure functional lazy language: variable, constructor, application, abstraction, case expressions, and local let expressions.

1 Introduction

The usual explanation of infinite objects relies on the use of greatest fixed-points of monotone operators, whose existence is justified by the impredicative proof of Tarski's fixed point theorem. The proof theory of such infinite objects, based on the so called co-induction principle, originally due to David Park [21] and explained with this name for instance in the paper [18], reflects this explanation. Constructively, to rely on such impredicative methods is somewhat unsatisfactory (see for instance the discussion in [13]) and this paper is a tentative attempt for a more direct understanding of infinite objects. Interestingly, the explicit consideration of proof objects plays an essential rôle here and this approach suggests an alternative reasoning system. In particular, the notion of constructors, or introduction rules, keeps the fundamental importance it has for proof systems about well-founded objects [15], while it appears as a derived notion in proof systems based on co-induction (where this notion is secondary to the notion of destructors, or elimination rules). As a consequence, the strong normalisation property does not hold any more, but it is still the case that any closed term reduces to a canonical form.

Briefly, we can describe our approach as follows. A co-inductive predicate, relation, ... is defined by its introduction rules. Following the proofs as programs principle, we represent them as constructors of a functional language with dependent types and each proof is now represented as a functional expression. Like

* This research has been done within the ESPRIT Basic Research Action "Types for Proofs and Programs". It has been paid by NUTEK, Chalmers and the University of Göteborg.

in a programming language, we can define a function by recursion, which corresponds to a proof where the result we want to prove is used recursively. This cannot be considered to be a valid proof in general, and has to satisfy some conditions in order to be correct. We describe a simple syntactical check that ensures this correctness, which we believe leads to a natural style of proofs about infinite (or lazy) objects.

Since one important application we have in mind is the mechanisation of reasoning about programs and processes, we analyse in our formalism some concrete examples from the literature [22, 18].

Besides to illustrate further the increasingly recognized importance of infinite proofs for programming language semantics, we hope to show also that the addition of infinite objects is an interesting extension of Type Theory. In particular, we can now represent a notion of processes in Type Theory.

2 General presentation

2.1 Type Theory of Well-Founded Objects

We recall briefly some basic notions of type theory of well-founded objects, that will be important for the extension to infinite objects. We use the word "expressions" or "terms" for designing syntactical representations of such objects. The books [20, 15] contain more detailed explanations, and the reference [3] describes the addition of case expressions and pattern-matching. We present first these definitions in general terms, and will explicit them more in details in a special instance when we present the guarded induction principle.

Computation Tree Semantics A(n inductive) **set** A is defined by its **constructors**. A closed term of type A can be thought of as a well-founded tree, built out of constructors. We identify sets and **propositions**. The constructors can be interpreted as **introduction rules**, and a closed proof of the proposition A is a well-founded proof tree built out of introduction rules.

Besides terms purely built out of constructors, one needs also to consider **noncanonical** expressions [15, 7]. The addition of such expressions is done in such a way however that any closed term of a closed set can be reduced to a **canonical form**, i.e. a term of the form $c(a_1, \ldots, a_n)$ where c is a constructor[2]. We can then associate in a natural way to any term a tree built out of constructors, and we require this tree to be well-founded. This tree is called the **computation tree** of a term. A **component** of a closed term is a (closed) term of the same type that appears in its computation tree. This defines an order relation on closed terms, called the **component ordering**.

What is essential is the fact that the component ordering is well-founded.

These notions can be traced back to Brouwer's idea of the "fully analysed" form of a proof [7].

[2] Our notations will follow [20].

Examples The set N of integers is defined by its constructors $0 : \mathsf{N}$ and $\mathsf{s} : (\mathsf{N})\mathsf{N}$. A closed element of type N is thus a finite object of the form $\mathsf{s}^k(0)$.

Let us consider a type P with constructors $\mathsf{out} : (\mathsf{N})(\mathsf{P})\mathsf{P}$, $\mathsf{in} : ((\mathsf{N})\mathsf{P})\mathsf{P}$ and $\mathsf{nil} : \mathsf{P}$. A closed element $p : \mathsf{P}$ has to be thought of as a well-founded tree built with the constructors out, in and nil. For instance, if $u(n) = \mathsf{out}(n, \mathsf{nil})$, the term $\mathsf{in}(u)$ has for components all the instances $\mathsf{out}(\mathsf{s}^k(0), \mathsf{nil})$ and nil.

The requirement that we should be able to think of all closed elements as a tree, with a definite branching (that may be infinite), imposes strong restriction on the type of the constructors. Thus, we cannot have a set X with a constructor of type $((X)X)X$ or of type $(((X)\mathsf{N})\mathsf{N})X$. However, a condition of strict positivity [8] on the type of the constructors is enough to ensure that we can think of elements as trees built out of constructors.

Noncanonical Constants We now give a general way of adding new noncanonical constant. These additions will be such that it will be possible at each "stages" to associate a well-founded proof tree to any closed object. A new constant f is first given a type $(x_1 : A_1, \ldots, x_n : A_n)A$, and then by its definition $f(x_1, \ldots, x_n) = e$, where e is an expression built on previously defined constants and case expressions. The definition may be recursive, but, using the semantics of a term as a well-founded tree, we can ensure that the recursive calls are well-founded and justify in such a way this recursivity. We notice, as in [6], that there is a simple syntactical check that ensures this: there exists a lexicographic ordering of the arguments of f, such that all recursive calls are well-founded for the lexicographic extension of the component ordering.

Examples The Ackerman function $A : (\mathsf{N})(\mathsf{N})\mathsf{N}$ defined by the equation

$$A(0, n) = \mathsf{s}(n),\ A(\mathsf{s}(m), 0) = A(m, \mathsf{s}(0)),\ A(\mathsf{s}(m), \mathsf{s}(n)) = A(m, A(\mathsf{s}(m), n)),$$

follows the schema of definition, since the recursive calls are always smaller for the lexicographic ordering. We can thus add it as a noncanonical constant.

Soundness As noticed in [15], to follow this semantics of well-founded trees will ensure that there is *no* closed term of type $\bot$, which is defined as a set with no constructor. Indeed, there is by definition no canonical element of this type, and hence no element that reduces to a canonical form.

This simple remark is important if we look at this set theory as a proof system. Indeed, it expresses a form of consistency of this proof system. So, as long as we add new rules that are justified w.r.t. this semantics in term of well-founded trees, we are sure of the consistency of our rules.

2.2 Infinite Objects

Analogy between proofs and processes It is tempting to think of an object of type P as a process p which has three possible behaviours: it can either emit an integer and becomes p_1, when it is of the form $\mathsf{out}(n, p_1)$, or express that it needs an integer as input, if it is of the form $\mathsf{in}(u)$, or show that it is inert, if it is of the form nil. In this reading, the computation tree of an element is the "behaviour tree" [19] of the process associated to it.

With this reading, the restriction to well-founded objects seems too strong. For the type P as defined above, this will mean that we consider only processes that eventually become inert. This forbids for instance a process $p = \mathsf{in}([n]\mathsf{out}(\mathsf{s}(n), p))$ that interactively asks for an integer and outputs its successor.

It is thus quite natural to consider also **lazy** elements that can be thought of as arbitrary, not necessarily well-founded, trees built out of constructors. In particular, a lazy term eventually reduce to constructor form, and there cannot be any lazy proof of $\perp$.

As we have seen, the consideration of such objects is common in the analysis of processes [19]. The consideration of not necessarily well-founded objects arouse also in proof theory, for the study of proofs in ω-logic [9].

The process $p = \mathsf{in}([n]\mathsf{out}(\mathsf{s}(n), p))$ recursively defined is a lazy element of the set P. It makes also sense of considering lazy elements of the set Ω, which has only one constructor $s : (\Omega)\Omega$. The well-founded version of this type is empty, but the set Ω contains the recursively defined lazy element $\omega = s(\omega)$. An object is called **productive** if we can associate a computation tree to it, without requiring this computation tree to be well-founded. If x is a (productive) object of type Ω, it should reduce to an element $x = s(x_1)$ because s is the only constructor of the set Ω, and similarly x_1 should reduce to an element $x_1 = s(x_2)$, and so on.

We can now see well-founded objects as special cases of productive objects. They are productive objects that are *accessible* for the component relation. If A is a data type, we will write $a \epsilon A$ for stressing that a is a well-founded element of A, and, in general, $a : A$ for expressing only that a is a productive element of A. Sometimes, we consider only well-founded elements of a data type A, for instance if A is the data type N of natural numbers, and it is then understood that $a : A$ means that a is well-founded.

Though this notion of productivity seems clear, at least in the case of finitely branching trees, the main problem will be to give a finitary precise definition of productivity. We will give this definition after reviewing some attempts in adding infinite objects to type theory. Though simple, it is surprising that the definition we shall present achieves this goal without infinitary considerations based on greatest fixed-points or infinite ordinals[3].

[3] This definition can be extracted from the paper [11], where the notion of "convergence" corresponds to our notion of productivity.

Problem with the addition of infinite objects Some problems in adding infinite objects in Type Theory are analysed by Martin-Löf in the reference [16]. One basic problem can be expressed as follows: how to add infinite objects without also adding partial objects, that is objects that do not reduce to a canonical form? We recall that this condition was indeed crucial as a guarantee of consistency of Type Theory seen as a proof system.

For instance, it is not correct to define a function $f : (\Omega)\Omega$ by the equation $f(s(x)) = f(x)$, because then $f(\omega)$ does not reduce to canonical form. In contrast, the definition $f(s(x)) = s(f(x))$ should be clearly allowed, because the element $f(x)$ is then productive if $x : \Omega$ is productive. Indeed, if x is productive, we have a chain of equalities

$$x = s(x_1),\ x_1 = s(x_2),\ x_2 = s(x_3), \ldots$$

which will give the chain equalities

$$f(x) = s(f(x_1)),\ f(x_1) = s(f(x_2)),\ f(x_2) = s(f(x_3)), \ldots$$

Is their a simple syntactical criteria that ensures the preservation of productivity, which is not too restrictive?

In our analysis, a definition of the primitive recursive form

$$f(s(x)) = g(x, f(x))$$

cannot be justified in general. Indeed, the justification of such a definition relies ultimately on the fact that we consider only well-founded objects [15].

In [16], a different view is followed, based on an unexpected analogy between the addition of infinite objects in type theory and non-standard extensions in non-standard analysis. This explanation rejects circular definitions such as $\omega = s(\omega)$, but allow non well-founded definitions such as

$$\omega_0 = s(\omega_1),\ \omega_1 = s(\omega_2), \ldots$$

In this approach, a definition like $f(s(x)) = f(x)$ is allowed. This implies the existence of closed terms that have no canonical form, namely $f(\omega_0)$. Despite this problem, it is still possible however to establish the consistency of Type Theory with such an extension [16].

In the next paragraph, we will suggest a proof principle which can also be seen as a way of defining functions over not necessarily well-founded objects. This new proof principle relies directly on the semantics of an object as a not necessarily well-founded tree built out of constructors.

A key example At this point, the basic difficulty is to find a way of defining functions that ensures that any instances of such functions on productive elements are productive. For this, the first step is of course to have a precise notion of productivity.

In order to find this definition, let us analyse a key example. We consider the function $f : (\mathsf{P})\mathsf{P}$ defined by the equations

$$f(\mathsf{nil}) = \mathsf{nil}, \quad f(\mathsf{in}(u)) = \mathsf{in}([n]f(u(n))), \quad f(\mathsf{out}(n,p)) = \mathsf{out}(n, f(p)).$$

It should be clear intuitively that $f(p)$ is productive if p is productive. How can we be convinced of this fact in a clear and rigourous way? One answer may be a definition of productivity as a greatest fixed-point. While this answer is formally satisfactory, it can be argued that its impredicative use of Tarski's fixed point theorem is not a satisfactory finitary explanation of infinite objects.

It can be noticed however that it is directly clear that $f(p)$ reduces to a canonical form if p is productive. Furthermore, we can see that all components of $f(p)$ are then of the form $f(q)$, for some productive $q : \mathsf{P}$, or nil. This remark suggests the definitions of the next section.

2.3 Guarded induction principle

Reducible elements In order to simplify the discussion, we suppose that we have introduced only two data types, the data type N of expressions built on the constructors $\mathsf{s} : (\mathsf{N})\mathsf{N}$ and $0 : \mathsf{N}$, and the data type of lazy expressions P built on constructors $\mathsf{nil} : \mathsf{P}$, $\mathsf{in} : ((n\epsilon\mathsf{N})\mathsf{P})\mathsf{P}$, and $\mathsf{out} : (n\epsilon\mathsf{N})(\mathsf{P})\mathsf{P}$. We hope that it is clear how this discussion extends to the consideration on any inductively defined data types.

Definition: We define what are the **direct components** of a closed expression $p : \mathsf{P}$. If p reduces to nil, it has no direct component. If p reduces to $\mathsf{out}(\mathsf{s}^k(0), q)$, it has for direct component q. If p reduces to $\mathsf{in}(u)$, it has for direct components all $u(\mathsf{s}^k(0))$. A **component** of p is p itself or a component of one of its direct component.

Definition: An element of type P is **productive** iff all its components reduce either to nil, or to an element of the form $\mathsf{in}(u)$, or to an element of the form $\mathsf{out}(\mathsf{s}^k(0), p)$.

We can then define when a close expression is **reducible** of type A, where A is a type built from the data type N and P. An expression c of type $(A)B$ is reducible iff the expression $c(a)$ is reducible of type B when a is reducible of type A. For the type N, it is simply to be convertible to a finite expression $\mathsf{s}^k(0)$. For the type P, it is to be productive.

Guarded definitions Let f be a constant of type

$$(x_1 : A_1, \ldots, x_p : A_p)A,$$

where A is a set (ground data type). We will give a sufficient condition on a recursive definition $f(x_1, \ldots, x_p) = e$ of f to ensure that f is a reducible expression. For this, we define when f is **guarded by** at least n constructors an expression e. It means intuitively that all occurences of f in e are of the form $f(u_1, \ldots, u_p)$ where f does not occur in any u_i, and are all guarded by only constructors and at least n constructors. This is by case analysis on e :

- if f does not occur in e, then f is guarded by at least n constructors in e, for all n,
- if e is of the form $c(u_1, \ldots, u_k)$ where c is a constructor, then f is guarded by at least n constructors in e iff $n \geq 1$ and f is guarded by at least $n-1$ constructors in all u_i, or $n = 0$ and f is guarded by at least 0 constructors in all u_i,
- if e is of the form $[x]u$, then f is guarded by at least n constructors in e iff f is guarded by at least n constructors in u,
- if e is a case expression $case(v, p_1 \rightarrow e_1, \ldots, p_k \rightarrow e_k)$, then f is guarded by at least n constructors in e iff f does not occur in v and f is guarded by at least n constructors in all e_i,
- if e is of the form $f(u_1, \ldots, u_p)$ and f does not occur in $u_1, \ldots, u_p$, then, f is guarded by at least 0 constructor in $f(u_1, \ldots, u_p)$.

Finally, we say that f is guarded in e iff f is guarded by at least n constructors in e for some $n \geq 1$.

Guarded induction principle The guarded condition is well-known for the recursive definition of processes [19]. The two important points here are first, its justification based on an inductive notion of productivity, and second, its use as a proof principle. In our setting, the importance of this notion comes from the following result.

Theorem: If $f : (x_1 : A_1, \ldots, x_n : A_n)A$, where A is a ground data type, has a guarded recursive definition

$$f(x_1, \ldots, x_n) = e,$$

where e is an expression built out only from f and reducible constants, then f is reducible.

Proof: We illustrate this proof on the previous example, which is hopefully generic enough. We consider $f : (\mathsf{P})\mathsf{P}$ defined by the equation

$$f(p) = case(p, \mathsf{nil} \rightarrow \mathsf{nil}, \mathsf{in}(u) \rightarrow \mathsf{in}([n]f(u(n))), \mathsf{out}(n, q) \rightarrow \mathsf{out}(n, f(q))).$$

Since p is reducible, $f(p)$ either reduces to nil, or to $\mathsf{in}([n]f(u(n)))$ if p reduces to $\mathsf{in}(u)$ or to $\mathsf{out}(n, f(q))$ if p reduces to $\mathsf{out}(n, q)$. Hence either $f(p)$ reduces to nil, or the direct components of $f(p)$ are all of the form $f(q)$, where q is reducible. Hence $f(p)$ is productive if p is productive. This means that f is reducible. **Q.E.D.**

This theorem can be read as a proof principle. In order to establish that a proposition ϕ follows from other propositions $\phi_1, \ldots, \phi_q$, it is enough to build a proof term e for it, using not only natural deduction, case analysis, and already proven lemmas, but also using the proposition we want to prove recursively, provided such a recursive call is guarded by introduction rules. We call this proof principle the "guarded induction principle". We hope to show by the examples given below that this reasoning principle is quite flexible and intuitive in practice.

The guarded induction principle will ensure that all closed expressions are reducible, and hence that they reduce to a canonical form. In particular, this implies that there will be no closed proof of $\bot$. This is a way of expressing the correctness of the guarded induction principle.

Some remarks on this proof principle First, it has to be noticed that this criteria cannot accept nested occurences of the function, contrary to the well-founded cases. Thus, we cannot define a function $f : (\Omega)\Omega$ by the equation

$$f(s(s(x))) = s(f(f(x))),$$

since the nested occurence of f in the right handside is not guarded. Indeed, in this case, it can be checked that $f(\omega)$ is not productive: since ω reduces to $s(s(\omega))$, the term $f(\omega)$ has for component $f(f(\omega))$ and this term does not reduce to canonical form.

Another remark is that we can combine this test with the previous test on well-founded recursive calls, if some arguments are explicitely assumed to be well-founded. This situation will occur in one example [18] analysed below, where an infinite proof is defined by well-founded recursion over an evaluation relation.

Finally, this guarded condition may seem too restrictive, especially in the definition of functions over infinite objects. Several programs on streams, even if they preserve productivity, do not obey in general this guarded condition [26]. Here is a simple example. If we consider the set of streams of integer S with only one constructor $\mathsf{cons} : (\mathsf{N})(\mathsf{S})\mathsf{S}$, we can define of the function $map : ((\mathsf{N})\mathsf{N})(\mathsf{S})\mathsf{S}$ by the guarded equation

$$map(f, \mathsf{cons}(x, l)) = \mathsf{cons}(f(x), map(f, l)),$$

and thus consider the equation

$$u = \mathsf{cons}(0, map(\mathsf{s}, u)),$$

which should represent the stream $\mathsf{cons}(0, \mathsf{cons}(\mathsf{s}(0), \ldots))$. This definition is not allowed because it is not guarded. Indeed, the occurence of u in the right handside appears in $map(\mathsf{s}, u)$ and map is *not* a constructor.

We think that the situation is similar to the one of well-founded objects, where the condition on structurally smaller recursive calls does not capture all usual definitions of programs defined over well-founded objects (though its scope is surprisingly large [3, 6]).

Though this does not seem to be the general case, some non guarded definitions can be turned easily in definitions that are guarded. For the previous attempt of the definition of the stream $\mathsf{cons}(0, \mathsf{cons}(\mathsf{s}(0), \ldots))$, we can instead first introduce the function $v : (\mathsf{N})\mathsf{S}$ by the guarded definition

$$v(n) = \mathsf{cons}(n, v(\mathsf{s}(n))),$$

and then $u = v(0)$[4].

Furthermore, the first intended application is for reasoning about infinite objects, and not for programming on them. For this application, the guarded condition is enough to give a proof system at least as powerful as the one based on co-induction, and seems more flexible on the examples we have tried. It is actually by trying to understand intuitively what was going on in proofs by co-induction that the guarded condition came out as a proof principle.

To summarize, what is important about the guarded condition is that it can be ensured by a simple syntactical check, that it can be directly justified, and that it seems to provide a powerful enough proof principle for reasoning about infinite objects.

2.4 Reformulation with rule sets

In this section we express in an abstract way how one can understand inductively a greatest fixed-point. We follow the terminology of [1].

We start with a set U of atoms and a set Φ of **rules**, which are pairs (X, x) such that $X \subseteq U$ and $x \in U$. We write $\Phi : X \mapsto x$ to mean that $(X, x) \in \Phi$. An element $(X, x) \in \Phi$ is called a rule of **conclusion** x and of **premisses** X. There is a monotone operator ϕ associated to Φ, given by

$$\phi(Y) = \{x \in U \mid \Phi : X \mapsto x \text{ for } X \subseteq Y\}.$$

The **kernel** of ϕ is given by

$$K(\phi) = \bigcup\{X \mid X \subseteq \phi(X)\}.$$

This is the greatest fixed point of ϕ.

[4] We introduce below a natural notion of equality between streams. This relation Eq is such that $\mathsf{Eq}(v(n), \mathsf{cons}(n, \mathit{map}(\mathsf{s}, v(n))))$. We will show also that, conversely, $\mathsf{Eq}(l, \mathsf{cons}(n, \mathit{map}(\mathsf{s}, l)))$ implies $\mathsf{Eq}(l, v(n))$. It can be proved that $v(n)$ and $\mathsf{cons}(n, \mathit{map}(\mathsf{s}, v(n)))$ are not convertible as expressions. Intuitively, any conversion derivation is finite, and any proof of equality of these two expressions has to be infinite.

We now give a purely inductive description of $K(\phi)$ in the case where Φ is **deterministic**, i.e. when $\Phi : X_1 \mapsto x$ and $\Phi : X_2 \mapsto x$ entail $X_1 = X_2$.

First, we define $S_{\Phi}(x)$ as the set of $y \in U$ such that there exists $\Phi : X \mapsto x$ with $y \in X$. Let $z \in S^*_{\Phi}(x)$ mean that $z = x$ or inductively that $z \in S^*_{\Phi}(y)$ for some $y \in S_{\Phi}(x)$. An element of $S_{\Phi}(x)$ is called a **direct component** of x, and an element of $S^*_{\Phi}(x)$ a **component** of x. Let $C(\phi) \subseteq U$ be the set of $x \in U$ such that there exists a rule of conclusion x. This defines the set of **canonical** elements. The alternative description of $K(\phi)$ is

$$K'(\phi) = \{x \in U \mid S^*_{\Phi}(x) \subseteq C(\phi)\},$$

that is, $K'(\phi)$ is the set of elements whose components are all canonical.

Theorem: $K(\phi) = K'(\phi)$.

Proof: If $A \subseteq \phi(A)$ and $x \in A$, then we have $A \subseteq C(\phi)$ and $S^*_{\Phi}(x) \subseteq A$, using the fact that Φ is deterministic, and hence all the components of x are canonical. This shows the inclusion $K(\phi) \subseteq K'(\phi)$. Conversely, the inclusion $K'(\phi) \subseteq \phi(K'(\phi))$ holds in general, and hence $K'(\phi) \subseteq K(\phi)$, without any hypothesis on Φ. **Q.E.D**

This theorem shows how it is possible to define the kernel of a rule set in a predicative way, namely as $K'(\phi)$, despite the fact that its usual definition as $K(\phi)$ is not predicative. (We take here "predicative" as defined for instance in [14]).

3 Simple examples of proofs and programs

3.1 Divergence

We introduce the following set of expressions

$$0 : \mathsf{Exp},\ \mathsf{s} : (\mathsf{Exp})\mathsf{Exp},\ \omega : \mathsf{Exp},$$

and the following inductively defined relation

$$\mathsf{e}_1 : \mathsf{Eval}(0,0),\ \mathsf{e}_2 : (x : \mathsf{Exp})\mathsf{Eval}(\mathsf{s}(x),\mathsf{s}(x)),\ \mathsf{e}_3 : \mathsf{Eval}(\omega,\mathsf{s}(\omega)),$$

and the following predicate

$$\mathsf{inf} : (x, y : \mathsf{Exp})(\mathsf{Eval}(x,\mathsf{s}(y)))(\mathsf{Inf}(y))\mathsf{Inf}(x).$$

The term

$$p_\infty : \mathsf{Inf}(\omega)$$

is defined by the guarded equation

$$p_\infty = \mathsf{inf}(\omega,\omega,\mathsf{e}_3,p_\infty),$$

and is thus a lazy proof of $\mathsf{Inf}(\omega)$.

Though this example is quite simple, it illustrates one difference between the present proof system and proofs based on co-induction. A proof that ω is divergent using co-induction will consist in finding a predicate P, which holds for ω, such that $P(x)$ implies that there exists y such $\mathsf{Eval}(x, y)$ and $P(y)$. Thus, one has to find an "invariant" predicate. By contrast, the present approach does not involve the search of suitable predicates, but analyses the problem by looking at the introduction rule for the predicate Inf[5].

3.2 Abstract divergence

In general, if we start with a set A with a binary relation R, one can describe inductively the predicate of accessibility

$$\mathsf{acc} : (x : A)((y : A)(R(x, y))\mathsf{Acc}(y))\mathsf{Acc}(x),$$

of which we consider only well-founded elements, and the predicate of divergence

$$\mathsf{inf} : (x, y : A)(R(x, y))(\mathsf{Inf}(y))\mathsf{Inf}(x).$$

Classically, these subsets form a partition of A. In the present intuitionistic framework, one cannot expect in general to have a proof of

$$(x : A)[\mathsf{Acc}(x) + \mathsf{Inf}(x)].$$

In particular, we cannot derive in our system some results of [12], which establish the equivalence of two notions of divergence using the fact that an element either diverges or converges. It seems quite interesting to investigate this problem more in detail from an intuitionistic point of view (our guess is that this equivalence is not really used, and the non equivalence indicates only that the stronger notion of divergence is the correct intuitionistic notion).

It is however possible to show that these subsets are disjoint, by defining

$$\phi : (x : A)(\mathsf{Acc}(x))(\mathsf{Inf}(x)) \perp$$

with the following equation

$$\phi(x, \mathsf{acc}(x, f), \mathsf{inf}(x, y, q, r)) = \phi(y, f(y, q), r),$$

which is well-founded because the recursive call of ϕ is smaller on its second argument, which is supposed to be well-founded.

---

[5] Of course, it may be that the proposition we try to prove cannot be proved by case analysis only, and we may have to find appropriate lemmas. We hope however that, both for well-founded and infinite objects, the process of finding these lemmas can be helped by such an analysis.

3.3 Representation of an unreliable medium

We want to build an element $m : \mathsf{P}$ that can be thought of as an unreliable medium: it asks first for an integer input, and either forgets it, or outputs it, and this recursively. For this, we introduce an infinite oracle set C with two constructors $0 : (\mathsf{C})\mathsf{C}$ and $1 : (\mathsf{C})\mathsf{C}$. An object of the set C can thus be thought of as an infinite stream of the form $0(1(0(0(\ldots))))$, and in this case, the computation tree of a term is similar to the binary development of a real number.

The following equations define a function $m : (\mathsf{C})\mathsf{P}$

$$m(0(x)) = \mathsf{in}([n]m(x)),\ m(1(x)) = \mathsf{in}([n]\mathsf{out}(n, m(x))),$$

since these equations satisfy the guarded condition.

What is important about this representation is that we will be able to define by a predicate on C when an element of C contains infinitely many ones, and hence to specify when an unreliable medium is fair.

3.4 Definition of co-recursion

We now show on one example how to translate co-induction and co-recursion in our proof system. We suppose given a map $f : (X)[X + X]$ and we want to build from this a map $corec(f) : (X)\mathsf{C}$ satisfying the usual co-recursive equations [22]. For this, we define first $\phi : (X + X)\mathsf{C}$ by the guarded equations

$$\phi(\mathsf{inl}(x)) = 0(\phi(f(x)))\quad \phi(\mathsf{inr}(x)) = 1(\phi(f(x))).$$

One can then check that $corec(f)(x) = \phi(f(x))$ is such that $corec(f)(x) = 0(corec(f)(y))$ when $f(x)$ is of the form $\mathsf{inl}(y)$ and $corec(f)(x) = 1(corec(f)(y))$ when $f(x)$ is of the form $\mathsf{inr}(y)$. Hence, we have a representation of co-recursion over the set C.

This indicates how one can develop a realisability semantics of co-induction with streams (see [27] and [24]) in such a way that an element of a coinductive type is interpreted by a productive element.

3.5 Fairness

We introduce an inductively defined predicate Event_1 on C, such that $\mathsf{Event}_1(x, y)$ means that x is of the form $x = 0(0(\ldots 0(1(y))\ldots))$. We have two introduction rules

$$\mathsf{d}_1 : (x : \mathsf{C})\mathsf{Event}_1(1(x), x),\qquad \mathsf{e}_1 : (x, y : \mathsf{C})(\mathsf{Event}_1(x, y))\mathsf{Event}_1(0(x), y).$$

A well-founded proof of $\mathsf{Event}_1(x, y)$ has to be thought of as a finite term of the form

$$\mathsf{e}_1(x_1, y, \ldots, \mathsf{e}_1(x_{n-1}, y, \mathsf{d}_1(y))\ldots),$$

with $x = 0(x_1),\ x_1 = 0(x_2), \ldots, x_{n-1} = 1(y)$.

Using the inductively defined predicate Event_1, we can now introduce the predicate $\mathsf{Inf}_1(x)$ which means that x contains infinitely many ones in its development. It has only one introduction rule:

$$\mathsf{inf}_1 : (x, y : \mathsf{C})(\mathsf{Event}_1(x, y))(\mathsf{Inf}_1(y))\mathsf{Inf}_1(x),$$

and a proof of $\mathsf{Inf}_1(x_0)$ should be thought of as an infinite proof term of the form

$$\mathsf{inf}_1(x_0, x_1, p_1, \mathsf{inf}_1(x_1, x_2, p_2, \mathsf{inf}_1(\ldots)))$$

where p_n is a proof of $\mathsf{Event}_1(x_{n-1}, x_n)$. This corresponds closely to the intuition of what it means for such a stream to have infinitely many ones.

A fair unreliable medium will then be defined as a medium $m(x) : \mathsf{P}$, together with a proof of $\mathsf{Inf}_1(x)$.

It may be interesting to see how far such ideas can be adapted to the representation of proofs about a process system like CBS, which can be simulated in a simple way in a lazy functional language [23].

3.6 Proof about the list of iterates

This example is taken from [22]. We define first a relation on the set of stream of integers with the only constructor

$$\mathsf{eq} : (n : \mathsf{N})(l_1, l_2 : \mathsf{S})(\mathsf{Eq}(l_1, l_2))\mathsf{Eq}(\mathsf{cons}(n, l_1), \mathsf{cons}(n, l_2)).$$

As a parenthesis, let us illustrate further our proof principle by showing that Eq is transitive. For this, we declare

$$trans : (l_1, l_2, l_3 : \mathsf{S})(\mathsf{Eq}(l_1, l_2))(\mathsf{Eq}(l_2, l_3))\mathsf{Eq}(l_1, l_3),$$

and define it by the guarded equation

$$trans(\mathsf{cons}(n, l_1), \mathsf{cons}(n, l_2), \mathsf{cons}(n, l_3), \mathsf{eq}(n, l_1, l_2, p), \mathsf{eq}(n, l_2, l_3, q))$$

$$= \mathsf{eq}(n, l_1, l_3, trans(l_1, l_2, l_3, p, q)).$$

Notice finally that if we have a closed infinite proof of $\mathsf{Eq}(l_1, l_2)$, then the two infinite terms l_1 and l_2 have the same computation tree. This relation Eq is analogous to bisimulation equivalence [19].

We end this parenthesis, and present the problem: it is to show that, if we define $v : (\mathsf{N})\mathsf{S}$ by the guarded equation

$$v(n) = \mathsf{cons}(n, v(\mathsf{s}(n))),$$

and $map : ((\mathsf{N})\mathsf{N})(\mathsf{S})\mathsf{S}$ is defined by the guarded equation

$$map(f, \mathsf{cons}(n, l)) = \mathsf{cons}(f(n), map(f, l)),$$

then we have $\mathsf{Eq}(l_0, v(0))$ if $\mathsf{Eq}(l_0, \mathsf{cons}(0, map(\mathsf{s}, l_0)))$.

For this, we define a function

$$f : (n : \mathsf{N})(l : \mathsf{S})(\mathsf{Eq}(l, \mathsf{cons}(n, map(\mathsf{s}, l))))\mathsf{Eq}(l, v(n))$$

by the guarded equation

$$f(n, \mathsf{cons}(n, l), \mathsf{eq}(n, l, \mathsf{cons}(\mathsf{s}(n), map(\mathsf{s}, l)), h))$$

$$= \mathsf{eq}(n, l, v(\mathsf{s}(n)), f(\mathsf{s}(n), l, h)).$$

We have then

$$f(0, l_0, h) : \mathsf{Eq}(l_0, v(0)) \quad [h : \mathsf{Eq}(l_0, \mathsf{cons}(0, map(\mathsf{s}, l_0)))].$$

We can read this proof as a program that transforms a (lazy) proof tree which establishes $\mathsf{Eq}(l_0, v(0))$ to a proof tree that establishes $\mathsf{Eq}(l_0, map(\mathsf{s}, l_0))$. Both proof trees furthermore are infinite and built only with the introduction rule

$$\frac{\mathsf{Eq}(l_1, l_2)}{\mathsf{Eq}(\mathsf{cons}(n, l_1), \mathsf{cons}(n, l_2))}.$$

3.7 Soundness of a type inference system

As test examples, we have represented in a mechanized system the problem of soundness of a type inference system analysed in [18]. This corresponds to using the present version of type theory with possibly infinite objects instead of Peter Aczel's non-well-founded set theory [2].

We shall not describe the proof in detail, but only emphasize some points, using freely the notation of [18]. In our formalism, it is directly justified to introduce an object cl_∞ with the computation rule

$$cl_\infty =< x, exp, E + \{f \mapsto cl_\infty\} > .$$

The relation $v : \tau$ given by the rule (15) of the paper [18] is seen in our formalism as the introduction rule for a relation between expressions and types. Thus, in the case of recursion, rule 6, page 217 (which is the only case where our proof differs), we see the problem of proving $cl_\infty : \tau$ as the problem of building an infinite proof tree ending with $cl_\infty : \tau$. But this is direct, using

$$cl_\infty =< x, exp, E + \{f \mapsto cl_\infty\} >$$

and the fact that it is allowed/guarded to use recursively $cl_\infty : \tau$.

4 Mechanization

We now discuss briefly the mechanization of the present system, and how to use it in the design an interactive proof search. This section is still tentative, and only partial implementations of the ideas described here have been tried on machine so far.

The starting point is to consider the logical framework as described in [20] as a type system that refines the type system of a lazy programming language. Thus the first step is to have a lazy functional language (like haskell or lml) with dependent types. In particular, we can, like in a lazy functional language, introduce new data types with their constructors. The typing relation $x : A$ will mean that x is a lazy element of the data type A, and we have to use another notation, for instance $x \epsilon A$, for expressing that x is a well-founded element of the data type A. An alternative notation is to have only one typing judgement, and to have two kind of data types, ones that have only well-founded elements, and ones that may have productive elements. We can then associate to any data type of the second kind its well-founded part.

In general, of course, the definition of recursive programs/proofs can lead to inconsistent reasonings. We need to introduce the notion of correct environment. The present paper gives a sufficient syntactic condition, to be guarded, for an environment to be valid w.r.t. the semantic of terms as productive objects. This check ensures in particular the consistency of an environment seen as a logical theory, and is complementary to the check of structurally smaller recursive calls [3, 6] for well-founded arguments.

We believe that this system leads to an intuitive interactive proof system, well-suited for providing a mechanical help in the development of proofs in relational (or natural) semantics [18]. The user introduces new sets, predicates, relations defined by their introduction rule. We remark that, in practice and probably because it is clearer, in [12, 4], the relations are not given by their elimination rules, but by their introduction rules.

When one wants to prove a result, or builds a noncanonical function, one first gives to it a name and a type. The use of case expression corresponds to the analysis of the hypotheses. This analysis generates subgoals that can be further analysed until we can write a solution. The possibility of declaring and proving local lemmas (that can be themselves recursively defined) corresponds to the addition of a local let construct in our proof term language. Recursive reasoning is allowed, and the system points out when it may lead to an inconsistency.

Conclusion

We hope to have shown that the guarded proof induction principle is a quite natural way of reasoning about infinite objects. The duality between the guarded conditions for infinite objects and the structurally smaller conditions [6, 3] complements the categorical duality between initial and final objects that is the basis of the notion of co-inductive definition [2, 17].

One main point of this paper, which goes back to the work of Lars Hallnäs [10], is that the impredicative notions that seem necessary in dealing with infinite objects, typically the use of greatest fixed-point or infinite ordinals, can be avoided altogether by explicit consideration of proof objects. Though it was not originally conceived with this remark in mind, the proof system we present can be seen as a further illustration of this basic idea[6].

Acknowledgement

The initial idea of this paper came through a discussion with Eike Ritter and Peter Dybjer about proof systems for infinite objects, and was precised by several discussions with Peter Dybjer, Martin Hofmann, Andy Moran and Lars Hallnäs. Many thanks also to the referees for their comments.

References

1. P. Aczel. An introduction to inductive definitions. In J. Barwise, editor, *Handbook of Mathematical Logic*, 739 - 782, (1977), Elsevier.
2. P. Aczel. *Non-Well-Founded Sets* CSLI Lecture Notes, Vol. 14 (LSCI, Stanford, 1988)
3. Th. Coquand. Pattern-Matching in Type Theory. Proceedings of the B.R.A. meeting on Proof and Types, (1992) Bastad.
4. P. Cousot and R. Cousot. Inductive definitions, semantics and abstract interpretation. POPL'91, (1991).
5. H. Curry and R. Feys. *Combinatory Logic, Vol. 1.* North-Holland Publishing Company.
6. O. Dahl. *Verifiable Programming.* Prentice Hall International, 1992.
7. M. Dummett. *Elements of Intuitionism.* Oxford University Press, 1977.
8. P. Dybjer. Inductive Families. To appear in Formal Aspects of Computing (1993).
9. J.Y. Girard. *Proof Theory and Logical Complexity.* Bibliopolis, 1988.
10. L. Hallnäs. An Intensional Characterization of the Largest Bisimulation. Theoretical Computer Science 53 (1987), 335 - 343.
11. L. Hallnäs. On the syntax of infinite objects: an extension of Martin-Löf's theory of expressions. LNCS 417, COLOG-88, P. Martin-Löf and G. Mints Eds., (1989), 94 - 103.
12. J. Hugues and A. Moran. A semantics for locally bottom-avoiding choice. Proceedings of the Glasogow Functional Programming Workshop'92, WICS (1992).
13. P. Lorenzen. Logical Reflection and Formalism. The Journal of Symbolic Logic, 23, 1958, 241 - 249.
14. P. Lorenzen and J. Myhill. Constructive Definition of Certain Sets of Numbers. The Journal of Symbolic Logic, 24, 1959, 37 - 49.
15. P. Martin-Löf. *Intuitionistic Type Theory.* Bibliopolis, 1984.

[6] One can see Martin-Löf's constructive explanation of the addition of non-standard elements through the explicit consideration of non-standard proof-objects [16] as yet another example of this idea.

16. P. Martin-Löf. Mathematics of Infinity. LNCS 417, COLOG-88, P. Martin-Löf and G. Mints Eds., (1989), 146 - 197.
17. N.P. Mendler, P. Panangaden and R.L. Constable. Infinite Objects in Type Theory. Proceeding of the first Logic In Computer Science 1986, 249 - 255.
18. R. Milner, M. Tofte. Co-induction in Relational Semantics Theoretical Computer Science 87 (1991), 209 - 220.
19. R. Milner. *Communication and Concurrency* Prentice Hall International, 1989.
20. B. Nordström, K. Petersson and J. Smith. *Programming in Martin-Löf's Type Theory. An Introduction.* Oxford University Press, 1990.
21. D. Park. Concurrency and automata on infinite sequences. in P. Deussen, editor, Proceedings of the 5th GI-conference on Theoretical Computer Science, LNCS 104, (1981), 167 - 183.
22. L. Paulson. Co-induction and Co-recursion in Higher-order Logic. Draft (1993), University of Cambridge.
23. K.V.S. Prasad. Programming with Broadcasts. CONCUR'93, LNCS 715, 173 - 187.
24. C. Raffalli. Fixed points and type systems (Abstract) proceeding of the third B.R.A. meeting on Proofs and Types (1992), Bastad, 309.
25. W. de Roever. On Backtracking and Greatest Fixpoints Formal Description of Programming Concepts, J. Neuhold (ed.), North-Holland, (1978), 621 - 639.
26. B.A. Sijtsma. On the productivity of recursive list functions. ACM Transactions on Programming Language and Systems, Vol. 11, No 4 (1989), 633 - 649.
27. M. Tatsuta. Realisability Interpretation of Coinductive Definitions and Program Synthesis with Streams. Proceedings of International Conference on Fifth Generation Computer Systems (1992) 666 - 673.

Conservativity between logics and typed λ calculi*

Herman Geuvers**

Faculty of Mathematics and Computer Science
University of Nijmegen, Netherlands

1. Introduction

When looking at systems of typed λ calculus from a logical point of view, there are some interesting questions that arise. One of them is whether the formulas-as-types embedding from the logic into the typed λ calculus is complete, that is, whether the types that are inhabited in the typed λ calculus are provable (as formulas) in the logic. It is well-known that this is not a vacuous question: the 'standard' formulas-as-types embedding from higher order predicate logic into the Calculus of Constructions is not complete. (See [Berardi 1989], [Geuvers 1989] or [Geuvers 1993].) Another interesting issue is whether the typed λ calculus approach can help to solve questions about the logics or vice versa. An example of such a fruitful interaction is the proof of (strong) normalization for the Calculus of Constructions, which has as corollary in higher order predicate logic that cut elimination terminates. In this paper we want to treat questions of conservativity between systems of typed λ calculi (and hence between the logical systems that correspond with them according to the formulas-as-types embedding). On the one hand this is an issue of interest for the typed λ calculi themselves. (Can new type forming operators create inhabitants of previously empty types?) On the other hand, however, this is a nice example of how the formulas-as-types embedding can help to solve questions about logics by making use of typed λ calculi and vice versa.

If one sees a typed λ calculus as a logical system, one takes one specific universe ('sort' in the terminology of Pure Type Systems) to be interpreted as the universe of all formulas. Let's call this universe Prop. Now suppose that S_1 is a system of typed λ calculus containing the universe Prop, and suppose that S_2 is a system that extends S_1.

1.1. DEFINITION. The type system S_2 is a *conservative extension* of S_1 if for every context Γ and type A one has

$$\left.\begin{array}{r}\Gamma \vdash_{S_1} A : \mathsf{Prop}\\ \Gamma \vdash_{S_2} M : A\end{array}\right\} \Rightarrow \exists N[\Gamma \vdash_{S_1} N : A].$$

* Partially sponsored by the ESPRIT Basic Research Action "TYPES"
** e-mail: herman@cs.kun.nl

The 'logical' intuition should be clear: if the formula A, taken from the smaller system, is provable in the larger system, then it is already provable in the smaller system. To make the connection with logics a bit more precise we recall that, if L_1 and L_2 are logics and L_2 extends L_1, then L_2 is a *conservative extension* of L_1 if for all formulas φ and sets of fomulas Δ one has

$$\left.\begin{array}{r}\Delta \cup \{\varphi\} \text{ is a set of formulas of } L_1\\ \Delta \vdash_{L_2} \varphi\end{array}\right\} \Rightarrow \Delta \vdash_{L_1} \varphi.$$

Now, let H be the formulas-as-types embedding from L_1 into S_1 and from L_2 into S_2. This means that for every finite set of formulas Δ' in L_i there is a specific context $\Gamma_{\Delta'}$ in S_i, in which all the declarations are made that are necessary for forming the types $H(\psi)$ (for $\psi \in \Delta$) in S_i. Furthermore this embedding H is *sound*:

$$\Delta \vdash_{L_i} \varphi \Rightarrow \exists N[\Gamma_{\Delta\cup\{\varphi\}}, \mathbf{p}{:}H(\Delta) \vdash_{S_i} N : H(\varphi)].$$

Here the $\mathbf{p}{:}H(\Delta)$ denotes a vector of variable-declarations $p_i : H(\psi_i)$ for each $\psi_i \in \Delta$. Hence the Δ is taken to be finite, which is not a real restriction. In the formulas-as-types embedding, the term N of type $H(\varphi)$ is defined by induction on the derivation of $\Delta \vdash \varphi$, so the formulas-as-types embedding not only maps formulas to types, but also derivations to proof-terms.

The formulas-as-types embedding is not always *complete*, where completeness means (in the terminology above) that for each formula φ and finite set of formulas Δ, taken from L_i one has

$$\Gamma_{\Delta\cup\{\varphi\}}, \mathbf{p}{:}H(\Delta) \vdash_{S_i} N : H(\varphi) \Rightarrow \Delta \vdash_{L_i} \varphi.$$

Some well-known examples of the formulas-as-types embedding are not complete, like the embedding of higher order predicate logic into the Calculus of Constructions. In this paper we are more interested in embeddings that are complete, in which case we usually speak of a *formulas-as-types isomorphism*. This is because of the following.

1.2. Proposition. If the formulas-as-types embedding H is complete, then

$$S_2 \text{ is a conservative extension of } S_1 \Leftrightarrow L_2 \text{ is a conservative extension of } L_1.$$

This proposition can be useful in two ways, both of which will be applied in this paper. Note therefore that in the definition of conservativity (Definition 1.1) there is no requirement about a function that takes an inhabitant $M : \varphi$ in the larger system and returns an inhabitant $N : \varphi$ in the smaller system. However, if there is such a function, then the conservativity result will usually be much easier to prove for the typed λ calculi, because one just has to define the function and to show (by induction on the derivation or by induction on the structure of the term) that it preserves derivability. This is a purely *syntactic* conservativity proof. If it is not clear how such a function should be defined, it is better to look at the logics, in which case one can forget about the proof terms all together and just look at provability. In this latter case a semantic approach suits very well to prove conservativity.

Here we study the conservativity relations inside the cube of typed λ calculi, a collection of eight type systems defined by Barendregt (see [Barendregt 1992]) to give a fine structure for the Calculus of Constructions. There is a close connection between the cube of typed λ calculi and a cube of logical systems, due to the formulas-as-types embedding from the latter into the first. To make this embedding more readily understandable it is often described in two steps, first from the logic to a typed λ calculus that is in direct correspondence with the logic and then from this latter typed λ calculus to a type system of the cube. (See [Barendregt 1992] but also [Geuvers 1993].) To strip our discussions about typed λ calculi from the need to first having to justify all kinds of meta theoretic reasoning, we work in the framework of 'Pure Type Systems'. (See [Geuvers and Nederhof 1991], [Barendregt 1992] or [Geuvers 1993].) This gives a general method for describing typed λ calculi. Moreover we can use all the well-known meta-theory for Pure Type Systems (PTSs).

The main result in this paper is that, if S_2 is a system in the cube that contains the system S_1, then S_2 is a conservative extension of S_1, unless S_2 is the Calculus of Constructions (CC) and S_1 is the second order dependent typed λ calculus λP2. But more interesting than this general result is maybe the proof, which is divided into four cases. The first case is to show that CC is not conservative over λP2. The second case is to show that the extension of a system by adding type dependency is conservative. The third is to show that an extension of a first order system (i.e. a system in the bottom plane of the cube) is always conservative. This leaves over one special case, which is to show that $\lambda\omega$ is conservative over the polymorphic λ calculus, $\lambda 2$. The second and third case are dealt with by defining a mapping from terms in the larger system to the terms in the smaller system, which gives us a purely syntactic conservativity proof. The fourth case is more difficult, because it is not clear how to do this proof by purely syntactic means. We therefore define a semantics for the logical systems of higher and second order propositional logic (which are isomorphic to $\lambda\omega$ and $\lambda 2$ by the formulas-as-types embedding) and show the conservativity on the level of the logics.

2. A fine structure for the Calculus of Constructions

2.1. Pure Type Systems

Our studies of the Calculus of Constructions and its subsystems will be done in the framework of 'Pure Type Systems'. This provides a generic way of describing systems of typed λ calculus. In fact one can only describe systems that have as type forming operator just the Π and as reduction rule just β. As the Calculus of Constructions is such a system, the Pure Type Systems (or PTSs) is the right framework for us.

The Pure Type Systems are formal systems for deriving judgements of the form

$$\Gamma \vdash M : A,$$

where both M and A are in the set of so called *pseudoterms*, a set of expressions from which the derivation rules select the ones that are typable. The Γ is a finite sequence of *declarations*, statements of the form $x : B$, where x is a variable and B is a pseudoterm. The idea is that a term M can only be of type A (notation $M : A$) relative to a typing of the free variables that occur in M and A. Before giving the precise definition of Pure Type Systems we define the set of pseudoterms T over a base set $\mathcal{S}$. (The dependency of T on $\mathcal{S}$ is usually ignored.)

2.1. DEFINITION. For $\mathcal{S}$ some set, the set of pseudoterms over $\mathcal{S}$, T, is defined by

$$\mathsf{T} ::= \mathcal{S} \mid \mathsf{Var} \mid (\Pi\mathsf{Var}{:}\mathsf{T}.\mathsf{T}) \mid (\lambda\mathsf{Var}{:}\mathsf{T}.\mathsf{T}) \mid \mathsf{T}\mathsf{T},$$

where Var is a countable set of expressions, called variables. Both Π and λ bind variables and hence we have the usual notions of *free variable* and *bound variable.* We adopt the λ-calculus notation of writing $\mathrm{FV}(M)$ for the set of free variables in the pseudoterm M.
On T we have the usual notion of β-reduction, generated from

$$(\lambda x{:}A.M)P \longrightarrow_\beta M[P/x],$$

where $M[P/x]$ denotes the substitution of P for x in M (done with the usual care to avoid capturing of free variables), and compatible with application, λ-abstraction and Π-abstraction. We also adopt from the untyped λ calculus the conventions of denoting the transitive reflexive closure of $\longrightarrow_\beta$ by $\twoheadrightarrow_\beta$ and the transitive symmetric closure of $\twoheadrightarrow_\beta$ by $=_\beta$.

The typing of terms is done under the assumption of specific types for the free variables that occur in the term.

2.2. DEFINITION. 1. A *declaration* is a statement of the form $x : A$, where x is a variable and A a pseudoterm,

2. A *pseudocontext* is a finite sequence of declarations such that, if $x : A$ and $y : B$ are different declarations of the same pseudocontext, then $x \not\equiv y$,
3. If $\Gamma = x_1{:}A_1, \ldots, x_n{:}A_n$ is a pseudocontext, the *domain of* Γ, $\mathsf{dom}(\Gamma)$ is the set $\{x_1, \ldots, x_n\}$; for $x_i \in \mathsf{dom}(\Gamma)$.
4. For Γ a pseudocontext, a variable y is Γ*-fresh* (or just *fresh* if it is clear which Γ we are talking about) if $y \notin \mathsf{dom}(\Gamma)$.

2.3. DEFINITION. A *Pure Type System* (PTS) is given by a set $\mathcal{S}$, a set $\mathcal{A} \subset \mathcal{S} \times \mathcal{S}$ and a set $\mathcal{R} \subset \mathcal{S} \times \mathcal{S} \times \mathcal{S}$. The PTS that is given by $\mathcal{S}$, $\mathcal{A}$ and $\mathcal{R}$ is denoted by

$\lambda(\mathcal{S}, \mathcal{A}, \mathcal{R})$ and is the typed λ calculus with the following deduction rules.

$$\text{(sort)} \quad \vdash s_1 : s_2 \qquad \text{if } (s_1, s_2) \in \mathcal{A}$$

$$\text{(var)} \quad \frac{\Gamma \vdash A : s}{\Gamma, x{:}A \vdash x : A} \qquad \text{if } x \text{ is } \Gamma\text{-fresh}$$

$$\text{(weak)} \quad \frac{\Gamma \vdash A : s \quad \Gamma \vdash M : C}{\Gamma, x{:}A \vdash M : C} \qquad \text{if } x \text{ is } \Gamma\text{-fresh}$$

$$(\Pi) \quad \frac{\Gamma \vdash A : s_1 \quad \Gamma, x{:}A \vdash B : s_2}{\Gamma \vdash \Pi x{:}A.B : s_3} \qquad \text{if } (s_1, s_2, s_3) \in \mathcal{R}$$

$$(\lambda) \quad \frac{\Gamma, x{:}A \vdash M : B \quad \Gamma \vdash \Pi x{:}A.B : s}{\Gamma \vdash \lambda x{:}A.M : \Pi x{:}A.B}$$

$$\text{(app)} \quad \frac{\Gamma \vdash M : \Pi x{:}A.B \quad \Gamma \vdash N : A}{\Gamma \vdash MN : B[N/x]}$$

$$\text{(conv)} \quad \frac{\Gamma \vdash M : A \quad \Gamma \vdash B : s}{\Gamma \vdash M : B} \qquad A =_\beta B$$

If $s_2 \equiv s_3$ in a triple $(s_1, s_2, s_3) \in \mathcal{R}$, we write $(s_1, s_2) \in \mathcal{R}$. The equality in the conversion rule (conv) is the β-equality on the set of pseudoterms T.
The elements of $\mathcal{S}$ are called *sorts*, the elements of $\mathcal{A}$ (usually written as $s_1 : s_2$) are called *axioms* and the elements of $\mathcal{R}$ are called *rules*.
If $\lambda(\mathcal{S}, \mathcal{A}, \mathcal{R})$ is a PTS, the set of *terms* of $\lambda(\mathcal{S}, \mathcal{A}, \mathcal{R})$, $\mathsf{Term}(\lambda(\mathcal{S}, \mathcal{A}, \mathcal{R}))$, is defined by

$$\mathsf{Term}(\lambda(\mathcal{S}, \mathcal{A}, \mathcal{R})) = \{A \mid \exists \Gamma, B[\Gamma \vdash A : B \vee \Gamma \vdash B : A]\}.$$

This is not the place to go into a detailed treatment of the meta-theoretic properties of PTSs. We refer to [Geuvers and Nederhof 1991], [Barendregt 1992] or [Geuvers 1993] for details. We only give the most important properties without proof.

2.4. PROPOSITION. In an arbitrary PTS $\lambda(\mathcal{S}, \mathcal{A}, \mathcal{R})$, the following holds.

- Substitution
  If $\Gamma_1, x{:}A, \Gamma_2 \vdash M : B$ and $\Gamma_1 \vdash N : A$, then $\Gamma_1, \Gamma_2[N/x] \vdash M[N/x] : B[N/x]$.
- Stripping

$$
\begin{array}{ll}
(i) & \Gamma \vdash s : R,\ s \in \mathcal{S} \Rightarrow R =_\beta s' \text{ with } s : s' \in \mathcal{A} \text{ for some } s' \in \mathcal{S},\\
(ii) & \Gamma \vdash x : R,\ x \in \mathsf{Var} \Rightarrow R =_\beta A \text{ with } x : A \in \Gamma \text{ for some term } A,\\
(iii) & \Gamma \vdash \Pi x{:}A.B : R \Rightarrow \Gamma \vdash A : s_1, \Gamma, x{:}A \vdash B : s_2 \text{ and } R =_\beta s_3\\
& \qquad \text{with } (s_1, s_2, s_3) \in \mathcal{R} \text{ for some } s_1, s_2, s_3 \in \mathcal{S},\\
(iv) & \Gamma \vdash \lambda x{:}A.M : R \Rightarrow \Gamma, x{:}A \vdash M : B, \Gamma \vdash \Pi x{:}A.B : s \text{ and}\\
& \qquad R =_\beta \Pi x{:}A.B \text{ for some term } B \text{ and } s \in \mathcal{S},\\
(v) & \Gamma \vdash MN : R \Rightarrow \Gamma \vdash M : \Pi x{:}A.B, \Gamma \vdash N : A \text{ with } R =_\beta B[N/x]\\
& \qquad \text{for some terms } A \text{ and } B.
\end{array}
$$

- Subject Reduction
  If $\Gamma \vdash M : A$ and $M \twoheadrightarrow_\beta N$, then $\Gamma \vdash N : A$.
- Confluence
  If $\Gamma \vdash M : A$, $\Gamma \vdash N : A$ and $M =_\beta N$, then there is a term Q with $\Gamma \vdash Q : A$ and $M \twoheadrightarrow_\beta Q$, $N \twoheadrightarrow_\beta Q$.

The definition of Pure Type System gives rise to an interesting notion of morphism between typed λ calculi which can be described by taking into account only the sorts, axioms and rules of the system.

2.5. DEFINITION. Let $\lambda(\mathcal{S}, \mathcal{A}, \mathcal{R})$ and $\lambda(\mathcal{S}', \mathcal{A}', \mathcal{R}')$ be PTSs. A *morphism from* $\lambda(\mathcal{S}, \mathcal{A}, \mathcal{R})$ *to* $\lambda(\mathcal{S}', \mathcal{A}', \mathcal{R}')$ is a mapping f from $\mathcal{S}$ to $\mathcal{S}'$ that *preserves axioms and rules*, that is

$$
\begin{gathered}
s_1{:}s_2 \in \mathcal{S} \Rightarrow f(s_1){:}f(s_2) \in \mathcal{S}',\\
(s_1, s_2, s_3) \in \mathcal{R} \Rightarrow (f(s_1), f(s_2), f(s_3)) \in \mathcal{R}'.
\end{gathered}
$$

A PTS-morphism f from $\lambda(\mathcal{S}, \mathcal{A}, \mathcal{R})$ to $\lambda(\mathcal{S}', \mathcal{A}', \mathcal{R}')$ immediately extends to a mapping from the pseudoterms of $\lambda(\mathcal{S}, \mathcal{A}, \mathcal{R})$ to the pseudoterms of $\lambda(\mathcal{S}', \mathcal{A}', \mathcal{R}')$ and hence to a mapping from pseudocontexts to pseudocontexts. This mapping preserves substitution and β-equality and also derivability:

2.6. LEMMA. If f is a PTS-morphism from ζ to ζ', then

$$\Gamma \vdash_\zeta M : A \Rightarrow f(\Gamma) \vdash_{\zeta'} f(M) : f(A).$$

2.2. The cube of typed λ calculi

2.7. DEFINITION. The Barendregt's cube of typed λ calculi consists of eight PTSs. Each of them has

$$
\begin{aligned}
\mathcal{S} &:= \{\star, \Box\},\\
\mathcal{A} &:= \{\star : \Box\}.
\end{aligned}
$$

The set of rules $\mathcal{R}$ for each system are as given in the following table.

$\lambda{\to}$	$(\star,\star)$			
$\lambda 2$	$(\star,\star)$		$(\square,\star)$	
$\lambda\underline{\omega}$	$(\star,\star)$			$(\square,\square)$
$\lambda\omega$	$(\star,\star)$		$(\square,\star)$	$(\square,\square)$
λP	$(\star,\star)$	$(\star,\square)$		
λP2	$(\star,\star)$	$(\star,\square)$	$(\square,\star)$	
λP$\underline{\omega}$	$(\star,\star)$	$(\star,\square)$		$(\square,\square)$
λPω	$(\star,\star)$	$(\star,\square)$	$(\square,\star)$	$(\square,\square)$.

The system λPω is the Calculus of Constructions, sometimes called the *Pure* Calculus of Constructions to distinguish it from its variants and extensions. We refer to it as CC. The systems of the cube are usually presented as follows.

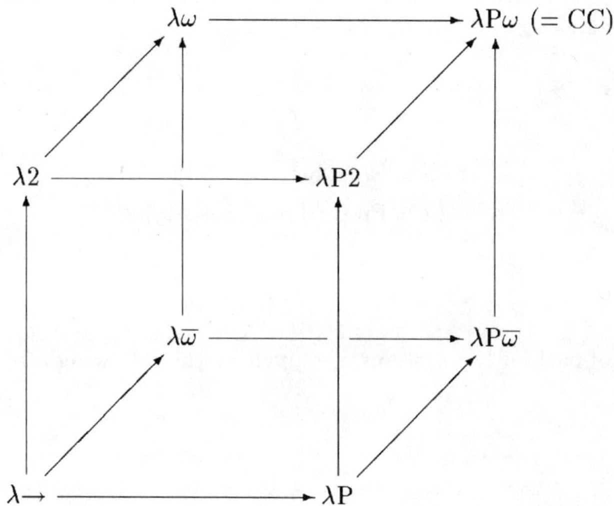

where an arrow denotes inclusion of one system in another.

The systems $\lambda{\to}$ and $\lambda 2$ are also known as the simply typed lambda calculus and the polymorphically typed λ calculus (due to Girard, as system F, and Reynolds). The system $\lambda\omega$ is a higher order version of $\lambda 2$, also known as Girard's system Fω. The presentation of these systems as a PTS is quite different from the original one. If one is just interested in those systems alone it is in general more convenient to study them in their original presentation. The PTS framework is more convenient for systems with *type dependency*, that is the feature that a type $A{:}\star$ may itself contain a subterm M with $M{:}B{:}\star$. This situation only occurs in the presence of the rule $(\star,\square)$. In that case there is no other syntax for the systems which is essentially more convenient then the PTS format. The system λP is very close to the system LF [Harper et al. 1987]. In fact LF is obtained from λP by replacing in the conversion rule the side condition $A =_\beta B$ by $A =_{\beta\eta} B$. The system λPω is the Calculus of Constructions, due to [Coquand 1985]. (See also [Coquand and Huet 1988].) The system $\lambda P2$ was defined under the same name in [Longo and Moggi 1988].

The formulas-as-types embedding from logical systems into the systems of the cube is best understood by first defining a cube of eight 'logical typed λ calculi'. These are systems for which there is a clear one-to-one correspondence between the original logical system and the typed λ calculus. This correspondence is given by the formulas-as-types embedding. This embedding assigns to every formula φ a type $\tilde{\varphi}$ and to every proof in natural deduction style a term such that a proof of φ becomes a term of the type $\tilde{\varphi}$. That this embedding is one-to-one means that every term of the type $\tilde{\varphi}$ is the image of a proof of φ.

2.8. DEFINITION ([Berardi 1990]). The *logic cube* consists of eight PTSs, each of them having as sorts and axioms

$$\mathcal{S} = \mathsf{Prop}, \mathsf{Set}, \mathsf{Type}^p, \mathsf{Type}^s,$$
$$\mathcal{A} = \mathsf{Prop} : \mathsf{Type}^p, \mathsf{Set} : \mathsf{Type}^s.$$

The rules of each of the systems are given by the following table

λPROP				
	(Prop, Prop)			
λPROP2				
	(Prop, Prop)		$(\mathsf{Type}^p, \mathsf{Prop})$	
λPROP$\underline{\omega}$				$(\mathsf{Type}^p, \mathsf{Type}^p)$
	(Prop, Prop)			
λPROPω				$(\mathsf{Type}^p, \mathsf{Type}^p)$
	(Prop, Prop)		$(\mathsf{Type}^p, \mathsf{Prop})$	
λPRED	(Set, Set)	$(\mathsf{Set}, \mathsf{Type}^p)$		
	(Prop, Prop)	(Set, Prop)		
λPRED2	(Set, Set)	$(\mathsf{Set}, \mathsf{Type}^p)$		
	(Prop, Prop)	(Set, Prop)	$(\mathsf{Type}^p, \mathsf{Prop})$	
λPRED$\underline{\omega}$	(Set, Set)	$(\mathsf{Set}, \mathsf{Type}^p)$	$(\mathsf{Type}^p, \mathsf{Set})$	$(\mathsf{Type}^p, \mathsf{Type}^p)$
	(Prop, Prop)	(Set, Prop)		
λPREDω	(Set, Set)	$(\mathsf{Set}, \mathsf{Type}^p)$	$(\mathsf{Type}^p, \mathsf{Set})$	$(\mathsf{Type}^p, \mathsf{Type}^p)$
	(Prop, Prop)	(Set, Prop)	$(\mathsf{Type}^p, \mathsf{Prop})$	

The systems are presented in a picture as follows.

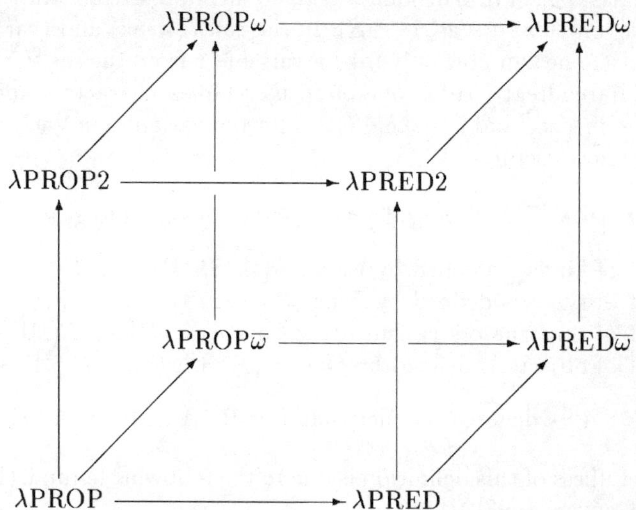

where an arrow denotes inclusion of one system in another.

That the type systems described above indeed correspond to logical systems will not be discussed here. See [Barendregt 1992], [Tonino and Fujita 1992] and [Geuvers 1993] for details. To get the idea we give some examples.

2.9. EXAMPLES. 1. $A{:}\mathsf{Set}, R{:}A{\to}A{\to}\mathsf{Prop}, \varphi{:}\mathsf{Prop} \vdash$
$\lambda p{:}(\Pi x, y{:}A.Rxy{\to}Ryx{\to}\varphi).\lambda x{:}A.\lambda q{:}Rxx.pxxqq :$
$(\Pi x, y{:}A.Rxy{\to}Ryx{\to}\varphi){\to}(\Pi x{:}A.Rxx{\to}\varphi)$ in λPRED.
The term $R : A{\to}A{\to}\mathsf{Prop}$ is understood as a binary relation on A. It should be clear how the term $\lambda x{:}A.\lambda q{:}Rxx.pxxqq$ corresponds to a proof in natural deduction style of the proposition
$(\forall x, y \in A[R(x,y) \supset R(y,x) \supset \varphi]) \supset (\forall x \in A[R(x,x){\to}\varphi])$.

2. In any system that contains λPROP2, $\bot$ can be defined as $\Pi\alpha{:}\mathsf{Prop}.\alpha(:\mathsf{Prop})$. One has indeed $\varphi{:}\mathsf{Prop} \vdash \lambda p{:}\bot.p\varphi : \bot{\to}\varphi$.

3. In λPRED2 one has $A{:}\mathsf{Set} \vdash$
$\lambda R{:}A{\to}A{\to}\mathsf{Prop}.\lambda p{:}(\Pi x, y{:}A.Rxy{\to}Ryx{\to}\bot).\lambda x{:}A.\lambda q{:}Rxx.pxxqq :$
$\Pi R{:}A{\to}A{\to}\mathsf{Prop}.(\Pi x, y{:}A.Rxy{\to}Ryx{\to}\bot){\to}(\Pi x{:}A.Rxx{\to}\bot)$, stating that any binary relation that is antisymmetric is areflexive.

The systems of Barendregt's cube and the logic cube enjoy some more special properties that will be used. First of all, the type of a term is unique up to β-conversion. (The proof is by induction on terms, see [Geuvers 1993] or [Barendregt 1992].)

2.10. PROPOSITION (Uniqueness of Types). For a system in one of the two cubes one has that if $\Gamma \vdash M : A$ and $\Gamma \vdash M : B$, then $A =_\beta B$.

Another nice thing is that, if variables are treated with some care, then the terms can be classified into disjoint sets. One therefore divides the set of variables Var into disjoint subsets Var^s ($s \in \mathcal{S}$). In the rules (weak) and (var), if $\Gamma \vdash A : s$ is the premise, one can now only take a variable x from the set Var^s. In the type systems of Barendregt's cube, one often uses Greek characters and capitals for the variables in $\mathsf{Var}^\Box$ and latin characters for the variables in $\mathsf{Var}^\star$. The following definition is now useful.

2.11. Definition. Let us consider any system of Barendregt's cube.

1. The set of kinds is defined by $\mathsf{Kind} := \{A \mid \exists\Gamma[\Gamma \vdash A : \Box]\}$.
2. The set of types is defined by $\mathsf{Type} := \{A \mid \exists\Gamma[\Gamma \vdash A : \star]\}$.
3. The set of constructors is defined by $\mathsf{Constr} := \{P \mid \exists A, \Gamma[\Gamma \vdash P : A : \Box]\}$.
4. The set of objects is defined by $\mathsf{Obj} := \{P \mid \exists A, \Gamma[\Gamma \vdash P : A : \star]\}$.

Here $\Gamma \vdash P : A : \star$ denotes the fact that $\Gamma \vdash P : A$ and $\Gamma \vdash A : \star$.

The usefulness of this definition is due to the following lemma. (For a detailed proof see [Geuvers 1993].)

2.12. Lemma (Classification). Let us consider any system of Barendregt's cube.

$$\mathsf{Kind} \cap \mathsf{Type} = \emptyset,$$
$$\mathsf{Constr} \cap \mathsf{Obj} = \emptyset.$$

The formulas-as-types embedding of a logic into the corresponding system of the logic cube is an isomorphism (for details see [Geuvers 1993]), so we can restrict our study of the formulas-as-types embedding into the systems of Barendregt's cube to the study of the *collapsing mapping* H that maps the systems of the logic cube into the ones of the cube of typed λ calculi.

2.13. Definition. The collapsing mapping H is defined as the family of PTS-morphisms from logic cube to Barendregt's cube given by

$$H(\mathsf{Prop}) = \star,$$
$$H(\mathsf{Set}) = \star,$$
$$H(\mathsf{Type}^p) = \Box,$$
$$H(\mathsf{Type}^s) = \Box.$$

It is immediate that the collapsing mapping H does not really do anything for the systems of the left plane of the cube. The sorts Prop and Type^p are renamed as $\star$ and $\Box$, but there are no additional rules. This implies that the formulas-as-types embedding from propositional logics into a system of the left plane of the cube is an isomorphism. For the right plane of the cube the situation is more interesting, because the sorts Prop and Set, respectively Type^p and Type^s are mapped to the same sort in the Barendregt's cube. The question of *completeness* of H becomes a real issue here.

2.14. DEFINITION. For L_i a system of the logic cube and S_i the corresponding system in Barendregt's cube, we say that $H : L_i \rightarrow S_i$ is *complete* if for all contexts Γ in L_i and φ with $\Gamma \vdash_{L_i} \varphi : \mathsf{Prop}$, one has

$$H(\Gamma) \vdash_{S_i} M : H(\varphi) \Rightarrow \exists N[\Gamma \vdash_{L_i} N : \varphi].$$

Completeness is of course important because typed λ calculi like the Calculus of Constructions are intended to be used as systems for formalizing mathematics, which is done by reasoning in the embedded higher order predicate logic. One then tacitly assumes that completeness holds, at least for the specific set of formulas that one is interested in.

However, the mapping H identifies the universe of sets (Set) and the universe of propositions (Prop), which is a strange feature in a logical system. For example, it implies that an axiom that states a property for all propositions, can also be applied to sets after the embeding H. In the higher order case (third order and higher) this can be used to construct counterexamples to completeness. A short counterexample, due to [Geuvers 1989] is found by considering the proposition $\Pi x{:}A.\phi$, with $x \notin \mathrm{FV}(\phi)$, and assuming $Q(\Pi x{:}A.\phi)$ for a basic predicate $Q : \mathsf{Prop}{\rightarrow}\mathsf{Prop}$. Then the proposition

$$\exists\psi{:}\mathsf{Prop}.Q(\psi{\rightarrow}\phi)$$

is not provable in λPREDω, whereas in CC, a term of type $\exists\psi{:}\star.Q(\psi{\rightarrow}\phi)$ can easily be found. (Take for ψ just $A : \star$.) Another counterexample, which is not so much of purely syntactical nature, is due to [Berardi 1989]. It is found by considering the extensionality axiom

$$\mathsf{ext} := \Pi\phi,\psi{:}\mathsf{Prop}.(\phi \leftrightarrow \psi){\rightarrow}(\phi = \psi).$$

Let Γ be the context $A : \mathsf{Set}, a, a' : A, z : a \neq a', y : \mathsf{ext}$. (Here, the equality denotes the so called 'Leibniz' equality, defined by taking for $t, u : B$, $t = u$ to be $\Pi P : B{\rightarrow}\mathsf{Prop}.Pt{\rightarrow}Pu$. This equivalence relation identifies terms that have the same properties.) Now, if one looks at the behaviour of ext in CC after the embedding H, it can be observed that H(ext) also applies to A. Hence, in CC we can derive in the context $H(\Gamma)$ that $A = A{\rightarrow}A$ holds. But this implies that A is a λ-algebra (this statement can be formalised precisely), which is of course not the case in λPREDω. More details about incompleteness of $H : \lambda\mathrm{PRED}\omega \rightarrow \mathrm{CC}$ can be found in [Barendregt 1992] and [Geuvers 1993].

The two counterexamples to completeness of H that are discussed above, apply to nth order predicate logic for any $n > 2$. Hence the embedding $H : \lambda\mathrm{PRED}n \rightarrow \lambda\mathrm{P}n$ is incomplete for any $n > 2$. (These systems λPREDn and λPn are found by a straightforward extension of the second order systems, allowing quantification over the collection of domains of order $\leq n$.) In contrast, the embedding $H : \lambda\mathrm{PRED} \rightarrow \lambda\mathrm{P}$ is complete, as was proved in [Berardi 1989] and [Barendsen and Geuvers 1989]. For the embedding $H : \lambda\mathrm{PRED2} \rightarrow \lambda\mathrm{P2}$ the question of completeness is still open.

3. Conservativity relations inside the cube

We now want to address the question of conservativity inside the cube of typed λ calculi and the logic cube. We first look at the cube of typed λ calculi, because the situation for the logic cube is very similar. There are four results that do the whole job, resulting in the following picture.

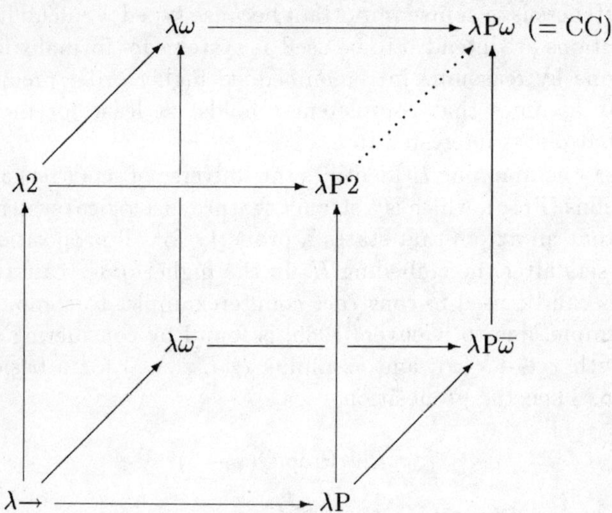

where an arrow denotes a conservative inclusion and a dotted arrow denotes a non-conservative inclusion. By transitivity of conservativity (if system 3 is conservative over system 2 and system 2 is conservative over system 1, then system 3 is conservative over system 1), it is no problem to fill in the picture further. (Draw the arrows between two non-adjacent systems) We can collect all this in the following Proposition.

3.1. THEOREM. For S_1 and S_2 two systems in the cube of typed lambda calculi such that $S_1 \subseteq S_2$:

$$S_2 \text{ is conservative over } S_1 \Leftrightarrow S_2 \neq \text{CC} \vee S_1 \neq \lambda\text{P2}.$$

PROOF. It suffices to prove the following four results.

1. If $S_2 \supseteq S_1$, with S_1 a system of the lower plane in the cube, then S_2 is conservative over S_1.(Proposition 3.2.)
2. If S_2 is a system in the right plane of the cube, and S_1 is the adjacent system in the left plane, then S_2 is conservative over S_1.(Proposition 3.6.)
3. $\lambda P\omega$ is not conservative over λP2,
4. $\lambda\omega$ is conservative over λ2. (Corollary 4.20.)

The fourth is a consequence of Corollary 4.20, saying that PROPω is conservative over PROP2, and of the fact that PROPω and PROP2 are isomorphic to, respectively, $\lambda\omega$ and λ2 via the formulas-as-types embedding. The conservativity of PROPω over PROP2 will be proved in detail later by using semantical methods.

The third was verified in detail by [Ruys 1991], following an idea from Berardi. The idea is to look at a context Γ in λP2 that represents Arithmetic. Then Γ with λP2 is as strong as second order Arithmetic and Γ with $\lambda\text{P}\omega$ is as strong as higher order Arithmetic. Hence we can use Gödel's Second Incompleteness Theorem to show that in λP2 one can not derive from Γ that Γ is consistent in λP2. On the other hand in $\lambda\text{P}\omega$ one can derive from Γ that Γ is consistent in λP2. Hence the non-conservativity. □

We first prove the Proposition about conservativity of systems over systems in the lower plane. The Proposition was also proved in [Verschuren 1990] in a slightly different way.

3.2. Proposition. We consider the cube of typed λ calculi. Let S_1 be a system of the lower plane and S_2 be another system of the cube such that $S_1 \subseteq S_2$. Then

$$\left.\begin{array}{r}\Gamma \vdash_{S_1} B : \star\\ \Gamma \vdash_{S_2} M : B\\ \Gamma \text{ and } M \text{ in normal form}\end{array}\right\} \Rightarrow \Gamma \vdash_{S_1} M : B.$$

Proof. By induction on the structure of M.

var. Say $M \equiv x$. Then $x : A \in \Gamma$, with $A =_\beta B$. Hence, $\Gamma \vdash_{S_1} x : A$, and by one application of (conv), we can conclude that $\Gamma \vdash_{S_1} x : B$.

applic. Say $M \equiv xP_1 \cdots P_n$. Then, by Stripping, $x{:}A \in \Gamma$ with $A =_\beta \Pi y_1{:}C.D$ for some C and D. Now, A is in normal form (because Γ is) and so A is itself a Π-term, say $A \equiv \Pi y_1{:}C_1.D_1$. So, $x{:}\Pi y_1{:}C_1.D_1 \in \Gamma$. Now, $\Gamma \vdash_{S_1} \Pi y_1{:}C_1.D_1 : \star$ (in the lower plane, i.e. without the rule $(\square, \star)$), but then also

$$\Gamma \vdash_{S_1} C_1 : \star.$$

Of course we also have

$$\Gamma \vdash_{S_2} P_1 : C_1,$$

so by IH (note that P_1 is in normal form), $\Gamma \vdash_{S_1} P_1 : C_1$. Hence $\Gamma \vdash_{S_1} xP_1 : D_1[P_1/y_1]$. We can now go further with P_2: We know that $D_1[P_1/y_1] \twoheadrightarrow_\beta \Pi y_2{:}C_2.D_2$. Now, $\Gamma \vdash_{S_1} D_1[P_1/y_1] : \star$ and hence $\Gamma \vdash_{S_1} \Pi y_2{:}C_2.D_2 : \star$ by Subject Reduction. So

$$\Gamma \vdash_{S_1} C_2 : \star.$$

Also

$$\Gamma \vdash_{S_2} P_2 : C_2,$$

so again we can apply IH to obtain $\Gamma \vdash_{S_1} P_2 : C_2$ and hence we have $\Gamma \vdash_{S_1} xP_1P_2 : D_2[P_2/y_2]$. Continuing in this way upto n we find that $\Gamma \vdash_{S_1} xP_1 \cdots P_n : D_n[P_n/y_n]$ with $D_n[P_n/y_n] =_\beta B$. By one application of conversion (using $\Gamma \vdash_{S_1} B : \star$) we conclude $\Gamma \vdash_{S_1} xP_1 \cdots P_n : B$.

abstr. Say $M \equiv \lambda x{:}A.N$. Then $B \twoheadrightarrow_\beta \Pi x{:}A.C$ for some C (note that A is in normal form). So $\Gamma \vdash_{S_1} \Pi x{:}A.C : \star$ by Subject Reduction and $\Gamma, x{:}A \vdash_{S_2} N : C$ (by Stripping and the conversion rule). By IH we conclude $\Gamma, x{:}A \vdash_{S_1} N : C$. Now we are done: By one λ-abstraction and one conversion we conclude $\Gamma \vdash_{S_1} \lambda x{:}A.N : B$. □

The side condition Γ in normal form has just been added for convenience (in giving the proof.) It is not essential and it may be dropped.

As a corollary one finds that a system of the cube is conservative over all its subsystems of the lower plane. If S_1 in the lower plane and $S_1 \subseteq S_2$, then

$$\left.\begin{array}{r}\Gamma \vdash_{S_1} A : \star \\ \Gamma \vdash_{S_2} M : A\end{array}\right\} \Rightarrow \exists N[\Gamma \vdash_{S_1} N : A].$$

This can even be made more precise, because the term N can be computed directly from the term M as follows.

3.3. Corollary. If $S_1 \subseteq S_2$, with S_1 in the lower plane, then

$$\left.\begin{array}{r}\Gamma \vdash_{S_1} A : \star \\ \Gamma \vdash_{S_2} M : A\end{array}\right\} \Rightarrow \Gamma \vdash_{S_1} \mathrm{nf}(M) : A,$$

where $\mathrm{nf}(M)$ denotes the β-normal form of M.

We now give a proof of the conservativity of the right plane over the left plane. The idea is to define a mapping that removes all type dependencies. This mapping will go from a system in the right plane to the adjacent system in the left plane and is the identity on terms that are already well-typed in the left plane. Hence the conservativity. The proof is originally independently due to [Paulin 1989] and [Berardi 1990]. The first described the mapping from $\lambda P\omega$ to $\lambda\omega$ in the first place to use it for program extraction; the second described the collection of four mappings (which is a straightforward generalisation of the mapping from $\lambda P\omega$ to $\lambda\omega$) to give this conservativity proof. The mappings are very much related to similar mappings one can define from predicate logic to propositional logic to prove conservativity of the first over the second.

3.4. Definition ([Paulin 1989], [Berardi 1990]). Let S_2 be a system of the right plane and S_1 the adjacent system in the left plane. The mapping $[-] : \mathsf{Term}(S_2) \to \mathsf{Term}(S_1)$ is defined as follows.

$$\begin{aligned}
[\square] &= \square, \\
[\star] &= \star, \\
[x] &= x, \text{ for } x \text{ a variable}, \\
[\Pi x{:}A.B] &= [B] \text{ if } A{:}\star, B{:}\square, \\
&= \Pi x{:}[A].[B] \text{ else}, \\
[\lambda x{:}A.M] &= [M] \text{ if } A{:}\star, M{:}B{:}\square, \text{ (for some } B), \\
&= \lambda x{:}[A].[M] \text{ else}, \\
[PM] &= [P] \text{ if } M{:}A{:}\star, P{:}B{:}\square, \text{ (for some } A, B), \\
&= [P][M] \text{ else},
\end{aligned}$$

3.5. REMARK. The side conditions in the definition are justified by the Classification Lemma (2.12).

The mapping $[-]$ extends straightforwardly to contexts. The following proposition justifies the statement in the definition that the mapping $[-]$ goes from the right plane to the left plane.

3.6. PROPOSITION ([Paulin 1989], [Berardi 1990]). Let S_2 be a system in the right plane and S_1 the adjacent system in the left plane of the cube.

$$\Gamma \vdash_{S_2} M : A \Rightarrow [\Gamma] \vdash_{S_1} [M] : [A]$$

PROOF. By a straightforward induction on the derivation of $\Gamma \vdash_{S_2} M : A$. □

3.7. COROLLARY ([Paulin 1989],[Berardi 1990]). For S_2 a system in the right plane and S_1 the adjacent system in the left plane of the cube we have that S_2 is conservative over S_1.

PROOF. The only thing to check is that for $M \in \mathsf{Term}(S_1)$, $[M] \equiv M$. This is done by an easy induction on the structure of M. □

Corollary 3.7 can be made a bit more precise by stating how the term in the smaller system is computed from the term in the larger system. For S_2 in the right plane and S_1 the adjacent system in the left plane one has

$$\left.\begin{array}{r}\Gamma \vdash_{S_1} A : \star \\ \Gamma \vdash_{S_2} M : A\end{array}\right\} \Rightarrow \Gamma \vdash_{S_1} [M] : A,$$

The conservativity relations in the logic cube (Definition 2.8) are as follows. (An arrow denotes a conservative extension, a dotted arrow a non-conservative extension.)

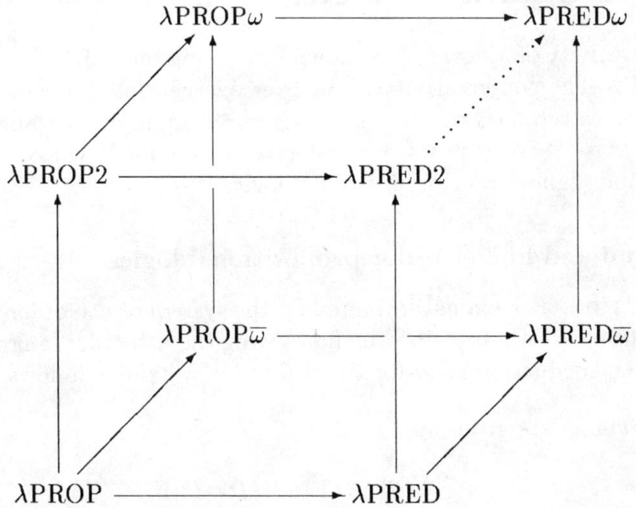

3.8. PROPOSITION. For L_1 and L_2 two systems in the logic cube such that $L_1 \subseteq L_2$:

$$L_2 \text{ is conservative over } L_1 \Leftrightarrow L_2 \neq \lambda\text{PRED}\omega \vee L_1 \neq \lambda\text{PRED2}.$$

PROOF. The proof is completely analoguous to the proof for the cube of typed lambda calculi. What has to be proved for conservativity is that, if $L_1 \subset L_2$ and Γ is a context of L_1 with $\Gamma \vdash A : \mathsf{Prop}$, then

$$\Gamma \vdash_{L_2} M : A \Rightarrow \exists N[\Gamma \vdash_{L_1} N : A].$$

The proof of non-conservativity of λPREDω over λPRED2 is the same as for CC over λP2, by using Gödel's incompleteness theorem. The proof of conservativity of any system over a subsystem in the lower plane is again by normalization (of the proof terms).
The proof of conservativity of the right plane over the left plane can be done by defining a mapping that forgets predicates, analogously to the one defined in Definition 3.4. A slightly shorter proof can be given by making use of the conservativities in the Barendregt's cube, as follows: Let L_1 be a system in the left plane and let Γ be a context and A be a term such that $\Gamma \vdash_{L_1} A : \mathsf{Prop}$. Furthermore, let L_2 be the adjacent system in the right plane and let M be an inhabitant of A in L_2, that is $\Gamma \vdash_{L_2} M : A$. If S_1 is the system in Barendregt's cube that corresponds with L_1 and S_2 is the system in Barendregt's cube that corresponds with L_2, then $H(\Gamma) \vdash_{S_2} H(M) : H(A)$ and hence $\exists N[H(\Gamma) \vdash_{S_1} N : H(A)]$ by the conservativity in Barendregt's cube. Because the formulas-as-types embedding H is an isomorphism on the left plane of the cube, we can conclude that $\exists N[\Gamma \vdash_{L_1} N : A]$.
The proof of conservativity of λPROPω over λPROP2 is given in the following section. □

4. The conservativity of $\lambda\omega$ over $\lambda 2$

The conservativity of $\lambda\omega$ over $\lambda 2$ is shown by proving that PROPω is conservative over PROP2. The conservativity of $\lambda\omega$ over $\lambda 2$ then follows from the fact that the formulas-as-types embedding is an isomorphism. In order to be very specific about the conservativity proof, we first give the detailed syntax of the systems of second and higher order propositional logic.

4.1. Second and higher order propositional logics

4.1. DEFINITION. For n a natural number, the system of nth order propositional logic, notation PROPn is defined by first giving the nth order language and then describing the deduction rules for the nth order system as follows.

1. The *domains* are given by

$$\mathcal{D} ::= \mathsf{Prop} \mid (\mathcal{D} \rightarrow \mathcal{D}).$$

We let brackets associate to the right, so $\mathsf{Prop}{\to}(\mathsf{Prop}{\to}\mathsf{Prop})$ is denoted by $\mathsf{Prop}{\to}\mathsf{Prop}{\to}\mathsf{Prop}$ and every domain can be written as $D_1{\to}\ldots{\to}D_p{\to}\mathsf{Prop}$, with $D_1,\ldots,D_p$ domains.

2. The *order of a domain D*, $\mathsf{ord}(D)$, is defined by

$$\mathsf{ord}(\mathsf{Prop}) = 2,$$
$$\mathsf{ord}(D_1{\to}\ldots{\to}D_p{\to}\mathsf{Prop}) = max\{\mathsf{ord}(D_i) \mid 1 \leq i \leq p\} + 1.$$

The orders are defined in such a way that in n-th order logic one can quantify over domains of order $\leq n$. Hence Prop is of order 2, because in second order propositional logic one can quantify over the set of all formulas. The domain $\mathsf{Prop}{\to}\mathsf{Prop}$ should be understood as the collection of sets of formulas (truth values), identifying a function P from Prop to Prop with the set of formulas φ for which $P\varphi$ holds.

3. For n a fixed positive natural number, the terms of the nth order language are defined as follows. (Each term is an element of a specific domain, which relation is denoted by ϵ).
   - There are countably many variables of domain D for any D with $\mathsf{ord}(D) \leq n$,
   - If $M \;\epsilon\; D_2$, x a variable of domain D_1 and $\mathsf{ord}(D_1{\to}D_2) \leq n$, then $\lambda x \epsilon D_1.M \;\epsilon\; D_1{\to}D_2$,
   - If $M \;\epsilon\; D_1{\to}D_2$, $N \;\epsilon\; D_1$, then $MN \;\epsilon\; D_2$,
   - If $\varphi \;\epsilon\; \mathsf{Prop}$, x a variable of domain D with $\mathsf{ord}(D) \leq n$, then $\forall x \epsilon D.\varphi \;\epsilon\; \mathsf{Prop}$.
   - If $\varphi \;\epsilon\; \mathsf{Prop}$ and $\psi \;\epsilon\; \mathsf{Prop}$, then $\varphi \supset \psi \;\epsilon\; \mathsf{Prop}$.
4. The terms φ for which $\varphi \;\epsilon\; \mathsf{Prop}$ are called *formulas* and Form denotes the set of formulas.
5. On the terms we have the well-known notion of definitional equality by β-conversion. This equality is denoted by $=$. The definitional equality allows us to identify for example the application of the function $\lambda x{:}\mathsf{Prop}.x \supset x$ (of domain $\mathsf{Prop}{\to}\mathsf{Prop}$) to φ with the a formula $\varphi \supset \varphi$.
6. For n a specific positive natural number, we now describe the deduction rules of the nth order predicate logic (in natural deduction style) that allow us to build derivations. So in the following let φ and ψ be formulas of the nth order language.

$$(\supset\text{-I})\ \frac{\begin{matrix}[\varphi]^i\\ \vdots\\ \psi\end{matrix}}{\varphi \supset \psi}\,i \qquad (\supset\text{-E})\ \frac{\varphi \supset \psi \quad \varphi}{\psi}$$

$$(\forall\text{-I})\ \frac{\psi}{\forall x \epsilon D.\psi}(*) \qquad (\forall\text{-E})\ \frac{\forall x \epsilon D.\psi}{\psi[t/x]}\ \text{if } t \;\epsilon\; D$$

$$(\text{conv})\ \frac{\psi}{\varphi}\ \text{if } \varphi = \psi$$

The formula occurrences that are between brackets ([–]) in the $\supset$-I rule are *discharged*. So, in an application of the $\supset$-I rule, several occurrences of ϕ (possibly zero) may be discharged. The superscript i in the $\supset$-I rule is taken from a countable set of indices I. The index i corresponds to one specific application of the $\supset$-I rule, so from the index that is on top of a discharged formula, we can see at which application of $\supset$-I it has been discharged.
$(*)$: in the $\forall$-I rule we make the usual restriction that the variable x may not occur free in a non-discharged assumption of the derivation.
For Γ a set of formulas of PROPn and φ a formula of PROPn, we say that φ *is derivable from Γ in* PROPn, notation $\Gamma \vdash_{\text{PROP}n} \varphi$, if there is a derivation with root φ and all non-discharged formulas in Γ.

The system of higher order proposition logic, notation PROPω, is the union of all PROPn.

4.2. REMARK. The choice for the connectives $\supset$ and $\forall$ may seem minimal. It is however a well-known fact that in second and higher order systems, the intuitionistic connectives &, $\vee$, $\neg$ and $\exists$ can be defined in terms of $\supset$ and $\forall$ as follows. (Let φ and ψ be formulas).

$$\begin{aligned}
\varphi \mathbin{\&} \psi &:= \forall \alpha \epsilon \mathsf{Prop}.(\varphi \supset \psi \supset \alpha) \supset \alpha,\\
\varphi \vee \psi &:= \forall \alpha \epsilon \mathsf{Prop}.(\varphi \supset \alpha) \supset (\psi \supset \alpha) \supset \alpha,\\
\bot &:= \forall \alpha \epsilon \mathsf{Prop}.\alpha,\\
\neg\varphi &:= \varphi \supset \bot,\\
\exists x \in D \varphi &:= \forall \alpha \epsilon \mathsf{Prop}.(\forall x \epsilon D.\varphi \supset \alpha) \supset \alpha.
\end{aligned}$$

Similarly we can define an equality judgement (the β-equality $=$, the *definitional equality of the language*, is purely syntactical) by taking the so called Leibniz equality: for $t, q \in D$,

$$t =_D q := \forall P \epsilon D \rightarrow \mathsf{Prop}.Pt \supset Pq,$$

which says that two objects are equal if they have the same properties. (It is not difficult to show that $=_D$ is symmetric).

It is not difficult to check that all the standard logical rules hold for &, $\vee$, $\bot$, $\neg$, $\exists$ and $=$. In the following we shall freely use these symbols.

4.3. REMARK. In each PROPn ($n \geq 2$), the *comprehension* property is satisfied. That is, for all $\varphi(\mathbf{x}) : \mathsf{Prop}$ with $\mathbf{x} = x_1, \ldots, x_p$ a sequence of free variables, possibly occurring in φ ($x_i \in D_i$), we have

$$\exists P \in D_1 \rightarrow \cdots D_p \rightarrow \mathsf{Prop}.\forall \mathbf{x} \epsilon \mathbf{D}(\varphi \leftrightarrow P x_1 \cdots x_p).$$

(Take $P \equiv \lambda x_1 \in D_1 \ldots . \lambda x_p \in D_p.\varphi(\mathbf{x})$.)

The presentation of propositional logics above can be extended to predicate logics, which is done in [Geuvers 1993]. There also the classical variants of the systems are studied. Here we restrict to the constructive versions of the propositional logics, because PROPω and PROP2 are the ones that correspond to the type systems $\lambda\omega$ and $\lambda 2$.

4.2. Extensionality

The definitional equality on the terms is β-equality. There is no objection to taking $\beta\eta$-equality instead: all the properties still hold. In fact it would make a lot of sense to do so, because we tend to view λ-abstraction as the necessary mechanism to make comprehension work. (And so both $P \in \mathsf{Prop}{\rightarrow}\mathsf{Prop}$ and $\lambda x \in \mathsf{Prop}.Px$ describe the collection of formulas φ for which $P\varphi$ holds).

This is related to the issue of *extensionality*: terms of domain $D{\rightarrow}\mathsf{Prop}$ are to be understood as predicates on D or also as subsets of D, an element t being in the set $P \in D{\rightarrow}\mathsf{Prop}$ if Pt holds. But if we take this set-theoretic understanding seriously, we have to identify predicates that are extensionally equal:

$$(\forall \mathbf{x}.(f\mathbf{x} \supset g\mathbf{x} \;\&\; g\mathbf{x} \supset f\mathbf{x})) \supset f =_D g. \quad (1)$$

Of course, this formula is in general not provable in our systems. However, in the standard models where predicates are interpreted as real sets, the formula is satisfied, so it is an important extension. A difficulty is, that extensionality in the form of (1) is in general not even expressible: if $\mathsf{ord}(D) = n$ in PROPn, then we can not express extensionality for f and g of domain D, because $f =_D g$ is not a formula of PROPn (it uses a quantification over $D{\rightarrow}\mathsf{Prop}$). This means that we have to express extensionality by a schematic rule.

4.4. Definition. The *extensionality scheme*, (EXT), is

$$(\mathrm{EXT})\ \frac{f\mathbf{x} \supset g\mathbf{x} \quad g\mathbf{x} \supset f\mathbf{x} \quad \varphi[f/y]}{\varphi[g/y]}\ (*)$$

where f and g are arbitrary terms of the same domain $D_1{\rightarrow}\cdots{\rightarrow}D_n{\rightarrow}\mathsf{Prop}$. When writing $\varphi[f/y]$, we assume that this substitution is correct, that is, no free variables become bound and f and y are of the same domain. $(*)$ signifies the usual restriction that the variables of $\mathbf{x}$ may not occur free in a non-discharged assumption of the derivations of $f\mathbf{x} \supset g\mathbf{x}$ and of $g\mathbf{x} \supset f\mathbf{x}$.
The extension of a system with the rule (EXT) will be denoted by adding the prefix E-, so E-PROPn is extensional nth order propositional logic.

4.5. Notation. For $f, g \in D = D_1{\rightarrow}\cdots{\rightarrow}D_n{\rightarrow}\mathsf{Prop}$, if it is allowed to quantify over $D_1, \ldots, D_n$ in the system, then we can compress the first two premises in the rule (EXT) to $\forall \mathbf{x}.(f\mathbf{x} \supset g\mathbf{x} \;\&\; g\mathbf{x} \supset f\mathbf{x})$. For convenience this will also be denoted by $f \sim_D g$, so

$$f \sim_D g := \forall \mathbf{x}.(f\mathbf{x} \supset g\mathbf{x} \;\&\; g\mathbf{x} \supset f\mathbf{x}),$$

where the D will usually be omitted if it is clear from the context.

4.6. Lemma. The extensionality scheme for $D = \mathsf{Prop}$ is admissible in any of the propositional logics, i.e.

$$\varphi \supset \psi, \psi \supset \varphi, \chi[\varphi/\alpha] \vdash \chi[\psi/\alpha]$$

is always provable.

Proof. By an easy induction on the structure of χ. □

The following is now immediate by the fact that in PROP2 the only extensionality scheme that can be expressed is the one for $D = \mathsf{Prop}$.

4.7. Corollary. In the system E-PROP2 of extensional second order propositional logic one can prove the same as in PROP2. That is

$$\Gamma \vdash_{\text{E-PROP2}} \varphi \Leftrightarrow \Gamma \vdash_{\text{PROP2}} \varphi.$$

4.3. Algebraic semantics for intuitionistic propositional logics

In this section we describe a semantics for our systems of intuitionistic propositional logic in terms of Heyting algebras. It is well-known how this is done for the full first order propositional logic, giving rise to a completeness result. For second and higher order propositional logic we need to refine the notion of Heyting algebra to also allow interpretations for the universal quantifier. It will be shown that *complete* Heyting algebras are strong enough to satisfy our purpose: complete Heyting algebras have arbitrary meets and joins, so for example $\forall f \mathrel{\epsilon} \mathsf{Prop}{\rightarrow}\mathsf{Prop}.\varphi$ can be interpreted as $\bigwedge\{[\![\varphi]\!]_{[f:=F]} \mid F \in A{\rightarrow}A\}$. It is however not so easy to show the completeness of complete Heyting algebras over E-PROPn (for any n), because the Lindenbaum algebra defined from E-PROPn is not a complete Heyting algebra.

The proof of completeness that is given below uses Theorem 13.6.13 of [Troelstra and Van Dalen 1988], which states that any Heyting algebra can be embedded in a complete Heyting algebra such that $\supset$, $\perp$ and all existing $\bigvee$ and $\bigwedge$ are preserved (and hence the ordering is preserved). The embedding i that is constructed in the proof is also faithful with respect to the ordering, that is, if $i(a) \leq i(b)$ in the image, then $a \leq b$ in the original Heyting algebra. All this implies completeness of complete Heyting algebras with respect to E-PROPn, for any n. This will be shown in detail in the rest of this section. Hence we have conservativity of E-PROP$(n+1)$ over E-PROPn.

At this point we do not know how (if at all possible) to conclude the conservativity of PROP$(n+1)$ over PROPn from the conservativity of E-PROP$(n+1)$ over E-PROPn. However, we do have the conservativity of PROPn over PROP2 for any n, because PROP2 and E-PROP2 are the same system (Corollary 4.7).

It is obvious that extensionality is required in the syntax because the model notion is extensional: if, for example, $F, G : A{\rightarrow}A$ (where A is the carrier set of the algebra) and $F(a) = G(a)$ for all $a \in A$, then $F = G$.

The method of showing conservativity by semantical means seems to be quite essential here. Syntactic conservativity proofs (like the others in this paper) use mappings from the 'larger' system to the 'smaller' system that are the identity on the smaller system. Such a mapping also constitutes a mapping from derivations to derivations, that is the identity on derivations of the smaller system. This was the case for the proof of conservativity of the upper plane of the cube over the lower plane, where the proof-term in the smaller system is just obtained by normalizing the proof-term in the larger system. For the case of propositional logics, this method is impossible: there are formulas of PROP2 that have more and more cut-free derivations when we go higher in the hierarchy of propositional logics. In Section 5 these issues will be discussed in some more detail.

4.8. DEFINITION. A *Heyting algebra* (or just Ha) is a tuple $(A, \wedge, \vee, \bot, \supset)$ such that $(A, \wedge, \vee)$ is a lattice with least element $\bot$ and $\supset$ is a binary operation with

$$a \wedge b \leq c \Leftrightarrow a \leq b \supset c,$$

where the ordering $\leq$ is defined by $a \leq b := a \wedge b = a$.

Remember that $(A, \wedge, \vee)$ is a lattice if the binary operations $\wedge$ and $\vee$ satisfy the following requirements.

$$\begin{aligned} a \wedge a &= a, & a \vee a &= a, \\ a \wedge b &= b \wedge a, & a \vee b &= b \vee a, \\ a \wedge (b \wedge c) &= (a \wedge b) \wedge c, & a \vee (b \vee c) &= (a \vee b) \vee c, \\ a \vee (a \wedge b) &= a, & a \wedge (a \vee b) &= a. \end{aligned}$$

Another way of defining the notion of lattice is by saying that it is a poset $(A, \leq)$ with the property that each pair of elements $a, b \in A$ has a least upperbound (denoted by $a \vee b$) and a greatest lowerbound (denoted by $a \wedge b$).

4.9. DEFINITION. A *complete Heyting algebra* (cHa) is a tuple $(A, \bigwedge, \bigvee, \bot, \supset)$ such that $(A, \bigwedge, \bigvee)$ is a complete lattice and $(A, \wedge, \vee, \bot, \supset)$ is a Heyting algebra. So $\bigvee$ and $\bigwedge$ are mappings from $\wp(A)$ to A such that for $X \subset A$, $\bigvee X$ is the least upperbound of X and $\bigwedge X$ is the greatest lower bound of X. The binary operations $\wedge$ and $\vee$ are defined by (for $a, b \in A$) $a \wedge b := \bigwedge\{a, b\}$ and $a \vee b := \bigvee\{a, b\}$.

An important feature of Heyting algebras which is forced by the presence of the binary operation $\supset$, is that they satisfy the infinitary distributive law:

$$(D) \quad \text{If } \bigvee X \text{ exists, then } a \wedge \bigvee X = \bigvee\{a \wedge b \mid b \in X\}.$$

The inclusion $\supseteq$ holds in any lattice; for the inclusion $\subseteq$ it is enough to show that $a \wedge c \subseteq \bigvee\{a \wedge b \mid b \in X\}$ for any $c \in X$, which is true due to the properties of $\supset$. Two other important facts are the following.

4.10. FACT. 1. If a complete lattice satisfies the infinitary distributive law (D), it can be turned into a cHa by defining

$$b \supset c := \bigvee\{d \mid d \wedge b \leq c\}.$$

2. Any Heyting algebra is distributive, i.e. any Ha satisfies

$$a \wedge (b \vee c) = (a \wedge b) \vee (a \wedge c).$$

For the first statement one has to show that $a \wedge b \leq c \Leftrightarrow a \leq \bigvee\{d \mid d \wedge b \leq c\}$. From left to right is easy; from right to left, notice that if $a \leq \bigvee\{d \mid d \wedge b \leq c\}$, then $a \wedge b \leq b \wedge \bigvee\{d \mid d \wedge b \leq c\}$ and the latter is (by D) equal to $\bigvee\{b \wedge d \mid d \wedge b \leq c\}$, which is just c. The second is easily verified.

We are now ready to give the algebraic semantics for the systems E-PROPn. In the following let $(A, \bigwedge, \bigvee, \perp, \supset)$ be a cHa. We freely use the notions $\vee$ and $\wedge$, as they were given in Definition 4.9. The interpretation of the terms of E-PROPn will be in A and its higher order function spaces. We therefore let $\lceil - \rceil$ be the mapping that associates the right function space to a domain D, so

$$\lceil \mathsf{Prop} \rceil = A,$$
$$\lceil D_1 \rightarrow D_2 \rceil = \lceil D_1 \rceil \rightarrow \lceil D_2 \rceil,$$

where the second $\rightarrow$ describes function space. In the following we shall freely speak of the 'interpretation of E-PROPn in $(A, \bigwedge, \bigvee, \perp, \supset)$', where of course this interpretation includes the mapping of higher order terms into the appropriate higher order function spaces based on A.

Note that, as there are no constants in the formal systems of propositional logics, a model of E-PROPn is just a cHa: we do not need a valuation for the constants. (The extension with constants is no problem though. In that case a model is a pair $(\Theta, \mathcal{C})$, with Θ a cHa and $\mathcal{C}$ a mapping that assigns values to the constants.)

4.11. DEFINITION. The interpretation of E-PROPn in the cHa $(A, \bigwedge, \bigvee, \perp, \supset)$, $[\![-]\!]$, is defined modulo a valuation ρ for free variables that maps variables of domain D into $\lceil D \rceil$. So let ρ be a valuation. Then $[\![-]\!]_\rho$ is defined inductively as follows.

$$[\![\alpha]\!]_\rho = \rho(\alpha), \text{ for } \alpha \text{ a variable},$$
$$[\![PQ]\!]_\rho = [\![P]\!]_\rho([\![Q]\!]_\rho),$$
$$[\![\lambda x \epsilon D.Q]\!]_\rho = \boldsymbol{\lambda} t \in \lceil D \rceil . [\![Q]\!]_{\rho(x:=t)},$$
$$[\![\varphi \supset \psi]\!]_\rho = [\![\varphi]\!]_\rho \supset [\![\psi]\!]_\rho,$$
$$[\![\forall x \epsilon D.\varphi]\!]_\rho = \bigwedge\{[\![\varphi]\!]_{\rho(x:=t)} \mid t \in \lceil D \rceil\}.$$

Note that $[\![P]\!]_\rho([\![Q]\!]_\rho)$ denotes a set-theoretic function application and $\boldsymbol{\lambda}$ denotes set-theoretic abstraction.

It is easily seen that $[\![-]\!]_\rho$ satisfies the usual substitution property and that interpretations are stable under $\beta\eta$-equality, i.e.

$$[\![P]\!]_{\rho(x:=[\![Q]\!]_\rho)} = [\![P[Q/x]]\!]_\rho$$

and

$$P =_{\beta\eta} Q \Rightarrow [\![P]\!]_\rho = [\![Q]\!]_\rho.$$

4.12. DEFINITION. For Γ a set of formulas of E-PROPn, φ a formula of E-PROPn and Θ a cHa, φ *is Θ-valid in* Γ, notation $\Gamma \models_\Theta \varphi$, if for all valuations ρ,

$$\bigwedge\{[\![\psi]\!]_\rho \mid \psi \in \Gamma\} \leq [\![\varphi]\!]_\rho.$$

If Γ is empty we say that φ *is Θ-valid* if $\models_\Theta \varphi$.

In the following we just write $[\![\Gamma]\!]_\rho$ for $\bigwedge\{[\![\psi]\!]_\rho \mid \psi \in \Gamma\}$.

Our definition is a bit different from the one in [Troelstra and Van Dalen 1988], where $\Gamma \models_\Theta \varphi$ is defined by

$$\forall\rho((\forall\psi \in \Gamma[[\![\psi]\!]_\rho = \top]) \Rightarrow [\![\varphi]\!]_\rho = \top).$$

Our notion implies the one above, but not the other way around. However, they are the same if $\Gamma = \emptyset$ and they also yield the same *consequence relation.*

4.13. DEFINITION. Let Γ be a set of formulas of E-PROPn and φ a formula of E-PROPn. We say that φ *is a consequence of* Γ, notation $\Gamma \models \varphi$, if $\Gamma \models_\Theta \varphi$ for all cHas Θ.

4.14. PROPOSITION (Soundness). For Γ a set of formulas of E-PROPn and φ a formula of E-PROPn,

$$\Gamma \vdash_{\text{E-PROP}n} \varphi \Rightarrow \Gamma \models \varphi.$$

PROOF. Let Θ be a cHa. By induction on the derivation of $\Gamma \vdash \varphi$ we show that for all valuations ρ, $[\![\Gamma]\!]_\rho \leq [\![\varphi]\!]_\rho$. None of the six cases is difficult. We treat the cases for the last rule being ($\supset$-E) and ($\forall$-I).

($\supset$-E) Say φ has been derived from $\psi \supset \varphi$ and ψ. Let ρ be a valuation. Then by IH $[\![\Gamma]\!]_\rho \leq [\![\psi]\!]_\rho$ and $[\![\Gamma]\!]_\rho \leq [\![\psi \supset \varphi]\!]_\rho$. The second implies $[\![\Gamma]\!]_\rho \wedge [\![\psi]\!]_\rho \leq [\![\varphi]\!]_\rho$. So, by $[\![\Gamma]\!]_\rho \leq [\![\psi]\!]_\rho$ we conclude $[\![\Gamma]\!]_\rho \leq [\![\varphi]\!]_\rho$.

($\forall$-I) Say $\varphi \equiv \forall f \epsilon D.\psi$ and $\Gamma' \subseteq \Gamma$ is the finite set of non-discharged formulas of the derivation with conclusion ψ. Then by IH, $\forall\rho[[\![\Gamma']\!]_\rho \leq [\![\psi]\!]_\rho]$, so $\forall\rho\forall F \in \lceil D\rceil[[\![\Gamma']\!]_\rho \leq [\![\psi]\!]_{\rho(f:=F)}]$, because $f \notin \text{FV}(\Gamma')$. This immediately implies that $[\![\Gamma]\!]_\rho \leq [\![\forall f \epsilon D.\psi]\!]_\rho$. □

To show completeness we first construct the Lindenbaum algebra for E-PROPn. This is a Ha but not yet a cHa. The construction in [Troelstra and Van Dalen 1988] tells us how to turn it into a cHa which has all the desired properties.

4.15. DEFINITION. For $n \in \mathbb{N} \cup \{\omega\}$, we define the *Lindenbaum algebra for* E-PROPn, $\mathcal{L}_n$. First we define the equivalence relation $\sim$ on Form(E-PROPn) by

$$\varphi \sim \psi := \vdash_{\text{E-PROP}n} \varphi \supset \psi \;\&\; \psi \supset \varphi.$$

We denote the equivalence class of φ under $\sim$ by $[\varphi]$. $\mathcal{L}_n$ is now defined as the Ha $(A, \wedge, \vee, \bot, \supset)$ where

$$\begin{aligned} A &= (\text{Form(E-PROP}n))_{\sim}, \\ [\varphi] \wedge [\psi] &= [\varphi \mathbin{\&} \psi], \\ [\varphi] \vee [\psi] &= [\varphi \vee \psi], \\ [\varphi] \supset [\psi] &= [\varphi \supset \psi], \\ [\bot] &= [\bot]. \end{aligned}$$

Note that the &, $\vee$, $\supset$ and $\bot$ on the right of the $=$ are the logical connectives: $\supset$ is basic and the others were defined in Remark 4.2 by

$$\begin{aligned} \varphi \mathbin{\&} \psi &:= \forall \alpha \epsilon \mathsf{Prop}.(\varphi \supset \psi \supset \alpha) \supset \alpha, \\ \varphi \vee \psi &:= \forall \alpha \epsilon \mathsf{Prop}.(\varphi \supset \alpha) \supset (\psi \supset \alpha) \supset \alpha, \\ \bot &:= \forall \alpha \epsilon \mathsf{Prop}.\alpha. \end{aligned}$$

Each $\mathcal{L}_n$ is obviously a Ha: $[\varphi] \leq [\psi]$ iff $\varphi \vdash_{\text{E-PROP}n} \psi$.

4.16. Lemma. For Γ a finite set of sentences of E-PROPn and φ a sentence of E-PROPn,

$$\Gamma \vdash_{\text{E-PROP}n} \varphi \;\Leftrightarrow\; [\bigwedge \Gamma] \leq [\varphi] \text{ in } \mathcal{L}_n.$$

Proof. Immediate by the construction of $\mathcal{L}_n$. □

4.17. Theorem ([Troelstra and Van Dalen 1988]). Each Ha Θ can be embedded into a cHa $c\Theta$ such that $\wedge$, $\vee$, $\bot$, $\supset$ and existing $\bigwedge$ and $\bigvee$ are preserved and $\leq$ is reflected.

Proof. Let $\Theta = (A, \wedge, \vee, \bot, \supset)$ be a Ha. A *complete ideal of* Θ, or just *c-ideal*, is a subset $I \subset A$ that satisfies the following properties.

1. $\bot \in I$,
2. I is *downward closed* (i.e. if $b \in I$ and $a \leq b$, then $a \in I$),
3. I is *closed under existing sups* (i.e. if $X \subset I$ and $\bigvee X$ exists, then $\bigvee X \in I$).

Now define $c\Theta$ to be the lattice of c-ideals, ordered by inclusion. Then $c\Theta$ is a complete lattice that satisfies the infinitary distributive law D, and hence $c\Theta$ is a cHa by defining

$$I \supset J := \bigvee\{K \mid K \wedge I \subset J\}.$$

To verify this note the following.

- $c\Theta$ has infs defined by $\bigwedge_{q \in Q} I_q = \bigcap_{q \in Q} I_q$.
- $c\Theta$ has sups defined by $\bigvee_{q \in Q} I_q = \{\bigvee X \mid X \subset \bigcup_{q \in Q} I_q, \bigvee X \text{ exists}\}$: the set $\{\bigvee X \mid X \subset \bigcup_{q \in Q} I_q, \bigvee X \text{ exists}\}$ is indeed a c-ideal and it is also the least c-ideal containing all I_q.
- $I \cap \bigvee_{q \in Q} I_q = \bigvee\{I \cap I_q \mid q \in Q\}$ and so D holds.

The embedding i from Θ to $c\Theta$ is now defined by

$$i(a) = \{x \in A \mid x \leq a\}.$$

The embedding preserves $\perp$, $\supset$ and all existing $\bigwedge$, $\bigvee$. For the preserving of $\bigvee$, let $X \subset A$ such that $\bigvee X$ exists in Θ. We have to show that $i(\bigvee X) = \bigvee_{x \in X} i(x)$, i.e. show that

$$\{y \in A \mid y \leq \bigvee X\} = \{\bigvee Y \mid Y \subset \bigcup_{x \in X} i(x), \bigvee Y \text{exists}\}.$$

For the inclusion from left to right, note that $X \subset \{y \in A \mid \exists x \in X[y \leq x]\}$ and so $X \subset \bigcup_{x \in X} i(x)$. This implies that $\bigvee X \in \{\bigvee Y \mid Y \subset \bigcup_{x \in X} i(x), \bigvee Y \text{exists}\}$ and so we are done because the latter is a c-ideal. For the inclusion from right to left, let $z = \bigvee Y_0$ with $Y_0 \subset \bigcup_{x \in X} i(x)$. Then $z \leq \bigvee X$ so we are done.

Finally, the embedding i reflects the ordering, i.e.

$$i(a) \subset i(b) \Rightarrow a \leq b. \square$$

4.18. Corollary (Completeness). For Γ a finite set of sentences of E-PROPn and φ a sentence of E-PROPn,

$$\Gamma \models \varphi \Rightarrow \Gamma \vdash_{\text{E-PROP}n} \varphi.$$

Proof. Following the Theorem, we embed the Lindenbaum algebra of E-PROPn, $\mathcal{L}_n$, in $c\mathcal{L}_n$. This cHa $c\mathcal{L}_n$ is complete with respect to the logic. So, for Γ a finite set of sentences and φ a sentence of E-PROPn, we have

$$\Gamma \models \varphi \;\Rightarrow\; \Gamma \models_{c\mathcal{L}_n} \varphi \;\Rightarrow\; [\bigwedge \Gamma] \leq [\varphi] \text{ in } \mathcal{L}_n \;\Rightarrow\; \Gamma \vdash_{\text{E-PROP}n} \varphi. \square$$

4.19. Corollary (Conservativity). For any $n \geq 2$, E-PROP$(n+1)$ is conservative over E-PROPn, and hence E-PROPω is conservative over E-PROPn.

Proof. For Γ a finite set of sentences and φ a sentence of E-PROPn,

$$\Gamma \vdash_{\text{E-PROP}(n+1)} \varphi \Rightarrow \Gamma \models \varphi \Rightarrow \Gamma \vdash_{\text{E-PROP}n} \varphi$$

by soundness and completeness of the cHas for any of the E-PROPn.

The conservativity of E-PROPω over E-PROPn is now immediate: any derivation in E-PROPω is a derivation in E-PROPm for some $m \in \mathbb{N}$. $\square$

4.20. Corollary. For any $n \in \mathbb{N} \cup \{\omega\}$, PROP$n$ is conservative over PROP2.

Proof. By the fact that PROPn is a subsystem of E-PROPn and the fact that PROP2 and E-PROP2 are the same system. $\square$

The formulas-as-types embedding (from PROPω to $\lambda\omega$, respectively from PROP2 to $\lambda 2$) is an isomorphism, so we can immediately conclude the following.

4.21. Theorem. The type system $\lambda\omega$ is conservative over $\lambda 2$, that is, for all $\lambda 2$-contexts Γ and $\lambda 2$-types σ we have

$$\Gamma \vdash_{\lambda\omega} M : \sigma \Rightarrow \exists N[\Gamma \vdash_{\lambda 2} N : \sigma].$$

5. Discussion and concluding remarks

5.1. Semantical versus syntactical proofs of conservativity

We have seen that a proof of conservativity between typed λ calculi can be helpful to prove conservativity between logics. An example is the proof of conservativity of λPRED2 over λPRED, which immediately implies the conservativity of second order predicate logic over minimal first order predicate logic. Due to the syntactic nature of the proof (which is done by normalizing the proof terms), it is convenient to use the typed λ calculus format for the conservativity proof. For the proof of conservativity of $\lambda\omega$ over $\lambda 2$, a semantical proof was used. At this point it is not clear to us how a purely syntactical proof can be given for this case. For example, the method of normalizing the proof terms does not work here because of the following.

5.1. FACT. There are Γ, A and M, with Γ a context of $\lambda 2$, A a type of $\lambda 2$ and M a term of $\lambda\omega$, such that

$$\Gamma \vdash_{\lambda\omega} M : A \text{ and } \Gamma \nvdash_{\lambda 2} \mathrm{nf}(M) : A.$$

One example is found by taking Γ to be the empty context and A to be the type of functions from numerals to numerals, so $A \equiv N \rightarrow N$, where $N \equiv \Pi\alpha : \star.(\alpha\rightarrow\alpha)\rightarrow\alpha\rightarrow\alpha$. Then one can take for M a representation of a recursive function that is λ-definable in $\lambda\omega$, but not λ-definable in $\lambda 2$. (Such terms exist, due to [Girard 1972], where it is shown that in $\lambda\omega$ more recursive functions are λ-definable then in $\lambda 2$.) Then $\vdash_{\lambda\omega} M : N\rightarrow N$, but not $\vdash_{\lambda 2} \mathrm{nf}(M) : N\rightarrow N$, because the normal form of M λ-defines the same recursive function as M.

An easier counterexample is found by taking, for example, the context Γ to be $x : \Pi\alpha{:}\star.\Pi\beta{:}\star.\beta\rightarrow\beta$. Then $\Gamma \vdash_{\lambda\omega} x(\Pi P{:}\star\rightarrow\star.P\bot) : \Pi\beta{:}\star.\beta\rightarrow\beta$, which is a term in normal form and not typable in $\lambda 2$.

It would be interesting to see how a syntactic proof of the conservativity of $\lambda\omega$ over $\lambda 2$ could be given. This would give an algorithm that computes for every $\lambda\omega$-term M that has a $\lambda 2$-type A, a $\lambda 2$-term N that also has the type A.

For the proof of conservativity of $\lambda 2$ over $\lambda\rightarrow$ (and hence of conservativity of second order propositional logic over minimal first order propositional logic), we used normalization here. This is not really necessary. It is possible to give a semantical proof, using, for example, the algebraic semantics that we discussed for second and higher order propositional logic. It is also possible to give a syntactic proof by defining a mapping from propositions and proofs of second order propositional logic to first order propositional logic that preserves derivability. This is done in [Pitts 1992].

5.2. Decidability

One of the consequences of conservativity of PROPω over PROP2 is that the system PROPω is not decidable. This follows from the undecidability of PROP2, which was proved by [Löb 1976] and also by [Gabbay 1981]. Similarly, all the logics PROPn and E-PROPn are undecidable (for $n \in \mathbb{N} \cup \omega$), because they are all conservative over PROP2. In [Löb 1976] this is proved by giving a sound and complete translation of first order predicate logic into PROP2. The conservativity of PROPω over PROP2 shows that this translation does not extend to a sound and complete embedding of higher order predicate logic into PROPω. (Otherwise the 'first order parts' in PROPω and PROP2 could be used to show non-conservativity, in the style of the non-conservativity proof of λPREDω over λPRED2.)

5.3. Conservativity of λP2 over λP

The conservativity of λP2 over λP, and similarly the conservativity of λPRED2 over λPRED, may look a bit strange at first. Why does Gödel's Second Incompleteness Theorem not apply here? (Showing that the consistency of HA, first order arithmetic, can not be proved in HA itself; it can be proved in HA2, hence the non-conservativity of λPRED2 over λPRED.) The answer is that the logic λPRED is too minimal to be able to represent enough arithmetic to apply Gödel's Theorem. Remember that λPRED only has the connectives $\rightarrow$ and $\forall$, and because we are in a first order system, the other connectives are not representable. Hence an axiom like $\forall x \in \mathbb{N}[x \neq 0 \Rightarrow \exists y \in \mathbb{N}[x = Sy]]$ is not representable. The system λP has the same weakness.

We conjecture here that λP2 is not conservative over λP$^\perp$, where λP$^\perp$ is λP extended with a type constant $\perp$, a term operator $c_\perp$ and the rules

$$(\perp)\ \frac{}{\vdash \perp : \star} \qquad (\perp\text{-I})\ \frac{\Gamma \vdash A : \star}{\Gamma \vdash c_\perp A : A}.$$

Of course, λP$^\perp$ is not really a subsystem of λP2, so it would be more precise to say that the (canonical) embedding from λP$^\perp$ into λP2 that maps $\perp$ to $\Pi\alpha{:}\star.\alpha$ is complete. This terminology is not used here, because we think it is clear that this is meant by the conservativity.

The motivation for this conjecture is that in λP$^\perp$, we can represent first order arithmetic, by using a classical interpretation of the connectives. So, for $\Gamma \vdash A, B : \star$ (with possibly $x{:}C$ free in A), define $\neg A :\equiv A{\rightarrow}\perp$, $A \mathbin{\&} B :\equiv \neg(A{\rightarrow}\neg B)$, $A \vee B :\equiv \neg A{\rightarrow}B$ and $\exists x : C.A :\equiv \neg(\Pi x{:}C.\neg A)$. Then, classical first order arithmetic can be represented in λP$^\perp$ (and similarly in λP2). The consistency of this system can be stated in λP$^\perp$, but it can only be proved in λP2. Hence the non-conservativity of λP2 over λP$^\perp$.

References

[Barendregt 1992] H.P. Barendregt, Typed lambda calculi. In *Handbook of Logic in Computer Science*, eds. Abramski et al., Oxford Univ. Press.

[Barendsen and Geuvers 1989] E. Barendsen and H. Geuvers, λP is conservative over first order predicate logic, Manuscript, Faculty of Mathematics and Computer Science, University of Nijmegen, Netherlands,

[Berardi 1988] S. Berardi, Towards a mathematical analysis of the Coquand-Huet calculus of constructions and the other systems in Barendregt's cube. Dept. Computer Science, Carnegie-Mellon University and Dipartimento Matematica, Universita di Torino, Italy.

[Berardi 1989] S. Berardi, Talk given at the 'Jumelage meeting on typed lambda calculus', Edinburgh, September 1989.

[Berardi 1990] S. Berardi, Type dependence and constructive mathematics, Ph.D. thesis, Universita di Torino, Italy.

[De Bruijn 1980] N.G. de Bruijn, A survey of the project Automath, In *To H.B. Curry: Essays on Combinatory Logic, Lambda Calculus and Formalism*, eds. J.P. Seldin, J.R. Hindley, Academic Press, New York, pp 580-606.

[Coquand 1985] Th. Coquand, Une théorie des constructions, Thèse de troisième cycle, Université Paris VII, France, January 1985.

[Coquand 1990] Th. Coquand, Metamathematical investigations of a calculus of constructions. In *Logic and Computer Science*, ed. P.G. Odifreddi, APIC series, vol. 31, Academic Press, pp 91-122.

[Coquand and Huet 1988] Th. Coquand and G. Huet, The calculus of constructions, *Information and Computation*, 76, pp 95-120.

[Coquand and Huet 1985] Th. Coquand and G. Huet, Constructions: a higher order proof system for mechanizing mathematics. *Proceedings of EUROCAL '85, Linz*, LNCS 203.

[Gabbay 1981] D.M. Gabbay, *Semantical investigations in Heyting's intuitionistic logic*, Synthese Library, vol 148, Reidel, Dordrecht.

[Geuvers 1989] J.H. Geuvers, Talk given at the 'Jumelage meeting on typed lambda calculus', Edinburgh, September 1989.

[Geuvers and Nederhof 1991] J.H. Geuvers and M.J. Nederhof, A modular proof of strong normalisation for the calculus of constructions. *Journal of Functional Programming*, vol 1 (2), pp 155-189.

[Geuvers 1993] J.H. Geuvers, Logics and Type systems, PhD. Thesis, University of Nijmegen, Netherlands.

[Girard 1972] J.-Y. Girard, Interprétation fonctionelle et élimination des coupures dans l'arithmétique d'ordre supérieur. Ph.D. thesis, Université Paris VII, France.

[Girard et al. 1989] J.-Y. Girard, Y. Lafont and P. Taylor, *Proofs and types*, Camb. Tracts in Theoretical Computer Science 7, Cambridge University Press.

[Harper et al. 1987] R. Harper, F. Honsell and G. Plotkin, A framework for defining logics. *Proceedings Second Symposium on Logic in Computer Science*, (Ithaca, N.Y.), IEEE, Washington DC, pp 194-204.

[Howard 1980] W.A. Howard, The formulas-as-types notion of construction. In *To H.B. Curry: Essays on Combinatory Logic, Lambda Calculus and Formalism*, eds. J.P. Seldin, J.R. Hindley, Academic Press, New York, pp 479-490.

[Löb 1976] M. Löb, Embedding first order predicate logic in fragments of intuitionistic logic, *J. Symbolic Logic* vol 41, 4, pp. 705–719.

[Longo and Moggi 1988] G. Longo and E. Moggi, Constructive Natural Deduction and its "Modest" Interpretation. Report CMU-CS-88-131.

[Paulin 1989] Ch. Paulin-Mohring, Extraction des programmes dans le calcul des constructions, Thèse, Université Paris VII, France.

[Pitts 1992] A.M. Pitts, On an interpretation of second order quantification in first order intuitionistic propositional logic. *J. Symbolic Logic* vol 57, 1, pp.33–52.

[Ruys 1991] M. Ruys, $\lambda P\omega$ is not conservative over $\lambda P2$, Master's thesis, University of Nijmegen, Netherlands, November 1991.

[Tonino and Fujita 1992] H. Tonino and K.-E. Fujita, On the adequacy of representing higher order intuitionistic logic as a pure type system, *Annals of Pure and Applied Logic* vol 57, pp 251–276.

[Troelstra and Van Dalen 1988] A. Troelstra and D. van Dalen, ***Constructivism in mathematics, an introduction, Volume I/II***, Studies in logic and the foundations of mathematics, vol 121 and volume 123, North-Holland.

[Verschuren 1990] E. Verschuren, Conservativity in Barendregt's cube, Master's thesis, University of Nijmegen, Netherlands, December 1990.

Logic of refinement types

Susumu Hayashi

Department of Applied Mathematics and Informatics
Ryukoku University
Seta, Ohtsu, Shiga, 520-21, JAPAN
hayashi@rins.st.ryukoku.ac.jp

To the memory of Prof. Ken Hirose

Abstract. Refinement types are subsets of ordinary types, which are intended to be specifications of programs. Ordinary types correspond to constructive propositions by Curry-Howard isomorphism. Refinement types correspond to "classical" propositions by a semantics resembling interpretations of logics in categorical/algebraic logic. In this paper, we will study the logic of refinement types in the type system ATTT which was introduced in [9] as a framework for an "optimized" Curry-Howard isomorphism.

1 Introduction

ATTT is a conservative extension of Girard-Reynolds' second order polymorphic lambda calculus $\lambda 2$ (or F in more popular name). The aim of ATTT is to serve yet another type theoretic basis for program extraction or program development. In [9], the theory of pure ATTT was presented and its basic metatheory was developed. In this paper, we will study logics in ATTT. The main purpose of this paper is to show how logic is represented by refinements of ATTT. We will show that the refinements of each type is an "internally" complete Heyting algebra (cHa). Using the cHa structure, second order intuitionistic logic is naturally interpreted by refinements via the technique of categorical logic [15]. The second order formulas provable in the intuitionistic second order logic are provably true in ATTT under this interpretation. Conversely, the first order formulas provably true in ATTT under this interpretation are provable in the intuitionistic first order logic. We conjecture that this holds for the second order case as well and will give a sufficient condition.

The logic of refinements mentioned above is "non-informative" in the sense of Coq system [3] or "rank zero" in the sense of PX system [8]. Thus, it is a substitute of logics of Coq's propositions and PX's rank zero formulas. This means that the interpretation of formulas does not keep any computational information contrary to the ordinary BHK-interpretation (Brouwer-Heyting-Kolmogorov-interpretation) of constructive logic. Besides this non-informative interpretation, some BHK-style interpretations of logic can be coded in ATTT. They are essentially realizability interpretations. We will show that both of recursive realizability and modified realizability are represented naturally in ATTT.

Then, we will show that informative induction principle is derivable by non-informative induction principle in ATTT.

We also introduce a notion of refinement classifier resembling subobject classifier of topos, and, by means of this notion, we will compare our approach to program/proof development in ATTT with related works [2], [3], [16], [20].

2 Refinement types

In this section, we will briefly review the notion of refinement types and develop cHa-structures of the refinements. The notion of refinement type was first introduced in [5]. We independently introduced a very similar notion for a rather different aim [9].[1]

2.1 Types versus refinement types

A type is a collection of data which have the same uniform structure. A set is a collection of data which have the same property. Property which defines a set can be so complicated that we cannot effectively decide if a data belongs to the set. On the other hand, types of programming languages are supposed to be simple. For examples, integers, elements of free algebras, records and functions are all types. But, the primes are not a type. It is a *set*. We summarize this intuition by the following "doctrine": the border of types are smooth and the border of sets are rugged.[2] "The function f returns the next prime number to its real argument" is a specification of a function f. The boundary of the collection of data satisfying this specification is rugged, as it uses the primes in it.

Intuitively, specifications must be identified with sets. Thus, we think that the specifications should be distinguished from data types, even in the type theories for program extraction based on Curry-Howard isomorphism. This consideration led us to introduce a new kind of "types" called *refinement types*. Refinement types have rugged boundaries and are intended to serve as specifications. This refinement types refine the boundaries of types, i.e., they distinguish elements more refinedly than types. More precisely, a refinement types of type A is intended to be a *subset* of the ordinary type A. Note that a refinement type, or refinement in short, is not a subtype of A, since it may have a rugged boundary (Fig. 1).

ATTT is a type system with refinement types designed as "ATTT = $\lambda 2$ + refinement types." In a sense , ATTT is "$\lambda 2$ + logic." In set theory, sets are defined by the aid of logical formulas. We do not introduce formulas but directly define set (refinements) by means of the rules for refinements in the framework of type theory. In categorical/algebraic logic, logics are coded through sets (subobject), e.g. the statement "$F(x)$ implies $G(x) \vee H(x)$" can be interpreted as

[1] As our framework looked very similar to Freeman and Pfenning, we call our notion by the same name. The exact relationship is still unknown, but it seems fair to say that these are essentially the same notion.

[2] I learnt this doctrine from Rod Burstall. According him, it's due to JÀRobinson.

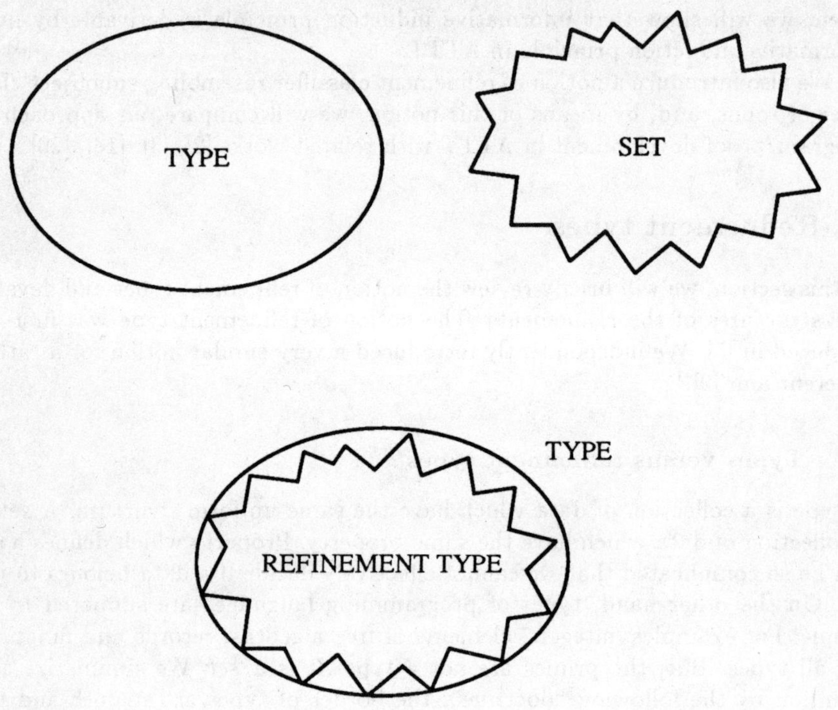

Fig. 1. Type, Set and Refinement Type

set-theoretic inclusion $\{x|F(x)\} \subset \{x|G(x)\} \cup \{x|H(x)\}$. Thus we may think that the set part (refinement part) of ATTT is a kind of logic *without* formulas. This resembles the philosophy of Martin-Löf's type theory (at least his philosophy in 80's). The difference is that Martin-Löf used Curry-Howard isomorphism to represent logic but we use the approach via categorical/algebraic logic. Note that we have *not* abandoned Martin-Löf's philosophy. The categorical/algebraic logic approach is used only for non-informative part. For informative part, we follow Martin-Löf's philosophy. In a sense, we use Curry-Howard isomorphism, when we sit in outside Martin-Löf's subset type, and use categorical/algebraic logic approach, when we sit in inside Martin-Löf's subset type.

More formally, ATTT is described as follows. The types and terms of ATTT are exactly the ones of $\lambda 2$. If A is a type of $\lambda 2$ (and so of ATTT), we introduce the refinement kind of A, which we will write *refine*(A). A refinement kind is a sort of "kind" in the sense of GTS. The elements of the refinement kind *refine*(A) is intended to be the refinements of the type A. Each refinement kind *refine*(A) is closed under the formation rules of singleton $\{a\}_A$ $(a \in A)$, and unions $R_1 \vee R_2$, $\bigvee x \in A.R$ and intersections $R_1 \wedge R_2$, $\bigwedge x \in A.R$. Furthermore, if R_1 is in *refine*(A) and R_2 is in *refine*(B), then $R_1 \to R_2$ is in *refine*$(A \to B)$. This refinement type of functions represents the constructive implication. Natural introduction and elimination rules for these refinements are included. A subtle point is the introduction rule for the refinement $R_1 \to R_2$. If $e \in R_2$ for $x \in R_1$, then the term $\lambda x \in A.e$ is introduced in $R_1 \to R_2$, and not $\lambda x \in R_1.e$.[3] The description of ATTT above would be enough to understand the development below. Thus we will not explain the details. See [9] for more details.

2.2 Refinement application

For the discussions below, we will introduce a notion *refinement application*. A future of ATTT is that the realizability relation "a realizes F" is not only a judgment but also a refinement type. The relation is expressed as

$$F \wedge \{a\}.$$

This refinement is realized by a, if and only if, a belongs to F. If we consider a refinement of A as a predicate on A as we will do later, $F \wedge \{a\}$ is considered the application of F to a. So we call this refinement application and write $F\{a\}$.

Note that Martin-Löf's propositional equality $I(F, a, a)$ is a proposition which expresses realizability relation. The refinement application resemble this. The difference is $F\{a\}$ is realized by a, and $I(F, a, a)$ is realized by a fixed constant.

2.3 The algebra of refinements

The refinement kind *refine*(A) is intended to be the subsets of the type A. So it has a lattice theoretic structure. $\bigwedge$ and $\bigvee$ are "internal" infimum and supremum, respectively. Actually, they are an "internally" complete Heyting algebra. Namely, they are distributed "internally" complete lattice. To show it, we define an pre-order relation on *refine*(A). The relation itself is a refinements of *refine*$(A \to A)$.

Definition 1 (subset refinement) Let R_1 and R_2 be refinements of a type A. The *subset refinement* $R_1 \leq R_2$ is defined as follows:

$$R_1 \leq R_2 \stackrel{\text{def}}{=} \bigwedge x \in R_1.(R_1\{x\} \to R_2\{x\}).$$

The subset refinement is a refinement of type $A \to A$. Intuitively, the subset refinement says that R_1 is a subset of R_2. For this refinement the following proposition holds.

[3] This rule is justified by the observation that terms of ATTT are exactly those of $\lambda 2$ and the former lambda term is a term of $\lambda 2$ but the latter is not. This rule also reflects modified realizabilities. Recently, Pfenning introduced a type theory with intersection types which has a function-introduction rule similar to ours for a different good reason [19].

Proposition 1 *Let $A \in Type$, $R_1 \in refine(A)$ and $R_2 \in refine(A)$ be derivable under a context Γ. Then, the following are equivalent:*

1. *$\Gamma, x \in R_1 \vdash x \in R_2$ is derivable.*
2. *$\Gamma \vdash Id_A \in R_1 \leq R_2$ is derivable.*
3. *$\Gamma \vdash e \in R_1 \leq R_2$ is derivable for some term e.*

Id_A is the identical function $\lambda x \in A.x$. Note that the second condition shows that the identity function is the standard witness of the refinement. In this sense, the subset refinement is self-realizing or non-informative.

It is easy to see the subset refinement defines an pre-order relation on *refine*(A). Note that this fact can be stated *internally*. Namely, the followings are derivable in an appropriate context:

1. $\bigwedge R \in refine(A).R \leq R$,
2. $\bigwedge R_1 \in refine(A). \bigwedge R_2 \in refine(A). \bigwedge R_3 \in refine(A).R_1 \leq R_2 \supset R_2 \leq R_3 \supset R_1 \leq R_3$.

Note that "$\supset$" is the ordinary implication defined by the function space. Since the subset refinement is self-realizing, the implication may be replaced by non-informative implication explained later.

Since the subset relation is a pre-order, we have to consider the "equivalence relation" induced from the pre-order. This can be also internalized. Let's call such an equivalence relation *extensional equality refinement*, $R_1 \geq\leq R_2$ in notation. It's defined by

$$R_1 \geq\leq R_2 \stackrel{\text{def}}{=} (R_1 \leq R_2) \wedge (R_2 \leq R_1).$$

2.4 The refinements are internally complete Heyting algebra

The finite intersection and union are infimum and supremum, respectively. These facts can be stated internally as well as externally. As we have big intersections and unions, the refinements of a type are *internally* complete. For example, we can derive the followings for the big intersection:

$$\ldots, i \in I \vdash Id_A \in (\bigwedge i \in I.R) \leq R$$

$$\frac{\ldots, X \in refine(A), i \in I \vdash e \in X \leq R}{\ldots, X \in refine(A) \vdash X \leq \bigwedge x \in A.R} (i \text{ is not free in } e)$$

Note that we have to be careful with what kind of indexes $i \in I$ are allowed. It depends on what kind of formation rules for the intersection and union are allowed. But, once a formation rule is introduced, there is no difficulty to prove the properties above.

A complete Heyting algebra is a complete lattice with the following distribution law:

$$a \wedge \bigvee i \in I.b_i = \bigvee i \in I.(a \wedge b_i).$$

The distribution law is provable in ATTT.

Lemma 1 (the distribution lemma) *Assume i is not free in R. In the contexts where R and S are refinements of a type A, the following refinement is provably inhabited.*

$$R \wedge \bigvee i \in I.S \geq\leq \bigvee i \in I.(R \wedge S).$$

Note that I must be an index set (in the context) for which the formation of the big intersection allowed.

This lemma is not quite trivial. The $\geq$-direction is trivial, but the $\leq$-direction is not. In some type theories with intersection and union types, the distribution law is included as an axiom, as the $\leq$-direction is not derivable from the other axioms and rules. In ATTT, the $\leq$-direction is easily derivable by the following lemma:

Lemma 2 *The following are derived rules of ATTT:*

1.

$$\frac{\Gamma \vdash e_0 \in \bigvee x \in A.B}{\Gamma \vdash e_0 \in \bigvee x \in A.(B \wedge \{e_0\})}$$

2.

$$\frac{\Gamma \vdash e_0 \in \bigvee x \in A.B \qquad \Gamma, x \in A, y \in B \wedge \{e_0\} \vdash e_1 \in C}{\Gamma \vdash e_1[y := e_0] \in C[y := e_0]},$$

where x is not in $FV(e_1) \cup FV(C)$.

The second one is a consequence of the first one.

2.5 implication refinement

In cHa, implication $a \supset b$ is defined as the greatest element c such that $a \wedge c \leq b$ holds. By the same vain, we define the *implication refinement.*

Definition 2 (implication refinement) Let R_1 and R_2 be refinements of a type A. Then we define the *implication refinement* $R_1 \breve{\supset} R_2$ by

$$\bigvee R \in \mathit{refine}(A). \bigvee w \in R_1 \wedge R \leq R_2.R.$$

Note that the implication refinement is of type A and the subset refinement is of type $A \rightarrow A$. For the implication refinement, the following two are equivalent:

$$\Gamma, a \in R_1 \vdash a \in R_2,$$

$$\Gamma, a \in A \vdash a \in R_1 \breve{\supset} R_2.$$

This implies the equivalence of the followings:

$$\Gamma, a \in R_1\{a\} \vdash a \in R_2\{a\},$$

$$\Gamma, a \in A \vdash a \in (R_1 \breve{\supset} R_2)\{a\}.$$

By the commutativity, we can prove that $(R_1 \check{\supset} R_2)\{a\}$ and $R_1\{a\} \check{\supset} R_2\{a\}$ are extensionally equal refinements. If we abuse the notation, we have

$$\Gamma, R_1\{a\} \vdash R_2\{a\},$$

$$\Gamma, a \in A \vdash R_1\{a\} \check{\supset} R_2\{a\}.$$

This shows that the implication refinement satisfies the standard rules for implication.

2.6 Absurdity refinement and truth refinement

The absurdity refinement of a type A, $\bot_A$, is the least refinement and the negation refinement is defined from it and the implication.

$$\bot_A \stackrel{\text{def}}{=} \bigwedge R \in \mathit{refine}(A).R,$$

$$\check{\neg} R \stackrel{\text{def}}{=} R \check{\supset} \bot_A.$$

Obviously, the absurdity refinement implies any refinement of the same type. The truth refinement $\top_A$, which is the greatest refinement is also definable by

$$\top_A \stackrel{\text{def}}{=} \bigvee R \in \mathit{refine}(A).R.$$

Normally, Heyting algebra is assumed to have at least two elements. But, we do not assume it in this paper. As a type may be empty in a semantics for $\lambda 2$, we cannot prove the truth refinement is not the same as the absurdity refinement.

Note that $\bot$ is not unique in ATTT. We have the absurdity $\bot$ for each refinement kind. Later, we will show the refinement of the unit type *unit* classifies the refinements. Thus, $\bot_{unit}$ is the most general absurdity in a sense. If $x \in A$ holds, then $R\{x\}$ for any refinement R of A under the assumption $\bot_{unit}$.

Proposition 2 *The following is derivable in ATTT:*

$$A \in \mathit{Type}, x \in A, R \in \mathit{refine}(A), w \in \bot_{unit} \vdash A \leq R.$$

This means that any refinement is true, if we assume $\bot_{unit}$.

3 Interpreting logic by refinements

In this section, we give an interpretation of second order logic by refinements. A refinement kind of a type A is the power set of A. Thus, refinement kinds resemble the algebras of subobjects in a category. We give an interpretation of second order predicate logic in ATTT using the technique of categorical logic by Makkai and Reyes [15]. But, our interpretation is not completely the same as theirs. Makkai and Reyes considered first order logic. We will consider second order logic. They used external intersections and unions, but we will use internal ones. Furthermore, products are assumed in [15]. We define product by the polymorphic product (see [9]). The polymorphic products are not real products but semi-products in the sense of [7] and [10], since $\lambda 2$-part of ATTT does not have η-conversion.[4]

3.1 The Makkai-Reyes-style interpretation

In spite of the differences mentioned above, Makkai-Reyes technique works well in our case by small modifications. Let's illustrate the interpretation briefly. Let D be a fixed type. This is intended to be the domain of first order objects (ground type). Let F be second order formulas whose *first order* free variables are among $x_1, \ldots, x_n$. Their interpretations are refinements of the type D^n (n-times product of D). F may have second order free variables. We assign refinements with appropriate types to the variables and the interpretation of F is defined depending on this assignment.

Interpretation of predicates Let's see how to interpret predicates by refinements. Since refinements are sets, they represent unary predicates. Thus, we use the polymorphic products and paring to interpret n-ary predicates. For example, a binary predicate $P(x, y)$ is interpreted as a refinement R of the polymorphic product $D \times D$. More precisely, we assign a refinement R of the type $D \times D$ to P, and interpret the formula $P(x, y)$ by

$$\{\langle x, y\rangle \in D \times D | R\{\langle x, y\rangle\}\}.$$

The pair $\langle x, y\rangle$ is the polymorphic Church pairing and the subset notation is an abbreviation of

$$\bigvee x \in D. \bigvee y \in D. \bigvee w \in R\{\langle x, y\rangle\}.\{\langle x, y\rangle\}_{D\times D}.$$

See [9] for details.

Interpretation of logical operators Conjunction, disjunction, implication and negation of formulas are interpreted as intersection, union, implication and negation of refinements. Note that implication is interpreted by implication refinement defined above. It is straightforward, but there is a problem.

If F and G have different free variables, this interpretation does not work, since their interpretations are of refinements of different types. Then, we embed refinements into a bigger refinements. Assume we are to form the union of the interpretations of F and G, say R_F and R_G. If F has a free variable x_1 as $F(x_1)$ and G has another free variable x_2 as $G(x_1, x_2)$. Then, $R_F \in \mathit{refine}(D)$ and $R_G \in \mathit{refine}(D \times D)$. Thus, we must embed the interpretation of $F(x_1)$ into $D \times D$ as $\{\langle x_1, x_2\rangle \in D \times D | R_F\{x_1\}\}$.

---

[4] Note that we can define a refinement $\bigvee a \in A. \bigvee b \in B.\{\langle a, b\rangle\}$ of a polymorphic product $A \times B$, which is the "real" product. But, this trick would be incorrect, as a product of types should be a type.

Next we interpret the universal and existential quantifiers. This is the point at which our interpretation diverges from Makkai-Reyes interpretation. Makkai and Reyes interpret first order quantifiers by images and co-images of subobject morphisms. We interpret them by the big intersection and union over the type D. Let $F(x_1, \ldots, x_n)$ be a formula and let R_F be its interpretation, which is a refinement of D^n. The interpretation of the formula $\forall x_i.F(x_1, \ldots, x_n)$ is the refinement

$$\bigwedge x_i \in D.\{\langle x_1, \ldots, x_{i-1}, x_{i+1}, \ldots, x_n\rangle \in D^{n-1} | R\{\langle x_1, \ldots, x_n\rangle\}\}.$$

First order existential quantifier is interpreted in the similar way by union.

Since we have unions and intersections over refinement kinds, second order quantifiers are interpreted in the same way. For example, let P be a binary predicate variable. Then $forallP.F$ is interpreted by $\bigwedge P \in \mathit{refine}(D^2).R_F$. Note that P is a refinement of the polymorphic product D^2, which may have more elements than the real pairs. Thus, P may contain elements which are not pairs. But, this is not a problem, since P always appears in the form $P\{\langle s, t\rangle\}$ in F. This completes the definition of the interpretation of logic by refinements.

3.2 Provably true formulas in ATTT

A refinement R of a type A is said to be true, if and only if $Id_A \in \top_A \leq R$ holds. [5] If this judgment is provable in ATTT, we will say the refinement R is provably true in ATTT. If the interpretation of a formula F is provably true in ATTT, then we say the formula is provably true in ATTT.

Intuitionistic second order logic are provably true Then, the following is easily proved:

Proposition 3 *The intuitionistic second order predicate logic (ISOL) is sound w.r.t. the interpretation. Namely, if a closed formula F of ISOL is provable, then it is provably true in ATTT under the context $D \in Type, x \in D$, where the type variable D is used as the domain of first order objects.*

The intuitionistic predicate logic assumes that the domain is non-empty. Thus, the assumption $x \in D$ is necessary. If we use a free logic instead, this is not necessary.

What are provably true formulas? It is natural to ask what are provably true formulas in ATTT. We conjecture that provably true formulas in ATTT are exactly the formulas provable in ISOL. This means that our interpretation is adequate to ISOL and amounts to the following:

Conjecture 1 *The converse of proposition 3 holds. Namely, if a closed formula F of ISOL is provably true in ATTT under the context mentioned in proposition 3, then F is provable in ISOL.*

[5] More exactly speaking, we have to respect in which context the refinement is true.

Somehow related result is in [14]. Although, we have not been able to prove the conjecture yet, it is easy to prove the conjecture restricted to first order formulas. Namely, the following proposition holds:

Proposition 4 *If a closed* first order *formula ϕ is provably true in ATTT under the context mentioned in the proposition above, then ϕ is provable in the intuitionistic* first order *predicate logic (IFOL).*

The idea of our proof is very simple. But, full details are rather clumsy. Thus, we illustrate only the idea, below.

Our proof consists three steps. First, we show that any provably true first order formula ϕ is valid in the sense of Tarski semantics by means of a term model of $\lambda 2$. Secondly, we formalize the proof of this fact in the intuitionistic second order arithmetic (HAS) augmented with an auxiliary sort γ. The auxiliary sort is intended as the generic domain, i.e., we do not pose any axiom or rules for this except the ones of ISOL. Let us call this system HAS(γ). Then, we can show that ϕ^γ, that is ϕ made the sort to be γ, is provable in HAS(γ). Lastly, we show that if ϕ^γ is provable in HAS(γ) then ϕ is provable in IFOL. Thus, ϕ is provable in IFOL.

The first step is easy. If the judgment "the interpretation is true" is provable in ATTT under the context, we can interpret it in the set-theoretical semantics introduced in [9]. Let *Const* be a arbitrary set of new constants. We augment $\lambda 2$ by *Const* as a new type. Namely, we introduce a new type constant D and regard the constants from *Const* as new constants of D. Let denote the augmented system by $\lambda 2(D)$. Let $\mathbf{M}$ be the *closed* term model of $\lambda 2(D)$.

In [9], we took BMM-model as the basis of semantics of ATTT. But, $\mathbf{M}$ is not a BMM-model but a $\lambda 2$-algebra in the sense of [11]. This difference is not so important, since any concrete $\lambda 2$-algebra also gives a semantics of ATTT in the sense of [9]. The reason why we considered only BMM-model in [9] was only for simplicity.

The model $\mathbf{M}$ consists of the collection of the set of closed normal terms of $\lambda 2(D)$. We denote the set of closed normal terms of type A by $\mathbf{M}(A)$. By interpreting *refine*(A) as the power set of the closed normal terms of type A, it becomes a model of ATTT (see [9]). Assume that a first order formula ϕ is provably true in ATTT, interpreting D is the domain of the first order objects. Since the normal closed terms of D are only the new constants, $\mathbf{M}(D)$ is identical to *Const*. Let $x_1, \ldots, x_n$ be the free variables of ϕ. Then, it is easy to check that R_ϕ (the interpretation of ϕ) coincides with the set of the list of constants $\langle c_1, \ldots, c_n \rangle$ where $\phi[c_1/x_1, \ldots, c_n/x_n]$ is valid in the sense of Tarski semantics whose domain is *Const*. Since *Const* is arbitrary, this means that ϕ is valid in any frame (a tautology) in the sense of Tarski semantics. Thus, ϕ is provable in the classical first order logic by the completeness theorem. Note that the argument above is all constructive except the completeness theorem.

The second step involves messy formalization.[6] Let us clarify the system HAS(γ) in which we do the formalization. HAS(γ) is a second order theory with two sorts, ν and γ. The sort ν is intended to be the sort of natural numbers and the sort γ is intended to be arbitrary (generic). The constants of ν is only 0, and γ does not have any constants. The only function symbol is s (successor) for ν. The arity of a predicate variable is a list $(s_1, \ldots, s_n)$ of sorts (n is possibly zero). Thus we can talk about functions from ν to γ, etc. The equality for each sort is defined by Leibniz equality. (This is only for simplicity. We may have equality symbols, instead.) The logic is the two-sorted intuitionistic second order logic, and the axioms are the Peano axiom for the sort of natural numbers ν.

Now, we formalize the argument of the first step in HAS(γ). Note that only "pointwise" formalization is possible, since we need normalization theorem of $\lambda 2$. Namely, we formalize the proof for each ϕ. First, we augment ATTT with D just as $\lambda 2(D)$. Let us denote the augmented system by ATTT(D). Assume that a first order formula ϕ is provably true in ATTT. Then it is also provably true in ATTT(D), regarding the new type D as the domain of the first order objects. Then there is a fragment of $\lambda 2(D)$ for which the strong normalization property of the terms is provable in HAS(γ) and all terms in the proof of the truth of ϕ fall in the fragment (see, e.g., [21]). Thus, we have a closed term model of the fragment of ATTT(D) formalized in HAS(γ). Since the set of constants *Const* is arbitrary, we may regard it as the sort γ. Recall that the Makkai-Reyes-style interpretation coincided with the Tarski semantics. Thus, we can conclude that ϕ^γ is provable in HAS(γ).

The third step consists of the following lemma:

Lemma 3 *A first order formula ϕ is provable in intuitionistic first order logic, if ϕ^γ is provable in HAS(γ).*

This is an easy consequence of an infinitary normalization theorem of intuitionistic second order arithmetic, which is proved by Tait-Girard computability predicate technique, e.g., [6]. A proof of ϕ^γ of HAS(γ) can be normalized using ω-rule. Since ϕ^γ is a first order formula only with the sort γ, subformula property holds, i.e., the sort appearing in the normal proof is only γ. This means that the proof is of intuitionistic first order logic, regarding the sort γ as the ground sort. This completes the proof.

The only third step fails for the second order case. Since second order logic does not have subformula property, our proof fails to prove the lemma above for second order case. But, we conjecture that the lemma will hold for second order formulas as well.

Conjecture 2 *A formula ϕ of second order predicate logic is provable in intuitionistic second order predicate logic, iff ϕ^γ is provable in HAS(γ).*

---

[6] It is possible to avoid the formalization by means of Kripke semantics. Then, we have to introduce a notion of Kripke semantics for $\lambda 2$ as did by Mitchell and Moggi and extend any first order Kripke frame to a Kripke frame of $\lambda 2$ by "free construction." This is not easier than the formalization.

Note that this lemma has an intrinsic meaning: if a second order formula is constructively valid under the assumption of the existence of the natural numbers, then it is provable in second order intuitionistic logic. Since this seems very plausible, the conjecture must be true.

Remark 1 The reduction to the original conjecture to the conjecture on HAS(γ) seem unnatural, as the original conjecture does not involve natural numbers. But, if the conjecture on HAS(γ) is once proved, then it will be straightforward to change it to a proof of the original conjecture via Kripke semantics of $\lambda 2$. In such a proof, arithmetic part and even formalization part will vanish. Actually, it is possible to give a sufficient condition by means of Kripke frames of $\lambda 2$. But, the sufficient condition by means of HAS(γ) is easier to understand and has an intrinsic meaning as noted above.

3.3 The excluded middle

The law of excluded middle for refinements

$$\Pi A \in Type. \bigwedge R \in refine(A).(\top_A \leq R \vee \dot{\neg} R)$$

or

$$\Pi A \in Type. \bigwedge R \in refine(A).(\neg\neg R \leq R).$$

is not derivable in ATTT by the the adequacy result above. Thus, the Heyting algebra of a refinement kind is not boolean. But, they are compatible with boolean laws. Even if we add the law of excluded middle above as an axiom, the system is still conservative over $\lambda 2$. In [9], we defined a translation from ATTT to $\lambda 2$ which is identical on the $\lambda 2$ fragment of ATTT. We may add the excluded middle above as an axiom, whose realizer is the identity function. Then the two forms of the classical axioms above are both translated to $Id_A \in A \rightarrow A$. This resembles the logic of PX system, which is compatible with classical logic as stressed in [8].

3.4 The refinement classifier and comparisons to the other approaches

The Makkai-Reyes-style interpretation given above look rather different from the standard way of interpreting logic in higher order type systems as Coq system. Thus, it seems difficult to compare our approach to the standard ones. But, we can encode logic similarly to the standard way by the notion of refinement classifier. Upon the idea, we can compare our approach to the others.

The refinement classifier Refinements resembles subobjects in toposes. A topos has a subobject classifiers by which subobjects are classified. Namely, a subobject of an object is represented by a map from the object to the subobject classifier. Intuitively, a subobject classifier is the power set of a singleton set. It can be considered as the set of truth values. Introducing a singleton type, say *unit*, consisting the only element $\star$, the refinement kind *refine*(*unit*) is a refinement classifier. Note that this is the kind of non-informative propositions, and so corresponds to *Prop* in the sense of Coq system rather than the *Prop* in the sense of the original Calculus of Constructions.

We will write the refinement kind *refine*(*unit*) by Ω and call it the *refinement classifier*. Assume that $R \in \mathit{refine}(A)$. Then we define a term of the type $A \to \Omega$. Then the following correspondence between $A \to \Omega$ and *refine*(A) is obtained:

$$R \in \mathit{refine}(A) \longmapsto \lambda x \in A. \bigvee w \in R\{x\}.\{\star\},$$

$$\phi \in A \to \Omega \longmapsto \bigvee x \in A. \bigvee w \in \phi(x)\{\star\}.\{x\}.$$

But, $A \to \Omega$ is illegal in ATTT in [9]. Thus, we have to extend ATTT to include such a type by allowing the following formation rule and corresponding introduction rule.

$$\frac{\Gamma \vdash A \in \mathit{Type} \qquad \Gamma \vdash B \in \mathit{RKind}}{\Gamma \vdash A \to B \in \mathit{RKind}}$$

This extension is not essential. In such a extension, any term of *RKind* has the form $A_1 \to \ldots A_n \to \mathit{refine}(B)$, where $A_1, \ldots, A_n$ are types. Then, we can regard it as $\mathit{refine}(A_1 \times \ldots \times A_n \times B)$, by regarding $\lambda x_1 \in A_1. \cdots \lambda x_n \in A_n.R$ as $\{\langle x_1, \ldots x_n, y\rangle \in A_1 \times \cdots A_n \times B | R\{y\}\}$. Note that this is a standard technique to encode functions from first order objects to predicates in the second order logic. Thus, the extension still keep the second order character.

Comparisons to the other approach Upon the notion of refinement classifier, we compare our approach to the others. In impredicative higher order type theories as Calculus of Constructions, *Type* (or often denoted as *Prop*) is often used as a substitute for the collection of the truth values. It is also regarded as the collection of the data types. This confusion leads to inefficiency of the extracted code and makes it difficult to understand encoded logic. Thus, Coq system separate these two notions by introducing two kinds *Prop* and *Set*. The kinds *Prop* and *Set* belong to the sorts (in the sense of GTS) *Type* and *Type_Set*, respectively. Note the messy confusion of symbols. *Prop* of Coq corresponds to our Ω and *Set* of Coq corresponds to our *Type*, the kind of the types. *Type* of ATTT belongs to the sort *Kind* and refinement kinds *refine*(A) belong to the sort *RKind*. Thus, *Type* of Coq is our *Kind* and *Type_Set* is our *RKind*.

The superficial divergences of our approach from Coq's are

1. . ATTT is a second order system, but Coq is a higher order system.
2. . The types of Coq can depend on data, as it is based on Calculus of Construction. The types of ATTT cannot depend on data, as it is based on $\lambda 2$.

There is still another twist. Coq has an extraction algorithm, by which the data-dependency of types (and other logical information) is stripped out so that the extracted codes are of Girard's F_ω. At the specification level, Coq has data-dependent types, but, at the object code level, it does not. The types of ATTT are the ones of $\lambda 2$ at the both levels. In ATTT, we directly talk about object level codes and their types, i.e. the terms and types of $\lambda 2$. On the other hand, the users of Coq talk about them indirectly through the extraction procedure. This is a fate of the systems based on realizability as Coq and PX. This might not be a bad doom, as the indirectness can make users think their programs abstractly and good extraction procedure can sometime produce better codes than the users expect. This contrast between direct and indirect approaches may be compared with the contrast between assembler languages and compiler languages.

Another approach closely related to Coq is "deliverable" by Burstall and McKinna ([2], [16]). They take a direct approach. They do not consider any extraction algorithm, but directly talk about codes. To represent data types and talk about them and codes, they use Luo's Extended Calculus of Constructions ECC ([12], [13]). ECC has *Prop* and a predicative cumulative hierarchy of kinds *Type*(0), *Type*(1),.... They use *Prop* as the truth values and *Type*(i) as data types. Thus, *Prop* corresponds to our Ω. But, there is a difference. *Prop* is an element and also a subset of *Type*(0). This implies that the collection of truth values and each truth value is a data type. It would be possible to regard the collection of truth values as a data type by regarding them as formulas. But, a proposition (truth value) is a refinement of a unit type from our point of view. Thus, it has a rugged border, and so it is not a data type. When it comes to data-dependency of types, deliverable approach allows it. The predicative hierarchy allows such types.

The approach most closed to ours is Erik Poll's programming logic $\lambda\omega_L$ [20]. As programming language, he uses Girard's F_ω, $\lambda\omega$ in his notation. As logic, he uses the other copy of $\lambda\omega$. His $*_s$ is *Type* and $*_p$ is Ω of ATTT. These two copies of the same type theory resembles two copies of Calculus of Constructions in the Coq system. Then he introduce function types from a data type A to $*_p$ to represent predicates. This corresponds to the refinement kind *refine*(A) or $A \rightarrow \Omega$. The data-dependency of types is not allowed as he uses F_ω. In a sense, $\lambda\omega_L$ is a higher order version of ATTT without refinements. The difference is that Poll uses predicates, on the other hand, we use sets (refinement types). Since propositions and data types, and so programs and proofs, are more clearly separated in $\lambda\omega_L$ than ECC, $\lambda\omega_L$ might be a better framework for the deliverable approach.

As illustrated above, the four approaches are closely related in rather intricate ways. They do not seem very different from a theoretical point of view. The difference in practice of proof/program developments should be investigated.

4 Informative interpretations of logic

The logic of refinements given above is a non-informative interpretation. In this section, we examine two informative interpretations in ATTT.

4.1 Two informative interpretations of implication

Type theories based on "proofs as program" notion can be regarded as axiomatizations of realizability notions. For example, Martin-Löf's type theory can be regarded as an axiomatization of extensional recursive realizability as exploited in [1].

In PX system, realizers of non-informative formulas are always the empty list which are passed by extracted codes. In Coq system, realizers of non-informative formulas are the null sequence which literally disappear in extracted codes. These two treatments of non-informativeness reflect the different realizability interpretations used by those systems. PX uses recursive realizability and Coq uses modified realizability.

The difference of these realizabilities appears in the interpretation of implication. Let P be a non-informative formula and let A be an informative formula. In recursive realizability,

$$r \text{ realizes } P \supset A \stackrel{\text{def}}{=} r \downarrow \wedge P \supset r(nil) \text{ realizes } A.$$

In modified realizability,

$$r \text{ realizes } P \supset A \stackrel{\text{def}}{=} r \downarrow \wedge P \supset r \text{ realizes } A.$$

(Normally, only terminating terms are used in modified realizability. Then, the condition $r \downarrow$ may be omitted.) In ATTT, user can choose both interpretations locally. Let R_1 and R_2 be refinements. The standard intuitionistic implication is defined by $R_1 \to R_2$. This interpretation takes R_1 informative.

The following interpretations take R_1 non-informative:

1. $\bigwedge w \in R_1.R_2$,
2. $\{x \in unit | R_1\} \to R_2$,

w is a fresh variable which does not appear in R_2. The first one represents the implication of the modified realizability, and the second one represents the implication of the recursive realizability. In this sense, ATTT embodies both realizabilities in a single framework.

4.2 Induction principles

Induction principle is a very important component of a system of constructive programming, since it is the device to derive recursive programs. Below, we will examine two kinds of induction principles, one is non-informative and the other is informative.

The non-informative one is purely logical. The informative one is not only logical but also representing recursion scheme as well. For example, informative mathematical induction represents primitive recursion and its correctness. We will show that informative induction principle can be derived from non-informative induction principle in ATTT. This is a future which distinguishes ATTT from the other type theories.

4.3 Monotone inductive definition of refinements

First, we will examine non-informative induction principles. They are induction principles over refinements. The monotone inductive definition of refinements are easily defined as in the second order logic. Let R be a refinement variable of type A and let $\Psi(R)$ be a refinement of A. Then, $\mu R.\Psi(R)$ is

$$\bigwedge S \in \mathit{refine}(A). \bigwedge w \in (\Psi(S) \leq S).S.$$

If $\Psi(S) \leq S$ holds, then $\mu R.\Psi(R) \leq S$ obviously holds. If Φ is monotone, i.e., $R_1 \leq R_2 \supset \Phi(R_1) \leq \Phi(R_2)$, holds, then $\Phi(\mu R.\Psi(R)) \geq\leq \mu R.\Psi(R)$ holds. In this sense, $\mu R.\Psi(R)$ is the least fixed point of a monotone operator $\Phi(R)$.

4.4 The type of natural numbers

Recursive data types as integers, list, etc. are definable in $\lambda 2$. For example, natural numbers are definable as Church integers. But, we do not use this as data types. We should introduce such types as primitive type as in [3]. For simplicity, we consider only *Nat*, here.

To extend ATTT by *Nat*, we introduce a type constant *Nat* and two constants $0 \in Nat$ and $S \in Nat \to Nat$. Then, we add the primitive recursor *rec*

$$rec \in \Pi X \in Type.X \to (Nat \to X \to X) \to Nat \to X$$

together with the standard reductions.

To say *Nat* is built by 0 and S, we introduce the following axiom:

$$Nat \ \leq \mu R.(\{0\}_{Nat} \vee S''R),$$

where $S''R$ is the image of R by S, which is defined by

$$f''R \stackrel{\text{def}}{=} \bigvee x \in R.\{f(x)\}.$$

Since *Nat* is not a refinement, "$Nat \ \leq \mu R. \ldots$" is not the order on refinements. This is defined by $\bigwedge x \in Nat.\{x\}_{Nat} \to (\mu R. \ldots)\{x\}$.

As the axiom is self-realizing by the identity function, the axiom may be put in the context with a variable, which is a virtual witness of the axiom.

Note that we did not introduce the informative mathematical induction. The last axiom is a kind of mathematical induction, but it is non-informative mathematical induction (NIMI). The informative mathematical induction (IMI) should be

$$\Pi A \in Type. \bigwedge P \in Nat \to \Omega.P(0) \to \Pi n \in Nat.(P(n) \to P(Sn)) \to \Pi n \in Nat.P(n).$$

In ATTT, IMI is provable from the axioms above.

Theorem 1 *The following is derivable in ATTT:*

$$\lambda A \in Type.\lambda a \in Nat.\lambda f \in Nat \to A \to A.\lambda n \in Nat.recAafn \in IMI.$$

Note that we have to put the abstractions, since ATTT does not have η-conversion. Note that this theorem asserts that the λ-term above is the realizer of IMI. Let $e(n)$ be the term $recAafn$. It is enough to prove $e(n) \in P(n)$ under the assumptions. To prove this, it is sufficient to prove the refinement $P(n)\{e(n)\}$. We can prove this by the non-informative mathematical induction NIMI. The proof is essentially the same as the soundness proof of mathematical induction for realizabilities.

This example shows that informative induction follows from non-informative induction in ATTT. This ability of ATTT distinguishes it from the other type theories and illustrates its set theoretical nature.

There is one thing missing in the axioms above. It is Peano's fourth axiom "$0 = 1$ implies $\bot$." There are several formulations of the axiom, since we have several ways to define implication and absurdity. One of the strongest formulation would be

$$\Pi A \in \mathit{Type}. \bigwedge w \in 0 = 1 . \bot_A .$$

The type of this refinement is $\Pi A \in \mathit{Type}.A$. This is rather problematic as pointed out in [18]. If the refinement is realized by f, then $f(A)$ is a polymorphic element of A. In PX system, this problem did not arise, as it is a monotype system whose domain is inhabited. But, we are now in a type theoretic framework and so cannot use such a solution. In Coq system [18], "abort"-command is introduced which belongs polymorphically to any type A. This solution seems to lead us to a type theory with non-terminating programs. Coq system offers a solution, but it is not very clear to me.

This approach resembles the resent works on controls in Curry-Howard isomorphisms by Griffin, Murthy, Nakano. Especially, Nakano's calculus accommodate catch/throw mechanism in a natural constructive framework [17]. As "abort" is a throw to the top-level, there might be a natural way to interpret this problem by Nakano's calculus.

Anyway, the problem does not seem to have been settled satisfactory. Thus, we do not use it but consider a less ambitious formulation

$$\Pi A \in \mathit{Type}. \bigwedge w \in 0 = 1 . A \to \bot_A ,$$

which is equivalent to

$$\bigwedge w \in 0 = 1 . \bot_{unit} .$$

In Coq system, essentially the same statement is proved by a proof by cases, which is similar to Martin-Löf's proof of the 4th axiom in his type theory. If we introduce a principle to define refinement-valued functions by cases, we can do the same thing in ATTT. Assume that we can define the following program from Nat to Ω.

$$\lambda x \in \mathit{Nat}.(\mathit{if}\ x = 0\ \mathit{then}\ \top_{unit}\ \mathit{else}\ \bot_{unit}).$$

By assuming $0 = 1$, we can convert $\top_{unit}$ to $\bot_{unit}$. This proves the axiom above by means of conversion rule or an appropriate equality rule. Note that the program above have the type $\mathit{Nat} \to \mathit{refine}(\mathit{unit})$. If we extend the type of the recursor *rec* so that it permits refinement kinds as well as the type A, then we can do such a definition by cases. This does not seem bad. But we do not do so here. We simply add the axiom to the system.

Note that type A is assumed to be non-empty, when we deduce $\perp_A$:

$$\Pi A \in \mathit{Type}. \bigwedge w \in 0 = 1.A \rightarrow \perp_A.$$

This means that "have an element of A and return it as the default value if something is wrong." The non-emptiness assumption would not cause a big problem in practical cases. Such an A would be the type of a specification. A specification of a program of a type whose elements are not known would be meaningless. Thus we may suppose the type is inhabited.

Acknowledgments

I am very grateful to Henk Barendregt, Rod Burstall and Tobias Nipkow for inviting me to the BRA workshop "Types for Proofs and Programs" and for opportunity to present the paper in this volume. I thank Kees Hemerik, Christine Paulin, Erik Poll, Benjamin Werner, Mariko Yasugi for discussions on the subjects of the paper and/or Coq system which helped me to clarify the nature of ATTT.

References

1. M.J. Beeson, *Foundations of Constructive Mathematics*, Springer-Verlag, 1985.
2. R.M. Burstall and J. H. McKinna, *Deliverables: an approach to program in Constructions*, Technical Report ECS-LFCS-91-133, Department of Computer Science, The University of Edinburgh, 1991.
3. Dowek, C. et al., *The Coq Proof Assistant User's Guide*, Version 5.6, Technical Report No. 134, INRIA, December, 1991.
4. Th. Coquand and G. Huet, Calculus of Constructions, *Information and Computation*, vol. 76, pp. 95-120, 1988.
5. T. Freeman and F. Pfenning, *Refinement Types for ML*, ACM SIGPLAN'91, Conference on Programming Language Design and Implementation, Toronto, Ontario, ACM Press, 1991.
6. S. Hayashi, On derived rules of intuitionistic second order arithmetic, *Commentariorum Mathematicorum Universitatis Sancti Pauli*, vol. XXVI, pp. 77-103, 1977.
7. S. Hayashi, Adjunction of semifunctors: categorical structures in non-extensional lambda calculus, *Theoretical Computer Sciences,*, vol. 41, pp.95-104, 1986.
8. S. Hayashi and H. Nakano, *PX: A Computational Logic*, The MIT Press, 1988.
9. S. Hayashi, *Singleton, Union and Intersection Types for Program Extraction*, Lecture Notes in Computer Science No. 526, pp. 701-730, T.Ito and A.R.Meyer, eds., Springer-Verlag, 1991, an extended version to appear in Information and Computation.
10. R. Hoofman, The theory of semi-functors, *Mathematical Structures in Computer Science*, vol. 3, pp.93-128, 1993.

11. B. Jacobs, Semantics of the second order lambda calculus, *Mathematical Structures in Computer Science*, vol. 1, pp. 327-360, 1991.
12. Z. Luo. *ECC, an Extended Calculus of Constructions*, in Proceedings of the Fourth Annual IEEE Symposium on Logic in Computer Science, Asilomar, California, 1989.
13. Z. Luo. *An Extended Calculus of Constructions*, Ph. D. thesis, Department of Computer Science, The University of Edinburgh, 1990.
14. Z. Luo. *A problem of adequacy: conservativity of Calculus of Constructions over higher order logic*, Technical Report ECS-LFCS-90-121, Department of Computer Science, The University of Edinburgh, 1990.
15. M. Makkai and G. Reyes. *First Order Categorical Logic*, Lecture Note in Mathematics No. 611, 1977, Springer-Verlag.
16. J. H. McKinna. *Deliverables: A Categorical Approach to Program Development in Type Theory*, Ph. D. thesis, Department of Computer Science, The University of Edinburgh, 1992.
17. , H. Nakano. *A Constructive Formalization of the Catch and Throw Mechanism*, in Proceedings of the Seventh Annual IEEE Symposium on Logic in Computer Science, Santa Cruz, 1992.
18. C. Paulin-Mohring and B. Werner, Synthesis of ML programs in the System Coq, Journal of Symbolic Computation, 1993.
19. F. Pfenning, Intersection Types for a Logical Framework, in this volume, 1992.
20. Erik Poll, A programming logic for F_ω, Computing Science Notes, 92/25, Department of Mathematics and Computing Science, Eindhoven University of Technology, 1992.
21. A.S. Troelstra, *Metamathematical investigations of intuitionistic arithmetic and analysis*, Lecture Notes in Mathematics, vol. 344, Springer-Verlag, 1973.

Proof-Checking a Data Link Protocol*

L. Helmink[1], M.P.A. Sellink[2], F.W. Vaandrager[3]

[1] Philips Research Laboratories, helmink@prl.philips.nl
[2] Utrecht University, alex@phil.ruu.nl
[3] CWI and University of Amsterdam, fritsv@cwi.nl

Abstract. A data link protocol developed and used by Philips Electronics is modeled and verified using I/O automata theory. Correctness is computer-checked with the Coq proof development system.

Key words: Communication Protocols, I/O Automata, Proof-Checking, Protocol Verification, Type Theory.

1 Introduction

The data-link layer of a telecommunication protocol is verified and proof-checked. The protocol has been designed to communicate messages of arbitrary length over unreliable channels. The messages are transmitted in small packets or *frames*. The protocol does not rely on fairness of data transmission channels, i.e., repeated transmission of a frame does not guarantee its eventual arrival. For this reason, the number of retransmission attempts is limited and the protocol is called Bounded Retransmission Protocol.

Reliable communication protocols are vital to the telecommunication industry. They are also of increasing importance to the electronics business because more and more products consist of communicating subsystems and because many products integrate technology from the fields of computers, telecommunication devices, and consumer electronics. The pressure for reliability of the protocols involved poses an important challenge to verification techniques.

Design, implementation and testing of communication protocols is a complicated and error-prone activity. For many protocol-based products, erroneous protocol behavior is met by error-recovery procedures or by issuing a new software release. For some products however, error situations are not acceptable and software maintenance is impossible. Correctness of protocols is usually examined by careful testing of implementations.

Thorough testing increases confidence but testing is only semi-decidable: it may reveal the presence of errors but not the absence of errors. Protocol verification is required to obtain a higher degree of confidence. The protocol is modeled

* The work of the first author is partially supported by ESPRIT Basic Research Action 6453: 'Types for Proofs and Programs'. The work of the third author took place in the context of the ESPRIT Basic Research Action 7166: 'CONCUR2'.

in a mathematical structure and correctness is guaranteed by showing that the protocol satisfies the required behavior under all circumstances. Verification is not restricted to implementations but can also be applied to designs that have not yet been implemented. It should be stressed however that although verification excludes *design* errors, it cannot replace testing of implementations.

A hand-written protocol verification may itself contain certain errors that can be eliminated by computer tools. Verification errors can be classified into two categories: wrong assumptions and wrong deductions, corresponding to errors in the protocol model and to errors in its correctness proof, respectively. Errors of the first type are the responsibility of the modeler. Errors of the second type can be eliminated using computer tools for proof development or proof-checking. There is an additional advantage to the use of computer tools in protocol verification. Protocol verification is a labour-intensive and a non-trivial activity: much effort of skilled experts is required. With the current state-of-the-art, it is cost-effective only for those (parts of) protocols that are truly critical. Computer tools will enable more efficient verification of protocols.

In this paper we describe a verification and the associated proof-checking of a simplified and stylized version of a Philips telecommunication protocol. First, the protocol is proven correct using the input/output automaton model of Lynch and Tuttle [19], a formalism based on extended finite state machines. Next, the verification is proof-checked in type theory with the Coq system [9]. The objective of this work is twofold. The first objective is to prove correctness of the protocol with the highest possible level of confidence. The second objective of this work is to bring to light all technical issues that are involved in obtaining this result.

A starting point for the work described here was an algebraic specification of the protocol in PSF [22], a language based on process algebra. This specification was developed and validated using PSF simulation tools. The PSF description was translated into I/O automata theory and a suitable correctness criterion was defined. The protocol was verified by proving that it satisfies the correctness criterion. This specification and verification were then translated into type theory and checked with the Coq proof development system.

This paper is divided into the following parts: Section 2 gives an informal description of the protocol. Next, Section 3 explains the verification of the protocol. Section 4 discusses the proof-checking with the Coq system. Section 5 concludes with a discussion of the results.

2 Protocol Outline

Like most data link protocols, the Bounded Retransmission Protocol can be regarded as an extended version of the Alternating Bit Protocol. The protocol uses a stop-and-wait approach known as 'positive acknowledgement with retransmission' [27]: after transmission of a frame the sender waits for an acknowledgement before sending a new frame. The protocol procedures are similar to the LAPB link control procedures of the X.25 protocol [6] (for X.25 acknowledged mode and window size = 1, viz. one outstanding unacknowledged frame). Incoming frames are checked for errors. Correctly received frames are acknowledged while erroneous frames are simply discarded. If the acknowledgement fails to appear, the sender times out and retransmits the frame. An alternating bit is used to detect duplication of a frame. Real-time aspects are limited to the use of time-outs to detect loss of frames and loss of acknowledgements. Three service primitives are offered by the protocol: a request and confirm service at the sender side, and an indication service at the receiver side.

- $REQ(s)$
  The request service to transmit a finite list s of data. Each datum will be transferred in a separate message frame.

- $CONF(c)$ ($c \in$ {C_OK, C_NOT_OK, C_DONT_KNOW})
  The confirmation service that informs the sender about the result of a request.
  - $c =$ C_OK : the request has been dispatched successfully.
  - $c =$ C_NOT_OK : the request has not been dispatched completely.
  - $c =$ C_DONT_KNOW : the request may or may not have been handled completely. This situation only occurs when the last frame is sent but not acknowledged.

- $IND(d, i)$ (d a datum and $i \in${I_FIRST, I_INCOMPLETE, I_OK})
  The indication service to pass a new frame to the receiver application.
  - $i =$ I_FIRST : the packet is the first one of a message; more data to follow.
  - $i =$ I_INCOMPLETE : the packet is an intermediate one; more data to follow.
  - $i =$ I_OK : the packet is the last one of a series, completing the transmission of a message.

- *IND_NOT_OK*
  The indication service to report loss of contact to the sender. Only part of a message has been received.

The protocol control procedures will be described by means of a sender S, a receiver R, and two communication channels K and L (Figure 1). We will assume that K and L are lossy channels: message frames are either lost or they arrive without corruption in the order in which they are sent. Messages can be communicated over ports *REQ, CONF, F, G, A, B, IND*. A data frame consists of a datum preceded by a header with three information bits named *first*, *last* and *toggle*: $(first, last, toggle, datum)$. Bits *first* and *last* indicate if a packet is the first or last frame of a series, respectively. For a single-frame message both are set. *toggle* plays the role of alternating bit to distinguish between subsequent data frames. Acknowledgement frames consist of these three information bits only: $(first, last, toggle)$.

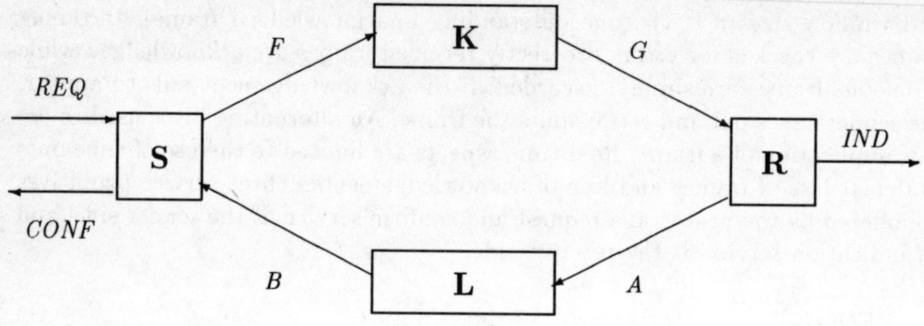

Fig. 1. Bounded Retransmission Protocol.

First consider a faultless transmission where no frames are lost. Suppose the sender S receives a request to transmit data $d_1 \dots d_n$: $REQ(d_1 \dots d_n)$. Here we will assume n>2; the cases n=1 or n=2 are similar. A frame (true, false, *toggle*, d_1) is sent on port F. Channel K passes on the frame to receiver R over port G. R then issues an $IND(d_1$, I_FIRST) to port IND, and sends an acknowledgement frame (true, false, *toggle*) on port A, which is passed on by channel L to port B. The acknowledgement frame consists of the header of the data frame. Upon receipt of the acknowledgement, the sender transmits the second datum: (false, false, $\neg$*toggle*, d_2), where *toggle* has flipped. The receiver issues $IND(d_2$, I_INCOMPLETE) and acknowledges the frame: (false, false, $\neg$*toggle*). This procedure is repeated until the last frame is sent with *first*=false, *last*=true, and *datum*=d_n. The receiver sends $IND(d_n$, I_OK) to report completion of the message and acknowledges receipt. The sender then informs the application of the successful dispatch of the transmission request with *CONF*(C_OK).

Now consider a transmission where data or acknowledgement frames are lost. First we take the sender's point of view. Upon sending a frame the sender S starts a timer t_1 and waits until either the frame is acknowledged or the timer goes off. If the acknowledgement is received, the timer is switched off and the next frame is sent. The timer is attuned to exceed the round trip time for sending a data frame and receipt of its acknowledgement. If the timer goes off no acknowledgement can come anymore and the frame is retransmitted.

The number of retransmission attempts is bounded by a parameter max, and if this maximum number of retransmissions has been reached, the sender gives up. The confirmation service is invoked in one of two ways: if the data frame in question is not the last frame of a series, then *CONF*(C_NOT_OK) confirms failure of message transfer. For the last data frame, a *CONF*(C_DONT_KNOW) is called: there is no way the sender can tell if the last frame was lost and never arrived, or if its acknowledgement was lost.

Finally consider the loss of frames from the receiver's point of view. Suppose a lost data frame is not the first one, i.e. the receiver is expecting a data frame follow-up. Upon receipt of a data frame, the receiver starts a timer t_2 and goes to a waiting state. When a data frame arrives it is acknowledged and timer t_2 is switched off. If the data frame has a flipped *toggle* then it is new and it is also indicated to the upper layers. When no data frame arrives, timer t_2 goes off eventually and service *IND_NOT_OK* is called. Timer t_2 will only go off if the sender has aborted the transmission, and therefore $t_2 > \mathsf{max}{*}t_1$.

3 Verification

3.1 I/O Automata Theory

In this section we give a brief account of those parts of I/O automata theory that we need for the purposes of the paper. For a more extensive introduction to the I/O automata model we refer to [19, 20].

I/O automata An *action signature* S is a triple $(in(S), out(S), int(S))$ of three disjoint sets of respectively *input actions*, *output actions* and *internal actions*. The derived sets of *external actions*, *locally controlled actions* and *actions* of S are defined respectively by

$$\begin{aligned} ext(S) &= in(S) \cup out(S), \\ local(S) &= out(S) \cup int(S), \\ acts(S) &= in(S) \cup out(S) \cup int(S). \end{aligned}$$

We say that S is *finite* if $acts(S)$ is a finite set.

An *I/O automaton* A consists of the following five components:

- an action signature $sig(A)$ (we will write $in(A)$ for $in(sig(A))$, $out(A)$ for $out(sig(A))$, etc.),
- a set $states(A)$ of *states*,
- a nonempty set $start(A) \subseteq states(A)$ of *start states*,
- a set $steps(A) \subseteq states(A) \times acts(A) \times states(A)$ of *transitions*, with the property that for every state s and input action a in $in(A)$ there is a transition (s, a, s') in $steps(A)$,
- an equivalence relation $part(A)$ on $local(A)$, having at most countably many equivalence classes.

We let $s, s', u, u', ..$ range over states, and $a, ..$ over actions. We write $s \xrightarrow{a}_A s'$, or just $s \xrightarrow{a} s'$ if A is clear from the context, as a shorthand for $(s, a, s') \in steps(A)$.

An action a is said to be *enabled* in a state s, if $s \xrightarrow{a} s'$ for some s'. Since every input action is enabled in every state, I/O automata are said to be *input enabled.* The intuition behind the input-enabling condition is that input actions are under control of the environment, and that the system that is modeled by an I/O automaton cannot prevent the environment from doing these actions. The partition $part(A)$ describes, what intuitively are the 'components' of the system, and will be used to define fairness.

Composition Intuitively, the composition of a collection of I/O automata is their Cartesian product, with the added requirement that automata synchronize the performance of shared actions. This synchronization models communication between system components: if a is an output action of A and an input action of B, then the simultaneous performance of a models communication from A to B. Since we do not want synchronization between output action of different I/O automata, or synchronizations involving internal actions, we require that the I/O automata are *compatible* in the sense that they do not share these actions.

Formally, we say that action signatures $S_1, \ldots, S_n$ are *compatible* if, for all $i, j \in \{1, \ldots, n\}$ satisfying $i \neq j$, $out(S_i) \cap out(S_j) = \emptyset$ and $int(S_i) \cap acts(S_j) = \emptyset$. We say that a number of I/O automata are *compatible* if their action signatures are compatible. The *composition* $S = \prod_{i=1}^{n} S_i$ of a finite collection of compatible action signatures $S_1, \ldots, S_n$ is defined to be the action signature with

- $in(S) = \bigcup_{i=1}^{n} in(S_i) - \bigcup_{i=1}^{n} out(S_i)$,
- $out(S) = \bigcup_{i=1}^{n} out(S_i)$,
- $int(S) = \bigcup_{i=1}^{n} int(S_i)$.

The *composition* $A = ||_{i=1}^{n} A_i$ of a finite collection of compatible I/O automata $A_1, \ldots, A_n$ is the I/O automaton defined as follows:

- $sig(A) = \prod_{i=1}^{n} sig(A_i)$,
- $states(A) = states(A_1) \times \cdots \times states(A_n)$,
- $start(A) = start(A_1) \times \cdots \times start(A_n)$,
- $steps(A)$ is the set of triples $(\mathbf{s}, a, \mathbf{s}')$ in $states(A) \times acts(A) \times states(A)$ such that, for all $1 \leq i \leq n$, if $a \in acts(A_i)$ then $\mathbf{s}[i] \xrightarrow{a}_{A_i} \mathbf{s}'[i]$ else $\mathbf{s}[i] = \mathbf{s}'[i]$,
- $part(A) = \bigcup_{i=1}^{n} part(A_i)$.

Notice that A is an I/O automaton indeed: $start(A)$ is nonempty because all the sets $start(A_i)$ are nonempty, A is input enabled because all the automata A_i are input enabled, and $part(A)$ is a partition of $local(A)$. We will sometimes write $A_1 || \cdots || A_n$ for $||_{i=1}^{n} A_i$.

Hiding If S is an action signature and $I \subseteq out(S)$, then the action signature HIDE I IN S is defined as the triple $(in(S), out(S) - I, int(S) \cup I)$. If A is an I/O automaton and $I \subseteq out(A)$, then HIDE I IN A is the I/O automaton obtained from A by replacing $sig(A)$ by HIDE I IN $sig(A)$, and leaving all the other components unchanged.

Traces and fair traces Let A be an I/O automaton. An *execution fragment* of A is a finite or infinite alternating sequence $s_0 a_1 s_1 a_2 s_2 \cdots$ of states and actions of A, beginning with a state, and if it is finite also ending with a state, such that for all i, $s_i \xrightarrow{a_{i+1}} s_{i+1}$. An *execution* of A is an execution fragment that begins with a start state. A state s of A is *reachable* if it is the final state of some finite execution of A.

Suppose $\alpha = s_0 a_1 s_1 a_2 s_2 \cdots$ is an execution fragment of A. Then the *trace* of α is the subsequence of $a_1 a_2 \cdots$ consisting of the external actions of A. With *traces*$^*(A)$ we denote the set of traces of finite executions of A. For s, s' states of A and β a finite sequence of external actions of A, we define $s \stackrel{\beta}{\Longrightarrow}_A s'$ iff A has a finite execution fragment with first state s, last state s' and trace β.

A *fair execution* of an I/O automaton A is defined to be an execution α of A such that the following conditions hold for each class C of *part*(A):

1. If α is finite, then no action of C is enabled in the final state of α.
2. If α is infinite, then either α contains infinitely many occurrences of actions from C, or α contains infinitely many occurrences of states in which no action from C is enabled.

This says that a fair execution gives fair turns to each class of *part*(A), and therefore to each component of the system being modeled. A state of A is said to be *quiescent* if only input actions are enabled in this state. Intuitively, in a quiescent state the system is waiting for an input from the environment. A finite execution is fair if and only if its final state is quiescent. We denote the set of traces of fair executions of A by *fairtraces*(A). Also, we write *qtraces*(A) for the set of traces of finite fair executions of A.

Safety, deadlock freeness and implementation Let A and B be I/O automata with the same input and output actions, respectively. Then we say that

- A is *safe* with respect to B iff *traces*$^*(A) \subseteq$ *traces*$^*(B)$,
- A is *deadlock free* with respect to B iff *qtraces*$(A) \subseteq$ *qtraces*(B),
- A *implements* B iff *fairtraces*$(A) \subseteq$ *fairtraces*(B).

If A is safe with respect to B then all finite behaviors of A are allowed by B. Thus A may still have behaviors that are not allowed by B, but these are all infinite, and so it cannot be concluded from a finite observation that A violates the requirements imposed by B.

Because in I/O automata input actions are always enabled, they will typically not have deadlocks in the sense of states without any outgoing transitions. Instead we define deadlock freeness as a relation between I/O automata. If A is deadlock free with respect to B, this means that whenever it is possible to reach a quiescent state of A via some trace, we can also reach a quiescent state of B with the same trace. Thus A can only become inactive when this is allowed by B.

In I/O automata theory, inclusion of fair traces is commonly used as implementation relation. Intuitively, one may think of B as defining a set of constraints, which A must obey. Note that A does not need exhibit *all* of the behaviors in *fairtraces*(B); merely a subset is sufficient. However, by requiring that A and B have the same input actions, and since input actions must always be enabled, trivial implementations are excluded. Here it is important to note that the concept of fairness used within the I/O automata model is *feasible* in the sense of [1]: each finite execution of an I/O automaton can be extended to a fair execution (for instance, by giving turns in a roundrobin way to all classes that are continuously enabled). As a consequence it also follows that A implements

B implies that A is safe with respect to B. In general, A implements B does not imply that A is deadlock free with respect to B. This is because a quiescent execution of A may be matched by a *divergent* fair execution of B, i.e., an infinite execution in which after some point only internal actions occur. However, it is easy to see that the implication does hold if B is *divergence free* in the sense that it has no divergent fair executions.

Refinements In the literature, a whole menagerie of so-called simulation techniques has been proposed to prove that the set of (finite, quiescent, fair,...) traces of one automaton is included in that of another. We refer to [21] for an overview and for further references. In this paper we only need a very simple type of simulation, which is called *weak refinement.*

Let A and B be I/O automata with the same input and output actions, respectively. A *weak refinement* from A to B is a function r from $states(A)$ to $states(B)$ such that:

1. If $s \in start(A)$ then $r(s) \in start(B)$.
2. If s is a reachable state of A and $s \xrightarrow{a}_A s'$, then $r(s) \stackrel{\beta}{\Longrightarrow}_B r(s')$ where β equals a if $a \in ext(A)$, and is empty otherwise.

Lemma 1. *If there exists a weak refinement from A to B then A is safe with respect to B.*

The converse implication does not hold, i.e. there exist I/O automata A and B such that A is safe with respect to B, but no weak refinement from A to B can be given. In those cases one has to use other, more general simulations. Also, if there exists a weak refinement from A to B then it is not in general the case that A is deadlock free with respect to B, or that A implements B. However, in the protocol that we analyze in this paper we will establish a weak refinement that maps quiescent executions to quiescent executions, and fair executions to fair executions, and these additional properties immediately imply absence of deadlock and the implementation relation.

The precondition/effect style In the I/O automata approach, the automata that model the basic building blocks of a system are usually specified in the so-called *precondition/effect* style. In this section we will briefly describe the syntax of this language.

We start from a typed signature Σ together with a Σ-algebra $\mathcal{A}$ which gives meaning to the function and constant symbols in Σ. To describe properties, we use a first-order language over signature Σ and a set V of (typed) variables, with equality and inequality predicates, and the usual logical connectives. If ξ is a valuation of variables in their domains, and b is a formula, then we write $\mathcal{A}, \xi \models b$ if b holds in $\mathcal{A}$ under valuation ξ.

An *I/O automaton generator* G consists of five components:

- a finite action signature $sig(G)$,

- a finite set $vars(G)$ of (typed) *state variables*,
- a satisfiable formula $init(G)$, in which variables from $vars(G)$ may occur free,
- for each action $a \in acts(G)$, a *transition type*, i.e., an expression of the form

  $a(y_1, \ldots, y_n)$
    Precondition:
      b
    Effect:
      $x_1 := e_1$
      $\vdots$
      $x_m := e_m$

  where the y_i are (typed) variables, b is a formula in which variables from $vars(G) \cup \{y_1, \ldots, y_n\}$ may occur free, and which is true if $a \in in(G)$, $vars(G) = \{x_1, \ldots, x_m\}$, and the e_j are expressions with the same type as x_j, in which the variables $vars(G) \cup \{y_1, \ldots, y_n\}$ may occur,
- an equivalence relation $part(A)$ on $local(G)$.

Each I/O automaton generator G denotes an I/O automaton A in the obvious way: states of A are interpretations of the variables of $vars(G)$ in their domains; start states of A are those states that satisfy formula $init(G)$; for each (input, output or internal) action $a \in acts(G)$ with a transition type as above, and for each choice of values $v_1, \ldots, v_n$ taken from the domains of $y_1, \ldots, y_n$, respectively, A contains an (input, output or internal) action $a(v_1, \ldots, v_n)$; A has a transition

$$s \xrightarrow{a(v_1,\ldots,v_n)} s'$$

iff there exists a valuation ξ such that

- for all $x \in vars(G)$, $\xi(x) = s(x)$,
- for $1 \leq i \leq n$, $\xi(y_i) = v_i$,
- $\mathcal{A}, \xi \models b$, and
- for $1 \leq j \leq m$, e_j evaluates to $s'(x_j)$ under ξ;

$part(G)$ trivially induces a partition on $local(A)$.

Let $a \in acts(G)$ be an action with a transition type as above. We define the formulas $enabled(a)$ and $quiescent(G)$ by

$$enabled(a) \triangleq \exists y_1, \ldots, y_n \,.\, b$$

$$quiescent(G) \triangleq \bigwedge_{a \in acts(G)} \neg enabled(a)$$

It follows that a state s of the automaton associated to G is quiescent iff it satisfies formula $quiescent(G)$.

The reader will observe that the translation from I/O automata generators to I/O automata is quite straightforward. In fact, Lynch and Tuttle [19, 20] do not even bother to distinguish between these two levels of description. For the formalization of I/O automata theory in Coq the distinction between the semantic and syntactic levels is of course important, which is why we have discussed it here. The definition of I/O automata generators has been inspired by similar definitions in the work of Jonsson (see, for instance, [15]). In the sequel we will, like Lynch and Tuttle, often refer to I/O automata when we actually mean I/O automata generators.

3.2 Protocol Specification

In this section, we present the formal specification of the Bounded Retransmission Protocol. Following a brief description of the many-sorted algebra that we use, we will first give I/O automata for each of the components of the protocol, and then define the full protocol as the composition of these I/O automata. At the end of this section we will moreover present the definition of an I/O automaton that gives the intended external behavior of the protocol. Since the BRP protocol has been explained already in considerable detail in Section 2, we will not repeat that explanation here, and confine ourselves in this section to the formal definitions, together with a brief discussion of some of the notation and certain modeling assumptions.

Data types We start the specification of the protocol with a description of the various data types that play a role. We assume a typed signature Σ and a Σ-algebra $\mathcal{A}$ which consist of the following components:

- a type **Bool** of booleans with constant symbols true and false, and a standard repertoire of function symbols ($\wedge$, $\vee$, $\neg$, $\rightarrow$), all with the standard interpretation over the booleans. Also, we require, for all types **S** in Σ, an equality, inequality, and if-then-else function symbol, with the usual interpretation:

$$.=. : \mathbf{S}\times\mathbf{S} \rightarrow \mathbf{Bool}$$
$$.\neq. : \mathbf{S}\times\mathbf{S} \rightarrow \mathbf{Bool}$$
$$\mathsf{if}\ .\ \mathsf{then}\ .\ \mathsf{else}\ . : \mathbf{Bool}\times\mathbf{S}\times\mathbf{S} \rightarrow \mathbf{S}$$

  Note the (harmless) overloading of the constants and function symbols of type **Bool** with the propositional connectives used in formulas. We will frequently view boolean valued expressions as formulas, i.e., we use b as an abbreviation of b=true.
- a type **Nat** of natural numbers, with constant symbol 0, successor function symbol succ, and function symbol $\leq$: **Nat**$\times$**Nat** $\rightarrow$ **Bool**, all with the usual interpretation. We also need a constant symbol max, which denotes the maximum number of retransmissions within the protocol.
- a type **Data** of data elements that the protocol has to transmit. We find it convenient to assume the presence of a constant symbol $\perp$ of type **Data**, which denotes the *undefined* data element.

- a type **List** of finite lists over the domain of **Data**, with a constant symbol ϵ, denoting the empty list, and a function symbol add : **Data**×**List** → **List**, denoting the operation of prefixing a list with a data element. Besides these constructors, there are function symbols hd : **List** → **Data**, tl : **List** → **List**, and one : **List** → **Bool**. hd takes the first element of a list, tl returns the remainder of a list after removal of the first element, and one returns true iff the argument list has length one. These operations are fully characterized by the axioms (where s is a variable of type **List**, and d, e are variables of type **Data**):

$$
\begin{array}{ll}
\mathsf{hd}(\epsilon) = \bot & \mathsf{one}(\epsilon) = \mathsf{false} \\
\mathsf{hd}(\mathsf{add}(d, s)) = d & \mathsf{one}(\mathsf{add}(d, \epsilon)) = \mathsf{true} \\
\mathsf{tl}(\epsilon) = \epsilon & \mathsf{one}(\mathsf{add}(d, \mathsf{add}(e, s))) = \mathsf{false} \\
\mathsf{tl}(\mathsf{add}(d, s)) = s &
\end{array}
$$

- a type **Conf** of *confirmation messages*, with constant symbols C_NOT_OK, C_OK and C_DONT_KNOW.
- a type **Ind** of *indication messages*, with constant symbols I_OK, I_FIRST and I_INCOMPLETE.
- a type **Spc** of *program counter values of the sender*, with constant symbols SF, WA, SC, ET2 and WT2.
- a type **Rpc** of *program counter values of the receiver*, with constant symbols WF, SI, SA, RTS and NOK.

The intended meaning of all these constants will be explained further on in this section. We assume that the interpretation of **Conf**, **Ind**, **Spc** and **Rpc** is free, in the sense that, for each of these types, different constants symbols are mapped to different elements in their domain ("no confusion"), and each element in the domain is denoted by some constant symbol ("no junk").

Notation In the presentation below, we use the following conventions:

- We omit the precondition of an input action (since this equals true by definition).
- In the effect part of transition types we omit assignments of the form $x := x$.
- We write if c then $[z_1 := f_1, \ldots, z_k := f_k]$ as an abbreviation for

$$
\begin{array}{c}
z_1 := \mathsf{if}\ c\ \mathsf{then}\ f_1\ \mathsf{else}\ z_1 \\
\vdots \\
z_k := \mathsf{if}\ c\ \mathsf{then}\ f_k\ \mathsf{else}\ z_k
\end{array}
$$

- We never mention the partition of the local action types because in all I/O automata generators that we consider it is trivial in the sense that there is just only block which contains all the locally controlled actions. (Note that the composition of the I/O automata denoted by these generators will not have a trivial partition!)

– We write $pc \in \{\mathsf{SF}, \mathsf{WA}, \mathsf{SC}\}$ for $pc{=}\mathsf{SF} \vee pc{=}\mathsf{WA} \vee pc{=}\mathsf{SC}$, etc.
– To improve readability we sometimes use Lamport's list notation for conjunction.

The sender We will now present the I/O automaton S, which models the sender of the protocol. An important state variable of S is *pc*, which gives the current value of the program counter of the sender. This variable, which is of type **Spc**, may have five different values:

- SF: Send a Frame at port F,
- WA: Wait for an Acknowledgement to arrive at port B,
- SC: Send a Confirmation message to the upper layer,
- ET2: Enable Timer 2, and
- WT2: Wait for Timeout of Timer 2.

We have modeled the arrival of a request (*REQ*) as an input action, since it is clearly under control of the environment. However, once we have taken this decision the I/O automata model forces us to specify, for all possible states, what happens if an *REQ* action occurs. In our modeling, the sender discards an incoming request if it is busy handling the previous request, something which is recorded by the boolean state variable *busy*.

T3 is a time out action that occurs when S wants to send a frame into channel K but does not succeed because other agents (not specified here) are using the channel. After the occurrence of a *T3* action, S will send a confirmation message C_DONT_KNOW or C_NOT_OK.

When S sends a frame into channel K by doing F, it simultaneously starts a timer by setting boolean state variable *timer1_on* to true. This timer will timeout if an acknowledgement for the frame does not arrive in time. Since we cannot explicitly model real-time aspects in the I/O automata model, we deal with this timing behavior in a different way. Under the assumptions that (1) the transmission of a frame through channels K and L takes a bounded time, and (2) R will always acknowledge an incoming frame in a bounded time, and (3) the timer is set properly, a timeout will occur iff a frame gets lost in channel K or in channel L. Thus one could say that the loss of a message in the channel "causes" a timeout action. In our specification we have made these causal links visible by introducing output actions *E1K* and *E1L* for channels K and L, respectively, which occur when a message gets lost, and corresponding input actions *E1K* and *E1L* of sender S, whose occurrence sets a boolean state variable *timer1_enabled*. By taking *timer1_enabled* to be part of the precondition of the timeout action *T1*, this gives us the desired causal links.

If something goes wrong during the handling of a request, and S sends a C_DONT_KNOW or C_NOT_OK confirmation message, then before dealing with a new request, S will wait long enough to make sure that the receiver R is prepared to receive new frames. Also here, since we cannot deal with real-time directly within our model, we describe the causal links that result from these real-time constraints. After sending a C_DONT_KNOW or C_NOT_OK confirmation message, the sender does an output action $E2$, which corresponds to starting a new timer (that is not specified here). Since it depends on the state of R when this timer will timeout, $E2$ is made into an input action of R. At the appropriate moment R will generate the timeout action $T2$ for the timer started by S, so that S can proceed and handle the next request.

We now give the code for I/O automaton S.

Input: *REQ*, *B*, *E1K*, *E1L*, *T2*
Output: *CONF*, *F*, *E2*
Internal: *T1*, *T3*

State Variables:		**Initialization:**
pc:	**Spc**	$\wedge$ *pc*=SF
busy,first,toggle:	**Bool**	$\wedge \neg$*busy*
list:	**List**	$\wedge$ *first*
timer1_on:	**Bool**	$\wedge \neg$*timer1_on*
timer1_enabled:	**Bool**	$\wedge \neg$*timer1_enabled*
rn:	**Nat**	$\wedge$ *rn*=0

REQ(*s* : **List**)
  Effect:
    if ¬*busy* ∧ *s*≠ε then [*list* := *s*
                busy := true]

F(*f* : **Bool**, *l* : **Bool**, *t* : **Bool**, *d* : **Data**)
  Precondition:
    pc=SF ∧ *busy* ∧
    f=*first* ∧ *l*=one(*list*) ∧ *t*=*toggle* ∧ *d*=hd(*list*)
  Effect:
    pc := WA
    timer1_on := true
    rn := succ(*rn*)

T3
  Precondition:
    pc=SF ∧ *busy*
  Effect:
    pc := SC

E1K
  Effect:
    timer1_enabled := true

E1L
  Effect:
    timer1_enabled := true

B(*f* : **Bool**, *l* : **Bool**, *t* : **Bool**)
  Effect:
    pc := if one(*list*) then SC else SF
    first := one(*list*)
    toggle := ¬*toggle*
    timer1_on := false
    list := tl(*list*)
    if ¬(one(*list*)) then [*rn* := 0]

T1
  Precondition:
    timer1_on ∧ *timer1_enabled*
  Effect:
    pc := if *rn*≤max then SF else SC
    timer1_on := false
    timer1_enabled := false

CONF(*c* : **Conf**)
  Precondition:
    pc=SC ∧ *c*=if *list*=ε then C_OK else
                if one(*list*) ∧ *rn*≠0 then C_DONT_KNOW else C_NOT_OK
  Effect:
    pc := if *list*=ε then SF else ET2
    busy := false
    list := ε
    rn := 0

E2
Precondition:
pc=ET2
Effect:
pc := WT2
first := true
toggle := ¬*toggle*

T2
Effect:
pc := SF

Channel *K* I/O automaton K models in a straightforward way the behavior of a faulty message buffer with input channel F, output channel G, and capacity one. Messages that arrive when the buffer is full are discarded. In Lemma 2 we will show that actually such a situation never occurs during a run of the protocol.

Input: F
Output: G, *E1K*
State Variables: *full*,*first*,*last*,*toggle*: **Bool**
datum: **Data**
Initialization: ¬*full*

$F(f : \mathbf{Bool}, l : \mathbf{Bool}, t : \mathbf{Bool}, d : \mathbf{Data})$
Effect:
if ¬*full* then [*full* := true
first := f
last := l
toggle := t
datum := d]

$G(f : \mathbf{Bool}, l : \mathbf{Bool}, t : \mathbf{Bool}, d : \mathbf{Data})$
Precondition:
full ∧ f=*first* ∧ l=*last* ∧ t=*toggle* ∧ d=*datum*
Effect:
full := false

E1K
Precondition:
full
Effect:
full := false

Channel *L* I/O automaton L is the same as K, except that L handles frames that consist of 3 instead of 4 fields, and its actions have different names.

Input: A
Output: B, *E1L*
State Variables: *full*,*first*,*last*,*toggle*: **Bool**
Initialization: ¬*full*

$A(f : \mathbf{Bool}, l : \mathbf{Bool}, t : \mathbf{Bool})$
Effect:
if ¬*full* then [*full* := true
first := f
last := l
toggle := t]

$B(f : \mathbf{Bool}, l : \mathbf{Bool}, t : \mathbf{Bool})$
Precondition:
full ∧ f=*first* ∧ l=*last* ∧ t=*toggle*
Effect:
full := false

E1L
Precondition:
full
Effect:
full := false

The receiver The most important state variable of I/O automaton R is pc, which gives the value of the program counter of the receiver. This variable, which is of type **Rpc**, can have five possible values:

- WF: Wait for a Frame to arrive at port G,
- SI: Send an Indication message to the upper layer,
- SA: Send an Acknowledgement message at port A,
- RTS: Return control bits of received frame To Sender via port A, and
- NOK: send an indication message NOT_OK to the upper layer.

The subtle part in the definition of R is again the part concerned with timing. The receiver has a timer of its own, which is started at the moment an acknowledgement message is sent by setting a boolean variable *timer2_on* to true. The timer will time out if after some time still no new frame has arrived at port G and it is clear that the sender has interrupted the transmission a list. When a timeout occurs, the receiver sets *ctoggle* to false to indicate that it will not reject the next frame on basis of its toggle bit, and it generates an indication NOT_OK in case some messages have not yet been received. If R has set the timer and S generates an *E2* action, then a transmission has been interrupted and a timeout action may occur. For convenience we identify in our model *E2* with the timeout action. However, if an *E2* action occurs and the receiver's timer has not been set, then this action should not be interpreted as a timeout, but just as a signal that an action *T2* can be generated at the sender side.

We now present the code for I/O automaton R.

Input: $G, E2$
Output: $A, IND, IND\_NOT\_OK, T2$

State Variables:		**Initialization:**
pc:	**Rpc**	$\wedge$ *pc*=WF
first,toggle,ctoggle:	**Bool**	$\wedge$ *first*
ffirst,flast,ftoggle:	**Bool**	$\wedge \neg$*ctoggle*
fdatum:	**Data**	$\wedge \neg$*timer2_on*
timer2_on:	**Bool**	$\wedge \neg$*timer2_enabled*
timer2_enabled:	**Bool**	

$G(f : \mathbf{Bool}, l : \mathbf{Bool}, t : \mathbf{Bool}, d : \mathbf{Data})$
  Effect:
    if *pc*=WF then [*pc* := if *ctoggle* → *t*=*toggle* then SI else RTS
      ffirst := *f*
      flast := *l*
      ftoggle := *t*
      fdatum := *d*
      if *ctoggle* → *t*=*toggle* then [*timer2_on* := false]]

$IND(d : \mathbf{Data}, i : \mathbf{Ind})$
  Precondition:
    pc=SI ∧ *d*=*fdatum*
    ∧ *i*=if *flast* then I_OK else (if *ffirst* then I_FIRST else I_INCOMPLETE)
  Effect:
    pc := SA

first := *flast*
ctoggle := true
toggle := ¬*ftoggle*

$A(f : \mathbf{Bool}, l : \mathbf{Bool}, t : \mathbf{Bool})$
Precondition:
pc∈{SA, RTS} ∧ *f*=*ffirst* ∧ *l*=*flast* ∧ *t*=*ftoggle*
Effect:
if *pc*=SA then [*timer2_on* := true]
pc := WF

IND_NOT_OK
Precondition:
pc=NOK
Effect:
pc := WF
first := true
timer2_on := true

E2
Effect:
timer2_enabled := true
if *timer2_on* then [*ctoggle* := false
if ¬*first* then [*pc* := NOK
timer2_on := false]]

T2
Precondition:
timer2_enabled ∧ *pc*=WF
Effect:
timer2_enabled := false

The full protocol I/O automaton *BRP* is defined as the parallel composition of I/O automata S, K, L and R, with all communication between these components hidden:

$$BRP \triangleq \text{HIDE } I \text{ IN } (S||K||L||R)$$

where $I \triangleq \{F(f,l,t,d), G(f,l,t,d), A(f,l,t), B(f,l,t), E1K, E1L, E2, T2$
$\mid f,l,t \text{ in domain } \mathbf{Bool}, d \text{ in domain } \mathbf{Data}\}$.

The correctness criterion We specify the collection of allowed behaviors of the Bounded Retransmission Protocol via an I/O automaton P, which has the same input and output actions as *BRP*, but no internal actions. If a *REQ*(s) action occurs in the initial state, then the regular behavior of P is to output the elements of s one by one, tagging the first datum with an indication I_FIRST, intermediate data with I_INCOMPLETE, and the last datum with I_OK. After sending the last datum P generates a confirmation message C_OK to indicate that the request has been carried out successfully, and return to its initial state. Requests that arrive at a time when the previous request has not yet been processed are ignored. While a request is being processed, something may go wrong at any point and, instead of the C_OK message a C_DONT_KNOW or a C_NOT_OK confirmation message may be sent. The C_DONT_KNOW message will only occur, however, if at most one data element has not been delivered, and the C_NOT_OK will only occur if at least one data element has not been delivered. If a C_NOT_OK or C_DONT_KNOW message is sent somewhere in the middle of the processing of a request, i.e., after the first but before the last data element has been delivered, P generates a NOT_OK message. After such a message P returns to its initial state, except if it has just received a new request, which will then be processed.

Below we present the code of I/O automaton P. In the next section we will establish that BRP is an implementation of P.

Input: REQ
Output: IND, IND_NOT_OK, $CONF$
State Variables: *busy,first,error*: **Bool**   **Initialization:** $\wedge \neg busy$ $\wedge$ *first* $\wedge \neg error$
list: **List**

$REQ(s : \textbf{List})$
Effect:
if $\neg busy \wedge s \neq \epsilon$ then $[busy := \text{true}$
$list := s]$

$IND(d : \textbf{Data}, i : \textbf{Ind})$
Precondition:
$busy \wedge \neg error \wedge list \neq \epsilon \wedge d = \text{hd}(list)$
$\wedge\ i = $ if one($list$) then I_OK else (if *first* then I_FIRST else I_INCOMPLETE)
Effect:
first := one(*list*)
list := tl(*list*)

$CONF(c : \textbf{Conf})$
Precondition:
$busy \wedge \neg error$
$\wedge$ (c=C_OK $\rightarrow$ $list = \epsilon$)
$\wedge$ (c=C_DONT_KNOW $\rightarrow$ ($list = \epsilon \vee$ one($list$)))
$\wedge$ (c=C_NOT_OK $\rightarrow$ $list \neq \epsilon$)
Effect:
busy := false
error := $\neg$*first*
list := ϵ

IND_NOT_OK
Precondition:
error
Effect:
first := true
error := false

3.3 Protocol Correctness Proof

Invariants In order to establish a weak refinement from BRP to P we must first gain insight into what are the reachable states of BRP. To this end, we present a number of *invariants* of the protocol, i.e., properties that are valid for all reachable states. Most of these invariants are proved by a routine induction on the length of the executions to the reachable states. The full, handwritten proofs of the invariants together occupy about 16 pages of ASCII text. We used numbering of assertions, as advocated by Lamport [16], although, due to the fact that the proofs went rarely more than 4 levels deep, we found it easier to use explicit names, like 3.1.1.1, instead of the implicit ones, like ⟨4⟩1. As an illustration we have included the full proof of the invariant *INVR* (Lemma 3). In order to distinguish between the state variables of different components of *BRP*, we prefix each state variable by the name of the component it originates from.

Lemma 2. *The following property INV1 is an invariant of BRP.*

$$\begin{array}{lll}
\wedge\ S.pc \in \{\mathsf{SF}, \mathsf{SC}, \mathsf{ET2}\} & \rightarrow & R.pc = \mathsf{WF} \\
\wedge\ S.timer1_enabled & \rightarrow & S.pc = \mathsf{WA} \wedge R.pc = \mathsf{WF} \wedge \neg K.full \wedge \neg L.full \\
\wedge\ K.full & \rightarrow & S.pc = \mathsf{WA} \wedge R.pc = \mathsf{WF} \wedge \neg L.full \\
\wedge\ R.pc \in \{\mathsf{SI}, \mathsf{SA}, \mathsf{RTS}\} & \rightarrow & S.pc = \mathsf{WA} \\
\wedge\ R.timer2_enabled & \rightarrow & S.pc = \mathsf{WT2} \wedge R.pc \in \{\mathsf{WF}, \mathsf{NOK}\} \wedge \\
 & & \neg K.full \wedge \neg L.full \\
\wedge\ L.full & \rightarrow & S.pc = \mathsf{WA} \wedge R.pc = \mathsf{WF} \wedge \neg K.full
\end{array}$$

Invariant *INV1* relates the control variables of the different components of the protocol. The invariant already allows us to make several important observations on the behavior of the protocol. The third clause implies that sender S will never send a frame into channel K when the channel is busy delivering another frame. Similarly, receiver R will never send a frame into channel L when L already contains a frame. Thus the protocol does not need communication channels with a buffering capacity of more than one. Clause three and six together give that there will never be a message in both K and L at the same time. Thus, an implementation of the protocol may use a single bidirectional medium to implement both channels. If channel L delivers a frame to the sender S, then S is in fact waiting for this frame to arrive. Similarly, if channel K delivers a frame to receiver R, then the receiver is waiting for this frame. It follows rather directly from invariant *INV1* that in each reachable state of the protocol at most one of the four components enables a locally controlled action. This means that the protocol operates in a is fully sequential way.

Invariants *INVR* of Lemma 3 gives some relationships between the state variables of R.

Lemma 3. *The following property INVR is an invariant of BRP.*

$$\begin{array}{lll}
\wedge\ R.pc = \mathsf{NOK} & \rightarrow & \neg R.ctoggle \\
\wedge\ R.pc = \mathsf{SI} & \rightarrow & R.ctoggle \rightarrow R.ftoggle = R.toggle \\
\wedge\ R.pc \in \{\mathsf{RTS}, \mathsf{SA}\} & \rightarrow & R.ctoggle \wedge R.ftoggle \neq R.toggle
\end{array}$$

Proof. Let s' be a reachable state of *BRP*. By induction on the length n of the shortest execution of *BRP* that ends in s', we prove $s' \models INVR$. If $n = 0$, then s' is a start state. Hence $s' \models R.pc = \mathsf{WF}$, which implies $s' \models INVR$.

For the induction step, suppose that s' is reachable via an execution with length $n + 1$. Then there exists a state s that is reachable via an execution of length n and $s \xrightarrow{a} s'$, for some action a. By induction hypothesis, $s \models INVR$. We prove $s' \models INVR$ by a routine case distinction on a. In the proof we will use several times that, by Lemma 2, $s \models INV1$.

1. Assume a is an action in which R does not participate. Then $s' \models INVR$ trivially follows from $s \models INVR$ and the observation that a does not change any of the state variables mentioned in $INVR$.
2. Assume $a = G(f,l,t,d)$
   2.1) $s \models K.full$ (by 2 and precondition G)
   2.2) $s \models R.pc{=}\mathsf{WF}$ (by 2.1 and $INV1$)
   2.3) Assume $s \models R.ctoggle \rightarrow t{=}R.toggle$
   2.3.1) $s' \models R.ctoggle \rightarrow t{=}R.toggle$ (by 2 and 2.3 since G does not change $R.ctoggle$ and $R.toggle$)
   2.3.2) $s' \models R.pc{=}\mathsf{SI} \wedge R.ftoggle{=}t$ (by 2, 2.2, 2.3 and effect G)
   2.3.3) $s' \models INVR$ (by 2.3.1 and 2.3.2)
   2.4) Assume $s \not\models R.ctoggle \rightarrow t{=}R.toggle$
   2.4.1) $s' \models \neg(R.ctoggle \rightarrow t{=}R.toggle)$ (by 2 and 2.4 since G does not change $R.ctoggle$ and $R.toggle$)
   2.4.2) $s' \models R.pc{=}\mathsf{RTS} \wedge R.ftoggle{=}t$ (by 2, 2.2, 2.4 and effect G)
   2.4.3) $s' \models INVR$ (by 2.4.1 and 2.4.2)
   2.5) $s' \models INVR$ (by 2.3 and 2.4)
3. Assume $a = IND(d,i)$
   3.1) $s' \models R.pc{=}\mathsf{SA} \wedge R.ctoggle \wedge R.ftoggle{\neq}R.toggle$ (by 3 and effect IND)
   3.2) $s' \models INVR$ (by 3.1)
4. Assume $a = A(f,l,t)$
   4.1) $s' \models R.pc{=}\mathsf{WF}$ (by 4 and effect A)
   4.2) $s' \models INVR$ (by 4.1)
5. Assume $a = E2$
   5.1) $s \models S.pc{=}\mathsf{ET2}$ (by 5 and precondition $E2$)
   5.2) $s \models R.pc{=}\mathsf{WF}$ (by 5.1 and $INV1$)
   5.3) Assume $s \models R.timer2\_on \wedge \neg R.first$
   5.3.1) $s' \models R.pc{=}\mathsf{NOK} \wedge \neg R.ctoggle$ (by 5, 5.3 and effect $E2$)
   5.3.2) $s' \models INVR$ (by 5.3.1)
   5.4) Assume $s \not\models R.timer2\_on \wedge \neg R.first$
   5.4.1) $s' \models R.pc{=}\mathsf{WF}$ (by 5, 5.2, 5.4 and effect $E2$)
   5.4.2) $s' \models INVR$ (by 5.4.1)
   5.5) $s' \models INVR$ (by 5.3 and 5.4)
6. Assume $a = T2$
   6.1) $s \models R.pc{=}\mathsf{WF}$ (by 6 and precondition $T2$)
   6.2) $s' \models R.pc{=}\mathsf{WF}$ (by 6, 6.1 and effect $T2$)
   6.3) $s' \models INVR$ (by 6.2)
7. Assume $a = IND\_NOT\_OK$
   7.1) $s' \models R.pc{=}\mathsf{WF}$ (by 7 and effect IND_NOT_OK)
   7.2) $s' \models INVR$ (by 7.1)
8. $s' \models INVR$ (by 1-7)

The next invariant $INVL$ implies that when an acknowledgement message arrives at the sender, the three bits of this acknowledgement are determined by the state of the sender, and hence provide no information. The only information conveyed by an acknowledgement is the fact of its arrival itself, the rest is redundant.

Lemma 4. *The following property INVL is an invariant of BRP.*

$$\begin{array}{lll} L.\mathit{full} & \rightarrow & L.\mathit{first}=R.\mathit{ffirst}=S.\mathit{first} \wedge L.\mathit{last}=R.\mathit{flast}=\mathrm{one}(S.\mathit{list}) \wedge \\ & & R.\mathit{ctoggle} \wedge L.\mathit{toggle}=\neg R.\mathit{toggle}=S.\mathit{toggle} \end{array}$$

The following invariant is not used in the proof of the refinement, but is interesting because it implies that, when a frame arrives at the receiver, the first field of this frame is determined by the state of the receiver and the other fields of the frame. Hence the first bit of the frame conveys no information and is redundant.

Lemma 5. *The following property INVK′ is an invariant of BRP.*

$$K.\mathit{full} \rightarrow K.\mathit{first}=\mathsf{if}\ (R.\mathit{ctoggle} \rightarrow K.\mathit{toggle}=R.\mathit{toggle})\ \mathsf{then}\ R.\mathit{first}\ \mathsf{else}\ R.\mathit{ffirst}$$

Safety We have now prepared the ground for the first main results of this paper: the existence of a weak refinement from *BRP* to *P*. Since states of *BRP* and *P* are fully determined by the values of their state variables, we can define a weak refinement from *BRP* to *P* by expressing the values of the state variables of *P* in terms of those of *BRP*. The weak refinement function, which is given in Theorem 6, turns out to be surprisingly simple: *P.list* is either *S.list* or tl(*S.list*), *P.busy* is just *S.busy*, *P.first* is just *R.first*, and *P.error* holds iff the receiver's program counter equals NOK or will necessarily do so after the next locally controlled action.

Theorem 6. *The function REF defined by the following formula is a weak refinement from BRP to P.*

$$\begin{array}{lll} \wedge\ P.\mathit{list} & = & \mathsf{if}\ S.\mathit{pc}\in\{\mathsf{ET2},\mathsf{WT2}\} \vee (R.\mathit{ctoggle} \rightarrow S.\mathit{toggle}=R.\mathit{toggle})\ \mathsf{then}\ S.\mathit{list} \\ & & \qquad \mathsf{else}\ \mathsf{tl}(S.\mathit{list}) \\ \wedge\ P.\mathit{busy} & = & S.\mathit{busy} \\ \wedge\ P.\mathit{first} & = & R.\mathit{first} \\ \wedge\ P.\mathit{error} & = & R.\mathit{pc}=\mathsf{NOK} \vee (S.\mathit{pc}=\mathsf{ET2} \wedge R.\mathit{timer2\_on} \wedge \neg R.\mathit{first}) \end{array}$$

Proof. 5 pages densely filled with ASCII.

Corollary 7. *BRP is safe with respect to P.*

Deadlock freeness

Theorem 8. *For each reachable and quiescent state s of BRP, REF(s) is a quiescent state of P.*

Corollary 9. *BRP is deadlock free with respect to P.*

Implementation We now come to the main result of this section, which says that the Bounded Retransmission Protocol correctly implementation specification P. Given that we have already shown that BRP is safe and deadlock free, the essential fact that remains to be established is that BRP is divergence free, i.e., will always eventually produce some allowed output after a given input. As is usual with liveness properties, we show this by presenting a weight function that maps states onto a well-founded domain (the natural numbers in our case) and demonstrating that after an input all actions, except possible further inputs and the required outputs, decrease the weight.

For each state s of BRP, define $weight(s)$ as the result of evaluating the following expression in s:

$$\begin{aligned}
&(6\mathsf{max}+5)\cdot \mathsf{length}(S.list) + 6\cdot(\mathsf{max}+1 \dot{-} S.rn) + \iota(S.timer1_on)\\
&+ 4\cdot\iota(S.pc{=}\mathsf{ET2}) + 2\cdot\iota(S.pc{=}\mathsf{WT2}) + \iota(S.pc \in \{\mathsf{SF},\mathsf{WA}\})\\
&+ 4\cdot\iota(K.full)\\
&+ 3\cdot\iota(R.pc{=}\mathsf{SI}) + 2\cdot\iota(R.pc \in \{\mathsf{SA},\mathsf{RTS}\}) + \iota(R.pc{=}\mathsf{NOK})\\
&+ \iota(L.full)
\end{aligned}$$

Besides some standard arithmetic operations, we have used here a function $\mathsf{length} : \mathbf{List} \rightarrow \mathbf{Nat}$, which gives the length of a list, and a function $\iota : \mathbf{Bool} \rightarrow \mathbf{Nat}$ defined by

$$\iota(\mathsf{false}) = 0 \qquad \iota(\mathsf{true}) = 1$$

Lemma 10. *Suppose s, s' are reachable states of BRP and $s \xrightarrow{a} s'$ for some action a, with $a \notin in(BRP)$ and a not of the form $CONF(c)$, for some c. Then $weight(s) > weight(s')$.*

Theorem 11. *BRP implements P.*

Proof. Assume that $\beta \in fairtraces(BRP)$. We must prove $\beta \in fairtraces(P)$.

Let $\alpha = s_0 a_1 s_1 a_2 s_2 \cdots$ be a fair execution of BRP with trace β.

If α is finite then α is quiescent and it follows by Corollary 9 that P has a quiescent execution with trace β. Since each quiescent execution is also fair, this implies $\beta \in fairtraces(P)$. So we may assume w.l.o.g. that α is infinite.

Using the fact that REF is a weak refinement (Theorem 6) we can easily construct an execution α' of P with trace β. It remains to prove that α' is fair. For this we distinguish between two cases.

1. β contains infinitely many $CONF$ actions. Since $part(P)$ contains only one class, and execution α' contains infinitely many occurrences of actions from that class, α' is fair.
2. β contains only finitely many $CONF$ actions. Call an input action a_i in α *discarded* if $s_{i-1} = s_i$. Then between any pair of non-discarded inputs in α there must be a $CONF$ action, because a non-discarded input always changes $S.busy$ from false to true, and $CONF$ is the only action that can set $S.busy$ to false again. Thus there is a point N in α after which

there are no more *CONF* actions and moreover all inputs are discarded. By Lemma 10 it follows that, for all $i > N$, if a_i is a locally controlled action then $weight(s_{i-1}) > weight(s_i)$ else $weight(s_{i-1}) = weight(s_i)$. Thus there must be a point $M \geq N$ after which α only contains discarded inputs. Moreover, all states from that point on are equal and quiescent, otherwise α would not be fair. By Lemma 8, $S.busy$=false for all quiescent states of BRP. It follows that α has an infinite suffix $s_M\ REQ(\epsilon)\ s_M\ REQ(\epsilon)\ s_M \cdots$. But this means that the corresponding execution α' of P has an infinite suffix $s_q\ REQ(\epsilon)\ s_q\ REQ(\epsilon)\ s_q \cdots$. Moreover, by Lemma 8 state s_q is quiescent. This implies that α' is fair.

4 Proof-Checking

In this Section, we report on the proof-checking of the protocol verification of Section 3. We have checked the proofs of all the invariants (Lemmas 2, 3, 4 and 5, as well as some other invariants that we needed as lemmas but that are not discussed here), the proof that *REF* is a weak refinement (Theorem 6), and the proof that *REF* preserves quiescence (Theorem 8). We did not proof-check "meta-results" such as Lemma 1 and Corollaries 7 and 9. Also, we have not checked the "liveness" result of Theorem 11. Proof-checking these results as well would have required a considerable effort with, at least in the case of the Bounded Retransmission Protocol, only a small payoff. Still we think that the formalization and mechanical checking of these type of results will be an important topic of future research.

4.1 Coq Proof Development System

Coq is a proof assistant for higher-order logic. It is based on the *Calculus of Inductive Constructions* [24], which is a polymorphic type theory allowing dependent types and inductive types. Constructing a proof in Coq is an interactive process. The user specifies the proof strategy (e.g. which deduction rule should be applied) and Coq does all the calculations.

Notation Coq is based on type theory, which means that (apart from some built in 'pretty printing' rules) all applications are denoted in pre-fix. In this paper we adapt the ASCII input and output of Coq in order to improve the readability. We write

$\lambda x{:}A\,.\,b$	for	`[x:A]b`
$\forall x{:}A\,.\,B$	for	`(x:A)B` when `x` is a free variable in `B`
$A_1 \rightarrow A_2$	for	`A1->A2`
$x = y$	for	`eq A x y` (or `<A>x=y`)
$A \wedge B$	for	`and A B` (or `A/\B`)
$A \vee B$	for	`or A B` (or `A\/B`)
$A \times B$	for	`prod A B` (or `A*B`)
$\sim A$	for	`A->False` (or `~A`)
$x \neq y$	for	$\sim(x = y)$

Note that we omit the type information in $x = y$. The reader can easily deduce this type from the context.

The Tactics theorem prover The Coq system makes use of the *Curry-Howard isomorphism*, which states that λ-terms can be used to encode natural deduction proofs. For instance the well-known S-combinator

$$\lambda x : A \rightarrow (B \rightarrow C) \,.\, \lambda y : A \rightarrow B \,.\, \lambda z : A \,.\, x\ z\ (y\ z)$$

encodes under the Curry-Howard isomorphism the following natural deduction proof. (Cancelled hypotheses are placed between square brackets.)

$$\dfrac{\dfrac{\dfrac{\dfrac{\dfrac{[A \rightarrow (B \rightarrow C)]^3 \quad [A]^1}{B \rightarrow C} \qquad \dfrac{[A \rightarrow B]^2 \quad [A]^1}{B}}{C}}{A \rightarrow C}\,1}{(A \rightarrow B) \rightarrow (A \rightarrow C)}\,2}{(A \rightarrow (B \rightarrow C)) \rightarrow ((A \rightarrow B) \rightarrow (A \rightarrow C))}\,3$$

In order to give the reader a flavor of a proof session in Coq we give the list of commands (*tactics*) needed to construct the proofterm above. At the right we expose how the proofterm is built step by step. Note that proofterm is constructed 'top-down'. The terms $Hyp_1, \ldots, Hyp_5$ represent the subgoals that are generated during the proof session. (We omit the types in the proofterm in order to save space.)

Goal $(A \rightarrow (B \rightarrow C)) \rightarrow ((A \rightarrow B) \rightarrow (A \rightarrow C))$.	proofterm: Hyp_1
Intros x y z.	proofterm: $\lambda xyz.\, Hyp_2$
Apply x.	proofterm: $\lambda xyz.\, x\ Hyp_3\ Hyp_4$
Assumption.	proofterm: $\lambda xyz.\, x\ z\ Hyp_4$
Apply y.	proofterm: $\lambda xyz.\, x\ z\ (y\ Hyp_5)$
Assumption.	proofterm: $\lambda xyz.\, x\ z\ (y\ z)$

Tactics can be composed to so called *tacticals*. The tactical $tac_0\ ;\ tac_1$ first applies tac_0 on the current goal and then applies tac_1 on all the subgoals generated by tac_0. More generally, the tactical $tac_0\ ;\ [tac_1 | \cdots | tac_N]$ first applies tac_0 and then applies tac_i on the i-th subgoal generated by tac_0 $(i = 1, \ldots, N)$. (When tac_0 does not generate N subgoals, this tactical fails.) The following tactical generates the same S-combinator.

Intros x y z ; Apply x ; [Assumption | Apply y ; Assumption].

Details about the use of Coq can be found in the Coq manual [9].

One of the most important features of Coq is the so called *program abstraction*. From a proof of $\forall x : A.\, \exists y : B.\, P(x, y)$ one can extract a function (program) $f : A \longrightarrow B$ such that $\forall x : A.\, P(x, f(x))$. We do not need this facility for our purposes.

Inductive types In our encodings we extensively use inductive types. For details about this notion we refer to [24]. In this paper we restrict ourselves to some examples. When we define $nat : Set$, $O : nat$ and $S : nat \to nat$ then $\underbrace{S(\cdots(S}_{n}\ O))$ is of type nat for all $n \geq 0$ but there might still be other terms of type nat. In Coq we have the alternative possibility

$$\begin{array}{ll} nat & := \mathsf{Ind}(X : Set)\{X \mid X \to X\} \\ O & := \mathsf{Constr}(1, nat) \\ S & := \mathsf{Constr}(2, nat). \end{array}$$

which is the result of the Coq command:

Inductive Definition nat : Set = O : nat | S : nat → nat.

This should be read as 'nat is the smallest set X closed under two constructors, one of type X and one of type $X \to X$'. When we choose for the second option then nat contains no other terms then those constructed from O and S. In other words: for arbitrary $P : nat \to *$ and $x : nat$ we are able to construct a term of type $P\,x$ from terms $\wp_o : P\,O$ and $\wp_s : \forall y : nat\,.\,P\,y \to P\,(S\,y)$. This term is written as $<P>\mathsf{Match}\ x\ \mathsf{with}\ \wp_o\ \wp_s$ in the system. The reduction behavior of this term is determined by the construction of x from O and S.

$$\begin{array}{l} <P>\mathsf{Match}\ O\ \mathsf{with}\ \wp_o\ \wp_s \ \twoheadrightarrow \wp_o \\ <P>\mathsf{Match}\ S\,y\ \mathsf{with}\ \wp_o\ \wp_s \twoheadrightarrow \wp_s\ y\ (<P>\mathsf{Match}\ y\ \mathsf{with}\ \wp_o\ \wp_s) \end{array}$$

Note that this reductions are well typed, i.e. reduction of a term does not change its type. When $* \equiv Prop$ (which is a predefined notion of Coq, representing the type of all propositions) then P is a predicate over nat and $\wp_o$ and $\wp_s$ are just the usual proofs for the zero-case and the successor-case. When $* \equiv Set$ (another predefined notion, representing the type of all sets) and P is a constant function on nat, say $P \equiv \lambda n : nat\,.\,A$ for some $A : Set$, then $\wp_o : A$ and $\wp_s : nat \to A \to A$ and $\lambda x : nat\,.\ <P>\mathsf{Match}\ x\ \mathsf{with}\ \wp_o\ \wp_s$ represents the function from nat to A that is defined by primitive recursion from $\wp_o$ and $\wp_s$. In other words: $\lambda a : A\,.\,\lambda g : nat \to A \to A\,.\,\lambda x : nat\,.\ <P>\mathsf{Match}\ x\ \mathsf{with}\ a\ g$ is a recursor. With this mechanism one can define any primitive recursive function (and even more because one can use higher order recursion).

We conclude this subsection with the illustration of how one can use inductive types to encode logical conjunction and disjunction. Define

$$\begin{array}{ll} and & := \lambda A, B : Prop.\mathsf{Ind}(X : Prop)\{A \to B \to X\} \\ or & := \lambda A, B : Prop.\mathsf{Ind}(X : Prop)\{A \to X \mid B \to X\} \\ conj & := \lambda A, B : Prop.\mathsf{Constr}(1, (and\ A\ B)) \\ or\_introl & := \lambda A, B : Prop.\mathsf{Constr}(1, (or\ A\ B)) \\ or\_intror & := \lambda A, B : Prop.\mathsf{Constr}(2, (or\ A\ B)) \end{array}$$

then $(and\ A\ B)$ contains no other terms (proofs) then those constructed from $(conj\ A\ B)$ and $(or\ A\ B)$ contains no other terms then those constructed from $(or\_introl\ A\ B)$ or $(or\_intror\ A\ B)$. This exactly reflects the intuitionistic meanings of conjunction and disjunction. The only way to prove $A \wedge B$ is proving both A and B, and the only way to prove $A \vee B$ is proving A or B.

4.2 Protocol Specification

The hand-written proof is written in many sorted predicate logic. For each sort there is an equality relation. We use the built-in encoding of polymorphic Leibniz equality

$$eq := \lambda A{:}Set\,.\,\lambda a{:}A\,.\,\mathsf{Ind}(X{:}A \rightarrow Prop)\{X\ a\}$$

to represent these equalities. Furthermore we use the standard encodings for conjunction and disjunction, briefly explained in the previous subsection. The types *Prop* and *Set*, also mentioned in the previous subsection, are predefined notions (constants) of Coq, comparable with the star (∗) in systems of the Barendregt-cube [2]. The logical implication and the functional implication are both identified with the arrow of type theory. (As a consequence our proof is intuitionistically valid.)

There are at least two ways to encode the functional behavior of a function $F : A \longrightarrow B$. For instance the sum $+ : \mathbf{Nat} \longrightarrow \mathbf{Nat} \longrightarrow \mathbf{Nat}$ can be defined by

$$\begin{array}{lll} sum & : nat \rightarrow nat \rightarrow nat & \\ s_1 & : \forall x{:}nat\,. & sum\ O\ x \quad = x \\ s_2 & : \forall x,y{:}nat\,. & sum\ (S\,y)\ x = S\,(sum\ y\ x) \end{array}$$

In this case *sum* is just a variable without any computational power. Computing the value of $(sum\ n\ m)$ can be done by the Coq command '*Rewrite* s_1.' or '*Rewrite* s_2.' depending on the value of n. The alternative is to define *sum* as an abbreviation.

$$sum := \lambda x,y{:}nat\,.\,<\!\lambda z{:}nat\,.\,nat\!>\!\mathsf{Match}\ x\ \mathsf{with}\ y\ \lambda z{:}nat\,.\,S \qquad (1)$$

The advantage of the second approach is that one does not have to give any command for computing the value of $(sum\ n\ m)$. Computation in this case is just normalization, and done automatically by the system. Note that Coq can not reduce $(sum\ n\ O)$ to n when n is a variable. In such a case one can do a case analysis on n. We try to use the second approach as much as possible.

In Coq it is allowed to omit the λ-abstraction in $<\!P\!>$Match x with... when $P\,x$ does not actually depend on x. So $<nat>$ Match x with... can replace $<\lambda z : nat\,.\,nat>$ Match x with... in (1). In the sequel we will omit such λ-abstractions.

The main result in the hand-written proof is that there exists a *weak refinement* from automaton *BRP* to automaton *P*. We modified our encodings several times in order to get a better formulation in Coq of this weak refinement property. In the approach that we have chosen eventually, we can represent the function $REF : states(BRP) \longrightarrow states(P)$ by a λ-term like in (1).

Data types The specification of the Bounded Retransmission Protocol makes use of several data types. We represent these types by inhabitants of *Set*.

– the sort **Bool** is represented by the inductive type

$$\begin{aligned} bool &:= \mathsf{Ind}(X\!:\!Set)\{X \mid X\} \\ true &:= \mathsf{Constr}(1, bool) \\ false &:= \mathsf{Constr}(2, bool) \end{aligned}$$

All functions on booleans can be represented by λ-terms. We will write

$\neg x$	for	<*bool*>Match x with *false true*	(negation)
$x \equiv y$	for	<*bool*>Match x with y $(\neg y)$	(equality)
$x \not\equiv y$	for	$\neg(x \equiv y)$	(inequality)
$x \sqcap y$	for	<*bool*>Match x with y *false*	(conjunction)
$x \sqcup y$	for	<*bool*>Match x with *true* y	(disjunction)

– The sort **Data** is represented by the variable $data : Set$. Furthermore we defined a variable *Undefined* : *data* which represents the element $\perp \in$ **Data**.
– The sort **List** is defined as the inductive type with constructors *NIL* and *ADD*, representing ϵ and add respectively. In formula:

$$\begin{aligned} LIST &:= \mathsf{Ind}(X\!:\!Set)\{X \mid data \to X \to X\} \\ NIL &:= \mathsf{Constr}(1, LIST) \\ ADD &:= \mathsf{Constr}(2, LIST) \end{aligned}$$

Functions like hd, tl, ϵ and one can all be represented by λ-terms. For instance

$$\begin{aligned} one := \lambda L\!:\!LIST\,.\ &<\!bool\!>\mathsf{Match}\ L\ \mathsf{with} \\ &false \\ &\lambda d\!:\!data\,.\,\lambda y\!:\!LIST\,.\,\lambda b\!:\!bool\,.\ <\!bool\!>\mathsf{Match}\ y\ \mathsf{with} \\ &\quad true \\ &\quad \lambda d\!:\!data\,.\,\lambda y\!:\!LIST\,.\,\lambda b\!:\!bool\,.\,false \end{aligned}$$

The equalities from Subsection 3.2 are satisfied. All the right-hand-sides are just the normal forms of the left-hand-sides.
– The finite sets **Spc**, **Rpc**, **Conf** and **Ind** are encoded as inductive types in the same style as the booleans. Some versions of Coq can not distinguish inductive types that have the same structure. Choosing different names for such types just introduces different names for the same expression. In particular, finite sets that have the same cardinality are not distinguished. For instance *Spc* and *Rpc* are two abbreviations for the same type $\mathsf{Ind}(X : Set)\{X \mid X \mid X \mid X \mid X\}$. We can prove $SF = WF$ by reflexivity because SF and WF are both the first element of a set of five elements. A typing error $\pi_{Rpc}(\pi_R(x)) = WA$ in one of the invariants was overlooked for a long time.

Similar to the binary operators $\equiv$ and $\not\equiv$ on *bool*, we have defined λ-terms representing $\equiv$ and $\not\equiv$ on *Spc, Rpc, Conf* and *Ind*.

Note: $SF = WF : Prop$ and $SF \equiv WF : bool$.

The actions We define finite sets *act_BRP* and *act_P* representing the sets of actions. We can not use the same name for actions of different automata. Hence we add a prime (′) by those action of automaton P that already occurred in automaton BRP. Constructors of *act_BRP* are $REQ : LIST \rightarrow act\_BRP$, $F : bool \rightarrow bool \rightarrow bool \rightarrow data \rightarrow act\_BRP$, etc. Elements of *act_P* are $REQ' : LIST \rightarrow act\_P$, etc. We add an extra element τ to the inductive set *act_P*. Next we define a term ev (evaluate) which maps actions of BRP to the corresponding actions of P. ($REQ \overset{ev}{\longmapsto} REQ'$, etc.) Internal actions of BRP are mapped to τ.

$$
\begin{array}{ll}
ev := \lambda a : act\_BRP\,.\, \langle act\_P\rangle \mathsf{Match}\ a\ \mathsf{with} & REQ' \\
& \lambda B_1, B_2, B_3 : bool\,.\,\lambda d : data\,.\,\tau \\
& \tau \\
& \lambda B_1, B_2, B_3 : bool\,.\,\tau \\
& \tau \\
& \tau \\
& \tau \\
& CONF' \\
& \tau \\
& \tau \\
& \lambda B_1, B_2, B_3 : bool\,.\,\lambda d : data\,.\,\tau \\
& \lambda B_1, B_2, B_3 : bool\,.\,\tau \\
& IND' \\
& INDn'.
\end{array}
$$

Note that we simply postulate which actions are internal in automaton BRP. One could think of encoding whole the theory about input- and output actions. Given the status of the actions in the components, the status of the actions in the product automaton could then be computed. However, this part of the hand-written proof is not the kind of reasoning where automatic verification pays off.

The state spaces The following step is the definition of types *states_BRP* and *states_P* representing the state spaces of the two automata BRP and P. The state space of BRP is encoded as a cartesian product of cartesian products. $states\_S := Spc \times bool \times \cdots \times bool \times LIST \times nat$. Analogously we define *states_K*, *states_L* and *states_R*. Now $states\_BRP := states\_S \times states\_K \times states\_L \times states\_R$. Finally $states\_P := LIST \times bool \times bool \times bool$.

We use the standard inductive type *prod* [9] with constructor *pair* for the encoding of the cartesian product. When A and B are sets and $(a,b) \in A \times B$ then (a,b) is represented in Coq by $(pair\ A\ B\ a\ b)$. Hence $(a,b,c) \in A \times B \times C$ is represented by $(pair\ A\ (B \times C)\ a\ (pair\ B\ C\ b\ c))$ which is already a bit less friendly. An element of *states_BRP* would cover the whole page. However, we can represent a function $F : A \longrightarrow B \longrightarrow C \longrightarrow (A \times B \times C)$ such that $F(a)(b)$ maps c to (a,b,c) by a λ-term in the style of (1).

$$F := \lambda x : A\,.\,\lambda y : B\,.\,\lambda z : C\,.\,pair\ A\ (B \times C)\ x\ (pair\ B\ C\ y\ z)$$

Then (a, b, c) can be represented by $(F\ a\ b\ c)$. This way we define functions *st_S*, *st_K*, *st_L*, *st_R*, *st_BRP* and *st_P* mapping the components of the state spaces to the corresponding elements in the cartesian products. Furthermore we define projection functions $\pi_{toggle} : states\_S \rightarrow bool$, $\pi_R : states\_BRP \rightarrow states\_R$, etc. For instance

$$\pi_{toggle}\ (st\_S\ B_1\ B_2\ B_3\ B_4\ B_5\ L\ n) \twoheadrightarrow B_3$$
$$\pi_R\ (st\_BRP\ S\ K\ L\ R) \twoheadrightarrow R$$

The weak refinement The mapping *REF* can now be represented by the λ-term below.

$ref := \lambda x : states\_BRP\ .\ (st\_P$

<*LIST*>Match $\pi_{Spc}\ (\pi_S\ x) \equiv ET2\ \sqcup$

$\pi_{Spc}\ (\pi_S\ x) \equiv WT2\ \sqcup$

$\neg\, \pi_{ctoggle}\ (\pi_R\ x)\ \sqcup$

$\pi_{toggle}\ (\pi_S\ x) \equiv \pi_{toggle}\ (\pi_R\ x)$

with $\pi_{list}\ (\pi_S\ x)\quad (tl\ (\pi_{list}\ (\pi_S\ x)))$

$\pi_{busy}\ (\pi_S\ x)$

$\pi_{first}\ (\pi_R\ x)$

$\pi_{Rpc}\ (\pi_R\ x) \equiv NOK$

$\sqcup$

$\pi_{Spc}\ (\pi_S\ x) \equiv ET2\ \sqcap$

$\pi_{timer2\_on}\ (\pi_R\ x)\ \sqcap$

$\neg\ (\pi_{first}\ (\pi_R\ x)))$.

The step relation The next step is the definition of types $step : act\_BRP \rightarrow states\_BRP \rightarrow states\_BRP \rightarrow Prop$ and $step' : act\_P \rightarrow states\_P \rightarrow states\_P \rightarrow Prop$ representing the notion of 'step'. The intended meaning of $step\ a\ s_1\ s_2$ is $s_1 \xrightarrow{a} s_2$. We use an inductive type again.

$$
\begin{aligned}
step := \mathsf{Ind}(X : act\_BRP \rightarrow states\_BRP \rightarrow states\_BRP \rightarrow Prop)\{ & \\
&\forall \sigma : LIST\ .\ \forall s : Spc\ .\ \forall B_1, B_2, B_3, B_4 : bool\ .\\
&\forall L : LIST\ .\ \forall n : nat\ .\\
&\forall s_K : states\_K\ .\ \forall s_L : states\_L\ .\ \forall s_R : states\_R\ .\\
&false = (empty\ \sigma) \rightarrow\\
&(X(REQ\ \sigma)\\
&\quad(st\_BRP\ (st\_S\ s\ false\ B_1\ B_2\ B_3\ B_4\ L\ n)\ s_K\ s_L\ s_R)\\
&\quad(st\_BRP\ (st\_S\ s\ true\ B_1\ B_2\ B_3\ B_4\ \sigma\ n)\ s_K\ s_L\ s_R))\\
|&\\
\vdots&\\
|&\ \cdots\}
\end{aligned}
$$

This enables us to do a case analysis on H when we have a proof $H : (step\ a\ s_1\ s_2)$ in our context and we want to prove $\phi(s_1, s_2)$ for some $s_1, s_2 : states\_BRP$. The first constructor of *step* leads to the following subgoal:

$$\begin{array}{l}
\forall \sigma : LIST\,.\,\forall s : Spc\,.\,\forall B_1, B_2, B_3, B_4 : bool\,.\\
\forall L : LIST\,.\,\forall n : nat\,.\\
\forall s_K : states_K\,.\,\forall s_L : states_L\,.\,\forall s_R : states_R\,.\\
\;false = (empty\ \sigma) \rightarrow\\
\;\phi((st_BRP\ (st_S\ s\ false\ B_1\ B_2\ B_3\ B_4\ L\ n)\ s_K\ s_L\ s_R),\\
\quad (st_BRP\ (st_S\ s\ true\ B_1\ B_2\ B_3\ B_4\ \sigma\ n)\ s_K\ s_L\ s_R))
\end{array}$$

This is the result of matching s_1 and s_2 with the terms of type *states_BRP* on which X is applied in the first–constructor–case of *step* (describing the behavior of the request action).

In our approach we encode directly how the actions affect the product automaton BRP. This way we avoid the problem of encoding how the composition of the automaton BRP out of its components S, K, L and R is organized. The fact that local actions that have the same name are synchronized in the product automaton is difficult to express.

Some actions are split in more than one case. For instance the action B is split into B_1 with extra precondition one(*list*)=true and B_2 with extra precondition one(*list*)=false. This way we obtain 24 constructors for *step*.

Reachability Reachability is encoded as an inductive type, having two constructors. The first constructor encodes the reachability of the initial state. The second constructor encodes the preservation of *reach* under *step*.

$$\begin{array}{rl}
reach := \mathsf{Ind}(X : states_BRP \rightarrow Prop)\{ & \\
& \forall s : states_BRP\,.\,(start\ s) \rightarrow (X\ s)\\
\mid & \forall a : act_BRP\,.\,\forall s_1, s_2 : states_BRP\,.\\
& \quad (step\ a\ s_1\ s_2) \rightarrow (X\ s_1) \rightarrow (X\ s_2)\}
\end{array}$$

where *start* is the predicate on *states_BRP* that holds only for the initial state, also defined inductively:

$$\begin{array}{rl}
start := \mathsf{Ind}(X : states_BRP \rightarrow Prop)\{ & \\
& \forall B_1, B_2, B_3, B_4, B_5, B_6, B_7, B_8, B_9, B_{10}, B_{11} : bool\,.\\
& \forall L : LIST\,.\,\forall d_1, d_2 : data\,.\\
& \;(X\ (st_BRP\\
& \quad (st_S\ SF\ false\ true\ B_1\ false\ false\ L\ O)\\
& \quad (st_K\ B_2\ B_3\ B_4\ false\ d_1)\\
& \quad (st_L\ B_5\ B_6\ B_7\ false)\\
& \quad (st_R\ WF\ B_8\ B_9\ B_{10}\ d_2\ true\ B_{11}\ false\ false\ false)))\}.
\end{array}$$

Assume that we want to prove $\phi(s_0)$ for some s_0:*states_BRP* and that we have a proof R:$(reach\ s_0)$. Eliminating the inductive type *reach* returns two subgoals:

$$\begin{array}{l}
(i)\ : \forall s : states_BRP\,.\,(start\ s) \rightarrow \phi(s)\\
(ii) : \forall a : act_BRP\,.\,\forall s_1, s_2 : states_BRP\,.\\
\qquad (step\ a\ s_1\ s_2) \rightarrow (reach\ s_1) \rightarrow \phi(s_1) \rightarrow \phi(s_2)
\end{array}$$

The first goal can be proved via '*Intros s H ; Elim H*' and the second goal can be proved via '*Intros a* s_1 s_2 *H ; Elim H*' which leads to proving $(reach\ s_1) \rightarrow \phi(s_1) \rightarrow \phi(s_2)$ by a case analysis on the proofterm H of type $(step\ a\ s_1\ s_2)$.

The weak refinement property Assume that we have in *BRP* a transition $s_1 \xrightarrow{a} s_2$ for some external *BRP*-action a, then we must have a transition $REF(s_1) \xrightarrow{a} REF(s_2)$ in automaton P. We are able to express this as

$$(step\ a\ s_1\ s_2) \rightarrow (step'\ (ev\ a)\ (ref\ s_1)\ (ref\ s_2)) \tag{2}$$

When a is an internal action then (2) evaluates to

$$(step\ a\ s_1\ s_2) \rightarrow (step'\ \tau\ (ref\ s_1)\ (ref\ s_2))$$

which we can not prove for there are no constructors of the form $step'\ \tau \ldots$ in the definition of $step'$. When we add a constructor of type $\forall s : states\_P\,.\,(step'\ \tau\ s\ s)$ then we can prove $(step\ a\ s_1\ s_2) \rightarrow (step'\ \tau(ref\ s_1)\ (ref\ s_2))$ iff we can prove $(ref\ s_1) = (ref\ s_2)$. This is exactly what we required so (2) also encodes the weak refinement property when a is internal.

Of course (2) does not have to hold for states that can not be reached. Hence we can add an extra precondition. Furthermore we quantify over the states and the action:

$$\begin{gathered}\forall a : act\_BRP\,.\,\forall s_1, s_2 : states\_BRP\,.\,(reach\ s_1) \rightarrow \\ (step\ a\ s_1\ s_2) \rightarrow (step'\ (ev\ a)\ (ref\ s_1)\ (ref\ s_2))\end{gathered} \tag{3}$$

A weak refinement mapping also has to map initial states to initial states. This is encoded as

$$\forall s : states\_BRP\,.\,(start\ s) \rightarrow (start'\ (ref\ s)) \tag{4}$$

The invariants For proving (3) we have to use the invariants. These invariants are proven valid in the reachable states only. Their formulation is rather straightforward. Below we give the encoded version of invariant *INVR* of Lemma 3. Note that the expression is prefixed by the precondition $(reach\ x)$.

$$\begin{aligned}invr := {} & \forall x : states\_BRP\,.\,(reach\ x) \rightarrow \\ & \quad \pi_{Rpc}(\pi_R\ x) = NOK \rightarrow \\ & \quad \pi_{ctoggle}(\pi_R\ x) = false \\ & \quad \wedge \\ & \quad \pi_{Rpc}(\pi_R\ x) = SI \rightarrow \\ & \quad \pi_{ctoggle}(\pi_R\ x) = true \rightarrow \\ & \quad \pi_{ftoggle}(\pi_R\ x) = \pi_{toggle}(\pi_R\ x) \\ & \quad \wedge \\ & \quad (\pi_{Rpc}(\pi_R\ x) = RTS \vee \pi_{Rpc}(\pi_R\ x) = SA) \rightarrow \\ & \quad (\pi_{ctoggle}(\pi_R\ x) = true \wedge \pi_{ftoggle}(\pi_R\ x) = \neg(\pi_{toggle}(\pi_R\ x)))\end{aligned}$$

4.3 Correctness Proof

Goals Proofs of the invariants and the refinement are essentially by induction over the transitions and split in the corresponding 25 cases (one initial state and 24 transition steps have to be considered). As is to be expected, transitions that do not affect variables that occur in an invariant prove in Coq simply by assumption with the induction hypothesis. Other cases resolve into further subgoals.

In this application of I/O automata, most predicates are equality assertions over state variables and the proofs involve much propositional reasoning. This is best illustrated by means of an example subgoal: Figure 2 shows a Coq goal that occurs when proving invariant *INVR* (Lemma 3). After elimination of reachable states (Section 4.2), Coq has filled in the variables and terms in proper places in the states before and after the transition, in the precondition, and in the invariant. The assertion to prove is on top, below that are the assumptions. This case corresponds to action G in case ($ctoggle \rightarrow t{=}toggle$). The latter condition is expressed by assumption H. Other preconditions of this transition arise as equalities over state variables that have been filled in automatically in the states before and after this transition. H_0 and H_1 assume reachability of these states. H_2 contains the induction hypothesis for the invariant property. The goal to prove is that the property holds for states after a G step.

The goal in Figure 2 decomposes in a number of subgoals. Figure 3 focuses on a particular subgoal. The proposition occurs in the rightmost conjunction of the invariant, viz. $R.pc{\in}\{\mathsf{RTS},\mathsf{SA}\} \rightarrow R.ftoggle{\neq}R.toggle$. H_5 assumes the precondition of this implication. The proof uses assumption H. The induction hypothesis (H_2 in Figure 2) has been decomposed into its constituent conjuncts. Applications of projection functions in the goal and in the assumptions have been reduced to retrieve the appropriate terms.

Many of the goals and subgoals that occur while proving the invariants in this exercise consist of a logical combination of equality statements. The same observation holds for those assumptions in the context that have not yet been eliminated and can be of relevance to the unfinished proof. In nearly all these cases the equality statements are over elements from finite sets. This holds for preconditions of transition steps as well as for predicates in the invariants.

The induction mechanism is often used in this exercise. Induction serves two purposes in the definition of a set: it states that the given elements are the only inhabitants of the set (*no junk* property) and it states that all elements are different (*no confusion* property). Inductively defined finite sets play an important role in the Coq checking of this verification, both to do analysis by cases as well as to distinguish between elements. Analysis by cases is provided directly in Coq via elimination of a variable over the elements of inductive set. Inequality of different elements of an inductively defined finite set is not directly available in Coq but must be derived with the *Match* mechanism. Because the verification described here uses this type of reasoning extensively, it will be

$(RTS = NOK \rightarrow$
$\pi_{ctoggle}(st\_R\ RTS\ f\ l\ t\ d\ B_4\ B_5\ B_6\ B_7\ B_8) = \mathit{false})$
$\wedge$
$(RTS = SI \rightarrow$
$\pi_{ctoggle}(st\_R\ RTS\ f\ l\ t\ d\ B_4\ B_5\ B_6\ B_7\ B_8) = \mathit{true} \rightarrow$
$\pi_{ftoggle}(st\_R\ RTS\ f\ l\ t\ d\ B_4\ B_5\ B_6\ B_7\ B_8) =$
$\pi_{toggle}(st\_R\ RTS\ f\ l\ t\ d\ B_4\ B_5\ B_6\ B_7\ B_8))$
$\wedge$
$((RTS = RTS \vee RTS = SA) \rightarrow$
$\pi_{ctoggle}(st\_R\ RTS\ f\ l\ t\ d\ B_4\ B_5\ B_6\ B_7\ B_8) = \mathit{true}$
$\wedge$
$\pi_{ftoggle}(st\_R\ RTS\ f\ l\ t\ d\ B_4\ B_5\ B_6\ B_7\ B_8) =$
$\neg\pi_{toggle}(st\_R\ RTS\ f\ l\ t\ d\ B_4\ B_5\ B_6\ B_7\ B_8))$

==============================

H_2 : $(WF = NOK \rightarrow$
$\pi_{ctoggle}(st\_R\ WF\ B_1\ B_2\ B_3\ d_1\ B_4\ B_5\ B_6\ B_7\ B_8) = \mathit{false})$
$\wedge$
$(WF = SI \rightarrow$
$\pi_{ctoggle}(st\_R\ WF\ B_1\ B_2\ B_3\ d_1\ B_4\ B_5\ B_6\ B_7\ B_8) = \mathit{true} \rightarrow$
$\pi_{ftoggle}(st\_R\ WF\ B_1\ B_2\ B_3\ d_1\ B_4\ B_5\ B_6\ B_7\ B_8) =$
$\pi_{toggle}(st\_R\ WF\ B_1\ B_2\ B_3\ d_1\ B_4\ B_5\ B_6\ B_7\ B_8))$
$\wedge$
$((WF = RTS \vee WF = SA) \rightarrow$
$\pi_{ctoggle}(st\_R\ WF\ B_1\ B_2\ B_3\ d_1\ B_4\ B_5\ B_6\ B_7\ B_8) = \mathit{true}$
$\wedge$
$\pi_{ftoggle}(st\_R\ WF\ B_1\ B_2\ B_3\ d_1\ B_4\ B_5\ B_6\ B_7\ B_8) =$
$\neg\pi_{toggle}(st\_R\ WF\ B_1\ B_2\ B_3\ d_1\ B_4\ B_5\ B_6\ B_7\ B_8))$
H_1 : $reach\ \ (st\_BRP\ s_S\ (st\_K\ f\ l\ t\ \mathit{false}\ d)\ s_L$
$(st\_R\ RTS\ f\ l\ t\ d\ B_4\ B_5\ B_6\ B_7\ B_8))$
H_0 : $reach\ \ (st\_BRP\ s_S\ (st\_K\ f\ l\ t\ \mathit{true}\ d)\ s_L$
$(st\_R\ WF\ B_1\ B_2\ B_3\ d_1\ B_4\ B_5\ B_6\ B_7\ B_8))$
H : $\sim(B_6 = \mathit{true} \rightarrow B_5 = t)$
s_L : $states\_L$
s_S : $states\_S$
$d\ d_1$: $data$
$B_1\ B_2\ B_3\ B_4\ B_5\ B_6\ B_7\ B_8$: $bool$
$f\ l\ t$: $bool$
S : $step\ a\ s_1\ s_2$
$s_1\ s_2$: $states\_BRP$
a : act_BRP
R : $reach\ x$
x : $states\_BRP$

Fig. 2. Characteristic Coq subgoal for this application. The assertion to prove is on top, the assumptions are below. The goal forms part of the obligation to prove that transition G preserves invariant $INVR$ (Lemma 3). H_2 assumes the invariant property holds for states that enable this transition step. The assertion to prove is that the property holds for states after the transition.

$t = \neg B_5$

$$
\begin{array}{ll}
\hline\hline
H_5 & : RTS = RTS \vee RTS = SA \\
H_4 & : (WF = RTS \vee WF = SA) \rightarrow (B_6 = true \wedge B_3 = \neg B_5) \\
H_3 & : WF = SI \rightarrow B_6 = true \rightarrow B_3 = B_5 \\
H_2 & : WF = NOK \rightarrow B_6 = false \\
H_1 & : reach\ \ (st\_BRP\ s_S\ (st\_K\ f\ l\ t\ false\ d)\ s_L \\
 & \qquad\qquad\qquad (st\_R\ RTS\ f\ l\ t\ d\ B_4\ B_5\ B_6\ B_7\ B_8)) \\
H_0 & : reach\ \ (st\_BRP\ s_S\ (st\_K\ f\ l\ t\ true\ d)\ s_L \\
 & \qquad\qquad\qquad (st\_R\ WF\ B_1\ B_2\ B_3\ d_1\ B_4\ B_5\ B_6\ B_7\ B_8)) \\
H & : \sim(B_6 = true \rightarrow B_5 = t) \\
s_L & : states\_L \\
s_S & : states\_S \\
d\ d_1 & : data \\
\multicolumn{2}{l}{B_1\ B_2\ B_3\ B_4\ B_5\ B_6\ B_7\ B_8 : bool} \\
f\ l\ t & : bool \\
S & : step\ a\ s_1\ s_2 \\
s_1\ s_2 & : states\_BRP \\
a & : act\_BRP \\
R & : reach\ x \\
x & : states\_BRP
\end{array}
$$

Fig. 3. A subgoal of the goal in Figure 2. The proof uses assumption H.

illustrated by means of a small example. We inductively define a finite set S and a predicate that discriminates its elements:

Inductive Definition $S : Set = a : S \mid b : S \mid c : S$.

Definition $neq\_S = \lambda x, y{:}S\,.$ <*Prop*>Match x with
(<*Prop*>Match y with *False True True*)
(<*Prop*>Match y with *True False True*)
(<*Prop*>Match y with *True True False*)

I.e., $(neq\_S\ x\ y)$ reduces to *False* if $x{=}y{=}a$ or $x{=}y{=}b$ or $x{=}y{=}c$ and it reduces to *True* otherwise. It serves to prove the desired inequalities $\sim(a{=}b)$, $\sim(a{=}c)$, etc. Instead of deriving and naming all n^2 lemmas for an n-ary set, we prove the following generalized lemma to derive contradictions:

$$\forall x, y{:}S\,.\,(x = y) \rightarrow (neq\_S\ x\ y) \rightarrow \forall P{:}Prop\,.\,P$$

Such a lemma is derived for all inductive sets. Suppose the lemma is named *absurd_S*. The latter is then used extensively to resolve goals with an inconsistent equality assumption in the context, say $a{=}b$. The following Coq tactical solves such goals immediately:

$$Apply\ (absurd\_S\ a\ b)\ ;\ [Assumption \mid Simpl\ ;\ Exact\ I] \tag{5}$$

For invariants that are proved by induction over transition steps, sometimes a majority of the subgoals prove by contradiction because they assume $a=b$ for different a and b from an inductive set.

Tacticals Both tactics and tacticals have been used in the proof-checking. Coq tacticals are composed of tactics and they can be used to apply at once a combination of rules. They can also be used to accomplish a limited form of proof search. Such tacticals have been written for five of the invariants in this application. One generic tactical was developed to decompose and investigate several lemmas. After case distinction over 25 cases (initial state and 24 transition steps), the tactical attempts to decompose these cases by elimination of logical connectives until only simple goals are left, where the assertion to prove is an equality assertion. For our invariants, typically some 50-100 simple goals are left then. Many of these are solved automatically by assumption, reflexivity or by means of an inconsistent equality statement in the context. For the invariants above, only a handful of non-trivial goals then remain to be solved by the user.

To achieve a form of search, the tacticals are mainly composed of combinations of the ";" and "*Orelse*" tacticals explained below.

$tactical_1$; $tactical_2$; $tactical_3$

This applies $tactical_2$ to the subgoals generated by $tactical_1$ and $tactical_3$ to those that are generated by $tactical_2$.

$tactical_1$ *Orelse* $tactical_2$ *Orelse* $tactical_3$

This tries to apply $tactical_1$. If that fails, $tactical_2$ is applied. If that fails, $tactical_3$ is applied. Coq tactical building blocks are fairly elementary. A definition mechanism or parameterization is not provided. This could be convenient for this application, since it would allow often recurring tacticals like (5) to be written very compactly.

The current Coq tactical language has no variables and pattern matching. As a consequence, tacticals must be tailored to the overall structure of goals if they are used for proof search. Because of this, writing a tactical proof often is as much effort as writing the corresponding tactic proof. Currently, the advantage of such tacticals is mainly that it is easier to adapt them than to adapt tactic proofs: tactical proofs are less affected when invariants or automata are modified.

5 Discussion

The main objectives of this work have been fulfilled: the protocol has been verified and the verification (at least the safety part of it) has been proof-checked. Although the Bounded Retransmission Protocol is small, it is by no means trivial and the efforts involved are considerable. While the PSF specification and simulation activity have been carried out in only two man-weeks, the manual verification took roughly two man-months (including write-up) and the proof-checking took more than three man-months. Part of the latter effort is due to a learning effect. Analysis of the Bounded Retransmission Protocol is not completed: the original protocol has an additional *disconnect* service that allows the sender and the receiver to disrupt an ongoing communication. This service has been neglected here and will be verified later. Apart from this, the protocol as described and verified in this paper contains most of the characteristics of the real protocol. It should be noted however that the model simplifies the real-time aspects of the protocol by the way timers are encoded. We could have modeled these real-time aspects more realistically by using a real-time extension of the I/O automata model (see [5]), but then the verification would have been much more involved.

Importance of the verification The verification has answered a number of questions about the protocol. Foremost, it proves that the data link protocol is free of design errors. An important result of the work is that it has corrected several inconsistencies, ambiguities, and omissions in the semi-formal original specification of the protocol. For instance, the exercise has pinned down the behavior of the *toggle* bit between subsequent messages and has formalized many assumptions that were previously left implicit. In addition, the correctness criterion given in the I/O automaton model formalizes the protocol service requirements, i.e., the required external behavior of the protocol.

The automaton specification also serves as a precise functional description for protocol implementations. In this description, all kind of important questions for implementors have been answered, like : "Can I send an empty message?", "How to respond if a request comes before the previous request is completed?", "What is the start value of the *toggle* bit for subsequent messages?". These issues are important if protocol implementations have to be developed by different programmers at different locations, as is the case with this protocol.

Other protocol properties are confirmed by the automaton model. For instance, invariant $INVK'$ (Lemma 5) proves that the use of the bit named *first* in data frames is redundant, because the receiver can always predict its value. This is consistent with the situation in the X.25 LAPB protocol [6] that has no comparable field and that uses a *more_data* bit only, which corresponds to the (inverted) bit named *last* in the Bounded Retransmission Protocol. Further, the automaton model confirms that the *first*, *last* and *toggle* bits from the header of acknowledgements are irrelevant for correctness.

Proof-checking with Coq The experiences with the Coq system are positive. The Coq system 5.8 is robust and reliable and is well-documented. Most shortcomings are related to the ASCII interface: it is easy to lose the overall picture when dealing with large contexts and large proofs.

The Coq proof-checking confirms that the verification is correct. It was not first-time right though and the proof-checking has corrected a number of draft versions. Both the verification and the specification have been revised several times. Other corrections relate to various errors and inaccuracies in versions of the manuscript proof. Preliminary versions of six invariants required modification. One invariant proved false and required weakening. In four cases the original invariants were probably valid but the proof-checking revealed that they needed strengthening (induction loading) to admit a proof. In several cases small modifications to the automaton were necessary to admit a missing proof. Much of the checking was done while parts of the proof were still under development and certain errors must therefore be ascribed to the iterative approach that characterizes the development of automata proofs. Usually the manuscript proof was followed, unless obvious simplifications were seen. For one invariant the use of tacticals simplified a handwritten proof by abstaining from the application of two other invariants that were used in the manuscript proof.

If this application is characteristic of I/O automata proofs — and this seems to be the case — then I/O automata verifications could benefit from proof search procedures. Many (sub-)proofs are truly elementary. It must be stressed that this quality does not come for free. In I/O automata verifications the crucial and most difficult part is *finding* the proper automata, the weak refinement relation and the invariants. This is an iterative process that can benefit from proof search support. Proof search can be used in two ways: it can speed up the checking of manuscript proofs but it can also speed up their development. The Coq system is currently designed as a proof-checker and not as a theorem prover. Accordingly, the system was used in this exercise to check versions of the manuscript proof and the system was not explicitly exploited in the development of the proof. The tacticals written for this application indicate that it is feasible to reduce conjectures of invariants to a few non-trivial or impossible subgoals for the user. Most proof obligations in this application require very specific and elementary reasoning. It seems that additional tactical building blocks can be of great help for future I/O automata verifications. Such tacticals can facilitate the proof-checking but they may also be used in the development of the proofs.

Modeling I/O automata in type theory Modeling the Bounded Retransmission Protocol automata, the invariants and the weak refinement proof in type theory (Coq's Inductive Calculus of Constructions) posed no problem. The translation into type theory that has been used skips much of the generic notions of I/O automata introduced in Section 3.1, like action signatures and explicit sets of states and transitions, but instead directly encodes these notions for this particular application. An important question is if this encoding is satisfactory or how it can be improved upon. An advantage of the current mapping to type theory is that it closely follows the application and directly supports the checking of the invariants and the refinement proof. While this encoding thus facilitates the operational checking, it also amalgamates the automata theory and the application which makes it difficult to reuse much of the Coq text for other applications.

An interesting option is to use a more general encoding of automata theory, together with a compact application description similar to the specification in Section 3.2. This can lead to an approach that is more flexible because it allows reuse of the theory part for different applications. Also, the simpler application description is less error-prone. The current encoding is tailored towards the proving of invariants and weak refinement relations. Absence of deadlock has to be defined specifically for this application and cannot be reconstructed easily from the transition steps. In an approach that explicitly models the meta theory of I/O automata, such properties can be defined independent of the particular application. A disadvantage of that approach is the extra theory level that enforces more elaborate and indirect proofs. Automatic translation of a combined meta theory encoding together with a particular application description into one application-specific encoding seems desirable, in order to obtain the advantages of the latter. The translation can be within Coq or part of a preprocessor. One may even want to use different translations for different purposes. Some of these options are currently investigated by the authors.

Related work Recently, there has been a growing interest in proof-checking protocol correctness proofs, see for instance [4, 8]. Since it is impossible to give here a complete overview of all the work in this area, we will only mention some papers that are directly related to our work, either by the choice of the concurrency formalism or by the choice of the proof-checking system.

Nipkow [23] verified two implementations of a memory system and a mutual exclusion algorithm using the theorem prover Isabelle [25]. The verifications were done both in a setting of algebraic data types (using data refinement) and in the I/O automaton model (using simulation relations). Loewenstein and Dill [17] verified a multiprocessor cache protocol using simulation relations and HOL, the Higher-Order Logic of [11]. This case study is similar in spirit to the one of Nipkow but more involved. Engberg, Grønning and Lamport [10] report on a tool that translates proofs in Lamport's Temporal Logic of Actions to input for LP, the Larch Prover of [13]. A few simple examples were verified using the tool, including a spanning tree algorithm. In these examples the mechanically checkable proofs written in the translator were only two to three times longer than careful hand proofs. Søgaard-Andersen et.al. [26] formalized a simple I/O automata verification of a communication protocol using the LP verification system. They report that, after all the basic machinery of the I/O automata model has been formalized, as well as the basic data types employed by the protocol, the use of LP even leads to a reduction in the size of the proofs. However, their example is quite simple (there is no need to establish state invariants) and it remains to generalize these results to larger examples. Bezem and Groote [3] have used Coq to check a verification of the alternating bit protocol in process algebra. Their proofs are essentially based on rewriting. Recently, Groote and Van de Pol [12] have also verified the Bounded Retransmission Protocol in process algebra using Coq. Whether one prefers process algebra or the I/O automata model appears to be a matter of taste, and in order to evaluate the relative merits of both approaches we will have to consider more and bigger examples. Martin Hofmann [14] in Edinburgh has checked a verification of the Alternating Bit Protocol with LEGO [18]. His verification is based on a functional approach and uses stream transformers.

All of the above researchers arrive at approximately the same conclusion: mechanically checking of protocol verifications is feasible and highly promising, but the current proof-checkers are not optimal: we need an improved user interface (along the lines of [10]) and better proof search procedures.

Acknowledgements

The authors wish to thank Thijs Winter for specifying and simulating the protocol. Doeko Bosscher investigated the state space of the protocol using the Concurrency Workbench [7], and in this way corrected an error in an early version of the specification. Final gratitude goes to Jan Friso Groote, Rob Jansen and Hans Oerlemans for several discussions on the subject.

References

1. K. Apt, N. Francez, and S. Katz. Appraising fairness in languages for distributed programming. *Distributed Computing*, 2:226–241, 1988.
2. H. Barendregt. Lambda calculi with types. In S. Abramsky, D. Gabbay, and T. Maibaum, editors, *Handbook of Logic in Computer Science*, pages 117–309. Oxford University Press, 1992.
3. M. Bezem and J. Groote. A formal verification of the alternating bit protocol in the calculus of constructions. Logic Group Preprint Series 88, Dept. of Philosophy, Utrecht University, Mar. 1993.
4. G. v. Bochmann and D. Probst, editors. *Proceedings of the 4th International Conference on Computer Aided Verification*, volume 663 of *Lecture Notes in Computer Science*. Springer-Verlag, 1992.
5. D. Bosscher, I. Polak, and F. Vaandrager. Verification of an audio control protocol. Report CS-R94XX, CWI, Amsterdam, 1994. In preparation.
6. CCITT Fascicle VIII.3. *CCITT Recommendation X.25. Interface between DTE and DCE for Terminals Operating in the Packet Mode on Public Data Networks*, 1988.
7. R. Cleaveland, J. Parrow, and B. Steffen. The concurrency workbench: A semantics based tool for the verification of concurrent systems. *ACM Trans. Prog. Lang. Syst.*, 1(15):36–72, 1993.
8. C. Courcoubetis, editor. *Proceedings of the 5th International Conference on Computer Aided Verification,* Elounda, Greece, June/July 1993, volume 697 of *Lecture Notes in Computer Science*. Springer-Verlag, 1993.
9. G. Dowek, A. Felty, H. Herbelin, G. Huet, C. Murthy, C. Parent, C. Paulin-Mohring, and B. Werner. The Coq proof assistant user's guide. Version 5.8. Technical report, INRIA – Rocquencourt, May 1993.
10. U. Engberg, P. Grønning, and L. Lamport. Mechanical verification of concurrent systems with TLA. In Bochmann and Probst [4].
11. M. Gordon. HOL: a proof generating system for higher-order logic. In G. Birtwistle and P. Subrahmanyam, editors, *VLSI Specification, Verification and Synthesis.* Kluwer Academic Publishers, 1988.
12. J. Groote and J. van de Pol. A bounded retransmission protocol for large data packets. Logic Group Preprint Series 100, Dept. of Philosophy, Utrecht University, Oct. 1993.

13. J. Guttag and J. Horning. *Larch: Languages and Tools for Formal Specification.* Springer-Verlag, 1993.
14. M. Hofmann. *Extensional Concepts in Intensional Type Theory.* PhD thesis, University of Edinburgh, 1994. Forthcoming.
15. B. Jonsson. *Compositional Verification of Distributed Systems.* PhD thesis, Department of Computer Systems, Uppsala University, 1987. DoCS 87/09.
16. L. Lamport. How to write a proof. Research Report 94, Digital Equipment Corporation, Systems Research Center, Feb. 1993.
17. P. Loewenstein and D. Dill. Verification of a multiprocessor cache protocol using simulation relations and higher-order logic (summary). In E. Clarke and R. Kurshan, editors, *Proceedings of the 2nd International Conference on Computer-Aided Verification,* New Brunswick, NJ, USA June 1990, volume 531 of *Lecture Notes in Computer Science*, pages 302–311. Springer-Verlag, 1991.
18. Z. Luo, R. Pollack, and P. Taylor. How to use LEGO. Technical Report LFCS-TN-27, University of Edinburgh, Edinburgh, Scotland, Oct. 1989.
19. N. Lynch and M. Tuttle. Hierarchical correctness proofs for distributed algorithms. In *Proceedings of the* 6th *Annual ACM Symposium on Principles of Distributed Computing,* pages 137–151, Aug. 1987. A full version is available as MIT Technical Report MIT/LCS/TR-387.
20. N. Lynch and M. Tuttle. An introduction to input/output automata. *CWI Quarterly,* 2(3):219–246, Sept. 1989.
21. N. Lynch and F. Vaandrager. Forward and backward simulations – part I: Untimed systems. Report CS-R9313, CWI, Amsterdam, Mar. 1993.
22. S. Mauw and G. Veltink, editors. *Algebraic Specification of Communication Protocols.* Cambridge Tracts in Theoretical Computer Science 36. Cambridge University Press, 1993.
23. T. Nipkow. Formal verification of data type refinement — theory and practice. In J. de Bakker, W. d. Roever, and G. Rozenberg, editors, *Proceedings REX Workshop on Stepwise Refinement of Distributed Systems: Models, Formalism, Correctness,* Mook, The Netherlands, May/June 1989, volume 430 of *Lecture Notes in Computer Science*, pages 561–591. Springer-Verlag, 1990.
24. C. Paulin-Mohring. Inductive definitions in the system Coq. Rules and properties. In M. Bezem and J. Groote, editors, *Proceedings of the* 1st *International Conference on Typed Lambda Calculi and Applications, TCLA'93,* Utrecht, The Netherlands, volume 664 of *Lecture Notes in Computer Science*, pages 328–345. Springer-Verlag, 1993.
25. L. Paulson. Isabelle: The next 700 theorem provers. In P. Odifreddi, editor, *Logic and Computer Science.* Academic Press, 1989.
26. J. Søgaard-Andersen, S. Garland, J. Guttag, N. Lynch, and A. Pogosyants. Computer-assisted simulation proofs. In Courcoubetis [8], pages 305–319.
27. A. Tanenbaum. *Computer networks.* Prentice-Hall International, Englewood Cliffs, 1981.

Elimination of extensionality in Martin-Löf type theory

Martin Hofmann

Department of Computer Science, University of Edinburgh
JCMB, KB, Mayfield Rd., Edinburgh EH9 3JZ, Scotland

Abstract. We construct a syntactic model of intensional Martin-Löf type theory in which two pointwise propositionally equal functions are propositionally equal themselves. In the model types are interpreted as types equipped with equivalence relations; the identity type at each type is interpreted as the associated relation. The interpretation function from the syntax to the model gives rise to a procedure which replaces all instances of the identity type by suitable relations defined by induction on the type structure and thereby eliminates instances of an axiom which states that pointwise propositionally equal functions are propositionally equal themselves. We also sketch how "quotient types" can be interpreted.

1 Martin-Löf's identity type

Martin-Löf introduced the *identity type* in order to internalise the notion of definitional equality [11]. For any two terms M, N of some type A a type $\mathrm{Eq}_A(M, N)$ is introduced, which should ideally be inhabited iff M and N are definitionally equal. This is achieved by the following rules.

$$\frac{\Gamma \vdash A}{\Gamma,\ x, y{:}A \vdash \mathrm{Eq}_A(x, y)}\ \textsc{Eq-Form}$$

$$\frac{\Gamma \vdash M : A}{\Gamma \vdash \mathrm{refl}_A(M) : \mathrm{Eq}_A(M, M)}\ \textsc{Eq-Intro}$$

$$\frac{\begin{array}{l}\Gamma,\ x, y{:}A,\ p{:}\mathrm{Eq}_A(x, y) \vdash C(x, y, p)\\ \Gamma,\ x{:}A \vdash M : C(x, x, \mathrm{refl}_A(x))\end{array}}{\Gamma,\ x, y{:}A,\ p{:}\mathrm{Eq}_A(x, y) \vdash \mathrm{J}_C(M) : C(x, y, p)}\ \textsc{Eq-Elim-J}$$

$$\frac{\begin{array}{l}\Gamma,\ x{:}A,\ p{:}\mathrm{Eq}_A(x, x) \vdash C(x, p)\\ \Gamma,\ x{:}A \vdash M : C(x, \mathrm{refl}_A(x))\end{array}}{\Gamma,\ x{:}A,\ p{:}\mathrm{Eq}_A(x, x) \vdash \mathrm{K}_C(M) : C(x, p)}\ \textsc{Eq-Elim-K}$$

and equality rules

$$\begin{array}{ll}\mathrm{J}_C(M)(x, x, \mathrm{refl}_A(x)) = M(x) & \textsc{Eq-Comp-J}\\ \mathrm{K}_C(M)(x, \mathrm{refl}_A(x)) = M(x) & \textsc{Eq-Comp-K}\end{array}$$

Notation. Here and in the sequel we write $\Gamma \vdash A$ to express that A is a type in context Γ. Round brackets with commas are used to denote free variables and substitution in an informal way. So $\mathrm{Eq}_A(x, y)$ could also be written Eq_A if we do not want to emphasize the two particular free variables, and $\mathrm{Eq}_A(M, N)$ is a shorthand for $\mathrm{Eq}_A[x := M][y := N]$. We also use parentheses with informal pattern-matching for the definition of types and terms, so for example $C(x : A, y : B(x)) := \ldots$ defines a type C in the context $x : A, y : B(x)$. If the types A and B are clear from the context we also write $C(x, y) := \ldots$ or even $C(y) := \ldots$ since x can be inferred from the type of y. If several variables of one and the same type are declared in a context we write the type only once. So $x, y : A$ declares two variables of type A. We occasionally omit subscripts in type and term formers like Eq_A if they are clear from the context.

The eliminator J is the one originally used by Martin-Löf [11]. It expresses in an intensional way that the only elements of an identity type are those of the form $\mathrm{refl}_A(-)$: A predicate (C) over an identity type which holds for the canonical elements $\mathrm{refl}_S(-)$ holds everywhere. The homogeneous eliminator K has later been added by Streicher [13] with the aim to make any two elements of an identity type propositionally equal. The proof that with K any two terms of an identity type are propositionally equal is straightforward and may e.g. be found in [13]. One can show that this property fails in the pure theory without K. Various applications for K and metatheoretical properties of K can be found in loc. cit.

We say that two terms M, N of type A in context Γ are *propositionally equal* if there exists a term P such that

$$\Gamma \vdash P : \mathrm{Eq}_A(M, N)$$

is derivable. On the other hand if

$$\Gamma \vdash M = N : A$$

is derivable we call M and N *definitionally equal*. This latter equality also makes sense for types.

Except in the empty context the propositional equality is strictly coarser than definitional equality. This means that if

$$\Gamma \vdash P : \mathrm{Eq}_A(M, N)$$

it is not necessarily the case that

$$\Gamma \vdash M = N : A$$

The reason is that P might have been obtained by induction on some free variable in Γ. If one forces the two notions of equality to agree by adding the *equality reflection rule*

$$\frac{\Gamma \vdash P : \mathrm{Eq}_A(M, N)}{\Gamma \vdash M = N : A}$$

as is done in extensional type theory [9] then type checking becomes undecidable. Intuitively this is because the proof term P is lost upon application of this rule. For this and other reasons the equality reflection rule was later rejected by Martin-Löf. The identity type without the reflection *rule* is called *intensional*. It is the subject of this paper.

In the empty context equality reflection is admissible, though. Indeed if

$$\vdash P : \mathrm{Eq}_A(M, N)$$

then by strong normalisation we must have that P is of the form $\mathrm{refl}_A(\_)$ and thus $\vdash M = N$. This property is called *equality reflection principle*. It is commonly considered as the characteristic property of propositional identity [7] and is thus required to be respected by possible extensions to the theory. Below we will argue against the equality reflection principle and propose to "specify" propositional equality by a Leibniz principle.

1.1 The strength and the weakness of the intensional identity type

The above formulation of the identity type captures most of the rules governing definitional equality. Apart from reflexivity, symmetry, and transitivity, in particular the substitution rule for dependent types

$$\frac{\begin{array}{l}\Gamma, x : A \vdash B(x) \\ \Gamma \vdash M = N : A \\ \Gamma \vdash U : B(M)\end{array}}{\Gamma \vdash U : B(N)}\ \textsc{Dep-Subst}$$

is reflected in that from J we can define an operator Subst_B, such that if $M, N : A$ and $P : \mathrm{Eq}_A(M, N)$ then if $U : B(M)$ then $\mathrm{Subst}_B(P, U)$ is an element of type $B(N)$. We first define the type C with which J gets instantiated by

$$C(x, y{:}A,\ p{:}\mathrm{Eq}_A(x, y)) := B(x) \to B(y)$$

and the premise to J by

$$H(x : A) := \lambda u : B(x).u) : C(x, x, \mathrm{refl}_A(x))$$

Now we can define Subst_B as

$$\mathrm{Subst}_B(P, U) := \mathrm{J}_C(H)(M, N, P)\, U$$

In other words, in order to get a function from $B(x)$ to $B(y)$ in the presence of a proof $P{:}\mathrm{Eq}_A(x, y)$ it is enough to give an inhabitant of that type with x and y identified, and here the identity function does the job.

From the equality rule Eq-Comp-J we can deduce that

$$\mathrm{Subst}_B(\mathrm{refl}(M), U) = U$$

Moreover, using J and K we can show that these Subst functions are *coherent*, i.e. they do not depend on the proof P and any diagram formed out of these functions commutes up to propositional equality

Also all the congruence rules for definitional equality hold for the identity type, with the exception of the ξ-rule

$$\frac{\Gamma,\ x{:}A \vdash M = N : B(x)}{\Gamma \vdash \lambda x{:}A.M = \lambda x{:}A.N : \Pi x{:}A.B}$$

which is not provable for propositional equality. This means that from a proof of pointwise equality of two (dependent) functions

$$\Gamma,\ x{:}A \vdash P(x) : \mathrm{Eq}_{B(x)}(F(x), G(x))$$

we cannot in general conclude their propositional equality, i.e. we cannot find an inhabitant of the type

$$\Gamma \vdash \mathrm{Eq}_{\Pi x:A.B(x)}(\lambda x{:}A.F(x), \lambda x{:}A.G(x))$$

The reason for this lies in the equality reflection *principle*, i.e. equality reflection in the empty context. If the ξ-rule held propositionally then e.g. from a proof

$$x : \mathrm{N} \vdash P(x) : \mathrm{Eq}_{\mathrm{N}}(F(x), G(x))$$

that F and G are pointwise equal functions on the natural numbers we could deduce an inhabitant of

$$\vdash \mathrm{Eq}_{\mathrm{N}\to\mathrm{N}}(\lambda x{:}\mathrm{N}.F(x), \lambda x{:}\mathrm{N}.G(x))$$

But then, since equality reflection holds in the empty context, we could conclude that F and G are definitionally equal. This is a contradiction because definitional equality is decidable and pointwise equality of functions is undecidable.

This argument not only shows that the propositional ξ-rule is not derivable, but also that any extension to the theory which includes the propositional ξ-rule must necessarily violate the equality reflection principle, i.e. there may be terms which are propositionally equal in the empty context without being definitionally equal.

We thus propose to give up the reflection principle as the defining property of propositional equality and instead to understand propositional equality as *substitutability in every context* in the sense that whenever M is propositionally equal to N and $C(M)$ is inhabited then so is $C(N)$ in a canonical way.

Now two pointwise equal functions are indeed substitutable for one another in every context except in one arising from the identity type itself. Clearly if $F(x)$ and $G(x)$ are pointwise propositionally equal and $C(f) = \mathrm{Eq}(f, \lambda x{:}A.F(x))$ then $C(\lambda x{:}A.F(x))$ is inhabited by reflexivity, but $C(\lambda x{:}A.G(x))$ is not, for this would entail the propositional ξ-rule.

So we propose to add a new family of constants to the theory

$$\frac{\Gamma, x : A \vdash P : \mathrm{Eq}_{B(x)}(F(x), G(x))}{\Gamma \vdash \mathrm{Ext}_{A,B}(P) : \mathrm{Eq}_{\Pi x:A.B(x)}(\lambda x : \sigma.F(x), \lambda x : \sigma.G(x))}$$

which both achieves (via Subst) substitutability of pointwise equal functions in every context, and repairs the just mentioned problem with the particular context $\mathrm{Eq}(-, \lambda x.G(x))$. This is essentially the solution proposed by Turner in [14]. Its serious drawback, immediately pointed out by Martin-Löf in a subsequent discussion also in [14] is that this introduces noncanonical elements in each type, since we have not specified, how the eliminators J and K should behave when applied to a proof having Ext as outermost constructor. For example, consider the (constant) family $f : A \to B \vdash \mathrm{N}$. Now if $x : A \vdash P(x) : \mathrm{Eq}(F\,x, G\,x)$ for two functions $F, G : \mathrm{N} \to \mathrm{N}$ then $\mathrm{Subst}\,(\mathrm{Ext}\,(P), 0)$ is an element of N in the empty context which does not reduce to canonical form. One might try to find suitable reduction rules for Ext under which this term would for example reduce to 0. Yet no satisfactory set of such rules has been found to date. Notice, however, that we can show that the term in question is ***propositionally equal*** to 0 because using J we can "replace" $\mathrm{Ext}\,(P)$ by an instance of refl.

In loc. cit. Turner proposes to add the (definitional) equation

$$\mathrm{Ext}\,(H) = \mathrm{refl}_{\Pi x:A.B(x)}(\lambda x : A.F(x))$$

where

$$H(x : A) := \mathrm{refl}_{B(x)}(F(x))$$

i.e. if we use Ext only to establish equality of definitionally equal terms then we may use refl straightaway. The equation is incomplete e.g. because even in its presence the above term is not equal to 0 or any other canonical natural number. As an example for the use of K we show how this equation holds ***propositionally***. We instantiate K with

$$C(f : \Pi x{:}A.B(x),\ p{:}\mathrm{Eq}(f, f)) := \mathrm{Eq}(p, \mathrm{refl}(f))$$

and thus reduce the task of proving the equation for $P := \mathrm{Ext}\,(\ldots)$ to the task of proving it for $P := \mathrm{refl}(\ldots)$ in which case it is an instance of reflexivity. This property does not seem to be provable using J alone because the family we are eliminating over only makes sense for Eq restricted to the diagonal.

Let us now come back to the problem of the noncanonical elements introduced by Ext . The solution we are going to describe in this paper consists of a post-hoc translation of proofs containing Ext into ones in the pure theory in which every occurrence of the identity type will be replaced by an equality relation defined by induction on the type structure. On basic inductive types like N this relation will be the identity type itself, but for example on the type $\mathrm{N} \to \mathrm{N}$ it will be pointwise equality and so on.

This translation is performed by constructing a syntactic model for type theory including Ext in which types are types with relations and dependent types are dependent types together with dependent relations and substitution functions. The interpretation of the identity type in the model is basically the relation associated to each type, which is why the propositional ξ-rule holds in the model. Of course in the translation every functional variable in a context comes equipped with an additional assumption that it respects these relations, so contexts must be translated, too.

Given this translation we may view the type theory with Ext as a meta- or macro-language for a theory in which equality is defined along the type structure and in which every substitution must be validated by a tedious proof of substitutivity. Through the interpretation in the model (which can be implemented on a machine) these substitutivity proofs are generated automatically.

For the nondependent case and predicate logic this method is well-known, in [2] it is attributed to Gandy, cf. also [6]. The idea of interpreting type theory with extensionality assumptions in pure intensional type theory was put forward by Martin-Löf during the discussion in [14], but to the best of our knowledge this idea has never been pursued.

The paper is organised as follows. In the next section we look at the nondependent case first and then lay down the interpretation of contexts, dependent types, and terms. In sections 3 and 4 we describe the interpretation of the dependent product and of the intensional identity types for which the propositional ξ-rule holds. This intensional identity type comes in two versions. In the first one the equality rules EQ-COMP-J and EQ-COMP-K only hold propositionally. This means that although in the model the two terms on either side of these equations are not equal, the corresponding identity type receives a nonempty interpretation. In the second more complicated version the two equations do hold. With the simpler version we can thus interpret a theory where the rules EQ-COMP-J and EQ-COMP-K are replaced by constants witnessing their propositional companions.

Section 5 sketches the interpretation of other type formers in particular universes and quotient types. In some of these problems similar to those with the identity type occur. Certain equations only hold propositionally. So when doing proofs in the "macro-language" we have to accept that we sometimes have to use explicit instances of Subst where in the pure theory an automatic conversion by rule DEP-SUBST does the job.

Section 6 contains several conclusive remarks and mentions an existing Lego-implementation of the model.

2 The setoid model

We shall now describe the syntactic model in detail, and show that its structure suffices to interpret all of intensional type theory including Ext. The underlying syntactic system is intensional Martin-Löf type theory without universes as described in [11]. Our presentation is clearly influenced by "categorical type theory" as described e.g. in [4, 12]; we try, however, to avoid categorical terminology as far as possible and we assume (almost) no knowledge of category theory. For the *cognoscenti*: we construct a "category with attributes" in the sense of Cartmell [1], see also [5].

For expository reasons we start with the interpretation of nondependent types which later appear as special cases.

2.1 Setoids

Definition 1. A *setoid* S is a quadruple $(S_{\mathrm{set}}, S_{\mathrm{rel}}, S_{\mathrm{sym}}, S_{\mathrm{trans}})$ where S_{set} is a type in the empty context

$$\vdash S_{\mathrm{set}}$$

together with a "binary relation" S_{rel}

$$s, s'{:}S_{\mathrm{set}} \vdash S_{\mathrm{rel}}(s, s')$$

which is proven symmetric and transitive by S_{sym} and S_{trans}

$$s, s'{:}S_{\mathrm{set}},\ p{:}S_{\mathrm{rel}}(s, s') \vdash S_{\mathrm{sym}}(p) : S_{\mathrm{rel}}(s', s)$$

$$s, s', s''{:}S,\ p{:}S_{\mathrm{rel}}(s, s'),\ p'{:}S_{\mathrm{rel}}(s', s'') \vdash S_{\mathrm{trans}}(p, p') : S_{\mathrm{rel}}(s, s'')$$

Two setoids are equal if all their four components are definitionally equal.

Examples of setoids. Every type T in the empty context gives rise to a setoid $\nabla(T)$ by $\nabla(T)_{\mathrm{set}} := T$, $\nabla(T)_{\mathrm{rel}}(t, t'{:}T) := \mathrm{Eq}_T(t, t')$. If S and T are setoids then their product $S \times T$ is defined by $(S \times T)_{\mathrm{set}} := S_{\mathrm{set}} \times T_{\mathrm{set}}$ and $(S \times T)_{\mathrm{rel}}((s, t), (s', t')) := S_{\mathrm{rel}}(s, s') \times T_{\mathrm{rel}}(t, t')$. The definition of the remaining components is obvious.

Definition 2. A *morphism* from setoid S to setoid T is a pair $f = (f_{\mathrm{fun}}, f_{\mathrm{resp}})$ where

$$s{:}S_{\mathrm{set}},\ \bar{s}{:}S_{\mathrm{rel}}(s, s) \vdash f_{\mathrm{fun}}(s, \bar{s}) : T_{\mathrm{set}}$$

and

$$\begin{gathered} s{:}S_{\mathrm{set}},\ \bar{s}{:}S_{\mathrm{rel}}(s, s),\ s'{:}S_{\mathrm{set}},\ \bar{s}'{:}S_{\mathrm{rel}}(s', s'),\ p{:}S_{\mathrm{rel}}(s, s') \vdash \\ f_{\mathrm{resp}}(p) : T_{\mathrm{rel}}(f_{\mathrm{fun}}(s, \bar{s}), f_{\mathrm{fun}}(s', \bar{s}')) \end{gathered}$$

Two morphisms are equal if their two components are definitionally equal.

Notice that the first component of a setoid morphism has two arguments. An element s of S_{set} and a proof $\bar{s} : S_{\mathrm{rel}}(s, s)$. As a convention we always use overlined variable names for such reflexivity assumptions. The morphisms between S and T can be internalised by the following definition of function space.

$$(S \Rightarrow T)_{\mathrm{set}} := \Pi s{:}S_{\mathrm{set}}.S_{\mathrm{rel}}(s, s) \to T_{\mathrm{set}}$$

and

$$\begin{aligned} &(S \Rightarrow T)_{\mathrm{rel}}(f, f') := \\ &\qquad \Pi s{:}S_{\mathrm{set}}.\Pi \bar{s}{:}S_{\mathrm{rel}}(s, s).\Pi s'{:}S_{\mathrm{set}}.\Pi \bar{s}'{:}S_{\mathrm{rel}}(s', s'). \\ &\qquad\quad S_{\mathrm{rel}}(s, s') \to T_{\mathrm{rel}}(f\ s\ \bar{s}, f'\ s'\ \bar{s}') \end{aligned}$$

Again we leave out the remaining components. By straightforward calculation we now obtain

Proposition 3. *If the underlying type theory has surjective pairing and an η-rule for the Π-type then the setoids form a cartesian closed category with terminal object.*

Thus setoids carry enough structure to interpret the simply typed λ-calculus. If surjective pairing and η-conversion are not available then we still get a model for λ-calculus without these rules. Our aim in the rest of this paper is to generalise this to a full model of Martin-Löf type theory in which the identity type at each setoid is interpreted as the corresponding relation.

2.2 Notation for contexts and telescopes

The contexts of setoids we are going to define are built upon ordinary syntactic contexts. We thus introduce some notation to describe various manoeuvres with contexts. We must make a compromise here between formal correctness and readability. A fully formal treatment would be possible only in terms of de Bruijn indices which we have not introduced.

The empty context is denoted $\underline{1}$. If $\Gamma \vdash A$ we write (Γ, A) for the context extension of Γ by A. By convention the empty context is omitted and parentheses associate to the left so that $\Gamma = (A_1, \cdots, A_n)$ is a generic context of length n. In this situation $(x_1, \cdots, x_n) : \Gamma$ introduces explicitly named variables to access the components of Γ. We have for $i = 1 \cdots n$

$$(x_1, \cdots, x_n) : \Gamma \vdash x_i : A_i$$

We may also introduce an indeterminate tuple of variables by $\gamma : \Gamma$. Then if $\Gamma = \underline{1}$ no variable is introduced and if $\Gamma = (\Gamma', A)$ then $\gamma.1$ is a tuple of variables for Γ' and $\gamma.2 : A$. For example if $\Gamma = (A_1, \ldots A_n)$ as before then

$$\gamma : \Gamma \vdash \gamma.1.1.2 : A_{n-2}$$

These two notations can be mixed as in

$$(\gamma, x) : (\Gamma, A) \vdash x : A$$

or even

$$\gamma : \Gamma,\ x : A \vdash x : A$$

If we want to emphasize free variables we may also write

$$\gamma : \Gamma \vdash A(\gamma)$$

instead of $\Gamma \vdash A$ and also write more explicitly $\underline{\Sigma}\gamma : \Gamma.A(\gamma)$ for the context extension (Γ, A). Note that $\underline{\Sigma}$ is a meta-operator on contexts and not part of the theory itself.

Similar conventions are adopted for tuples of terms. If $\Delta = (A_1, \cdots A_n)$ then we write

$$\Gamma \vdash (M_1, \cdots, M_n) : \Delta$$

if $\Gamma \vdash M_1 : A_1$, $\Gamma \vdash M_2 : A_2(M_1)$, etc. . We also use an indeterminate notation

$$\Gamma \vdash M : \Delta$$

where automatically $M = ()$ if $\Delta = \underline{1}$ and $M = (M.1, M.2)$ if $\Delta = \underline{\Sigma}\delta' : \Delta'.A(\delta')$ and then

$$\Gamma \vdash M.1 : \Delta'$$
$$\Gamma \vdash M.2 : A(M.1)$$

Such a tuple of terms $\Gamma \vdash M : \Delta$ is called a *context morphism* from Γ to Δ.

We single out specific tuples of types as so-called *telescopes*[1] or *contexts relative to a context*. We write $\Gamma \vdash \Delta$ if Δ is a context relative to Γ. We always have $\Gamma \vdash ()$ and if $\Gamma \vdash \Delta$ and $\Gamma, \Delta \vdash A$ then $\Gamma \vdash (\Delta, A)$. The above conventions on names, variables, and terms extend accordingly to telescopes. For example we write

$$x, y : \mathrm{N} \vdash \underline{\Sigma}(z, p) : (\underline{\Sigma} z : \mathrm{N}.\mathrm{Eq}\,(x, z)).\mathrm{Eq}\,(y, z)$$

as an abbreviation for the three judgements

$$\begin{array}{l} x, y : \mathrm{N} \vdash \mathrm{N} \\ x, y : \mathrm{N},\ z : \mathrm{N} \vdash \mathrm{Eq}\,(x, z) \\ x, y : \mathrm{N},\ z : \mathrm{N},\ p : \mathrm{Eq}\,(x, z) \vdash \mathrm{Eq}\,(y, z) \end{array}$$

and

$$x, y : \mathrm{N} \vdash M : \underline{\Sigma}(z, p) : (\underline{\Sigma} z : \mathrm{N}.\mathrm{Eq}\,(x, z)).\mathrm{Eq}\,(y, z)$$

as an abbreviation for

$$\begin{array}{l} x, y : \mathrm{N} \vdash M.1.1.2 : \mathrm{N} \\ x, y : \mathrm{N} \vdash M.1.2 : \mathrm{Eq}\,(x, M.1.1.2) \\ x, y : \mathrm{N} \vdash M.2 : \mathrm{Eq}\,(y, M.1.1.2) \end{array}$$

Remember that $M.1.1.1 = ()$.

2.3 Contexts of setoids

We are now ready to define the interpretation of contexts in the model. It may seem strange that it comes before the definition of (dependent) types, but as we shall see the contexts can be defined independently of the types and thus the inherent circularity in the definition of type dependency can be unravelled.

Definition 4. A *context of setoids* is a triple $\Gamma = (\Gamma_{\mathrm{set}}, \Gamma_{\mathrm{rel}}, \Gamma_{\mathrm{refl}})$ where Γ_{set} is a context and Γ_{rel} is a (syntactic) context relative to $(\Gamma_{\mathrm{set}}, \Gamma_{\mathrm{set}})$, i.e.

$$\gamma : \Gamma_{\mathrm{set}},\ \gamma' : \Gamma_{\mathrm{set}} \vdash \Gamma_{\mathrm{rel}}(\gamma, \gamma')$$

and finally Γ_{refl} is a tuple of terms proving reflexivity of Γ_{rel}, i.e.

$$\gamma : \Gamma_{\mathrm{set}} \vdash \Gamma_{\mathrm{refl}}(\gamma) : \Gamma_{\mathrm{rel}}(\gamma, \gamma)$$

Two contexts of setoids are equal if their three components are definitionally equal. The set of contexts of setoids is denoted Con.

[1] This term was introduced by N. De Bruijn.

Examples. If $\vdash A$ and $a, a' : A \vdash R(a, a')$ then we get a context of setoids Γ by putting

$$\begin{aligned} \Gamma_{\text{set}} &:= \underline{\Sigma} a : A.R(a,a) \\ \Gamma_{\text{rel}}((a,p),(a',p')) &:= (R(a,a')) \\ \Gamma_{\text{refl}}(a,p) &:= (p) \end{aligned}$$

So in particular every setoid gives rise to a context of setoids. As can be seen in this example the relation associated to a context of setoids is supposed to be reflexive because such a context is meant to contain a reflexivity assumption for every variable which is projected out by $-_{\text{refl}}$.

We could require the relation Γ_{rel} to be symmetric and transitive, too; but for reasons which become clear later in 3.1; these additional assumptions could never be used so they can be omitted.

Another example is the empty context of setoids $\bullet$ defined by $\bullet_{\text{set}} = \underline{1}$, $\bullet_{\text{rel}} = \underline{1}$, $\bullet_{\text{refl}} = ()$.

Next we define morphisms between contexts of setoids which are to interpret substitutions and weakenings.

Definition 5. Let Γ and Δ be contexts of setoids. A *morphism* from Γ to Δ is a pair $f = (f_{\text{fun}}, f_{\text{resp}})$ where

$$\gamma : \Gamma_{\text{set}} \vdash f_{\text{fun}}(\gamma) : \Delta_{\text{set}}$$

and

$$\gamma, \gamma' : \Gamma_{\text{set}},\ p : \Gamma_{\text{rel}}(\gamma, \gamma') \vdash f_{\text{resp}}(p) : \Delta_{\text{rel}}(f_{\text{fun}}(\gamma), f_{\text{fun}}(\gamma'))$$

such that reflexivity is preserved up to *definitional* equality, i.e.

$$\gamma : \Gamma \vdash f_{\text{resp}}(\Gamma_{\text{refl}}(\gamma)) = \Delta_{\text{refl}}(f_{\text{fun}}(\gamma))$$

is provable. Two morphisms between contexts of setoids are equal if their two components are definitionally equal. The set of these morphisms is denoted by $\text{Mor}\,(\Gamma, \Delta)$.

Examples. For every context of setoids Γ we have the *identity morphism* $\text{Id}_\Gamma \in \text{Mor}\,(\Gamma, \Gamma)$ given by

$$\begin{aligned} (\text{Id}_\Gamma)_{\text{fun}}(\gamma) &:= \gamma \\ (\text{Id}_\Gamma)_{\text{resp}}(p) &:= p \end{aligned}$$

Similarly, if $g \in \text{Mor}\,(\Delta, \Theta)$ and $f \in \text{Mor}\,(\Gamma, \Delta)$ we define the *composition* $g \circ f \in \text{Mor}\,(\Gamma, \Theta)$ by

$$\begin{aligned} (g \circ f)_{\text{fun}}(\gamma) &:= g_{\text{fun}}(f_{\text{fun}}(\gamma)) \\ (g \circ f)_{\text{resp}}(p) &:= g_{\text{resp}}(f_{\text{resp}}(p)) \end{aligned}$$

as componentwise substitution. Finally there is a unique element $!_\Gamma$ in $\mathrm{Mor}\,(\Gamma, \bullet)$ defined by

$$(!_\Gamma)_{\mathrm{fun}}(\gamma) := ()$$
$$(!_\Gamma)_{\mathrm{resp}}(\gamma) := ()$$

Clearly in all three cases reflexivity is preserved so that morphisms have been defined, and thus we get the following proposition by straightforward calculation.

Proposition 6. *The contexts of setoids together with their morphisms form a category with terminal object* $\bullet$.

2.4 Families of setoids

The most important ingredient needed to interpret Martin-Löf type theory is the correct definition of type dependency. So we must say what a family of setoids indexed over a context of setoids is. We first introduce a useful abbreviation. If $\Gamma \in \mathrm{Con}$ and $\gamma_1, \ldots, \gamma_n : \Gamma_{\mathrm{set}}$ then

$$\Gamma_{\mathrm{conn}}(\gamma_1, \ldots, \gamma_n)$$

denotes the context consisting of all types $\Gamma_{\mathrm{rel}}(\gamma_i, \gamma_j)$ for $i, j = 1 \ldots n, i \neq j$. So for example if $\gamma, \gamma' : \Gamma_{\mathrm{set}}$ then

$$\Gamma_{\mathrm{conn}}(\gamma, \gamma') = (\Gamma_{\mathrm{rel}}(\gamma, \gamma'),\ \Gamma_{\mathrm{rel}}(\gamma', \gamma))$$

Definition 7. Let Γ be a context of setoids. A *family of setoids above* Γ is a 6-tuple $S = (S_{\mathrm{set}}, S_{\mathrm{rel}}, S_{\mathrm{rewrite}}, S_{\mathrm{sym}}, S_{\mathrm{trans}}, S_{\mathrm{ax}})$ where

- S_{set} is a type depending on Γ_{set}

$$\gamma : \Gamma_{\mathrm{set}} \vdash S_{\mathrm{set}}(\gamma)$$

- S_{rel} is a dependent relation on S_{set}

$$\gamma, \gamma' : \Gamma_{\mathrm{set}},\ s : S_{\mathrm{set}}(\gamma),\ s' : S_{\mathrm{set}}(\gamma') \vdash S_{\mathrm{rel}}(s, s')$$

- S_{rewrite} is a "rewriter" which allows to substitute connected elements of Γ_{set} in S_{set}

$$\gamma, \gamma' : \Gamma_{\mathrm{set}},\ p : \Gamma_{\mathrm{conn}}(\gamma, \gamma'),\ s : S_{\mathrm{set}}(\gamma),\ \bar{s} : S_{\mathrm{rel}}(s, s) \vdash$$
$$S_{\mathrm{rewrite}}(p, s, \bar{s}) : S_{\mathrm{set}}(\gamma')$$

such that S_{rel} is symmetric and transitive and such that $S_{\mathrm{rewrite}}(p, s)$ is always S_{rel}-related to s. More precisely we require terms

$$\begin{array}{ll}\gamma, \gamma' : \Gamma_{\mathrm{set}}, & \\ p : \Gamma_{\mathrm{conn}}(\gamma, \gamma'), & \\ s : S_{\mathrm{set}}(\gamma),\ s' : S(\gamma'), & \\ q : S_{\mathrm{rel}}(s, s') & \vdash S_{\mathrm{sym}}(p, q) : S_{\mathrm{rel}}(s', s)\end{array}$$

$$\begin{array}{ll}\gamma, \gamma', \gamma'' : \Gamma_{\mathrm{set}}, & \\ p : \Gamma_{\mathrm{conn}}(\gamma, \gamma', \gamma''), & \\ s : S_{\mathrm{set}}(\gamma),\ s' : S_{\mathrm{set}}(\gamma'),\ s'' : S_{\mathrm{set}}(\gamma''), & \\ q : S_{\mathrm{rel}}(s, s'),\ q' : S_{\mathrm{rel}}(s', s'') & \vdash S_{\mathrm{trans}}(p, q, q') : S_{\mathrm{rel}}(s, s'')\end{array}$$

$$\begin{array}{l}\gamma, \gamma' : \Gamma_{\mathrm{set}}, \\ p : \Gamma_{\mathrm{conn}}(\gamma, \gamma'), \\ s : S_{\mathrm{set}}(\gamma),\ \bar{s} : S_{\mathrm{rel}}(s, s) \vdash S_{\mathrm{ax}}(p, s, \bar{s}) : S_{\mathrm{rel}}(s, S_{\mathrm{rewrite}}(p, s, \bar{s}))\end{array}$$

Two families are equal if all their six components are definitionally equal. We denote the set of families of setoids over context Γ by $\mathrm{Fam}(\Gamma)$.

The idea behind the rewriter "S_{rewrite}" is to allow substitution inside a dependent family if the indexing elements are "equal", i.e related. It will be the main ingredient in the interpretation of the identity elimination rule in the setoid model. The reflexivity assumption $\bar{s} : S_{\mathrm{rel}}(s, s)$ in S_{ax} is needed for otherwise from S_{ax} one could conclude that any two elements of $S_{\mathrm{set}}(\gamma)$ are S_{rel}-related. The rewriter S_{rewrite} could also be defined without this assumption.

Example. If Γ is a context of setoids and S is a setoid as defined in Section 2 then we can form a constant family of setoids indexed over Γ whose underlying set and relation are just their weakened companions taken from S, whereas the reindexer is the identity. In fact the nondependent setoids are in 1-1 correspondence to families of setoids over the empty context. More examples arise from the operations on families of setoids we are going to describe.

The task is now to show that this notion of families is stable under all constructions needed to interpret Martin-Löf type theory, i.e. to show that all six components of a family can be defined by induction along a type expression. This means that apart from the various type formers we are interested in, we must interpret context comprehension and substitution. This will be done in the rest of this section. A fully formal account of what exactly is needed in order to interpret Martin-Löf type theory can e.g. be found in [12].

2.5 Context comprehension

In the setoid model contexts are interpreted as contexts of setoids, whereas types (in contexts) will be interpreted as families of setoids above the interpretation of their context. So the first operation we have to define is context comprehension, i.e. the interpretation of the rule

$$\frac{\Gamma \vdash A}{\Gamma, x : A \text{ is a context}}$$

Let S be a family of setoids indexed over Γ. Its comprehension, denoted $\Gamma.S$, is the context of setoids defined by

$$\begin{array}{ll} \Gamma.S_{\text{set}} & := \underline{\Sigma}(\gamma, s) : (\underline{\Sigma}\gamma \in \Gamma_{\text{set}}.S_{\text{set}}(\gamma)).S_{\text{rel}}(s, s) \\ \Gamma.S_{\text{rel}}((\gamma, s, p), (\gamma', s', p')) := & (\Gamma_{\text{rel}}(\gamma, \gamma'),\ S_{\text{rel}}(s, s')) \\ \Gamma.S_{\text{refl}}(\gamma, s, p) & := (\Gamma_{\text{refl}}(\gamma), p) \end{array}$$

Thus a typical context of setoids Γ of length 2 takes the form

$$\begin{array}{ll} \Gamma_{\text{set}} & = s_1 : (S_1)_{\text{set}}, \bar{s}_1 : (S_1)_{\text{rel}}(s_1, s_1), \\ & \quad s_2 : (S_2)_{\text{set}}(s_1, \bar{s}_1), \bar{s}_2 : (S_2)_{\text{rel}}(s_1, \bar{s}_1,\ s_2, s_2) \\ \Gamma_{\text{rel}}(s_1, \bar{s}_1, s_2, \bar{s}_2,\ s_1', \bar{s}_1', s_2', \bar{s}_2') & = p_1 : (S_1)_{\text{rel}}(s_1, s_1'), \\ & \quad p_2 : (S_2)_{\text{rel}}(s_1, \bar{s}_1, s_1', \bar{s}_1', s_2, s_2') \\ \Gamma_{\text{refl}}(s_1, \bar{s}_1, s_2, \bar{s}_2) & = (\bar{s}_1, \bar{s}_2) \end{array}$$

where we have used the standard notation for contexts to exemplify the use of the abbreviations.

Canonical projection. We define a morphism $\mathrm{p}(S) \in \mathrm{Mor}\,(\Gamma.S, \Gamma)$ by

$$\begin{array}{l} \mathrm{p}(S)_{\text{fun}}(\gamma, s, \bar{s}) := \gamma \\ \mathrm{p}(S)_{\text{resp}}(p, q) \quad := p \end{array}$$

It follows immediately from the definition of $(\Gamma.S)_{\text{refl}}$ that this is indeed a morphism.

2.6 Sections of families

Instead of defining arbitrary morphisms between families we restrict ourselves to "sections" which will be used to interpret terms and can be viewed as family morphisms from the constant (unit) family corresponding to the context itself into a family.

Definition 8. If S is a family over a context of setoids Γ then a section of S is a pair $M = (M_{\text{el}}, M_{\text{resp}})$ where

$$\gamma : \Gamma_{\text{set}} \vdash M_{\text{el}}(\gamma) : S_{\text{set}}(\gamma)$$

and

$$\gamma, \gamma' : \Gamma_{\text{set}},\ p : \Gamma_{\text{rel}}(\gamma, \gamma') \vdash M_{\text{resp}}(p) : S_{\text{rel}}(M_{\text{el}}(\gamma), M_{\text{el}}(\gamma'))$$

We denote the set of sections of S by $\mathrm{Sect}\,(S)$. Two sections are equal if both components are definitionally equal.

Every section induces a context morphism from its context to the comprehension of its type. More precisely, if $M \in \mathrm{Sect}(S)$ then we get a morphism $\overline{M} \in \mathrm{Mor}(\Gamma, \Gamma.S)$ by

$$\begin{aligned} \overline{M}_{\mathrm{fun}}(\gamma) &:= (\gamma, M_{\mathrm{el}}(\gamma), M_{\mathrm{resp}}(\Gamma_{\mathrm{refl}}(\gamma))) \\ \overline{M}_{\mathrm{resp}}(p) &:= (p, M_{\mathrm{resp}}(p)) \end{aligned}$$

We check that reflexivity is preserved:

$$\begin{aligned} &\overline{M}_{\mathrm{resp}}(\Gamma_{\mathrm{refl}}(\gamma)) = \\ &(\Gamma_{\mathrm{refl}}(\gamma),\ M_{\mathrm{resp}}(\Gamma_{\mathrm{refl}}(\gamma))) = \\ &\Gamma.S_{\mathrm{refl}}(\gamma, M_{\mathrm{el}}(\gamma), M_{\mathrm{resp}}(\Gamma_{\mathrm{refl}}(\gamma))) = \\ &\Gamma.S_{\mathrm{refl}}(\overline{M}_{\mathrm{fun}}(\gamma)) \end{aligned}$$

So although no equational constraints are placed on sections they nevertheless induce proper morphisms.

We have

$$\mathrm{p}(S) \circ \overline{M} = \mathrm{Id}_{\Gamma}$$

which explains the term "section". We can also get back sections from certain context morphisms as is shown in the next section.

2.7 Weakening and substitution

In a model, substitution and weakening are defined as additional operations rather than inductively as in the syntax. First, in this way substitution is defined for arbitrary families and sections, not only for the syntactically expressible ones. Second, with an explicit presentation of substitution it becomes easier to prove the correctness of the interpretation of the Π-type and other constructions which involve substitution. Of course, one must then show that the interpretation of syntactic substitution agrees with the semantical substitution applied to the interpretation of the original non-substituted syntactic object. For this, one must establish that all semantic type and term formers commute with semantic substitution.

Instead of defining the substitution of an element (a section) into a family we define substitution for arbitrary morphisms between contexts of setoids which gives both simultaneous substitution by several terms and weakening as special cases. This technique is reminiscent of categorical models of type theory. Under this interpretation it is helpful to think of morphisms of contexts as of tuples of terms ("context morphisms" or "substitutions").

So let S be a family of setoids indexed over Δ and f be a morphism from Γ to Δ. We obtain a family of setoids over Γ denoted $S[f]$ by precomposing with f, i.e. by putting

$$S[f]_{\mathrm{set}}(\gamma : \Gamma_{\mathrm{set}}) := S_{\mathrm{set}}(f_{\mathrm{fun}}(\gamma))$$

$$S[f]_{\mathrm{rel}}(s : S_{\mathrm{set}}(f_{\mathrm{fun}}(\gamma)),\ s' : S_{\mathrm{set}}(f_{\mathrm{fun}}(\gamma'))) := S_{\mathrm{rel}}(s, s')$$

$$\begin{aligned} &S[f]_{\mathrm{rewrite}}(p : \Gamma_{\mathrm{conn}}(\gamma, \gamma'),\ s : S_{\mathrm{set}}(f_{\mathrm{fun}}(\gamma)),\ \bar{s} : S_{\mathrm{rel}}(s, s)) := \\ &\quad S_{\mathrm{rewrite}}(f_{\mathrm{resp}}(p), s, \bar{s}) \end{aligned}$$

Here by a slight abuse of notation we have applied f_{resp} to $p : \Gamma_{\mathrm{conn}}(\gamma, \gamma')$. This is understood componentwise. The other components of $S[f]$ are defined similarly by precomposition.

Substitution along a morphism of the form $\overline{M}$ arising from a section corresponds to real substitution as in

$$\frac{\Gamma,\ x : S \vdash T(x)}{\Gamma \vdash T(M)}$$

whereas substitution along a morphism $\mathrm{p}(S)$ interprets weakening

$$\frac{\Gamma \vdash T}{\Gamma,\ x : S \vdash T}$$

If no confusion can arise we abbreviate $T[\mathrm{p}(S)]$ for $S, T \in \mathrm{Fam}(\Gamma)$ simply by T^+ and also write $T[M]$ instead of $T[\overline{M}]$ if $T \in \mathrm{Fam}(\Gamma.S)$ and $M \in \mathrm{Sect}\,(S)$.

There is also a context morphism arising from substitution which is a bit difficult to understand at first. It goes from $\Gamma.S[f]$ to $\Delta.S$ and we denote it by $q(f, S)$. Its function component is defined by

$$q(f,S)_{\mathrm{fun}}(\gamma : \Gamma_{\mathrm{set}},\ s : S_{\mathrm{set}}(f_{\mathrm{fun}}(\gamma)),\ \bar{s} : S_{\mathrm{rel}}(s,s)) := (f_{\mathrm{fun}}(\gamma), s, \bar{s}) : \Delta.S_{\mathrm{set}}$$

It is used to perform substitutions in variables other than the last one as in

$$\frac{\begin{array}{l}\Gamma \vdash A\\ \Gamma,\ x : A \vdash B\\ \Gamma,\ x : A,\ y : B \vdash C\\ \Gamma \vdash M : A\end{array}}{\Gamma,\ y : B(M) \vdash C(M, y)}$$

In the model, A is a family of setoids over Γ, B is one over $\Gamma.A$, and C is a family over $\Gamma.A.B$. M is a section of A. The conclusion is then obtained as

$$C[q(M, B)]$$

It is a characteristic property of substitution that the square of morphisms f, $\mathrm{p}(S)$, $\mathrm{p}(S[f])$, $q(f, S)$ is a pullback.

Extraction of sections from morphisms. If $f \in \mathrm{Mor}\,(\Gamma, \Delta.S)$ then we construct a section $\mathrm{Fst}(f) \in \mathrm{Sect}\,(S[\mathrm{p}(S) \circ f])$ as follows. The $-_{\mathrm{el}}$-part of $\mathrm{p}(S) \circ f$ sends $\gamma : \Gamma_{\mathrm{set}}$ to $\delta := f_{\mathrm{fun}}(\gamma).1.1.2 : \Delta_{\mathrm{set}}$. Now $f_{\mathrm{fun}}(\gamma).1.2$ is an element of $S_{\mathrm{set}}(\delta)$. So we put

$$\mathrm{Fst}(f)_{\mathrm{el}}(\gamma) := f_{\mathrm{fun}}(\gamma).1.2$$

The $-_{\mathrm{resp}}$-component is defined analogously. We have

$$f = q(f', S) \circ \overline{\mathrm{Fst}(f)}$$

and

$$M = \mathrm{Fst}(\overline{M})$$

so sections and right-inverses to canonical projections are in 1-1 correspondence. If $f \in \mathrm{Mor}\,(\Gamma, \Delta)$, $S \in \mathrm{Fam}\,(\Delta)$ and $M \in \mathrm{Sect}\,(S[f])$ then

$$\mathrm{Cons}(f, M) := q(f, S) \circ \overline{M} \in \mathrm{Mor}\,(\Gamma, \Delta.S)$$

and $\mathrm{Fst}(\mathrm{Cons}(f, M)) = M$. This may explain the operator name Fst.

Substitution and weakening on sections. Let $f \in \mathrm{Mor}\,(\Gamma, \Delta)$ and $S \in \mathrm{Fam}\,(\Delta)$. If M is a section of S then

$$M[f] := \mathrm{Fst}(\overline{M} \circ f)$$

is a section of $S[f]$. Its element component is

$$M[f]_{\mathrm{el}}(\gamma : \Gamma_{\mathrm{set}}) = M_{\mathrm{el}}(f_{\mathrm{fun}}(\gamma))$$

The $-_{\mathrm{resp}}$-component is defined similarly. In this way we interpret substitution on terms. The abbreviations introduced before apply analogously to substitution on sections.

Variables. The final ingredient we require to interpret all manoeuvres with variables and substitutions is the extraction of the last variable in a context, i.e. the interpretation of

$$\Gamma,\ x : S \vdash x : S$$

In our setup this is a section of S^{+}, since the type S on the rhs is actually weakened. We obtain this section as

$$\mathrm{var}^{S} := \mathrm{Fst}(\mathrm{Id}_{\Gamma.S})$$

Its first component is

$$\mathrm{var}^{S}{}_{\mathrm{el}}(\gamma : \Gamma_{\mathrm{set}}, s : S_{\mathrm{set}}(\gamma), \bar{s} : S_{\mathrm{rel}}(s, s)) = s$$

as expected. The other variables are obtained as suitable weakenings of this.

It should be stressed that our substitution inherits the split property from the syntax. This means that for $f \in \mathrm{Mor}\,(\Gamma, \Delta)$ and $g \in \mathrm{Mor}\,(\Delta, \Theta)$ and S a family above Θ we have the equality of families

$$S[g][f] = S[g \circ f]$$

and also

$$S[\mathrm{Id}_{\Theta}] = S$$

The structure of the model is now set out, we have defined domains of interpretation for contexts, types, and terms and related them through appropriate operations. It remains to show that the model contains the base types and is closed under the type constructors we are interested in. Since Martin-Löf's type theory is an open system there can be arbitrarily many such constructors. For the purpose of this paper we confine ourselves to the interpretation of the dependent product, and the intensional identity type (together with Ext). In Section 5 we sketch the interpretation of other type constructors like inductive types and universes.

3 Dependent product

Let Γ be a context of setoids, S be a family over Γ and T be a family over $\Gamma.S$. We want to define a family over Γ which "internalises" the sections of T, in order to interpret the Π-type. We denote this family by $\Pi(S,T)$. Its type component is given by

$$\Pi(S,T)_{\mathrm{set}}(\gamma : \Gamma_{\mathrm{set}}) := \Pi s : S_{\mathrm{set}}(\gamma).\Pi \bar{s} : S_{\mathrm{rel}}(s,s).T_{\mathrm{set}}(\gamma, s, \bar{s})$$

The relation is defined by

$$\begin{aligned} &\Pi(S,T)_{\mathrm{rel}}(U : \Pi(S,T)_{\mathrm{set}}(\gamma),\ V : \Pi(S,T)_{\mathrm{set}}(\gamma')) := \\ &\quad \Pi s : S_{\mathrm{set}}(\gamma)\Pi \bar{s} : S_{\mathrm{rel}}(s,s)\Pi s' : S_{\mathrm{set}}(\gamma')\Pi \bar{s}' : S_{\mathrm{rel}}(s',s'). \\ &\qquad S_{\mathrm{rel}}(s,s') \to T_{\mathrm{rel}}(U\, s\, \bar{s}, V\, s'\, \bar{s}') \end{aligned}$$

We leave out the definition of the other components, but mention that the proof of transitivity requires the component S_{rewrite}. This means that if we had defined families of setoids without the rewriter, it would have been impossible to define the dependent product. We also need the $-_{\mathrm{refl}}$ operation in the definition of various parts.

Next we define introduction and elimination for the dependent product, that is the interpretation of the two rules:

$$\frac{\Gamma, x : S \vdash M(x) : T(x)}{\Gamma \vdash \lambda x{:}S.M(x) : \Pi x{:}S.T(x)} \qquad \frac{\Gamma \vdash M : \Pi x{:}S.T(x) \quad \Gamma \vdash N : S}{\Gamma \vdash (M\, N) : T(N)}$$

So if $M \in \mathrm{Sect}\,(T)$ we construct

$$\Pi_{\mathrm{intro}}(S,T,M) \in \mathrm{Sect}\,(\Pi(S,T))$$

and conversely if $M \in \mathrm{Sect}\,(\Pi(S,T))$ and $N \in \mathrm{Sect}\,(S)$ we construct

$$\Pi_{\mathrm{elim}}(S,T,M,N) \in \mathrm{Sect}\,(T[N])$$

The element parts are

$$\Pi_{\mathrm{intro}}(S,T,M)_{\mathrm{el}}(\gamma : \Gamma_{\mathrm{set}}) := \lambda s : S_{\mathrm{set}}(\gamma).\lambda \bar{s} : S_{\mathrm{rel}}(s,s).M_{\mathrm{el}}(\gamma, s, \bar{s})$$

and

$$\Pi_{\mathrm{elim}}(S,T,M,N)_{\mathrm{el}}(\gamma : \Gamma_{\mathrm{set}}) := M_{\mathrm{el}}(\gamma)\, N_{\mathrm{el}}(\gamma)\, N_{\mathrm{resp}}(\Gamma_{\mathrm{refl}}(\gamma))$$

The relational parts are defined similarly. Now for $M \in \mathrm{Sect}\,(T)$ and $N \in \mathrm{Sect}\,(S)$ we have the equation

$$\Pi_{\mathrm{elim}}(S,T,\Pi_{\mathrm{intro}}(S,T,M),N) = M[N]$$

which interprets the β-equality rule. If the underlying type theory has an η-rule then a corresponding equation holds as well.

3.1 Compatibility with substitution.

As argued in 2.7 we must now show that substitution commutes with product formation, as well as with introduction and elimination. In categorical jargon this is referred to as the "Beck-Chevalley condition" or "stability under substitution". Consider the following situation: $\Gamma \in \mathrm{Con}$, S above Γ, and T above $\Gamma.S$ as before; Γ' another context and f a context morphism from Γ' to Γ. Now we may form the product of T and then substitute along f:

$$\Pi(S,T)[f]$$

or first substitute f into both S and T and then take the product:

$$\Pi(S[f],\ T[q(f,S)])$$

It can be shown by careful examination or by machine-supported normalisation that these families are indeed equal. It is crucial for this result that all morphisms preserve reflexivity ($-_{\mathrm{refl}}$), since this operation is part of the definition of the dependent product.

To clarify the delicacy of stability under substitution in the setoid model we give two type formers A and B which are not stable under substitution. Both simply map families over some context Γ to families over Γ. We define for $S \in \mathrm{Fam}(\Gamma)$

$$A(S)_{\mathrm{set}}(\gamma : \Gamma_{\mathrm{set}}) := \Pi\gamma' : \Gamma_{\mathrm{set}}.\Gamma_{\mathrm{conn}}(\gamma,\gamma') \to S_{\mathrm{set}}(\gamma')$$

By S_{rewrite} the family $A(S)$ will be "isomorphic" to S up to S_{rel}, but no matter how the other components of $A(S)$ are defined, the type constructor $A(-)$ cannot be stable under substitution because for $f \in \mathrm{Mor}(\Gamma,\Delta)$ and $S \in \mathrm{Fam}(\Delta)$ we have

$$A(S)[f]_{\mathrm{set}}(\gamma) = \Pi\delta' \in \Delta_{\mathrm{set}}.\Delta_{\mathrm{conn}}(f_{\mathrm{fun}}(\gamma),\delta') \to S_{\mathrm{set}}(\delta')$$

whereas

$$A(S[f])_{\mathrm{set}}(\gamma) = \Pi\gamma' \in \Gamma_{\mathrm{set}}.\Gamma_{\mathrm{conn}}(\gamma,\gamma') \to S_{\mathrm{set}}(f_{\mathrm{fun}}(\gamma'))$$

For the other example we assume an operation $\Gamma_{\mathrm{sym}} : \Pi\gamma,\gamma' : \Gamma_{\mathrm{set}}.\Gamma_{\mathrm{rel}}(\gamma,\gamma') \to \Gamma_{\mathrm{rel}}(\gamma',\gamma)$ to be defined for each context Γ. This is in fact possible for all contexts defined from $\bullet$ by successive applications of comprehension. Now if for $S \in \mathrm{Fam}(\Gamma)$ we define

$$\begin{array}{ll} B(S)_{\mathrm{set}} & := S_{\mathrm{set}} \\ B(S)_{\mathrm{rel}} & := S_{\mathrm{rel}} \\ B(S)_{\mathrm{sym}}((p_1,p_2):\Gamma_{\mathrm{conn}}(\gamma,\gamma'),\ q:S_{\mathrm{rel}}(s,s')) & := S_{\mathrm{sym}}((\Gamma_{\mathrm{sym}}(p_2),\Gamma_{\mathrm{sym}}(p_1)),\ q) \end{array}$$

i.e. we use Γ_{sym} to "permute" the proof (p_1,p_2), then again we lose stability under substitution because for $f \in \mathrm{Mor}(\Gamma,\Delta)$ and $S \in \mathrm{Fam}(\Delta)$ the family $B(S)[f]$ contains the term

$$\Delta_{\mathrm{sym}}(f_{\mathrm{resp}}(p_2))$$

whereas $B(S[f])$ contains

$$f_{\text{resp}}(\Gamma_{\text{sym}}(p_2))$$

and these are in general not equal. This is the reason why (in contrast to an earlier version of this paper) we do not require the relations in a context to be symmetric and transitive and why we use Γ_{conn} instead of Γ_{rel} as a premise to all operations associated with a family. We could of course require that context morphisms have to preserve symmetry and transitivity, but then also sections would have to do so and it would no longer be possible to internalise them in a Π-type.

In both examples we have used "local components" of Γ. In contrast, all type- and term operators the definition of which uses only Γ_{refl} and the components of the participating families will be stable under substitution.

4 The identity type

We can now reap the fruits of the laborious model constructions carried out above and define the identity setoid which satisfies the extensionality principle. The basic idea is that the identity setoid will be given by the relation associated to each family and the identity elimination operator will be based on the "rewriter" S_{rewrite}.

Suppose we are given a context of setoids Γ and a family of setoids S over Γ. We first form the context consisting of Γ and two copies of S. In our notation this is $\Gamma.S.S^{+}$. The identity setoid, denoted $\text{Eq}\,(S)$, is a family over this. There is a rather simple definition of this family if we are prepared to accept that in the model the equality rule Eq-Comp-J for the identity type holds only up to propositional equality, i.e. the interpretations of

$$\text{J}_C(M)(x, x, \text{refl}_A(x))$$

and

$$M(x)$$

are not equal, but the interpretation of the corresponding identity type is inhabited in the model. If we want the equality rule to hold in the model definitionally we must do a bit more work. In this paper we describe the first (simplified) identity family in detail because it explains the idea and only hint in 4.3 at the construction of the correct identity family since it is rather complicated and best understood using a proof checker like Lego interactively.

4.1 The simplified case

In the simplified case we put

$$\text{Eq}\,(S)_{\text{set}}((\gamma, s_1, \bar{s}_1, s_2, \bar{s}_2) : (\Gamma.S.S^{+})_{\text{set}}) := S_{\text{rel}}(s_1, s_2)$$

and

$$\text{Eq}\,(S)_{\text{rel}}(p, q) = \mathbf{1}$$

i.e. any two elements of $\mathrm{Eq}\,(S)_{\mathrm{set}}$ are related. Clearly this is symmetric and transitive. To define the rewriter $\mathrm{Eq}\,(S)_{\mathrm{rewrite}}$ we make use of transitivity and symmetry of S_{rel}. We shall now embark on the definition of the combinators associated with the identity type.

Reflexivity. In the model $\mathrm{refl}_S(x)$ is a section of $\mathrm{Eq}\,(S)[\overline{\mathrm{var}^S}]$[2]. It is defined by

$$\mathrm{refl}\,(S)_{\mathrm{el}}((\gamma, s, \bar{s}) : \Gamma.S) := \bar{s}$$

The $-_{\mathrm{resp}}$ component is trivial since any two elements of the identity setoid are related.

Identity elimination. The main ingredient of the definition of the J-eliminator for $\mathrm{Eq}\,(S)$ is the rewriter $-_{\mathrm{rewrite}}$. We must do a bit of work, though, in order to get the various contexts and substitutions right. Let C be a family of setoids indexed over $\Gamma.S.S^{+}.\mathrm{Eq}\,(S)$. Substituting $\mathrm{refl}\,(S)$ into C gives

$$C(\mathrm{refl}\,(S)) := C[q(\mathrm{var}^S, \mathrm{Eq}\,(S))][\mathrm{refl}\,(S)]$$

Let M be a section of this family. We must construct a section $\mathrm{J}(C, M)$ of C from this. We define

$$\begin{aligned}
&\mathrm{J}(C, M)_{\mathrm{el}}((\gamma, s_1, \bar{s}_1, s_2, \bar{s}_2, p, \bar{p}) : \Gamma.S.S^{+}.\mathrm{Eq}\,(S)) := \\
&\quad C_{\mathrm{rewrite}}(\\
&\qquad ((\Gamma_{\mathrm{refl}}(\gamma),\ \bar{s}_1,\ p,\ \star),\ (\Gamma_{\mathrm{refl}}(\gamma),\ \bar{s}_1,\ S_{\mathrm{sym}}((\Gamma_{\mathrm{refl}}(\gamma), \Gamma_{\mathrm{refl}}(\gamma)), p),\ \star)), \\
&\qquad M_{\mathrm{el}}(\gamma, s_1, \bar{s}_1), \\
&\qquad M_{\mathrm{resp}}(\Gamma_{\mathrm{refl}}, \bar{s}_1))
\end{aligned}$$

Here $\star$ denotes the unique element of the unit type $\mathbf{1}$. The first argument to C_{rewrite} is a proof that

$$x := (\gamma, s_1, \bar{s}_1, s_1, \bar{s}_1, \bar{s}_1, \star)$$

and

$$y := (\gamma, s_1, \bar{s}_1, s_2, \bar{s}_2, p, \star)$$

are connected elements of $(\Gamma.S.S^{+}.\mathrm{Eq}\,(S))_{\mathrm{set}}$. The assumption M gives an element of $C_{\mathrm{set}}(x)$ (second argument) and a proof that it is related to itself (third argument). C_{rewrite} then gives the desired element of $C_{\mathrm{set}}(y)$.

We omit the $-_{\mathrm{resp}}$ part of $\mathrm{J}(C, M)$. Its main ingredient is C_{ax} — the proof that rewriting does not alter the C_{rel}-class. The definition of the other eliminator K is analogous.

As announced above this eliminator does not satisfy the rule Eq-Comp-J, i.e. we do not have

$$\mathrm{J}(C, M)[q(\mathrm{var}^S, \mathrm{Eq}\,(S))][\mathrm{refl}\,(S)] = M$$

The reason for this is that C_{rewrite} applied to a proof by reflexivity is not necessarily the identity function. However, by virtue of C_{ax}, the propositional companion to Eq-Comp-J, is inhabited in the model.

---

[2] Notice that $\overline{\mathrm{var}^S} \in \mathrm{Mor}\,(\Gamma.S, (\Gamma.S.S^{+})_{\mathrm{set}})$ is the "diagonal".

4.2 Extensionality

Let Γ and S be as before, T above $\Gamma.S$ and U, V sections of T. Moreover, assume a section M of

$$\mathrm{Eq}\,(S)(U,V) := \mathrm{Eq}\,(T)[V^{+}][U]$$

i.e. a proof that U and V are equal. We must show that their respective abstractions are equal as well — we need a section $\mathrm{Ext}\,(M)$ of

$$\mathrm{Eq}\,(\Pi(S,T))[\Pi_{\mathrm{intro}}\,(T,V)^{+}][\Pi_{\mathrm{intro}}\,(T,U)]$$

The element part of M is basically (modulo some currying of Σ-types) a term of type

$$\gamma : \Gamma_{\mathrm{set}},\ s : S_{\mathrm{set}}(\gamma),\ \bar{s} : S_{\mathrm{rel}}(s,s) \vdash S_{\mathrm{rel}}(U_{\mathrm{el}}(\gamma,s,\bar{s}),\ V_{\mathrm{el}}(\gamma,s,\bar{s}))$$

The element we are looking for amounts to an inhabitant of

$$\begin{array}{l}\gamma : \Gamma_{\mathrm{set}},\ s : S_{\mathrm{set}}(\gamma),\ \bar{s} : S_{\mathrm{rel}}(s,s),\ s' : S_{\mathrm{set}}(\gamma),\ \bar{s}' : S_{\mathrm{rel}}(s,s) \vdash \\ \quad S_{\mathrm{rel}}(U_{\mathrm{el}}(g,s,\bar{s}),\ V_{\mathrm{el}}(g,s',\bar{s}'))\end{array}$$

We obtain that by using either U_{resp} or V_{resp} and transitivity. The $-_{\mathrm{resp}}$ part is again trivial.

4.3 The unsimplified case

For the rule Eq-Comp-J to hold definitionally in the model we need a sum type in the original type theory given by the following rules.

$$\frac{\Gamma \vdash A \quad \Gamma \vdash B}{\Gamma \vdash A+B} \qquad \frac{\Gamma \vdash M : A}{\Gamma \vdash \mathrm{inl}(M) : A+B} \quad \frac{\Gamma \vdash M : B}{\Gamma \vdash \mathrm{inr}(M) : A+B}$$

$$\frac{\begin{array}{l}\Gamma,\ x : A+B \vdash C(x) \\ \Gamma,\ x : A \vdash L(x) : C(\mathrm{inl}(x)) \\ \Gamma,\ x : B \vdash R(x) : C(\mathrm{inr}(x)) \\ \Gamma \vdash M : A+B\end{array}}{\Gamma \vdash \mathrm{cases}(L,R,M) : C(M)} \qquad \begin{array}{c}\overline{\Gamma \vdash \mathrm{cases}(L,R,\mathrm{inl}(M)) = L(M) : C(\mathrm{inl}(M))} \\ \\ \overline{\Gamma \vdash \mathrm{cases}(L,R,\mathrm{inr}(M)) = R(M) : C(\mathrm{inr}(M))}\end{array}$$

With this sum type we can treat reflexivity as a special case and then interpret J as the identity. More precisely we put

$$\begin{array}{l}\mathrm{Eq}\,(S)_{\mathrm{set}}((\gamma,s_1,\bar{s}_1,s_2,\bar{s}_2) : (\Gamma.S.S^{+})_{\mathrm{set}}) := \\ \quad (\Sigma p : \mathrm{Eq}(s_1,s_2).\mathrm{Eq}(\mathrm{Subst}\,(p,\bar{s}_1),\ \bar{s}_2))\ +\ S(s_1,s_2)\end{array}$$

So an element of the identity family either proves that the two arguments are equal or that they are related. The relation on the identity family is chosen to be trivial. The rewriting component is again defined using symmetry and transitivity. A rewritten element of the identity family always is in the right component of the sum.

For reflexivity we choose the left component.

$$\mathrm{refl}\,(S)_{\mathrm{el}}((\gamma, s, \bar{s}) : \Gamma.S) := \mathrm{inl}(\mathrm{refl}(s), \mathrm{refl}(\bar{s}))$$

Now the elimination rule J can be defined by case distinction. If the element $p : \mathrm{Eq}\,(S)(\gamma, s_1, \bar{s}_1, s_2, \bar{s}_2)$ is of the form $\mathrm{inl}((a, b))$ then we use the J-operator from the original type theory, whereas in the other case we use C_{rewrite} as in the other definition above. Now the equation EQ-COMP-J can be deduced from the equations for the sum type and the EQ-COMP-J-equation from the original type theory.

Similarly one may define K and Ext.

5 Interpretation of other type constructors

In this section we sketch the interpretation of type constructors other than Π and Eq. Some interpretations, in particular the one of the Σ-type below, only approximate their syntactical companions. Often, a problem similar to the one encountered with the simplified definition of the identity setoid occurs: a certain equality rule only holds propositionally. So in the interpretation one would have to replace all instances of the β-rule for equality by propositional equalities and suitably interspersed Subst-operations.

Inductive types like the natural numbers or the booleans lift straightforwardly to the setoid model; the relation is simply the identity type. The computation rule for the natural numbers will only be valid for closed terms and otherwise hold propositionally.

Parametrised inductive types like lists or trees remain to be investigated.

Universes. If the underlying type theory has a universe

$$\Gamma \vdash U$$

$$\Gamma,\ x : U \vdash \mathrm{El}(x)$$

then in the setoid model a universe can be defined as the discrete setoid (∇) on the type

$$\Sigma S : U.\Sigma S_r : \mathrm{El}(S) \to \mathrm{El}(S) \to U. \qquad \text{type and relation}$$
$$(\Pi s, s' : \mathrm{El}(S).\mathrm{El}(S_r\ s\ s') \to \mathrm{El}(S_r\ s'\ s)) \times \qquad \text{symmetry}$$
$$(\Pi s, s', s'' : \mathrm{El}(S).\mathrm{El}(S_r\ s\ s') \to \mathrm{El}(S_r\ s'\ s'') \to \mathrm{El}(S_r\ s\ s'')) \qquad \text{transitivity}$$

This universe is then closed under Π, Eq, and Σ, provided the original one (U) is. So in particular we can obtain a model of the Calculus of Constructions, i.e. Martin-Löf type theory with a universe closed under impredicative quantification.

Quotient types. The relation on a family of setoids being arbitrary we can e.g. interpret a type of rationals with underlying set $\mathrm{N} \times \mathrm{N}$ and suitable relation. More generally it is possible to interpret in the model a *quotient type former* which allows to form the quotient of a type by an arbitrary internal equivalence relation. This will be spelled out in more detail in the author's forthcoming thesis [3].

Streams. Among the numerous applications of the propositional ξ-rule we just single out the following. In the presence of Ext the type $\mathrm{N} \rightarrow A$ may serve as a type of streams (infinite lists) over A which has the property that any two bisimilar streams are propositionally equal and thus can be substituted for one another in every context.

Sigma types. Our definition of contexts and context morphisms is based on an equational constraint (preservation of reflexivity). So we cannot expect that they can easily be internalised in the setoid model by some sort of Σ-type. The obvious guess for a Σ-type in the setoid model has (for Γ, S, T as in the definition of the Π-type) as underlying set

$$\Sigma(S,T)_{\mathrm{set}}(\gamma : \Gamma_{\mathrm{set}}) = \Sigma s : S_{\mathrm{set}}(\gamma).\Sigma\bar{s} : S_{\mathrm{rel}}(s,s).T_{\mathrm{set}}(\gamma, s, \bar{s})$$

and as relation

$$\Sigma(S,T)_{\mathrm{rel}}((s,\bar{s},t),(s',\bar{s}',t')) = S_{\mathrm{rel}}(s,s') \times T_{\mathrm{rel}}(t,t')$$

We can now define pairing and the first projection and more generally interpret the weak Σ-elimination rule [10]. In order to define a second projection or equivalently the dependent Σ-elimination rule we must use T_{rewrite} and thus we cannot get the equation

$$(M,N).2 = N$$

but only interpret the corresponding propositional identity. If we insist on a full Σ-type we could move to telescopes of setoids, i.e. a family of setoids would be a list of the form $(\Gamma, S_1, \ldots, S_n)$ where the S_i are families in the old sense and S_1 is above Γ, S_2 is above $\Gamma.S_1$ and so forth. For general reasons this structure is a model, and has strong Σ-types.

6 Summary and conclusive remarks

We have now developed a full model of intensional Martin-Löf type theory. This means that along the lines described in [12] we can define a semantic function $[\![-]\!]$ which maps ordinary contexts to contexts of setoids, types in contexts to families of setoids over the interpretation of their contexts and finally terms to sections. This interpretation is sound in the sense that whenever some judgement J is derivable in the theory with Ext, then $[\![J]\!]$ is derivable in the pure theory by mimicking the derivation of J in the setoid model. The converse does not hold, i.e. if $[\![J]\!]$ is derivable then J itself need not be derivable in the theory with Ext. Consider for example the judgement J

$$\vdash \mathrm{refl_N}(0) : \mathrm{Eq_N}(0,\ \mathrm{Subst}\,(\mathrm{Ext}\,(P), 0))$$

where P is a proof that two functions on the natural numbers are pointwise propositionally equal. Clearly $[\![J]\!]$ is provable because Subst (Ext (P), 0) equals 0 in the setoid model. Intuitively this is so because $[\![\mathrm{Subst}\,(\mathrm{Ext}\,(p), 0)]\!]$ is a term of type $[\![\mathrm{N}]\!] = \mathrm{N}$ in the empty context. So it must be a normal form of type N, but it can hardly be a successor. On the other hand J itself is not derivable as indicated in the Introduction.

So a precise "specification" of the setoid model is not straightforward. For the moment we can only offer the semantic equations themselves. In future work we would like to establish a correspondence between the setoid model and derivations in extensional type theory, i.e. with the equality reflection rule.

We have argued that we can now use the type theory with Ext and eliminate all occurrences of Ext by a post-hoc interpretation in the setoid model. But is there any use in actually performing this interpretation? Certainly the terms obtained from this interpretation can be executed, whereas the terms containing Ext cannot. But if one is merely interested in execution one may just as well use the much simpler realisability interpretation into untyped lambda calculus where Ext can be realised by the identity.

In our opinion the real value of model constructions like the one we have described lies in the syntactic justification of rules like Ext or quotient types, and in the insight that formal proof development in type theory does not necessarily mean to carry around lots of different equalities and substitutivity proofs, since in principle the translation into setoids may always be performed.

There are at least two more solutions to the extensionality problem. One consists of adding a new universe of propositions which does not affect the types at all. One is then free to add any propositional assumptions one likes, provided one can give a model or other proof of consistency, but one loses the possibility of computational use of proofs, in particular the possibility to reindex dependent types along propositional equalities. If one is interested in formalisations of algebra where dependent types play a subordinate rôle, this is a very simple yet sound approach.

The other solution is again a syntactic model construction, which differs from the given one in that we interpret families of setoids as nondependent sets where a non-reflexive relation singles out the different fibres. The identity type becomes the unit type under this interpretation. In this model the type part and the relation part are completely separated, so that the relation part can be projected away. What remains is a kind of realisability interpretation of type theory. Dependent types are interpreted as simple types, dependent product as the arrow type and the identity type becomes the unit. Both constructions will be described in more detail in [3], too.

The setoid model has been implemented in the Lego system [8]. This means that the combinators we have defined are actually available and setoids can be built using these combinators according to some derivation in type theory. Also we have used Lego to check all the equations which are required to hold. For the future it might be useful to have a "parser" which translates actual lambda terms into such combinators.

Acknowledgements

I wish to thank Thorsten Altenkirch, Don Sannella, Thomas Streicher, and an anonymous referee for helpful comments on earlier versions of this paper.

References

1. J. Cartmell. *Generalized algebraic theories and contextual categories.* PhD thesis, Univ. Oxford, 1978.
2. Solomon Feferman. Theories of Finite Type. In Jon Barwise, editor, *Handbook of Mathematical Logic*, chapter D.4, pages 934–935. North-Holland, 1977.
3. Martin Hofmann. *Extensional concepts in intensional type theory.* PhD thesis, Univ. of Edinburgh, forthcoming 1994.
4. Bart Jacobs. *Categorical Type Theory.* PhD thesis, University of Utrecht, 1991.
5. Bart Jacobs. Comprehension categories and the semantics of type theory. *Theoretical Computer Science*, 107:169–207, 1993.
6. Horst Luckhardt. *Extensional Gödel Functional Interpretation. A Consistency Proof of Classical Analysis*, volume 306 of *Lecture Notes in Mathematics.* Springer, Berlin, 1973.
7. Zhaohui Luo. *An Extended Calculus of Constructions.* PhD thesis, University of Edinburgh, July 1990.
8. Zhaohui Luo and Randy Pollack. LEGO Proof Development System: User's Manual. Technical Report ECS-LFCS-92-211, University of Edinburgh, May 1992.
9. Per Martin-Löf. *Intuitionistic Type Theory.* Bibliopolis·Napoli, 1984.
10. John Mitchell and Gordon Plotkin. Abstract Types have Existential Type. *ACM Transactions on Programming Languages and Systems*, 10(3):470–502, 1988.
11. B. Nordström, K. Petersson, and J. M. Smith. *Programming in Martin-Löfs Type Theory, An Introduction.* Clarendon Press, Oxford, 1990
12. Thomas Streicher. *Semantics of Type Theory.* Birkhäuser, 1991.
13. Thomas Streicher. *Semantical Investigations into Intensional Type Theory.* Habilitationsschrift, LMU München, to appear 1993.
14. David Turner. A new formulation of constructive type theory. In P. Dybjer, editor, *Proceedings of the Workshop on Programming Logic*, pages 258–294. Programming Methodology Group, Univ. of Göteborg, May 1989.

Programming with Streams in Coq
A case study : the Sieve of Eratosthenes*

François Leclerc[1] and Christine Paulin-Mohring[2]

[1] CRIN URA CNRS 262, BP 239, 54506 Vandoeuvre-les-Nancy cedex, France
[2] LIP URA CNRS 1398, ENS Lyon, 46 Allée d'Italie, 69364 Lyon cedex 07, France.

Abstract. Kahn and MacQueen [13, 14] proposed considering a parallel dataflow program as a network of functional transformers over infinite lists (also called streams). Recently, type theory and the "proofs as programs" paradigm have proved useful for the validation of functional programs.
We propose to relate both approaches, by studying a special dataflow program (the Sieve of Eratosthenes) in two strongly-typed lambda-calculi (system F and the Calculus of Constructions).
The originality of our approach is the introduction of a type of parameterized streams which uses the mechanism of dependent types in the Calculus of Constructions. The Sieve of Eratosthenes consists of an infinite list which gives both the integer and the proof that it is the first prime since the last output.

Introduction

This paper studies an example of the conjunction of three fruitful ideas :

1. Kahn and MacQueen's proposition to model a parallel dataflow program as a functional transformation over infinite lists.
2. The "proofs as programs" paradigm which interprets a formula as a specification and a proof of the formula as the construction of a program correct with respect to the specification.
3. Higher-Order quantification which makes it possible to build types corresponding to infinite structures.

Higher-order type theory is often presented as a good framework for the formal development of correct programs [3, 5, 6, 20, 18]. The usual programs which are validated in these theories are functional programs which are specified as a finite transformation from an input satisfying some property into an output related by some condition to the input.

* This research started during F. Leclerc's DEA project at LIP (spring 91). It was partly supported by ESPRIT Basic Research Actions "Logical Frameworks" and "Types for Proofs and Programs" and by MRE Programme de Recherches Coordonnées and CNRS GDR "Programmation".

Various computers programs such as protocols or top-level loops (special cases of so called reactive systems) involve another kind of specification. Depending on the action of the external world, they continuously produce reactions. Such processes are not supposed to stop by themselves but should be able to always produce outputs.

Kahn and MacQueen [13, 14] proposed modeling these systems as functional transformations over infinite lists (also called streams). This approach is well-suited for type theory, which aims to validate functional programs. Impredicative type theories like system F or the Calculus of Constructions provide a way to represent infinite structures internally as coinductive types. We propose to investigate the paradigm of programming with streams in these two theories.

We study the Sieve of Eratosthenes which is the standard example used in this domain.

Organization of the paper We recall the basic ideas of the impredicative encoding of coinductive types in system F which was first presented in [24]. Our presentation will stress the analogy with the dual notion of inductive definitions. We briefly explain the "proofs as programs" paradigm and how a correct program can be built as a constructive proof of a given specification in the Calculus of Constructions. This approach motivates the main contribution of this paper which is to propose a representation of streams which internalizes the specification of the outputs. The adequacy of this representation is illustrated by the development of two versions of the Sieve of Eratosthenes which have been completely formalized and checked using the proof assistant Coq [7]. We conclude with a discussion on the computational behavior of our programs.

Notations Our aim is to give the main ideas for the construction of the programs. We will not be too formal but the examples were completely checked in the Coq system [7].

We shall write terms either from the system F or from the Calculus of Constructions, with the following notations. Quantification is written $\forall x : M.N$, implication is written $M \rightarrow N$, both associate to the right. The lambda-abstraction is written $\lambda x : M.N$ or $\Lambda X.M$ for an abstraction over type or predicate variables. The application of a term M to a term N is written $(M\ N)$, it associates to the left, we shall sometimes omit the external parentheses [3]. The type annotation after the ":" in quantification or abstraction will be omitted when it is clear from the context. Also the notation $\lambda x, y.t$ will be used for multiple abstraction $\lambda x.\lambda y.t$.

We shall write $A(X)$ to emphasize the occurrence of the variable X in a term A. In that case $A(M)$ denotes the result of substituting M for all occurrences of the variable X in A.

[3] In the system Coq a predicate is defined as a particular functional term which associates a proposition to objects, consequently we use the application notation $(P\ t_1 \ldots t_n)$ which intuitively represents the instance of the predicate P for the terms $t_1, \ldots, t_n$.

We write $M \simeq N$ when the terms M and N are convertible for β equivalence.

The same names will sometimes be used for different constructions when the ambiguity can be solved from the context.

1 Impredicative encoding of coinductive types

The system F is an extension of simply typed lambda-calculus with quantification over second-order type variables. It was independently introduced by Girard and Reynolds.

A particularity of this calculus is the possibility to represent data types internally. For instance, one can build a type only with arrows and second-order quantification such that there is a bijection between the set of natural numbers and closed normal terms inhabiting this type. Furthermore, a large class of functions over natural numbers will also be represented inside this calculus.

The representation of inductive data types like integers or lists in system F can be seen as an encoding of smallest fixpoints of monotonic operators. A general presentation of this can be found in [2] or [11].

But inductive types only represent finite terms. Infinite data are also important in computer science. A standard example is infinite lists of elements of a given type A. This type can be represented using different methods. One possibility is to take the type $\mathsf{Nat} \to A$ of functions from Nat to A.

We investigate another representation as the greatest fixpoint of the monotonic operator $F(X) = A*X$. This approach can be generalized to other possibly infinite structures (trees, lists which are finite or infinite, etc). It is a particular case of coinductive types which can be uniformly represented using the impredicativity of system F. We present here a general scheme of definition of coinductive types. We emphasize two aspects. First, this encoding corresponds to a particular application of Tarski's theorem. Second, from the computational point of view, elements of inductive types can be seen as abstract processes. This encoding was first studied by G. Wraith [24].

1.1 Encoding an existential quantification

The impredicative encoding of coinductive types uses an existential quantification over type variables. This quantification can be represented using only universal quantification. We recall this encoding.

Let X be a type variable and $A_1, \ldots, A_n$ be types possibly depending on X. We introduce the notation :

$\exists X.A_1 \wedge \ldots \wedge A_n$ for the type $\forall C.(\forall X.A_1 \to \cdots \to A_n \to C) \to C$.

It is easy to build a term elim (defined as $\lambda m.m$) of type $(\exists X.A_1 \wedge \ldots \wedge A_n) \to \forall C.(\forall X.A_1 \to \cdots \to A_n \to C) \to C$.

For X a type and $t_1, \ldots, t_n$ terms of type respectively $A_1, \ldots, A_n$ we can build a term of type $\exists X.A_1 \wedge \ldots \wedge A_n$ (take $\Lambda C.\lambda H.(H\ X\ t_1 \ldots t_n)$) this term will be written $(X, t_1, \ldots, t_n)$.

One easily checks that the equality (elim $(X, t_1, \ldots, t_n)\ C\ f) \simeq (f\ X\ t_1 \ldots t_n)$ holds.

Even if it is interesting to encode everything just using higher order universal quantification, we should mention that this encoding is not completely satisfactory because we can find more terms in the type $\exists X.A$ than terms built from tuples (X, a). A very simple example is with $A = X$.

The term $\Lambda C.\lambda H : \forall X.X \rightarrow C.(H\ C \rightarrow C\ \lambda x : C.x)$ is in closed normal form and in the type $\exists X.X$ but it is not convertible to a term (X, a). This is a well-known feature of the impredicative encoding of data types which also appears for usual pairs (see for instance [22]).

This is not really a problem (it just means that the type contains more elements than the one we are expecting). In order to avoid this phenomenon, we can extend system F with a type constructor for existential quantification and special rules. In the system Coq, we can use the general mechanism of inductive definitions to define an existential with all the expected properties.

In the following we only use the notations $\exists X.A$, (X, a), elim and the types and equality introduced above without using the exact implementation of these operators.

1.2 Coinductive types in System *F*

The representation of fixpoints of monotonic operators can be seen as an application of Tarski general fixpoint theorem. A coinductive type is the greatest fixpoint of a monotonic operator $A(X)$ which is computed as the least upper bound of the X such that $X < A(X)$. The order is just inclusion which is encoded via implication. The least upper bound is the union which is encoded via an existential type.

Basic definitions In system F, the types in which a variable X occurs positively are generated by the entry *Pos* of the following syntax :

$$\begin{array}{lcl} Pos & ::= & M \mid X \mid \forall Y.Pos \mid Neg \rightarrow Pos \\ Neg & ::= & M \mid \forall Y.Neg \mid Pos \rightarrow Neg \end{array}$$

with the restriction that X does not occur in M.

Let $A(X)$ be a correct type in which X occurs positively, let Y be a type variable and f a variable of type $X \rightarrow Y$; then it is possible to build a term $A[f]$ of type $A(X) \rightarrow A(Y)$ by induction over $A(X)$.

Let $A(X)$ be a correct type of system F in which X occurs positively. We can define both μ and ν the smallest and the greatest fixpoint of this operator. We outline in the following table the main constructions associated to both types.

Inductive types	**Coinductive types**
$\mu \equiv \bigcap_X A(X) \subset X$ $\equiv \forall X.(A(X) \to X) \to X$	$\nu \equiv \bigcup_X X \subset A(X)$ $\equiv \exists X.(X \to A(X)) \wedge X$
$\mathsf{iter} : \forall X.(A(X) \to X) \to \mu \to X$ $\equiv \Lambda X.\lambda f, m.(m\, X\, f)$ $\mathsf{in} : A(\mu) \to \mu$ $\mathsf{in}\, a \equiv \Lambda X.\lambda f.(f\, (A[\mathsf{iter}\, X\, f]\, a))$	$\mathsf{build} : \forall X.(X \to A(X)) \to X \to \nu$ $\equiv \Lambda X.\lambda f, x.(X, f, x)$ $\mathsf{out} : \nu \to A(\nu)$ $\mathsf{out}\, m \equiv \mathsf{elim}\, m\, A(\nu)$ $\Lambda X.\lambda f, x.(A[\mathsf{build}\, X\, f]\, (f\, x))$
$\mathsf{iter}\, X\, F\, (\mathsf{in}\, m) \to F\, (A[\mathsf{iter}\, X\, F]\, m)$	$\mathsf{out}\, (\mathsf{build}\, X\, F\, x) \to A[\mathsf{build}\, X\, F]\, (F\, x)$

Natural numbers and Streams The typical example of an inductive definition is the type of natural numbers. It is the smallest fixpoint of the operator $1 + X$ which can be encoded in system F as $\forall C.C \to (X \to C) \to C$. The typical example of a coinductive definition is the type of streams of elements of a type A. It is the greatest fixpoint of the operator $A * X$ which can be encoded as $\forall C.(A \to X \to C) \to C$. In both cases, we can find more direct encodings than the one presented above. We outline the main constructions in the following table.

Natural numbers	**Streams**
$\mathsf{Nat} \leftrightarrow 1 + \mathsf{Nat}$ $\equiv \forall X.X \to (X \to X) \to X$	$\mathsf{Str} \leftrightarrow A * \mathsf{Str}$ $\equiv \exists X.(X \to A) \wedge (X \to X) \wedge X$
$\mathsf{iter} : \forall X.X \to (X \to X)$ $\to \mathsf{Nat} \to X$ $\equiv \Lambda X.\lambda x, f.\lambda n.(n\, X\, x\, f)$ $0 : \mathsf{Nat}$ $\equiv \Lambda X.\lambda x, f.x$ $\mathsf{S} : \mathsf{Nat} \to \mathsf{Nat}$ $\equiv \lambda n.\Lambda X.\lambda x, f.(f\, (n\, X\, x\, f))$	$\mathsf{build} : \forall X.(X \to A) \to (X \to X)$ $\to X \to \mathsf{Str}$ $\equiv \Lambda X.\lambda h, t, x.(X, h, t, x)$ $\mathsf{hd} : \mathsf{Str} \to A$ $\equiv \lambda s.(s\, A\, \Lambda X.\lambda h, t, x.(h\, x))$ $\mathsf{tl} : \mathsf{Str} \to \mathsf{Str}$ $\mathsf{tl}\, s \equiv \mathsf{elim}\, s\, \mathsf{Str}\, \Lambda X.\lambda h, t, x.(\mathsf{build}\, X\, h\, t\, (t\, x))$
$g : T \quad h : T \to T$ $f : \mathsf{Nat} \to T \equiv (\mathsf{iter}\, T\, g\, h)$ $f\, 0 \simeq g$ $f\, (\mathsf{S}\, n) \simeq h\, (f\, n)$	$g : T \to A \quad h : T \to T$ $f : T \to \mathsf{Str} \equiv (\mathsf{build}\, T\, g\, h)$ $\mathsf{hd}\, (f\, x) \simeq (g\, x)$ $\mathsf{tl}\, (f\, x) \simeq f\, (h\, x)$

1.3 Examples

The nth element of a stream. Computing the nth element of a stream is done by induction on n. We define a function nth which has type $\mathsf{Nat} \to \mathsf{Str} \to A$. We want it to satisfy the following equations :

$$\mathsf{nth}\ 0\ s \simeq \mathsf{hd}\ s \qquad \mathsf{nth}\ (\mathsf{S}\ n)\ s \simeq \mathsf{nth}\ n\ (\mathsf{tl}\ s)$$

This is achieved by the following definition :

$$\mathsf{nth} \equiv (\mathsf{iter}\ \mathsf{Str} \to A\ \mathsf{hd}\ \lambda H : \mathsf{Str} \to A.\lambda s : \mathsf{Str}.(H\ (\mathsf{tl}\ s)))$$

This is an example of an iterative definition over a higher-order type ($\mathsf{Str} \to A$).

Stream of natural numbers starting from n. We can represent the stream of natural numbers $(n\; n+1\; n+2 \ldots)$. We define a function Enu which has type Nat $\rightarrow$ Str. We want it to satisfy the following equations :

$$\mathsf{hd}\ (\mathsf{Enu}\ n) \simeq n \qquad \mathsf{tl}\ (\mathsf{Enu}\ n) \simeq \mathsf{Enu}\ (\mathsf{S}\ n)$$

This is achieved with the definition : $\mathsf{Enu} \equiv (\mathsf{build\ Nat}\ \lambda x.x\ \mathsf{S})$.

Following the same pattern we can represent the constant stream which only contains the value n as :

$$\mathsf{Con} \equiv (\mathsf{build\ One}\ \lambda x.n\ \lambda x.x\ \mathsf{o})$$

with One a type (for instance $\forall X.X \rightarrow X$) with at least one element o.

From a function to a stream. Given a function f of type Nat $\rightarrow A$, one can define the stream repr by (build Nat f S O). Let $\tilde{n}$ be the term of type Nat obtained by applying n times the successor function to 0. It is easy to check that nth $\tilde{n}$ repr $\simeq$ $f\ \tilde{n}$. This shows a strong correspondence between streams and functions from Nat to A.

1.4 Properties of streams

Representation A "canonical element" of type streams will be a quadruple (X, H, T, x) with X a type, H a function of type $X \rightarrow A$, T a function of type $X \rightarrow X$ and x a term of type X. Such a stream is obtained by (build $X\ H\ T\ x$). Its head will be $(H\ x)$ and its tail a quadruple $(X, H, T, (T\ x))$. The nth element of this stream is $(H\ (T^n\ x))$ where $(T^0\ x) = x$ and $(T^{n+1}\ x) = (T^n\ (T\ x))$. The stream (X, H, T, x) can be seen as an abstract representation of a process built on a type X, a current state x and functions H and T that computes the output of the stream and the modification of the state.

We can say that this representation is abstract because when we have an element of type stream, we cannot access its particular implementation.

Of course an infinite list can be implemented as many different objects of type stream. For instance, if s is a stream then (build Str hd tl s) and (build Nat λn : Nat.(nth $n\ s$) S) are also streams which produce the same elements.

Iterative versus primitive recursive definitions The impredicative encoding of natural numbers gives naturally the definition of functions using an iterative scheme $f\ (\mathsf{S}\ n) = h\ (f\ n)$. The more general scheme of primitive recursive definition :

$$f\ (\mathsf{S}\ n) = h\ n\ (f\ n)$$

is obtained using iteration and pairing. It is well known that this encoding is not satisfactory because $f\ (\mathsf{S}\ n)$ reduces to $h\ n\ (f\ n)$ only if n is a closed natural numbers and also in that case the number of reduction steps will be proportional to n. There is of course an analogous problem for streams. The basic iterative scheme of definition is :

$$\mathsf{tl}\ (f\ x) = f\ (h\ x)$$

With just this scheme, it is not immediate to program a function conc for the concatenation of an element a at the head of a stream s. The equations for such a definition will be :

$$\text{hd}\ (\text{conc}\ a\ s) = a \qquad \text{tl}\ (\text{conc}\ a\ s) = s$$

More generally we would like to program a stream as some process (X, h, t, x) which at some step becomes a new given stream. This new scheme can be obtained using disjunct sum and iteration.

We write $X + \text{Str} \equiv \forall C.(X \rightarrow C) \rightarrow (\text{Str} \rightarrow C) \rightarrow C$ the type representing the disjunct union of X and Str. We call inl (resp. inr) the left (resp. right) injection of type $X \rightarrow X + \text{Str}$ (resp. $\text{Str} \rightarrow X + \text{Str}$). The analogue of primitive recursion will be an operation build_pr of type :

$$\forall X.(X \rightarrow A) \rightarrow (X \rightarrow (X + \text{Str})) \rightarrow X \rightarrow \text{Str}.$$

We would like the following equalities to hold :

$$
\begin{array}{lll}
(1) & \text{hd}\ (\text{build\_pr}\ X\ h\ t\ x) = (h\ x) & \\
(2) & \text{tl}\ (\text{build\_pr}\ X\ h\ t\ x) = \text{build\_pr}\ X\ h\ t\ y & \text{if}\ (t\ x) = (\text{inl}\ y) \\
(3) & \text{tl}\ (\text{build\_pr}\ X\ h\ t\ x) = s & \text{if}\ (t\ x) = (\text{inr}\ s)
\end{array}
$$

If f is of type $X \rightarrow Y$ and g of type $\text{Str} \rightarrow Y$, we write $[f, g]$ the function of type $(X + \text{Str}) \rightarrow Y$ such that $[f, g]\ (\text{inl}\ x) \simeq (f\ x)$ and $[f, g]\ (\text{inr}\ y) \simeq (g\ y)$. We can mimic the behavior of build_pr by taking :

$$
\begin{array}{l}
\text{build\_pr} \equiv \Lambda X.\lambda h : X \rightarrow A.\lambda t : X \rightarrow (X + \text{Str}).\lambda x : X. \\
\qquad (\text{build}\ X + \text{Str}\ [h, \text{hd}]\ [t, \lambda s : \text{Str}.(\text{inr}\ (\text{tl}\ s))]\ (\text{inl}\ x))
\end{array}
$$

The equalities (1) and (2) will be satisfied as convertibility rules. But if $(t\ x) = (\text{inr}\ s)$, the streams tl (build_pr $X\ h\ t\ x$) and s will not be convertible but will only have the same behavior.

Using build_pr, the stream (conc $a\ s$) can be defined as :

$$(\text{build\_pr One}\ \lambda x.a\ \lambda x.(\text{inr}\ s)\ o)$$

The definition of the analogue of primitive recursion for coinductive types in typed lambda-calculus is presented in [17, 9]. We will not need it in our development of the sieve of Eratosthenes.

Termination properties In system F, every program terminates. If s is a stream, it implies that for each n, nth $n\ s$ has a value. Consequently an element of type Str define a total function from Nat to A.

2 Logical specification of streams

2.1 Proofs and Programs

Logical Frameworks such as the Calculus of Constructions or Martin-Löf's Intuitionistic Type Theory include both a programming language in a functional style and a logic to reason about these objects.

From proofs to Programs Using the type of natural numbers with 0 and the successor function S, a predecessor function can be defined which satisfies the defining equations :

$$\mathsf{pred}\ 0 = 0 \qquad \mathsf{pred}\ (\mathsf{S}\ n) = n$$

For instance, one can inductively prove the following properties :

$$\forall n : \mathsf{Nat}.(n = 0) \vee (n = \mathsf{S}(\mathsf{pred}\ n)) \quad \forall n : \mathsf{Nat}.(\mathsf{pred}\ n) \leq n$$

What is specific to these type theories, is the possibility to mix computational and logical informations. For instance one may specify a predecessor function as a transformation of a natural number n into a natural number m such that $(n = m = 0) \vee n = (\mathsf{S}\ m)$.

This specification translates to an existential formula :

$$\forall n : \mathsf{Nat}.\exists m : \mathsf{Nat}.(n = m = 0) \vee (n = \mathsf{S}\ m)$$

From this proof one can extract both the predecessor function and a proof of correctness of this function. The main advantage of this method is that one build only one object (the proof of the existential formula) in order to get both a program and a proof of correctness of this program. Giving the specification first forces the user to only build a correct program.

From programs to proofs One can object that sometimes, like for the very simple case of the predecessor function, one knows the function better than the proof, and that we are not sure that our proof corresponds to the expected algorithm.

One can solve this problem. C. Parent [19] designed a tactic which from the specification and the program generates "proof obligations" which are simple logical formulae which have to be verified in order to complete the proof of the specification.

For the example of the predecessor function, one can just start with the specification $\forall n : \mathsf{Nat}.\exists m : \mathsf{Nat}.(n = m = 0) \vee (n = \mathsf{S}\ m)$ and the pred function. The `Program` tactic generates the two trivial subgoals $0 = 0 = 0 \vee (0 = \mathsf{S}\ m)$ and $\mathsf{S}\ n = n = 0 \vee (\mathsf{S}\ n = \mathsf{S}\ n)$.

The methodology of extracting programs from proofs which is the theoretical basis of this tactic gives us a powerful tool to justify the correctness of programs by just giving a specification and completing proofs of basic properties of this specification.

The chosen example is very simple to remain readable but the same methodology applies to non-trivial algorithms.

A drawback of this method is the necessity to extract a program out of the proof but this is done in a complete mechanical way. Certainly some programs are not as efficient as they would be if written directly but automatic optimizations can be performed.

We definitely think this is a good methodology for program development, at least when we have the initial specification. For these reasons, a natural question was to investigate if this methodology of including the logical part inside programs could also be used in order to justify the correctness of streams. The answer is yes and we propose two possible parameterized types of streams which are quite general and are used in the developments of the Sieve of Eratosthenes.

2.2 Parameterized streams in the Calculus of Constructions

In system F, a stream is represented as a process which produces infinitely many objects of type A.

One way to include logical information is to require the type A to be a specification. For instance say that A will be an existential property $\exists p.A'(p)$. But if A' only depends on p we cannot specified very interesting behavior because all the elements of the stream will obey the same specification.

For instance we could say that all the elements of the stream are prime but this is also true for the infinite stream containing only 2. The specification should be more precise. The predicate $A'(p)$ should also depend on other parameters.

Indexed Streams A natural idea is to have the specification depending on the index of the element in the stream.

Given a specification $(A\ k)$ on natural numbers, we define a type of indexed stream Str.

Intuitively, with n an integer, an element of type $(\mathsf{Str}\ n)$ is a stream whose first element has index n. The head of this stream will be an element of $(A\ n)$ and the tail of the stream will be a stream indexed by $(\mathsf{S}\ n)$ that is an element of $(\mathsf{Str}\ (\mathsf{S}\ n))$.

This type can easily be represented in the Calculus of Constructions as a coinductive predicate over natural numbers. The encoding of coinductive predicates is a simple extension of the case of coinductive types in system F.

A predicate over natural numbers in the Calculus of Constructions is represented as a function from Nat to Set (the type of specifications).

The terms related to the indexed streams are given in the following table.

$\mathsf{Str} \equiv \lambda n:\mathsf{Nat}.\exists P.(\forall m.(P\ m) \rightarrow (A\ m)) \wedge (\forall m.(P\ m) \rightarrow (P\ (\mathsf{S}\ m))) \wedge (P\ n)$ $: \mathsf{Nat} \rightarrow Set$
$\mathsf{build} : \forall n:\mathsf{Nat}.\forall P:\mathsf{Nat}\rightarrow Set.$ $(\forall m.(P\ m) \rightarrow (A\ m)) \rightarrow (\forall m.(P\ m) \rightarrow (P\ (\mathsf{S}\ m))) \rightarrow (P\ n) \rightarrow (\mathsf{Str}\ n)$ $\equiv \lambda n.\Lambda P.\lambda h.\lambda t.\lambda x.(P,h,t,x)$
$\mathsf{hd} : \forall m.(\mathsf{Str}\ m) \rightarrow (A\ m)$ $\equiv \lambda m.\lambda s.(\mathsf{elim}\ s\ (A\ m)\ \Lambda P.\lambda h.\lambda t.\lambda x.(h\ m\ x))$ $\mathsf{tl} : \forall m.(\mathsf{Str}\ m) \rightarrow (\mathsf{Str}\ (S\ m))$ $\equiv \lambda m.\lambda s.(\mathsf{elim}\ s\ (\mathsf{Str}\ (\mathsf{S}\ m))\ \Lambda P.\lambda h.\lambda t.\lambda x.(\mathsf{build}\ (\mathsf{S}\ m)\ P\ h\ t\ (t\ m\ x)))$

The following convertibility rules are satisfied. With m, P, h, t and x of the appropriate types :

$$\begin{aligned}\mathsf{hd}\ m\ (\mathsf{build}\ m\ P\ h\ t\ x) &\simeq h\ m\ x\\ \mathsf{tl}\ m\ (\mathsf{build}\ m\ P\ h\ t\ x) &\simeq \mathsf{build}\ (\mathsf{S}\ m)\ P\ h\ t\ (t\ m\ x)\end{aligned}$$

We can now prove the following property by induction over n.

$$\forall n.\forall m : \mathsf{Nat}.(\mathsf{Str}\ m) \rightarrow (A\ (n+m))$$

We call this proof nth. We can check that its computational behavior is similar to that of the nth function in system F.

2.3 General parameterized Streams

The type of indexed streams looks nice but when we tried to specify the filter function which gives in a stream only the elements which satisfy a condition, it was not at all satisfactory.

The natural way to specify this operator is to say that since the previous output, no input of the stream did satisfy the specification. To solve this problem we ask each element of the stream to carry an extra argument which is a parameter suitable for the specification of the outputs.

We have a specification $(A\ q)$ depending on a parameter q of type U. The parameterized streams are objects of type $(\mathsf{Str}\ p)$, also depending on a parameter of type U. The head of an object in $(\mathsf{Str}\ p)$ is an element of type $(A\ p)$, the tail function associates to an object in $(\mathsf{Str}\ p)$, a new index q and an object in $(\mathsf{Str}\ q)$.

The indexed stream is a particular case of this scheme where the parameter is just the index itself and is incremented by one at each step.

For the filter operator, the parameter in the stream can be the index of the element in the initial stream. $(A\ p)$ could express that there exists an object a in the initial stream with an index q which satisfies the condition and such that from p to q no elements in the initial stream did satisfy the condition. The index q will be the parameter of the tail of the stream.

We do not give all the precise definitions for such a type of streams. It will be done in a particular case for the development of the partial version of the sieve of Eratosthenes.

Comparison The type of indexed stream could also be defined in a functional way as objects which associate to n a proof of $(A\ n)$. It is not clear how to represent in a functional way the parameterized streams. The functional representation of streams assumes we have a global knowledge of the infinite list. The coinductive representation corresponds to only give a method to build an arbitrary finite initial part of the list. It is clear from the parameterized specification where the new state depends on what was known after computing the initial segment.

3 The sieve of Eratosthenes in system F

We now present the development of the Sieve of Eratosthenes in system F.

3.1 Description of the algorithm

The algorithm is simple, we describe it equationally.

An auxiliary operation is the sieve function itself which takes a number p and a stream s and gives back the stream of the elements of s which cannot be divided by p. The operation sieve has type $\mathsf{Nat} \rightarrow \mathsf{Str} \rightarrow \mathsf{Str}$. It can be described by the following equation :

$$\begin{aligned}(\mathsf{sieve}\ p\ s) = {} & \mathsf{if}\ \mathsf{div}\ p\ (\mathsf{hd}\ s)\ \mathsf{then}\ \mathsf{sieve}\ p\ (\mathsf{tl}\ s) \\ & \mathsf{else}\ \mathsf{conc}\ (\mathsf{hd}\ s)\ (\mathsf{sieve}\ p\ (\mathsf{tl}\ s))\end{aligned}$$

The sieve is used in an operation of type $\mathsf{Str} \rightarrow \mathsf{Str}$ that we call primes. This operation takes a stream s, keep its head p and applies to the tail of this stream the sieve operation using p. The primes function is characterized by the following equations.

$$\mathsf{hd}\ (\mathsf{primes}\ s) = (\mathsf{hd}\ s) \qquad \mathsf{tl}\ (\mathsf{primes}\ s) = \mathsf{primes}\ (\mathsf{sieve}\ (\mathsf{hd}\ s)\ (\mathsf{tl}\ s))$$

The primes numbers are obtained by applying the primes operation to the stream (Enu 2).

If the scheme for the definition of the stream of prime numbers follows the general pattern of an iterative definition, it is not the case for the sieve function. The head of the stream (sieve s) will be the first element of s which can be divided by p. Nothing in the algorithm makes sure that this search terminates. Starting from a different stream than (Enu 2) we could loop forever. To say that the result of the sieve has type Str implies in particular that there are infinitely many primes numbers. It is not surprising that we cannot just translate this algorithm in system F.

3.2 A total version of the sieve

We propose two solutions to avoid this problem. The first one is to introduce an explicit bound (from mathematical results we know how to compute one) for the search of the next number which cannot be divided by p. The second one is not to manipulate streams of natural numbers but streams of a type Nat^{+} which contains an extra dummy element dum. The output will be a stream with primes numbers separated by the dummy element. Nothing in the type of the output avoids that, from some point onwards, every output will be dummy. A similar idea of introducing a silent step was also used by C. Raffalli [23].

We call this last algorithm, the total version of the sieve of Eratosthenes. We can program in system F a function div^{+} of type $\mathsf{Nat}^{+} \rightarrow \mathsf{Nat}^{+} \rightarrow \mathsf{bool}$, such that $(\mathsf{div}^{+}\ p\ q) = \mathsf{true}$ when p or q is the dummy element or when p divides q (division on natural numbers is primitive recursive and can be represented in system F). The operation sieve has type $\mathsf{Nat}^{+} \rightarrow (\mathsf{Str}\ \mathsf{Nat}^{+}) \rightarrow (\mathsf{Str}\ \mathsf{Nat}^{+})$. It can be described by the following equations :

$$\begin{aligned}\mathsf{hd}\ (\mathsf{sieve}\ p\ S) &= \mathsf{if}\ (\mathsf{div}^{+}\ p\ (\mathsf{hd}\ S))\ \mathsf{then}\ \mathsf{dum}\ \mathsf{else}\ (\mathsf{hd}\ S) \\ \mathsf{tl}\ (\mathsf{sieve}\ p\ S) &= \mathsf{sieve}\ p\ (\mathsf{tl}\ S)\end{aligned}$$

This follows an iterative scheme which is easily translated into system F code. With f the function $\lambda q.\text{if } (\text{div}^+\ p\ q) \text{ then dum else } q$:

$$\text{sieve} \equiv (\text{build } (\text{Str Nat}^+)\ \lambda s : (\text{Str Nat+}).(f\ (\text{hd } s))\ \text{tl})$$

The primes operation has type $(\text{Str Nat}^+) \rightarrow (\text{Str Nat}^+)$. The equations are not changed :

$$\text{hd } (\text{primes } s) = (\text{hd } s) \qquad \text{tl } (\text{primes } s) = \text{primes } (\text{sieve } (\text{hd } s)\ (\text{tl } s)))$$

The primes numbers are obtained by applying the primes operation to the stream of successive elements in Nat^+starting from 2 namely with inj the injection function from Nat to Nat^+.

$$\text{Si} \equiv (\text{build Nat inj S } 2)$$

We may remark that we will also get the stream of primes numbers starting from three by applying the primes operation to the stream of odd numbers starting from three. This stream can be constructed as :

$$(\text{build Nat inj } \lambda n : \text{Nat.}(\text{S } (\text{S } n))\ 3)$$

4 The sieve of Eratosthenes in Coq

We now want to have a verified version of the sieve of Eratosthenes, showing that it gives us all prime numbers.

Instead of doing a proof of the previous program we shall build a new one that will give us as an output a natural number and a proof of its primality. Of course the problem will also be to specify that it gives all prime numbers.

We study the proof counterpart of the total sieve which answers for each number if it is prime or not and also gives the constructions corresponding to a stream which only contains the prime numbers.

4.1 Specification

If we analyze the algorithm, we can see that its specification does not concern really primality but can be parameterized by the initial stream the primes operation is applied to.

Let this stream be called Si. We shall denote $\text{Si}\,(n)$ its n-th element. The output of the sieve program will be the elements of Si which cannot be divided by any of the previous elements in the stream. Of course if Si is the stream of natural numbers starting from two or the stream of odd numbers starting from three, the fact that they cannot be divided by a previous element is equivalent to the fact that they are prime.

This analysis led us to the definition of the relation divinf on natural numbers. The meaning of divinf k n is that $\text{Si}\,(n)$ can be divided by at least one $\text{Si}\,(p)$ for $p < k$. The definition of divinf is :

$$\text{divinf } k\ n \equiv \exists p.(p < k \wedge \text{div Si}\,(p)\ \text{Si}\,(n))$$

A few logical lemmas about divinf will be used.

4.2 A total sieve development

We first develop a verified version of the sieve of Eratosthenes which corresponds to a total sieve.

We use the type of indexed streams defined previously. The definition depends on a specification $(A\ n)$. The development of the sieve uses several different specifications. So the constructions Str, hd and tl are abstracted with respect to this specification. We use the notation (Str A), (hd A) and (tl A) to explicitly instantiate the definition with a particular specification.

We introduce the specification (divspec k n) which says "either (divinf k n) or $\neg$(divinf k n) holds".

The output of the sieve program will be an indexed stream based on the predicate λn : Nat.(divspec n n). It will indicate for the nth element of the stream whether there exists $k < n$ such that Si (k) divides Si (n).

The function sieve. The sieve transformation itself corresponds to a proof of :

$$\forall n.(\mathsf{Str}\ (\mathsf{divspec}\ k)\ n) \rightarrow (\mathsf{Str}\ (\mathsf{divspec}\ (\mathsf{S}\ k))\ n)$$

To prove this property, we just use build with the predicate (Str (divspec k)); we have to prove the two following lemmas :

$$\forall n.(\mathsf{Str}\ (\mathsf{divspec}\ k)\ n) \rightarrow (\mathsf{divspec}\ (\mathsf{S}\ k)\ n)$$

and

$$\forall n.(\mathsf{Str}\ (\mathsf{divspec}\ k)\ n) \rightarrow (\mathsf{Str}\ (\mathsf{divspec}\ k)\ (\mathsf{S}\ n))$$

This last lemma is proved by the tl term applied to the specification (divspec k).

For the first one, assuming we have a stream s in (Str (divspec k) n) we look at the head of the stream. It gives us a proof of (divspec k n), so we know whether Si (n) can be divided or not by Si (l) with $l < k$. In order to decide if Si (n) can be divided by Si (l) with $l <$ (S k), it is enough to check if Si (k) divides Si (l). The proof can easily be completed this way.

The function primes. The primes function corresponds to a proof of :

$$\forall k : \mathsf{Nat}.(\mathsf{Str}\ (\mathsf{divspec}\ k)\ k) \rightarrow (\mathsf{Str}\ \lambda n : \mathsf{Nat}.(\mathsf{divspec}\ n\ n)\ k)$$

It means that starting from a stream indexed by k and which gives for each n whether Si (n) can be divided by Si (m) for $m < k$ we can build a "diagonal" stream also indexed by k which gives for each n whether Si (n) can be divided by Si (m) for $m < n$.

This is proved by build applied to the predicate $(P\ n) \equiv$ (Str (divspec n) n). We can remark that the predicate is directly suggested by the form of the specification to prove.

We have to prove the lemma :

$$\forall n : \mathsf{Nat}.(\mathsf{Str}\ (\mathsf{divspec}\ n)\ n) \rightarrow (\mathsf{divspec}\ n\ n)$$

which is just proved by the hd function for the specification (divspec n).

We also have to prove :

$$\forall k : \mathsf{Nat}.(\mathsf{Str}\ (\mathsf{divspec}\ k)\ k) \rightarrow (\mathsf{Str}\ (\mathsf{divspec}\ (\mathsf{S}\ k))\ (\mathsf{S}\ k))$$

Let s be a term of type (Str (divspec k) k) We apply the sieve function developed previously. We get a stream in (Str (divspec (S k)) k). We apply to this term the tl function (for the specification (divspec (S k))). It gives the expected result in (Str (divspec (S k)) (S k)).

Final program Because we have trivially a proof of $\neg$(divinf 0 n) we may build the initial stream as a proof of (Str (divspec 0) 0).

Applying the primes operation to this initial stream gives us a proof of :

$$(\mathsf{Str}\ \lambda n : \mathsf{Nat}.(\mathsf{divspec}\ n\ n)\ 0).$$

Using the nth function we have a proof of $\forall n$.(divspec n n).

Our specification follows the operational behavior of the sieve algorithm. We have to justify that with an appropriate input it gives us the primality condition.

This can easily be done by doing a proof of the following properties :

$$(\forall p.\mathsf{Si}\,(p) = p + 2) \rightarrow (\neg(\mathsf{divinf}\ n\ n) \leftrightarrow (\mathsf{is\_prime}\ n + 2))$$

$$(\forall p.\mathsf{Si}\,(p) = 2p + 3) \rightarrow (\neg(\mathsf{divinf}\ n\ n) \leftrightarrow (\mathsf{is\_prime}\ 2n + 3))$$

These properties only involve arithmetical properties of the division and are not necessary for running the program.

4.3 A partial filter development

We are now interested in a program that will only gives as outputs the numbers that cannot be divided by previous elements.

Specification It is not easy to specify this problem using the index of this number in the actual stream. A more natural specification will be to relate the output to its index in the initial stream Si and also to the index of the previous element.

For this we use a general parameterized type of streams which is defined as follow. Let $(A\ n\ m)$ be a specification depending on two natural numbers n and m. We give the type of the build and the out function. In this case the out function gives for a stream parameterized by p, a new parameter q, its head which is a proof of $(A\ p\ q)$ and its tail which is a stream parameterized by $(\mathsf{S}\ q)$[4].

$\mathsf{Str} \equiv \lambda p:\mathsf{Nat}.\exists P.(\forall p.(P\ p) \rightarrow \exists q:\mathsf{Nat}.(A\ p\ q) \wedge (P\ (\mathsf{S}\ q))) \wedge (P\ p)$ $:\ \mathsf{Nat} \rightarrow Set$
$\mathsf{build}\ :\ \forall p:\mathsf{Nat}.\forall P:\mathsf{Nat} \rightarrow Set.$ $(\forall p.(P\ p) \rightarrow \exists q:\mathsf{Nat}.(A\ p\ q) \wedge (P\ (\mathsf{S}\ q))) \rightarrow (P\ p) \rightarrow (\mathsf{Str}\ p)$ $\mathsf{out}\ :\ \forall p.(\mathsf{Str}\ p) \rightarrow \exists q:\mathsf{Nat}.(A\ p\ q) \wedge (\mathsf{Str}\ (\mathsf{S}\ q))$

As before, we shall use the type Str, the operators **build** and **out** with different specifications A explicitly given as arguments.

If n and m are two natural numbers and $(P\ k)$ is a property on natural numbers, we introduce a property which says that $n \leq m$ and P holds between n and m :

$$(\mathsf{between}\ n\ m\ P) \equiv (n \leq m) \wedge \forall x.(n \leq x < m) \rightarrow (P\ x)$$

For the development of the partial sieve, the specification will be :

$$(\mathsf{ASieve}\ k\ p\ q) \equiv \neg(\mathsf{divinf}\ k\ q) \wedge (\mathsf{between}\ p\ q\ (\mathsf{divinf}\ k))$$

$(\mathsf{ASieve}\ k\ p\ q)$ means $\mathsf{Si}\,(q)$ cannot be divided by a $\mathsf{Si}\,(l)$ for $l < k$ and that the element of Si between indexes p and q can be divided by a $\mathsf{Si}\,(l)$ for $l < k$.

Bounded search We have to search for an element in the stream which satisfies some property.

We know the existence of a bound N for the number of steps in the search.

To program this, we use that some order is well-founded. The order depends on the bound N, it is defined as :

$$n \prec_N m \equiv m < n \wedge m < N$$

It is clear that there cannot be any infinite decreasing chain for $\prec_N$ because if $\ldots n_k \prec_N \ldots \prec_N n_1 \prec_N n_0$ we have :

$$n_0 < n_1 < \ldots < n_k < \ldots < N$$

We shall use a principle of well-founded induction namely the property WF-$\prec_N$:

$$\forall P:\mathsf{Nat} \rightarrow Set.(\forall n.(\forall m.(m \prec_N n) \rightarrow (P\ m)) \rightarrow (P\ n)) \rightarrow \forall n.(P\ n)$$

This property can be proved directly by induction over the bound N. The proof uses the properties $\forall n,m:\mathsf{Nat}.\neg(m \prec_0 n)$ and $\forall N,n,m:\mathsf{Nat}.((\mathsf{S}\ m) \prec_{(S\ N)} (\mathsf{S}\ n)) \rightarrow m \prec_N n$. We do not give here the detail of the proof. We only indicate the program extracted of this proof written in a ML-like form :

[4] The general case would have been to give the tail as a stream parameterized by q, but in our case q will always be equal to $(\mathsf{S}\ q')$ and the specification can more naturally be written as a relation between p and q' than as a relation between p and q

```
let rec Wfind = fun
   O     F n -> (F n (fun m -> error))
| (S N) F n ->
   (F n (fun m ->
        Wfind N (fun p Hp -> F (S p) (fun m -> Hp (m-1))) (m-1)))
```

This primitive recursive functional looks slightly more complicated than the general recursive program which does the same task :

```
let rec Wfrec F n = F n (Wfrec F)
```

This second program does not make use of the bound N for the search. In Coq, we can choose to use the direct proof of the induction principle $\prec_N$ and we will get a strongly normalizable program. We can also just prove that the order we use is well-founded and then use the principle :

$$\forall R.(\mathsf{well\_founded}\ R) \rightarrow \forall P.(\forall n.(\forall m.(R\ m\ n) \rightarrow (P\ m)) \rightarrow (P\ n)) \rightarrow \forall n.(P\ n)$$

This axiom is interpreted via a realisability interpretation as the program WFrec. It does not make use of the proof of the well-foundness of the relation.

The sieve program To be able to write the sieve program we need more information on the stream Si, namely that for each k it contains infinitely many elements that cannot be divided by $\mathsf{Si}\,(l)$ for $l < k$.

We add such an hypothesis which is expressed as the formula :

$$\forall k, n : \mathsf{Nat}.\exists N : \mathsf{Nat}.\exists p : \mathsf{Nat}.((n \leq p < N) \land \neg(\mathsf{divinf}\ k\ \mathsf{Si}\,(p)))$$

If we want a program written in a total language we need to explicitly give the bound N; if we only want to develop the program using a general fixpoint this property can be non informative and will only be used for proving the well-foundness of the order.

The sieve program will be a proof of :

$$\begin{aligned}\forall p, q : \mathsf{Nat}.\,&(\mathsf{between}\ p\ q\ (\mathsf{divinf}\ p))\\ &\rightarrow \forall r : \mathsf{Nat}.(\mathsf{Str}\ (\mathsf{ASieve}\ p)\ r) \rightarrow (\mathsf{Str}\ (\mathsf{ASieve}\ (\mathsf{S}\ q))\ r)\end{aligned}$$

In order to do that, we assume (betweeen $p\ q$ (divinf p)). We apply build with the predicate (Str (ASieve p)). We have to prove :

$$\forall r.(\mathsf{Str}\ (\mathsf{ASieve}\ p)\ r) \rightarrow \exists t : \mathsf{Nat}.(\mathsf{ASieve}\ (\mathsf{S}\ q)\ r\ t) \land (\mathsf{Str}\ (\mathsf{ASieve}\ p)\ (\mathsf{S}\ t))$$

For this, we use the fact that there exists N such that $\exists x : \mathsf{Nat}.r \leq x < N \land \neg(\mathsf{divinf}\ (\mathsf{S}\ q)\ \mathsf{Si}\,(x))$ and use well-founded induction over the order $\prec_N$. Because N depends on r, the hypothesis that N bounds the search from r should also appear as an extra hypothesis in the induction hypothesis. We introduce the notation :

$$(\mathsf{bound}\ p\ r\ N) \equiv \exists x : \mathsf{Nat}.r \leq x < N \land \neg(\mathsf{divinf}\ p\ x)$$

Our induction hypothesis will be :

$$\forall u : \mathsf{Nat}.(u \prec_N r) \rightarrow (\mathsf{bound}\ (\mathsf{S}\ q)\ u\ N) \rightarrow$$
$$(\mathsf{Str}\ (\mathsf{ASieve}\ p)\ u) \rightarrow \exists t : \mathsf{Nat}.(\mathsf{ASieve}\ (\mathsf{S}\ q)\ u\ t) \wedge (\mathsf{Str}\ (\mathsf{ASieve}\ p)\ (\mathsf{S}\ t))$$

Let s be of type (Str (ASieve p) r). Applying the **out** function, we get a parameter t, a proof of (ASieve $p\ r\ t$) and a stream *stl* of type (Str (ASieve p) (S t)).

From (ASieve $p\ r\ t$), we know ¬(divinf $p\ t$) and (**between** $r\ \dot{t}$ (divinf p)).

Because of the hypothesis (**between** $p\ q$ (divinf p)) we have ¬(divinf (S q) t) if Si (q) does not divide Si (t). We perform a case analysis.

Case Si (q) *divides* Si (t). In that case we apply the induction hypothesis to (S t) and the stream *stl*. We have to check the induction hypotheses are correct. We have (**between** r (S t) (divinf (q))). This implies both (S t) $< N$ and (bound(S q) (S t) N).

From the induction hypothesis we get a new parameter u and proofs of (ASieve (S q) (S t) u) and (Str (ASieve p) (S u)). To complete the proof, we need to show that (ASieve (S q) $r\ u$) holds but this is an easy consequence of the various hypotheses.

Case Si (q) *does not divide* Si (t). This case is simple because it is enough to show that the problem is solved with t as the expected parameter.

This ends the proof of this case and of the **sieve** program.

The primes function The **primes** function is now not really difficult to prove. Its specification is :

$$\forall k : \mathsf{Nat}.(\mathsf{Str}\ (\mathsf{ASieve}\ k)\ k) \rightarrow (\mathsf{Str}\ \lambda n, m : \mathsf{Nat}.(\mathsf{ASieve}\ n\ n\ m)\ k)$$

The proof applies **build** with the predicate λk : Nat.(Str (ASieve k) k). We have to show that :

$$\forall p : \mathsf{Nat}.(\mathsf{Str}\ (\mathsf{ASieve}\ p)\ p) \rightarrow \exists q : \mathsf{Nat}.(\mathsf{ASieve}\ p\ p\ q) \wedge (\mathsf{Str}\ (\mathsf{ASieve}\ (\mathsf{S}\ q))\ (\mathsf{S}\ q))$$

Let s be of type (Str (ASieve p) p), we apply an **out** step. It gives us q, a proof of (ASieve $p\ p\ q$) and the tail stream *stl* of type (Str (ASieve p) (S q)). From (ASieve $p\ p\ q$) we get a proof of (**between** $p\ q$ (divinf p)), consequently we are able to apply the **sieve** function to *stl* and directly get as expected a proof of (Str (ASieve (S q)) (S q)).

The final step As previously we build from Si a proof of (Str (ASieve 0) 0) to which we apply the **primes** operation. Now if we have a proof of (ASieve $p\ p\ q$), it implies that Si (q) cannot be divided by Si (k) with $k < p$ and $\forall x.p \leq x < q \rightarrow$ (divinf $p\ x$) this implies that Si (q) cannot be divided by Si (k) with $k < q$ which is the expected result for testing primality.

5 Computational interpretation of parameterized streams

The main difference between a representation of infinite lists with a function on natural numbers and with a coinductive type resides in the computational interpretation of these two objects.

A function f from Nat to A computes from each natural number n a result $(f\ n)$ in a non specified way. The representation of f as an infinite list S using a coinductive type, computes $(f\ n)$ by evaluating nth $n\ S$ which first computes $(f\ 0), (f\ 1), \ldots, (f\ (n-1))$. This representation can be efficient in case we need all these values because in general we could find a more efficient way to compute the whole sequence than separately each value.

For instance any function f from Nat to A defined in a iterative way by the equations :

$$f\ 0 = g \qquad f\ (\mathsf{S}\ n) = h\ (f\ n)$$

can be implemented as the stream (build $A\ \lambda x : A.x\ \lambda y : A.(h\ y)\ g$). Assume the function h is computed in a constant time, each computation of $(f\ n)$ takes a time proportional to n. But the computation of the initial sequence $(f\ 0), \ldots, (f\ n)$, will take a time proportional to n^2 with a functional representation and only a linear time with the stream representation.

5.1 Analysis of the computational behavior of the sieve

A natural question is to analyze the efficiency of our two versions of the Sieve algorithm. Actually the programs we propose do not correspond exactly to the usual dataflow description. We show the two ways to modify them and obtain efficient code at the end.

Eliminating access to the initial stream One drawback of our representation comes from the naive way we wrote our specifications. In the case of the indexed or parameterized stream, we say for the index or the parameter n whether the corresponding element in the initial stream could be divided or not. But when we did have to test for the division then it was necessary to access the elements using the notation $\mathsf{Si}\,(n)$. This does not correspond to the dataflow vision where we only manipulate the elements as they arrive. But this choice was only done because the development of the proofs was simpler that way, actually the formalized examples in Coq are optimized.

The idea is very simple. Instead of carrying out in the specification whether the element in the initial stream corresponding to the parameter satisfies a property, we also include in the stream the object of the initial stream when we will need it.

In the case of the indexed stream the specification was :

(divspec $k\ n$) $\equiv$ (divinf $k\ n$) $\vee \neg$(divinf $k\ n$) which says whether $\mathsf{Si}\,(n)$ can be divided or not by $\mathsf{Si}\,(k)$ for $k < l$. In the case $\mathsf{Si}\,(n)$ can be divided, we know we will never need to access this value. But in the other case, it will be necessary to access the value of $\mathsf{Si}\,(n)$ to test for the possibility of other division, so we can decide to keep this value in the stream itself. For doing that, it is enough to modify the specification and take :

$$(\mathsf{divspec}\ k\ n) \equiv (\mathsf{divinf}\ k\ n) \vee \exists p.p = \mathsf{Si}\,(n) \wedge \neg(\mathsf{divinf}\ k\ n)$$

A stream built on this specification will give for each n either the indication $(\mathsf{divinf}\ k\ n)$ or a natural number p which is provable equal to $\mathsf{Si}\,(n)$ and such that $\neg(\mathsf{divinf}\ k\ n)$. Obviously the two specifications are logically equivalent but the second one is computationally more efficient because we do not have to reaccess the element in the initial stream for the division test.

For parameterized streams, the problem is the same. If we want to translate accurately the behavior of the dataflow program, we need to modify the specification ASieve to include the integer corresponding to the parameter. For this it is enough to take

$$(\mathsf{ASieve}\ k\ p\ q) \equiv \exists P.P = \mathsf{Si}\,(q) \wedge \neg(\mathsf{divinf}\ k\ q) \wedge (\mathsf{between}\ p\ q\ (\mathsf{divinf}\ k))$$

Eliminating the computation of parameters If the specification is modified as it is proposed above, then we get an efficient algorithm for the sieve which really mimics the behavior of the dataflow program.

Now we observe how the stream itself is implemented. If we perform the extraction process naively on these programs, we remove all parts concerning proofs of correctness (that is the proofs of properties involving divinf or between). The remaining process used to encode the stream is built on a state with two components, one for the parameter and one for the number itself. This is not satisfactory because we expect the program to work with only the stream containing the numbers, the parameter itself is only used for the specification.

The process of extraction should be able to remove this part which is never used in a computational way, at least in the optimized algorithm we suggested above. This problem is a bit technical and we do not discuss it extensively here.

We cannot use the sort *Prop* of the system Coq as is proposed in [21], because its realisability interpretation does not correspond to what we need here. What is possible is to have a third sort, call it for instance *Par* such that if M is of type *Par*, and $(P\ x)$ is an informative predicate depending on x of type M then the type extracted from $(x : M)(P\ x)$ is the type extracted from $(P\ x)$ which does not depend on x and a program p realizes (i.e. is correct with respect to) $(x : M)(P\ x)$ if and only if for all x of type M, p realizes $(P\ x)$.

Another way to introduce annotations in a specification to constrain the computational use of some hypothesis was also proposed by Hayashi [12] who formalizes ideas initiated by Takayama. In this proposition a new quantification is introduced, with the computational interpretation proposed above.

Berardi and Boerio [1] also propose methods to automatically extract the optimized version without modifying the underlying logic.

The two methods with explicit annotations of the informative contents can be simply applied to the formalism of the Calculus of Constructions and will give exactly what we expect for the resulting program. Also the explicit marking of the specification will prevent the programmer of a computational use of the parameters. The automatic methods are less constraining and more promising but have to be adapted to this formalism.

6 Conclusion

In this paper we investigate programming with infinite lists in strongly typed lambda-calculus by developing the example of the sieve of Eratosthenes. The complete proofs were developed in the system Coq.

6.1 Comparison with related work

Analogous investigations have been done for other theories. Mendler [16, 17], proposed an extension of Nuprl's type theory with the introduction of new constructors for coinductive types and build and out functions. As in our approach, infinite objects are introduced which are represented by total objects. We use an impredicative encoding while he extends the theory with new combinators. Dybjer and Sander [8] adopt a point of view where streams are described in a language with general recursion. Properties of these programs are defined using relations defined coinductively. In our example, proofs and programs are put together and we only build one stream represented as a coinductive predicate. In [15], Paulson investigates the encoding of induction and coindunction in higher-order logic. The method uses also a formalization of Tarski's theorem. It was completely written using Isabelle proof assistant. In this formalism, the functions are not interpreted in a computational way. In his thesis [23] Raffalli proposes an extension of Krivine's AF_2 with two operators for smallest and greatest fixpoints. In this framework, proofs are no longer necessarily strongly normalizable. The streams are represented by lambda-terms which are indeed infinite objects. One difference between his approach and ours is that his specifications are written equationally and specified the computational behavior of the program rather than logical properties such as "to be prime". Coquand [4] also proposes an extension of type theory where we can build infinite objects with recursive definitions which are guarded (a recursive call can only appear under a sequence of constructors of the coinductive type). His approach does not introduce any partial objects or greatest fixpoint construction in the logic and provides a natural way of writing infinite objects like in functional programming languages. To establish the meta-theory of this system is not clear.

6.2 Remarks

Our methodology was to enrich the type of streams and build a type of parameterized streams which includes the specification in the process itself. In the Sieve of Eratosthenes, instead of having a infinite list of natural numbers we also provide for each output a justification that it is the first prime number greater than the previous element in the list.

One surprising fact is that the impredicative encoding was satisfactory from the logical point of view and did not require adding new axioms to complete the proof. While during our first investigation on programming with the impredicative encoding of inductive types, we immediately needed induction axioms and non-confusion properties ($0 \neq 1$). From the computational point of view, the parameterized formulation of streams points out the need for a more sophisticated way to indicate which part of the type is computational or not than the one provided in Coq at the moment.

In strongly typed theory an element in the type stream is always infinite. Consequently, a filter function which takes an infinite list as input and gives as output only elements satisfying a condition cannot be directly written. The two solutions described in this paper are introducing silent steps and explicitly using one extra hypothesis which assumes infinite elements satisfying the condition in the input. It is not clear how to adapt these techniques to introduce systematic encoding of streams described in a mutually recursive way, as they appear for instance in the formulation of the alternating bit protocol.

The type of infinite lists defined coinductively captures all the possible implementations of a process generating infinitely many elements by transformation of a state. Various implementations may have different computational behavior and be more or less efficient. What are the exact tools we need to master the behavior of the streams remains to be understood.

We do not claim this is the only methodology to justify programs involving streams but at least it is a proposition which deserves further investigations. The main advantages of our method are the following. Once we have found the right representation of streams and the correct predicate for the intermediate steps, the development of the proof itself (and consequently of the underlying program) becomes direct and natural. Also we end up with a certified program and the specification may involves arbitrary logical properties.

References

1. L. Boerio. Extending pruning techniques to polymorphic second order λ-calculus. In *Proceedings ESOP'94*, 1994.
2. C. Böhm and A. Berarducci. Automatic synthesis of typed λ-programs on term algebras. *Theoretical Computer Science*, 39, 1985.
3. R.L. Constable et al. *Implementing Mathematics with the Nuprl Proof Development System*. Prentice-Hall, 1986.
4. Th. Coquand. Infinite objects in type theory. In *[10]*, 1993.
5. Th. Coquand and G. Huet. Constructions: A higher order proof system for mechanizing mathematics. In *EUROCAL'85*, Linz, 1985. Springer-Verlag. LNCS 203.
6. Th. Coquand and G. Huet. Concepts mathématiques et informatiques formalisés dans le calcul des constructions. In The Paris Logic Group, editor, *Logic Colloquium'85*. North-Holland, 1987.
7. G. Dowek, A. Felty, H. Herbelin, G. Huet, C. Murthy, C. Parent, C. Paulin-Mohring, and B. Werner. The Coq Proof Assistant User's Guide Version 5.8. Rapport Technique 154, INRIA, May 1993.

8. P. Dybjer and H. Sander. A functional programming approach to the specification and verification of concurrent systemsnd verification of concurrent systems. *Formal Aspects of Computing*, 1:303–318, 1989.
9. H. Geuvers. Inductive and coinductive types with iteration and recursion. Faculty of Mathematics and Informatics, Catholic University Nijmegen, 1991.
10. H. Geuvers, editor. *Informal Proceedings of the 1993 Workshop on Types for Proofs and Programs*, 1993.
11. J.-Y. Girard, Y. Lafont, and P. Taylor. *Proofs and Types*. Cambridge Tracts in Theoretical Computer Science 7. Cambridge University Press, 1989.
12. S. Hayashi. Singleton, union, intersection types for program extraction. In *Proceedings of TACS'91*, 1991.
13. G. Kahn. The semantics of a simple language for parallel programming. In *Information Processing 74*. North-Holland, 1974.
14. G. Kahn and D. MacQueen. Coroutines and networks of parallel processes. In B. Gilchrist, editor, *Information Processing 77*. North-Holland, 1977.
15. L.C. Paulson. Co-induction and co-recursion in higher-order logic. available by anonymous ftp.
16. N. Mendler. *Inductive Definition in Type Theory*. PhD thesis, Cornell University, 1988.
17. N. Mendler. Predicative types universes and primitive recursion. In *Sixth Annual IEEE Symposium on Logic in Computer Science*, pages 173–184. Amsterdam, The Netherlands, IEEE Computer Society Press, 1991.
18. B. Nordström, K. Petersson, and J. Smith. *Programming in Martin-Löf's Type Theory*. International Series of Monographs on Computer Science. Oxford Science Publications, 1990.
19. C. Parent. Developing certified programs in the system Coq- The Program tactic. Technical Report 93-29, Ecole Normale Supérieure de Lyon, October 1993. also in Proceedings of the BRA Workshop Types for Proofs and Programs, may 93.
20. M. Parigot, P. Manoury, and M. Simonot. Propre : A programming language with proofs. In A. Voronkov, editor, *Logic Programming and automated reasoning*, number 624 in LNCS, St. Petersburg, Russia, July 1992. Springer-Verlag.
21. C. Paulin-Mohring. Extracting F_ω's programs from proofs in the Calculus of Constructions. In *Sixteenth Annual ACM Symposium on Principles of Programming Languages*, Austin, January 1989. ACM.
22. C. Paulin-Mohring. *Extraction de programmes dans le Calcul des Constructions*. PhD thesis, Université Paris 7, January 1989.
23. Ch. Raffalli. *L'arithmétique fonctionnelle du second ordre avec points fixes*. PhD thesis, Université Paris VII, 1994.
24. G. C. Wraith. A note on categorical data types. In D.H. Pitt, D.E. Rydeheard, P. Dybjer, A.M. Pitts, and A. Poigné, editors, *Category Theory and Computer Science*. Springer-Verlag, 1989. LNCS 389.

The ALF proof editor and its proof engine *

Lena Magnusson and Bengt Nordström

University of Göteborg/Chalmers, S-412 96 Göteborg, Sweden

Abstract. Alf is an interactive proof editor. It is based on the idea that to prove a mathematical theorem is to build a proof object for the theorem. The proof object is directly manipulated on the screen, different manipulations correspond to different steps in the proof. The language we use is Martin-Löf's monomorphic type theory. This is a small functional programming language with dependent types. The language is open in the sense that it is easy to introduce new inductively defined sets. A proof is represented as a mathematical object and a proposition is identified with the set of its proof objects. The basic part of the proof editor can be seen as a proof engine with two basic commands, one which builds an object by replacing a placeholder in an object by a new object, and another one which deletes a part of an object by replacing a sub-object by a placeholder. We show that the validity of the incomplete object is preserved by admissible insertions and deletions.

1 Background

During the years we have learned that there is no such thing as "the logic of programming". Different kinds of programs require different kind of reasoning. Programs are manipulating different kinds of objects, and it would be very awkward to code these objects into a fixed set of objects. Objects have their own logic, it is for instance very different to reason about ongoing processes and fixed objects like natural numbers and lists. We also need a different kind of logic when we are interested in computational aspects of a program (like complexity and storage requirements). We don't think we will ever find *the* logic of programming.

The idea behind a logical framework is to have a flexible formal logic, in which it is possible to introduce new kinds of objects, including objects for proofs. The logical framework we are using is Martin-Löf's monomorphic type theory, which can be seen as a small functional language with dependent types. We express problems as types and solutions (proofs) as programs.

The fundamental notion of proof is a process which leads to a conviction of something to hold (an assertion, or equivalently, a judgement). You have a series of steps, in each step you make an assertion which holds because earlier assertions have been made. A proof object should be a mathematical object which represents this proof process. The proof object must be derivable from

* This research has been done within the ESPRIT Basic Research Action "Types for Proofs and Programs". It has been paid by NUTEK, Chalmers and the University of Göteborg.

the proof process. But we need something more: If a proof object represents a proof then it must be possible to compute a proof process from the proof object.

The traditional way of using a computer for interactive proof checking is to formalize the proof process and then letting the computer check each step. The user types in commands in some imperative language and the effect of executing a command is to update some internal data base which represents assertions being made. We call this indirect editing. It is like we cannot see the objects being built, instead we have to make experiments on it to see what we have.

To directly build something with a computer is to have an impression that the objects which are built (and changed) are directly manipulated on the screen using the keyboard and the mouse. It is like we have a hand (represented by the cursor) on the screen to select parts and to grasp for different tools which can manipulate the object. A change of the object is immediately shown on the screen.

The idea we use is to use a proof object as a true representative of a proof. The process of proving the proposition A is represented by the process of building a proof object of A. There is a close connection between the individual steps in proving A and the steps to build a proof object of A. For instance the act of applying a rule is done by building an application of a constant, to assume that a proposition A holds is to make an abstraction of a variable of the type A and to refer to an assumption is to use the corresponding variable. To delete a part of a proof object corresponds to regretting some eaarlier steps in the proof. Notice that the deleted steps don't have to be the last steps in the derivation, by moving the pointer around in the proof object it is possible to undo any of the preceeding steps without altering the effect of following steps. However, the deletion of a sub-object may cause the deletion of other parts which are depending on this.

We are interested in an interactive direct proof checker. So if we represent the proof process by the process of building a proof object it must be possible to deal with *incomplete* proof objects, i.e. proof objects which represents incomplete proofs.

The proof editor we are using can be seen as an interactive structure-oriented editor for Martin-Löf's monomorphic type theory. An object which has been created by the editor is always meaningful (well typed), which means that the object really represents a proof. Before we explain how a partial proof is represented, we will explain how a complete proof is represented. To do this we need to explain Martin-Löf's monomorphic type theory.

2 Martin-Löf's type theory

There are four judgement forms in type theory:

- A *type*. We know that A is a type when we know what it means to be an object in A.
- $A = B$. Two types are equal when they have the same objects, so an object in A must be an object of B and conversely. Identical objects in A must also be identical in B and vice versa.

- $a \in A$. a is an object in A.
- $a = b \in A$. a and b are identical objects in A.

These judgements are decidable.

In general, a judgement may depend on a context, i.e. a list of assumptions. For instance, the general form of the third judgement is therefore:

$$a \in A \quad [x_1 \in A_1, \ldots, x_n \in A_n]$$

where a and A may depend on $x_1, \ldots, x_n$ and for $j \leq n$, A_j may depend on $x_1, \ldots, x_{j-1}$. Notice that the order of the assumptions is in general important, since the type of one assumption may depend on earlier assumptions.

2.1 How to form types

The type structure is very simple, there are two ways of forming ground types and one way of forming function types. We will use the notation $b\{x{:=}a\}$ for the expression obtained by substituting the expression a for all free occurrences of the variable x in the expression b.

- Set is a type. This is the type whose objects are (inductively defined) sets.
  Set formation
  $$\mathsf{Set}\ \mathit{type}$$
- If $A \in \mathsf{Set}$, i.e. if A is a set, then *El*(A) is a type. The objects in this type are the elements of the set A. We will write A instead of *El*(A), since it will always be clear from the context whether we mean A as a set (i.e. as an object in Set) or as a type.
  El-formation
  $$\frac{A \in \mathsf{Set}}{\mathit{El}(A)\ \mathit{type}}$$
- If A is a type and B is a family of types for $x \in A$ then $(x \in A)B$ is the type which contains functions from A to B as objects. All free occurrences of x in B become bound in $(x \in A)B$.
  Fun formation
  $$\frac{A\ \mathit{type} \qquad B\ \mathit{type}\ [x \in A]}{(x \in A)B\ \mathit{type}}$$
  To know that an object c is in the type $(x \in A)B$ means that we know that when we apply it to an object a in A we get an object $c(a)$ in $B\{x{:=}a\}$ and that we get identical objects in $B\{x{:=}a_1\}$ when we apply it to identical objects a_1 and a_2 in A.

2.2 How to form objects in a type

Objects in a type are formed from constants and variables using application and abstraction. We already mentioned how to apply a function to an object:

Application

$$\frac{c \in (x \in A)B \qquad a \in A}{c(a) \in B\{x{:=}a\}}$$

Functions can be formed by abstraction, if $b \in B$ under the assumption that $x \in A$ then $[x]b$ is an object in $(x \in A)B$. All free ocurrences of x in b become bound in $[x]b$.

Abstraction

$$\frac{b \in B \;\; [x \in A]}{[x]b \in (x \in A)B}$$

The abstraction is explained by the ordinary β-rule which defines what it means to apply an abstraction to an object in A.

β – rule

$$\frac{a \in A \qquad b \in B \;\; [x \in A]}{([x]b)(a) = b\{x{:=}a\} \in B\{x{:=}a\}}$$

The traditional η-, α- and ξ-rules can be justified.

We will sometimes use the notation $(A)B$ or $A \to B$ when B does not contain any free occurrences of x. We will write $(x_1 \in A_1, \ldots, x_n \in A_n)B$ instead of $(x_1 \in A_1) \ldots (x_n \in A_n)B$ and $b(a_1, \ldots, a_n)$ instead of $b(a_1) \ldots (a_n)$ in order to increase the readability. Similarly, we will write $[x_1] \ldots [x_n]e$ as $[x_1, \ldots, x_n]e$.

An object is *saturated* if it is not a function, i.e. if its type is Set or *El*(A), for $A \in$ Set. The *arity* of an object is the number of arguments it can be applied to in order for the result to be saturated. It is an important property that a well-typed object has a unique arity.

2.3 Experimental additions to the language

In order to make type theory more similar to a standard functional language we have extended it in various ways:

explicit substitution. This has been suggested by Martin-Löf in various lectures in Göteborg, Båstad and Leiden during 1993. The syntax we use is

$$d\{x{:=}e\}$$

where d and e are well-typed expressions and x is a variable. The expression can be read as d where x is e. A detailed description can be found in Alvaro Tasistro's licentiate thesis [23].

case-expressions We have implemented a version of case-expressions. The system generates an exhaustive, non-overlapping list of patterns following ideas from Thierry Coquand [4]. In this implementation, case-expressions may only occur on the outer level of a definiens, they are thus not allowed inside abstractions or applications.

named contexts In order to have a weak notion of abstract data type, we have given the user a possibility to declare constants in an explicit (possibly named) context. The licenciate thesis by Gustavo Betarte [1] reports on an experiment with this facility.

2.4 Definitions

Most of the generality and strength of the language comes from the possibilities of introducing new constants. It is in this way that we can introduce the usual mathematical objects like natural numbers, integers, functions, tuples etc. It is also possible to introduce more complicated inductive sets like sets for proof objects.

A distinction is made between primitive and defined constants. The value of a *primitive constant* is the constant itself. So the constant has only a type, it doesn't have a definition. It gets its meaning in other ways (outside the theory). Such a constant is also called a constructor. Examples of primitive constants are N, s and $\mathsf{0}$, they can be introduced by the following declarations:

$$\begin{aligned}&\mathsf{N} \in \mathsf{Set}\\&\mathsf{s} \in \mathsf{N} \to \mathsf{N}\\&\mathsf{0} \in \mathsf{N}\end{aligned}$$

A *defined constant* is defined in terms of other objects. When we apply a defined constant to all its arguments in an empty context, e.g. $c(e_1, \ldots, e_n)$, then we get an expression which is a definiendum, i.e. an expression which computes in one step to its definiens (which is a well-typed object).

A defined constant can either be explicitly or implicitly defined. We declare an *explicitly defined constant* c by giving it as an abbreviation of a well-typed object:

$$c = a \in A$$

The constant c is a definiendum in itself, not only when it is applied to its arguments. For instance we can make the following explicit definitions:

$$\begin{aligned}1 &= \mathsf{s}(\mathsf{0})) \in \mathsf{N}\\I_N &= [x]x \in \mathsf{N} \to \mathsf{N}'\\I &= [A][x]x \in (A \in \mathsf{Set}, A)A\end{aligned}$$

The last example is the monomorphic identity function which when applied to an arbitrary set A yields the identity function on A.

It is easy to check whether an explicit definition is correct, you just check that the definiens is an object in the correct type.

We declare an *implicitly defined constant* by showing what definiens it has when we apply it to its arguments. This is done by pattern-matching and the definition is sometimes recursive. Here are some examples:

$$\begin{aligned} + &\in \mathsf{N} \rightarrow \mathsf{N} \rightarrow \mathsf{N} \\ &+(0, y) = y \\ &+(\mathsf{s}(x), y) = \mathsf{s}(+(x, y)) \\ \mathsf{natrec} &\in \mathsf{N} \rightarrow (\mathsf{N} \rightarrow \mathsf{N} \rightarrow \mathsf{N}) \rightarrow \mathsf{N} \rightarrow \mathsf{N} \\ &\mathsf{natrec}(d, e, 0) = d \\ &\mathsf{natrec}(d, e, \mathsf{s}(a)) = e(a, \mathsf{natrec}(d, e, a)) \end{aligned}$$

The last example is a specialized version of the primitive recursion operator.

Whether a definition of this kind is meaningful can in general only be checked outside the theory. We must be sure that all well-typed expressions of the form $c(e_1, \ldots, e_n)$ is a definiendum with a unique well-typed definiens. The system now generates a complete set of nonoverlapping patterns, but there is no check that the definition is well-founded. We could syntactically restrict the definiens to guarantee well-foundedness, but we know that these kind of restrictions will be too limited. However, this is only a poor excuse that some limited check has not been implemented.

3 The representation of proofs, theories, theorems, derived rules etc.

We are representing proofs as mathematical objects, the type of a proof object represents the proposition which is the conclusion of the proof. Variables are used as names of assumptions and constants are used as rules. To apply a rule to a number of subproofs is done by applying a constant to the corresponding subproof objects.

A theory is presented by a list of typings and definitions of constants. When we read the constant as a name of a rule, then a primitive constant is usually a formation or introduction rule, an implicitly defined constant is an elimination rule (with the contraction rule expressed as the step from the definiendum to the definiens) and finally, an explicitly defined constant is a lemma or derived rule. As an example of this, consider the definition of conjunction.

The formation rule for conjunction expresses that $A \,\&\, B$ is a proposition if A and B are propositions:

$$\frac{A\ prop \qquad B\ prop}{A \,\&\, B\ prop}$$

We express this by introducing the primitive constant & by the following typing:

$$\& \in (\mathsf{Set},\ \mathsf{Set})\mathsf{Set}$$

We use the type of sets to represent the type of propositions. A canonical proof of the problem $A \,\&\, B$ is on the form $\&\mathbf{I}(a, b)$, where a is a proof of A and b a proof of B. This reflects the explanation that a proof of $A \,\&\, B$ consists of a proof of A and a proof of B. If we are in a context where A and B are propositions we can define $A \& B$ by introducing the primitive constant

$$\&\mathbf{I} \in (A, B)A \& B$$

Another notation for this is:

$$\frac{A \qquad B}{A \& B}$$

This is the introduction rule for conjunction. If we are in an empty context we must declare the parameters A and B explicitly:

$$\&\mathbf{I} \in (A \in \mathsf{Set},\ B \in \mathsf{Set},\ A,\ B)A \& B$$

The elimination rules for conjunction

$$\frac{A \& B}{A} \qquad \frac{A \& B}{B}$$

are expressed by introducing the implicitly defined constants $\&\mathbf{E}_l$ and $\&\mathbf{E}_l$ by the following declarations:

$$\begin{aligned}
\&\mathbf{E}_l &\in (A \in \mathsf{Set},\ B \in \mathsf{Set},\ A \& B)A \\
&\&\mathbf{E}_l(A, B, \&\mathbf{I}(a, b)) = a \\
\&\mathbf{E}_r &\in (A \in \mathsf{Set},\ B \in \mathsf{Set},\ A \& B)B \\
&\&\mathbf{E}_r(A, B, \&\mathbf{I}(a, b)) = b
\end{aligned}$$

The equalities are the contraction rules for & and these are essential for the correctness of the elimination rule. Since all proofs of $A \& B$ is equal to a proof on the form $\&\mathbf{I}(a, b)$, where a is a proof of A and b a proof of B, we know from the contraction rule that we get a proof of A if we apply $\&\mathbf{E}_r$ to an arbitrary proof of $A \& B$, and similarly for $\&\mathbf{E}_l$.

Notice the difference with the Edinburgh LF encoding of logic, where the elimination rules (like all rules) are expressed as *primitive* constants. This means that in LF the logical constants are not inductively defined by their introduction rules and hence does not reflect Heyting's explanation. He defines a logical constant by giving their introduction rules and the elimination rules are just consequences of this definition.

To summarize, we have the following declarations and definitions for conjunction. We use the symbol $\downarrow$ in front of arguments which are not printed, e.g. the term $\&\mathbf{I}(A,\ B,\ a,\ b)$ will be written $\&\mathbf{I}(a,\ b)$.

$$\begin{aligned}
\& &\in (\mathsf{Set},\ \mathsf{Set})\mathsf{Set} \\
\&\mathbf{I} &\in (\downarrow A \in \mathsf{Set},\ \downarrow B \in \mathsf{Set},\ A,\ B)A \& B \\
\&\mathbf{E}_l &\in (\downarrow A \in \mathsf{Set},\ \downarrow B \in \mathsf{Set},\ A \& B)A \\
&\&\mathbf{E}_l(\&\mathbf{I}(a, b)) = a \\
\&\mathbf{E}_r &\in (\downarrow A \in \mathsf{Set},\ \downarrow B \in \mathsf{Set},\ A \& B)B \\
&\&\mathbf{E}_r(\&\mathbf{I}(a, b)) = b
\end{aligned}$$

4 Representation of incomplete objects

When we are proving a proposition A in a theory then we are building a proof object of type A in an environment consisting of a list of declaration of constants. This is presented on the screen by having two windows, a theory window containing declarations of constants and a scratch area containing objects being edited.

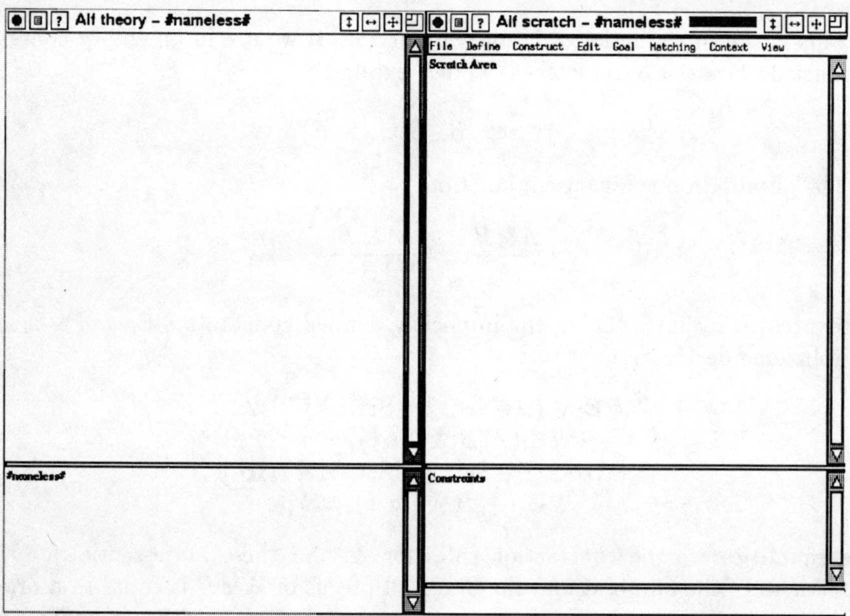

The objects which are being built in the scratch area are always correct relative to the current theory.

4.1 Editing objects

When we are making a top-down proof of a proposition A, then we try to reduce the problem A to some subproblems $B_1, \ldots, B_n$ by using a rule c which takes proofs of $B_1, \ldots, B_n$ to a proof of A. Then we continue by proving $B_1, \ldots, B_n$. For instance, we can reduce the problem A to the two problems $C \supset A$ and C by using modus ponens. In this way we can continue until we have only axioms and assumptions left. This process corresponds exactly to how we can build a mathematical object from the outside and in. Suppose that we want to build an object like

$$f(g_1(a_1, a_2), g_2(b)).$$

Then we start from its outer form to build $f(?_1, ?_2)$, where $?_1$ and $?_1$ are placeholders for not yet filled-in objects, then continue to fill in g_1 or g_2 etc. This means that the type or the problem to solve is constant while the solution to it is edited. It is an important property of the formal system that it is possible to compute the expected type of the placeholders. It is because of this that we can look at the editing operations as a way of decomposing a problem into subproblems.

Let's see what kind of structure we need to represent incomplete objects. We will first introduce placeholders $?_1, \ldots ?_n$ to be used for parts of the objects which are to be filled in. The expression

$$? \in A$$

expresses a state of an ongoing process of finding an object in the type A. We say that the expected type of ? is A. Objects are built up from variables and constants using application and abstraction. Therefore there are four ways of refining a placeholder:

- The placeholder is replaced by a constant c. This is correct if the type of c is equal to A.
- The placeholder is replaced by a variable x. The type of x must be equal to A. But we cannot replace a placeholder with any variable of the correct type, the variable must have been abstracted earlier. We keep track of this by associating not only a type but also a *local context* to each place holder. The placeholders stand for open expressions and their local context expresses what variables the substituted expression may depend on. The general form of the local context is $x_1 \in A_1, \ldots, x_n \in A_n$, where A_i is a type which may depend on the variables $x_1, \ldots x_{i-1}$.
- The placeholder is replaced by an abstraction $[x]?_1$. We must have that

  $$[x]?_1 \in A$$

  which holds if A is equal to a functional type $(y \in B)C$. The type of the variable x must be B and we must keep track of the fact that $?_1$ may be substituted by an expression which may depend on the variable x. So the local context of $?_1$ must be the local context of ? extended with the typing $x \in B$. So after this refinement we have that

  $$?_1 \in C\{y := x\}$$

  and $?_1$ has a local context which contains $x \in B$. This corresponds to making a new assumption, when we are constructing a proof. We reduce the general problem $(y \in B)C$ to the problem $C\{y := x\}$ under the assumption that $x \in B$. The assumed object x can be used to construct a solution to C, i.e. we may use the knowledge that we have a solution to the problem B when we are constructing a solution to the problem C.
  Notice that the placeholder will in general be replaced by an open term, this is a motivation for having open terms as first-class objects.

- Finally, the placeholder can be replaced by an application $c(?_1, \ldots ?_n)$ where c is a constant, or $x(?_1, \ldots ?_n)$, where x is a variable. In the case that we have a constant, we must have that $c(?_1, \ldots ?_n) \in A$, which holds if the type of the constant c is equal to $(x_1 \in A_1, \ldots, x_n \in A_n)B$ and $?_1 \in A_1, ?_2 \in A_2\{x_1 := ?_1\}, \ldots, x_n \in A_n\{x_1 := ?_1, \ldots, x_{n-1} := ?_{n-1}\}$ and
$$B\{x_1 := ?_1, \ldots, x_{n-1} := ?_{n-1}\} = A$$
So, we have reduced the problem A to the subproblems $A_1, A_2\{x_1 := ?_1\}, \ldots, A_n\{x_1 := ?_1, \ldots, x_{n-1}\}$ and further refinements must satisfy the constraint $B\{x_1 := ?_1, \ldots, x_{n-1} := ?_{n-1}\} = A$. The number n of new placeholders can be computed from the arity of the constant c and the expected arity of the placeholder. As an example, if we start with $? \in A$ and A is not a function type and if we apply the constant c of type $(x \in B)C$, then the new term will be
$$c(?_1) \in A$$
where the new placeholder $?_1$ must have the type B (since all arguments to c must have that type) and furthermore the type of $c(?_1)$ must be equal to A, i.e. the following equality must hold:
$$C\{x := ?_1\} \equiv A.$$
As will be described later, these kind of constraints will in general be simplified by the system. So, the editing step from $? \in A$ to $c(?_1) \in A$ is correct if $?_1 \in B$ and $C\{x := ?_1\} \equiv A$. This operation corresponds to applying a rule when we are constructing a proof. The rule c reduces the problem A to the problem B.

To summarize, an ongoing proof process (or an ongoing construction of a mathematical object) is represented by:

- A list of definitions, in which the definiens is a partial object.
- A list of placeholders $?_1, \ldots, ?_n$, each with an expected type and a local context (i.e. a list of typed variables).
- A set of constraints, which is a set of definitional equalities containing the placeholders. All refinements of the placeholders must satisfy the constraints.

The proof engine, which is the abstract machine representing an ongoing proof process (or an ongoing construction of a mathematical object) has two parts, the theory (which is a list of constant declarations) and the scratch area. Objects are built up in the scratch area and moved to the theory part when they are completed. There are two basic operations which are used to manipulate the scratch area. The *insertion* command replaces a placeholder by a new (possible incomplete) object and the *deletion* command replaces a sub-object by a placeholder. In this paper we will concentrate on describing these operations. But before we do this we will go through a small example how the system actually works.

An example in ALF

As a small example of a proof we prove one half of the distributivity of conjunction over disjunction in propositional logic. A variant of this example was used already by Gentzen [10] to motivate natural deduction. We have already defined the constants for conjunction; we repeat them here together with the corresponding definitions for disjunction as given to ALF. At present, ALF does not support infix operators, so we will write propositions with the logical operations in prefix form as in $\mathsf{And}(A, \mathsf{Or}(B, C))$.

```
And..∈..(A,B ∈ Set) Set
   AndI..∈..(↓A,↓B ∈ Set; A; B) And(A,B)
AndEl..∈..(↓A,↓B ∈ Set; And(A,B)) A
   AndEl(AndI(h1,h2))..≡..h1
AndEr..∈..(↓A,↓B ∈ Set; And(A,B)) B
   AndEr(AndI(h1,h2))..≡..h2
Or..∈..(A,B ∈ Set) Set
   OrIl..∈..(↓A,↓B ∈ Set; A) Or(A,B)
   OrIr..∈..(↓A,↓B ∈ Set; B) Or(A,B)
OrE..∈..(↓A,↓B,↓C ∈ Set; (A)C; (B)C; Or(A,B)) C
   OrE(h,h1,OrIl(h3))..≡..h(h3)
   OrE(h,h1,OrIr(h3))..≡..h1(h3)
```

This picture and the ones to follow in this section are screen dumps from a session with ALF. The vertical arrows in front of some arguments indicate that these arguments should be suppressed, as is done in the contraction rules. These arguments can typically be inferred by the system, so the user may completely ignore them.

The theorem we want to prove is

$$(A, B, C \in \mathsf{Set}; \mathsf{And}(A, \mathsf{Or}(B, C)))\mathsf{Or}(\mathsf{And}(A, B), \mathsf{And}(A, C))$$

This is a function type. An object of this type expects four arguments: three sets A, B and C and a proof of $\mathsf{And}(A, \mathsf{Or}(B, C))$. Given this input, the function must produce an element of (a proof of) the set (the proposition)

$$\mathsf{Or}(\mathsf{And}(A, B), \mathsf{And}(A, C))$$

We shall do this in two different ways:

1. By defining a function *distr1* as an abbreviation, or in ALF terminology, an explicit constant. This will be done by using the elimination rules to analyze the last argument and then the introduction rules to build up the result.

2. By defining a function *distr2* as an implicit constant, where the argument is analyzed directly by pattern matching and the elimination rules are not needed.

Using the first method, we instruct the system that we intend to define an explicit constant with the name *distr1*. The system responds with a template for the definition:

$$\text{distr1} \equiv ?_{\text{distr1}} \in ?_{\text{distr1.T}}$$

The definition has two placeholders, one for the definiens and one for its type. We proceed by filling in the type:

$$\text{distr1} \equiv ?_{\text{distr1}} \in (A, B, C \in \textbf{Set};\ \text{And}(A, \text{Or}(B, C)))\ \text{Or}(\text{And}(A, B), \text{And}(A, C))$$

The definiens is built top-down. The first step is to form an abstraction

$$\text{distr1} \equiv [A, B, C, h]?_e \in (A, B, C \in \textbf{Set};\ \text{And}(A, \text{Or}(B, C)))\ \text{Or}(\text{And}(A, B), \text{And}(A, C))$$

where the $?_e$ should have type $\mathsf{Or}(\mathsf{And}(A, B), \mathsf{And}(A, C))$. To construct an element in this type we must analyze the second projection of h using the *OrE* rule:

$$\text{distr1} \equiv [A, B, C, h]\text{OrE}(?_{h1}, ?_{h2}, \text{AndE}_r(h))$$

The three first arguments are inferred by the system and not displayed. We have to fill in the remaining two arguments. The type of the fourth argument is $(B)\mathsf{Or}(\mathsf{And}(A, B), \mathsf{And}(A, C))$. An object in this type is again a function, which gets a proof of B as input. Using this input, it is easy to construct the result using the left introduction rule for Or. Similarly, the second argument can be completed using the right Or-introduction rule, giving the complete proof

$$\begin{aligned}\text{distr1} \equiv [A, B, C, h]\text{OrE}(&[h_1]\text{OrI}_l(\text{AndI}(\text{AndE}_l(h), h_1)),\\ &[h_1]\text{OrI}_r(\text{AndI}(\text{AndE}_l(h), h_1)),\\ &\text{AndE}_r(h))\end{aligned}$$

The omitted steps in this proof all consist of simple direct manipulations with the mouse; nothing is typed on the keyboard (except the name *distr1*).

In the second method, using pattern matching instead of elimination rules, the initial situation in building the proof is the following:

```
distr2 ∈ (A,B,C ∈ Set; And(A,Or(B,C))) Or(And(A,B),And(A,C))
  distr2(A,B,C,h) ≡ ?distr2.0.E
```

Here we can now ask the system to analyze the possible forms of an argument. We perform this pattern matching on the last argument, giving

```
distr2 ∈ (A,B,C ∈ Set; And(A,Or(B,C))) Or(And(A,B),And(A,C))
  distr2(A,B,C,AndI(h1,h2)) ≡ ?distr2.0.0.E
```

There is only one constructor for And, so h must evaluate to $\mathsf{AndI}(h_1, h_2)$, where $h_1 \in A$ and $h_2 \in \mathsf{Or}(B, C)$. We proceed by analyzing h_2, which must reduce to one of two possible forms:

```
distr2 ∈ (A,B,C ∈ Set; And(A,Or(B,C))) Or(And(A,B),And(A,C))
  distr2(A,B,C,AndI(h1,OrIl(h))) ≡ ?distr2.0.0.0.E
  distr2(A,B,C,AndI(h1,OrIr(h))) ≡ ?distr2.0.0.1.E
```

So, the pattern matching separates the task of defining *distr2* into two mutually exhaustive cases. In both cases it is immediate to construct the right hand side using constructors and the variables on the left hand side:

```
distr2 ∈ (A,B,C ∈ Set; And(A,Or(B,C))) Or(And(A,B),And(A,C))
  distr2(A,B,C,AndI(h1,OrIl(h))) ≡ OrIl(AndI(h1,h))
  distr2(A,B,C,AndI(h1,OrIr(h))) ≡ OrIr(AndI(h1,h))
```

The proof is complete.

The pattern matching approach is the outcome of experiments with the ALF system [4] and is not present in type theory proper as presented by Martin-Löf. In fact, the two proofs presented here are just instances of two different disciplines. In the first, one defines for each set once and for all an elimination rule, capturing proof by structural induction over elements of the set.[2] These elimination rules are defined as implicit constants and are justified by reflection on the definition of the set. Having done this, all proofs involving elements of this set are defined as explicit constants. In the second discipline, only the set with its introduction rules is defined at the outset and later proofs are done by pattern-matching, involving a reflection on the arguments specially adapted to the particular proposition one wants to prove. Interestingly, the two disciplines are not proof-theoretically equivalent. One can exhibit propositions that can be

[2] The elimination rules for And and Or given here can be slightly generalized, using dependent sets. In this generalization, the two And-elimination rules are replaced by just one rule.

proved by pattern-matching but are false in certain models of type theory with the standard elimination rules [12]. It is presently a research topic to gain a better understanding of this phenomenon.

5 The scratch area

We will now present how partial objects are represented and manipulated by insertion and deletion in the scratch area. The representation of partial objects is designed in such a way that the two operations insert and delete becomes mainly a matter of type checking the partial objects. The type checking algorithm produces a list of equations, which in the case of complete objects becomes a decision procedure since the convertibility of the equations is decidable. In the case of an incomplete object, the problem of solving the list of equations becomes a unification problem, since place holders may occur in the equations. Therefore, the *same* algorithm is used for type checking complete objects as well as incomplete ones.

The direct manipulation of insertion in an object can be achieved by using a general user interface for theorem provers ([14]) which has been adopted to proof editors such as Coq ([7]) and Isabelle ([18]). The insertion operation corresponds to the refinement command in these provers which can be called by an interface instead of a user. However, since the delete operation we refer to may resume in a completely *new state* of the proof engine, it must be supported by the proof engine and is not simply a matter of interface. The desire for this operation is expressed in [14] where it is referred to as local undo.

We will define a valid scratch area to be such that *the partial objects in the scratch area are instantiated to complete, type correct objects exactly when all remaining placeholders have type correct instantiations which satisfies the constraints.* Then we will show that the operations on the scratch area preserves the validity. This idea of inserting and deleting subobjects can be applied to other formalisms with explicit proof objects.

To summarize, what we need to be able to do in the scratch area are

1. Represent partial objects.
2. Replace a placeholder by a partial object (*insertion*).
3. Replace a (partial) object by a placeholder (*deletion*).

which requires that we can do the following

1. Type check partial objects. We use a type checking algorithm which reduces the problem of checking if an object has a given type, to the problem of checking if a set of equations holds. This idea was first used in Automath [6]. If the equations only contain complete objects, we can check the equalities by convertibility, and we have a decision procedure. If the objects are partial (i.e. contain placeholders) we have instead a unification problem, since we want to find instantiations of all placeholders in the equations, such that

the equations hold. This unification problem can not always be solved, [3] since we may have higher order placeholders and placeholders as arguments to functions defined by pattern matching, which requires an instantiation of the placeholder before the matching can be performed. Therefore, the unification may leave unsolved equations as constraints restricting further instantiations.

2. Check if a replacement of a placeholder by an object is type correct relative to the expected type and the constraints, and reject the replacement if it leads to an (detectably) inconsistent set of constraints.
3. Automatic instantiations caused by the content of the deleted subobject must be withdrawn. This requires that we separate instantiations caused by unification from the user instantiations. If we only had the insertion operation we could perform the unification instantiations on the object directly.

We will start by giving an example which illustrates why we cannot define the validity of a scratch area as an "absolute property", rather as a property which depends on future instantiations. The example shows a partial object, in which either the constraint is satisfied but then it is not possible to give instantiations to the remaining placeholders, or the placeholders are instantiated but then the constraint is not satisfied.

Ex. Assume we define a set $\mathsf{Seq}(A, n)$ (denoting a sequence of type A and length n) with the two constructors atom and cons

$\mathsf{Seq} \in (\mathsf{Set}; \mathsf{N})\mathsf{Set}$

$\mathsf{atom} \in (A \in \mathsf{Set}; a \in A)\mathsf{Seq}(A, 1)$

$\mathsf{cons} \in (A \in \mathsf{Set}; a \in A; n \in \mathsf{N}; l \in \mathsf{Seq}(A, n))\mathsf{Seq}(A, s(n))$

and an append function with the type

$\mathsf{append} \in (A \in \mathsf{Set}; n, m \in \mathsf{N}; l_1 \in \mathsf{Seq}(A, n); l_2 \in \mathsf{Seq}(A, m))\mathsf{Seq}(A, n + m)$.

Assume we want to find an element in $\mathsf{Seq}(\mathsf{N}, 2)$ by using the append function:

$\mathsf{append}(\mathsf{N}, ?n, ?m, ?s_1, ?s_2) \in \mathsf{Seq}(\mathsf{N}, 2)$

where $?n, ?m, ?s_1$ and $?s_2$ are placeholders, with the typings

$?n, ?m \in \mathsf{N}$,

$?s_1 \in \mathsf{Seq}(\mathsf{N}, ?n)$ and

$?s_2 \in \mathsf{Seq}(\mathsf{N}, ?m)$.

Now, we will do a refinement which leads to a scratch area which is impossible to complete, but which can not be detected by the computation of the constraints. If $?s_1$ is refined by cons, we get the object

$\mathsf{append}(\mathsf{N}, ?n, ?m, \mathsf{cons}(\mathsf{N}, ?a, ?n_1, ?s), ?s_2) \in \mathsf{Seq}(\mathsf{N}, 2)$

and the type checking will produce the equalities

$?n = s(?n_1)$ and $?n + ?m = 2$.

[3] In [8] and [20] it is shown that higher order unification [13] can be generalized to dependent types. However, in our situation it seems difficult even to ensure that flexible-flexible pairs are always unifiable, since a flexible term may be defined by pattern matching.

The first equation will instantiate $?n$, leaving us with the constraint

$$s(?n_1)+?m = 2.$$

Now, we can see that since a sequence always has positive length, it is impossible to both instantiate the remaining placeholders and satisfy the constraint.

So we have here an example where a user refinement leads to a "dead end", which cannot be detected by the constraints. Of course, if the placeholders are further instantiated the constraint *will* be violated, but it was impossible to detect at the point when the erroneous step was made. This is also an argument for why the deleting operation is important.

Now, we will define what a scratch area is, but first we must define exactly what we mean by a partial object. We are forced to restrict all objects in definitions to be β-normal, since we can only type check β-normal objects. The reason is that given an object $([x]b)a$ and a type B, we can not uniquely infer the type family $(x \in A)B'$, which when applied to a gives the type B, due to dependent function types (see [21]).

Definition A *partial object* is a β-normal object which may contain placeholders everywhere except as the head of an application.

The reason we can not allow a placeholder as the head of an application is that we must know the type of the head to compute the argument types.

Definition A *scratch area* is represented by a tuple $\langle\mathcal{D}, \langle\mathcal{P}, \mathcal{C}\rangle\rangle$, where

- $\mathcal{D}$ is a set of definitions, in which the definiens are partial objects,
- $\mathcal{P}$ is a list of placeholders (instantiated or not) together with their types and contexts.
- $\mathcal{C}$ is a list of constraints.

We require all placeholders in $\mathcal{D}$ to be distinct and typed in $\mathcal{P}$, and all placeholders in $\mathcal{C}$ to be in $\mathcal{P}$.

The intuitive meaning of this representation is that the partial objects in $\mathcal{D}$ corresponds to the user instantiations, the instantiated placeholders in $\mathcal{P}$ is instantiations caused by unification, and $\mathcal{C}$ is the unsolved constraints. The uninstantiated placeholders in $\mathcal{P}$ is what is left to instantiate. When the partial object is presented to the user, then the instantiated placeholders are expanded.

Definition Let $\langle\mathcal{D}, \langle\mathcal{P}, \mathcal{C}\rangle\rangle$ be a scratch area. If every placeholder in $\mathcal{P}$ is instantiated such that the constraints in $\mathcal{C}$ are satisfied, then the scratch area is *complete*. A *solution* to $\langle\mathcal{P}, \mathcal{C}\rangle$ is an instantiation of the placeholders which makes the scratch area complete.

Note that if $\mathcal{P}$ is empty, then the definitions in $\mathcal{D}$ can not contain any placeholders and are therefore complete.

Since we allow several definitions in the scratch area, which can be manipulated simultaneously, we must ensure that the set of definitions are not circular in an illegal way, i.e. there must be a non-circular dependency order between the definitions. Mutually recursive definitions will be considered as one combined definition. Also, explicit constant definitions may not be recursive, whereas implicit definitions may.

Definition A set of definitions is *well-ordered* if the dependency graph of the definitions becomes acyclic when recursive dependencies of implicit constants are removed from the graph.

Definition A scratch area $\langle \mathcal{D}, \langle \mathcal{P}, \mathcal{C} \rangle \rangle$ is *valid* if
- The definitions in $\mathcal{D}$ are well-ordered.
- $\langle \mathcal{P}, \mathcal{C} \rangle$ has the same set of solutions as the union of the unification problems we get from type checking each definition in $\mathcal{D}$

The point is that we can type check instantiations locally, i.e. it is enough to check that an instantiation of a placeholder has the expected type, and we must not type check the entire definition every time a placeholder is instantiated. As a consequence of the definition of a valid scratch area, we get the following property;

Corollary 1. *All definitions in a complete scratch area are type correct.*

Proof. If the scratch area is complete, then we have a solution to all unification problems of type checking the definitions in $\mathcal{D}$, and since placeholders are distinct, we can divide this solution into solutions for each definition separately, which means that the instantiated definitions are complete and type correct.

6 Operations on incomplete proofterms

As mentioned, the two main operations on the scratch area is to replace a placeholder by a partial object and the converse, to replace a partial object by a placeholder. Placeholders (together with their types and local contexts) are generated when the user *refines* a placeholder. Consider again the distributivity example, where we had the definition

$$\mathsf{distr} = ?d \in (A, B, C \in \mathsf{Set}; \mathsf{And}(A, \mathsf{Or}(B, C)))\mathsf{Or}(\mathsf{And}(A, B), \mathsf{And}(A, C)).$$

The first step was to form an abstraction, yielding the new definition

$$\mathsf{distr} = [A, B, C, h]?e \in (A, B, C \in \mathsf{Set}; \mathsf{And}(A, \mathsf{Or}(B, C)))\\ \mathsf{Or}(\mathsf{And}(A, B), \mathsf{And}(A, C))$$

where the new placeholder $?e$ of type $\mathsf{Or}(\mathsf{And}(A, B), \mathsf{And}(A, C))$ in the local context $[A, B, C \in \mathsf{Set}; h \in \mathsf{And}(A, \mathsf{Or}(B, C))]$ is generated. The type and the context can be computed from the original type. Then the new placeholder is added to the scratch area and the old is replaced by the partial object $[A, B, C, h]?e$. In the next step $?e$ is refined with the constant OrE. Here, the number of required arguments and their types can be computed from the types of OrE and $?e$, yielding a list of new placeholders

$$?A, ?B, ?C \in \mathsf{Set}$$
$$?h1 \in (?A)?C$$

$?h2 \in (?B)?C$
$?h3 \in \mathsf{Or}(?A, ?B)$

and $?e$ is replaced by the partial object $\mathsf{OrE}(?A, ?B, ?C, ?h1, ?h2, ?h3)$. When $\mathsf{OrE}(?A, ?B, ?C, ?h1, ?h2, ?h3)$ is checked to be of proper type, the first three arguments are instantiated by unification.

When a part of an object is deleted, a new placeholder is created and its type can be computed from its position in the object. However, to ensure that all placeholders have their most general type after deletion, we may have to change the type of other placeholders as well. For example, given the definition of append in section 5, we can have a object

$\mathsf{append}(\mathsf{N}, \mathsf{s}(?n), ?m, ?s_1, ?s_2) \in \mathsf{Seq}(\mathsf{N}, 2)$,

where the placeholder $?s_1$ must be of type $\mathsf{Seq}(\mathsf{N}, \mathsf{s}(?n))$. If we replace $\mathsf{s}(?n)$ by a new placeholder $?n_1$, we must recompute the type of $?s_1$ to get the most general type $\mathsf{Seq}(\mathsf{N}, ?n_1)$. Actually, if we did not change the type of s_1, unification would again instantiate $?n_1$ to $\mathsf{s}(?n)$, and it would be impossible to delete any dependent argument. Another way to solve this problem of implicit sharing is to give an internal name to each dependent argument, and use the name instead in the object ([16]). However, the second approach becomes rather inefficient when objects grow large.

Before we describe the operations, we will explain the type checking algorithm briefly.

6.1 Typechecking

The algorithm takes as input a context, a type and a β-normal object and returns a list of constraints which must be satisfied for type correctness, or a failure. If the list is empty, the object is type correct. The algorithm starts by checking if the context is valid, then checks if the type is a valid type in that context, before calling the actual type checking algorithm. This algorithm consists of mainly three parts; type checking *TC*, type conversion and conversion *Conv*. The first part computes a list of *type equations*. These type equations are simplified one by one with the type conversion algorithm, which reduces a type equation to a list of object equations or reports a failure. The object equations are simplified one by one with the conversion algorithm, which reduces an object equation to simpler equations and finally removes trivial equations.

The algorithm will be computed in an *environment*, where constants are declared. Since the environment stays constant during type checking, we will assume a valid environment throughout this presentation. The environment is denoted by Σ below.

When an object is on β-normal form, we know that the head of an application is always a constant or a variable, and its type can be looked up in the environment or context, respectively. Therefore, we have an algorithm *CT* (for *C*ompute *T*ype), which is called by *TC* in the case of an application, and it returns the computed type and the equations that must hold for the arguments to be type correct. @ denotes concatenation of two lists.

$TC(a, A, \Gamma)$ checks if a is of type A in context Γ:

$$\frac{}{TC(x, A, \Gamma) \Rightarrow [A = A' \;\; \Gamma]}\ \text{TC-Var}\ (x{\in}A' \in \Gamma) \qquad \frac{}{TC(c, A, \Gamma) \Rightarrow [A = A' \;\; \Gamma]}\ \text{TC-Const}\ (c{\in}A' \in \Sigma)$$

$$\frac{TC(b, B\{y{:=}x\}, [\Gamma, x{\in} A]) \Rightarrow \xi}{TC([x]b, (y \in A)B, \Gamma) \Rightarrow \xi}\ \text{TC-Abs}$$

$$\frac{CT(f, \Gamma) \Rightarrow \langle \xi_1, (x \in A')B \rangle \quad TC(e, A', \Gamma) \Rightarrow \xi_2}{TC(fe, A, \Gamma) \Rightarrow \xi_1 @ \xi_2 @ [B\{x{:=}e\} = A \;\; \Gamma]}\ \text{TC-App}$$

$$\frac{}{CT(x, \Gamma) \Rightarrow \langle [\,], A \rangle}\ \text{CT-Var}\ (x{\in}A \in \Gamma) \qquad \frac{}{CT(c, \Gamma) \Rightarrow \langle [\,], A \rangle}\ \text{CT-Const}\ (c{\in}A \in \Sigma)$$

$$\frac{CT(f, \Gamma) \Rightarrow \langle \xi_1, (x \in A)B \rangle \quad TC(e, A, \Gamma) \Rightarrow \xi_2}{CT(fe, \Gamma) \Rightarrow \langle \xi_1 @ \xi_2, B\{x{:=}e\} \rangle}\ \text{CT-App}$$

Type conversion is computed in the following way, first the types are reduced to (outermost) constructor form, which pushes substitutions inside the type constructors. Then, if the types have the same form, the parts of the types are checked recursively. If they have not the same form type conversion returns a failure (constructors are assumed to be one-to-one).

Conversion The conversion algorithm is similar to the one presented in [3]. The algorithm proceeds as follows;

1. If the objects are syntactically equal - we are done.
2. If the objects have a function type, then both objects are applied to a fresh variable, and conversion is called recursively.
3. Try to reduce both objects to *head normal form.*
4. If both objects are rigid (i.e the head is a variable or a constructor and can not be changed by any instantiation), the simpler head conversion is invoked.
5. Otherwise, (i.e. at least one object is flexible), we leave the equation as a constraint.

(2) guarantees that the objects are *saturated*, and (4) implies that the object is of the form $b(a_1, \ldots, a_n)$ where b is either a variable or a constructor. (Note that this is a stronger restriction on b than β-normal, where b may be any constant, and since constants may have reduction rules associated with them, the object may be further reduced). The only possibility for two saturated objects on head normal form to be equal, is that the heads are identical and the arguments are pairwise convertible. Therefore, this is exactly what the head conversion algorithm checks. There are two advantages of performing the rule (2), first η-conversion need not be checked separately ($[x](fx)$ will be equal to f when applied to a variable) and second, we know that a function defined by pattern matching will be applied to all its arguments and this simplifies the matching.

$Conv(a, b, A, \Gamma)$ checks if a and b are convertible. The head-normal-form reduction ($\xrightarrow{hnf}$) returns a labeled object, where the labels are either *Rigid* or *Flex*. The reason is that we can not determine if an object is rigid or flexible just by looking at the form, since an application of an implicit constant can be either rigid ($+(x, y)$, where x, y are variables) or flexible ($+(?x, y)$). This is decided during reduction.

$$\frac{}{Conv(a, a, A, \Gamma) \Rightarrow []}\ \text{Conv-Id} \qquad \frac{Conv(az, bz, B\{x{:=}z\}, [\Gamma, z \in A]) \Rightarrow \xi}{Conv(a, b, (x \in A)B, \Gamma) \Rightarrow \xi}\ \begin{array}{l}\text{Conv-fun}\\ (z \notin Dom(\Gamma))\end{array}$$

$$\frac{a \xrightarrow{hnf} Rigid(a') \quad b \xrightarrow{hnf} Rigid(b') \quad HConv(a', b', \Gamma) \Rightarrow \langle \xi, A \rangle}{Conv(a, b, A, \Gamma) \Rightarrow \xi}\ \text{Conv-rigid}$$

$$\frac{a \xrightarrow{hnf} Flex(a') \text{ or } b \xrightarrow{hnf} Flex(b')}{Conv(a, b, A, \Gamma) \Rightarrow [a' = b' \in A \;\; \Gamma]}\ \text{Conv-flexible}$$

$$\frac{}{HConv(b, b, \Gamma) \Rightarrow \langle [], A \rangle}\ \begin{array}{l}\text{HConv-head}\\ (\ b \in \{x, c\}\ )\end{array}$$

$$\frac{HConv(f, g, \Gamma) \Rightarrow \langle \xi_1, (x \in A)B \rangle \quad Conv(a, b, A, \Gamma) \Rightarrow \xi_2}{HConv(fa, gb, \Gamma) \Rightarrow \langle \xi_1 @ \xi_2, B\{x{:=}a\} \rangle}\ \text{HConv-app}$$

The conversion algorithm correspond exactly to the rigid-rigid transformation in Elliot's unification algorithm for dependent function types. It computes a well-formed list of equations, so if all equations hold then all equations are well-typed.

Assuming that the substitution calculus in [23] is normalizing, we can show the following properties:

Proposition 1 *The type checking algorithm is sound and complete relative to Martin-Löf's substitution calculus, for β-normal, complete objects and types.*

This result will appear in the forthcoming Ph.D thesis of the first author.

Lemma 2. *If the input to the conversion algorithm is well-typed, then the resulting list of equations have the same set of solutions as the input equation.*

Proof. The Conv-Id rule is trivial and the Conv-fun rules is justified by the extensionality rule of the calculus. Due to normalization, objects are equal if and only if their (head) normal forms are equal, so the Conv-rigid rule preserves the set of solutions. Finally, since constructors are assumed to be one-to-one, and free variables are unique, the equation $b(a_1, \ldots, a_n) = b(a'_1, \ldots, a'_n)$ holds iff $a_1 = a'_1 \wedge \cdots \wedge a_n = a'_n$ hold, and if the heads are distinct, there is no solution (and the conversion algorithm returns fail).

6.2 Insertion

We will define when a placeholder can be replaced by an object, and how the list of constraints is simplified.

Definition Let $\langle \mathcal{D}, \langle \mathcal{P}, \mathcal{C} \rangle \rangle$ be a valid scratch area and let $?u$ be a placeholder occurring in a definition c, and $?u$ is not instantiated in $\mathcal{C}$. Then the insertion of object e in place of $?u$ is *admissible* if the following holds

1. Type checking e with type A_u in Γ_u produces a list of constraints $\mathcal{C}_u$, where A_u and Γ_u is the type and context of $?u$, respectively.
2. e contains no constants which depends on c, unless c is an implicit constant then c and other mutually defined constants may occur in e.
3. Simplifying the new list of constraints, where $?u$ is replaced by e everywhere and $\mathcal{C}_u$ is added, does not produce a detectable inconsistency.

If the conditions hold, then the placeholder is removed and $?u$ is replaced by e everywhere.

Definition A solved constraint is an equation $?u = e \in A\ \Gamma$ (or $e =?u \in A\ \Gamma$), where $?u$ does not occur in e.

Simplification of constraints: Simplification of the constraints proceeds by applying the following rule of transformation, until the rule is no longer applicable.

1. Pick a solved constraint $?u = e \in A\ \Gamma$ in $\mathcal{C}$
2. Type check e with the expected type $A_u\ \Gamma_u$, yielding a list of constraints $\mathcal{C}_u$
3. Replace $?u$ by e everywhere in $\mathcal{C}$ and $\mathcal{P}$, and add $\mathcal{C}_u$ to $\mathcal{C}$.
4. Update $?u$ by e in $\mathcal{P}$.
5. For each constraint in $\mathcal{C}$, replace the constraint by the result of applying the conversion algorithm. If the conversion returns fail, the list of constraints is inconsistent.

We will illustrate why we need to type check the instantiation from the solved constraint with the following example. Suppose we want to prove the proposition $\exists x.\forall y.R(x, y)$ for some reflexive relation R, so we suppose we have a constant $\mathsf{refl} \in (x \in A)R(x, x)$. After using the exist- and forall- introduction rules, we are in the situation

$$c =?c \in R(?x, y) \quad [y \in A]$$

and want to fill in the placeholders $?c$ and $?x$, where $?x$ is of type A and has an empty local context. Refining $?c$ with the constant refl creates a new placeholder $?u$ of type A in context $[y \in A]$. Type checking the insertion of $\mathsf{refl}(?u) with expected type R(?x, y)$ produces the equation

$$R(?u, ?u) = R(?x, y) \in Set \quad [y \in A]$$

which is simplified to

$$?x = y \in A \quad [y \in A] \text{ and } ?u = y \in A \quad [y \in A].$$

Since $?x$ is defined in the empty context, the instantiation is not valid, it violates the scoping rules. We conjecture that it is enough to check that the free variables of a solved constraint is included in the placeholders local context, rather than type checking the instantiation. This is enough if we can show that the type in a solved constraint is always the same as the expected type of the placeholder.

Lemma 3. *The simplification of a list of constraints preserves the set of solutions.*

Proof. We can only guarantee termination if the constraints arè consistent, since otherwise the objects in the equations may not be well-typed, and ill-typed objects may be reduced in the conversion algorithm. However, if the constraints are consistent, then the transformation will terminate since for each transformation the number of un-instantiated placeholders decreases, and the conversion algorithm produces a result which is either empty, identical to the original constraint or replaced with a list of constraints corresponding to the arguments compared pairwise which are all strictly smaller in complexity then the original constraint.

Finally, since $?u = e$ must hold in any solution, we can replace $?u$ by e without changing the set of solutions.

Proposition 2 *The validity of a scratch area is invariant under admissible insertions.*

Proof. Let $\langle \mathcal{D}, \langle \mathcal{P}, \mathcal{C} \rangle \rangle$ be a valid scratch area and let $\langle \mathcal{D}', \langle \mathcal{P}', \mathcal{C}' \rangle \rangle$ be the scratch area after the admissible insertion of e for $?u$ in definition c. By assumption $\mathcal{D}$ is well-ordered and since e can not contain any constants that depend on c in an illegal way, the insertion can not create a cycle. Hence, $\mathcal{D}'$ is well-ordered.

Let $\mathcal{U}$ ($\mathcal{U}'$) denote the union of the unification problem we get from type checking each definition in $\mathcal{D}$ ($\mathcal{D}'$), respectively. Let us call a list of constraints *updated by* $(?u, e)$ if $?u$ is replaced by e in the list, and the constraints from type checking e with the type of $?u$ is added to the list. Then we know that the solutions of $\langle \mathcal{P}, \mathcal{C} \rangle$ updated by $(?u, e)$ are the same as the solutions of $\langle \mathcal{P}', \mathcal{C}' \rangle$ by lemma 3, and since $\mathcal{U}'$ is the same set of equations as $\mathcal{U}$ updated by $(?u, e)$, they have the same solutions. By assumption, we have that $\mathcal{U}$ and $\langle \mathcal{P}, \mathcal{C} \rangle$ have the same solutions, and hence, $\mathcal{U}'$ and $\langle \mathcal{P}', \mathcal{C}' \rangle$ do to.

6.3 Deletion

To delete the object e in definition c, in a scratch area $\langle \mathcal{D}, \mathcal{P}, \mathcal{C} \rangle$ we only have to do the following steps

1. Create a new placeholder and replace e by it.
2. Delete the placeholders in e from $\mathcal{P}$, and remove all instantiations in $\mathcal{P}$.
3. Delete $\mathcal{C}$.
4. Recompute the types of all placeholders in c.
5. Retype check all definitions in $\mathcal{D}$, yielding a list of constraints $\mathcal{C}_{new}$.
6. Simplify $\mathcal{C}_{new}$.

Proposition 3 *The validity of a scratch area is invariant under deletion.*

Proof. Since the definitions in are noncyclic by assumption, we can not create a cycle by deleting a subobject. We have that the new list of constraints has the same set of solutions as the simplified list, by lemma 3.

In the implementation of ALF, the operations on the scratch area is optimized by having one visible part of the scratch area, in which *all* instantiations are updated in the definitions, and one invisible part where only the user instantiations are updated. This speeds up the insertion operation, and does not effect the deletion operation.

7 Proof Experiments and Experiences

The experiments done so far are relatively small. Nora Szasz has given a formal proof [22] that Ackermann's function is not primitive recursive. Veronica Gaspes showed [9] functional completeness of combinatorial logic, i.e. that every function can be compiled into an expression only involving the basic combinators **S**, **K** and **I**. Björn von Sydow [24] showed the fundamental theorem of arithmetic, i.e. that every integer is a product of a unique multiset of primes. Karlis Cerans and K.V.S. Prasad has made experiments with expressing proofs in various process calculii.

The proof engine is implemented in Standard ML and the window interface is written in C++ using the Interviews package. The next version is being written in Haskell and is substantially smaller. The current system is still incomplete, but people who are interested to try it are welcome to get a copy by anonymous ftp from ftp.cs.chalmers.se. A user manual can also be obtained in that way.

8 Comparision with other work

This editor is in a tradition of editors which started with Stanford and Edinburgh LCF [11]. Later descendants to this system are Coq and Lego. Coq [7] was developed in INRIA-Rocquencourt by Gerard Huet and his group and is based on Coquand's and Huet's Calculus of Constructions [5]. Lego [15] started as an offspring of Coq, but is now a completely new system. None of these systems use direct manipulation of the proof object, instead a proof is built up by giving commands to a proof engine.

The first implementation of Martin-Löf's type theory was made in 1982 by Kent Petersson [19] who replaced PPλ, the logic of the Edinburgh LCF with the polymorphic type theory as described in [17]. A group in Cornell under Robert Constable implemented the NuPrl system, a proof editor for a version of Martin-Löf's type theory with a modern user interface. This system is also based on indirect building of a proof [2].

9 Acknowledgements

This is joint work with Thierry Coquand. We want to thank him for many discussions. The first version of ALF was designed by Thierry Coquand and Bengt

Nordström in 1991, Thierry implemented the first proof engine and Lennart Augustsson implemented the user interface. The current proof engine is implemented by Lena. Johan Nordlander has programmed the user interface. We also want to thank the members of the programming logic group at Chalmers for many discussions on these topics. In particular we want to thank Björn von Sydow for writing the section describing the distributivity example.

References

1. Gustavo Betarte. A case study in machine-assisted proofs: The integers form an integral domain. Licentiate Thesis, Chalmers University of Technology and University of Göteborg, Sweden, November 1993.
2. R. L. Constable et al. *Implementing Mathematics with the NuPRL Proof Development System.* Prentice-Hall, Englewood Cliffs, NJ, 1986.
3. Thierry Coquand. An algorithm for testing conversion in type theory. In *Logical Frameworks.* Cambridge University Press, 1991.
4. Thierry Coquand. Pattern matching with dependent types. In *Proceeding from the logical framework workshop at Båstad*, June 1992.
5. Thierry Coquand and Gérard Huet. The Calculus of Constructions. Technical Report 530, INRIA, Centre de Rocquencourt, 1986.
6. N.G. de Bruijn. Generalizing automath by means of a lambda-typed lambda calculus. In *Mathematical Logic and Theoretical Computer Science, Lecture Notes in pure and applied mathematics*, pages 71–92. 1987.
7. G. Dowek, A. Felty, H. Herbelin, H. Huet, G. P. Murthy, C. Parent, C. Paulin-Mohring, and B. Werner. The coq proof assistant user's guide version 5.6. Technical report, Rapport Technique 134, INRIA, December 1991.
8. Conal M. Elliot. Higher-order unification with dependent function types. In N. Derikowitz, editor, *Proceedings of the 3rd International Conference on Rewriting Techniques and Applications*, pages 121–136, April 1989.
9. Veronica Gaspes. Formal Proofs of Combinatorial Completeness. In *To appear in the informal proceedings from the logical framework workshop at Båstad, June 1992.*
10. Gerhard Gentzen. Investigations into Logical Deduction. In E. Szabo, editor, *The Collected Papers of Gerhard Gentzen.* North-Holland Publishing Company, 1969.
11. M. Gordon, R. Milner, and C. Wadsworth. *Edinburgh LCF*, volume 78 of *Lecture Notes in Computer Science.* Springer-Verlag, 1979.
12. Martin Hofmann. A model of intensional martin-löf type theory in which unicity of identity proofs does not hold. Technical report, Dept. of Computer Science, University of Edinburgh, June 1993. Draft.
13. Gérard Huet. A unification algorithm for typed λ-calculus. *Theoretical Computer Science*, 1(1):27–57, 1975.
14. G. Kahn. L. Thery, Y. Bertot. Real Theorem Provers Deserve Real User-Interfaces. Technical report, INRIA, Rocquencourt, 1992.
15. Z. Luo and R. Pollack. LEGO Proof Development System: User's Manual. Technical report, LFCS Technical Report ECS-LFCS-92-211, 1992.
16. Lena Magnusson. Refinement and local undo in the interactive proof editor ALF. In *The Informal Proceeding of the 1993 Workshop on Types for Proofs and Programs*, May 1993.

17. Bengt Nordström, Kent Petersson, and Jan M. Smith. *Programming in Martin-Löf's Type Theory. An Introduction.* Oxford University Press, 1990.
18. Lawrence C. Paulson and Tobias Nipkow. Isabelle tutorial and user's manual. Technical report 189, Universtiy of Cambridge Computer Laboratory, Cambridge, January 1990.
19. Kent Petersson. A Programming System for Type Theory. PMG report 9, Chalmers University of Technology, S–412 96 Göteborg, 1982, 1984.
20. David Pym. A unification algorithm for the logical framework. Technical Report ECS-LFCS-92-229, University of Edinburgh, August 1992.
21. Anne Salvesen. Polymorphism and Monomorphism in Martin-Löf's Type Theory. Technical report, Norwegian Computing Center, P.b. 114, Blindern, 0316 Oslo 3, Norway, December 1988.
22. Nora Szasz. A Machine Checked Proof that Ackermann's Function is not Primitive Recursive. Licentiate Thesis, Chalmers University of Technology and University of Göteborg, Sweden, June 1991. To appear in G. Huet and G. Plotkin, editors, Logical Frameworks, Cambridge University Press.
23. Alvaro Tasistro. Formulation of Martin-Löf's Theory of Types with Explicit Substitution. Licentiate Thesis, Chalmers University of Technology and University of Göteborg, Sweden, May 1993.
24. Björn von Sydow. A machine-assisted proof of the fundamental theorem of arithmetic. Pmg memo, Chalmers University of Technology, 1992.

Encoding Z-style Schemas in Type Theory

Savi Maharaj

LFCS, Department of Computer Science, University of Edinburgh
JCMB, The King's Buildings, Edinburgh EH9 3JZ.
email: Savi.Maharaj@dcs.ed.ac.uk

Abstract. A distinctive feature of the Z specification language is its Schema Calculus which allows specifications to be packaged and put together to form new specifications. We investigate methods of transporting the Schema Calculus to the type theory UTT. We first attempt a direct encoding of schemas as Σ-types. This turns out to be unsatisfactory because encoding the operations of the Schema Calculus requires the ability to perform computations on the syntax of schemas, so we develop methods in which this syntax is also represented. These methods also depend upon Σ-types but use them in an unconventional fashion. We define a notion of implementation of a schema and use the LEGO proof-checker to prove some theorems about the interaction between implementations and our encodings of the operations of the Z Schema Calculus.

1 Introduction

The Z language [2, 5] is a formal notation based on set theory which provides an expressive, unambiguous language for writing specifications of programs. One of its main strengths is a structuring mechanism called the Schema Calculus[5] which allows specification modules to be put together in various ways to build new specifications. However there are elements which could be added to Z in order to make the language the basis of a complete program development methodology. For instance it is necessary to define what it means to implement a Z specification. It would also be helpful for proof support systems for Z to enable users to exploit the logical properties of the Schema Calculus itself.

The Unifying Theory of dependent Types (UTT) [9], and its implementation in the LEGO proof-checker [10], can also be viewed as a system for formal software development. Like set theory UTT can be used as a language for writing specifications. As a constructive type theory it also provides us with a notion of "program" which we can use to define an implementation. The LEGO proof-checker allows us to carry out machine-checked proofs in UTT. However UTT lacks some of the user-friendly properties of the specification languages used in industry.

In this paper we focus our attention on the structuring mechanism provided by Z, the Schema Calculus, which we attempt to interpret independently of the set theory within which it is used to structure theories. We investigate ways of transferring the Schema Calculus onto UTT as a base language instead of set theory. This is done by encoding a portion of the Schema Calculus in UTT. Our encoding enriches UTT by providing a way of writing structured specifications in UTT in the style of Z. This work can also be viewed as an alternative semantics for the Schema Calculus, based on type theory rather than set theory. This makes the Schema Calculus more independent than was originally envisaged by the designers of Z while preserving its essential features.

The encoding enables us to use LEGO to explore the properties of the operations of the Schema Calculus and their interaction with our definition of implementation. One of our aims is to gather a library of LEGO proofs of general properties of the Schema Calculus operations which we can re-use for proving properties of specifications or doing program verification.

For instance, the Schema Calculus provides an operation whereby two schemas S and T can be conjoined to produce a new schema $S \wedge T$. We would like to know whether if we have an implementation of schema $S \wedge T$ we can always derive from it implementations of S and of T — a kind of elimination rule. Conversely, if a program implements both S and T, or is an extension of implementations of these, does it then yield an implementation of $S \wedge T$? — a kind of introduction rule.

In Section 2 we introduce a small fragment of the Schema Calculus notation, just enough to illustrate the work that we have done. Then in Section 3 we discuss the ways in which we have tried to represent the Schema Calculus in LEGO, showing the problems that have motivated the development of each subsequent technique. We give the definitions that we finally settle upon and describe some results that we've proved. In Section 4 we give an example of the kind of reasoning that is made possible by my encoding. In Section 5 we discuss the relationship between our work and other semantic accounts of the Schema Calculus. We also compare our encoding with systems providing proof support for Z. Finally we discuss our conclusions in Section 6.

2 The Z notation

The Z notation consists of a core language based on set theory, and a structuring mechanism consisting of modules called *schemas* which can be combined in various ways using operations that make up the *Schema Calculus*.

Here is an example of a simple Z schema:

S

$x : \mathbb{N}$
$y : \mathit{list}\ \mathbb{N}$

$x \leq \mathit{length}\ y$

The schema consists of a *signature* and a *predicate*.

One of the operations of the Schema Calculus is schema conjunction; this involves *join*ing the signatures of two schemas and conjoining their predicates to give a new predicate over the joined signature. When two signatures are joined occurrences of the same identifier in both signatures are identified with each other.

Example:

$$\begin{array}{|l}
\hline T \\
x : \mathbb{N} \\
z : \mathit{list}\ \mathbb{N} \\
\hline
x \geq \mathit{length}\ z \\
\hline
\end{array}$$

Conjoining S and T gives the schema:

$$\begin{array}{|l}
\hline S \wedge T \\
x : \mathbb{N} \\
y : \mathit{list}\ \mathbb{N} \\
z : \mathit{list}\ \mathbb{N} \\
\hline
(x \leq \mathit{length}\ y) \wedge (x \geq \mathit{length}\ z) \\
\hline
\end{array}$$

Other operations, which we won't describe here, include disjunction, implication, negation, inclusion of one schema within another, composition of schemas, and piping. Most of these make use of the *join* operation to combine signatures.

3 Representing the Schema Calculus in UTT

The Schema Calculus is the most distinctive feature of Z — it is what makes Z superior to using just set theory as a specification language. As a mechanism for structuring specifications it has proved its worth since the Z language is widely used in industry. We think it is rewarding to study this system independently of the set theory which it is used to structure, and in particular, to investigate whether this system may be usefully transported to another "core language" — that of constructive type theory.[1]

It must be pointed out that in standard Z the Schema Calculus and core language are interdependent, since it is possible to use schemas as types. We diverge from Z in isolating the Schema Calculus. The relationship between our work and standard Z will be discussed in Section 5.

For the purposes of our encoding, we first select a part of UTT to be our core language. This includes a selection of inductive types such as *nat*, *bool* and polymorphic *list*. See [10] and [9, 7] for discussions of, respectively, the practical and the theoretical aspects of introducing such inductive datatypes into the LEGO implementation of UTT. We take our definitions of these types and of basic functions that act upon them from the LEGO library [6]. The library functions and lemmas that we use are described in Appendix B.

[1] In previous work [11] we explored ways of "implementing" Z in LEGO by encoding set theory.

For many inductive types it is possible to define a computational (*bool*-valued) equality predicate on that type. We use the symbol $\stackrel{bool}{=}$ to denote such equality predicates. There are various propositional (*Prop*-valued) equalities which can be defined in UTT; of these we use Paulin-Mohring's inductive equality [3] which we denote by the symbol $=$.

Having defined a core language, we then introduce a new type representing schemas. Most of this section is concerned with the search for a suitable UTT type for this purpose. The type chosen should allow us to define all the operations of the Schema Calculus. Our intention is that UTT will play a double role in the encoding — it will act as the object language in which schemas are given meaning, but it will also be the metalanguage in which the Schema Calculus operations are defined, thereby enabling us to prove theorems about these operations *within* LEGO.

We make use of the fact that we are working in a constructive type theory to define a notion of program and an *implementation* relation between programs and schemas. Again we explore various possibilities for these definitions. Having made a final choice, we use LEGO to prove some theorems about the interaction between the implementation relation and the Schema Calculus operations.

Method 1: Schemas as Σ types We can use Σ-types to represent schemas in a manner similar to the way type theory is used in [8]. Then the schema S presented above is encoded in UTT as:

$$S\_sig \stackrel{def}{=} nat \times list\ nat$$
$$S\_pred \stackrel{def}{=} \lambda\, str : S\_sig.\, (\pi_1 str) \leq length\ (\pi_2 str)$$
$$S \stackrel{def}{=} \Sigma\, str : S\_sig.\, S\_pred\ str$$

This allows us to define an implementation: an implementation of S is just an object whose type is S, that is, a program of type *S_sig* paired with a proof that this satisfies the predicate *S_pred*. But how do we go about defining the operations of the Schema Calculus? In order to implement the *join* operation we need to compare the identifiers and types used in our schemas, that is, we need a computational equality on identifiers and on types. But with schemas as Σ-types we have no representation for the identifiers in schemas. Though we do have a representation of types (as UTT types) we cannot define a computational equality on these.

It may appear that our problem with identifiers would be solved by adding record types to the type theory. In fact this is not so, since the problem is not the absence of labels for the components of the Σ-type, but the impossibility of treating such labels as terms in the type theory that can be acted upon by functions defined in the type theory. What we need to do therefore is to encode the *syntax* of Z identifiers and types as terms in UTT that we can use to do computations.

Method 2: Syntactic names and types in signatures We introduce two new inductive types to represent identifiers and type names. The identifiers will be derived from the specification that is being encoded. For our example we have:

Definition 1 Ident.

$$Ident ::= \text{`}x\text{'} \mid \text{`}y\text{'} \mid \text{`}z\text{'}$$
$$: Type$$

We also introduce a new inductive type of Z type names. Here, *Given_Type* is an inductive type consisting of type names over which a specification is parameterised.

Definition 2 Ztype.

$$\begin{aligned} Ztype ::= {} & natT \mid boolT \mid givenT\ Given\_Type \mid \\ & funT\ (Ztype, Ztype) \mid prodT\ (Ztype, Ztype) \end{aligned}$$
$$: Type$$

We define a signature as a list of pairs of these syntactic identifiers and types:

Definition 3 Signature.

$$Signature \overset{def}{=} list\ (Ident \times Ztype) : Type$$

Since we still want to be able to relate these specifications to programs written in UTT, we must define the relationship between these syntactic signatures and types in UTT. To do this we define a semantic function, *Typ* that maps these syntactic types to UTT types: e.g. $Typ\ natT = nat$. Then we extend this to a function *Typify* of type $Signature \rightarrow Type$[2] which forms a product of the types obtained by applying *Typ* to all of the *Ztype*s in a given signature, together with the unit type in the case of the empty signature. This essentially allows us to recapture our previous definition of a signature as a product of types.

We can then define a schema as consisting of a syntactic signature *sig* paired with a predicate over the semantic signature *Typify sig*:

Old definition 1 (Schema)

$$Schema \overset{def}{=} \Sigma\, sig : Signature.\, (Typify\ sig) \rightarrow Prop$$
$$: Type$$

We give the names *.sig* and *.pred*, respectively, to the first and second projections from a *Schema*.

We define an implementation of such a schema $(sig, pred)$ as a program of type *Typify sig* paired with a proof that it satisfies the predicate *pred*. This closely resembles the notion of implementation in Method 1.

---

[2] Actually UTT has a countable hierarchy of type universes. We select a particular universe, which, for simplicity, we refer to as *Type*.

Old definition 2 (Implementation)

$$Implementation \stackrel{def}{=} \lambda\, S\!:\!Schema.\, \Sigma\, str\!:\, Typify\ S.sig.\ S.pred\ str$$
$$:Schema \rightarrow Type$$

Implementations of a schemas S are objects of type (*Implementation* S).

In order to work with these syntactic functions we need to define several functions. One of these is *lookup* which, when given an identifier and a tuple *str* of type *Typify sig* for some signature *sig*, attempts to locate the identifier in *sig* and then projects the value in the corresponding position in *str*. Failure is handled by returning the value *void*. Typechecking will detect when *lookup* fails since the value returned in the case of failure will be of the wrong type. For example, in the following definition of the schema S, if we remove the identifier 'x' from *S_sig* (or if we paired it with some other type), then the definition of *S_pred* will fail to typecheck.[3]

The main use of *lookup* is in writing schema predicates. This is illustrated by the new definition of the schema S.

$$S\_sig \stackrel{def}{=} [(`x', natT), (`y', listT\ natT)]$$
$$S\_pred \stackrel{def}{=} \lambda\, str\!:\, Typify\ S\_sig.\, (lookup\ `x'\ str) \leq length\ (lookup\ `y'\ str)$$
$$S \stackrel{def}{=} (S\_sig, S\_pred)$$

Another example of a schema is the trivial, unsatisfiable, *Absurd_schema* which consists of the empty signature and the predicate $\lambda\, str\!:\, Typify\ [\,].\ absurd$.

Now we can begin to define the operations of the Schema Calculus. Consider the operation of conjoining two schemas S and S'. First we must form a new signature *newsig* by joining the signatures of S and S'. These two signatures may be inconsistent, in that there may be an identifier which occurs in both of them that is paired with different *Ztypes* in each occurrence, so we must find some way of handling this possibility. Next we must form a new predicate over the semantic signature *Typify newsig* by conjoining the two old predicates. To do this we have to make use of coercions which map programs in the new semantic signature back to programs in *Typify sig* and *Typify sig'* since these types are the domains of the old predicates.

First we define the *join* function. This takes two signatures *sig* and *sig'* yields a new signature *newsig* together with a coercion back from *newsig* to *sig*. The coercion takes a tuple of type *Typify newsig* and produces a tuple of type *Typify sig* by projecting only those components that correspond to identifiers present in *sig*. No coercion back to the second signature *sig'* is computed since this may not exist if *sig* and *sig'* happen to be inconsistent.

Another operation *coerce* attempts to find coercions between arbitrary signatures. The type of *coerce* reflects the fact that it is partial: if no coercion exists it returns *in*2 *void*.

---

[3] This is accomplished by defining *lookup* in terms of another function *lookup_aux* which returns a dependent pair consisting of a type and a value of that type. We then use the second projection of this result.

$$coerce : \Pi\, S, S' : Signature.\, ((Typify\ S) \rightarrow (Typify\ S')) + unit$$

Now we can define schema conjunction. To conjoin S and S' we first *join* their signatures to form a new signature *newsig*. Then we attempt to coerce *newsig* back to the signature of S'. This will fail if S and S' happen to be inconsistent, in which case we return *Absurd_schema* as our result. Otherwise we return a schema made up of *newsig* and the predicates of S and S' conjoined and composed with coercions as appropriate.

The definition is as follows. We use square brackets here to enclose local definitions of identifiers, a useful feature of LEGO syntax. The function *case* is an elimination rule for the sum datatype: when applied to any $f : s \rightarrow u$ and $g : t \rightarrow u$, where s, t, and u are types, *case* returns a function of type $(s + t) \rightarrow u$.

Old definition 3 (And_schema)

$$\begin{array}{l} And\_schema \stackrel{def}{=} \lambda\, S, S' : Schema. \\ \quad [tmp \stackrel{def}{=} join\ S\ S'] \\ \quad [newsig \stackrel{def}{=} (\pi_1 tmp)] \\ \quad [coercion1 \stackrel{def}{=} (\pi_2 tmp)] \\ \quad [coercion2 \stackrel{def}{=} coerce\ newsig\ S'.sig] \\ case \\ \quad (\lambda\, f : (Typify\ newsig) \rightarrow (Typify\ S'.sig). \\ \qquad (newsig, \lambda\, s : Typify\ newsig.\, (S.pred\ (coercion1\ s)) \wedge (S'.pred\ (f\ s)))) \\ \quad (\lambda\, x : unit.\, Absurd\_schema) \\ \quad coercion2 \\ : Schema \rightarrow Schema \rightarrow Schema \end{array}$$

With this method we can define all the operations of the Schema Calculus. However we need to compute lots of coercions and reasoning about these turns out to be difficult. For instance, *coerce* makes use of a simple function called *coerce_Ztypes* which takes two *Ztype*s z and z' and attempts to find mappings to and from *Typ* z and *Typ* z'. This function has the type:

$$\Pi\, z, z' : Ztype.\, (((Typ\ z) \rightarrow (Typ\ z')) \times ((Typ\ z') \rightarrow (Typ\ z))) + unit$$

This function is defined by induction on *Ztype*s in a straightforward way. It succeeds when z and z' are identical, in which case it returns functions that are extensionally equal to the identity function on the appropriate type. So we tried to prove the following result:

$$\begin{array}{l} \forall\, z : Ztype.\ \exists f, f' : (Typ\ z) \rightarrow (Typ\ z). \\ \qquad (coerce\_Ztypes\ z\ z = in1\ (f, f')) \wedge (\forall\, x : Typ\ z.\, (f\ x = x) \wedge (f'\ x = x)) \end{array}$$

However we found that in order to prove it we needed to assume extensionality for functions. The reason for this has to do with way that *coerce_Ztype* is defined on *Ztypes* of the form $funT\ z\ z'$. The coercions that are found in this case are of type $((Typ\ z) \rightarrow (Typ\ z')) \rightarrow ((Typ\ z) \rightarrow (Typ\ z'))$ They map a function f to another function created by pre- and post-composing f with coercions between z and z and between z' and z'. This function is only extensionally equal to f.

Extensionality is not part of UTT and we would prefer not to have to assume it. Perhaps we can avoid it if we find a way of avoiding having to find coercions. We needed coercions because schema predicates were defined over specific signatures and therefore needed to be composed with coercions before they could be applied to other signatures. So what if we allow our predicates to be defined over all signatures? This leads us to explore a third method of representing Z schemas.

Method 3: Syntactic names in programs The idea here is to introduce a new type of programs, over which schema predicates will be defined. Whereas before we used UTT's typing rules to determine whether a program matched a signature, we will now have to explicitly define a matching relation between programs and signatures.

We continue to use the types *Ident*, *Ztype* and *Signature* and the semantic function *Typ*. However instead of representing programs as tuples, we use a more syntactic representation in which values are associated with syntactic names and types. We call these programs *Structures* since they are reminiscent of Structures in the programming language SML.

Definition 4 Structure.

$$Structure \stackrel{def}{=} list\ (\Sigma\, p : Ident \times Ztype.\ Typ\ (\pi_2 p)) : Type$$

We have to write some functions to handle these syntactic programs. First we define a function which simply extracts a *Signature* from a *Structure*:

Definition 5 extract_sig.

$$\begin{array}{l} extract\_sig \stackrel{def}{=} map\ \lambda\, x : str\_item.\ \pi_1 x \\ : Structure \rightarrow Signature \end{array}$$

The next function, *matches*, checks whether the names and identifiers in a *Structure* are exactly the same as those in a given *Signature*.

Definition 6 matches.

$$\begin{array}{l} matches \stackrel{def}{=} \lambda\, S : Signature.\ \lambda\, str : Structure.\ S \stackrel{bool}{=} (extract\_sig\ str) \\ : Signature \rightarrow Structure \rightarrow bool \end{array}$$

We redefine *lookup* to work with our new representation of programs.

Definition 7 lookup.

$$
\begin{array}{l}
lookup \stackrel{def}{=} \lambda\, x : sig\_item. \\
\quad list\_iter\ (in1\ void) \\
\qquad\qquad (\lambda\, y : str\_item.\ \lambda\, prev : (unit + str\_item). \\
\qquad\qquad\quad if\ (x \stackrel{bool}{=} (\pi_1 y))\ (in2\ y)\ prev) \\
: sig\_item \rightarrow Structure \rightarrow (unit + str\_item)
\end{array}
$$

The next function *restrict*, attempts to cut down a structure so that it has only those components specified in a given *Signature*; *restrict* fails if the *Signature* requires components that are not in the *Structure*.

Definition 8 restrict.

$$
\begin{array}{l}
restrict \stackrel{def}{=} \lambda\, str : Structure. \\
\quad list\_iter\ (in2\ nil\_str) \\
\qquad\qquad (\lambda\, x : sig\_item.\ \lambda\, prev : (unit + Structure). \\
\qquad\qquad\quad case\ \lambda\_ : unit.\, in1\ void \\
\qquad\qquad\qquad\quad \lambda\, s : Structure.\ case\ \ \lambda\_ : unit.\, in1\ void \\
\qquad\qquad\qquad\qquad\qquad\qquad\qquad \lambda\, si : str\_item.\, in2\ (cons\ si\ s) \\
\qquad\qquad\qquad\qquad\qquad\qquad\qquad (lookup\ x\ str) \\
\qquad\qquad\qquad\quad prev) \\
: Structure \rightarrow Signature \rightarrow (unit + Structure)
\end{array}
$$

An example of a syntactic program is the following:

$$prog \stackrel{def}{=} [(\text{'}x\text{'}, natT, 0), (\text{'}b\text{'}, boolT, true)] : Structure$$

If we define *sig* to be the signature $[(\text{'}b\text{'}, boolT)]$ then (*matches sig prog*) evaluates to *false* and (*restrict prog sig*) evaluates to the *Structure* $[(\text{'}b\text{'}, boolT, true)]$.

Our new definition of the type *Schema* is:

Definition 9 Schema.

$$Schema \stackrel{def}{=} Signature \times (Structure \rightarrow Prop) : Type$$

We redefine the projections *.sig* and *.pred* to use this new representation of schemas.

Schema predicates become more complicated since we have to explicitly allow for the possibility that *lookup* might fail. The predicates and relations that we use in writing schema predicates need to be redefined with this in mind. For instance in the definition of the schema S we replace $\leq : nat \rightarrow nat \rightarrow Prop$ with $\preceq : (unit + str\_item) \rightarrow (unit + nat) \rightarrow Prop$ which is defined as the proposition *absurd* in the case where either of its first arguments happens to be *in*1 *void*. We also replace $length : \Pi\, t : Type.\,(list\ t) \rightarrow nat$ with $Length : (unit + str\_item) \rightarrow (unit + nat)$. Here is the new definition of this schema:

$$
\begin{array}{l}
S\_sig \stackrel{def}{=} [(\text{`}x\text{'}, natT), (\text{`}y\text{'}, listT\ natT)] \\
S\_pred \stackrel{def}{=} \lambda\, str : Structure. \\
\qquad\qquad (lookup\ (\text{`}x\text{'},\ natT)\ str) \preceq Length\ (lookup\ (\text{`}y\text{'},\ (listT\ natT))\ str) \\
S \stackrel{def}{=} (S\_sig, S\_pred)
\end{array}
$$

Another example is the new definition of *Absurd_Schema*:

Definition 10.

$$Absurd\_schema \stackrel{def}{=} ([\,], \lambda\, s : Structure.\ absurd) : Schema$$

We need to place some conditions on schemas in order to exclude some badly behaved predicates. We would like predicates to remain true of structures if they are enriched by adding new components. Therefore we don't want to allow, for instance, a predicate that says that a certain identifier does not occur in a structure.

The first property we require of a schema says that any structure *str* which satisfies the schema's predicate must be capable of being restricted by the schema's signature, yielding a structure *str′* which must also satisfy the schema's predicate.

Definition 11.

$$
\begin{array}{l}
Condition1 \stackrel{def}{=} \lambda\, S : Schema. \\
\quad \forall\, str : Structure.\,(S.pred\ str) \Rightarrow case\ \ \lambda\, \_ : unit.\ absurd \\
\qquad\qquad\qquad\qquad\qquad\qquad\qquad\quad \lambda\, str' : Structure.\ S.pred\ str' \\
\qquad\qquad\qquad\qquad\qquad\qquad\qquad\quad (restrict\ str\ S.sig) \\
: Schema \rightarrow Prop
\end{array}
$$

The second condition is almost the converse of the first. This says that if a structure *str* can be restricted successfully by a schema's signature to give another structure which satisfies that schema's predicate, then *str* itself must satisfy the schema's predicate.

Definition 12.

$$
\begin{array}{l}
Condition2 \stackrel{def}{=} \lambda\, S : Schema. \\
\quad \forall\, str : Structure.\ case\ \ \lambda\, \_ : unit.\ trueProp \\
\qquad\qquad\qquad\qquad\qquad \lambda\, str' : Structure.\,(S.pred\ str') \Rightarrow S.pred\ str \\
\qquad\qquad\qquad\qquad\qquad (restrict\ str\ S.sig) \\
: Schema \rightarrow Prop
\end{array}
$$

A valid schema is one that satisfies both *Condition*1 and *Condition*2.

Definition 13 Valid_schema.

$$Valid\_schema \stackrel{def}{=} \lambda\, S : Schema.\,(Condition1\ S) \wedge (Condition2\ S)$$
$$: Schema \rightarrow Prop$$

The user will need to prove that this condition is satisfied whenever a new schema is defined. We have done this for the example schema S; the proof is lengthy but straightforward. We will also have to show that all our basic schemas and schema operations have or preserve this property.

Proposition 14 Absurd_schema_valid.

$$Valid\_schema\ Absurd\_schema$$

Proof. Trivial.

With these more syntactic programs, our definitions of schema operations become much simpler since there is no longer any need to compute or keep track of coercions. The function *join*, for instance, gets redefined in a simpler way. This definition makes use of a simple *bool*-valued function *member_ident* which checks whether a given identifier occurs in a given signature and is defined in an obvious way.

Definition 15 join.

$$\begin{array}{l} join \stackrel{def}{=} \lambda\, S, T : Signature. \\ \quad list\_iter\ T \\ \qquad\qquad \lambda\, x : sig\_item.\ \lambda\, prev : Signature. \\ \qquad\qquad\qquad if\ (member\_ident\ (\pi_1 n)\ prev)\ prev\ (cons\ x\ prev) \\ \qquad\qquad S \\ : Signature \rightarrow Signature \rightarrow Signature \end{array}$$

Here is the new definition of schema conjunction. We make use of a new function $consistent : Signature \rightarrow Signature \rightarrow bool$ which checks whether two signatures are consistent. We omit the definition of this function because it is long. Its behaviour is partially characterised by Lemma 34 in Appendix A.

Definition 16 And_schema.

$$\begin{array}{l} And\_schema \stackrel{def}{=} \lambda\, S, S' : Schema. \\ \quad if\ (consistent\ S.sig\ S'.sig) \\ \qquad ((join\ S.sig\ S'.sig),\ \lambda\, s : Structure.\,(S.pred\ s) \wedge (S'.pred\ s)) \\ \qquad Absurd\_schema \\ : Schema \rightarrow Schema \rightarrow Schema \end{array}$$

We show that schema conjunction preserves the property *Valid_schema*. The lemmas referred to in this proof are given in Appendix A.

Proposition 17 And_preserves_validity.

$$\begin{array}{l} \forall S, T{:}\,Schema. \\ \quad (unique\_idents\ S.sig) \Rightarrow (unique\_idents\ T.sig) \Rightarrow \\ \quad\quad (Valid\_schema\ S) \Rightarrow (Valid\_schema\ T) \Rightarrow \\ \quad\quad\quad Valid\_schema\ (And\_schema\ S\ T) \end{array}$$

Proof. We introduce all the hypotheses and then consider the two possible values of (*consistent* *S.sig* *T.sig*). In the case where this is equal to *false*, *And_schema S T* reduces to *Absurd_schema* for which we use Proposition 14.

In the case where S and T are consistent our goal is reduced to finding a proof of the following. Here the ? is the name of an existential variable, standing for the proof that we have to construct.

$$\begin{array}{l} ?{:}\ Valid\_schema \\ \quad ((join\ S.sig\ T.sig), \lambda\, str{:}\,Structure.\,(S.pred\ str) \wedge (T.pred\ str)) \end{array}$$

We expand the definition of *Valid_schema* and then do an and-introduction which gives us two subgoals. The first of these is the following:

$$\begin{array}{l} ?_{28}{:}\forall\, str{:}\,Structure.\,((S.pred\ str) \wedge (T.pred\ str)) \Rightarrow \\ \quad (case\ \lambda\,\_{:}\ unit.\ absurd \\ \quad\quad \lambda\, str'{:}\,Structure.\,((S.pred\ str') \wedge (T.pred\ str')) \\ \quad\quad (restrict\ str\ (join\ S.sig\ T.sig))) \end{array}$$

In other words we are being asked to show that if a structure *str* satisfies the predicates of both S and T, then it can be successfully restricted by the signature (*join S.sig T.sig*) to give a new structure *str′* which also satisfies *S.pred* and *T.pred*.

First we introduce into the proof context a structure *str* and a hypothesis H_2 stating that *str* satisfies *S.pred* and *T.pred*. From H_2 and from the assumptions that S and T are valid schemas we can conclude that *str* can be successfully restricted by each of the signatures *S.sig* and *T.sig*. We can then use Lemma 30 to derive that *str* can be successfully restricted by (*join S.sig T.sig*), giving a new structure *str′*.

Now we have to show that *str′* satisfies *S.pred* and *T.pred*. We use Lemma 31 to show that (*restrict str′ S*) is equal to (*restrict str S*). Since S is a valid schema, and *str* satisfies *S.pred*, we can conclude that *str′* must also satisfy *S.pred*. We show that *str′* also satisfies *T.pred* in a similar way, using instead Lemma 32 to show that (*restrict str′ T*) equals (*restrict str T*). This concludes the proof of the first subgoal.

The second subgoal is almost the converse of the first:

$$\begin{array}{l} ?_{29}{:}\forall\, str{:}\,Structure. \\ \quad (case\ \lambda\,\_{:}\ unit.\ trueProp \\ \quad\quad \lambda\, str'{:}\,Structure.\,((S.pred\ str') \wedge (T.pred\ str')) \Rightarrow \\ \quad\quad\quad\quad ((S.pred\ str) \wedge (T.pred\ str)) \\ \quad\quad (restrict\ str\ (join\ S.sig\ T.sig))) \end{array}$$

Here we have to show that if a structure *str* can be successfully restricted to the signature (*join* $S.sig$ $T.sig$) giving a new structure *str′*, such that *str′* satisfies the predicates of S and T, then *str* must satisfy these predicates as well.

We introduce a structure *str*. Next we use a LEGO library lemma *in1_or_in2* to examine the two possible results of restricting *str* to (*join* $S.sig$ $T.sig$). In the case where the result is (*in1 void*), our goal is reduced to proving *trueProp*, which is trivially true.

The remaining case is where *str* can be restricted successfully, giving a new structure *str′*. In this case we are reduced to having to show:

$$?_{242}: ((S.pred\ str') \wedge (T.pred\ str')) \Rightarrow ((S.pred\ str) \wedge (T.pred\ str))$$

We use Lemmas 44 and 45 to show that *str* can be successfully restricted by $S.sig$ and $T.sig$, respectively. We use Lemma 31 to show that (*restrict str′* $S.sig$) equals (*restrict str* $S.sig$), and we use Lemma 32 to show the corresponding result for $T.sig$. With these in our proof context, we can then use the assumptions that S and T are valid to complete the proof. □

An implementation of a schema S is a structure *str* paired with a proof of (*Implements* S *str*) where *Implements* is defined as

Definition 18 Implements.

$$\begin{aligned}
&Implements \stackrel{def}{=} \lambda\, S : Schema.\ \lambda\, str : structure. \\
&\qquad\qquad\qquad (matches\ S.sig\ str = true) \wedge (S.pred\ str) \\
&: Schema \rightarrow Structure \rightarrow Prop
\end{aligned}$$

This states that an implementation of a schema is a *Structure* which exactly matches the schema's signature and which satisfies the schema's predicate. It may turn out that requiring an exact match with the signature is too restrictive, but for now this is the definition that we use.

We have succeeded in proving introduction and elimination rules for the operation *And_schema*. They hold for valid schemas under the reasonable condition that identifiers can appear at most once in any of the signatures and structures involved. This condition is expressed by the following predicate.

Definition 19 unique_idents.

$$\begin{aligned}
&unique_idents \stackrel{def}{=} \\
&\quad list_rec\ trueProp \\
&\qquad\qquad \lambda\, x : sig_item.\ \lambda\, l : Signature.\ \lambda\, prev : Prop. \\
&\qquad\qquad\qquad\qquad ((member\ x\ l) = false) \wedge prev \\
&: Signature \rightarrow Prop
\end{aligned}$$

These results make use of a predicate named *restricts_to_impl*, defined below, which says two things: that a given *Structure* can be successfully restricted to the signature of a given *Schema*, and that the new *Structure* obtained by this *restriction* is an implementation of the given *Schema*.

Definition 20 restricts_to_impl.

$$\begin{array}{l} \mathit{restricts\_to\_impl} \stackrel{def}{=} \lambda\, S\!:\!\mathit{Schema}.\ \lambda\, \mathit{str}\!:\!\mathit{Structure}.\\ \quad \mathit{case}\ \lambda\, \_\!:\mathit{unit}.\ \mathit{absurd}\\ \qquad \lambda\, \mathit{str}'\!:\!\mathit{Structure}.\ \mathit{Implements}\ S\ \mathit{str}'\\ \qquad (\mathit{restrict}\ \mathit{str}\ S.\mathit{sig})\\ :\mathit{Schema} \rightarrow \mathit{Structure} \rightarrow \mathit{Prop} \end{array}$$

The following result gives a kind of introduction rule for schema conjunction. If we are given a *Structure str* which can be restricted to give implementations of two *Schema*s S and S', then we can conclude from this theorem that *str* can be restricted to an implementation of *And_schema* S S'.

Proposition 21 And_schema_intro.

$$\begin{array}{l} \forall\, S, T\!:\!\mathit{Schema}.\ \forall\, \mathit{str}\!:\!\mathit{Structure}.\\ \quad (\mathit{Valid\_schema}\ S) \Rightarrow (\mathit{Valid\_schema}\ T) \Rightarrow\\ \quad (\mathit{unique\_idents}\ S.\mathit{sig}) \Rightarrow (\mathit{unique\_idents}\ T.\mathit{sig}) \Rightarrow\\ \quad (\mathit{unique\_idents}\ (\mathit{extract\_sig}\ \mathit{str})) \Rightarrow\\ \qquad (\mathit{restricts\_to\_impl}\ S\ \mathit{str}) \Rightarrow\\ \qquad (\mathit{restricts\_to\_impl}\ T\ \mathit{str}) \Rightarrow\\ \qquad \mathit{restricts\_to\_impl}\ (\mathit{And\_schema}\ S\ T)\ \mathit{str} \end{array}$$

Proof. We begin by case analyses on the results of restricting *str* to $S.sig$ and to $T.sig$. In the cases where either of these restrictions fails we can easily obtain a contradiction with the appropriate hypothesis. For instance, if we have that (*restrict str* $S.sig$) is equal to *in*1 *void*, we can use this to reduce the hypothesis (*restricts_to_impl* S *str*) to a proof of *absurd*.

So the interesting case is where *str* can be successfully restricted to both $S.sig$ and $T.sig$, yielding new structures *strS* and *strT*, respectively. Here is part of what our current proof context looks like:

$$\begin{array}{l} H_1\!: \mathit{restrict}\ \mathit{str}\ S.\mathit{sig} = \mathit{in2}\ \mathit{strS}\\ H_4\!: \mathit{restrict}\ \mathit{str}\ T.\mathit{sig} = \mathit{in2}\ \mathit{strT}\\ H_2\!: \mathit{Implements}\ S\ \mathit{strS}\\ H_5\!: \mathit{Implements}\ T\ \mathit{strT} \end{array}$$

Lemma 30 tells us that *str* can be successfully restricted to the signature (*join* S T), yielding a new structure t. We add these facts to our proof context.

Eventually we wish to show that this structure t is an implementation of the schema *And_schema* S T. As a first step towards proving this we make the following two claims:

$$\begin{array}{l} ?88\!: S.\mathit{pred}\ \mathit{str}\\ ?89\!: T.\mathit{pred}\ \mathit{str} \end{array}$$

By applying Lemma 38, *join_is_consistent*, to these two claims, as well as to the appropriate hypotheses, we obtain a proof that (*consistent* $S.sig$ $T.sig$)

equals *true*. This allows us to conclude that the signature of (*And_Schema S T*) is equal to (*join S.sig T.sig*). Since we know that t is the result of restricting *str* to this signature, our goal can be reduced to the following two subgoals:

?118: *is_true* (*matches* (*join S.sig T.sig*) t)
?119: (*S.pred t*) $\wedge$ (*T.pred t*)

We prove the first of these by using Lemma 40. Before we prove the second we make use of Proposition 17 to construct a proof that *And_schema S T* has the property *Valid_schema*. We use this proof, together with the fact that t is obtained by restricting *str* to the signature of (*And_schema S T*), and together with our two claims, to prove the second subgoal.

Next we have to prove the claims. These follow easily from the facts that schemas S and T have the property *Valid_schema*, and that *str* can be successfully restricted to give implementations of these schemas. □

The next two results can be thought of as left and right elimination rules for schema conjunction.

Proposition 22 And_schema_elim_l.

$\forall$ *S*, *T* : *Schema*. $\forall$ *str* : *Structure*.
(*Valid_schema S*) $\Rightarrow$
(*unique_idents S.sig*) $\Rightarrow$ (*unique_idents T.sig*) $\Rightarrow$
(*is_true* (*consistent S.sig T.sig*)) $\Rightarrow$
(*Implements* (*And_schema S T*) *str*) $\Rightarrow$ *restricts_to_impl S str*

Proof. By using LEGO's introduction tactics and rewriting with the hypothesis stating that *S.sig* and *T.sig* are consistent we arrive at a context including:

str : *Structure*
H : *Implements* ((*join S.sig T.sig*), λ *s* : *Structure*. (*S.pred s*) $\wedge$ (*T.pred s*))
str

Our goal at this point is:

? : *restricts_to_impl S str*

Next we make a claim, $?_{25}$ that *str* can be successfully restricted by *S.sig*, yielding a structure *str'*. We have

H_1 : *restrict str S.sig* = *in2 str'*

We rewrite with H_1 and reduce our goal to having to show that *str'* is an implementation of S, that is, that it matches *S.sig* and satisfies *S.pred*. We prove the first of these by applying Lemma 40. The second follows from H and the assumption that S has the property *Valid_schema*.

All that remains is to prove the claim, $?_{25}$. We prove this by Lemma 44, which then asks us to show that *str* can be successfully restricted by the signature (*join S.sig T.sig*). This follows from Lemma 46 and the fact that by H, *str* matches (*join S.sig T.sig*). □

Proposition 23 And_schema_elim_r.

$$\begin{array}{l} \forall S, T{:}\,Schema.\ \forall str{:}\,Structure. \\ \quad (Valid\_schema\ T) \Rightarrow \\ \quad (unique\_idents\ S.sig) \Rightarrow (unique\_idents\ T.sig) \Rightarrow \\ \quad (is\_true\ (consistent\ S.sig\ T.sig)) \Rightarrow \\ \quad\quad (Implements\ (And\_schema\ S\ T)\ str) \Rightarrow restricts\_to\_impl\ T\ str \end{array}$$

Proof. We prove this the same way we prove Proposition 22, using Lemma 45 instead of Lemma 44. □

By using the introduction rule and (a slightly more general version of) the elimination rules we can easily prove the following useful result.

Proposition 24 And_schema_commutes.

$$\begin{array}{l} \forall S, T{:}\,Schema.\ \forall str{:}\,Structure. \\ \quad (Valid\_schema\ S) \Rightarrow (Valid\_schema\ T) \Rightarrow \\ \quad (unique\_idents\ S.sig) \Rightarrow (unique\_idents\ T.sig) \Rightarrow \\ \quad (unique\_idents(extract\_sig\ str)) \Rightarrow \\ \quad (is\_true\ (consistent\ S.sig\ T.sig)) \Rightarrow \\ \quad\quad (restricts\_to\_impl\ (And\_schema\ S\ T)\ str) \Rightarrow \\ \quad\quad (restricts\_to\_impl\ (And\_schema\ T\ S)\ str) \end{array}$$

This says that, under reasonable conditions, any structure which yields an implementation of $And\_schema\ S\ T$ also yields an implementation of $And\_schema\ T\ S$.

4 Schema-level reasoning: an example

A technique that is commonly used in writing Z specifications is to specify a system by first writing a schema to describe the correct, or normal operation of the system, negating this schema to describe error conditions, and then disjoining these two schemas to specify a total operation. To support this pattern of specification building, we would like to prove, for instance, that the final schema produced by this process is, in some sense, total. Our encoding of the Schema Calculus allows us to prove results like this generally, for all schemas.

First we must define the operation of negating a schema. The negation of a schema S is a new schema whose signature is the same as that of S and whose predicate is true of all structures which can be successfully restricted to the signature of S and which satisfy the negation of the predicate of S.

Definition 25 Not_schema.

$$\begin{array}{l} Not\_schema \stackrel{def}{=} \lambda S{:}\,Schema. \\ (S.sig, \lambda str{:}\,Structure.\ case\ (\lambda\_{:}\,unit.\ absurd) \\ \qquad\qquad\qquad\qquad\qquad\qquad (\lambda str'{:}\,Structure.\neg(S.pred\ str')) \\ \qquad\qquad\qquad\qquad\qquad\qquad (restrict\ str\ S.sig)) \\ \ {:}\,Schema \rightarrow Schema \end{array}$$

We also need the operation of schema disjunction. When we combine two schemas by this operation we obtain a new schema whose signature is the *join* of the two original signatures, and whose predicate is true of exactly those structures which can be restricted successfully to the new signature (and therefore to both of the original signatures) and which satisfy one or other of the original predicates.

Definition 26 Or_schema.

$$
\begin{array}{l}
\mathit{Or\_schema} \stackrel{def}{=} \lambda\, S, S' : \mathit{Schema}. \\
\quad \mathit{if}\ (\mathit{consistent}\ S.\mathit{sig}\ S'.\mathit{sig}) \\
\qquad ((\mathit{join}\ S.\mathit{sig}\ S'.\mathit{sig}), \\
\qquad \lambda\, \mathit{str} : \mathit{Structure}.\ \mathit{case}\ (\lambda\, \_ : \mathit{unit}.\ \mathit{absurd}) \\
\qquad\qquad (\lambda\, \mathit{str}' : \mathit{Structure}.\ (S.\mathit{pred}\ \mathit{str}') \vee (S'.\mathit{pred}\ \mathit{str}')) \\
\qquad\qquad (\mathit{restrict}\ \mathit{str}\ (\mathit{join}\ (\pi_1 S)\ (\pi_1 S')))) \\
\qquad \mathit{Absurd\_schema} \\
\quad : \mathit{Schema} \rightarrow \mathit{Schema} \rightarrow \mathit{Schema}
\end{array}
$$

The "totality" theorem we will prove is the intuitionistic counterpart of the law of the excluded middle, expressed partly at the level of schemas. There are many variations on this statement that we can also prove, e.g. replacing the double negation by a double application of *Not_schema*, but this one seems likely to be the most useful.

Proposition 27 Totality.

$$
\begin{array}{l}
\forall\, S : \mathit{Schema}.\ \forall\, \mathit{str} : \mathit{Structure}. \\
\quad (\mathit{unique\_idents}\ S.\mathit{sig}) \Rightarrow (\mathit{is\_in2}\ (\mathit{restrict}\ \mathit{str}\ S.\mathit{sig})) \Rightarrow \\
\qquad \neg\neg(\mathit{restricts\_to\_impl}\ (\mathit{Or\_schema}\ S\ (\mathit{Not\_schema}\ S))\ \mathit{str})
\end{array}
$$

Proof. Unsurprisingly, this proof has the same basic structure as a proof of the analogous proposition: $\forall\, P : \mathit{Prop}.\, \neg\neg(P \vee \neg P)$. At various points we need to show that the signature of $(\mathit{Or\_schema}\ S\ (\mathit{Not\_schema}\ S))$ is the same as that of S, for which we use some of our lemmas about the *join* operation.

5 Comparison with other work on Z

Adequacy and other semantic accounts of Z

As a reference during this work we have used [5] which contains a lucid, semi-formal presentation of Z (though it does not claim to give a full semantics.) Hayes describes the operational behaviour of the schema-forming operators as they act upon the syntax of schema signatures and predicates. We believe that we have followed this account correctly as far as the effects on signatures is concerned. For predicates, however, we have had to make explicit the environments, or programs, to which they refer, which are left implicit in Hayes. We have also had to explicitly deal with the conditions in which schema combining operators fail.

These considerations make it difficult to know how to formulate the statement of adequacy for the formation of schema predicates with respect to Hayes' presentation. As for the provability of predicates, we know that since UTT provides an intuitionistic logic we will not be able to prove as many theorems as in the classical logic used by Z.

The standard semantic account of Z is [2], which has a complex relationship to the older semantics in [15]. These present a denotational account of Z. We believe that there is a close relationship between our notion of program (*Structure*) and the semantic representation of schemas in these accounts ("structures" in [15] and "sets of bindings" in [2]), and that our work may be viewed as an implementation of something closely related to these semantics. This would be an interesting possibility to explore. We conjecture that there is some restricted version of the Z of [2] (minus schemas as types; with a simpler type system; using intuitionistic logic instead of classical; using only computable functions) which is adequately represented by my encoding. More work needs to be done on explicating the relationship between our work and [2] before this can be stated formally.

Proof support for Z

Since the language we have encoded is not Z, we cannot claim to have provided proof support for Z. However our encoding provides proof support for specifications structured by means of the Schema Calculus and written in a simple core language based on type theory rather than set theory. Our encoding also provides a notion of implementation (via programs written in constructive type theory) and enables LEGO to be used to verify that programs are implementations of specifications. Furthermore, our encoding allows us to prove general properties about the Schema Calculus operators themselves which can then be re-used when verifying programs. It is a "deep" embedding of the Schema Calculus in UTT, as contrasted with "shallow" embeddings in which the Schema Calculus operators are implemented within a metalanguage which "macro expands" schema operators and supplies the expanded forms as input to the proof-checker. Shallow embeddings do not allow the structure of specifications to be exploited when doing proofs.

Other work aimed at providing proof support for Z include: the ProofPower system [14] which is based a deep embedding of Z in a HOL-like theorem-prover with a user interface that closely resembles Z notation — this embedding is not deep enough, however, to allow facts like the commutativity of schema conjunction to be proved [1]; a shallow embedding of Z in HOL carried out by Bowen and Gordon [1]; the work of Martin [12] who has encoded W, a logic for Z, in the metalogical framework 2OBJ; the Z/EVES project [13] which uses a theorem prover for ZF set theory; the Balzac project [4] at Imperial Software Technology about which we know very little.

6 Conclusions and Future Work

The techniques we describe in this paper are promising. We can extend what we have done to encode all the operations of the Schema Calculus and prove more results of the kind demonstrated. These give us a framework for reasoning about specifications at the schema level. We can also attempt to extend our core language by adding new *Ztypes*, or even use a completely different core language such as an encoding of set theory.

To test the usability of this encoding we can encode and prove some theorems about a moderate-sized specification. This will reveal whether we have made useful choices in defining, for instance, an implementation, and whether our theorems about schema operations are appropriate for doing structured reasoning about specifications.

A major task would be to find out the relationship between our type-theoretic semantics for Z schemas and other proposed semantics. However even if we cannot do this in a formal way, we can still use examples to show how our encoding allows us to mimic the use of the Z notation within the LEGO proof-checker.

Another possible line of development would be to explore possible definitions of *refinement* within our system and to use Lego to study the relationship between refinement and the Schema Calculus operations.

7 Acknowledgements

We have benefited from discussions with Stuart Anderson, Stephen Gilmore, Healfdene Goguen, Claire Jones and from comments made by two anonymous referees. This work was partly supported by the British Council and partly by the Esprit BRA "Types". In preparing this document we made use of Mike Spivey's LaTeX style file for Z.

References

1. J. Bowen and M. Gordon. Z and HOL, 1994. submitted to the '94 Z User Meeting.
2. S. Brien, J. Nicholls, et al. Z Base Standard version 1.0. Technical Report ZIP/PRG/92/121, Oxford University Computing Laboratory, 1992.
3. Dowek, Felty, et al. The Coq proof assistant user's guide, version 5.8. Technical report, INRIA-Rocquencourt, February 1993.
4. W. Harwood. Proof rules for Balzac. Technical Report WTH/P7/001, Imperial Software Technology, Cambridge, 1991.
5. I. Hayes. *Specification Case Studies.* Prentice-Hall International, 1987.
6. C. Jones and S. Maharaj. The LEGO library. Technical Report (forthcoming), LFCS, University of Edinburgh, 1994.
7. Z. Luo. *Computation and Reasoning: A Type Theory for Computer Science.* Oxford University Press (forthcoming).
8. Z. Luo. Program Specification and Data Refinement in Type Theory. Technical Report ECS-LFCS-91-131, LFCS, University of Edinburgh, 1991.

9. Z. Luo. A Unifying Theory of Dependent Types: the Schematic Approach. In *Logical Foundations of Computer Science—Tver '92.* Springer-Verlag, 1992.
10. Z. Luo and R. Pollack. LEGO Proof Development System: user's manual. Technical Report ECS-LFCS-92-211, LFCS, University of Edinburgh, 1992.
11. S. Maharaj. Implementing Z in LEGO. MSc thesis, University of Edinburgh, 1990.
12. A. Martin. Encoding W: A logic for Z in 2OBJ. In *FME '93: Industrial-Strength Formal Methods,* Lecture Notes in Computer Science. Springer-Verlag, 1993.
13. M. Saaltink. Z and EVES. Technical Report TR-91-5449-02, Odyssey Research Associates, Ottawa, Canada, 1991.
14. ProofPower server. Send email to ProofPower-server@win.icl.co.uk.
15. J.M. Spivey. *Understanding Z: a specification language and its formal semantics.* Cambridge University Press, 1988.

A More Proof Descriptions

Lemma 28 restrict_to_tail.

$$\forall\, sig : Signature.\ \forall\, x : sig\_item.\ \forall\, str : Structure.\\ \quad is\_in2\ (restrict\ str\ (cons\ x\ sig)) \Rightarrow is\_in2\ (restrict\ str\ sig)$$

Proof. We prove this easily by manipulating the definition of *restrict*. □

Lemma 29 join_cons_cases.

$$\forall\, sig, sig' : Signature.\ \forall\, x : sig\_item.\\ \quad (join\ (cons\ x\ sig)\ sig' = join\ sig\ sig') \lor\\ \quad (join\ (cons\ x\ sig)\ sig' = cons\ x\ (join\ sig\ sig'))$$

Proof. This is an easy proof that proceeds by first expanding the definition of *join*, then examining all possible values of $(member\_ident\ (\pi_1 x)\ (join\ sig\ sig'))$, and observing that the goal is satisfied in every case. □

Lemma 30 restrict_join.

$$\forall\, sig, sig' : Signature.\ \forall\, str : Structure.\\ \quad (is\_in2\ (restrict\ str\ sig)) \Rightarrow (is\_in2\ (restrict\ str\ sig')) \Rightarrow\\ \qquad is\_in2\ (restrict\ str\ (join\ sig\ sig'))$$

Proof. The proof is by a straightforward list induction on *sig*. In the case where *sig* is *nil*, $(join\ sig\ sig')$ reduces to sig', so the proof is immediate. In the case where *sig* is of the form $(cons\ x\ l)$ by making use of the induction hypothesis we get a proof context that includes the following:

$$H_1 : is\_in2\ (restrict\ str\ (cons\ x\ l))\\ H_2 : is\_in2\ (restrict\ str\ (join\ l\ sig'))$$

Next we use Lemma 29 to do a case analysis on the result of joining $(cons\ x\ l)$ and sig'. In the case where $(join\ (cons\ x\ l)\ sig')$ equals $(join\ l\ sig')$ the hypothesis H_2 proves the subgoal. In the next case we have

$$H_3 : join\ (cons\ x\ l)\ sig' = (cons\ x\ (join\ l\ sig'))$$

and our goal is

$$?: is\_in2\ (restrict\ str\ (join\ (cons\ x\ l)\ sig'))$$

We do a case analysis on the result of looking up x in *str*. In the case where *lookup* fails we obtain a contradiction with H_1 by using the lemma *in2_not_in1* from the sums library. In the case where *lookup* succeeds we first use Lemma 28 to get a proof that *str* can be successfully restricted to the signature (*join l sig'*). We complete the proof by rewriting with H_3, expanding the definition of *restrict* and then substituting in the results of looking up x in *str* and of restricting *str* to (*join l sig'*). □

Lemma 31 restrict_join_l.

$$\begin{array}{l}\forall\, sig, sig' : Signature.\ \forall\, str : Structure.\\ \quad (is\_true\ (consistent\ sig\ sig')) \Rightarrow\\ \quad (unique\_idents\ sig) \Rightarrow (unique\_idents\ sig') \Rightarrow\\ \quad (is\_in2\ (restrict\ str\ sig)) \Rightarrow (is\_in2\ (restrict\ str\ sig')) \Rightarrow\\ \qquad case\ (\lambda\_ : unit.\ absurd)\\ \qquad\quad (\lambda\, str' : Structure.\ restrict\ str'\ sig = restrict\ str\ sig)\\ \qquad\quad (restrict\ str\ (join\ sig\ sig'))\end{array}$$

Proof. Omitted.

Lemma 32 restrict_join_r.

$$\begin{array}{l}\forall\, sig, sig' : Signature.\ \forall\, str : Structure.\\ \quad (unique\_idents\ sig) \Rightarrow (unique\_idents\ sig') \Rightarrow\\ \quad (is\_in2\ (restrict\ str\ sig)) \Rightarrow (is\_in2\ (restrict\ str\ sig')) \Rightarrow\\ \qquad case\ (\lambda\_ : unit.\ absurd)\\ \qquad\quad (\lambda\, str' : Structure.\ restrict\ str'\ sig' = restrict\ str\ sig')\\ \qquad\quad (restrict\ str\ (join\ sig\ sig'))\end{array}$$

Proof. Omitted.

In the next lemma we use the predicate *type_consistent*. Two signatures have this property if any identifier which appears in both signatures is paired with the same type in each occurrence.

Definition 33 type_consistent.

$$\begin{array}{l}type\_consistent \stackrel{def}{=} \lambda\, S, T : Signature.\ \forall\, i : Ident.\ \forall\, z, z' : Ztype.\\ \qquad (is\_true\ (member\ (i, z)\ S)) \Rightarrow (is\_true\ (member\ (i, z')\ T)) \Rightarrow z = z'\\ : Signature \rightarrow Signature \rightarrow Prop\end{array}$$

Lemma 34 consistent_is_type_consistent.

$$\begin{array}{l}\forall\, sig, sig' : Signature.\\ \quad (unique\_idents\ sig) \Rightarrow (unique\_idents\ sig') \Rightarrow\\ \qquad (type\_consistent\ sig\ sig') \Leftrightarrow (is\_true\ (consistent\ sig\ sig'))\end{array}$$

Proof. Omitted.

Lemma 35 member_restrict_implies_member_orig.

$$\begin{aligned}&\forall\, sig: Signature.\ \forall\, str: Structure.\ \forall\, x: sig\_item.\\&\quad case\ \lambda\_: unit.\ trueProp\\&\qquad \lambda\, str': Structure.\ (is\_true\ (member\ x\ (extract\_sig\ str'))) \Rightarrow\\&\qquad\qquad (is\_true\ (member\ x\ (extract\_sig\ str)))\\&\qquad (restrict\ str\ sig)\end{aligned}$$

Proof. Omitted.

Lemma 36 restrict_equals_sig.

$$\begin{aligned}&\forall\, sig: Signature.\ \forall\, str: Structure.\\&\quad case\ \lambda\_: unit.\ trueProp\\&\qquad \lambda\, str': Structure.\ sig = extract\_sig\ str'\\&\qquad (restrict\ str\ sig)\end{aligned}$$

Proof. Omitted.

We introduce a predicate *self_consistent* which we use in the next lemma.

Definition 37 self_consistent.

$$\begin{aligned}&self\_consistent \stackrel{def}{=} \lambda\, S: Signature.\ type\_consistent\ S\ S\\&: Signature \rightarrow Prop\end{aligned}$$

Lemma 38 join_is_consistent.

$$\begin{aligned}&\forall\, S, T: Schema.\ \forall\, str: Structure.\\&\quad (Valid\_schema\ S) \Rightarrow (Valid\_schema\ T) \Rightarrow\\&\quad (unique\_idents\ S.sig) \Rightarrow (unique\_idents\ T.sig) \Rightarrow\\&\quad (self\_consistent\ (extract\_sig\ str)) \Rightarrow\\&\quad (S.pred\ str) \Rightarrow (T.pred\ str) \Rightarrow\\&\qquad is\_true\ (consistent\ S.sig\ T.sig)\end{aligned}$$

Proof. We introduce S, T, *str*, and the various hypotheses so that we are left having to show that $S.sig$ and $T.sig$ are consistent. We refine by Lemma 34, *consistent_is_type_consistent*, which gives us a new goal:

$$\begin{aligned}&?: \forall\, i: Ident.\ \forall\, z, z': Ztype.\\&\quad (is\_true\ (member\ (i, z)\ S.sig)) \Rightarrow (is\_true\ (member\ (i, z')\ T.sig)) \Rightarrow\\&\qquad z = z'\end{aligned}$$

We introduce i, z, z', and two hypotheses. From the assumptions that S and T are valid schemas and that their predicates are satisfied by *str*, we can deduce that *str* can be successfully restricted by $S.sig$ and $T.sig$, yielding structures *strS* and *strT*, respectively.

We now try to prove that z and z' are equal by using the assumption that the signature of *str* is self-consistent. We try to show that (i, z) and (i, z') are both in the signature of *str*.

We know that (i, z) is a member of *S.sig*. By Lemma 36, *restrict_equals_sig*, we know that the signature of *strS* equals *S.sig*, so (i, z) is a member of the signature (*extract_sig strS*). Since *strS* is obtained by restricting *str*, Lemma 35 can be used to show that (i, z) is a member of *str*. By a similar argument we also show that (i, z') is in *str*. □

Lemma 39 restrict_matches_sig.

$$\begin{array}{l} \forall\, sig : Signature.\ \forall\, str : Structure. \\ \quad is\_true\ (case\ \lambda\, \_ : unit.\ true \\ \qquad\qquad \lambda\, str' : Structure.\ matches\ sig\ str' \\ \qquad\qquad (restrict\ str\ sig)) \end{array}$$

Proof. Omitted.

Lemma 40 restriction_matches.

$$\begin{array}{l} \forall\, sig : Signature.\ \forall\, str : Structure. \\ \quad (is\_in2\ (restrict\ str\ sig)) \Rightarrow \\ \quad is\_true\ (case\ \lambda\, \_ : unit.\ false \\ \qquad\qquad \lambda\, str' : Structure.\ matches\ sig\ str' \\ \qquad\qquad (restrict\ str\ sig)) \end{array}$$

Proof. We introduce *sig*, *str* and a hypothesis H. Using H we introduce a new structure *str′* which is the result of restricting *str* to *sig*. We use this to reduce the remaining goal to showing that *str′* matches *sig*. This we then prove by Lemma 39. □

Lemma 41 member_join_l.

$$\begin{array}{l} \forall\, sig, sig' : Signature.\ \forall\, x : sig\_item. \\ \quad (is\_true\ (consistent\ sig\ sig')) \Rightarrow \\ \quad (unique\_idents\ S) \Rightarrow (unique\_idents\ sig') \Rightarrow \\ \quad (is\_true\ (member\ x\ sig)) \Rightarrow \\ \qquad is\_true\ (member\ x\ (join\ sig\ sig')) \end{array}$$

Proof. Omitted.

Lemma 42 restrict_join_back_l_lemma1.

$$\begin{array}{l} \forall\, sig : Signature.\ \forall\, str : Structure.\ \forall\, x : sig\_item. \\ \quad (is\_in2\ (lookup\ x\ str)) \Rightarrow \\ \quad (is\_in2\ (restrict\ str\ sig)) \Rightarrow \\ \qquad is\_in2\ (restrict\ str\ (cons\ x\ sig)) \end{array}$$

Proof. This follows easily from the definition of *restrict*. □

Lemma 43 restrict_join_back_l_lemma2.

$$\forall sig: Signature.\ \forall str: Structure.\ \forall x: sig\_item.$$
$$(is\_true\ (member\ x\ sig)) \Rightarrow$$
$$(is\_in2\ (restrict\ str\ sig)) \Rightarrow$$
$$is\_in2\ (lookup\ x\ str)$$

Proof. Omitted.

Lemma 44 restrict_join_back_l.

$$\forall sig, sig': Signature.\ \forall str: Structure.$$
$$(is\_true\ (consistent\ sig\ sig')) \Rightarrow$$
$$(unique\_idents\ sig) \Rightarrow (unique\_idents\ sig') \Rightarrow$$
$$(is\_in2\ (restrict\ str\ (join\ sig\ sig'))) \Rightarrow is\_in2\ (restrict\ str\ sig)$$

Proof. The proof is by list induction on *sig*. The base case follows easily from the definition of *restrict*. In the case where *sig* is of the form (*cons x l*) we introduce a structure *str* and several hypotheses, leaving the following proof context and goal:

$$H: \forall sig': Signature.\ \forall str': Structure.\ \ldots \Rightarrow$$
$$(is\_in2\ (restrict\ str'(join\ l\ sig'))) \Rightarrow is\_in2\ (restrict\ str'\ l)$$
$$H_1: is\_in2\ (restrict\ str\ (join\ (cons\ x\ l)\ sig'))$$
$$?_{15}: is\_in2\ (restrict\ str\ (cons\ x\ l))$$

Refining by Lemma 42 leaves us with the job of proving

$$?_{19}: is\_in2\ (restrict\ s\ l)$$
$$?_{20}: is\_in2\ (lookup\ x\ str)$$

To prove the first of these we use the induction hypothesis H, which then gives us the task of showing that *str* can be successfully restricted to (*join l sig'*). We then use Lemma 29 to give us the two possible values of (*join* (*cons x l*) *sig'*), and show that the subgoal follows from H_1 in either case.

Next we have to prove that looking up x in *str* is successful. By Lemma 43 we can show this by showing that x is a member of the signature (*join* (*cons x l*) *sig'*) and that *str* can be successfully restricted by this signature. The first of these follows from Lemma 41 and the second is in our list of hypotheses. □

Lemma 45 restrict_join_back_r.

$$\forall sig, sig': Signature.\ \forall str: Structure.$$
$$(is\_in2\ (restrict\ str\ (join\ sig\ sig'))) \Rightarrow is\_in2\ (restrict\ str\ sig')$$

Proof. We prove this easily by induction on *sig*. The case where *sig* is *nil* is immediate. In the case where *sig* is of the form (*cons x l*) we use Lemma 29 to examine the two possible values of (*join* (*cons x l*) *sig'*) and show that the goal follows from the induction hypothesis in either case. □

Lemma 46 restrict_matching_sig.

$$\forall\, sig : Signature.\ \forall\, str : Structure.\ (unique\_idents\ sig) \Rightarrow (is\_true\ (matches\ sig\ str)) \Rightarrow is\_in2\ (restrict\ str\ sig)$$

Proof. Omitted. We believe that this result should remain true if the condition ($unique\_idents\ S$) is removed, but we haven't found a proof of this.

B LEGO library functions and lemmas

$trueProp : Prop \stackrel{def}{=} \forall\, P : Prop.\ P \Rightarrow P$

$absurd : Prop \stackrel{def}{=} \forall\, P : Prop.\ P$

list_rec This lets us define functions from lists over a type s to a type t by supplying a base case of type t and a step function of type $\Pi\, head : s.\ \Pi\, tail : list\ s.\ \Pi\, prev : t.\ t$.

list_iter. This lets us define functions from lists over a type s to a type t by supplying a base case of type t and a step function of type $\Pi\, head : s.\ \Pi\, prev : t.\ t$.

$length : \Pi\, t \mid Type.\ (list\ t) \rightarrow nat$ The | here means that t is an implicit argument.

$if : \Pi\, t : Type.\ \Pi\, b : bool.\ \Pi\, tcase, fcase : t.\ t$ This allows us to define functions on *bool*s by case analysis.

$is\_in1 : \Pi\, s, t \mid Type.\ \Pi\, x : (s + t).\ Prop$ This is defined by $is\_in1\ x \stackrel{def}{=} \exists\, y : s.\ x = (in1\ y)$. Similarly we define is_in2.

$in2\_not\_in1 : \forall\, s, t : Type.\ \forall\, x : s.\ \neg(is\_in2\ (in1\ x))$

$in1\_or\_in2 : \forall\, s, t : Type.\ \forall\, x : (z + t).\ (is\_in1\ x) \vee (is\_in2\ x)$

The Expressive Power of Structural Operational Semantics with Explicit Assumptions*

Marino Miculan

Dipartimento di Matematica e Informatica
Università di Udine
via Zanon, 6 – I 33100 Udine – Italy
miculan@udmi5400.cineca.it

Abstract. We explore the expressive power of the formalism called *Natural Operational Semantics*, *NOS*, introduced by Burstall and Honsell for defining the operational semantics of programming languages. This formalism is derived from the Natural Semantics of Despeyroux and Kahn. It arises if we take seriously the possibility of deriving assertions in Natural Semantics under assumptions, i.e. using hypothetico-general premises in the sense of Martin-Löf. We investigate to what extent we can reduce to hypothetical premises the notions of store and environment of Plotkin's Structural Operational Semantics. We use this formalism to define the semantics of a functional language which features commands, blocks, procedures, complex declarations, structures and Abstract Data Types. We give the NOS together with the denotational semantics and prove the adequacy of the former w.r.t. the latter. We discuss some other difficulties which arose in the previous treatment of variables in connection with procedures.

Natural Operational Semantics can be easily encoded in formal systems based on λ-calculus type-checking, such as the Edinburgh Logical Framework. We briefly investigate this and discuss some of the design choices.

1 Introduction

In order to establish formally properties of programs, we have to represent formally their operational semantics. A very successful style of presenting operational semantics is the one introduced by Gordon Plotkin and known as *Structural Operational Semantics* (SOS) ([21]). The idea behind this approach is that all computational elaboration and evaluation processes can be construed as logical processes and hence can be reduced to the sole process of formal logical derivation within a formal system.

For example, the SOS of a functional language is a formal system for inferring assertions such as $\rho \vdash M \rightarrow m$, where m is the *value* of the *expression* M, and

* Work partially supported by Esprit BRA 6453, *Types for Proofs and Programs*, and italian MURST 40%, 60% grants.

ρ is the *environment* in which the evaluation is performed – usually a function mapping identifiers to values. The intended meaning of this proposition is "in the environment ρ, the evaluation of M gives m".

This style of specification does not have many of the defects of other formalisms (such as automata and definitional interpreters), since it is syntax-directed, abstract and easy to understand. It has been proved to be very successful in various areas of theoretical computer science. It was studied in depth by Kahn and many of his coworkers, and it has been used by Milner with the name of *Relational Semantics*. Nevertheless, the explicit presence of environments in propositions has some drawbacks in practical use:

- the abstraction power is limited: a function which maps identifiers to values amounts to von Neumann's computer's memory.
- Modularity is limited. Modularity of semantic descriptions is an ongoing area of research—see e.g. [17, 24]. Typically, in considering extensions of the language we may be forced to change the evaluation judgment itself. For instance, the judgment can take the form $\rho \vdash \langle M, \sigma \rangle \rightarrow \langle m, \sigma' \rangle$ in the case of expressions with side-effects [21]. Hence, previous rules and derivations are not any more compatible with the new assertion. However, even simple extensions which only introduce new kinds of identifiers and denotable objects (e.g. procedure identifiers and procedures) cause such problems, since the judgment can take the form: $\rho, \tau \vdash M \rightarrow m$.
- The system lacks conciseness: environments appear in all rules but are seldom used. For instance, in the "+" rule, $\frac{\rho \vdash N_1 \rightarrow n_1 \quad \rho \vdash N_2 \rightarrow n_2}{\rho \vdash N_1 + N_2 \rightarrow plus(n_1, n_2)}$, ρ plays no rôle: it is merely transferred from conclusion to premises (in a top-down proof development). The environment is effectively used only when we are dealing with identifiers, that is when we either declare an identifier or evaluate it, e.g. in the rule $\frac{\rho \vdash M \rightarrow m \quad [x \mapsto n]\rho \vdash N \rightarrow n}{\rho \vdash \mathbf{let}\ x = M\ \mathbf{in}\ N} \rightarrow n$ and the axiom $\rho \vdash x \rightarrow \rho(x)$.
- In order to reason formally about properties of the operational semantics, it is necessary to encode the formal system into some proof-editor/checker. However, in most of the proof assistants, representation of functions (such as the environments) can be rather cumbersome, and mechanized reasoning about these encodings can be very hard.

A possible solution to these drawbacks is the *Natural Operational Semantics* formalism (NOS) introduced in [4] as a refinement of the Natural Semantics originally proposed by Kahn and his coworkers ([6, 12]). This formalism arises if we take seriously the possibility of deriving under assumptions assertions in Natural Semantics, i.e. using hypothetico-general judgments in the sense of Martin-Löf ([19]). It is based in fact on Gentzen's Natural Deduction style of proof ([8]): hypothetical premises are used to make assumptions about the values of variables. In this paper we investigate to what extent we can reduce to hypothetical premises the fragments of the store and environment of Plotkin's Structural Operational Semantics. Thus, instead of evaluating an expression within a given environment, we compute its value under a set of assumptions on the values of its free variables. In other words, we replace explicit environments with implicit contextual structures, that is, the hypothetical premises in Natural Deduction.

For example, consider a functional language with two syntactic classes, *Expr*, the class of expressions (ranged over by M, N), and *Id*, the class of identifiers (ranged over by x, y), the former including the latter. The SOS of this language is a system for deriving judgments of the form $\rho \vdash M \rightarrow m$. Instead, in the NOS paradigm the judgments can be simplified to those of the form $M \Rightarrow m$, whose reading is "the value of expression M is m". There are no more contextual structures: the predicate is $\Rightarrow \subset Expr \times Expr$.

These assertions can be inferred using a Natural Deduction style proof system, that is a set of rules of the form

$$\frac{\begin{array}{ccc}(\Delta_1) & \ldots & (\Delta_k) \\ \vdots & & \vdots \\ M_1 \Rightarrow m_1 & \ldots & M_k \Rightarrow m_k\end{array}}{M \Rightarrow m} \text{(possible side-condition)}$$

where the sets of assertions $\Delta_1, \ldots \Delta_k$ are the *discharged assumptions*. Therefore, the evaluation of the expression M to the value m can be represented by the following derivation in N.D. style:

$$\Gamma = \{x_1 \Rightarrow n_1, \ldots, x_k \Rightarrow n_k\}$$

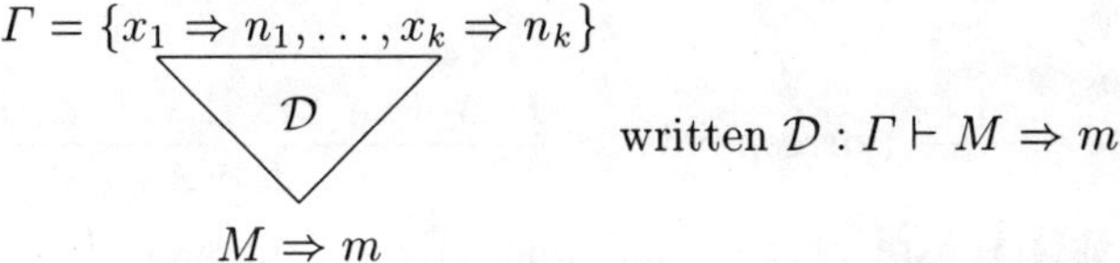

written $\mathcal{D} : \Gamma \vdash M \Rightarrow m$

$$M \Rightarrow m$$

where the hypotheses $\Gamma = \{x_1 \Rightarrow n_1, \ldots, x_k \Rightarrow n_k\}$ $(k \geq 0)$ can be interpreted as a set of variable bindings: the value of the variables involved in the evaluation of M. This derivation can be read as "in every environment which satisfies the assumptions in Γ, M is evaluated to m." This means that, given an environment ρ s.t. $\forall (x \Rightarrow m) \in \Gamma : \rho(x) = m$, there is a derivation of $\rho \vdash M \rightarrow m$ in the corresponding SOS proof system. An assumption about the value of a variable can be discharged when it is valid locally to a subcomputation. For instance, in the case of local declarations, in order to evaluate **let** $x = N$ **in** M, we can evaluate M assuming that the value of x is the same as that of N. This extra assumption is not necessary for evaluating **let** $x = N$ **in** M, so it can be discharged. The **let** rule is the rule in which the whole power of the ND style appears

$$\frac{\begin{array}{cc} & (x \Rightarrow n) \\ & \vdots \\ N \Rightarrow n & M \Rightarrow m\end{array}}{\textbf{let } x = N \textbf{ in } M \Rightarrow m}$$

whose reading is "if n is the value of N and, assuming the value of x is n then m is the value of M, then the value of **let** $x = N$ **in** M is m." (Unfortunately, the situation is not so simple, since this extra assumption can clash with a previous assumption on x which is valid globally. This will be discussed in detail in Sect.2.)

This truly N.D. approach has the benefit that all the rules which do not refer directly to identifiers appear in a simpler form than those in SOS style: no environment appears. For instance, the rule for the "+" function becomes

$$\frac{N_1 \Rightarrow n_1 \quad N_2 \Rightarrow n_2}{N_1 + N_2 \Rightarrow plus(n_1, n_2)}.$$

In this paper, we address the following question: what kind of programming languages can be treated conveniently using this formalism. We are interested in understanding to what extent we can reduce to assumptions the concepts of store, environment, binding and similar linear datatypes.

2 Analysis of the NOS style

In this section we try to convey briefly to the reader the main features of operational semantics in N.D. style. Recall that a N.D. style rule can be viewed as a concise description of a special kind of rule for deriving *sequents*, i.e. metapropositions of the form $\Gamma \vdash A$ ([8, 2]):

$$\begin{array}{c} (\Delta_1) \ldots (\Delta_k) \\ \vdots \qquad \vdots \\ \dfrac{A_1 \quad \ldots \quad A_k}{A} \end{array} \quad \text{corresponds to} \quad \frac{\Gamma, \Delta_1 \vdash A_1 \quad \ldots \quad \Gamma, \Delta_k \vdash A_k}{\Gamma \vdash A}$$

where $A, A_1, \ldots, A_k$ are propositions and $\Delta_1, \ldots, \Delta_k$ sets of propositions. Γ is any set of proposition. This rule means that, in order to prove that A is a consequence of a given Γ, we have to prove for $i = 1 \ldots k$ that A_i is a consequence of Γ, Δ_i. In other words, for proving each A_i we can use some local assumptions Δ_i, the global hypotheses Γ always remaining valid. This fact is at the core of the issues discussed in the following subsections.

2.1 The issue of local variables

Since the NOS rules are N.D. rules, if we have the following deduction $\mathcal{D}$:

$$\frac{\begin{array}{c}\Gamma, (\Delta_1) \\ \mathcal{D}_1 \\ M_1 \Rightarrow m_1\end{array} \quad \ldots \quad \begin{array}{c}\Gamma, (\Delta_k) \\ \mathcal{D}_k \\ M_k \Rightarrow m_k\end{array}}{M \Rightarrow m}$$

all the bindings in Γ are available in evaluating M_i, for $i = 1 \ldots k$. As a consequence of this, the **let** rule showed in Sect.1 above, is incorrect because previous (global) assumptions on locally defined variables can be used during the subevaluation, e.g. as follows:

$$\frac{0 \Rightarrow 0 \qquad \dfrac{1 \Rightarrow 1 \quad (x \Rightarrow 0)_{(1)}}{\textbf{let } x = 1 \textbf{ in } x \Rightarrow 0}}{\textbf{let } x = 0 \textbf{ in let } x = 1 \textbf{ in } x \Rightarrow 0}(1)$$

An attempt to overcome this problem could be that of using *higher-order syntax* à la Church. This technique originated with Church's idea to analyze $\forall x.P$ as $\forall(\lambda x.P)$ where $\forall$ has a higher order functionality: $\forall : (\mathit{Term} \rightarrow \mathit{Prop}) \rightarrow \mathit{Prop}$ [5]. It was further used by Martin-Löf [19] and thoroughly expanded in the Edinburgh Logical Framework [11]. This technique has been proved to work extremely well for pure functional languages (see [3] for a treatment of this in the context of λ-calculus and [9, 14] of more general functional languages). For example, the construct **lambda** $x.M$ could be compiled to **lam** $(\lambda x.M)$, where **lam** $: (\mathit{Expr} \rightarrow \mathit{Expr}) \rightarrow \mathit{Expr}$. However, higher-order syntax cannot be used directly in the case of languages with imperative features. In fact, it easily yields semantic inconsistencies, since it treats identifiers as placeholders for expressions. This is correct in pure functional languages, but does not hold in imperative languages. For instance, the application of the λ-abstraction containing a command[2] **lambda** $(\lambda x.[x := x + 1]x)$ to 0 would be reduced to the evaluation of $[0 := 0 + 1]0$, which is meaningless. Furthermore, there is no direct representation of loops like **while** b **do** $x := x + 1$. See [3] for more difficulties in handling Hoare's logic. Another problem is the absence of induction principles for encodings that employ higher-order syntax.

The difficulty of avoiding the capturing of local variables can be overcome by making explicit the textual substitution of variables in local evaluations [4]. This is similar to Gentzen's notion of *Eigenvariable* [8]. Recall the $\exists$-ELIM rule:

$$\frac{\exists x.A \quad \begin{array}{c}(A')\\ \vdots \\ B\end{array}}{B}$$

A' is obtained from A by replacing all the occurrences of x with x', where x' does not occur neither in any of A, x, B, nor in any assumption different from A'.

Simlarly, in evaluating **let** $x = N$ **in** M, we have to replace all the occurrences of x in M with a new identifier never used before, say x', which will be bound to the value of n. The **let** rule is definable as follows:

$$\frac{N \Rightarrow n \quad \begin{array}{c}(x' \Rightarrow n)\\ \vdots \\ M' \Rightarrow m'\end{array}}{\mathbf{let}\ x = N\ \mathbf{in}\ M \Rightarrow m}\ E(x, M, m)$$

where $E(x, M, m)$ is a typographic abbreviation for the *Eigenvariable Condition*: $E(x, M, m) \equiv$ "M', m' are obtained from M, m respectively by replacing *all* the occurrences of x with x', which does not appears neither in x, M, m nor in any assumption different from $(x' \Rightarrow n)$".

This treatment of local variables correctly obeys the standard stack discipline of languages with static scoping: when we have to define a local variable, we allocate a new cell (represented by x', a new variable) where we store the local value (this is achieved by assuming $x' \Rightarrow n$). This allocation is active only during the evaluation of M (the derivation tree of $M' \Rightarrow m'$); then, the cell is disposed (x' does not occur in any other place).

[2] $[\cdot]\cdot : \mathit{Comm} \times \mathit{Expr} \rightarrow \mathit{Expr}$ applies commands to expressions; see Sect.3.1,4 and [4]

2.2 What informations can assumptions represent?

The structural rules implicit in N.D. systems of monotonicity of hypothesis have another immediate consequence. We can reduce to assumptions only informations which can be dealt with using a static scoping discipline. In particular, a side-effect assignment of pointers which induces variables aliasing (or sharing) is difficult to encode, since we would necessitate of a vector. In fact, we cannot retrace all the bindings which are involved on a set of shared variables whenever one of them changes its value.

However, in languages which do not allow sharing, assignments can be reduced to definitions of new variables. Therefore, we focus on this kind of languages. Namely, those whose semantics can be defined without using both environment and store. These comprise all purely functional languages, but also some interesting extensions of these which have genuinely imperative features. This is in fact our thesis: only languages whose denotational semantics is definable by using only the notion of environment can be conveniently handled using NOS. In the following we describe some of these languages.

3 The language $\mathcal{L}_P$

In this section, we examine a functional language extended with imperative features as assignments which give it an imperative flavor. Its semantics can been successfully described by using the NOS paradigm. We give its syntax, its NOS and denotational semantics (App.A, B, C) and we prove that the former is adequate w.r.t. the latter. Finally, we will discuss the relation between the NOS and a SOS description.

3.1 Syntax

$\mathcal{L}_P$ is an untyped λ-calculus extended by a set of structured commands. These commands are embedded into expressions using the "modal" operator $[\mathbf{on}\cdot\ \mathbf{do}\cdot]\cdot$. The expression $[\mathbf{on}\ x_1 = M_1; \ldots; x_k = M_k\ \mathbf{do}\ C]M$ can be read as:

"execute C in the environment formed only by the bindings $x_1 = M_1; \ldots; x_k = M_k$; use resulting values of these identifiers to extend the global environment in which M has to be evaluated, obtaining the value of the entire expression."

C cannot have access to "external" variables other than $x_1 \ldots x_k$, so all possible side effects are concerned with only these variables. Moreover, the entire **on-do** expression above does not have any side effect: all environment changes due to C's execution are local to M.

$\mathcal{L}_P$ allows us to declare and use procedures. For the sake of simplicity, but w.l.o.g., these procedures will take exactly two arguments. The first argument is passed by value/result, the second by value [21]. Furthermore, the body of a procedure cannot access global variables, but only its formal parameters (and locally defined identifiers, of course). This means that when $P(x, M)$ is executed within the scope of the declaration $\mathbf{proc}\ P(y, z) = C\ \mathbf{in}\ D$, C is executed in the environment formed by only two bindings: $\{y \Rightarrow n, z \Rightarrow m\}$, where n, m are the values of x, M respectively. After C's execution, the new value of y is copied back into x. So, $P(x, M)$ can effect only x.

The restriction on global access forbids sharing of identifiers, so there is no need for a store. This does not drastically reduce the expressiveness of the imperative language. Donahue has shown that in this case, the call-by-value/result is a "good" simulation of the usual call-by-reference [7].

In [4] a different definition of procedure is given. There, procedures parameters are passed only by value, but procedures can have access to global variables. However, there is a problem with this approach, since the N.D. treatment of procedures does not immediately lend itself to support side effects on global variables. That approach does not work; for instance, the expression $[\mathbf{on}\ x = 0\ \mathbf{do}\ \mathbf{proc}\ P(z) = (x := z)\ \mathbf{in}\ x := 1; P(nil)]x$ would be evaluated to 1 instead of *nil*. This is due to the fact that the assignment made by $P(nil)$ on the global variable x is local to the environment of the procedure itself. In fact, executions of such procedures leave the global environment unchanged.

3.2 Natural Operational Semantics

The complete NOS formal system for $\mathcal{L}_P$ consists of 67 rules; see App.B.1.

In order to deal with λ-closures, command checking and execution, procedure checking and bookkeeping, we need to introduce some new constructors besides those of Sect.3.1 and new predicates besides $\Rightarrow$. As in [4], the use of these new constructors is reserved: a programmer cannot directly utilize these constructors to write down a program. Below we list the constructors and predicates, and we briefly describe the most important ones. For their formal meaning, see Theor.3.

Constructor	Functionality	
$[\_/\_]\_$	: *Expr* $\times$ *Id* $\times$ *Expr*	$\rightarrow$*Expr*
$\_\cdot\_$	: *Expr* $\times$ *Expr*	$\rightarrow$*Expr*
$[\_\vert\_]\_$	: *Declarations* $\times$ *Commands* $\times$ *Expr*	$\rightarrow$*Expr*
$[\_/\_]_c\_$	: *Commands* $\times$ *Id* $\times$ *Commands*	$\rightarrow$*Commands*
lambda	: *Id* $\times$ *Id* $\times$ *Commands*	$\rightarrow$*Procedures*
$[\_/\_]_{pe}\_$	: *Procedures* $\times$ *ProcId* $\times$ *Expr*	$\rightarrow$*Expr*
$[\_/\_]_{pc}\_$	: *Procedures* $\times$ *ProcId* $\times$ *Commands*	$\rightarrow$*Commands*

Judgment	Type	Judgment	Type
$\Rightarrow$	$\subset$ *Expr* $\times$ *Expr*	$\Rightarrow_p$	$\subset$ *ProcId* $\times$ *Procedures*
value	$\subset$ *Expr*	$free_e$	$\subset$ *Expr* $\times$ *IdSet*
closed	$\subset$ *Expr*	$free_c$	$\subset$ *Commands* $\times$ *IdSet*
$closed_p$	$\subset$ *ProcId*	$\rhd$	$\subset$ *Declarations* $\times$ *IdSet*

where *Procedures* is a new syntactic class defined as $q ::= \mathbf{lambda}\ x, y.C$, and *IdSet* is the subset of *Expr* defined as $l ::= nil \mid x \mid l_1 :: l_2$

The intuitive meaning of $[n/x]M$ is "the expression obtained from M by replacing all free occurrences of x with n." Just as for the **let** discussed in Sect.2, in order to evaluate $[n/x]M$ we have to evaluate M under the assumption that the value of x is n, and hence any previous assumption on x must be ignored. This is implemented by the substitution rule, no.1, which is very similar to the **let** rule of Sect.2. This rule is the core of the evaluation system. Many other evaluation rules, e.g. the one for **let**, are reduced to the substitution evaluation (rule no.3). In NOS, to each sort of identifiers and substitution operators (e.g. *Id* and $[\_/\_]\_$, *ProcId* and $[\_/\_]_{pe}\_$, *Id* and $[\_/\_]_{c}\_$, etc.) there corresponds a specific substitution rule, similar in shape to rule no.1. In fact, this mechanism is used whenever one has to deal with standard static scoping. One can even think of these rules as a polymorphic variant of the same set of rules. Of course, minor adjustments have to be accounted for (rules no.24, 33, 29) (see [4, 15]).

The operator $[\_/\_]\_$ is also used to record local environments in values of **lambda**-abstractions, i.e. the *closures*. An expression like **lambda**$x.M$ is evaluated into $[n_1/x_1]\ldots[n_k/x_k]$**lambda**$x.M$, where $x_1,\ldots,x_k$ are all the free identifiers of M but x, and $n_1,\ldots,n_k$ are their respective values. The construction of closures is performed by rules no.4 and no.5; its application by rules no.7, no.8

The intuitive meaning of $[R|C]M$ is the same as of [**on** R **do** C]M. This expression is introduced in order to apply the declaration R until it is empty (rule no.16); then, the command C is executed.

The judgment *value* encodes the assertion that an expression is a value, and so it cannot be further reduced nor its meaning is affected by a substitution.

The judgments *closed*, *closed*$_p$ are used during closure construction, in order to determine the bindings that we have to record (rules no.4, no.5, no.31). Informally, we can derive *closed* M if and only if M has no free variables. These judgments belong to static semantics: their rules do not use evaluation rules.

The judgments *free*, *free*$_c$, $\triangleright$ are used to check that command expressions [**on** D **do** C]M and procedures do not access global variable. Informally, we can infer $\Gamma \vdash$ *free* M l if and only if all the free variables of M appear at the leaves of the tree l (see Theor.3). On the other hand, $\triangleright$ collects the variables defined by a declaration D into a set (represented by a tree of identifiers).

The judgment $\Rightarrow_p$ is used for bookkeeping the bindings between procedure identifiers and procedural abstraction (see rules no.28, no.30).

3.3 Denotational Semantics

In appendix C.1 we sketch the denotational semantics for the language $\mathcal{L}_P$. Domains are introduced to represent all the entities we have defined. This semantics is self-explanatory. We follow the usual syntax ([23]); $\underline{\lambda}$ denotes the *strict abstraction*: for each meta-expression M with free variable x on pointed domain D, $(\underline{\lambda}x.M)\bot = \bot$. Furthermore, $\underline{\underline{\lambda}}$ is the *double-strict abstraction*: for each meta-expression $M \neq \bot$ with free variable x on pointed domain D with both $\bot$ and $\top$, $(\underline{\underline{\lambda}}x.M)\bot = \bot, (\underline{\underline{\lambda}}x.M)\top = \top$.

Moreover we use the standard domains without giving their definition. The domains used are *Unit* (the set composed by only one point), $\mathbb{T}$ (the boolean set composed by two points, *true* and *false*), $\mathbb{N}$ (the set of natural numbers).

3.4 Adequacy

In this section we will show that the NOS description of $\mathcal{L}_P$ appearing in appendix B.1 is adequate w.r.t. the denotational semantics; that is, we will give soundness and completeness results of one semantics w.r.t. the other. Due to lack of space, we will only sketch the proofs; for further details see [15].

Definition 1. A set of formulæ Γ is a *canonical hypothesis* if

- it contains only formulæ like "$x \Rightarrow n, P \Rightarrow_p q, closed(x), closed_p(P)$";
- if $x \Rightarrow n, x \Rightarrow m \in \Gamma$ then m and n are syntactically the same expression;
- if $P \Rightarrow_p q, P \Rightarrow_p q' \in \Gamma$ then q and q' are syntactically the same procedure;

where $x \in Id, P \in ProcId$ and $m, n \in Expr, q, q' \in Procedures$.

In the rest of section, Γ will denote a generic canonical hypothesis. Let G be a formula; with $\Gamma \vdash G$ we denote the N.D. derivation of G, whose undischarged assumptions are in Γ.

Definition 2. Let $M \in Expr, R \in Declarations, \Gamma$ a canonical hypothesis; then 1. the set of *free identifiers of* M is denoted by $\mathrm{FV}(M) \subset Id \cup ProcId$. FV is naturally extended to *Commands*, bearing in mind that $\mathrm{FV}(x := M) = \mathrm{FV}(M)$; 2. the set of *variables defined by* R is $\mathrm{DV}(M) \subset Id$, defined as $\mathrm{DV}(x_1 = M_1; \ldots; x_k = M_k) = \{x_1, \ldots, x_k\}$;
3. the set of Γ*-closed identifiers* $\mathrm{C}(\Gamma)$ is $\mathrm{C}(\Gamma) \stackrel{\text{def}}{=} \{x \in Id \mid closed(x) \in \Gamma\} \cup \{P \in ProcId \mid closed_p(P) \in \Gamma\}$;
4. the *closure* of Γ is $\overline{\Gamma} = \Gamma \cup \{closed(x) \mid (y \Rightarrow n) \in \Gamma, x \in \mathrm{FV}(n)\} \cup \{closed_p(P) \mid (y \Rightarrow n) \in \Gamma, P \in \mathrm{FV}(n)\}$;
5. Γ is a *well-formed hypothesis*, *wfh*, if $\Gamma = \overline{\Gamma}$.

Theorem 3. $\forall \Gamma, \forall M, m \in Expr \forall C \in Commands, \forall l \in IdSet:$
1. $\Gamma \vdash closed\ M \iff \mathrm{FV}(M) \subseteq \mathrm{C}(\Gamma)$
2. $\Gamma \vdash free\ m\ l \iff \mathrm{FV}(m) \cap Id \subseteq leaves(l) \wedge \mathrm{FV}(m) \cap ProcId \subseteq \mathrm{C}(\Gamma)$
$\Gamma \vdash free\ C\ l \iff \mathrm{FV}(C) \cap Id \subseteq leaves(l) \wedge \mathrm{FV}(C) \cap ProcId \subseteq \mathrm{C}(\Gamma)$
where $leaves(nil) = \emptyset, leaves(x) = \{x\}, leaves(l_1 :: l_2) = leaves(l_1) \cup leaves(l_2)$
3. $\Gamma \vdash value\ m \implies \overline{\Gamma} \vdash closed\ m$

Proof. By induction on the derivations and on the syntax of M, m, C. □

Note that not all closed expressions are values; e.g., ((**lambda** $x.x$) 0).

Definition 4. Let $I \subseteq Id \cup ProcId$ and let $\rho, \rho' \in \mathbb{E}$. We say that ρ and ρ' *agree on* I ($\rho \equiv_I \rho'$) if $\forall x \in I \cap Id : (access\ [\![x]\!]\ \rho = access\ [\![x]\!]\ \rho')$ and $\forall P \in I \cap ProcId : (procaccess\ [\![P]\!]\ \rho = procaccess\ [\![P]\!]\ \rho')$.

Note that all ρ, ρ' agree on the empty set, that is $\forall \rho, \rho' \in \mathbb{E} : \rho \equiv_\emptyset \rho'$.

Theorem 5. $\forall m \in Expr, \forall R \in Declarations, \forall \rho, \rho' \in \mathbb{E}$:
1. $\rho \equiv_{\mathrm{FV}(m)} \rho' \Rightarrow \mathcal{E}[\![m]\!]\rho = \mathcal{E}[\![m]\!]\rho'$
2. $\rho \equiv_{\mathrm{FV}(C)} \rho' \Rightarrow \mathcal{C}[\![C]\!]\rho = \mathcal{C}[\![C]\!]\rho'$
3. $\rho \equiv_{\mathrm{FV}(R)} \rho' \Rightarrow \mathcal{D}[\![R]\!]\rho = \mathcal{D}[\![R]\!]\rho'$

Proof. By simultaneous induction on the syntax of m, C, R. □

Theorem 6. $\forall \Gamma, \forall \rho, \rho' \in \mathbb{E}, \forall m \in Expr, \forall l \in IdSet$:
1. $\rho \equiv_{\mathrm{C}(\Gamma)} \rho' \wedge \Gamma \vdash closed\ m \Longrightarrow \mathcal{E}[\![m]\!]\rho = \mathcal{E}[\![m]\!]\rho'$
2. $\rho \equiv_{leaves(l)} \rho' \wedge \Gamma \vdash free\ C\ l \Longrightarrow \mathcal{C}[\![C]\!]\rho = \mathcal{C}[\![C]\!]\rho'$
3. $\rho \equiv_{\mathrm{C}(\Gamma)} \rho' \wedge \Gamma \vdash value\ m \Longrightarrow \mathcal{E}[\![m]\!]\rho = \mathcal{E}[\![m]\!]\rho'$

Proof. Follows from Theor.3, Theor.5. □

Corollary 7. $\Gamma \vdash value\ m \wedge \mathrm{C}(\Gamma) = \emptyset \Longrightarrow \forall \rho, \rho' \in \mathbb{E} : \mathcal{E}[\![m]\!]\rho = \mathcal{E}[\![m]\!]\rho'$

Definition 8. We say that $\rho \in \mathbb{E}$ *satisfies* Γ ($\rho \models \Gamma$) if $\forall (x \Rightarrow n) \in \Gamma$: $access\ [\![x]\!]\ \rho = \mathcal{E}[\![n]\!]\rho$, and $\forall (P \Rightarrow q) \in \Gamma : procaccess\ [\![x]\!]\ \rho = \mathcal{Q}[\![q]\!]\rho$.

This is another place where the conciseness of the N.D. formalism comes into play. The domain of environments satisfying a given Γ can be much larger than the set of variables which occur on the left of assumptions in Γ.

Theorem 9. $\forall M, m, \forall \Gamma\ wfh, \forall \rho : \rho \models \Gamma \wedge \Gamma \vdash M \Rightarrow m \Longrightarrow \mathcal{E}[\![M]\!]\rho = \mathcal{E}[\![m]\!]\rho$

Proof. By induction on the structure of derivation, using the previous results. □

Corollary 10 Soundness of NOS wrt DS. $\forall M, m \in Expr : \vdash M \Rightarrow m \Longrightarrow \mathcal{E}[\![M]\!] = \mathcal{E}[\![m]\!]$

Proof. Put $\Gamma = \emptyset$ in Theor.9, and notice that $\emptyset$ is a wfh and $\forall \rho \in \mathbb{E} : \rho \models \emptyset$. □

A completeness result is something like an "inverse" of Corollary 10. However, a literal converse of Corollary 10 cannot hold: for $M = m =$ (**lambda** $x.x0$) it is $\mathcal{E}[\![M]\!] = \mathcal{E}[\![m]\!]$ but of course $\not\vdash M \Rightarrow m$. In fact, only some expressions can appear as values (see Theor.3). We need a new definition:

Definition 11. Let $M \in Expr$. An hypothesis Γ is *suitable for* M (M-suit(Γ)), if $\forall x, P \in \mathrm{FV}(M) \exists (x \Rightarrow n), (P \Rightarrow_p q) \in \Gamma$ such that $\mathrm{FV}(n), \mathrm{FV}(q) \subseteq \mathrm{C}(\Gamma)$.

A hypothesis is suitable for M if it contains enough bindings to evaluate M.

Theorem 12 Completeness of NOS wrt DS. $\forall M \in Expr, \forall \Gamma\ wfh, \forall \rho \in \mathbb{E}$: *if* $\mathcal{E}[\![M]\!]\rho \neq \bot, \top$, M-suit(Γ) *and* $\rho \models \Gamma$, *then* $\exists m \in Expr : \Gamma \vdash M \Rightarrow m$.

Proof. The difficulty in the proof is this: given an expression M whose meaning, in a given environment, is a proper point of $\mathbb{V}$, and a suitable hypothesis Γ, we have to build up a deduction $\Gamma \vdash M \Rightarrow m$, for some m.[3] This cannot be done by induction on the syntactic structure of M, since our language is higher order; in fact, the evaluation of M can use M itself, and not only its subterms (see e.g. rule no.21). Nevertheless, the theorem can be proved by using the technique of *inclusive predicates*, developed by Milner and Plotkin [22]. □

[3] By Theor.9, this m has the same meaning as M

3.5 Adequacy w.r.t. the Structural Operational Semantics

In the previous subsection we have proved the adequacy of the NOS specification of $\mathcal{L}_P$ w.r.t. the denotational semantics. Actually, the same adequacy can be proved w.r.t. a Structural Operational Semantics (*à la Plotkin*, [21]). One can define a complete "input-output" SOS system for $\mathcal{L}_P$, that is a system for deriving two kinds of judgments: *evaluation of expressions*, $\rho \vdash_{SOS} M \to m$, and *execution of commands*, $\rho \vdash_{SOS} C \to \rho'$ where ρ, ρ' are finite environments, i.e. they are defined on a finite number of identifiers, and m is a value. In such a SOS system, there is no problem in handling substitutions, since we merely update the environment function in the subderivation:

$$\frac{\rho[x \mapsto n] \vdash_{SOS} M \to m}{\rho \vdash_{SOS} [n/x]M \to m}$$

Of course, this is not a linearized N.D. style system since we may delete a previous binding on x from the environment. These systems are equivalent, that is, $\forall \rho$ finite environment, $\forall \Gamma, \forall M, m \in \mathit{Expr}$:
1. if $\forall (x \Rightarrow n) \in \Gamma : \rho(x) = n$ and $\Gamma \vdash M \Rightarrow m$, then $\rho \vdash_{SOS} M \to m$
2. if $\rho \vdash_{SOS} M \to m$ and $\forall x \in \mathrm{FV}(M) : (x \Rightarrow \rho(x)) \in \Gamma$, then $\Gamma \vdash M \Rightarrow m$.
This is provable using techniques similar to those of previous subsection. Moreover, the completeness result (2) does not require the technique of inclusive predicates, but only a simpler structural induction on the derivation $\rho \vdash_{SOS} M \to m$.

4 Some remarks about language design

$\mathcal{L}_P$ is quite different from the language considered in [4]. There are several reasons for these changes. In some cases these are motivated by the desire to have a natural soundness result (see section 3.1 for remarks concerning procedures).

In our language, commands are embedded into expressions by the **on-do** construct. A simpler formalism for applying directly commands to expressions is used in [4], i.e. the "modal" operator $[\ ] : \mathit{Commands} \times \mathit{Expr} \to \mathit{Expr}$, so that $[C]M$ is an expression if $M \in \mathit{Expr}, C \in \mathit{Commands}$. Informally, the value of $[C]M$ is the value of M after the execution of C; C can affect any variable which is defined before its execution. Furthermore, as all expressions, $[C]M$ has no side-effects, that is evaluating $[C]M$ does not change the global environment any more than evaluating 0 or *nil*. C affects only the local environment which is used to evaluate M, but its side effects are not "filtered" by a declaration of accessible variables. In order to appreciate the difference in notation between the two approaches compare the following semantically equivalent expressions:

in the system of [4]: $\textbf{let}\ x = 0\ \textbf{in}\ [x := \mathit{nil}]x$; in $\mathcal{L}_P$: $[\textbf{on}\ x = 0\ \textbf{do}\ x := \mathit{nil}]x$

At first it seems that the latter is more complex and nothing has been gained. But the former expression might lead us to think that we can define functions with local state variables and more interesting expressions objects, but this is not the case! For instance, we can try to model a bank account defining a function `withdraw` which takes the amount to be withdrawn (an example taken from [1]):

```
let bal = 100; withdraw = lambda a.[bal:=bal-a]bal in
   let remaining = (withdraw 50) in
      (withdraw 30)
```

The system in [4] will evaluate it to 70 instead 20: the first withdraw has no effect. The reason is that in the closure of `withdraw`, `bal` is bound to 100, and this binding is reapplied to the local environment whenever `withdraw` is applied; this "reinitializes" `bal` to 100 each time (see rules no.5, no.6, no.8). Therefore, an application of `withdraw` cannot affect any following application.

Thus, [4]'s system may lead to misunderstanding the meaning of some expressions. We decide to avoid this by writing explicitly the variables which a command can affect, and making explicit that such variables are always reinitialized whenever the command is executed. By writing $[\mathbf{on}\, x_1 = M_1; \ldots; x_k = M_k\ \mathbf{do}\, C]M$ we immediately know that, *before* C is executed, the "interface variables" $x_1 \ldots x_k$ are initialized. Therefore, an obscure program, like the `withdraw` one, cannot be written in $\mathcal{L}_P$:the `withdraw` function should be declared as

```
let withdraw = lambda a.[on bal = 100 do bal:=bal-a]bal in ...
```

and hence its meaning is clearer. This aspect is however a major problem: neither in [4] system nor in $\mathcal{L}_P$ the `withdraw` function with the intended meaning of [1] can be written. We'll elaborate on this in Sect.7.

5 Some extensions of $\mathcal{L}_P$

In this section we briefly describe some further extensions of $\mathcal{L}_P$ concerning complex declarations, structures and imperative modules. Their semantics can be expressed without stores because there is no variable sharing. See appendix A, B and C for their syntax, NOS and DS respectively. We deal with each extension by itself, by simply adding new rules to the formal system without altering the previous ones. This illustrates modularity of NOS which allows us to add new rules for new constructs without changing the previous ones. For each extension, one can prove adequacy of NOS w.r.t. the denotational semantics ([15]), just by discussing only the new cases due to the extra rules.

5.1 Complex Declarations

$\mathcal{L}_D$ is obtained from $\mathcal{L}_P$ by adding expressions of the form $\mathbf{let}R\ \mathbf{in}M$ where R is a complex declaration like in Standard ML ([16]). In spite of the syntactic simplicity of these extensions, it appears to be unavoidable to define an entire evaluation system for declarations (rules no.72–88). The value of complex declarations are finite sets of bindings, represented by expressions called *syntactic environments*; they are trees whose leaves are of the form $x \mapsto n$ where $\mapsto$: *Id* $\times$ *Expr* $\rightarrow$ *Expr* is a new local constructor. We need to introduce furthermore several constructors and a judgment for applying such syntactic environments to expressions and declarations ($\{\_\}\_$, $\{\_\}_{d}\_$) and for inferring expression closures ($\langle\_\rangle\_$, $\gg$). Informally, one can derive $\Gamma \vdash R \gg I$ iff all expressions contained in R are closed in Γ and I is the set of identifiers defined by R. On the other hand, $\Gamma \vdash$ *closed* $\langle I \rangle M$ iff all free variables in M but the ones in I are *closed* in Γ. Once the rules will be laid down, these fact will be formally provable. Using this set of rules, we can define precisely when a complex **let** is closed without using any evaluation, since *closed* is a property belonging to static semantics. An adequacy theorem similar to Theor.3 can be proved for the system given in Sect.B.2. In [4] there is a simpler approach; it uses the complex declaration evaluation in order to determine the set of defined identifiers. This approach is not complete: there are closed expression whose *closed* property cannot be inferred in [4]'s system (e.g. **let** $o = ($**lambda** $x.xx); z = (oo)$ **in** z).

5.2 Structures and signatures

$\mathcal{L}_{M_F}$ extends $\mathcal{L}_P$ by adding a module system like that of Standard ML ([16]), where a module is "an environment turned into a manipulable object". Like SML, a module (here called *structure*) has a *signature*, and we can do *signature matching* in order to "cast" structures. However, there are some differences between SML and $\mathcal{L}_{M_F}$. First, in $\mathcal{L}_{M_F}$ structures and signatures are indeed expression. Therefore, they may be associated to identifiers with simple **let**s, without using special constructs. These **let**s can appear anywhere in expressions, not only at top level. Structures and signatures can be manipulated by common functions; however, there are not *functors* since the sharing specification is not implemented. The NOS should be self-explanatory.

5.3 Imperative modules (Abstract Data Types)

The extension $\mathcal{L}_{M_I}$ introduces modules *à la Morris* ([18]). In this formulation, a module is very close to an Abstract Data Type: it contains
1. a set of local variables, recording the *state* of the module; they are not accessible from outside the module;
2. some code for the initialization of the local variables above;
3. a set of procedures and functions which operate on these local variables and are the only part accessible from outside the module (the *interface*).

From outside a module we can only evaluate its functions, which do not produce side-effects, and execute its procedures, which can modify the state of the module (the value of local variables). In order to illustrate the idea, but w.l.o.g., we discuss only modules with exactly one local variable, one procedure with one argument (passed by value) and one function.

As for the previous languages, we do not need a representation of the store in defining the semantics of this kind of module ([7]). The rules for the specification of the imperative modules are certainly the most complex of those discussed in this paper. They are based on the principle of distributing as much as possible under the form of hypothetical assumption in deductions. In a module there are three informations: the state, the procedure and the function. Actually, only the state is subject to changes upon execution of the module procedure. We split

these three informations and record them using three different judgments (see rule no.114). The predicates of these assumptions are the following:
$\Rightarrow_m \subset$ *ModId* $\times$ (*Expr* $\times$ *ModId*) $\Rightarrow_{mp} \subset$ (*ModId* $\times$ *ProcId*) $\times \mathbb{Q}$
$\Rightarrow_{mf} \subset$ (*ModId* $\times$ *Id*) $\times$ *Expr*
We use a lot of syntactic sugar; for instance, we write $T.P \Rightarrow_{mp} \boldsymbol{\lambda} x, y.C$ instead of $\Rightarrow_{mp} ((T, P), \textbf{lambda}\, x, y.C)$.

When the state of a module changes (by executing its procedure), we have to substitute only the assumption involving $\Rightarrow_m$; the other two remain the same. Thus, while the procedure and the function are left associated to the original module identifier, the state becomes associated to a new *ModId*, and this substitution affects a part of the declaration to be evaluated (see rules no.116 no.115). The link between the new state and the procedures is maintained by the module identifier which appears on right of $\Rightarrow_m$ assumption: it is merely copied from the old assumption into the new one (rule no.116).

When a module procedure has to be executed ($T.P(M)$), first we look for the state of the module T, by requiring $T \Rightarrow_m (p, T')$. Here we find the original module identifier, T'. The invoked procedure is then associated to this identifier in the assumption $T'.P \Rightarrow_{mp} \textbf{lambda}\, x, y.C$. After having bound x and y respectively to module variable value (p) and actual parameter (m), we execute C and get back the new value of the state variable. Finally, we substitute T with the new module state.

Function evaluation is similar to procedure call, but simpler (rule no.117).

We can successfully implement the bank account examined in Sect.4 by using this kind of modules, e.g. as follows:

```
module account is
  bal = 100;
  proc withdraw(amount) = bal := bal - amount;
  func balance = bal
in ...
```

Now we can withdraw an amount A by executing `account.withdraw(`A`)`, and know how much money we have left by evaluating `account.balance`.

However, even this notion of module is too weak to adequately model "functions with local state" as are necessary, for instance, in realizing memoized functions. In fact, as soon as an instance of a module is packaged within a λ abstraction, its connection with its parent (definition) is severed.

6 Encoding NOS in the Edinburgh LF

From a logician's point of view, the Natural Operational Semantics of a language is just a formal logical system in Natural Deduction style. Therefore, it can be easily encoded in interactive proof-checkers based on type-checking of typed λ-calculus, such as the Edinburgh Logical Framework (LF, [11]). This was actually one of the main motivations for introducing and investigating the systems of this paper. A first outline about this can be found in [4]. In [15] a complete encoding of the NOS of the **while** subset of $\mathcal{L}_P$ appears.

The LF encoding of NOS has several significant consequences. When we encode the operational semantics in LF, we have to discuss details that are normally left out or too often taken for granted or even "swept under the rug". For instance, the complex side-condition of rule no.1 requires that "x is a new identifier", but we do not give a formal definition of this. When we encode NOS in LF, this condition has to be expressed formally and unambiguously. This is achieved by introducing two auxiliary judgments $\mathit{in}, \mathit{notin} : (\mathit{Term}\ \mathit{Id}) \to \prod_{S:\mathit{Sorts}}(\mathit{Term}\ S) \to \mathit{Type}$ where $\mathit{Sorts} : \mathit{Type}$ is the type of syntactic classes and $\mathit{Term} : \mathit{Sorts} \to \mathit{Type}$. The intuitive meaning of $(\mathit{in}\ x\ S\ p)$ is "the identifier x appears in the phrase p which belongs to the syntactic class S"; dually for *notin*. The rules for these judgments are given on the syntax of phrases in the obvious way—see [4, 15]. Thus, the complete substitution rule no.1 is as follows, where $\mathit{Id}, \mathit{Expr} : \mathit{Sorts}$:

$$M, m : \mathit{Id} \to \mathit{Expr}\ \frac{\mathit{value}\ n \qquad \forall w : \mathit{Id} \left\{\begin{array}{c}(\mathit{notin}\ x\ \mathit{Id}\ w)\\ \vdots \\ \mathit{notin}\ x\ \mathit{Expr}\ (M\ w)\end{array}\right. \qquad \forall x' : \mathit{Id} \left\{\begin{array}{c} \left(\begin{array}{c} \forall w : \mathit{Id}\ \dfrac{\mathit{in}\ w\ \mathit{Id}\ x}{\mathit{notin}\ w\ \mathit{Id}\ x'} \\ \forall w : \mathit{Id}\ \dfrac{\mathit{in}\ w\ \mathit{Expr}\ (M\ x)}{\mathit{notin}\ w\ \mathit{Id}\ x'} \\ \forall w : \mathit{Id}\ \dfrac{\mathit{in}\ w\ \mathit{Expr}\ (m\ x)}{\mathit{notin}\ w\ \mathit{Id}\ x'} \\ x' \Rightarrow n \end{array}\right) \\ \vdots \\ (M\ x') \Rightarrow (m\ x')\end{array}\right.}{[n/x](M\ x) \Rightarrow (m\ x)}$$

The middle subderivation requires that x does not occur in the expression context M. Evaluation is performed in the right-hand subderivation; here, x is replaced by x' assuming x' does not occur in any of $x, (M\ x), (m\ x)$. This is achieved by the three discharged rules about *in*, *notin*. The full power of LF is exploited: rules are treated just as any other judgment.

We can use this encoding with *proof editors* based on LF, such as LEGO ([13]), and *logic programming languages* based on LF, such as Elf ([20]). LEGO can be successfully used to develop derivations (= computation traces) and to verify properties about the semantics themselves, e.g. equivalence between constructs. During the phase of operational semantics developing, we can try our rules and look for inconsistencies. Thus, we have immediately a powerful tool for semantic development and consistency checking.

On the other hand, logic programming languages such as Elf can be used to get an interpreter prototype for free: immediately after we have encoded in Elf the LF representation, we can ask queries like `?- True(eval` M `V).` where M is (the encoding of) an expression. In resolving this goal, Elf instantiates `V` to M's value, and develops a term which represent the deduction $\vdash M \Rightarrow V$, that is the computation trace of the evaluation of M.

In these systems we can prove several meta-results about semantics. In [15] the equivalence between two different NOS of the same **while**-language is developed. One of these semantics is "natural", clear but inefficient. The rules for the **while** execution are the following:

$$\frac{M \Rightarrow \mathit{true} \quad [C]([\mathbf{while}\, M\, \mathbf{do}\, C]N) \Rightarrow n}{[\mathbf{while}\, M\, \mathbf{do}\, C]N \Rightarrow n} \qquad \frac{M \Rightarrow \mathit{false} \quad N \Rightarrow n}{[\mathbf{while}\, M\, \mathbf{do}\, C]N \Rightarrow n}$$

This semantics needs to backtrack and to re-evaluate the test expression if it does not match the required value in the assumption. The second semantics overcomes this drawback by introducing an auxiliary judgment, *dw* ("do while"):

$$\frac{M \Rightarrow_a m \quad dw\, m\, M\, C\, N\, n}{[\mathbf{while}\, M\, \mathbf{do}\, C]N \Rightarrow_a n} \quad \frac{[C]([\mathbf{while}\, M\, \mathbf{do}\, C]N) \Rightarrow_a n}{dw\, \mathit{true}\, M\, C\, N\, n} \quad \frac{N \Rightarrow_a n}{dw\, \mathit{false}\, M\, C\, N\, n}$$

Here, backtracking and double evaluation are not needed any more.

Adopting a technique used by Michaylov and Pfenning for functional languages ([14]), we can prove the equivalence between these two semantics by encoding in Elf a judgment, $\mathsf{naeq} : \prod_{M,m \in Expr}(M \Rightarrow m) \rightarrow (M \Rightarrow_a m) \rightarrow \mathsf{Type}$. This judgment represents the equivalence between "natural" and "algorithmic" computation traces. Asking Elf about queries of the form `?- naeq` D D' where one of D, D' is instantiated to a derivation in one semantics, the system automatically gives us the equivalent derivation in the other semantics. In this way we have defined a bijection between the computation traces of the two semantics.

We can think the former semantic as the "theoretical" semantics of the language, and the latter as the real implementation. Thus, the formal equivalence proved in Elf between them can be seen as the backbone of a proof of compiler correctness. (For compiler correctness in LF see also [10]).

7 Concluding remarks

In this paper we have described the expressive power of the Natural Operational Semantics formalism. We have seen that this formalism handles successfully languages which do not allow variable aliasing, or sharing, We have shown some of these languages: functional languages extended with a restricted form of commands and procedures, blocks, complex declarations, modules *à la ML* (structures and signatures) and modules *à la Morris.*

This formalism improves abstractness and modularizability of Plotkin's Structural Operational Semantics and Kahn's Natural Semantics. Furthermore, such a operational description can be easily encoded in LF. Such encodings can be used within implementations of LF (LEGO and Elf), giving us powerful tools for developing language semantics formally, for checking correctness of translators and for proving semantic properties.

Unfortunately, so far we have not been able to give the semantics of a truly imperative language using this formalism. It seems that one cannot represent simultaneously both the store and the environment by means of assumptions. Without encoding a store we cannot describe usual imperative phenomena like side-effects with aliasing, argument passage of parameters by-reference and so on. Therefore, this formalism seems not general enough to deal with expressions with side-effects, functions with local state variables or memoization, Pascal procedures (procedures with global variables and call-by-reference).

We think that exception handling can be added to $\mathcal{L}_{M_F}$ quite easily ([4]). The real lack of our languages w.r.t. ML is the absence of the store: ML is a store-based language. Therefore, in order to capture fully the semantics of ML (and encode it in LF) we have to find some representation of the store. This is a task remaining to be done. Ideally, we would like to extend the formalism as much as is needed to describe the semantics of an untyped λ-calculus extended by primitives for manipulating side-effects, like ML's `ref`, `!` and `:=` ([16]). The NOS of this language should be easily extended to that of ML.

A Syntax

A.1 Syntax of $\mathcal{L}_P$

Syntactic class *Id*
$x ::= i_0 \mid i_1 \mid i_2 \mid i_3 \mid \ldots$

Syntactic class *Expr*
$M ::= 0 \mid succ \mid plus \mid true \mid false \mid \leq$
$\mid nil \mid M :: N \mid hd \mid tl$
$\mid \mathbf{lambda}\, x.M \mid MN$
$\mid \mathbf{let}\; x = M \;\mathbf{in}\; N$
$\mid \mathbf{letrec}\; f(x) = M \;\mathbf{in}\; N$
$\mid [\mathbf{on}\; R \;\mathbf{do}\; C]M$

Syntactic class *ProcId*
$P ::= p_1 \mid p_2 \mid p_3 \mid \ldots$

Syntactic class *Declarations*
$R ::= \langle\rangle \mid x = M; R$

Syntactic class *Commands*
$C ::= x := M \mid C; D \mid \mathbf{nop}$
$\mid \mathbf{if}\; M \;\mathbf{then}\; C \;\mathbf{else}\; D$
$\mid \mathbf{beginnew}\; x = M;\; C \;\mathbf{end}$
$\mid \mathbf{proc}\; P(x, y) = C \;\mathbf{in}\; D$
$\mid \mathbf{while}\; M \;\mathbf{do}\; C \mid P(x, M)$

A.2 Syntax of $\mathcal{L}_D$

Syntactic class *Expr*
$M ::= \ldots \mid \mathbf{let}\; R \;\mathbf{in}\; M$

Syntactic class *Declarations*
$R ::= \ldots \mid R; S \mid R \;\mathbf{and}\; S$

A.3 Syntax of $\mathcal{L}_{M_F}$

Syntactic class *LongId*
$u ::= x \mid u.x$

Syntactic class *Commands*
$C ::= \ldots \mid u := M$

Syntactic class *Expr*
$M ::= \ldots \mid \mathbf{sig}\; x_1 \ldots x_k \;\mathbf{end}$
$\mid \mathbf{struct}\; x_1 = M_1; \ldots; x_k = M_k \;\mathbf{end}$
$\mid M : N \mid \mathbf{open}\; u \;\mathbf{in}\; M$

A.4 Syntax of $\mathcal{L}_{M_I}$

Syntactic class *ModId*
$T ::= t_1 \mid t_2 \mid t_3 \mid \ldots$
Syntactic class *Expr*
$M ::= \ldots \mid T.f$
Syntactic class *Commands*
$C ::= \ldots \mid T.P(M)$
$\mid$ **module** T **is** $x = M$;
proc $P(y) = C$; **func** $f = N$
in D

B Rules for the NOS

B.1 NOS of $\mathcal{L}_P$

Rules for judgment $\Rightarrow$ For the meaning of $E(\cdot,\cdot,\cdot)$, see Sect.2.1. For typographical reasons, **lambda** will be sometimes abbreviated with $\boldsymbol{\lambda}$ and $[\langle\rangle|C]N$ with $[C]N$.

$$\frac{\begin{matrix}(x' \Rightarrow n)\\ \vdots \\ \mathit{value}\ n\ M' \Rightarrow m'\end{matrix}}{[n/x]M \Rightarrow m}\ E(x,M,m) \qquad (1)$$

$$\frac{\mathit{value}\ m}{m \Rightarrow m} \qquad (2)$$

$$\frac{N \Rightarrow n \quad [n/x]M \Rightarrow m}{\mathbf{let}\ x = N\ \mathbf{in}\ M \Rightarrow m} \qquad (3)$$

$$\frac{\begin{matrix}(\mathit{closed}\ x)\\ \vdots \\ \mathit{closed}\ M\end{matrix}}{\mathbf{lambda}\ x.M \Rightarrow \mathbf{lambda}\ x.M} \qquad (4)$$

$$\frac{\begin{matrix}(\mathit{closed}\ y)\\ \vdots \\ y \Rightarrow n\ \mathbf{lambda}\ x.M \Rightarrow m\end{matrix}}{\mathbf{lambda}\ x.M \Rightarrow [n/y]m} \qquad (5)$$

$$\frac{M \Rightarrow m \quad N \Rightarrow n \quad m \cdot n \Rightarrow p}{MN \Rightarrow p} \qquad (6)$$

$$\frac{[n/x]M \Rightarrow p}{(\mathbf{lambda}\ x.M) \cdot n \Rightarrow p} \qquad (7)$$

$$\frac{\mathit{value}\ n \quad [m'/x](m \cdot n) \Rightarrow p}{([m'/x]m) \cdot n \Rightarrow p} \qquad (8)$$

$$\frac{\mathit{value}\ n}{(\mathit{plus} \cdot 0) \cdot n \Rightarrow n} \qquad (9)$$

$$\frac{(\mathit{plus} \cdot m) \cdot n \Rightarrow p}{(\mathit{plus} \cdot (\mathit{succ} \cdot m)) \cdot n \Rightarrow \mathit{succ} \cdot p} \qquad (10)$$

$$\frac{\begin{matrix}\mathbf{let}\ f = (\mathbf{lambda}\ x.\mathbf{letrec}\\ f(x) = N\ \mathbf{in}\ N)\ \mathbf{in}\ M \Rightarrow p\end{matrix}}{\mathbf{letrec}\ f(x) = N\ \mathbf{in}\ M \Rightarrow p} \qquad (11)$$

$$\frac{M \Rightarrow m \quad N \Rightarrow n}{M :: N \Rightarrow m :: n} \qquad (12)$$

$$\frac{\mathit{value}\ m}{\mathit{hd} \cdot (m :: n) \Rightarrow m} \qquad (13)$$

$$\frac{\mathit{value}\ n}{\mathit{tl} \cdot (m :: n) \Rightarrow n} \qquad (14)$$

$$\frac{D \rhd I \quad \mathit{free}\ C\ I \quad [D|C]N \Rightarrow n}{[\mathbf{on}\ D\ \mathbf{do}\ C]N \Rightarrow n} \qquad (15)$$

$$\frac{M \Rightarrow m \quad [m/x]([D|C]N) \Rightarrow n}{[x = M; D|C]N \Rightarrow n} \qquad (16)$$

$$\frac{N \Rightarrow n \quad [n/x]M \Rightarrow m}{[x := N]M \Rightarrow m} \qquad (17)$$

$$\frac{[C]([D]M) \Rightarrow m}{[C; D]M \Rightarrow m} \qquad (18)$$

$$\frac{M \Rightarrow \mathit{true} \quad [C]N \Rightarrow n}{[\mathbf{if}\ M\ \mathbf{then}\ C\ \mathbf{else}\ D]N \Rightarrow n} \qquad (19)$$

$$\frac{M \Rightarrow \mathit{false} \quad [D]N \Rightarrow n}{[\mathbf{if}\ M\ \mathbf{then}\ C\ \mathbf{else}\ D]N \Rightarrow n} \qquad (20)$$

$$\frac{\begin{matrix}M \Rightarrow \mathit{true}\\ [C]([\mathbf{while}\ M\ \mathbf{do}\ C]N) \Rightarrow n\end{matrix}}{[\mathbf{while}\ M\ \mathbf{do}\ C]N \Rightarrow n} \qquad (21)$$

$$\frac{M \Rightarrow \mathit{false} \quad N \Rightarrow n}{[\mathbf{while}\ M\ \mathbf{do}\ C]N \Rightarrow n} \qquad (22)$$

$$\frac{N \Rightarrow n \quad [[n/x]_c C]M \Rightarrow m}{[\mathbf{beginnew}\ x = N;\ C\ \mathbf{end}]M \Rightarrow m} \qquad (23)$$

$$\frac{\begin{array}{c}(x' \Rightarrow n)\\ \vdots\\ value\ n\ [C']M \Rightarrow m'\end{array}}{[[n/x]_c C]M \Rightarrow m} E(x, C, m) \quad (24)$$

$$\frac{value\ n}{(\leq \cdot 0) \cdot n \Rightarrow true} \quad (25)$$

$$\frac{value\ n}{(\leq \cdot (succ \cdot n)) \cdot 0 \Rightarrow false} \quad (26)$$

$$\frac{(\leq \cdot n) \cdot m \Rightarrow p}{(\leq \cdot (succ \cdot n)) \cdot (succ \cdot m) \Rightarrow p} \quad (27)$$

$$\frac{[[\mathbf{lambda}\, x, y.C/P]_{pc} D]M \Rightarrow m}{[\mathbf{proc}\ P(x, y) = C\ \mathbf{in}\ D]M \Rightarrow m} \quad (28)$$

$$\frac{\begin{array}{c}(P' \Rightarrow_p \boldsymbol{\lambda} x, y.C)\\ \vdots\\ free_c\ C\ (x, y) \quad [D']M \Rightarrow m'\end{array}}{[[\boldsymbol{\lambda} x, y.C/P]_{pc} D]M \Rightarrow m} E(P, D, m) \quad (29)$$

$$\frac{\begin{array}{c}P \Rightarrow \boldsymbol{\lambda} x, y.C \quad M \Rightarrow m \quad z \Rightarrow p\\ {[p/x][m/y][C]x \Rightarrow v} \quad [v/z]N \Rightarrow n\end{array}}{[P(z, M)]N \Rightarrow n} \quad (30)$$

$$\frac{\begin{array}{cc} & (closed\ P)\\ free\ C\ (x, y) & \vdots\\ P \Rightarrow_p \boldsymbol{\lambda} x, y.C & \boldsymbol{\lambda} z.M \Rightarrow m\end{array}}{\boldsymbol{\lambda} z.M \Rightarrow [\boldsymbol{\lambda} x, y.C/P]_{pe} m} \quad (31)$$

$$\frac{value\ n \quad [Q/P]_{pe}(m \cdot n) \Rightarrow p}{([Q/P]_{pe} m) \cdot n \Rightarrow p} \quad (32)$$

$$\frac{\begin{array}{c}(P' \Rightarrow_p Q)\\ \vdots\\ free_c\ C\ (x, y) \quad M' \Rightarrow m'\end{array}}{[\boldsymbol{\lambda} x, y.C/P]_{pe} M \Rightarrow m} E(P, M, m) \quad (33)$$

Rules for judgment *value*

$$\frac{}{value\ m}\ m \text{ is a constant} \quad (34)$$

$$\frac{M \Rightarrow m}{value\ m} \quad (35)$$

Rules for judgment $\triangleright$

$$\frac{}{\langle\rangle \triangleright nil} \quad (36)$$

$$\frac{D_l \triangleright I}{x = M; D_l \triangleright x :: I} \quad (37)$$

Rules for judgment *closed*

$$\frac{}{closed\ m}\ m \text{ is a constant} \quad (38)$$

$$\frac{closed\ M \quad closed\ N}{closed(MN)} \quad (39)$$

$$\frac{closed\ m \quad closed\ n}{closed(m \cdot n)} \quad (40)$$

$$\frac{\begin{array}{cc} & (closed\ x)\\ & \vdots\\ closed\ N & closed\ M\end{array}}{closed(\mathbf{let}\ x = N\ \mathbf{in}\ M)} \quad (41)$$

$$\frac{\begin{array}{cc}(closed\ f, closed\ x) & (closed\ f)\\ \vdots & \vdots\\ closed\ N & closed\ M\end{array}}{closed(\mathbf{letrec}\ f(x) = N\ \mathbf{in}\ M)} \quad (42)$$

$$\frac{\begin{array}{c}(closed\ x)\\ \vdots\\ closed\ M\end{array}}{closed(\mathbf{lambda}\, x.M)} \quad (43)$$

$$\frac{\begin{array}{cc} & (closed\ x)\\ & \vdots\\ closed\ n & closed\ M\end{array}}{closed([n/x]M)} \quad (44)$$

$$\frac{closed\ m \quad closed\ n}{closed(m :: n)} \quad (45)$$

$$\frac{D \triangleright I \quad free\ C\ I \quad closed\ [D|\mathbf{nop}]M}{closed\ [\mathbf{on}\ D\ \mathbf{do}\ C]M} \quad (46)$$

$$\frac{closed\ M}{closed\ [\langle\rangle|\mathbf{nop}]M} \quad (47)$$

$$\cfrac{\begin{array}{c}(closed\ x)\\ \vdots\\ closed\ N\ closed\ [R|\mathbf{nop}]M\end{array}}{closed\ [x = N; R|\mathbf{nop}]M} \quad (48)$$

$$\cfrac{\begin{array}{c}(closed_p\ P)\\ \vdots\\ free\ C\ (x,y)\quad closed\ M\end{array}}{closed\ [\mathbf{lambda}\, x,y.C/P]_{pe}M} \quad (49)$$

Rules for judgment *free*

$$\cfrac{}{free\ x\ (x,m)} \quad (50)$$

$$\cfrac{free\ x\ m}{free\ x\ (y,m)} \quad (51)$$

$$\cfrac{free\ M\ m\quad free\ N\ m}{free\ (M\ N)\ m} \quad (52)$$

$$\cfrac{free\ M\ m\quad free\ N\ x :: m}{free\ (\mathbf{let}\ x = M\ \mathbf{in}\ N)\ m} \quad (53)$$

$$\cfrac{free\ M\ x :: m}{free\ (\mathbf{lambda}\, x.M)\ m} \quad (54)$$

$$\cfrac{free\ M\ m\quad free\ N\ m}{free\ (M \cdot N)\ m} \quad (55)$$

$$\cfrac{free\ M\ m\quad free\ N\ m}{free\ (M :: N)\ m} \quad (56)$$

$$\cfrac{free\ n\ m\quad free\ M\ x :: m}{free\ ([n/x]M)\ m} \quad (57)$$

$$\cfrac{\begin{array}{c}(closed_p\ P)\\ \vdots\\ free\ C\ (x,y,m)\qquad free\ M\ m\end{array}}{free\ ([\mathbf{lambda}\, x,y.C/P]M)\ m} \quad (58)$$

$$\cfrac{free\ C\ m\quad free\ M\ m}{free\ ([C]M)\ m} \quad (59)$$

$$\cfrac{free\ C\ m\quad free\ D\ m}{free\ (C;D)\ m} \quad (60)$$

$$\cfrac{free\ M\ m\quad free\ C\ m\quad free\ D\ m}{free\ (\mathbf{if}\ M\ \mathbf{then}\ C\ \mathbf{else}\ D)\ m} \quad (61)$$

$$\cfrac{free\ M\ m\quad free\ C\ m}{free\ (\mathbf{while}\ M\ \mathbf{do}\ C)\ m} \quad (62)$$

$$\cfrac{free\ M\ m\quad free\ C\ x :: m}{free\ (\mathbf{beginnew}\ x = M; C\ \mathbf{end}\ )\ m} \quad (63)$$

$$\cfrac{\begin{array}{c}(closed_p\ P)\\ \vdots\\ free\ C\ (x,y,m)\qquad free\ D\ m\end{array}}{free\ (\mathbf{proc}\ P(x,y) = C\ \mathbf{in}\ D)\ m} \quad (64)$$

$$\cfrac{closed_p(P)\quad free\ x\ m\quad free\ M\ m}{free\ (P(x,M))\ m} \quad (65)$$

$$\cfrac{free\ n\ m\quad free\ C\ x :: m}{free\ ([n/x]C)\ m} \quad (66)$$

$$\cfrac{\begin{array}{c}(closed_p\ P)\\ \vdots\\ free\ C\ (x,y,m)\qquad free\ D\ m\end{array}}{free\ ([\mathbf{lambda}\, x,y.C/P]D)\ m} \quad (67)$$

B.2 NOS of $\mathcal{L}_D$

Rules for judgment $\Rightarrow$

$$\cfrac{R \Rightarrow_d r\quad \{r\}M \Rightarrow m}{\mathbf{let}\ R\ \mathbf{in}\ M \Rightarrow m} \quad (68)$$

$$\cfrac{M \Rightarrow m}{\{nil\}M \Rightarrow m} \quad (69)$$

$$\cfrac{[n/x]M \Rightarrow m}{\{x \mapsto n\}M \Rightarrow m} \quad (70)$$

$$\cfrac{\{r\}(\{s\}M) \Rightarrow m}{\{r :: s\}M \Rightarrow m} \quad (71)$$

Rules for judgment $\Rightarrow_d$

$$\frac{\begin{array}{c}(x' \Rightarrow n)\\ \vdots \\ value\ n\ R' \Rightarrow_d m\end{array}}{[n/x]_d R \Rightarrow_d m}\ E(x,n,R,m) \qquad (72)$$

$$\frac{M \Rightarrow m}{x = M \Rightarrow_d x \mapsto m} \qquad (73)$$

$$\frac{R \Rightarrow_d r \quad S \Rightarrow_d s}{R \textbf{ and } S \Rightarrow_d r :: s} \qquad (74)$$

$$\frac{R \Rightarrow_d r \quad \{r\}_d S \Rightarrow_d s}{R; S \Rightarrow_d r :: s} \qquad (75)$$

$$\frac{R \Rightarrow_d r}{\{nil\}_d R \Rightarrow_d r} \qquad (76)$$

$$\frac{[n/x]_d R \Rightarrow_d r}{\{x \mapsto n\}_d R \Rightarrow_d r} \qquad (77)$$

$$\frac{\{r\}_d(\{s\}_d R) \Rightarrow_d r}{\{r :: s\}_d R \Rightarrow_d r} \qquad (78)$$

Rules for judgment *closed*

$$\frac{closed\ M}{closed\ \{nil\} M} \qquad (79)$$

$$\frac{closed\ [n/x]M}{closed\ \{x \mapsto n\}M} \qquad (80)$$

$$\frac{closed\ \{r\}\{s\}M}{closed\ \{r :: s\}M} \qquad (81)$$

$$\frac{closed\ m}{closed\ x \mapsto m} \qquad (82)$$

$$\frac{R \gg m \quad closed\ \langle m \rangle M}{closed(\textbf{let } R \textbf{ in } M)} \qquad (83)$$

$$\frac{\begin{array}{c}(closed\ x)\\ \vdots \\ closed\ M\end{array}}{closed\ \langle x \rangle M} \qquad (84)$$

$$\frac{closed\ \langle m \rangle(\langle n \rangle M)}{closed\ \langle m :: n \rangle M} \qquad (85)$$

Rules for judgment $\gg$

$$\frac{}{\langle\rangle \gg nil} \qquad (86)$$

$$\frac{R \gg m \quad S \gg n}{R \textbf{ and } S \gg m :: n} \qquad (87)$$

$$\frac{\begin{array}{c}(closed\ x)\\ \vdots \\ closed\ M \quad R \gg n\end{array}}{x = M; R \gg x :: n} \qquad (88)$$

B.3 NOS of $\mathcal{L}_{M_F}$

Rules for judgment $\Rightarrow$

$$\frac{}{\textbf{struct end} \Rightarrow nil} \qquad (89)$$

$$\frac{M \Rightarrow m \quad [m/x]\textbf{struct } B_{str} \Rightarrow l}{\textbf{struct } x = M\ B_{str} \Rightarrow (x \mapsto m, l)} \qquad (90)$$

$$\frac{M \Rightarrow m \quad N \Rightarrow t \quad proj\ m\ (t)\ n}{M : N \Rightarrow n} \qquad (91)$$

$$\frac{u \Rightarrow m \quad (x \mapsto p)\ in\ m}{u.x \Rightarrow p} \qquad (92)$$

$$\frac{u \Rightarrow l \quad \{l\}M \Rightarrow m}{\textbf{open } u \textbf{ in } M \Rightarrow m} \qquad (93)$$

$$\frac{\begin{array}{c}M \Rightarrow m \quad u \Rightarrow l\\ upd\ l\ x\ m\ l' \quad [u := l']N \Rightarrow n\end{array}}{[u.x := M]N \Rightarrow n} \qquad (94)$$

Rules for judgment *value*

$$\frac{}{value(\textbf{sig } B_{sig})} \qquad (95)$$

Rules for judgment *closed*

$$\frac{}{closed\ \mathbf{sig}\ B_{sig}} \tag{96}$$

$$\frac{closed\ M \quad closed\ N}{closed\ M : N} \tag{97}$$

$$\frac{}{closed\ \mathbf{struct\ \ end}} \tag{98}$$

$$\frac{closed\ M\ closed(\mathbf{struct}\ B_{str}) \overset{\displaystyle (closed\ x)}{\vdots}}{closed(\mathbf{struct}\ x = M\ \ B_{str})} \tag{99}$$

$$\frac{closed\ u}{closed\ u.x} \tag{100}$$

$$\frac{closed\ u \quad closed\ M}{closed(\mathbf{open}\ u\ \mathbf{in}\ M)} \tag{101}$$

Rules for judgments *in*, *proj*, *upd*

$$\frac{}{m\ in\ (m :: l)} \tag{102}$$

$$\frac{m\ in\ l}{m\ in\ (p :: l)} \tag{103}$$

$$\frac{}{proj\ l\ (\mathbf{sig\ \ end}\ )\ nil} \tag{104}$$

$$\frac{(x \mapsto m)\ in\ l \quad proj\ l\ (\mathbf{sig}\ B_{sig})\ l'}{proj\ l\ (\mathbf{sig}\ x\ \ B_{sig})\ (x \mapsto m, l')} \tag{105}$$

$$\frac{}{upd\ (x \mapsto n, l)\ x\ m\ (x \mapsto m, l)} \tag{106}$$

$$\frac{upd\ l\ x\ m\ l'}{upd\ (y \mapsto n, l)\ x\ m\ (y \mapsto n, l')}\ x \neq y \tag{107}$$

B.4 NOS of $\mathcal{L}_{M_I}$

Rules for judgment *closed*

$$\frac{closed\ T}{closed\ T.f} \tag{108}$$

Rules for judgment $\gg$

$$\frac{\overset{\displaystyle (closed\ T)}{\vdots} \\ R \gg I}{[p/T]_m R \gg I} \tag{109}$$

Rules for judgment *free*

$$\frac{free\ R\ m \quad free\ M\ m}{free\ R.P(M)} \tag{110}$$

$$\frac{free\ R\ m}{free\ R.f\ m} \tag{111}$$

$$\frac{free\ p\ m \quad free\ N\ (R, m)}{free\ [p/R]_m N\ m} \tag{112}$$

$$\frac{\mathit{free}\ M\ m \quad \mathit{free}\ C\ (x,y) \quad \mathit{free}\ N\ (x) \quad \mathit{free}\ D\ (R,m)}{\mathit{free}\ (\textbf{module}\, R\ \textbf{is}\ x = M;\ \textbf{proc}\ P(y) = C;\ \textbf{func}\ f = N\textbf{in}\ D)\ m} \tag{113}$$

Rules for judgment $\Rightarrow$

$$\begin{pmatrix} R' \Rightarrow_m (m, R') \\ (R', P) \Rightarrow_{mp} \boldsymbol{\lambda} x, y.C \\ (R', f) \Rightarrow_{mf} \boldsymbol{\lambda} x.N \end{pmatrix}$$
$$\vdots$$
$$\frac{M \Rightarrow m \quad \mathit{free}\ C\ (x,y) \quad \mathit{free}\ N\ (x) \qquad\qquad [D']N \Rightarrow n'}{[\textbf{module}\, R\ \textbf{is}\ x = M_1;\ \textbf{proc}\ P(y) = C;\ \textbf{func}\ f = M_2\textbf{in}\ D]N \Rightarrow n}\ E(R, D, m) \tag{114}$$

$$\frac{\begin{matrix} R \Rightarrow_m (p, R') \quad (R', P) \Rightarrow_{mp} \textbf{lambda}\, x, y.C \\ M \Rightarrow m \quad [p/x][m/y][C]x \Rightarrow p' \quad [p'/R]_m N \Rightarrow n \end{matrix}}{[R.P(M)]N \Rightarrow n} \tag{115}$$

$$(R' \Rightarrow_m (p, T))$$
$$\vdots$$
$$\frac{\mathit{value}\ p \quad R \Rightarrow_m (\_, T) \qquad N' \Rightarrow n'}{[p/R]_m N \Rightarrow n}\ E(R, N, n) \tag{116}$$

$$\frac{R \Rightarrow_m (p, T) \quad (T, f) \Rightarrow_{mf} \textbf{lambda}\, x.M \quad [p/x]M \Rightarrow m}{R.f \Rightarrow m} \tag{117}$$

C Denotational semantics

C.1 Denotational semantics of $\mathcal{L}_P$

Semantic domains

$\mathbb{V} = (\mathbb{N} + \mathbb{T} + \mathbb{U} + \mathbb{P} + \mathbb{F})_\perp^\top$ $\quad\mathbb{P} = \mathbb{V} \times \mathbb{V}$
$\mathbb{N} = \mathit{Nat}$ (the domain of natural numbers) $\quad\mathbb{F} = \mathbb{V} \to \mathbb{V}$
$\mathbb{T} = \mathit{Truth}$ (the domain of truth values) $\quad\mathbb{E} = ((\mathit{Id} \to \mathbb{V}) \times (\mathit{ProcId} \to \mathbb{Q}))^\top$
$\mathbb{U} = \mathit{Unit}$ (the one-element domain) $\quad\mathbb{Q} = (\mathit{Id} \to \mathbb{V} \to \mathbb{E} \to \mathbb{E})^\top$

Operators

$$\begin{array}{lll}
\mathit{newenv} & = (\lambda x.\top, \lambda p.\top) & : \mathbb{E} \\
\mathit{update} & = \lambda x.\lambda n.\underline{\underline{\lambda}}(\rho_v, \rho_p).([x \mapsto n]\rho_v, \rho_p) & : \mathit{Id} \to \mathbb{V} \to \mathbb{E} \to \mathbb{E} \\
\mathit{access} & = \lambda x.\underline{\underline{\lambda}}(\rho_v, \rho_p).\rho_v(x) & : \mathit{Id} \to \mathbb{E} \to \mathbb{V} \\
\mathit{procupdate} & = \lambda p.\lambda q.\underline{\underline{\lambda}}(\rho_v, \rho_p).(\rho_v, [p \mapsto q]\rho_p) & : \mathit{ProcId} \to \mathbb{Q} \to \mathbb{E} \to \mathbb{E} \\
\mathit{procaccess} & = \lambda p.\underline{\underline{\lambda}}(\rho_v, \rho_p).\rho_p(p) & : \mathit{ProcId} \to \mathbb{E} \to \mathbb{Q} \\
\mathit{overlay} & = \underline{\underline{\lambda}}\rho_1.\underline{\underline{\lambda}}\rho_2.\lambda x.\textbf{if}\ \mathrm{is}\top(\rho_2(x)) \to \rho_1(x)\ [\!]\ \rho_2(x) & : \mathbb{E} \to \mathbb{E} \to \mathbb{E}
\end{array}$$

Semantic functions

$$\mathcal{E} : Expr \to \mathbb{E} \to \mathbb{V} \qquad \mathcal{D} : Declarations \to \mathbb{E} \to \mathbb{E}$$
$$\mathcal{C} : Commands \to \mathbb{E} \to \mathbb{E} \quad \mathcal{Q} : Procedures \to \mathbb{E} \to \mathbb{Q}$$

$$\mathcal{E}[\![x]\!] = \underline{\underline{\lambda}}\rho.access[\![x]\!]\rho \qquad \mathcal{E}[\![0]\!] = \underline{\underline{\lambda}}\rho.\text{in}\mathbb{N}(zero) \qquad \mathcal{E}[\![nil]\!] = \underline{\underline{\lambda}}\rho.\text{in}\mathbb{U}()$$

$$\mathcal{E}[\![true]\!] = \underline{\underline{\lambda}}\rho.\text{in}\mathbb{T}(true) \qquad \mathcal{E}[\![false]\!] = \underline{\underline{\lambda}}\rho.\text{in}\mathbb{T}(false)$$

$\mathcal{E}[\![\textbf{let } x = M \textbf{ in } N]\!] = \underline{\underline{\lambda}}\rho.\textbf{let } v = \mathcal{E}[\![M]\!]\rho \textbf{ in } \mathcal{E}[\![N]\!](update\ [\![x]\!]\ v\ \rho)$

$\mathcal{E}[\![\textbf{letrec } f(x) = M \textbf{ in } N]\!] = \underline{\underline{\lambda}}\rho.\textbf{let } g = fix(\underline{\underline{\lambda}}g.\underline{\underline{\lambda}}v.\mathcal{E}[\![M]\!](update\ [\![f]\!]\ g\ \rho)) \textbf{ in}$
$\qquad \mathcal{E}[\![N]\!](update\ [\![f]\!]\ g\ \rho)$

$\mathcal{E}[\![\textbf{lambda } x.M]\!] = \underline{\underline{\lambda}}\rho.\text{in}\mathbb{F}(\underline{\underline{\lambda}}v.\mathcal{E}[\![M]\!](update\ [\![x]\!]\ v\ \rho))$

$\mathcal{E}[\![M\ N]\!] = \underline{\underline{\lambda}}\rho.\textbf{cases } \mathcal{E}[\![M]\!]\rho \textbf{ of } \text{is}\mathbb{F}(f) \to f(\mathcal{E}[\![N]\!]\rho) [\!] \top \textbf{end}$

$\mathcal{E}[\![M :: N]\!] = \underline{\underline{\lambda}}\rho.\textbf{let } v_1 = \mathcal{E}[\![M]\!]\rho \textbf{ in let } v_2 = \mathcal{E}[\![N]\!]\rho \textbf{ in } \text{in}\mathbb{P}((v_1, v_2))$

$\mathcal{E}[\![[m/x]N]\!] = \underline{\underline{\lambda}}\rho.\textbf{let } v = \mathcal{E}[\![m]\!]\rho \textbf{ in } \mathcal{E}[\![N]\!](update\ [\![x]\!]\ v\ \rho)$

$\mathcal{E}[\![m \cdot n]\!] = \underline{\underline{\lambda}}\rho.\textbf{cases } \mathcal{E}[\![m]\!] \textbf{ of } \text{is}\mathbb{F}(f) \to f(\mathcal{E}[\![n]\!]\rho) [\!] \top \textbf{end}$

$\mathcal{E}[\![[\textbf{on } \bar{x} = \bar{M} \textbf{ do } C]N]\!] = \underline{\underline{\lambda}}\rho.\textbf{if } (maxfree\ [\![C]\!](\bar{x})) \to \mathcal{C}[\![C]\!](\mathcal{D}[\![\bar{x} = \bar{M}]\!]\rho) [\!] \top$

where $maxfree : Commands \to Id^* \to \mathbb{T}$; the meaning of "$maxfree\ [\![C]\!]\ s = true$" is simply "every free identifier of C is in s". *maxfree* is trivially defined on the syntactic structure of commands; we omit its definition.

$\mathcal{D}[\![\langle\rangle]\!] = \underline{\underline{\lambda}}\rho.newenv$

$\mathcal{D}[\![x = M; R]\!] = \underline{\underline{\lambda}}\rho.\textbf{let } v = \mathcal{E}[\![M]\!]\rho \textbf{ in}$
$\qquad \textbf{let } \tau = \mathcal{D}[\![R]\!](update\ [\![x]\!]\ v\ \rho) \textbf{ in}$
$\qquad\quad overlay\ \tau\ (update\ [\![x]\!]\ v\ newenv)$

$\mathcal{D}[\![[n/x]_d R]\!] = \underline{\underline{\lambda}}\rho.\textbf{let } v = \mathcal{E}[\![n]\!]\rho \textbf{ in } \mathcal{D}[\![R]\!](update\ [\![x]\!]\ v\ \rho)$

$\mathcal{C}[\![x := M]\!] = \underline{\underline{\lambda}}\rho.\textbf{let } v = \mathcal{E}[\![M]\!]\rho \textbf{ in } update\ [\![x]\!]\ v\ \rho$

$\mathcal{C}[\![\textbf{while } M \textbf{ do } C]\!] = fix(F)$

where $F : (\mathbb{E} \to \mathbb{E}) \to (\mathbb{E} \to \mathbb{E})$ $F = \underline{\lambda}f.\underline{\underline{\lambda}}\rho.\textbf{cases } \mathcal{E}[\![M]\!]\rho \textbf{ of}$
$\qquad \text{is}\mathbb{T}(t) \to \textbf{if } t \to f(\mathcal{C}[\![C]\!]\rho) [\!] \rho$
$\qquad [\!] \top$
$\qquad \textbf{end}$

$\mathcal{C}[\![\textbf{beginnew } x = M;\ C \textbf{ end}]\!] = \underline{\underline{\lambda}}\rho.\textbf{let } \rho' = update\ [\![x]\!]\ (\mathcal{E}[\![M]\!]\rho)\ \rho \textbf{ in}$
$\qquad \textbf{let } \rho'' = \mathcal{C}[\![C]\!]\rho' \textbf{ in}$
$\qquad\quad update\ [\![x]\!]\ (access\ [\![x]\!]\ \rho)\ \rho''$

$\mathcal{C}[\![\textbf{proc } P(x, y) = C \textbf{ in } D]\!] =$
$\underline{\underline{\lambda}}\rho.\textbf{let } \rho' = procupdate\ [\![P]\!]\ (\mathcal{Q}[\![\textbf{lambda } x, y.C]\!]\rho)\ \rho \textbf{ in}$
$\qquad \textbf{let } \rho'' = \mathcal{C}[\![D]\!]\rho' \textbf{ in}$
$\qquad\quad procupdate\ [\![P]\!]\ (procaccess\ [\![P]\!]\ \rho)\ \rho''$

$\mathcal{C}[\![P(x,M)]\!] = \underline{\underline{\lambda}}\rho.\textbf{let } v = \mathcal{E}[\![M]\!]\rho \textbf{ in } ((\mathit{procaccess}\ [\![P]\!]\ \rho)\ [\![x]\!]\ v\ \rho)$

$\mathcal{Q}[\![\textbf{lambda}\, x, y.C]\!] =$
$\underline{\underline{\lambda}}\rho.\textbf{if } \mathit{maxfree}\ [\![C]\!]\ ([\![x]\!], [\![y]\!])\mathit{emptysign})) \rightarrow$
$\quad \lambda i.\underline{\underline{\lambda}} v_y.\underline{\underline{\lambda}}\tau.\textbf{let } v_x = (\mathit{access}\ i\ \tau) \textbf{ in}$
$\quad\quad \textbf{let } \rho' = \mathcal{C}[\![C]\!](\mathit{update}\ [\![y]\!]\ v_y\ (\mathit{update}\ [\![x]\!]\ v_x\ \rho)) \textbf{ in}$
$\quad\quad\quad \mathit{update}\ i\ (\mathit{access}\ [\![x]\!]\ \rho')\ \tau$
$\quad [\!] \top$

$\mathcal{E}[\![[Q/P]_{pe}M]\!] = \underline{\underline{\lambda}}\rho.\mathcal{E}[\![M]\!](\mathit{procupdate}\ [\![P]\!]\ \mathcal{Q}[\![Q]\!]\rho\ \rho)$

C.2 Denotational semantics of $\mathcal{L}_D$

Semantic functions $\mathcal{O} : \mathit{SyntEnvir} \rightarrow \mathbb{E} \rightarrow \mathbb{E}$

$\mathcal{E}[\![\textbf{let } R \textbf{ in } N]\!] = \underline{\underline{\lambda}}\rho.\mathcal{E}[\![N]\!](\mathit{overlay}\ (\mathcal{D}[\![R]\!]\rho)\ \rho)$

$\mathcal{E}[\![\{r\}M]\!] = \underline{\underline{\lambda}}\rho.\mathcal{E}[\![M]\!](\mathcal{O}[\![r]\!]\rho) = \mathcal{E}[\![M]\!] \circ \mathcal{O}[\![r]\!]$

$\mathcal{D}[\![R \textbf{ and } S]\!] = \underline{\underline{\lambda}}\rho.\mathit{overlay}\ (\mathcal{D}[\![S]\!]\rho)\ (\mathcal{D}[\![R]\!]\rho)$

$\mathcal{O}[\![x \mapsto n]\!] = \underline{\underline{\lambda}}\rho.\mathit{update}\ (\mathcal{E}[\![n]\!]\rho)\ \rho$

$\mathcal{O}[\![r :: s]\!] = \mathcal{O}[\![s]\!] \circ \mathcal{O}[\![r]\!]$

C.3 Denotational semantics of $\mathcal{L}_{M_F}$

Semantic domains

$$\begin{array}{ll} \mathbb{V} = (\mathbb{N} + \mathbb{U} + \mathbb{P} + \mathbb{F} + \mathbb{B} + \mathbb{S})_\perp^\top & \mathbb{B} = \mathit{Id} \times \mathbb{V} \\ \mathbb{U} = \mathit{Unit} & \mathbb{S} = \mathit{Id}^* = \mathbb{ES} + \mathbb{CS} \\ \mathbb{P} = \mathbb{V} \times \mathbb{V} & \mathbb{ES} = \mathit{Unit} \\ \mathbb{F} = \mathbb{V} \rightarrow \mathbb{V} & \mathbb{CS} = \mathit{Id} \times \mathbb{S} \end{array}$$

Operators

$$\begin{array}{lll} \mathit{emptystruct} & = \mathrm{in}\mathbb{U}() & : \mathbb{V} \\ \mathit{consstruct} & = \lambda x.\underline{\underline{\lambda}} v.\underline{\underline{\lambda}} c.\mathrm{in}\mathbb{P}(\mathrm{in}\mathbb{B}([\![x]\!], v), c) & : \mathit{Id} \rightarrow \mathbb{V} \rightarrow \mathbb{V} \rightarrow \mathbb{V} \\ \mathit{emptysign} & = \mathrm{in}\mathbb{ES}() & : \mathbb{V} \\ \mathit{conssign} & = \lambda i.\lambda t.\mathrm{in}\mathbb{CS}((i,t)) & : \mathit{Id} \rightarrow \mathbb{S} \rightarrow \mathbb{S} \\ \mathit{accessstruct} & = \text{see below} & : \mathit{Id} \rightarrow \mathbb{V} \rightarrow \mathbb{V} \\ \mathit{applystruct} & = \text{see below} & : \mathbb{V} \rightarrow \mathbb{E} \rightarrow \mathbb{E} \\ \mathit{projection} & = \text{see below} & : \mathbb{V} \rightarrow \mathbb{S} \rightarrow \mathbb{V} \\ \mathit{longupdate} & = \text{see below} & : \mathit{LongId} \rightarrow \mathbb{V} \rightarrow \mathbb{E} \rightarrow \mathbb{E} \end{array}$$

$\mathit{projection} = \underline{\underline{\lambda}} s.\lambda t.\textbf{cases } t \textbf{ of}$
$\quad \mathrm{is}\mathbb{ES}() \rightarrow \mathrm{in}\mathbb{U}()$
$\quad [\!]\ \mathrm{is}\mathbb{CS}(i, t') \rightarrow$
$\quad\quad \textbf{let } v = \mathit{accessstruct}\ i\ s \textbf{ in}$
$\quad\quad\quad \textbf{let } s' = \mathit{projection}\ s\ t' \textbf{ in } \mathit{consstruct}\ i\ v\ s'$
$\quad \textbf{end}$

Semantic functions $\mathcal{E}[\![\textbf{struct end}]\!] = \underline{\underline{\lambda}}\rho.emptystruct$

$\mathcal{E}[\![x \mapsto n]\!] = \underline{\underline{\lambda}}\rho.\textbf{let } v = \mathcal{E}[\![n]\!]\rho \textbf{ in } \mathrm{in}\mathbb{B}([\![x]\!], v)$

$$\mathcal{E}[\![\textbf{struct } x = M\ B_{str}]\!] = \underline{\underline{\lambda}}\rho.\textbf{let } v_1 = \mathcal{E}[\![M]\!]\rho \textbf{ in}$$
$$\textbf{let } v_2 = \mathcal{E}[\![\textbf{struct } B_{str}]\!](update\ [\![x]\!]\ v_1\ \rho) \textbf{ in}$$
$$consstruct\ [\![x]\!]\ v_1\ v_2$$

$\mathcal{E}[\![\textbf{sig end}]\!] = \underline{\underline{\lambda}}\rho.\mathrm{in}\mathbb{S}(emptysign)$

$$\mathcal{E}[\![\textbf{sig } x\ B_{sig}]\!] = \underline{\underline{\lambda}}\rho.\textbf{cases } \mathcal{E}[\![\textbf{sig } B_{sig}]\!]\rho \textbf{ of}$$
$$\mathrm{is}\mathbb{S}(s) \to \mathrm{in}\mathbb{S}(conssig\ [\![x]\!]\ s)$$
$$[\!]\ \top$$
$$\textbf{end}$$

$$\mathcal{E}[\![M : N]\!] = \underline{\underline{\lambda}}\rho.\textbf{let } s = \mathcal{E}[\![M]\!]\rho \textbf{ in}$$
$$\textbf{cases } \mathcal{E}[\![N]\!]\rho \textbf{ of}$$
$$\mathrm{is}\mathbb{S}(t) \to projection\ s\ t$$
$$[\!]\ \top$$
$$\textbf{end}$$

$\mathcal{E}[\![\textbf{open } u \textbf{ in } M]\!] = \underline{\underline{\lambda}}\rho.\textbf{let } s = \mathcal{E}[\![u]\!]\rho \textbf{ in } \mathcal{E}[\![M]\!](applystruct\ s\ \rho)$

$\mathcal{E}[\![u.x]\!] = \underline{\underline{\lambda}}\rho.accessstruct\ [\![x]\!]\ (\mathcal{E}[\![u]\!]\rho)$

C.4 Denotational semantics of $\mathcal{L}_{M_I}$

Semantic domains

$$\begin{aligned} \mathbb{E} &= (\mathbb{IM} \times \mathbb{PM} \times \mathbb{MM})^\top & \mathbb{MM} &= ModId \to \mathbb{M} \\ \mathbb{IM} &= Id \to \mathbb{V} & \mathbb{M} &= (\mathbb{V} \times \mathbb{Q}_M \times \mathbb{F}_M)^\top \\ \mathbb{PM} &= ProcId \to \mathbb{Q} & \mathbb{Q}_M &= \mathbb{V} \to \mathbb{V} \to \mathbb{V} \\ \mathbb{Q} &= (Id \to \mathbb{V} \to \mathbb{E} \to \mathbb{E})^\top & \mathbb{F}_M &= \mathbb{V} \to \mathbb{V} = \mathbb{F} \end{aligned}$$

Operators

$$\begin{aligned} newenv &= (\lambda x.\top, \lambda p.\top, \lambda r.\top) &&: \mathbb{E} \\ update &= \lambda x.\lambda n.\underline{\underline{\lambda}}(\rho_v, \rho_p, \rho_m).([x \mapsto n]\rho_v, \rho_p, \rho_m) &&: Id \to \mathbb{V} \to \mathbb{E} \to \mathbb{E} \\ access &= \lambda x.\underline{\underline{\lambda}}(\rho_v, \rho_p, \rho_m).\rho_v(x) &&: Id \to \mathbb{E} \to \mathbb{V} \\ procupdate &= \lambda p.\lambda q.\underline{\underline{\lambda}}(\rho_v, \rho_p, \rho_m).(\rho_v, [p \mapsto q]\rho_p, \rho_m) &&: ProcId \to \mathbb{Q} \to \mathbb{E} \to \mathbb{E} \\ procaccess &= \lambda p.\underline{\underline{\lambda}}(\rho_v, \rho_p, \rho_m).\rho_p(p) &&: ProcId \to \mathbb{E} \to \mathbb{Q} \\ modupdate &= \lambda r.\lambda q.\underline{\underline{\lambda}}(\rho_v, \rho_p, \rho_m).(\rho_v, \rho_p, [r \mapsto m]\rho_m) &&: ProcId \to \mathbb{Q} \to \mathbb{E} \to \mathbb{E} \\ modaccess &= \lambda r.\underline{\underline{\lambda}}(\rho_v, \rho_p, \rho_m).\rho_m(r) &&: ProcId \to \mathbb{E} \to \mathbb{Q} \end{aligned}$$

Semantic functions

$\mathcal{C}[\![\textbf{module } R \textbf{ is } x = M;\ \textbf{proc } P(y) = C;\ \textbf{func } f = N \textbf{ in } D]\!] =$

$\underline{\underline{\lambda}}\rho.\textbf{if } maxfree\ [\![C]\!]\ (conssign\ [\![x]\!]\ (conssign\ [\![y]\!] emptysign)) \to$

$\quad \textbf{if } maxfree\ [\![N]\!]\ (conssign\ [\![x]\!]\ emptysign) \to$

$$
\begin{array}{l}
\textbf{let } m = \mathcal{E}[\![M]\!]\rho \textbf{ in} \\
\quad \textbf{let } q = \underline{\underline{\lambda}} v_x.\underline{\underline{\lambda}} v_y.\mathit{access}\ [\![x]\!]\ \mathcal{C}[\![C]\!](\mathit{update}\ [\![y]\!]\ v_y\ (\mathit{update}\ [\![x]\!]\ v_x\ \rho)) \textbf{ in} \\
\quad\quad \textbf{let } g = \underline{\underline{\lambda}} v_x.\mathcal{E}[\![N]\!](\mathit{update}\ [\![x]\!]\ v_x\ \rho) \textbf{ in} \\
\quad\quad\quad \textbf{let } \rho' = \mathit{modupdate}\ [\![R]\!]\ (m, q, g)\ \rho \textbf{ in} \\
\quad\quad\quad\quad \mathit{modupdate}\ [\![R]\!]\ (\mathit{modaccess}\ [\![R]\!]\ \rho)\ \mathcal{C}[\![D]\!]\rho'
\end{array}
$$

$$[\!]\ \top$$

$$[\!]\ \top$$

$$
\begin{array}{l}
\mathcal{C}[\![R.P(M)]\!] = \underline{\underline{\lambda}}\rho.\textbf{let } (n, q, g) = \mathit{modaccess}\ [\![R]\!]\ \rho \textbf{ in} \\
\qquad\qquad\qquad \textbf{let } n' = q\ n\ (\mathcal{E}[\![M]\!]\rho) \textbf{ in} \\
\qquad\qquad\qquad\quad \mathit{modupdate}\ [\![R]\!]\ (n', q, g)\ \rho
\end{array}
$$

$$\mathcal{E}[\![R.f]\!] = \underline{\underline{\lambda}}\rho.\textbf{let } (n, q, g) = \mathit{modaccess}\ [\![R]\!]\ \rho \textbf{ in } (g\ n)$$

$$
\begin{array}{l}
\mathcal{E}[\![[n/R]_m M]\!] = \underline{\underline{\lambda}}\rho.\textbf{let } (\_, q, g) = \mathit{modaccess}\ [\![R]\!]\ \rho \textbf{ in} \\
\qquad\qquad \textbf{let } m' = \mathcal{E}[\![n]\!]\rho \textbf{ in } \mathcal{E}[\![M]\!](\mathit{modupdate}\ [\![R]\!]\ (m', q, g)\ \rho)
\end{array}
$$

Acknowledgments

Many of the ideas in this paper were first presented in [15]. I am most grateful to Furio Honsell for his invaluable and patient support and for directing my thesis work. I wish to acknowledge Randy Pollack and Frank Pfenning for several useful discussions and for making accessible via `ftp` the LEGO and Elf systems respectively. I would like to thank also the anonymous referees for the useful comments on the earlier version of this paper.

References

1. H. Abelson and G. J. Sussman. *Structure and Interpretation of Computer Programs.* The MIT Electrical Engineering and Computer Science Series. MIT Press, Cambridge, Massachusetts, 1985.
2. A. Avron. Simple consequence relations. *Information and Computation*, 92:105–139, Jan. 1991.
3. A. Avron, F. Honsell, I. A. Mason, and R. Pollack. Using Typed Lambda Calculus to implement formal systems on a machine. *Journal of Automated Reasoning*, 9:309–354, 1992.
4. R. Burstall and F. Honsell. Operational semantics in a natural deduction setting. In G. Huet and G. Plotkin, editors, *Logical Frameworks*, pages 185–214. Cambridge University Press, June 1990.
5. A. Church. A formulation of the simple theory of types. *Journal of Symbolic Logic*, 5:56–68, 1940.
6. J. Despeyroux. Proof of translation in natural semantics. In *Proceedings of the First Conference on Logic in Computer Science*, pages 193–205. The Association for Computing Machinery, 1986.
7. J. E. Donahue. Locations considered unnecessary. *Acta Informatica*, 8:221–242, July 1977.

8. G. Gentzen. Investigations into logical deduction. In M. Szabo, editor, *The collected papers of Gerhard Gentzen*, pages 68–131. North Holland, 1969.
9. J. J. Hannan. Proof-theoretical methods for analysis of functional programs. Technical Report MS–CIS–89–07, Dep. of Computer and Information Science, University of Pennsylvania, Dec. 1988.
10. J. J. Hannan and F. Pfenning. Compiler verification in LF. In *Seventh Annual IEEE Symposium on Logic in Computer Science*, pages 407–418, Santa Cruz, California, June 1992. IEEE Computer Society Press.
11. R. Harper, F. Honsell, and G. Plotkin. A framework for defining logics. *Journal of the ACM*, 40(1):143–184, Jan. 1993.
12. G. Kahn. Natural Semantics. In *Proceedings of the Symposium on Theoretical Aspects of Computer Science*, number 247 in Lecture Notes in Computer Science, pages 22–39. Springer-Verlag, 1987.
13. Z. Luo, R. Pollack, and P. Taylor. *How to use LEGO (A Preliminary User's Manual).* Department of Computer Science, University of Edinburgh, Oct. 1989.
14. S. Michaylov and F. Pfenning. Natural Semantics and some of its Meta-Theory in Elf. In L.-H. Eriksson, L. Hallnäs, and P. Schroeder-Heister, editors, *Proceedings of the Second International Workshop on Extensions of Logic Programming*, number 596 in LNAI, pages 299–344, Stockolm, Sweden, Jan. 1991. Springer-Verlag.
15. M. Miculan. Semantica operazionale strutturata ad ambienti distribuiti – teoria e sperimentazione. Undergraduate thesis, Università di Udine, Udine, Italy, July 1992. In italian.
16. R. Milner, M. Tofte, and R. Harper. *The Definition of Standard ML.* MIT Press, Cambridge, Massachusetts, 1990.
17. E. Moggi. Notions of computation and monads. *Information and Computation*, 1, 1993.
18. J. H. Morris, Jr. Types are not sets. In *Conference Record of the ACM Symposium on Principles of Programming Languages*, pages 120–124, Boston, Oct. 1973. The Association for Computing Machinery.
19. B. Nordström, K. Petersson, and J. M. Smith. *Programming in Martin-Löf's Type Theory: An Introduction*, volume 7 of *International Series of Monograph on Computer Science.* Oxford University Press, 1990.
20. F. Pfenning. Elf: A language for logic definition and verified metaprogramming. In *Fourth Annual Symposium on Logic in Computer Science*, pages 313–322. IEEE, June 1989. Also available as ERGO Report 89–067, School of Computer Science, Carnegie Mellon Univ., Pittsburgh.
21. G. D. Plotkin. A structural approach to operational semantics. DAIMI FN-19, Computer Science Department, Århus University, Århus, Denmark, Sept. 1981.
22. G. D. Plotkin. Notes about semantics. Unpublished notes given at CSLI, Stanford, Aug. 1985.
23. D. A. Schmidt. *Denotational Semantics.* Allyn & Bacon, 1986.
24. A. K. Wright and M. Felleisen. A syntactic approach to type soundness. Technical Report TR91–160, rev.2, Department of Computer Science, Rice University, Houston, Texas, 1991.

Developing Certified Programs in the System Coq
The Program Tactic

C. Parent *

LIP, URA CNRS 1398, ENS Lyon
46 Allée d'Italie, 69364 Lyon cedex 07, France
e-mail : parent@lip.ens-lyon.fr

Abstract. The system *Coq* is an environment for proof development based on the Calculus of Constructions extended by inductive definitions. The specification of a program can be represented by a logical formula and the program itself can be extracted from the constructive proof of the specification. In this paper, we look at the possibility of inverting the extraction process. More precisely, we present a method which, given a specification and a program, builds the logical conditions to be verified in order to obtain a correctness proof of the program. We build a proof of the specification from the program from which the program can be extracted. Since some information cannot automatically be inferred, we show how to annotate the program by specifying some of its parts in order to guide the search for the proof.

1 Introduction

In this paper, we focus on the general problem of proving program correctness. Type theory is a particular framework for program development. Indeed, there is a constructive interpretation of proofs, i.e. proving a formula implies explicitly constructing a typed λ-term. This suggests a uniform framework for representing formulas, proofs and programs. Via the Curry-Howard isomorphism [How80], the notion of proofs and programs and the notion of types and specifications can be identified. To have a correct program in such a formalism, a proof of a logical formula $\forall x.P(x) \Rightarrow \exists y.Q(x,y)$ (called the specification) has to be derived. This follows Heyting's semantics of constructive proofs : a proof of $\forall x.P(x) \Rightarrow \exists y.Q(x,y)$ gives a method to transform an object i and a proof of $P(i)$ into an object o and a proof of $Q(i,o)$. In some cases, the specification (essentially the pre- and post-conditions P and Q) and the program p are naturally given. A first idea is to prove $\forall x.P(x) \Rightarrow Q(x,(p\ x))$. But, this is in general laborious and implies reasoning about the executions of p. We propose here a method which justifies p by building a proof of $\forall x.P(x) \Rightarrow \exists y.Q(x,y)$ from which p can be extracted. The program p is obtained by extraction from the proof by forgetting

* This research was partly supported by ESPRIT Basic Research Action "Types for Proofs and Programs" and by Programme de Recherche Coordonnées and CNRS Groupement de Recherche "Programmation".

everything concerning the logical correctness of the program, in particular proofs of logical assertions and intermediate properties of sub-programs. Our method of building a proof from a program will necessary leave "holes" i.e. logical properties that will have to be satisfied to ensure the correctness of the program. That is why we will introduce a language of annotated programs to guide the method by indicating the specification of sub-programs.

The system *Coq* is an implementation of a particular type theory called the Calculus of Constructions enhanced with inductive definitions [PM93, DFH+93]. As we explained earlier, proofs of specifications can be developed and programs can be extracted from these proofs [PM89b]. The extraction in *Coq* is based on a realizability notion [PM89a]. Realizability is an interpretation of the computational content of intuitionistic proofs as programs satisfying a given specification. Such a program is called a *realization* of the specification. Realizability allows to eliminate non computational parts of proofs, including dependent types, and to extract correct programs from proofs. Some other systems like PX and NuPrl offer similar possibilities of extraction [HN88, Con86]. Both of them use untyped theories. More precisely, PX uses an untyped theory and, in NuPrl, the theory is typed but the extracted terms are untyped. PX uses a notion of proofs-as-programs which is not Curry-Howard but there are two different levels (0 for proofs and 1 for programs). Then, a process of extraction is defined using a special notion of realizability called the *px*-realizability. A difference between the realizability used for the *Coq* extraction and the px-realizability is that the px-realizers are allowed not to terminate. In NuPrl, there is no distinction between proofs and programs. A process of extraction can be expressed : redundant information can be hidden using the fact that if a is of type $\{x : A|P\ x\}$ then a is also of type A, but a consequence of this is that typing becomes undecidable.

Coq is thus a good framework for our method of building proofs from programs. The plan of our presentation will be in a first section to briefly present the Pure Calculus of Constructions. In a second section, we show an example of proof development in *Coq* to focus on what we are looking for. In a third section, we present the extraction mechanism and deduce from this our method. In a fourth section, we add inductive types. In a fifth section, we discuss some optimizations and then conclude.

2 The Pure Calculus of Constructions

We present here the Pure Calculus of Constructions and not the Calculus of Constructions with Inductive Definitions because it is simpler. It appears that, for our method, the adjunction of inductive types is neither a difficulty nor the central problem. We will just briefly talk about inductive definitions in a later section.

The Calculus of Constructions is a typed lambda-calculus. Thus, it is a language of terms and types where terms can be seen as representing proofs or programs and types as representing specifications or data types.

Types can be defined by their arity. For example, the type of natural numbers can be defined as **nat:Set**. Objects on these types can be defined. For example, the successor function can be defined as **S:nat->nat**. Then, predicates on these objects can be defined. For example, the predicate less-or-equal can be defined as **le:nat->nat->Prop** and if **n:nat** then **(le n n):Prop**. Now, predicates and objects can be mixed in specifications. For example, **{n:nat|(le n (S O))}:Set** is a specification to express $\exists n.(n \leq 1)$. A proof of such a specification is inhabited by a pair consisting of a natural number and a proof that this natural number satisfies the specification. For example, a proof can be the pair **(O,(le O (S O)))**.

We saw two different arities **Set** and **Prop**. The basic difference between **Set** and **Prop** is their meaning : both of them are used to mark terms (since they are types), but the first one indicates that the term has a computational content and the second that the term has no computational content. These marks on terms allow the extraction to treat differently computational terms and non computational terms and to forget all the non computational ones.

We can now explain the different possible formations for terms and types[2]. First, terms are variables or constants (both can be first-order or higher-order), abstractions (on any order variables) or applications (for example, instantiations of predicates). For instance, **x=4** is an instantiation of the predicate **[y:nat](x=y)** with the constant **4**.

[x:A]B	Abstraction of **B** w.r.t. **x** of type **A** (usually noted $\lambda x^A B$)
(A B)	Application of **A** to **B**
(x:A)B	Product of **B** w.r.t. **x** of type **A** (usually noted $\forall x : A.B$)
A → B	Type of functions from **A** to **B** (≡ **(x:A)B** when **x** not in **B**)
Prop	Type of propositions
Set	Type of specifications and data types

Second, types are propositional variables, products on types (dependent or not) or applications. One can quantify over predicates. For instance, the expression **(P:nat→Set)(P O)→((n:nat)(P n)→(P (S n)))→(n:nat)(P n)** is a case
of quantification over predicates. One can instantiate **P** with **[n:nat](n≥O)** and obtain the expression **(O≥O)→((n:nat)(n≥O)→((S n)≥O))→(n:nat)(n≥O)**.

This defines a typed λ-calculus usually called λC, which is the highest point in Barendregt's cube [Bar91], and includes polymorphism, higher order and dependent types. *Coq* is a system which implements this calculus and in the next section, we present a simple example of development in this system.

3 An example of development in *Coq*

Let us consider the division algorithm as an example of a development in *Coq*. A division program would take two arguments a and b and give as outputs q

[2] The notations are given in the following.

and r such that they satisfy $a = b * q + r \wedge b > r$. But, a necessary condition is that $b > 0$, otherwise the condition on r cannot be satisfied. So, a specification of a division algorithm should be :

$$\forall b. b > 0 \Rightarrow \forall a. \exists q. \exists r. (a = b * q + r \wedge b > r) \quad (1)$$

Every constructive proof of such a specification gives an algorithm by extraction [PMW92]. If one gives a program, one gets the existence of such an algorithm and one has a skeleton of a possible proof. This skeleton allows to do the computational parts of the proof (i.e. to solve specifications). If the remaining logical assertions can be solved, such as proving loop invariants are preserved, then the initial program can be certified correct with respect to the initial specification.

An ML program corresponding to a naive algorithm for our example could be :

```
let div b a = divrec a where rec divrec = function
    0 -> (0,0)
  | Sn -> let (q,r) = divrec n in
            if (Sr<b) then (q,Sr) else (Sq,0) ;;
```

Let us do a mathematical proof of our specification and see the link with the ML program.

One wants to prove $\forall b. b > 0 \Rightarrow \forall a. \exists q. \exists r. (a = b * q + r \wedge b > r)$. Given b, $b > 0$, one wants to prove $\forall a. \exists q. \exists r. (a = b*q+r \wedge b > r)$. Let us do an induction on a.

First case : $a = 0$. Then, one needs to prove $\exists q. \exists r. (0 = b * q + r \wedge b > r)$. The values $q = 0$ and $r = 0$ are good candidates since $0 = b * 0 + 0 \wedge b > 0$.

Second case : one assumes $\exists q. \exists r. (n = b*q+r \wedge b > r)$ for a given n, and one wants to prove $\exists q. \exists r. (Sn = b * q + r \wedge b > r)$. Given q and r from the induction hypothesis, let us look for q' and r' such that $(Sn = b * q' + r' \wedge b > r')$. Two subcases : if $Sr < b$ then let us take $q' = q$ and $r' = Sr$. Then, one has to prove $(Sn = b * q + Sr \wedge b > r)$. But, $b > Sr$ by hypothesis and one knows by the induction hypothesis that $n = b * q + r$. So, this case is solved. If $Sr \geq b$ then let us take $q' = Sq$ and $r' = 0$. Then, one has to prove $(Sn = b * q + b \wedge b > 0)$. The second part of the conjunction is trivial. For the first one, one knows $b > r$ and $Sr \geq b$, so one can conclude $b = Sr$. And the second case is solved.

Remark that the structure of the proof is closely related to the structure of the program : induction on a, recursive call on n in the second case of the induction ....

Let us now see how this proof can be developed in *Coq* and how a program can be extracted. Then, the link between proofs and programs will appear once more. First, *Coq* allows the interactive development of proofs. One gives a specification as above (1) and then one can use predefined tactics to develop a proof. The reasoning follows a natural deduction style. There are introduction and elimination tactics and resolution tactics. All the steps of the mathematical proof can be expressed with these tactics : the introductions by `Intro`, the inductions by **Elim**, the introductions of the existential quantifiers by **Exists**... The proof of our example can then be expressed only using **Intro**, **Elim** and **Exists** and is developed in figure 1 (comments are expressed between (* and *)).

```
Intros b H a.                 (* H : b>0 *)
Elim a.
Exists 0. Exists 0.           (* b>0 and 0=b*0+0 *)
Auto.
Intros n H0.                  (* H0 : induction hypothesis *)
Elim H0.                      (* getting back q *)
Intros q H1.
Elim H1.                      (* getting back r *)
Intros r H2.
Elim (inf b (S r)).           (* deciding of the order of b and Sr *)
Intros Le.                    (* Le : b<=Sr *)
Exists (S q). Exists 0. (* easy to resolve : b>0 and Sn=b*(Sq)+0 *)
Intros Gt.                    (* Gt : b>Sr *)
Exists q. Exists (S r). (* easy to resolve : b>Sr and Sn=b*q+Sr *)
```

Fig. 1. A proof example in *Coq*

This proof is close to the mathematical one in the sense that one can retrieve the same steps of introductions, inductions .... Moreover, if one extracts the computational part from this *Coq* proof, one gets the program above. Our aim is now to take this program and to retrieve the computational parts of its corresponding proof leaving to the user logical properties to prove to ensure the correctness of the program.

4 Extraction and inversion of extraction

Let us first recall how proofs and programs are represented in *Coq*. Proofs are typed λ-terms marked with information on their computational contents (i.e. **Set** for informative terms or **Prop** for logical terms). A *Coq* formula P can be represented by a judgment $\Gamma \vdash P : A$ where A can be **Set** or **Prop** (for first order), **TypeSet** or **Type** (for higher order). A *Coq* proof t of a specification P can be represented by a judgment $\Gamma \vdash t : P$.

The extraction is a function from proof terms to program terms which consists in forgetting from a proof term all the logical parts to obtain a program term, i.e. a typed λ-term with only informative parts. The extraction function is a forgetful function. There is an extraction at the level of terms and at the level of types. Both of these aspects forget the logical parts, but it is perhaps not so clear at the level of types. For example, one can have a type of lists of given length (for the proof point of view). This type is extracted into the type of lists (for the program point of view). The information related to the length is lost.

To present the extraction, we introduce a new judgment $\Gamma \vdash t \rightarrow p : P$ when P : `Set` whose interpretation is in Γ, t is a proof of P and p can be extracted from t.

Though there is an extraction on types and on proof terms, we focus on the extraction on proof terms. Our rules of extraction[3] are thus directed by the syntax of proofs. A type is noted `L` when it is a logical - non-computational - type and `I` when it is an informative - computational - type.

$$\frac{x : A \in \Gamma}{\Gamma \vdash x \rightarrow x \ : \ A}$$

$$\frac{\Gamma, x : L \vdash t \rightarrow p \ : \ B(x)}{\Gamma \vdash [x : L]t \rightarrow p \ : \ (x : L)B(x)}$$

$$\frac{\Gamma, x : I \vdash t \rightarrow p \ : \ B(x)}{\Gamma \vdash [x : I]t \rightarrow [x : \mathcal{E}(I)]p \ : \ (x : I)B(x)}$$

$$\frac{\Gamma \vdash t \rightarrow p \ : \ (x : I)B(x) \quad \Gamma \vdash u \rightarrow q \ : I}{\Gamma \vdash (t\ u) \rightarrow (p\ q) \ : \ B(u)} \quad (\Gamma \vdash I : Set)$$

$$\frac{\Gamma \vdash t \rightarrow p \ : \ (x : I)B(x) \quad \Gamma \vdash P \ : \ I}{\Gamma \vdash (t\ P) \rightarrow (p\ \mathcal{E}(P)) \ : \ B(P)} \quad (\Gamma \vdash I : TypeSet^4)$$

$$\frac{\Gamma \vdash t \rightarrow p \ : \ (x : L)B(x) \quad \Gamma \vdash u \ : \ L}{\Gamma \vdash (t\ u) \rightarrow p \ : \ B(u)} \quad (\Gamma \vdash L : Prop \ or \ \Gamma \vdash L : Type)$$

It appears clearly that the extraction is directed by the structure of proof terms and that terms are disappearing from proof terms to program terms. Higher order predicates are "lost", in the sense that only their informative parts are kept. For example, the predicate $\exists n : nat.(n \ is \ odd)$ is extracted into nat. If it is easy to go from the first to the second, it seems hard to retrieve the first from the second.

Since we want to generate proofs from programs, since higher order predicates are essential for the proof, and since they disappear in program terms, we are going to modify the extraction a little bit, and more precisely the rule about higher order predicates. We modify it into the following one.

$$\frac{\Gamma \vdash t \rightarrow p \ : \ (x : I)B(x) \quad \Gamma \vdash P \ : \ I}{\Gamma \vdash (t\ P) \rightarrow (p\ \{P\}) \ : \ B(P)} \quad (\Gamma \vdash I : TypeSet)$$

[3] The extraction function is denoted by the symbol $\mathcal{E}$.

[4] $P : I : TypeSet$ means P is a higher order informative predicate.

This allows to keep at the level of program terms (in comments) ALL the information about higher order predicates. Now, since we want to generate proofs from programs, we have to transform these rules such that they were directed by the syntax of program terms.

We just want here to mention a trivial case which is the case of **coarse programs**.

Definition 1. A program p is coarse with respect to a specification S if its type is exactly this specification, i.e. if $\texttt{p:S}$ $(\equiv \mathcal{E}(\texttt{S}))$.

These are pointed out because they are very simple cases since they exactly correspond to the proof term.

In the following, we are going to give a new set of inference rules for a new judgment denoted by $\rightsquigarrow$. This set is supposed to be more deterministic, i.e. it will be directed by the syntax of program terms. For a judgment $\Gamma \vdash t' \rightsquigarrow p : S'$, if p is given it will be in general possible to infer t' and S' complete enough in the sense that if $\Gamma \vdash t \rightarrow p : S$ then t and t', and S and S' will be "equivalent" in a sense defined later.

Now, we can give the following rules[5] directed by the syntax of program terms with a new type of judgment denoted by $\rightsquigarrow$.

$$\frac{\boldsymbol{x} : A \in \Gamma}{\Gamma \vdash \boldsymbol{x} \rightsquigarrow \boldsymbol{x} \ : \ A}$$

$$\frac{\Gamma, \boldsymbol{y} : \boldsymbol{L}, \boldsymbol{x} : A \vdash t \rightsquigarrow p \ : \ B(\boldsymbol{y}, \boldsymbol{x})}{\Gamma \vdash [\boldsymbol{y} : \boldsymbol{L}][\boldsymbol{x} : A]t \rightsquigarrow [\boldsymbol{x} : \mathcal{E}(A)]p \ : \ (\boldsymbol{y} : \boldsymbol{L})(\boldsymbol{x} : A)B(\boldsymbol{y}, \boldsymbol{x})}$$

$$\frac{\Gamma \vdash t \rightsquigarrow p \ : \ (\boldsymbol{y} : \boldsymbol{L})(\boldsymbol{x} : A(\boldsymbol{y}))B(\boldsymbol{x}, \boldsymbol{y}) \quad \Gamma \vdash \boldsymbol{l} : \boldsymbol{L} \quad \Gamma \vdash u \rightarrow q \ : \ A(\boldsymbol{l})}{\Gamma \vdash (t\ \boldsymbol{l}\ u) \rightsquigarrow (p\ q) \ : \ B(u, \boldsymbol{l})}$$

$$\frac{\Gamma \vdash t \rightsquigarrow p \ : \ (\boldsymbol{y} : \boldsymbol{L})(\boldsymbol{x} : A(\boldsymbol{y}))B(\boldsymbol{x}, \boldsymbol{y}) \quad \Gamma \vdash \boldsymbol{l} : \boldsymbol{L} \quad \Gamma \vdash P \ : \ A(\boldsymbol{l})}{\Gamma \vdash (t\ \boldsymbol{l}\ P) \rightsquigarrow (p\ \{P\}) \ : \ B(P, \boldsymbol{l})}$$

Definition 2. A term t is logically more general than a term t', noted $t \succ_T t'$, iff $\exists \boldsymbol{x} : \boldsymbol{L}.\exists \boldsymbol{l}$ s.t. $t = [\boldsymbol{x} : \boldsymbol{L}](t'\ \boldsymbol{l})$.

Definition 3. A specification S is logically more general than a specification S', noted $S \succ_S S'$, iff $\exists \boldsymbol{x} : \boldsymbol{L}.\exists \boldsymbol{l}$ s.t. $S = (\boldsymbol{x} : \boldsymbol{L})S'(\boldsymbol{l})$.

Theorem 1 *If $\Gamma \vdash t \rightarrow p : S$ then $\exists t'.\exists S'$ s.t. $\Gamma \vdash t' \rightsquigarrow p : S'$ with $t \succ_T t'$ and $S \succ_S S'$.*

Proof. Proof by induction on the derivation of $\rightarrow$.

[5] We use a vectorial notation $(\boldsymbol{y} : \boldsymbol{L})$ for a list of variables $(y_1 : L_1) \ldots (y_n : L_n)$.

The new set of inference rules corresponds to a system where, from a program containing all the information on higher order predicates, a specification and a proof can be inferred. The theorem allows to prove that each proof having the same extracted program (annotated with all the information on higher order predicates) can be deduced from the inferred proof.

Practically, this means that if a user gives a program , then a specification S' and a proof t' can be inferred. Then, the initial specification S is logically more general than S' and $S = (\boldsymbol{x} : \boldsymbol{L})S'(\boldsymbol{l})$. To obtain the searched proof, $\boldsymbol{x}$ and $\boldsymbol{l}$ are needed. The $\boldsymbol{x}$ are known and the problem is to retrieve the $\boldsymbol{l}$. It can be resolved by unification : there are rigid constraints only on logical variables and it is easy.

The problem is now to know if these rules are deterministic from the program point of view. Let us see the four cases separately, each one illustrated with an example. The case of variables is trivial and we do not say anything about it.

4.1 λ-abstractions

We give once more the corresponding rule.

$$\frac{\Gamma, \boldsymbol{y} : \boldsymbol{L}, x : A \vdash t \rightsquigarrow p \ : \ B(\boldsymbol{y}, x)}{\Gamma \vdash [\boldsymbol{y} : \boldsymbol{L}][x : A]t \rightsquigarrow [x : \mathcal{E}(A)]p \ : \ (\boldsymbol{y} : \boldsymbol{L})(x : A)B(\boldsymbol{y}, x)}$$

As one knows the correspondence between the program `p` and the specification `S`, one knows that if the program is a λ-abstraction `[x:`$\mathcal{E}$`(A)]p` then the specification is a product `(`$\boldsymbol{y}$`:`$\boldsymbol{L}$`)(x:A)B(`$\boldsymbol{y}$`,x)`. These logical products in the specification correspond to logical λ-abstractions in the proof terms. These λ-abstractions can thus all be retrieve from the specification in a deterministic way.

Practically, logical introductions not indicated in the program have to be done at the proof level. The method consists in this case in doing as many introductions as they are non-informative products in the specification and then one last introduction.

Let us consider the problem on an example. Consider the previous division algorithm written in the *Coq* syntax[6] :

```
[b:nat][a:nat]
  <nat*nat>Match a with
    (* O *) <nat,nat>(O,O)
    (* S *) [n:nat][H:nat*nat]
             <nat*nat>let (q,r:nat) = H in
                 <nat*nat> if (inf b (S r)) then
                                <nat,nat>((S q),O)
                           else <nat,nat>(q,(S r)).
```

[6] The notation <P>Match x with is the case analysis.

whose specification is $\forall b.b > 0 \Rightarrow \forall a.\exists q.\exists r.(a = b * q + r \ \wedge \ b > r)$. Since the program is a λ-abstraction, this suggests to introduce the b and then generate a new specification $b > 0 \Rightarrow \forall a.\exists q.\exists r.(a = b * q + r \ \wedge \ b > r)$ for the program `[a:nat]`.... Now, to mimic the program, one would like to introduce the symbol a. But this introduction cannot be performed as the specification has not the shape $\forall a.\exists q.\exists r.(a = b * q + r \ \wedge \ b > r)$ but the shape $b > 0 \Rightarrow \forall a.\exists q.\exists r.(a = b*q+r \wedge b > r)$. In such a situation, one has to introduce the non-computational hypothesis $(b > 0)$ before the computational variable a.

4.2 Applications

There are two rules corresponding to the application of a program to a program or to a type.

$$\frac{\Gamma \vdash t \rightsquigarrow p \ : \ (\boldsymbol{y} : \boldsymbol{L})(x : A(\boldsymbol{y}))B(x, \boldsymbol{y}) \quad \Gamma \vdash \boldsymbol{l} : \boldsymbol{L} \quad \Gamma \vdash u \rightarrow q \ : \ A(\boldsymbol{l})}{\Gamma \vdash (t \ \boldsymbol{l} \ u) \rightsquigarrow (p \ q) \ : \ B(u, \boldsymbol{l})}$$

$$\frac{\Gamma \vdash t \rightsquigarrow p \ : \ (\boldsymbol{y} : \boldsymbol{L})(x : A(\boldsymbol{y}))B(x, \boldsymbol{y}) \quad \Gamma \vdash \boldsymbol{l} : \boldsymbol{L} \quad \Gamma \vdash P \ : \ A(\boldsymbol{l})}{\Gamma \vdash (t \ \boldsymbol{l} \ P) \rightsquigarrow (p \ \{P\}) \ : \ B(P, \boldsymbol{l})}$$

If the program is $(p \ q)$ then there are two cases : the argument is a higher order predicate (between comments) or not.

The first case is easy. Indeed, the problem is to find the higher order predicate and it is given in comments in the program. There is thus no problem.

The second case is harder. If one supposes the specification of p is known, then the problem is to retrieve the specification of q. With the given rules it is not possible because we do not want to be directed by the syntax of the proof term but rather by the syntax of the program term. One strategy is to look for a specification S of q with the inference rules of $\rightsquigarrow$. But, the specification S is then surely not the right one but an equivalent one in the sense of equivalence on specifications $(A(\boldsymbol{l}) = (\boldsymbol{x} : \boldsymbol{L}')(S \ \boldsymbol{l}'))$. Moreover, this implies to unify S with $A(\boldsymbol{x})$ and this is not deterministic.

In practice, this is what is done. In many practical cases, the unification gives a solution (by using heuristics). If this fails, then our method fails.

Thus, we have a method to retrieve proofs from programs which is deterministic (modulo some heuristics on unification) and complete since it inverts the extraction process. But, we suppose that all the higher order predicates are given. Naturally, it is not what we want to impose to the user. We want to allow the user not to give the higher order predicates and to find them mechanically. Once more, this is a problem of unification but now involving informative predicates. Since this is not decidable and since *Coq* uses first order unification, we will be able via heuristics to solve it in some cases but, it will fail in some other cases.

Let us take a successful example. Suppose one wants to prove :
$\forall n.\exists m.((Sm = n) \vee (n = m = 0))$. A program can be :

`[n:nat](nat_rec nat O [y:nat][H:nat]y)`

where **nat_rec** is the induction principle on natural numbers whose type is `(P:nat→Set)(P O)→((n:nat)(P n)→(P (S n)))→(n:nat)(P n)`. Note that we do not give explicitly the predicate `P` and that we only give the type `nat`.

Suppose `n` is introduced. Then, the specification is $\exists m.((Sm = n) \vee (n = m = 0))$ with the program :

`(nat_rec nat O [y:nat][H:nat]y)`

The desired result is two subgoals with two subprograms :

- $\exists m.((Sm = O) \vee (O = m = O))$ with `O`.
- $\forall n.\exists m.((Sm = n) \vee (n = m = O)) \rightarrow \exists m.((Sm = Sn) \vee (Sn = m = O))$ with `[y:nat][H:nat]y)`.

The program is an application with the constant **nat_rec** as head. Its specification is known and is `(P:nat→Set)(P O) → ((n:nat)(P n) → (P (S n))) → (n:nat)(P n)`. To generate the subgoals, one needs to instantiate the predicate `P` of **nat_rec**. Since one knows the specification to prove, one can use it to find this predicate. The head of the type of **nat_rec** i.e. `(P n)` and the specification $(\exists m.(Sm = n)) \vee (O = n)$ have thus to be unified (in this case, a higher-order unification is necessary). After that, `P` can be instantiated by $[n](\exists m.(Sm = n)) \vee (O = n)$ and allows to generate the two previous subgoals.

Thus, in many practical cases, our method will be able to generate a proof of a program for a given specification leaving logical properties to prove to ensure the correctness. We identify the cases of failure as unification problems for higher order predicates. A solution is a proposition of annotated programs. This will be presented in a next section but we first discuss the problem of adding inductive types.

5 Adding inductive types

We just talked about Pure Calculus of Constructions. The system *Coq* implements this calculus enhanced with inductive definitions. We will here discuss the addition of inductive definitions in our problem.

First of all, adding inductive definitions gives two more rules from the extraction point of view expressed in the following, one for constructors, one for dependent elimination. The notations are :

$\mathsf{Ind}(X : A)\{C_1(X)|\ldots|C_n(X)\}$: inductive type whose constructors are C_i.

$\mathsf{Constr}(i, Ind)$: i-th constructor of the inductive type Ind.

$C\{Ind, P, c\}$: term defined by induction over the structure of the type of constructor C (see [PM93]).

$\mathsf{Elim}_{Ind}(c, P)\{f_1|\ldots|f_n\}$: notation for $<P>Match\ c\ with\ f_1 \ldots f_n$ with $c : Ind$.

The rules are the following :

$$\frac{Ind \equiv \mathsf{Ind}(X:A)\{C_1(X)|\ldots|C_n(X)\}}{\Gamma \vdash \mathsf{Constr}(i, Ind) \rightsquigarrow \mathsf{Constr}(i, \mathcal{E}(Ind)) \ : C_i(Ind)}$$

$$\frac{\begin{array}{ll}\Gamma \vdash c \rightsquigarrow p \ : \ (Ind\ \boldsymbol{a}) & (\forall i = 1 \ldots n) \\ \Gamma \vdash P : (\boldsymbol{x} : \boldsymbol{A})(Ind\ \boldsymbol{x}) \to s' & \Gamma \vdash f_i \rightsquigarrow q_i \ : \ C_i\{Ind, P, \mathsf{Constr}(i, Ind)\}\end{array}}{\Gamma \vdash \mathsf{Elim}_{Ind}(c, P)\{f_1|\ldots|f_n\} \rightsquigarrow \mathsf{Elim}_{\mathcal{E}(Ind)}(p, \mathcal{E}(P))\{q_1|\ldots|q_n\} \ : \ (P\ \boldsymbol{a}\ c)}$$

The first rule is not as trivial as it seems. Indeed, the problem is to retrieve from the inductive type $\mathcal{E}(Ind)$ the inductive type Ind. This uses the property that for all S s.t. $S \succ_S C_i(Ind)$, the conclusion of S is the type Ind applied to logical arguments. With this property, the type Ind can be retrieved from the specification.

For the second rule, as for application of higher order predicates, we modify the elimination rule to keep elimination predicates.

$$\frac{\begin{array}{ll}\Gamma \vdash c \rightsquigarrow p \ : \ (Ind\ \boldsymbol{a}) & (\forall i = 1 \ldots n) \\ \Gamma \vdash P : (\boldsymbol{x} : \boldsymbol{A})(Ind\ \boldsymbol{x}) \to s' & \Gamma \vdash f_i \rightsquigarrow q_i \ : \ C_i\{Ind, P, \mathsf{Constr}(i, Ind)\}\end{array}}{\Gamma \vdash \mathsf{Elim}_{Ind}(c, P)\{f_1|\ldots|f_n\} \rightsquigarrow \mathsf{Elim}_{\mathcal{E}(Ind)}(p, \{P\})\{q_1|\ldots|q_n\} \ : \ (P\ \boldsymbol{a}\ c)}$$

If the predicates are given, it is trivial. But, as for applications, we want not to impose to the user to give the elimination predicates. The problem is thus to retrieve the right predicate and we will just show on examples what happens.

Let us take our first example of division algorithm. Suppose we take the sub-program (`inf` is a boolean function deciding the order of two natural numbers, `if` is a macro for the elimination on booleans) :

```
<nat*nat>if (inf b (S r)) then <nat,nat>((S q),O)
        else <nat,nat>(q,(S r))
```

The corresponding specification is $(b > r) \to (n = b * q + r) \to \exists q \exists r\ (Sn = b*q+r) \wedge (b > r)$. The program suggests to do a case analysis on `(inf b (S r))`.

If `(inf b (S r))` has type $(b < Sr) \vee (b \geq Sr)$ then the elimination predicate is `(P:bool->Set)(P (b<Sr))->(P (b>=Sr))->(B:bool)(P B)`. Since the goal is $(b > r) \to (n = b*q+r) \to \exists q \exists r\ (Sn = b*q+r) \wedge (b > r)$, `P` can be instantiated with $[B](b > r) \to (n = b*q+r) \to \exists q \exists r\ (Sn = b*q+r) \wedge (b > r)$. But, this is very heavy. The heuristic is to introduce in the context all the logical informations that do not depend on the elimination term. Indeed, a proof by induction on n of $A \Rightarrow B(n)$ generates a subgoal $(A \Rightarrow B(n)) \Rightarrow (A \Rightarrow B(Sn))$ when a proof by induction on n of $B(n)$ in the context A generates $B(n) \Rightarrow B(Sn)$ in the context A. Clearly, the two proofs are equivalent but the second one is easier. That is why we use this heuristic. In our example, we introduces all the logical hypotheses that do not depend on `(inf b (S r))`. Then, `P` can be instantiated with $[B]\exists q \exists r\ (Sn = b * q + r) \wedge (b > r)$. The generated subgoal are :

$$(b < Sr) \to \exists q \exists r\ (Sn = b * q + r) \wedge (b > r)$$

$$(b \geq Sr) \to \exists q \exists r\ (Sn = b * q + r) \wedge (b > r)$$

But, if `(inf b (S r))` has type `bool` then the elimination predicate is `(P:bool->Set)(P true)->(P false)->(B:bool)(P B)` and the generated subgoals are :

$$\exists q \exists r\ (Sn = b * q + r) \wedge (b > r)$$

$$\exists q \exists r\ (Sn = b * q + r) \wedge (b > r)$$

These subgoals are not useful since the information as to whether `(inf  b (S r))` is true or not is lost. The subgoals one would like to generate would rather be :

$$((inf\ b\ (S\ r)) = true) \to \exists q \exists r\ (Sn = b * q + r) \wedge (b > r)$$

$$((inf\ b\ (S\ r)) = false) \to \exists q \exists r\ (Sn = b * q + r) \wedge (b > r)$$

That is to introduce a dependency in the specification if the specification does not depend on the term of induction. So, if S is the current specification and t the proof term corresponding to m, then S is modified into $(t = t) \to S$. This just introduces a dependency without modifying the specification and allows to obtain probably more useful subgoals. Indeed, the problem comes from the fact that one looks for an adequate generalization of the goal and there are many ways of doing it. This choice is thus only a heuristic.

Finally, one obtains as many subgoals as constructors of m and the different programs corresponding to the different constructors of the type of m are the elements of lf. Note, one more time, the importance of retrieving the specification of a part of a program since, if the specification of m cannot be retrieved, then the specification cannot be generalized.

Note that the previous heuristic points out the fact that recursion without parameters may or may not correspond to proof by induction without parameters, depending on the computational meaning of those parameters. In the previous example, it corresponds to proof by induction with a logical parameter which implies the generalization of the goal.

Note that the heuristic of generalizing the goal is only used for proofs by case analysis and it does not affect the provability of the goal in this case since it consists in adding logical parameters to the case analysis.

Afterwards, we would like to mention here another problem due to the introduction of inductive definitions. In our description of the problematic case of applications, we described the problem of retrieving the specification of the head of the application. Suppose this head is now a recursion. Then, the problem has many solutions since there are many possible predicates for the recursion. Thus, once more, a heuristic is applied and the goal is generalized to reduce to a known case i.e. the case of recursion. This heuristic corresponds to the following rule :

$$\frac{\Gamma \vdash \mathsf{Elim}_I(m, P)\{lf\} : (x : A)\ B \quad \Gamma \vdash a : A}{\Gamma \vdash (\mathsf{Elim}_I(m, P)\{lf\}\ a) : B[x/a]}$$

To conclude, the addition of inductive types does not affect the validity of theorem 1. But, if we do not want the user to give all predicates, then there are once more heuristics which can fail. This leads us to the notion of annotated programs.

6 Adding annotations

We have already discussed the importance of indicating higher order predicates in programs. We saw it is in some cases possible to not give them in a program and to retrieve them automatically. We want here to give a new syntax to the user to annotate a program with higher order predicates or elimination predicates. Annotations are then comments which can be interpreted by the system. The new syntax for programs is that one can annotate any part of a program with the syntax `(: a specification :)`. Between `(:` and `:)`, one gives the specification one would like the program to have. This forces the system to take this information as a specification. The corresponding rule is :

$$\frac{\Gamma \vdash t \rightsquigarrow p : S \quad S \succ_S S'}{\Gamma \vdash t \rightsquigarrow p\ (:\ S\ :) : S'}$$

Note that these annotations can contain free variables. These free variables can be program variables but can be logical variables too. One must thus introduce another new syntax for λ-abstractions on logical variables `[{x:L}]`. The corresponding rule is :

$$\frac{\Gamma, x : L \vdash t \rightsquigarrow p : S}{\Gamma \vdash [x : L]t \rightsquigarrow [\{x : L\}]p : (x : L)S}$$ [7]

Note that these rules do not affect the validity of the theorem 1. This just adds two trivial rules.

Let us give an example. Suppose we take the division algorithm at a particular step. The specification is $(b > r) \rightarrow (n = b{*}q{+}r) \rightarrow \exists q \exists r\ (Sn = b{*}q{+}r) \wedge (b > r)$ and the program is `if (Sr<b)  then (q,Sr) else (Sq,0)`. In fact, in *Coq*, it is written :

```
<nat*nat>if (inf b (Sr)) then <nat,nat>((Sq),0)
                          else <nat,nat>(q,(Sr))
```

with the constant **inf** being the decidability of the ordering relation on natural numbers.

Suppose first **inf** is declared as a variable without any specification, i.e. it is just a boolean value. Then, the generated subgoals are :

$$(inf\ b\ (Sr)) = true \rightarrow \exists q \exists r\ (Sn = b * q + r) \wedge (b > r)$$

[7] A logical λ-abstraction in a program always corresponds to the first logical product in the specification. If one wants to mention the second logical product, one needs to indicate the first and the second corresponding λ-abstraction.

$$(inf\ b\ (Sr)) = false \rightarrow \exists q \exists r\ (Sn = b * q + r) \wedge (b > r)$$

But, then, one has to prove that :

$(inf\ b\ (Sr)) = true \rightarrow (b \leq (Sr))$

$(inf\ b\ (Sr)) = false \rightarrow (b > (Sr))$

which is not easy if **inf** has no specification.

In a second case, if **inf** is declared as a program already specified by $\forall n.\forall m.(n \leq m) \vee (n > m)$, then the generated subgoals are :

$$(b \leq (Sr)) \rightarrow \exists q \exists r\ (Sn = b * q + r) \wedge (b > r)$$
$$(b > (Sr)) \rightarrow \exists q \exists r\ (Sn = b * q + r) \wedge (b > r)$$

which are directly usable.

So, if **inf** is just a boolean function, one can explicitly indicate in the program the specification one wants for it by giving an annotation to this part of the program :

```
<nat*nat>if (inf b (Sr)) (: {(le b (Sr))}+{(gt b (Sr))} :)
          then <nat,nat>((Sq),O) else <nat,nat>(q,(Sr))
```

Then, this will generate the same subgoals as in the second case plus one needed to verify that the annotated program is consistent with its annotation. This last subgoal is the following :

$$(b \leq (Sr)) \vee (b > (Sr))$$

associated to the program `(inf b (Sr))`.

Now that we give this example, it is clear that the interpretation of annotations is that the specification of an annotated term is the annotation itself. This can be useful to direct the tactic in its choices i.e. to explicitly give predicates which could perhaps not be automatically found by the tactic.

7 Optimizations

Programs are written in a $F_\omega{}^{Ind}$ form which is not always very practical. We would like to have a language closer to ML. We have so introduced some optimizations in the formulation of the input program.

7.1 Constants

First, and this is not exactly an optimization, constants have a particular status. Two alternatives appear : the constant can be taken as an object hiding a more complex structure, an already specified program, and allowing us to not repeat work already done. This implies that one forgets this complex structure. But, in some cases, this structure can be useful. So, our decision was to try our method with the unexpanded constant and if it fails to retry with the expanded constant.

A future alternative could be to give the possibility to the user to control the expansion of constants.

7.2 Recursive programs

The basic notion of *Coq* induction follows a primitive recursive scheme (or structural induction). But normal programs use general recursion. *Coq* defines a well founded induction principle, which can be realized by a recursive program :

$$\forall P\ \forall R\ (wellfounded\ R) \rightarrow (\forall x\ (\forall y\ (R\ y\ x) \rightarrow (P\ y)) \rightarrow (P\ x)) \rightarrow \forall a.(P\ a)$$

The first optimization is only syntactic sugar. It introduces a notion of recursive programs (general induction). A new syntax allows to write directly general recursive programs and it is translated in the previous well founded induction principle. So one needs an ordering relation R on which the induction is based and that has to be explicitly given. Indeed, this ordering relation cannot be retrieved automatically from the program and is the basis of the well-foundedness of the induction. With this new syntax, one gives the ordering relation and uses directly general recursive programs.

The syntax is `<P>rec H (: order :)` for the ML `let rec H x = ...H y ...` with `P` the type of the result and `order` the ordering relation on which the well-founded induction is based.

Example : Euclidean division algorithm.

An Euclidean division algorithm can be expressed by the following program :

```
[b:nat](<nat*nat>rec div (: lt :)
        [a:nat](<nat*nat>if (inf b a) then
                (<nat*nat>let (q,r:nat) = (div (minus a b)) in
                             <nat,nat>((S q),r))
                     else <nat,nat>(O,a))).
```

if `lt` is the natural strict ordering relation on natural numbers, `div` and `minus` the division and subtraction on natural numbers and `inf` the decidability on the ordering relation on natural numbers.

The corresponding specification can be $\forall b.(b > 0) \Rightarrow \forall a.\exists q \exists r.(a = b * q + r) \wedge (b > r)$. The following proof obligations are generated :

- $(wellfounded\ lt)$ as a logical subgoal
- $\forall a.\exists q \exists r.(a = b * q + r) \wedge (b > r)$ associated to the program `(<nat*nat>if (inf b a) then ...`

7.3 Eliminations

This optimization is in fact the inversion of an optimization done during the extraction. Suppose you have an elimination in a recursive program. An optimization of the extraction method is the following : if an hypothesis appears in each different case of the elimination, the program is transformed by taking this hypothesis off from each case and placing it just before the elimination. It is the current way of writing programs. If the extracted program is `<A->B>Match n` `with [x:A]t1 ... [x:A]tm`, then the more natural optimized program has a different shape : `[x:A]<B>Match n with t1 ... tm`[8].

So, our optimization is to consider that every hypothesis which is external regarding an elimination and used in this elimination has to be placed back into each case of the elimination. This optimization is important because, if it is not done, it can generate much harder proofs.

Let us take the example of the Quicksort. It can be expressed by the specification $\forall l.\exists m.(sorted\ m) \wedge (permut\ l\ m)$ with the following program where `Splitting` represent a previous program which splits a list into two lists from a pivot point :

```
(<list>rec quick (: ltl :)
   [l:list](<list>Match l with
       (* nil *) nil
  (* cons a m *) [a:A][m:list][h:list]
                        <list>let (l1,l2:list) = (Splitting a m) in
                               (mil a (quick l1) (quick l2)))).
```

which is a macro for :

```
[x:list](well_founded_induction list list
  [l:list][quick:list->list](<list>Match l with
       (* nil *) nil
  (* cons a m *) [a:A][m:list][h:list]
                        <list>let (l1,l2:list) = (Splitting a m) in
                               (mil a (quick l1) (quick l2))) x).
```

and for the proof, one would like to have :

```
[x:list](well_founded_induction list list
  [l:list](<(list->list)->list>Match l with
     (* nil *) [quick1:list->list]nil
(* cons a m *) [a:A][m:list][h:(list->list)->list]
                     [quick2:list->list]
                      <list>let (l1,l2:list) = (Splitting a m) in
                             (mil a (quick2 l1) (quick2 l2))) x).
```

Indeed, in the second program, the **quick** hypothesis has type $\forall y.(ltl\ y\ l) \Rightarrow \exists m.(sorted\ m) \wedge (permut\ y\ m)$. This cannot be used in the proof since one knows nothing about `l`.

In the third program, the **quick** hypothesis has two different occurrences **quick1** and **quick2** depending on what is `l`. If `l` is `nil`, the **quick1** hypothesis has type $\forall y.(ltl\ y\ nil) \Rightarrow \exists m.(sorted\ m) \wedge (permut\ y\ m)$. If `l` is `(cons a m)`, the **quick2** hypothesis has type $\forall y.(ltl\ y\ (cons\ a\ m)) \Rightarrow \exists m.(sorted\ m) \wedge (permut\ y\ m)$. Then, in the second case of the induction, **quick2** can be used.

The optimization consists thus in taking the first program and transforming it into the third one.

[8] Note that this optimization can only be done with non recursive eliminations

7.4 Contraction of expressions

The purpose here is to allow programs to be given in a natural form.

Let us take the case of expressions like `if b then true else false`. These expressions are not natural in programs, that is to say that a programmer writes only `b`, but the proof has to be explicitly given like this to correspond to the right specifications. For example, if b is correct with respect to A, it can be correct with respect to another specification B. But, the proof C from which b is extracted is of type A, and not of type B. For example, if A is $n = m \vee n \neq m$ and B is $Sn = Sm \vee Sn \neq Sm$, the program b realizes A and B but a proof of A is not a proof of B. But, the program `if b then true else false` can be extracted from a proof of B. One has then to prove that $n = m \rightarrow Sn = Sm$ and $n \neq m \rightarrow Sn \neq Sm$.

So, the optimization consists in writing natural programs without `if b then true else false` and transforming them when necessary. This is just explained on this simple example but can be generalized and, then, automatic transformations of programs are generated.

7.5 Singleton types

Let us take the example of the Ackermann function to explain the problem of singleton types.

The definition of the function is the following :

$$ack(0, n) = n + 1$$
$$ack(n + 1, 0) = ack(n, 1)$$
$$ack(n + 1, m + 1) = ack(n, ack(n + 1, m))$$

To express this definition we use in fact a ternary predicate :

```
Inductive Definition Ack : nat->nat->nat->Prop =
     AckO : (n:nat)(Ack O n (S n))
   | AcknO : (n,p:nat)(Ack n (S O) p)->(Ack (S n) O p)
   | AckSS : (n,m,p,q:nat)(Ack (S n) m q)->(Ack n q p)
                                ->(Ack (S n) (S m) p).
```

Suppose now we want to prove that $\forall n.\forall m.\exists p.Ack(n, m, p)$. The type extracted from this expression is : $nat \rightarrow nat \rightarrow sig\ nat$[9]. Suppose we want to give the program corresponding to this proof. It will be (in a CAML form) :

```
let rec ack n m = match n with
          0     -> (fun m -> m+1)
        | n'+1 -> (match m with
                              0      -> ack n' 1
                            | m'+1 -> ack n' (ack (n'+1) m')) ;;
```

[9] *sig nat* is the notation for the singleton type corresponding to *nat*, that is to say the inductive type with one constructor of type $nat \rightarrow (sig\ nat)$.

This program written in a F_ω form[10] is :

```
[n:nat](<nat->nat>Match n with
      [m:nat](S m)
      [y:nat][H:nat->nat][m:nat]
            (<nat>Match m with
                  (H (S O))
                  [m':nat][H':nat](H H')))
```

The type of these last programs is : $nat \to nat \to nat$.

It is clear this type is not the same as the one extracted from the specification. But, suppose one develops the proof of this specification by hand, then the proof term will be (the Li represent logical parts which are not interesting from the program point of view, the _ non useful information for understanding the problem) :

```
[n:nat]
  (<[n0:nat](m:nat){p:nat|(Ack n0 m p)}>Match n with
   [m:nat](exist (Ack O m) (S m) L1)
   [y:nat][H:(m:nat){p:nat|(Ack y m p)}][m:nat]
     (<[n0:nat]{p:nat|(Ack (S y) n0 p)}>Match m with
      <_>let (x:nat,p:(Ack y (S O) x)) = (H (S O)) in
              (exist (Ack (S y) O) x L2)
      [m':nat][H':sig nat]
         <_>let (x:nat,p:(Ack (S y) y0 x)) = H' in
           <_>let (x':nat,p':(Ack y x x0)) = (H x) in
                  (exist (Ack (S y) (S y0)) x' L3)))
```

with *exist* being the constructor of the inductive type *sig*. This proof has the same type as the specification. But, if one uses an isomorphism between A and *sig* A, one would like the proof and the program to have the same structure. And, this is not the case, since there are eliminations in the proof corresponding to the extraction of the structure of some terms of type *sig nat* which do not appear in the natural program (since there are only terms of type *nat*). So, there are many transformations to do on the program to obtain a program able to generate the proof.

We define now a new notion of convertibility, a convertibility modulo $A \equiv sig\ A$ (that we will call **weak convertibility**). The sense is larger than the usual convertibility (that we will call **strong convertibility**) and allows to accept programs that have just to be modified. The method of transformation is based on a comparison of the program and its specification.

A first typical case is when the program is a λ-abstraction whose type is $A \to B$ when its specification type is $sig\ A \to C$[11]. The program is then transformed in a new λ-abstraction of type $sig\ A \to B$. For our example, let us take H of type $nat \to nat$ but the corresponding specification $\forall m.\exists p.Ack(y, m, p)$ is of

[10] The notation $[x : A]t$ denotes the λ-term $\lambda x : A.t$

[11] C because it is B modulo $A \equiv sig\ A$.

type *nat* → *sig nat*. So, the program is transformed with `[H:nat->(sig nat)]`. This implies that parts of programs will no longer be well typed and this fact will help us to transform programs.

Another case of transformation is when the program is an application. There are two cases :

1. the program is ill typed. This implies that arguments are not of the right type A but of type *sig* A and have to be replaced. For our example, consider `(H H')`. `H'` is of type *sig nat* and `H` of type *nat* → *sig nat*. This term is ill typed. So, it is transformed into :
   ```
   <sig nat>let (x:nat) = H' in (exist nat (H x)).
   ```
   We see the transformation is not complete. This is because of another problem. If we look at the specification of `(H x)` which is $\exists p.Ack(y+1, m', p)$ and at the specification it is associated to which is $\exists p.Ack(y+1, m'+1, p)$, we see there are not identical. The program is then once more transformed into :

   ```
   <sig nat>let (x:nat) = H' in <sig nat>let (x':nat) = (H x) in
                                     (exist nat x').
   ```

   This is in fact analogous to the transformation described in 7.4.
2. the program is well typed but of type A when its specification is of type *sig* A. For our example, let us take `(S m)`. It has type *nat* when its specification has type *sig nat*. The program is transformed into `(exist nat (S m))`.

This gives some typical cases of a method to transform programs which are weakly convertible but not strongly convertible to the specification. This allows to write programs in a more convivial form.

8 Results

8.1 Theoretical results

We give now some results about the "meta-theory" of the method described above.

Proposition 1 (Validity). *If a program* **p** *associated to a specification* **S** *leads to logical lemmas by the use of the Program tactic and if these lemmas are provable, then* **S** *is provable and the program extracted from the generated proof is the input program* **p** *modulo the weak convertibility.*

Proof. Trivial by the theorem 1. □

Remark. The generated logical lemmas are atomic since, for a specification $\forall x.(P\ x) \Rightarrow \exists y.(Q\ x\ y)$ and a program p, subspecifications of the initial specification associated to subprograms of the initial program are generated until only logical lemmas are left.

Indeed, the tactic iterates a method on the structure of the program term. A complete proof iterates this until only logical lemmas are left. Then, the user solves these lemmas. The user can influence the proof between two steps of the tactic by unfolding constants, generalizing goals ...

Proposition 2 (Completeness). *If a specification* S *is provable and if an associated program* p *explicitly contains all the information about higher order predicates then logical generated lemmas are provable.*

Proof. We will give an informal proof.

Suppose S is provable, then there exists a program extracted from a proof of S. The tactic can be applied with this program. It may succeed if all the logical informations can be retrieved. We saw problematic informations are informations about predicates. If one supposes that the input program of the tactic contains all the informations about predicates via annotations, then all logical informations can be retrieved by the tactic and logical lemmas can be generated. Then, since the program is a skeleton of the desired proof and since S is provable, logical lemmas are provable. □

8.2 Practical results

The method described above has been added to the system *Coq* (see [DFH+93]) with a tactic called the Program tactic. The entire library of *Coq* examples has been tested [Par92]. This means that we took every example of the library and try to use the Program tactic for each computational lemma or theorem of each example. This done, we have been able to rewrite all computational theorems with our tactic. We gave the programs and solved the logical lemmas.

We prove algorithms on graphs (Floyd, Dijkstra, Warshall), trees (insertion in avl trees), sorts (Quicksort, Mergesort, Heapsort), Ackermann function, natural numbers (euclidean division) and a tautology checker. Some of them were very quick to prove with our method since there were not a lot of logical lemmas (even sometimes none). Others (like the algorithms on graphs) were harder to prove (subtle logical lemmas) and require the use of annotations. The main problem was to find when where and how to use annotations.

9 Conclusion

This method can be compared to the approach of [Pol92] and to the deliverables of [BM92]. [Pol92] describes a development of proofs and programs hand in hand. There is a separation between the programming language and the logic language, which are two versions of the Calculus of Constructions. So, this is close to our approach but different in the sense that we first give the program and then develop automatically the proof. Moreover, there is a possibility of annotating programs to represent properties of these programs. With the deliverables approach, proofs and programs are also developed hand by hand. But, there is no separation between the programming language and the logical language. Proofs and programs are developed together using strong sums in the Luo's Extended Calculus of Constructions [Luo90]. This is what are called deliverables. There is a distinction between two kinds of deliverables : first-order ones which do not allow to express a relation between the input and the output, and second-order ones, which allow the expression of such a relation. Moreover, deliverables are more rigid than our approach in the sense that one cannot consider specifications not of the form $\forall x.(P\ x) \Rightarrow \exists y.(Q\ x\ y)$.

The method presented above allows to obtain a system in which one can write programs and prove them automatically to be correct with respect to a specification. In fact, this method is not completely automatic since one usually has to solve logical assertions on the program by hand. One has to comment programs with annotations, not in all cases but often. This allows to guide the proof but is not always trivial. One should have a more natural way of writing annotated programs, for example a possibility to suppress the type information in the programs and to replace it by annotations. The future versions of *Coq* with existential variables [Dow91, Dow] would allow to delay the instantiation of some parameters (like the ordering relation in the recursive programs) which could be fixed by the user when he solves the logical lemmas. Moreover, one could increase the synthesis power by using unification. This is under development in a future version of *Coq*. Finally, we hope to be able to use ProPre [MS92] which has been integrated into *Coq*. This allows to define functions via equations. This definition is transformed into a primitive recursive definition which can be used as input of our tactic. This can allow to write more easily input programs of our tactic. In the current state, this is possible but for only a restricted number of functions. We hope the number of functions easily expressible with Propre will increase and then allow us to use it in more general way.

References

[Bar91] H. Barendregt. Lambda Calculi with Types. Technical Report 91-19, Catholic University Nijmegen, September 1991.

[BM92] R. Burstall and J. McKinna. Deliverables : a categorical approach to program development in type theory. Technical Report 92-242, LFCS, October 1992. Also in [NPP92].

[Con86] R. L. Constable et al. *Implementing Mathematics with the Nuprl Proof Development System.* Prentice-Hall, 1986.

[DFH+93] G. Dowek, A. Felty, H. Herbelin, G. Huet, C. Murthy, C. Parent, C. Paulin-Mohring, and B. Werner. The Coq Proof Assistant User's Guide - Version 58. Technical Report 154, Projet Formel - INRIA-Rocquencourt-CNRS-ENS Lyon, May 1993.

[Dow91] G. Dowek. *Démonstration Automatique dans le Calcul des Constructions.* PhD thesis, Université Paris 7, 1991.

[Dow] G. Dowek. A Complete Proof Synthesis Method for the Cube of Type Systems. *Journal of Logic and Computation*, To appear.

[HN88] S. Hayashi and H. Nakano. *PX : A Computational Logic.* Foundations of Computing. MIT Press, 1988.

[How80] W.A. Howard. The formulaes-as-types notion of construction. In J.R. Hindley, editor, *To H.B.Curry : Essays on Combinatory Logic , lambda-calculus and formalism.* Seldin, J.P., 1980.

[Luo90] Z. Luo. *An Extended Calculus of Constructions.* PhD thesis, Department of Computer Science, University of Edinburgh, June 1990.

[MS92] P. Manoury and M. Simonot. *Des preuves de totalité de fonctions comme synthèse de programmes.* PhD thesis, Université PARIS 7, December 1992.

[NPP92] B. Nordström, K. Petersson, and G. Plotkin, editors. *Prooceedings of the 1992 worshop on types for proofs and programs*, June 1992.

[Par92] C. Parent. Automatisation partielle du développement de programmes dans le système Coq. Master's thesis, Ecole Normale Supérieure de Lyon, June 1992.

[PM89a] C. Paulin-Mohring. Extracting F_ω's programs from proofs in the Calculus of Constructions. In Association for Computing Machinery, editor, *Sixteenth Annual ACM Symposium on Principles of Programming Languages*, Austin, January 1989.

[PM89b] C. Paulin-Mohring. *Extraction de programmes dans le Calcul des Constructions.* PhD thesis, Université Paris VII, 1989.

[PM93] C. Paulin-Mohring. Inductive Definitions in the System Coq - Rules and Properties. In *Typed Lambda Calculi and Applications*, volume 664 of *LNCS*, March 1993. Also in research report 92-49, LIP-ENS Lyon, December 1992.

[PMW92] C. Paulin-Mohring and B. Werner. Synthesis of ML programs in the system Coq. *Journal of Symbolic Computation-special issue on automated programming*, 1992. To appear.

[Pol92] E. Poll. A programming logic for Fω. Technical Report 92/25, Eindhoven University of Technology, September 1992.

Closure Under Alpha-Conversion*

Randy Pollack

Laboratory for Foundations of Computer Science, University of Edinburgh, The King's Buildings, Edinburgh, EH9 3JZ, Scotland
rap@dcs.ed.ac.uk

1 Introduction

Consider an informal presentation of simply typed λ-calculus as in [Bar92]. Leaving out some of the details, let σ, τ range over simple types, x, y range over a class of term variables, and M, N, range over the Church-style terms. A *statement* has the form $M : \sigma$, where M is the *subject* of the statement and σ is its *predicate*. A *context*, ranged over by Γ, is a list of statements with only variables as subjects. A context is *valid* if it contains only distinct variables as subjects; defined inductively by

NIL-VALID $\quad \bullet\ \mathsf{valid}$

CONS-VALID $\quad \dfrac{\Gamma\ \mathsf{valid}}{\Gamma, x{:}\sigma\ \mathsf{valid}} \qquad x \notin \mathsf{Dom}\,(\Gamma)$

A statement, $M : \sigma$, is *derivable* from context Γ, notation $\Gamma \vdash M : \sigma$, if $\Gamma \vdash M : \sigma$ can be produced using the following rules.

VAR $\quad \dfrac{\Gamma\ \mathsf{valid}}{\Gamma \vdash x : \sigma} \qquad x{:}\sigma \in \Gamma$

LDA $\quad \dfrac{\Gamma, x{:}\sigma \vdash M : \tau}{\Gamma \vdash [x{:}\sigma]M : \sigma \rightarrow \tau}$

APP $\quad \dfrac{\Gamma \vdash M : \sigma \rightarrow \tau \qquad \Gamma \vdash N : \sigma}{\Gamma \vdash M\,N : \tau}$

Such a presentation is usually considered formal enough for everyday reasoning. It can be implemented literally as a type synthesis algorithm for $\lambda\rightarrow$: to compute a type for a variable, look it up in the context; to compute a type for a lambda abstraction, compute a type for its body in an extended context; to compute a type for an application, compute types for its left and right components, and

* This work was supported by the ESPRIT Basic Research Actions on Logical Frameworks and Types for Proofs and Programs, and by grants from the British Science and Engineering Research Council.

check that they match appropriately. Lets use the algorithm to compute a type for $a = [x{:}\tau][x{:}\sigma]x$.

$$\cfrac{\cfrac{\cfrac{\cfrac{\text{FAILURE: no rule applies because } x \in \mathsf{Dom}\,(x{:}\tau)}{x{:}\tau, x{:}\sigma \;\mathsf{valid}}}{x{:}\tau, x{:}\sigma \vdash x : ?}}{x{:}\tau \vdash [x{:}\sigma]x : \sigma \to ?}}{\vdash [x{:}\tau][x{:}\sigma]x : \tau \to \sigma \to ?} \qquad (1)$$

This system fails to derive the intended type $\tau \to \sigma \to \sigma$. Notice that $\vdash [x{:}\tau][y{:}\sigma]y : \tau \to \sigma \to \sigma$ is derivable, but the system is not closed under alpha-conversion of subjects.

What went wrong? In directly implementing this system we are taking informal notation too literally: there is no "x" in $[x{:}\tau][x{:}\sigma]x$; the names of bound variables are not meant to be taken seriously. The rule LDA should be read as "in order to type $[x{:}\sigma]M$, choose some suitable alpha-representative of $[x{:}\sigma]M$, ...".

Formal systems with variable binding are implemented on machines as the basis of programming languages and proof checkers, among other applications. It is clear that the concrete syntax that users enter into such implementations, and see printed by the implementation in response, should be formally related to the implemented formal system. Further, users and implementors need an exact and concise description of such a system; informal explanation is not good enough.

The concrete syntax should have good properties. Users of such implemented systems will construct large formal objects with complex binding. The implementation should help in this task, and anamolies of naming such as the small example above make the job more difficult. What do you say to an ML implementation that claims `fn x => fn x => x` is not well typed?

There are several approaches to naming in implementations of formal systems. Perhaps the best known is the use of explicit names, and Curry-style renaming in the definition of substitution. This technique can (probably) be formalized. The difficulty arises when we ignore the distinction between alpha-convertible terms, and treat then as equal.

It is well known that one solution to the problems of alpha-conversion is the use of de Bruijn "nameless variables" [dB72]. Although nameless variables have their partisans for use in metatheoretic study, even those partisans admit that the explanation of substitution of a term for a given variable is painful in such a presentation, although it can be, and has been, carried out elegantly [Alt93, Hue93][2]. However, the direct use of nameless variables is not a real possibility in pragmatic applications because human users find it difficult to write even small

[2] For an example of metatheory where nameless variables are very inconvenient, see the discussion of the Thinning Lemma in [MP93]

expressions using nameless variables. It is necessary to translate from named syntax to nameless, and then back again to named syntax for pretty printing, and this translation itself must be formalized.

I know of two recent proposals that take names seriously, but avoid the need for alpha-conversion. One proposal, by Coquand [Coq91], follows a style in logic to distinguish between free variables (parameters) and bound variables (variables). This idea has been used to formalize a large theory of Pure Type Systems, including reduction, conversion and typing [MP93]. This formalization does distinguish between alpha-convertible terms, and the typing judgement is indeed closed under alpha-conversion. The other proposal, by Martin-Löf [Tas93] goes much further, not only using explicit names, but also explicit substitutions, i.e. making the notion of substitution a part of the formal system (as originally proposed for nameless terms in [ACCL91]). Unfortunately the system of [Tas93], in its current formulation, is not closed under alpha-conversion; e.g. it fails to derive judgement (7) in section 3.

Finally, there is a recent proposal [Gor93] of a formalization mixing nameless terms and named variables in such a way that named terms are equal up to alpha-conversion.

1.1 The Constructive Engine

The Constructive Engine [Hue89] is an abstract machine for type checking the Calculus of Constructions. It is the basis for the proofcheckers Coq [DFH$^+$93] and LEGO [LP92]. Among its interesting aspects are:

1. the non-deterministic rules of the underlying type theory are converted into a deterministic, syntax-directed program
2. this syntax-directed program implements a relation equivalent to the type theory, but with very much smaller derivations
3. external *concrete* syntax with explicit variable names is translated into internal *abstract* syntax of *locally nameless* terms, that is, local binding by de Bruijn indexes, and global binding by explicit names
4. an efficient technique for testing conversion of locally nameless terms (with special attention to the treatment of definitions)

The basic ideas of the first and second of these points appeared in early writing of Martin-Löf. The first point has been studied extensively [Pol92, vBJMP94] for the class of Pure Type Systems. The second point is addressed in [vBJMP94, Pol94]. The fourth point (which is clearly the remaining limiting factor in pragmatic implementations of proof checkers) has not received any theoretical attention to my knowledge, although [Hue89, dB85] suggest interesting ideas.

In this note I focus on the third item above, the relationship between concrete syntax and abstract syntax in the Constructive Engine. The use of locally nameless style for internal representation of terms is one of the basic decisions of the Constructive Engine, but perhaps reflects more Huet's interest in experimenting with de Bruijn representation than any ultimate conviction that they are the "right" notation for implementing a type checker. I do not want to study the pros and cons of this representation for efficient typechecking, but only to muse over the relationship between concrete terms, their abstract representations, and their (abstract) types.

Plan of the paper. In the next section we discuss simply-typed lambda calculus, $\lambda\!\rightarrow$. After presenting several concrete and abstract presentations of its typing rules, we derive a Constructive Engine for $\lambda\!\rightarrow$, and consider some variations.

In section 3 we consider the same issue for Pure Type Systems (PTS). There is one new problem in the case of dependent types. We explain a constructive engine for dependent types, and show how to make it closed under alpha-conversion of terms.

Acknowledgement A careful and knowledgeable referee made many useful suggestions.

2 Simply typed lambda calculus

There is a crude way to close the relation $\vdash$ of the Introduction under alpha-conversion of subjects, by adding a rule

$$\text{ALPHA} \qquad \frac{\Gamma \vdash M : \sigma}{\Gamma \vdash N : \sigma} \qquad M \stackrel{\alpha}{=} N$$

where $M \stackrel{\alpha}{=} N$, alpha-conversion, must also be defined by some inductive definition. Such solutions are heavy, and not ideal for either implementation or formal meta-reasoning. Instead of reasoning about three or five rules, we'll have to reason about all the rules for $\stackrel{\alpha}{=}$ as well. Further, rules such as ALPHA, that are not syntax-directed, are hard to reason about: being non-deterministic, they allow many derivations of the same judgement, which sometimes prevents proof by induction on the structure of derivations.

2.1 A concrete presentation closed under alpha-conversion

Another approach is to formalize the informal meaning of the LDA rule suggested above: choose a sufficiently fresh variable name to substitute for x. Informally, replace LDA by

$$\frac{\Gamma, y{:}\sigma \vdash_s M[y/x] : \tau}{\Gamma \vdash_s [x{:}\sigma]M : \sigma \rightarrow \tau} \qquad y \notin M$$

Substitution of y for x in M must still be defined, and the usual definition involves alpha-conversion. We give a formulation suggested in [Coq91] and formalized in detail in [MP93]. Let p, q, r, range over an infinite set of *parameters*, and x, y, z over variables as before. Parameters and variables are disjoint sets[3]. Define two operations of replacement. Replacing a parameter by a term is entirely textual:

$$\begin{aligned} x[M/p] &= x \\ q[M/p] &= \text{if } p = q \text{ then } M \text{ else } q \\ ([x{:}\sigma]N)[M/p] &= [x{:}\sigma]N[M/p] \\ (N_1\, N_2)[M/p] &= (N_1[M/p])\,(N_2[M/p]) \end{aligned}$$

Replacing a variable by a term does respect the scope of variable binding but does not rename variables to prevent capture:

$$\begin{aligned} x[M/y] &= \text{if } y = x \text{ then } M \text{ else } x \\ q[M/y] &= q \\ ([x{:}\sigma]N)[M/y] &= [x{:}\sigma](\text{if } y = x \text{ then } N \text{ else } N[M/y]) \\ (N_1\, N_2)[M/y] &= (N_1[M/y])\,(N_2[M/y]) \end{aligned}$$

Now replace LDA by

S-LDA
$$\frac{\Gamma, p{:}\sigma \vdash_s M[p/x] : \tau}{\Gamma \vdash_s [x{:}\sigma]M : \sigma \to \tau} \qquad p \notin M$$

(where $p \in M$ means *textual* occurrence). In the side condition of this rule, it's not necessary to check that $p \notin \mathsf{Dom}(\Gamma)$ because failure of that condition prevents completing a derivation; just choose another parameter, since p does not occur in the conclusion of the rule. It *is* necessary to check $p \notin M$ so that the premiss doesn't bind instances of p that do not arise from x.

We could define beta-reduction, beta-conversion, prove Church-Rosser, subject reduction, etc. [MP93], but for our purposes alpha-conversion is enough:

α-REFL
$$M \stackrel{\alpha}{=} M$$

α-LDA
$$\frac{M[p/x] \stackrel{\alpha}{=} M'[p/y]}{[x{:}\sigma]M \stackrel{\alpha}{=} [y{:}\sigma]M'} \qquad p \notin M,\ p \notin M'$$

α-APP
$$\frac{M \stackrel{\alpha}{=} M' \qquad N \stackrel{\alpha}{=} N'}{M\,N \stackrel{\alpha}{=} M'\,N'}$$

Now we can state and prove $\vdash_s$ is closed under alpha-conversion

[3] Another informality! What is required is that the *terms* p and x be distinguishable, not necessarily that the underlying objects be. Depending on the formalization of terms we might use weaker conditions. In [MP93], where terms are an inductive type with distinct constructors for parameters and variables, we don't require parameters and variables to be distinct. In informal presentations of logic it is common for "term" to be an inductive *relation* on strings over some alphabet; in this case, of course, we require that (distinct) objects of the alphabet be distinct.

Lemma 1 Closure of $\vdash_s$ under alpha-conversion.
If $\Gamma \vdash_s M : \sigma$ and $M \stackrel{\alpha}{=} M'$ then $\Gamma \vdash_s M' : \sigma$

This can be proved following the same outline as a proof of subject reduction (closure under beta-reduction); in fact $\stackrel{\alpha}{=}$ is contained in parallel reduction, so this lemma is a corollary of subject reduction.

$\vdash_s$ still treats parameters seriously:

$$\vdash_s [x{:}\tau][x{:}\sigma]x : \tau \rightarrow \sigma \rightarrow \sigma \quad \text{but} \quad p{:}\tau, p{:}\sigma \not\vdash_s p : \sigma.$$

This is a different problem, if it is a problem at all. In $\vdash_s$ we have analysed the transition from local variable to global parameter, while the treatment of parameters themselves is the same as in $\vdash$.

An induction principle for $\vdash_s$. An interesting variation on the previous idea is to use generalized induction to truly remove the fresh name from derivations. Replace S-LDA by

$$\text{G-LDA} \qquad \frac{\forall p \notin \mathsf{Dom}\,(\Gamma)\ .\ \Gamma, p{:}\sigma \vdash_g M[p/x] : \tau}{\Gamma \vdash_g [x{:}\sigma]M : \sigma \rightarrow \tau}$$

Notice again the "side condition", this time appearing as an antecedent of the generalized premiss. We don't exclude those p that happen to occur in M, because we must derive $\Gamma, p{:}\sigma \vdash_g M[p/x] : \tau$ for infinitely many p (using that the class of variables is infinite), while M can contain only finitely many p. On the other hand, for $p \in \mathsf{Dom}\,(\Gamma)$, $\Gamma, p{:}\sigma \vdash_g M[p/x] : \tau$ is not derivable for reasons not having to do with M or τ, so this case must be excluded.

Both $\vdash_s$ and $\vdash_g$ derive more judgements than $\vdash$; in fact $\vdash_s$ and $\vdash_g$ are equivalent.

Lemma 2. *For all Γ, M and σ,*
$\Gamma \vdash_s M : \sigma \quad \Leftrightarrow \quad \Gamma \vdash_g M : \sigma$

This fact, to be proved, allows us to use structural induction over $\vdash_g$ as an induction principle for $\vdash_s$ that is stronger than structural induction over $\vdash_s$. Lemma 2 states that $\vdash_s$ and $\vdash_g$ are *extensionally* equivalent, i.e. have the same judgements. Consider proving some extensional property, $\mathcal{P}$, of $\Gamma \vdash_s M : \sigma$, by structural induction. In the case of S-LDA we must justify $\mathcal{P}(\Gamma \vdash_s [x{:}\sigma]M : \sigma \rightarrow \tau)$ from the induction hypothesis $\mathcal{P}(\Gamma, p{:}\sigma \vdash_s M[p/x] : \tau)$ for some *particular* p. Using lemma 2 it suffices to justify $\mathcal{P}(\Gamma \vdash_s [x{:}\sigma]M : \sigma \rightarrow \tau)$ from the stronger induction hypothesis $\forall p \notin \mathsf{Dom}\,(\Gamma)\ .\ \mathcal{P}(\Gamma, p{:}\sigma \vdash_s M[p/x] : \tau)$.

Informally, this strength comes from showing that the same judgements are derivable in a system with fewer derivations. It is clear that while there are infinitely many derivations of, for example, $\vdash_s [x{:}\sigma]x : \sigma \rightarrow \sigma$, each containing some particular parameter, $\vdash_g [x{:}\sigma]x : \sigma \rightarrow \sigma$ has only one derivation that does not contain any particular parameter. Loosely speaking, $\vdash_g$ has a "subformula property" that $\vdash_s$ lacks.

It is this induction principle which justifies our belief that in a judgement $\Gamma \vdash_s M : \sigma$, the occurrence of a parameter in Γ can be treated as binding its occurrences in M, hence the actual parameter used doesn't matter as long as it is sufficiently fresh. Such arguments are used many times in the formalization of named variables in [MP93, Pol94], and are used below in justifying the Constructive Engine.

Proof of lemma 2. Direction $\Leftarrow$ is by induction on the derivation of $\Gamma \vdash_g M : \sigma$.

Direction $\Rightarrow$ is not so easy. It can be proved by induction on the length of the subject, M, as, for every rule of $\vdash_g$, the subject of the conclusion is longer than the subject of any premiss. Such a proof does not extend to the case of Pure Type Systems to be considered in section 3. Here I give a proof that does extend, and is better than the proof given in [MP93]. [Pol94] describes these three different ways to prove such an equivalence in excrutiating detail.

We introduce the machinary of renaming. A *renaming* (ranged over by ϕ) is a function from parameters to parameters such that $\phi p = p$ for all but finitely many p. We extend the action of renamings compositionally to terms and contexts. It's easy to see that *bijective* renamings respect both $\vdash_s$ and $\vdash_g$; in particular, if ϕ is bijective and $\Gamma \vdash_g M : \sigma$, then $\phi\Gamma \vdash_g \phi M : \sigma$. It's a little difficult to construct bijective renamings in general, because not only the parameters that get moved have to be considered, but also those that are fixed; a combinatorial nightmare. However it's clear that any renaming that only swaps parameters, e.g. $\{q \mapsto p,\ p \mapsto q\}$, is bijective.

Now prove $\Gamma \vdash_g M : \sigma$ by structural induction on a derivation of $\Gamma \vdash_s M : \sigma$. All cases are trivial except the rule S-LDA

$$\text{S-LDA} \qquad \frac{\Gamma, p{:}\sigma \vdash_s M[p/x] : \tau}{\Gamma \vdash_s [x{:}\sigma]M : \sigma \rightarrow \tau} \qquad p \notin M$$

By induction hypothesis $\Gamma, p{:}\sigma \vdash_g M[p/x] : \tau$. To show $\Gamma \vdash_g [x{:}\sigma]M : \sigma \rightarrow \tau$ by G-LDA we need $\Gamma, r{:}\sigma \vdash_g M[r/x] : \tau$ for arbitrary parameter $r \notin \mathsf{Dom}(\Gamma)$.

Taking $\phi = \{r \mapsto p,\ p \mapsto r\}$, we have $\phi(\Gamma, p{:}\sigma) \vdash_g \phi(M[p/x]) : \tau$ is derivable by renaming the induction hypothesis. Thus we are finished if we can show

$$\phi(\Gamma, p{:}\sigma) = \Gamma, r{:}\sigma \qquad \text{and} \qquad \phi(M[p/x]) = M[r/x].$$

Notice $p \notin \mathsf{Dom}(\Gamma)$ (or the premiss of S-LDA could not be derivable), and we also know $r \notin \mathsf{Dom}(\Gamma)$. From these observations it's clear that the first equation holds. For the second equation, notice that if $r = p$ then ϕ is the identity renaming, and we are done, so assume $r \neq p$, and hence $r \notin M[p/x]$ (from the premiss of S-LDA and the assumption $r \notin \mathsf{Dom}(\Gamma)$). Now we use a lemma easily proved by structural induction on terms

$$\forall \phi, N, M, x \,.\, \phi M[\phi N/x] = \phi(M[N/x])$$

to reason

$$\begin{array}{rcll} \phi(M[p/x]) & = & \{p \mapsto r\}(M[p/x]) & (r \notin M[p/x]) \\ & = & (\{p \mapsto r\}M)[\{p \mapsto r\}p/x]) & (\text{lemma above}) \\ & = & M[r/x] & (p \notin M) \end{array}$$

as required. □

In the discussion before this proof I emphasised that lemma 2 is about extensional equivalence; we don't expect intensional properties of derivations, such as height, or occurrence of a particular parameter, to be preserved. However this proof is better than the statement of the lemma in the sense that it only renames derivations, leaving their shape intact; every one of the infinitely many branches above a G-LDA created by this proof has the same shape.

2.2 Some other systems for $\lambda\!\rightarrow$

We are now working towards a Constructive Engine for $\lambda\!\rightarrow$, and this will be a system for typing concrete terms with named variables that is closed under alpha-conversion. First we present an optimization that suggests a new idea for handling global variables. Following this idea we will see a presentation of $\lambda\!\rightarrow$ not mentioning substitution, that is closed under alpha-conversion.

An optimization. I think this optimization first appears in early writing of Martin-Löf, and it is also used in the Constructive Engine. It is interesting for our present purposes because it distinguishes between the variables that have always been global, i.e. bound by the context part of the judgement, and those that have only "locally" become global during construction of a derivation.

The inductive definition of $\vdash$ is very inefficient in duplicating the test that Γ valid on each branch of a derivation. For example

$$\dfrac{\dfrac{\vdots \atop x{:}\sigma\rightarrow\sigma, y{:}\sigma \ \mathsf{valid}}{x{:}\sigma\rightarrow\sigma, y{:}\sigma \vdash x : \sigma\rightarrow\sigma} \qquad \dfrac{\vdots \atop x{:}\sigma\rightarrow\sigma, y{:}\sigma \ \mathsf{valid}}{x{:}\sigma\rightarrow\sigma, y{:}\sigma \vdash y : \sigma}}{x{:}\sigma\rightarrow\sigma, y{:}\sigma \vdash x\,y : \sigma}$$

We can optimize $\vdash$ by moving the test for a valid context outside the typing derivation, that is, test once and for all that the given context is in fact valid, and then whenever a derivation extends the context (using the LDA rule), check that the extension preserves validity.

O-VAR $\qquad \Gamma \vdash_o x : \sigma \qquad\qquad x{:}\sigma \in \Gamma$

O-LDA $\qquad \dfrac{\Gamma, x{:}\sigma \vdash_o M : \tau}{\Gamma \vdash_o [x{:}\sigma]M : \sigma\rightarrow\tau} \qquad\qquad x \notin \mathsf{Dom}\,(\Gamma)$

O-APP $\qquad \dfrac{\Gamma \vdash_o M : \sigma\rightarrow\tau \qquad \Gamma \vdash_o N : \sigma}{\Gamma \vdash_o M\,N : \tau}$

Comparing with $\vdash$, notice that O-VAR does not check that Γ is valid, but O-LDA does maintain this property during derivations.

The sense in which $\vdash_o$ is correct is given by

Lemma 3 Correctness of $\vdash_o$ ***for*** $\vdash$.
$\Gamma \vdash M : \sigma \quad \Leftrightarrow \quad (\Gamma \text{ valid and } \Gamma \vdash_o M : \sigma)$

Thus, in the tiny example above, we only need to check

$$x{:}\sigma \to \sigma, y{:}\sigma \text{ valid} \quad \text{and} \quad \frac{\begin{matrix}\vdots \\ x{:}\sigma \to \sigma, y{:}\sigma \vdash_o x : \sigma \to \sigma \qquad x{:}\sigma \to \sigma, y{:}\sigma \vdash_o y : \sigma\end{matrix}}{x{:}\sigma \to \sigma, y{:}\sigma \vdash_o x\, y : \sigma}$$

Both directions of lemma 3 are easily proved by structural induction. However, there is a similar optimization, with a similar correctness lemma, for Pure Type Systems (see [vBJMP94, Pol94]). In that case, where correctness of a context and the typing judgement are mutually inductive, direction $\Rightarrow$ is trivial but direction $\Leftarrow$ is not. It is understandable that the latter is difficult, since it says there is a terminating algorithm for putting back all the redundant information removed from a $\vdash$-derivation[4].

The root of the problem We can view the systems presented so far as leaving unspecified how a context is searched for the type of a variable. This leaves open the possibility for various implementations, such as linear search, or hash-coding. The price we pay is the requirement for only one binding occurrence of a variable in a valid context. This is actually the root of our problem about closure under alpha-conversion, since we don't restrict to only one binding instance for a variable in a term. Informally our idea is to replace the rule O-VAR, which does not specify how to search Γ for an assignment to x, by

$$\Gamma \vdash x : \mathsf{assoc}\ x\ \Gamma$$

which searches Γ linearly ($\mathsf{assoc}\ x\ \Gamma$ returns the type of the *first* occurrence of x in Γ, viewing Γ as a list that conses on the right). More precisely, we replace O-VAR with two rules that search Γ from right to left.

I-START $\qquad \Gamma, x{:}\sigma \vdash_i x : \sigma$

I-WEAK $\qquad \dfrac{\Gamma \vdash_i x : \sigma}{\Gamma, y{:}\tau \vdash_i x : \sigma} \qquad x \neq y$

I-LDA $\qquad \dfrac{\Gamma, x{:}\sigma \vdash_i M : \tau}{\Gamma \vdash_i [x{:}\sigma]M : \sigma \to \tau} \qquad x \notin \mathsf{Dom}(\Gamma)$

I-APP $\qquad \dfrac{\Gamma \vdash_i M : \sigma \to \tau \qquad \Gamma \vdash_i N : \sigma}{\Gamma \vdash_i M\, N : \tau}$

$\vdash_i$ has fewer judgements than $\vdash_o$, for example $x{:}\sigma, x{:}\tau \vdash_o x : \sigma$ but $x{:}\sigma, x{:}\tau \not\vdash_i x : \sigma$. However only judgements of $\vdash_o$ that are incorrect for $\vdash$ are excluded: if Γ is valid, the order of search doesn't matter.

Lemma 4 Correctness of $\vdash_i$ ***for*** $\vdash$. *If Γ valid then*
$\Gamma \vdash_o M : \sigma \quad \Leftrightarrow \quad \Gamma \vdash_i M : \sigma$

[4] I owe this observation to Stefano Berardi.

Closure under alpha-conversion. The system $\vdash_i$ seems strange: why would we be more operational in presenting an abstract relation than required? The payoff is that now the side condition $x \notin \mathsf{Dom}(\Gamma)$ of rule I-LDA can also be dropped, giving the system of "liberal terms":

$$\text{LT-START} \qquad \Gamma, x{:}\sigma \vdash_{lt} x : \sigma$$

$$\text{LT-WEAK} \qquad \frac{\Gamma \vdash_{lt} x : \sigma}{\Gamma, y{:}\tau \vdash_{lt} x : \sigma} \qquad x \neq y$$

$$\text{LT-LDA} \qquad \frac{\Gamma, x{:}\sigma \vdash_{lt} M : \tau}{\Gamma \vdash_{lt} [x{:}\sigma]M : \sigma \rightarrow \tau}$$

$$\text{LT-APP} \qquad \frac{\Gamma \vdash_{lt} M : \sigma \rightarrow \tau \qquad \Gamma \vdash_{lt} N : \sigma}{\Gamma \vdash_{lt} M\,N : \tau}$$

We can consider two new relations now, $\vdash_{lt}$ and (Γ valid and $\vdash_{lt}$).

Notation 5. For relation $\vdash_x$, write $\Gamma \vdash_x^l M : \sigma$ for (Γ valid and $\Gamma \vdash_x M : \sigma$), the *local* version of $\vdash_x$

Clearly

$$\vdash \;=\; \vdash_i^l \;\subset\; \vdash_{lt}^l \;\subset\; \vdash_{lt}$$

where the containments are proper, as suggested by the following examples

$$y{:}\varsigma, x{:}\tau \vdash ([z{:}\tau][w{:}\xi]w)\,x : \xi \rightarrow \xi \tag{2}$$

$$y{:}\varsigma, x{:}\tau \vdash_{lt}^l ([x{:}\tau][x{:}\xi]x)\,x : \xi \rightarrow \xi \tag{3}$$

$$x{:}\varsigma, x{:}\tau \vdash_{lt} ([x{:}\tau][x{:}\xi]x)\,x : \xi \rightarrow \xi \tag{4}$$

In $\vdash$ a variable may not be bound twice on one branch, so judgement (3) is not $\vdash$-derivable. In $\vdash_{lt}^l$, a context must be valid, so (4) is not $\vdash_{lt}^l$-derivable, but there is no other restriction on variable re-use. In $\vdash_{lt}$ there is no restriction on variable re-use at all.

Notice that $\Gamma \vdash_{lt} M : \sigma$ iff $\vdash_{lt} \Gamma M : \Gamma\sigma$ (where if $\Gamma = x{:}\varsigma, y{:}\tau, \ldots$, then $\Gamma M = [x{:}\varsigma][y{:}\tau]\ldots M$ and $\Gamma\sigma = \varsigma \rightarrow \tau \rightarrow \ldots \sigma$), while $\vdash_{lt}^l$ doesn't have this property, which is why $\vdash_{lt}^l$ is called the local system of liberal terms.

With $\vdash_{lt}$ and $\vdash_{lt}^l$ we have systems for typing $\lambda\!\rightarrow$ which are closed under alpha-conversion and require no notion of substitution. (But of course we are also interested in reduction and conversion on the typed terms, and these require substitution.)

A criticism of $\vdash_{lt}$.As I suggested above, the non-operational abstraction "$x \in \Gamma$" that requires x is bound at most once in a valid context, is not well matched to our goal of presenting the typing relation, for the informal notion of term allows the same variable name to be bound more than once, and implicitly contains the idea of "linearly" searching from a variable instance through enclosing scopes to find the one binding that variable instance.

In fact, presentations of type systems in the style of our presentation of $\vdash$, where validity of a context means any variable name is bound at most once, are very common in the literature (for example [Bar92, Luo90, HHP92]). Why do type theory designers not use presentations in the style of $\vdash_{lt}$? The problem is that $\vdash_{lt}$ has bad properties of weakening. If $\Gamma \vdash M : \sigma$ and Γ' contains all the bindings of Γ, and is also valid, then $\Gamma' \vdash M : \sigma$ but $\vdash_{lt}$ doesn't have this property. This is a logical property which shows that global bindings should not be treated the same as local bindings. Both $\vdash$ and $\vdash_{lt}$ treat local and global bindings uniformly: $\vdash$ is unsatisfactory because it is too restrictive with local bindings, so is not closed under alpha-conversion; $\vdash_{lt}$ is unsatisfactory because it is too liberal with global bindings, so is not closed under weakening. Is $\vdash'_{lt}$ just right?

2.3 λ→ with nameless variables

A well-known technique to avoid questions of variable names is the use of de Bruijn nameless variables.

Pure nameless terms. Here is a presentation of λ→ for pure nameless (de Bruijn) terms.

DB-START $\quad \Gamma, \sigma \vdash_{db} 0 : \sigma$

DB-WEAK $$\frac{\Gamma \vdash_{db} n : \sigma}{\Gamma, \tau \vdash_{db} n+1 : \sigma}$$

DB-LDA $$\frac{\Gamma, \sigma \vdash_{db} M : \tau}{\Gamma \vdash_{db} [\sigma]M : \sigma \rightarrow \tau}$$

DB-APP $$\frac{\Gamma \vdash_{db} M : \sigma \rightarrow \tau \qquad \Gamma \vdash_{db} N : \sigma}{\Gamma \vdash_{db} M\,N : \tau}$$

Notice that there are no real choices to be made: there are no restrictions on the context, and, since there is no ambiguity possible, how we search the context is immaterial.

Locally nameless terms. Now consider terms whose local binding is by de Bruijn indexes, but whose global binding is by named variables. As before, x, y range over a class of variables that will be used for global, or free, variables. As usual, we define two operations of "substitution" (see [Hue89])

$M[N/k]$ replaces the kth *free* index with appropriately lifted instances of N, and lowers all free indexes higher than k since there is no longer a "hole" at k.

$M[k/x]$ replaces name x with the kth *free* index, lifting indexes greater or equal to k to make room for a new free index.

Here is a system for $\lambda\!\rightarrow$ typing of locally nameless terms.

$$\text{LN-VAR} \qquad \frac{\Gamma \text{ valid}}{\Gamma \vdash_{ln} x : \sigma} \qquad x{:}\sigma \in \Gamma$$

$$\text{LN-LDA} \qquad \frac{\Gamma, x{:}\sigma \vdash_{ln} M[x/0] : \tau}{\Gamma \vdash_{ln} [\sigma]M : \sigma \rightarrow \tau} \qquad x \notin M$$

$$\text{LN-APP} \qquad \frac{\Gamma \vdash_{ln} M : \sigma \rightarrow \tau \qquad \Gamma \vdash_{ln} N : \sigma}{\Gamma \vdash_{ln} M\,N : \tau}$$

This system is very similar in spirit to $\vdash_s$ of section 2.1. Its handling of global names is identical to that of $\vdash_s$ (and $\vdash$), and its central feature, the analysis of how a local variable becomes global, is very reminiscent of $\vdash_s$. In particular, any sufficiently fresh variable can be used for x in the LN-LDA rule, and we can formalize this observation by proving, exactly as in lemma 2, that the judgements of $\vdash_{ln}$ are not changed by replacing LN-LDA with

$$\frac{\forall x \notin \mathsf{Dom}(\Gamma)\,.\,\Gamma, x{:}\sigma \vdash_{ln} M[x/0] : \tau}{\Gamma \vdash_{ln} [\sigma]M : \sigma \rightarrow \tau}$$

From this observation, we have a stronger induction principle for $\vdash_{ln}$ than structural induction, as discussed in relation to lemma 2.

Of course $\vdash_{ln}$ is closed under alpha-conversion, because alpha-conversion and identity are the same for locally nameless terms. The Constructive Engine uses $\vdash_{ln}$ as the "kernel" of a system for typing conventional named terms that inherits closure under alpha-conversion from $\vdash_{ln}$.

Locally closed terms. We call a term *locally closed* if it has no free index occurrences. It is easy to see that if $\Gamma \vdash_{ln} M : \sigma$, then M is locally closed, and all the type systems for locally nameless terms used below have this property.

2.4 A Constructive Engine for $\lambda\!\rightarrow$

Since $\vdash_{ln}$ treats global names just as $\vdash$ does, we may use the optimization and transformations of section 2.2 on $\vdash_{ln}$. Analogous to $\vdash_i$ we have $\vdash_{iln}$

ILN-START $\quad \Gamma, x{:}\sigma \vdash_{iln} x : \sigma$

ILN-WEAK $\quad \dfrac{\Gamma \vdash_{iln} x : \sigma}{\Gamma, y{:}\tau \vdash_{iln} x : \sigma} \qquad x \neq y$

ILN-LDA $\quad \dfrac{\Gamma, x{:}\sigma \vdash_{iln} M[x/0] : \tau}{\Gamma \vdash_{iln} [\sigma]M : \sigma \rightarrow \tau} \qquad x \notin M,\ x \notin \mathsf{Dom}\,(\Gamma)$

ILN-APP $\quad \dfrac{\Gamma \vdash_{iln} M : \sigma \rightarrow \tau \qquad \Gamma \vdash_{iln} N : \sigma}{\Gamma \vdash_{iln} M\,N : \tau}$

Similar to lemmas 3 and 4,

$$\Gamma \vdash_{ln} M : \sigma \quad \Leftrightarrow \quad (\Gamma \text{ valid and } \Gamma \vdash_{iln} M : \sigma)$$

Again as in section 2.2 we define a system of "liberal terms" by replacing ILN-LDA with

LTLN-LDA $\quad \dfrac{\Gamma, x{:}\sigma \vdash_{ltln} M[x/0] : \tau}{\Gamma \vdash_{ltln} [\sigma]M : \sigma \rightarrow \tau} \qquad x \notin M$

In section 2.2 the step from $\vdash_i$ to $\vdash_{lt}$ changed the derivable judgements; in fact $\vdash_{lt}$ is closed under alpha-conversion, while $\vdash_i$ is not. In the present case $\vdash_{iln}$ is already closed under alpha-conversion, so the step to $\vdash_{ltln}$ does not change the derivable judgements. The main point is that x occurs in the conclusion of I-LDA but not in the conclusion of ILN-LDA.

Lemma 6 Correctness of $\vdash_{ltln}$.
$\Gamma \vdash_{ln} M : \sigma \quad \Leftrightarrow \quad$ (*Γ valid and $\Gamma \vdash_{ltln} M : \sigma$*)

Proof. It suffices to show $\Gamma \vdash_{iln} M : \sigma \Leftrightarrow \Gamma \vdash_{ltln} M : \sigma$. Direction $\Rightarrow$ is trivial. Prove direction $\Leftarrow$ by induction on a derivation of $\Gamma \vdash_{ltln} M : \sigma$ using the strong induction principle derived from the fact that LTLN-LDA can be replaced by

$$\frac{\forall x \notin \mathsf{Dom}\,(\Gamma)\,.\ \Gamma, x{:}\sigma \vdash_{ltln} M[x/0] : \tau}{\Gamma \vdash_{ltln} [\sigma]M : \sigma \rightarrow \tau}$$

without changing the derivable judgements, as in the proof of lemma 2. $\square$

The Constructive Engine. We are almost ready to present the Constructive Engine for $\lambda\!\rightarrow$. It is (a system of rules for) an inductive relation of the shape $\Gamma \vdash M \Rightarrow \overline{M} : \sigma$. Γ and M are concrete objects with named variables, which we think of as inputs to the engine. $\overline{M}$ and σ are the outputs, respectively the translation of M into locally nameless form, and the Γ-type of $\overline{M}$ in $\vdash_{ltln}$. For example, the rule for application terms is

$$\text{CE-APP} \qquad \frac{\Gamma \vdash M \Rightarrow \overline{M} : \sigma \rightarrow \tau \qquad \Gamma \vdash N \Rightarrow \overline{N} : \sigma}{\Gamma \vdash M\,N \Rightarrow \overline{M}\,\overline{N} : \tau}$$

This is read "to translate and compute a type for the named term $M\,N$ in context Γ (i.e. to evaluate the conclusion of the rule given its inputs), translate and compute types for M and N (i.e. evaluate the premisses of the rule, whose inputs are computed from the given inputs to the conclusion), and return a result computed from the results of the premisses". We have called such systems *translation systems* [Pol90].

There is one difficulty remaining, with the rule for lambda terms. Following the CE-APP example, it should be

$$\frac{\Gamma, x{:}\sigma \vdash M \Rightarrow \overline{M}[x/0] : \tau}{\Gamma \vdash [x{:}\sigma]M \Rightarrow [\sigma]\overline{M} : \sigma \rightarrow \tau} \qquad x \notin \overline{M}$$

but it is not clear how to compute $[\sigma]\overline{M}$ from $\overline{M}[x/0]$. Reading LTLN-LDA algorithmically the term $[\sigma]M$ is the input: to compute its type, strip off the lambda, put a variable x in the hole thus created, (i.e. $M[x/0]$) and compute a type for this in an extended context. In the translation system this is dualized: given the named term $[x{:}\sigma]M$, translate the named term M to locally nameless term $\overline{M}$, and then somehow construct a locally nameless version of $[x{:}\sigma]M$. To fix this problem, we consider one more system, the same as $\vdash_{ltln}$ except that LTLN-LDA is replaced by

$$\text{PCE-LDA} \qquad \frac{\Gamma, x{:}\sigma \vdash_{pce} N : \tau}{\Gamma \vdash_{pce} [\sigma](N[0/x]) : \sigma \rightarrow \tau}$$

(PCE is for *pre-constructive-engine*) and claim:

Lemma 7 Correctness of $\vdash_{pce}$.
$\Gamma \vdash_{ln} M : \sigma \quad \Leftrightarrow \quad$ (*Γ valid and* $\Gamma \vdash_{pce} M : \sigma$)

Proof. It suffices to show $\Gamma \vdash_{ltln} M : \sigma \;\Leftrightarrow\; \Gamma \vdash_{pce} M : \sigma$. First we have the equations

$$M[0/x][x/0] = M \qquad \text{if } M \text{ is locally closed} \tag{5}$$

$$M[x/0][0/x] = M \qquad \text{if } x \notin M \tag{6}$$

For direction $\Leftarrow$, if a PCE-derivation ends with

$$\text{PCE-LDA} \qquad \frac{\Gamma, x{:}\sigma \vdash_{pce} N : \tau}{\Gamma \vdash_{pce} [\sigma](N[0/x]) : \sigma \rightarrow \tau}$$

(hence N is locally closed) apply LTLN-LDA with $M = N[0/x]$, using equation (5) and the fact that $x \notin N[0/x]$ no matter what N is.

Conversely, assume a LTLN-derivation ends with

$$\text{LTLN-LDA} \qquad \frac{\Gamma, x{:}\sigma \vdash_{ltln} M[x/0] : \tau}{\Gamma \vdash_{ltln} [\sigma]M : \sigma \rightarrow \tau} \qquad x \notin M$$

Since $x \notin M$, using equation (6), apply PCE-LDA with $N = M[x/0]$. □

Now we can give the Constructive Engine for $\lambda\!\rightarrow$:

$$\text{CE-START} \qquad \Gamma, x{:}\sigma \vdash x \Rightarrow \overline{x} : \sigma$$

$$\text{CE-WEAK} \qquad \frac{\Gamma \vdash x \Rightarrow \overline{x} : \sigma}{\Gamma, y{:}\tau \vdash x \Rightarrow \overline{x} : \sigma} \qquad x \neq y$$

$$\text{CE-LDA} \qquad \frac{\Gamma, x{:}\sigma \vdash M \Rightarrow \overline{M} : \tau}{\Gamma \vdash [x{:}\sigma]M \Rightarrow [\sigma](\overline{M}[0/x]) : \sigma \rightarrow \tau}$$

$$\text{CE-APP} \qquad \frac{\Gamma \vdash M \Rightarrow \overline{M} : \sigma \rightarrow \tau \qquad \Gamma \vdash N \Rightarrow \overline{N} : \sigma}{\Gamma \vdash M\,N \Rightarrow \overline{M}\,\overline{N} : \tau}$$

This system has a clear operational reading. Further, it has a soundness property: if $\Gamma \vdash N \Rightarrow \overline{N} : \sigma$ is derivable then $\Gamma \vdash_{pce} \overline{N} : \sigma$ is derivable, for given a derivation of the former, just erase the named terms to get a derivation of the latter. If we show that the translation from named terms to locally nameless terms is correct (I will not do so) the correctness of this engine is established.

3 Dependent Types

We will work with the familiar class of Pure Type Systems [Bar91, Bar92, GN91, Ber90, MP93, vBJMP94, vBJ93], which, without further ado, we present as the system of rules in Table 1.

A new difficulty arises with alpha-conversion in dependent types: the binding dependency of a term and its type may be different. For example, we expect to be able to derive

$$A{:}*, P{:}A \rightarrow * \vdash [x{:}A][x{:}Px]x : \{x{:}A\}\{y{:}Px\}Px \tag{7}$$

but not to derive

$$A{:}*, P{:}A \rightarrow * \vdash [x{:}A][x{:}Px]x : \{x{:}A\}\{x{:}Px\}Px$$

This example suggests that the rule

$$\text{LDA} \qquad \frac{\Gamma[x{:}A] \vdash M : B \qquad \Gamma \vdash \{x{:}A\}B : s}{\Gamma \vdash [x{:}A]M : \{x{:}A\}B}$$

AX	$\bullet \vdash s_1 : s_2$	$\mathsf{Ax}(s_1{:}s_2)$
START	$\dfrac{\Gamma \vdash A : s}{\Gamma[x{:}A] \vdash x : A}$	$x \notin \mathsf{Dom}\,(\Gamma)$
WEAK	$\dfrac{\Gamma \vdash \sigma : C \qquad \Gamma \vdash A : s}{\Gamma[x{:}A] \vdash \sigma : C}$	σ is a sort or a variable, $x \notin \mathsf{Dom}\,(\Gamma)$
PI	$\dfrac{\Gamma \vdash A : s_1 \qquad \Gamma[x{:}A] \vdash B : s_2}{\Gamma \vdash \{x{:}A\}B : s_3}$	$\mathsf{Rule}(s_1, s_2, s_3)$
LDA	$\dfrac{\Gamma[x{:}A] \vdash M : B \qquad \Gamma \vdash \{x{:}A\}B : s}{\Gamma \vdash [x{:}A]M : \{x{:}A\}B}$	
APP	$\dfrac{\Gamma \vdash M : \{x{:}A\}B \qquad \Gamma \vdash N : A}{\Gamma \vdash M\,N : B[N/x]}$	
CONV	$\dfrac{\Gamma \vdash M : A \qquad \Gamma \vdash B : s \qquad A \simeq B}{\Gamma \vdash M : B}$	

Table 1. The typing judgement of a PTS.

using the same bound variable for the term and its type is not exactly what we intend.

A formalization of PTS that distinguishes between parameters and variables, along the lines discussed in section 2.1, is described in [MP93]. We use the following LDA rule:

$$\text{LDA} \qquad \frac{\Gamma, p{:}A \vdash M[p/x] : B[p/y] \qquad \Gamma \vdash \{y{:}A\}B : s}{\Gamma \vdash [x{:}A]M : \{y{:}A\}B} \; p \notin M,\ p \notin B$$

This system has closure under parallel reduction [Pol94]; writing $\twoheadrightarrow\!\!\!\!\!\!\shortmid\;\;$ for parallel reduction we have

Lemma 8. *If* $\Gamma \vdash M : A$, $\Gamma \twoheadrightarrow \Gamma'$, $M \twoheadrightarrow M'$ *and* $A \twoheadrightarrow A'$ *then* $\Gamma' \vdash M' : A'$

Since alpha-conversion is contained in parallel reduction, we have as a corollary

Corollary 9. *If* $\Gamma \vdash M : A$, $\Gamma \stackrel{\alpha}{=} \Gamma'$, $M \stackrel{\alpha}{=} M'$ *and* $A \stackrel{\alpha}{=} A'$ *then* $\Gamma' \vdash M' : A'$

However this proof, instantiating closure under parallel reduction with the degenerate case of alpha-conversion, is not intensionally satisfactory as it uses the rule CONV only for alpha-conversion. A presentation of PTS using nameless terms will never use CONV for alpha-conversion, and I would like to know $\vdash$ is the structurally isomorphic to such a nameless presentation, not just that it has isomorphic judgements.

VC-SRT	$\Gamma \vdash_{vc} s_1 : s_2$	$\mathsf{Ax}(s_1{:}s_2)$
VC-VAR	$\Gamma \vdash_{vc} x : \mathsf{assoc}\ x\ \Gamma$	
VC-PI	$\dfrac{\Gamma \vdash_{vc} A : s_1 \qquad \Gamma, x{:}A \vdash_{vc} B : s_2}{\Gamma \vdash_{vc} \{x{:}A\}B : s_3}$	$\mathsf{Rule}(s_1, s_2, s_3)$ $x \notin \mathsf{Dom}\,(\Gamma)$
VC-LDA	$\dfrac{\Gamma, x{:}A \vdash_{vc} b : B \qquad \Gamma \vdash_{vc} \{x{:}A\}B : s}{\Gamma \vdash_{vc} [x{:}A]b : \{x{:}A\}B}$	$x \notin \mathsf{Dom}\,(\Gamma)$
VC-APP	$\dfrac{\Gamma \vdash_{vc} a : \{x{:}B\}A \quad , \quad \Gamma \vdash_{vc} b : B}{\Gamma \vdash_{vc} a\, b : A[b/x]}$	
VC-CNV	$\dfrac{\Gamma \vdash_{vc} a : A \qquad \Gamma \vdash_{vc} B : s \qquad A \simeq B}{\Gamma \vdash_{vc} a : B}$	
NIL-VC	$\bullet \vdash_{vc}$	
CONS-VC	$\dfrac{\Gamma \vdash_{vc} \qquad \Gamma \vdash_{vc} A : s}{\Gamma, x{:}A \vdash_{vc}}$	$x \notin \mathsf{Dom}\,(\Gamma)$

Table 2. The system of valid contexts.

In section 2.2 we derived a system, $\vdash_{lt}$, for $\lambda\!\rightarrow$ without any variable renaming that was closed under alpha-conversion. I don't think we can do the same for PTS. If we follow the transformations of section 2.2, first optimizing to only check context validity once, then linearizing context search, we arrive at the system of Table 2. This system is correct, in the sense

$$\Gamma \vdash M : A \Leftrightarrow (\Gamma \vdash_{vc} \text{ and } \Gamma \vdash_{vc} M : A)$$

If we now try to drop the side conditions $x \notin \mathsf{Dom}\,(\Gamma)$ from VC-PI and VC-LDA, as in section 2.2, (call this system $\vdash_{bad}$) we find the following incorrect derivation

$$\dfrac{\dfrac{\Gamma, x{:}A, x{:}Px \vdash_{bad} x : Px}{\Gamma, x{:}A \vdash_{bad} [x{:}Px]x : \{x{:}Px\}Px}}{\Gamma \vdash_{bad} [x{:}A][x{:}Px]x : \{x{:}A\}\{x{:}Px\}Px}$$

3.1 The Constructive Engine

I remind you that this paper is not addressing the issue of making PTS syntax directed; the Constructive Engine we will derive now is not yet a program for typechecking PTS (in particular, the non-syntax-directed conversion rule remains), but does explain the interaction between named and nameless variables of an operational Constructive Engine.

Table 3 is a correct presentation of PTS using locally nameless terms, corresponding to $\vdash_{iln}$ of section 2.4. Now, as in section 2.4, we may drop the side

ILN-SRT	$\Gamma \vdash_{iln} s_1 : s_2$	$\mathsf{Ax}(s_1{:}s_2)$
ILN-VAR	$\Gamma \vdash_{iln} x : \mathsf{assoc}\ x\ A$	
ILN-PI	$\dfrac{\Gamma \vdash_{iln} A : s_1 \qquad \Gamma, x{:}A \vdash_{iln} B[x/0] : s_2}{\Gamma \vdash_{iln} \{A\}B : s_3}$	$\mathsf{Rule}(s_1, s_2, s_3)$ $x \notin B,\ x \notin \mathsf{Dom}\,(\Gamma)$
ILN-LDA	$\dfrac{\Gamma, x{:}A \vdash_{iln} b[x/0] : B[x/0] \qquad \Gamma \vdash_{iln} \{A\}B : s}{\Gamma \vdash_{iln} [A]b : \{A\}B}$	$x \notin b,\ x \notin B$ $x \notin \mathsf{Dom}\,(\Gamma)$
ILN-APP	$\dfrac{\Gamma \vdash_{iln} a : \{B\}A \qquad \Gamma \vdash_{iln} b : B}{\Gamma \vdash_{iln} a\, b : A[b/0]}$	
ILN-CNV	$\dfrac{\Gamma \vdash_{iln} a : A \qquad \Gamma \vdash_{iln} B : s \qquad A \simeq B}{\Gamma \vdash_{iln} a : B}$	
ILN-NIL	$\bullet \vdash_{iln}$	
ILN-CONS	$\dfrac{\Gamma \vdash_{iln} \qquad \Gamma \vdash_{iln} A : s}{\Gamma, x{:}A \vdash_{iln}}$	$x \notin \mathsf{Dom}\,(\Gamma)$

Table 3. The intermediate system of locally nameless terms.

condition $x \notin \mathsf{Dom}\,(\Gamma)$ from rules ILN-PI and ILN-LDA (getting the system $\vdash_{ltln}$), just as in lemma 6. Here we are using the locally nameless representation in an essential way for dependent types!

Continuing as in section 2.4, we use the argument of lemma 7 to replace LTLN-PI and LTLN-LDA by

PCE-PI	$\dfrac{\Gamma \vdash_{pce} A : s_1 \qquad \Gamma, x{:}A \vdash_{pce} B : s_2}{\Gamma \vdash_{pce} \{A\}(B[0/x]) : s_3}$	$\mathsf{Rule}(s_1, s_2, s_3)$
PCE-LDA	$\dfrac{\Gamma, x{:}A \vdash_{pce} b : B \qquad \Gamma \vdash_{pce} \{A\}B : s}{\Gamma \vdash_{pce} [A](b[0/x]) : \{A\}(B[0/x])}$	

giving a system, $\vdash_{pce}$, that can be made into a Constructive Engine as in section 2.4. This Constructive Engine (Table 4) is closed under alpha-conversion.

CE-SRT $\quad \Gamma \vdash s_1 \Rightarrow s_1 : s_2 \qquad \mathsf{Ax}(s_1{:}s_2)$

CE-VAR $\quad \Gamma \vdash x \Rightarrow x : \mathsf{assoc}\; x\; A$

CE-PI
$$\frac{\Gamma \vdash A \Rightarrow \overline{A} : s_1 \qquad \Gamma, x{:}A \vdash B \Rightarrow \overline{B} : s_2}{\Gamma \vdash \{x{:}A\}B \Rightarrow \{\overline{A}\}(\overline{B}[0/x]) : s_3} \qquad \mathsf{Rule}(s_1, s_2, s_3)$$

CE-LDA
$$\frac{\Gamma, x{:}A \vdash b \Rightarrow \overline{b} : \overline{B} \qquad \Gamma \vdash \{x{:}A\}B \Rightarrow \{\overline{A}\}\overline{B} : s}{\Gamma \vdash [x{:}A]b \Rightarrow [\overline{A}](\overline{b}[0/x]) : \{\overline{A}\}(\overline{B}[0/x])}$$

CE-APP
$$\frac{\Gamma \vdash a \Rightarrow \overline{a} : \{\overline{B}\}\overline{A} \qquad \Gamma \vdash b \Rightarrow \overline{b} : \overline{B}}{\Gamma \vdash a\, b \Rightarrow \overline{a}\, \overline{b} : \overline{A}[\overline{b}/0]}$$

CE-CNV
$$\frac{\Gamma \vdash a \Rightarrow \overline{a} : \overline{A} \qquad \Gamma \vdash B \Rightarrow \overline{B} : s \qquad \overline{A} \simeq \overline{B}}{\Gamma \vdash a \Rightarrow \overline{a} : \overline{B}}$$

CE-NIL $\quad \bullet \vdash_{iln}$

CE-CONS
$$\frac{\Gamma \vdash_{iln} \qquad \Gamma \vdash A \Rightarrow \overline{A} : s}{\Gamma, x{:}A \vdash_{iln}} \qquad x \notin \mathsf{Dom}\,(\Gamma)$$

Table 4. The Constructive Engine for PTS.

References

[ACCL91] M. Abadi, L. Cardelli, P.-L. Curien, and J.-J. Levy. Explicit substitutions. *Journal of Functional Programming*, 1(4):375–416, October 1991.

[Alt93] Thorsten Altenkirch. A formalization of the strong normalization proof for System F in LEGO. In *Proceedings of the International Conference on Typed Lambda Calculi and Applications, TLCA'93*, March 1993.

[Bar91] Henk Barendregt. Introduction to generalised type systems. *J. Functional Programming*, 1(2):125–154, April 1991.

[Bar92] Henk Barendregt. Lambda calculi with types. In Gabbai Abramsky and Maibaum, editors, *Handbook of Logic in Computer Science*, volume II. Oxford University Press, 1992.

[Ber90] Stefano Berardi. *Type Dependence and Constructive Mathematics.* PhD thesis, Dipartimento di Informatica, Torino, Italy, 1990.

[Coq91] Thierry Coquand. An algorithm for testing conversion in type theory. In G. Huet and G. D. Plotkin, editors, *Logical Frameworks.* Cambridge University Press, 1991.

[dB72] Nicolas G. de Bruijn. Lambda calculus notation with nameless dummies, a tool for automatic formula manipulation, with application to the church-rosser theorem. *Indag. Math.*, 34(5), 1972.

[dB85] Nicolas G. de Bruijn. Generalizing automath by means of a lambda-typed lambda calculus. In *Proceedings of the Maryland 1984-1985 Special Year in Mathematical Logic and Theoretical Computer Science*, 1985.

[DFH+93] Dowek, Felty, Herbelin, Huet, Murthy, Parent, Paulin-Mohring, and Werner. The Coq proof assistant user's guide, version 5.8. Technical report, INRIA-Rocquencourt, February 1993.

[GN91] Herman Geuvers and Mark-Jan Nederhof. A modular proof of strong normalization for the calculus of constructions. *Journal of Functional Programming*, 1(2):155–189, April 1991.

[Gor93] Andrew Gordon. A mechanism of name-carrying syntax up to alpha-conversion. In *Proceedings of the 1993 HOL User's Meeting, Vancouver*. Springer-Verlag, 1993. LNCS.

[HHP92] Robert Harper, Furio Honsell, and Gordon Plotkin. A framework for defining logics. *Journal of the ACM*, 40(1):143–184, 1992. Preliminary version in LICS'87.

[Hue89] Gérard Huet. The constructive engine. In R. Narasimhan, editor, *A Perspective in Theoretical Computer Science*. World Scientific Publishing, 1989. Commemorative Volume for Gift Siromoney.

[Hue93] G. Huet. Residual theory in λ-calculus: A complete Gallina development. 1993.

[LP92] Zhaohui Luo and Robert Pollack. LEGO proof development system: User's manual. Technical Report ECS-LFCS-92-211, LFCS, Computer Science Dept., University of Edinburgh, The King's Buildings, Edinburgh EH9 3JZ, May 1992. Updated version.

[Luo90] Zhaohui Luo. *An Extended Calculus of Constructions*. PhD thesis, Department of Computer Science, University of Edinburgh, June 1990.

[MP93] James McKinna and Robert Pollack. Pure type systems formalized. In M.Bezem and J.F.Groote, editors, *Proceedings of the International Conference on Typed Lambda Calculi and Applications, TLCA'93*, pages 289–305. Springer-Verlag, LNCS 664, March 1993.

[Pol90] Robert Pollack. Implicit syntax. Informal Proceedings of First Workshop on Logical Frameworks, Antibes, May 1990.

[Pol92] R. Pollack. Typechecking in pure type systems. In *Informal Proceedings of the 1992 Workshop on Types for Proofs and Programs, Båstad, Sweden*, pages 271–288, June 1992. available by ftp.

[Pol94] Robert Pollack. *The Theory of LEGO; A Proof Checker for the Extended Calculus of Constructions*. PhD thesis, University of Edinburgh, 1994. In preparation.

[Tas93] A. Tasistro. Formulation of Martin-Löf's theory of types with explicit substitutions. Master's thesis, Chalmers Tekniska Högskola and Göteborgs Universitet, May 1993.

[vBJ93] L.S. van Benthem Jutting. Typing in pure type systems. *Information and Computation*, 105(1):30–41, July 1993.

[vBJMP94] L.S. van Benthem Jutting, James McKinna, and Robert Pollack. Typechecking in pure type systems. In Henk Barendregt and Tobias Nipkow, editors, *Formal Proceedings of the Nijmegen Workshop on Types for Proofs and Programs, May '93*. Springer-Verlag, LNCS, 1994. This volume.

Machine Deduction

Christophe Raffalli *

Logic team of Paris VII, CNRS UA 753
Laboratory for Foundations of Computer Science, University of Edinburgh

Abstract. Machine Deduction is a type system designed to extract code for an abstract machine from proofs. This paper presents the basic definitions and results, and shows how we can replace a compilation of typed lambda-terms by a proof translation into our system.

1 Introduction.

The proofs as programs paradigm, using the Curry-Howard isomorphism [4], gives a way to associate a program to an intuitionistic proof. This program is almost always a functional program (in general a lambda-term [1]) which has to be compiled before being executed [15]. This ensures some correctness about the functional program extracted from the proof. But the correctness of the compiled code is relative to the proof of the compiler.

We study in this paper a type system for the code of an abstract machine (S.E.C. machine or Krivine's machine). This approach authorises a new kind of compilation: we translate the proof in natural deduction to a proof in our system and we extract the code from this new proof.

The two kinds of compilation can be represented by the following diagram:

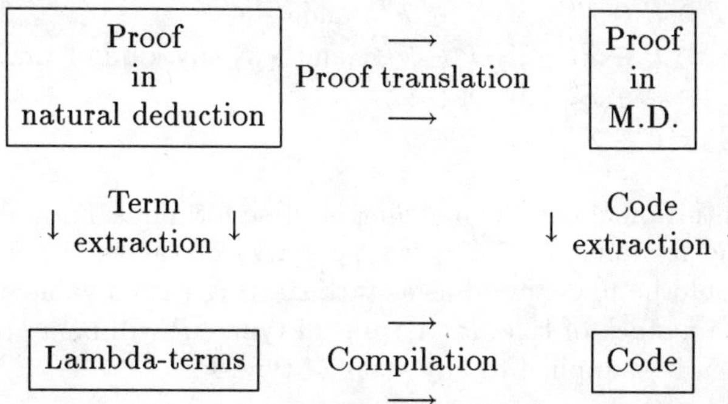

To achieve this goal we define a deduction system MD_{SEC}, for intuitionistic logic. This system is a second order system specially tailored to a translation of Leivant and Krivine's system AF_2[5, 8, 12, 9].

Secondly, we define an S.E.C. machine which is a modification of Krivine's machine (using arrays to store environment and adding some instructions to save

* email: cr@dcs.ed.ac.uk

and restore the stack). Then we introduce a semantics for intuitionistic logic in terms of this machine and we show how to extract code from a proof in our system in a way which is sound for this semantics.

Next, we show how to deal with data types, and how the previous notion of semantics ensures the correctness of programs on data types. In fact MD_{SEC}, may be seen as an extension of AF_2 in which terms are replaced by compiled code for the S.E.C. machine. However, the ability to use machine data types is the principal benefit of MD_{SEC}, because it allows us to consider the notion of computed data inside the system, with an associated type (see section 8).

Finally we give two proof translations, one for Krivine's call-by-name compilation of classical logic and another which is an alternative to call-by-value. This illustrates how our method ensures the correctness of the compiler through the use of data types like the natural numbers. We also briefly show how we can optimise our last compilation in this framework.

2 The deduction system.

We use classical second order formulas. First we define first order terms from a language $\mathcal{L}$ defined by an algebraic signature Σ. Then we define by induction two sets of formulas: $\mathcal{F}^{\Phi}$, the set of *value formulas* and $\mathcal{F}^{\Pi}$ the set of *stack formulas*:

Definition 1. We choose some infinite sets of predicate variables: $\mathcal{V}_n^{\Phi}$ the set *value variables* of arity n and $\mathcal{V}_n^{\Pi}$ the set of *stack variable* of arity n. And we define $\mathcal{F}^{\Phi}$ and $\mathcal{F}^{\Pi}$ as the least sets of word satisfying:

$$\begin{array}{rl}
\top, \bot \in \mathcal{F}^{\Pi} & \\
X(t_1, \ldots, t_n) \in \mathcal{F}^{\Pi} & \text{if } \ X \in \mathcal{V}_n^{\Pi} \\
F \wedge P \in \mathcal{F}^{\Pi} & \text{if } \ F \in \mathcal{F}^{\Phi} \ \text{ and } \ P \in \mathcal{F}^{\Pi} \\
\exists \chi P \in \mathcal{F}^{\Pi} & \text{if } \ P \in \mathcal{F}^{\Pi} \ \text{ and } \chi \text{ is any kind of variable} \\
A(t_1, \ldots, t_n) \in \mathcal{F}^{\Phi} & \text{if } \ A \in \mathcal{V}_n^{\Phi} \\
\neg P \in \mathcal{F}^{\Phi} & \text{if } \ P \in \mathcal{F}^{\Pi}
\end{array}$$

Here is some intuition about the meaning of these formulas: Formulas in $\mathcal{F}^{\Phi}$ will type values and formulas in $\mathcal{F}^{\Pi}$ will type stacks of values. Thus an object of type $F \wedge P$ should be understood as a stack starting with a value of type F and continuing with a stack of type P. A value of type $\neg P$ will be a program which terminates when it is applied to any stack of type P.

In all this paper, we will use the following notation to write formulas:

- M, N for arbitrary formulas.
- P, Q, R for stack formulas.
- F, G for value formulas.
- X, Y for stack variables.
- A, B for value variables.
- x, y for first order variables.
- t, u for first order terms.
- Γ, Δ for multisets of value formulas.
- $M[t/x]$ for the substitution of the first order variable x with a term t in the formula M.

* $M[\lambda x_1 \ldots \lambda x_n N/X]$ for the substitution of the the second order variable X of arity n with a formula N in the formula M. This substitution is defined as usual, but to be compatible with the definition of stack formulas and value formulas, we will substitute only stack formulas to stack variables and value formulas to value variables.
* χ for any kind of variable (first order, stack or value variables).
* φ, associated to χ, for an expression which is substitutable to χ (only in substitution of the form $M[\varphi/\chi]$):
  · φ is a term if χ is a first order variable
  · $\varphi = \lambda x_1 \ldots \lambda x_n P$ where $P \in \mathcal{F}^\Pi$ if χ is a stack variable or arity n
  · $\varphi = \lambda x_1 \ldots \lambda x_n F$ where $F \in \mathcal{F}^\Phi$ if χ is a value variable or arity n
* We will often omit parenthesis for variables and constants of arity 1.

We will consider only sequents of the following form, with $F_1, \ldots, F_n \in \mathcal{F}^\Phi$ and $P \in \mathcal{F}^\Pi$:

$$F_1, \ldots, F_n \mid P \vdash$$

In such a sequent, the "," and "|" must be understood as conjunction. So $F_1, \ldots, F_n \mid P \vdash$ means that we get a contradiction from $F_1 \wedge \ldots \wedge F_n \wedge P$. It also means that a program of this type will terminate in an environment of values of type $F_1, \ldots, F_n$ and with a stack of type P.

Here are the rules of the deduction system MD_{SEC}:

$$\frac{}{F_1, \ldots, F_{m-1}, \neg P, F_{m+1}, \ldots, F_n \mid P \vdash} Ax \qquad \frac{F_1, \ldots, F_n \mid P \vdash}{\Gamma \mid F_1 \wedge \ldots \wedge F_n \wedge P \vdash} \wedge_i$$

$$\frac{F_1, \ldots, F_m, \ldots, F_n \mid (F_m \wedge P) \vdash}{F_1, \ldots, F_m, \ldots, F_n \mid P \vdash} Co \qquad \frac{\Gamma \mid \neg Q \wedge P \vdash \quad \Gamma \mid Q \vdash}{\Gamma \mid P \vdash} \wedge_e$$

$$\frac{\Gamma \mid \top \vdash}{\Gamma \mid P \vdash} \top_e \qquad \frac{\Gamma \mid \neg(\neg P \wedge \top) \wedge P \vdash}{\Gamma \mid P \vdash} \top'_e$$

$$\frac{\Gamma \mid P \vdash \qquad \chi \notin \Gamma}{\Gamma \mid \exists \chi P \vdash} \exists_i \qquad \frac{\Gamma \mid \exists \chi P \vdash}{\Gamma \mid P[\varphi/\chi] \vdash} \exists_e$$

$$\frac{}{\Gamma \mid \bot \vdash} \bot_s$$

Note: the $\top$ connective is not useful when we use the existential quantifier. If we replace $\top$ by $\exists X\, X$ the rule $\top_e$ is derivable and the rule $\bot_s$ is still correct. We give a system using $\top$ to have also a complete propositional version.

Proposition 2. *This deduction system is correct and complete for intuitionistic logic. This means that we prove $\Gamma \mid P \vdash$ in our system if and only if $\Gamma, P \vdash$ is a valid sequent in second order intuitionistic logic (or classical logic).*

Proof. Correctness part: The proof of correction is done by induction on the derivation of $\Gamma \mid P \vdash$. In fact, it's sufficient to remark that all rules are correct (the rule $\top'_e$ could seem classical. But because formulas are to the left, this rule is in fact equivalent to $\neg(\neg\neg P \wedge P) \rightarrow \neg P$ which is intuitionisticaly true).

We won't give here the proof of completeness, because of its length and because we don't use this result for what follows in this paper. □

The meaning of the correctness part of this proposition is obvious: it implies the consistency of the system. However, the meaning of the completeness, which is relative to the syntactic restrictions over formulas is less clear. The fact our system is complete for both intuitionistic and classical logic is not surprising. Indeed there are sequents which can not written in MD, and for all MD formulas Glivenko's theorem holds (all formulas are negated because they are on the left part of the sequent, and we don't use universal quantification). The main result we can deduce from this is that all functions provably total in classical second order logic are also provably total in MD and therefore we can extract an algorithm for them (This will be proved with more efficient algorithms in section 7 and 8).

3 Programs and machine.

In this section, we describe an S.E.C. machine, similar to Krivine's machine extended with instruction to save and restore the stack. We define by induction the set of instructions $\mathcal{I}$, the set of programs $\mathcal{P}$, the set of environments $\mathcal{G}$, the set of values $\mathcal{V}$ and the set of stacks $\mathcal{S}$ as the least sets of words satisfying the following conditions:

$$
\begin{array}{rl}
\texttt{Erase}, \texttt{Stop}, \texttt{Save}, \texttt{Rest} \in \mathcal{I} & \\
\texttt{Jump}_n, \texttt{Pop}_n, \texttt{Push}_n \in \mathcal{I} & \text{if } \ n \in I\!N \\
\texttt{Push}[p] \in \mathcal{I} & \text{if } \ p \in \mathcal{P} \\
i_1;\ldots;i_n \in \mathcal{P} & \text{if } \ i_1,\ldots,i_n \in \mathcal{I} \\
() \in \mathcal{G} & \text{empty environment} \\
(\varphi_1,\ldots,\varphi_n) \in \mathcal{G} & \text{if } \ \varphi_1,\ldots,\varphi_n \in \mathcal{V} \\
\langle p/e \rangle \in \mathcal{V} & \text{if } \ p \in \mathcal{P} \ \text{ and } \ \varphi \in \mathcal{V} \\
\varepsilon \in \mathcal{S} & \text{empty stack} \\
\varphi \cdot \pi \in \mathcal{S} & \text{if } \ \varphi \in \mathcal{V} \ \text{ and } \ \pi \in \mathcal{S}
\end{array}
$$

Remark: These sets satisfy the following isomorphisms : $\mathcal{P} \cong \mathcal{I}^{<\omega}$ (where $\mathcal{I}^{<\omega}$ is the set of finite sequences of instructions), $\mathcal{G} \cong \mathcal{S} \cong \mathcal{V}^{<\omega}$ and $\mathcal{V} \cong (\mathcal{P} \times \mathcal{G})$.

Now, we define the transition function "tr" (this is a partial function), from $\mathcal{P} \times \mathcal{G} \times \mathcal{S}$ to itself. We give this definition in table 1. In this table, the first line of each cell is a pattern for the arguments of the "tr" function, and the second line gives the value of "tr" applied to this pattern.

For instructions `Save` and `Rest`, we use the canonical isomorphism between $\mathcal{S}$ and $\mathcal{G}$ to store a stack in place of an environment.

Table 1. Here is the complete transition table for the S.E.C. machine (tr):

input code / output code	input environment / output environment	input stack / output stack
$\mathtt{Pop}_m;p$	e	$\varphi_1 \cdots \varphi_m \cdot \pi$
p	$(\varphi_1, \ldots, \varphi_m)$	π
$\mathtt{Push}[p'];p$	e	π
p	e	$\langle p'/e \rangle \cdot \pi$
$\mathtt{Push}_m;p$	$(\varphi_1, \ldots, \varphi_n)$ with $(1 \leq m \leq n)$	π
p	$(\varphi_1, \ldots, \varphi_n)$	$\varphi_m \cdot \pi$
$\mathtt{Jump}_m;p$	$(\varphi_1, \ldots, \varphi_{m-1}, \langle p'/e' \rangle, \varphi_{m+1}, \ldots, \varphi_n)$	π
p'	e'	π
$\mathtt{Erase};p$	e	π
p	e	ε
$\mathtt{Stop};p$	e	π
$\mathtt{Stop};p$	e	π
$\mathtt{Save};p$	e	π
p	e	$\langle \mathtt{Rest}/\pi \rangle \cdot \pi$
$\mathtt{Rest};p$	$e = \pi'$	$\langle p'/e' \rangle \cdot \pi$
p'	e'	π'

Definition 3. We define the partial function $\mathrm{ex}(\varphi, \pi)$ from $\mathcal{V} \times \mathcal{S}$ to $\mathcal{S}$. Given a value $\varphi = \langle p/e \rangle$ and a stack π, let be $\{S_n\}_{n \in \mathbb{N}}$ the sequence defined by

* $S_0 = (p, e, \pi)$
* $S_{n+1} = \mathrm{tr}(S_n)$

Then, $\mathrm{ex}(\varphi, \pi)$ is defined if the previous sequence is well defined and if there exists an integer N such that $S_N = (\mathtt{Stop};p', e', \pi')$. In this case, we define $\mathrm{ex}(\varphi, \pi) = \pi'$.

Fact 4. *If* $\mathrm{tr}(p, e, \pi) = (p', e', \pi')$ *then* $\mathrm{ex}(\langle p/e \rangle, \pi)) = \mathrm{ex}(\langle p'/e' \rangle, \pi')$.

4 Semantics.

In this section, we define a semantics of the logic in terms of machines. This semantics associates to a value (resp. stack) formula the set of values (resp. stacks) of this type.

Definition 5. An interpretation σ, is given by:

* A mapping $x \mapsto |x|^\sigma$ from first order variables to $\mathcal{V}$.
* A mapping $f \mapsto |f|^\sigma$ from function constants of arity n to $\mathcal{V}^n \to \mathcal{V}$.
* A mapping $A \mapsto |A|^\sigma$ from program variables of arity n to $\mathcal{V}^n \to \mathcal{P}(\mathcal{V})$.
* A mapping $X \mapsto |X|^\sigma$ from stack variables of arity n to $\mathcal{V}^n \to \mathcal{P}(\mathcal{S})$.
* An element $|\bot|^\sigma$ of $\mathcal{S}^\sigma$.

Definition 6. Given $\Phi \in \mathcal{P}(\mathcal{V})$ and $\Pi \in \mathcal{P}(\mathcal{S})$, we define

$$\Phi \times \Pi = \{\varphi \cdot \pi \mid \varphi \in \Phi \quad \text{and} \quad \pi \in \Pi\}$$

Definition 7. Given Π in $\mathcal{P}(\mathcal{S})$, we define the set $\overline{\Pi}$ in $\mathcal{P}(\mathcal{V})$ by:

$$\overline{\Pi} = \{\varphi \in \mathcal{V} \mid \quad \text{for all} \quad \pi \in \Pi \quad \mathrm{ex}(\varphi, \pi) \in |\bot|^\sigma\}$$

We note that $\varphi \in \overline{\Pi}$ implies that $\mathrm{ex}(\varphi, \pi)$ is well defined for all $\pi \in \Pi$.

It is very important to note that the definition of $\overline{\Pi}$ depends on $|\bot|^\sigma$ which is in fact the set of all legal stacks when a program stops.

Given such an interpretation, we define by induction the interpretation for all first order terms, stack formulas and value formulas. The interpretation of a term is an element of $\mathcal{V}$, the interpretation of a stack formula is an element of $\mathcal{P}(\mathcal{S})$ and the interpretation of a value formula is an element of $\mathcal{P}(\mathcal{V})$:

$$\begin{aligned}
|f(t_1, \ldots, t_n)|^\sigma &= |f|^\sigma(|t_1|^\sigma, \ldots, |t_n|^\sigma) \\
|X(t_1, \ldots, t_n)|^\sigma &= |X|^\sigma(|t_1|^\sigma, \ldots, |t_n|^\sigma) \\
|A(t_1, \ldots, t_n)|^\sigma &= |A|^\sigma(|t_1|^\sigma, \ldots, |t_n|^\sigma) \\
|\top|^\sigma &= \{\varepsilon\} \\
|\neg P|^\sigma &= \overline{|P|^\sigma} \\
|F \wedge P|^\sigma &= |F|^\sigma \times |P|^\sigma \\
|\exists X P|^\sigma &= \bigcup_{\Pi \in \mathcal{V}^n \to \mathcal{P}(\mathcal{S})} |P|^{\sigma[\Pi/X]} \quad (n \text{ is the arity of } X) \\
|\exists A P|^\sigma &= \bigcup_{\Phi \in \mathcal{V}^n \to \mathcal{P}(\mathcal{V})} |P|^{\sigma[\Phi/A]} \quad (n \text{ is the arity of } A) \\
|\exists x P|^\sigma &= \bigcup_{\varphi \in \mathcal{V}'} |P|^{\sigma[\varphi/x]}
\end{aligned}$$

We introduce also the following notation:

- If $\Gamma = F_1, \ldots, F_n$, we write $|\Gamma|^\sigma$ for $\{(\varphi_1, \ldots, \varphi_n) \mid \varphi_i \in |F_i|^\sigma\}$.
- For any interpretation σ, we write $\sigma[\Phi/\chi]$ for the usual modification of the interpretation of only one variable.
- To deal with second order, we also write $|\lambda x_1 \ldots \lambda x_n\, M|^\sigma$ (with $M \in \mathcal{F}^\Phi$ or $M \in \mathcal{F}^\Pi$) for the function defined $\varphi_1, \ldots, \varphi_n \mapsto |M|^{\sigma[\varphi_1/x_1]\ldots[\varphi_n/x_n]}$.

Fact 8. *For all interpretations σ, for all value formulas F, and for all stack formulas P, we have:*

$$\begin{aligned}
|F[\varphi/\chi]| &= |F|^{\sigma[|\varphi|^\sigma/\chi]} \\
|P[\varphi/\chi]| &= |P|^{\sigma[|\varphi|^\sigma/\chi]}
\end{aligned}$$

5 The type system.

We can also use proofs to associate programs to formulas. As in Krivine's and Leivant's system AF_2, we choose a set $\mathcal{E}$ of equational axioms on first order terms and add a rule for these equations. Here are the rules with their algorithmic contents:

$$\frac{}{\texttt{Jump}_m : F_1, \ldots, F_{m-1}, \neg P, \ldots, F_n \mid P \vdash} Ax \qquad \frac{p : F_1, \ldots, F_n \mid (F_m \wedge P) \vdash}{\texttt{Push}_m ; p : F_1, \ldots, F_n \mid P \vdash} Co$$

$$\frac{p : F_1, \ldots, F_n \mid P \vdash}{\texttt{Pop}_n ; p : \Gamma \mid F_1 \wedge \ldots \wedge F_n \wedge P \vdash} \wedge_i \qquad \frac{p : \Gamma \mid \neg Q \wedge P \vdash \quad q : \Gamma \mid Q \vdash}{\texttt{Push}[q] ; p : \Gamma \mid P \vdash} \wedge\neg_e$$

$$\frac{p : \Gamma \mid \top \vdash}{\texttt{Erase} ; p : \Gamma \mid P \vdash} \top_e \qquad \frac{p : \Gamma \mid \neg(\neg P \wedge \top) \wedge P \vdash}{\texttt{Save} ; p : \Gamma \mid P \vdash} \top'_e$$

$$\frac{p : \Gamma \mid P \vdash \qquad \chi \notin \Gamma}{p : \Gamma \mid \exists \chi\, P \vdash} \exists_i \qquad \frac{p : \Gamma \mid \exists \chi\, P \vdash}{p : \Gamma \mid P[\varphi/\chi] \vdash} \exists_e$$

$$\frac{}{\texttt{Stop} : \Gamma \mid \bot \vdash} \bot_s \qquad \frac{p : \Gamma \mid P[t/x] \vdash \quad \mathcal{E} \vdash t = u}{p : \Gamma \mid P[u/x] \vdash} Eq$$

Now we can prove that this code extraction is sound for the interpretation semantics previously defined:

Proposition 9. *Let σ be an interpretation satisfying: $\mathcal{E} \vdash t = u$ implies $|t|^\sigma = |u|^\sigma$ for all first order terms. If we prove $p : \Gamma \mid P \vdash$ then for all $e \in |\Gamma|^\sigma$, we have*

$$\langle p/e \rangle \in |\neg P|^\sigma$$

Proof. We prove this result by induction on the proof:

* If the last rule is Ax:

$$\frac{}{\texttt{Jump}_m : F_1, \ldots, F_{m-1}, \neg P, F_{m+1}, \ldots, F_n \mid P \vdash} Ax$$

  Let $e = (\varphi_1, \ldots, \varphi_n) \in \mathcal{V}$ be such that $\varphi_i \in |F_i|^\sigma$. We have $\text{ex}(\langle \texttt{Jump}_m/e \rangle, \pi) = \text{ex}(\varphi_m, \pi)$. So $\langle \texttt{Jump}_m/e \rangle \in |\neg P|^\sigma$, because $\varphi_m \in |\neg P|^\sigma$.

* If the last rule is Co

$$\frac{p : F_1, \ldots, F_m, \ldots F_n \mid (F_m \wedge P) \vdash}{\texttt{Push}_m ; p : F_1, \ldots, F_m, \ldots F_n \mid P \vdash} Co$$

  We have to prove $\langle \texttt{Push}_m ; p/e \rangle \in |\neg P|^\sigma$. We choose $e \in |F_1, \ldots, F_n|^\sigma$ and $\pi \in |P|^\sigma$. By definition, we have $e = \langle \varphi_1 \ldots \varphi_m \ldots \varphi_n \rangle$ with for all i, $\varphi_i \in |F_i|^\sigma$. Thus we get $\text{ex}(\langle \texttt{Push}_m ; p/e \rangle, \pi) = \text{ex}(\langle p/e \rangle, \varphi_m \cdot \pi)$. Hence, we get the expected result using $\langle p/e \rangle \in |\neg(F_m \wedge P)|^\sigma$ (by induction hypothesis) and $\varphi_m \cdot \pi \in |F_m \wedge P|^\sigma$.

* If the last rule is $\wedge_i$

$$\frac{p : F_1, \ldots, F_n \mid P \vdash}{\texttt{Pop}_n;p : \Gamma \mid F_1 \wedge \ldots \wedge F_n \wedge P \vdash} \wedge_i$$

We denote $\Gamma' = F_1, \ldots, F_n$. We have to prove $\langle \texttt{Pop}_n;p/e \rangle \in |\neg(F_1 \wedge \ldots \wedge F_n \wedge P)|^\sigma$ for all $e \in |\Gamma|^\sigma$. We choose $e \in |\Gamma|^\sigma$ and $\pi \in |F_1 \wedge \ldots \wedge F_n \wedge P|^\sigma$. By definition, we have $\pi = \varphi_1 \cdots \varphi_n \cdot \pi'$ with for all i, $\varphi_i \in |F_i|^\sigma$ and $\pi' \in |P|^\sigma$. Then, $\mathrm{ex}(\langle \texttt{Pop}_n;p/e \rangle, \pi) = (\langle p/e' \rangle, \pi')$ with $e' = (\varphi_1, \ldots, \varphi_n)$, and we get the result using $e' \in |\Gamma'|^\sigma$, $\langle p/e' \rangle \in |\neg P|^\sigma$ (induction hypothesis) and $\pi' \in |P|^\sigma$.

* If the last rule is $\wedge\neg_e$

$$\frac{p : \Gamma \mid \neg Q \wedge P \vdash \quad q : \Gamma \mid Q \vdash}{\texttt{Push}[q];p : \Gamma \mid P \vdash} \wedge\neg_e$$

We have to prove $\langle \texttt{Push}[q];p/e \rangle \in |\neg P|^\sigma$. We choose $e \in |\Gamma|^\sigma$ and $\pi \in |P|^\sigma$. We have $\mathrm{ex}(\langle \texttt{Push}[q];p/e \rangle, \pi) = \mathrm{ex}(\langle p/e \rangle, \langle q/e \rangle \cdot \pi)$. Thus, we get the result because by induction hypothesis we have $\langle p/e \rangle \in |\neg(\neg Q \wedge P)|^\sigma$ and $\langle q/e \rangle \in |\neg Q|^\sigma$, so we have $\langle q/e \rangle \cdot \pi \in |\neg Q \wedge P|^\sigma$.

* If the last rule is $\top_e$

$$\frac{p : \Gamma \mid \top \vdash}{\texttt{Erase};p : \Gamma \mid P \vdash} \top_e$$

Let $e \in |\Gamma|^\sigma$ be, we have to prove $\langle \texttt{Erase};p/e \rangle \in |\neg P|^\sigma$. By definition, for all $\pi \in |P|^\sigma$, we have $\mathrm{ex}(\langle \texttt{Erase};p/e \rangle, \pi) = \mathrm{ex}(\langle p/e \rangle, \varepsilon)$. Hence, we get the desired result because $\langle p/e \rangle \in |\neg \top|^\sigma$ (induction hypothesis).

* If the last rule is $\bot_s$

$$\frac{}{\texttt{Stop} : \Gamma \mid \bot \vdash} \bot$$

For all $e \in |\Gamma|^\sigma$ and $\pi \in |\bot|^\sigma$, we have $\mathrm{ex}(\langle \texttt{Stop}/e \rangle, \pi) = \pi \in |\bot|^\sigma$. So we have $\langle \texttt{Stop}/e \rangle \in |\neg\bot|^\sigma$.

* If the last rule is $\top_c$

$$\frac{p : \Gamma \mid \neg(\neg P \wedge \top) \wedge P \vdash}{\texttt{Save};p : \Gamma \mid P \vdash} \top_c$$

Let $e \in |\Gamma|^\sigma$ be, we have to prove that $\langle \texttt{Save};p/e \rangle \in |\neg P|^\sigma$. Let $\pi \in |P|^\sigma$ be, so we have $\mathrm{ex}(\langle \texttt{Save};p/e \rangle, \pi) = \mathrm{ex}(\langle p/e \rangle, \varphi \cdot \pi)$, with $\varphi = \langle \texttt{Rest}/\pi \rangle$. If we prove $\varphi \in |\neg(\neg P \wedge \top)|^\sigma$, we get $\varphi \cdot \pi \in |\neg(\neg P \wedge \top) \wedge P|^\sigma$ and with the induction hypothesis, we get the desired result.

Now let us prove that $\varphi \in |\neg(\neg P \wedge \top)|^\sigma$. Let us choose $\pi' \in |\neg P \wedge \top|^\sigma$. By definition, $\pi' = \langle p'/e' \rangle \cdot \varepsilon$ with $\langle p'/e' \rangle \in |\neg P|^\sigma$. But we have $\mathrm{ex}(\langle \texttt{Rest}/\pi \rangle, \pi') = \mathrm{ex}(\langle p'/e' \rangle, \pi)$. Hence we get the expected result because $\langle p'/e' \rangle \in |\neg P|^\sigma$ and $\pi \in |P|^\sigma$.

* If the last rule is $\exists_i$

$$\frac{p : \Gamma \mid P \vdash \qquad \chi \notin \Gamma}{p : \Gamma \mid \exists\chi\, P \vdash}\ \exists_i$$

Let σ be an interpretation and choose $e \in |\Gamma|^\sigma$, we have to prove that $\langle p/e\rangle \in |\neg\exists\chi\, P|^\sigma$. But this says that for all possible interpretations φ for the variable χ, we have $\langle p/e\rangle \in \overline{|P|^{\sigma[\varphi/\chi]}}$, and this is true by induction hypothesis.

* If the last rule is $\exists_e$

$$\frac{p : \Gamma \mid \exists\chi\, P \vdash Q}{p : \Gamma \mid P[\varphi/\chi] \vdash Q}\ \exists_e$$

By induction hypothesis, for all interpretations σ and for all $e \in |\Gamma|^\sigma$, $\langle p/e\rangle \in |\neg\exists\chi\, P|^\sigma$, so we have $\langle p/e\rangle \in \overline{|P|^{\sigma[|\varphi|^\sigma/\chi]}}$, for all expressions φ substitutable to χ, and by the proposition 8, we have $|P[\varphi/\chi]|^\sigma = |P|^{\sigma[|\varphi|^\sigma/\chi]}$. Hence we get $\langle p/e\rangle \in |\neg P[\varphi/\chi]|^\sigma$.

* If the last rule is Eq

$$\frac{p : \Gamma \mid P[t/x] \vdash \quad \mathcal{E} \vdash t = u}{p : \Gamma \mid P[u/x] \vdash}\ Eq$$

By hypothesis on σ and by 8, we get $|P[t/x]|^\sigma = |P[u/x]|^\sigma$. So we get the desired result. □

We may have a stronger correctness result for closed formulas whose interpretation does not depend upon the interpretation of $\perp$:

Definition 10. We will say that M is a control formula, if $|M|^\sigma$ is independent of the interpretation σ (we can apply this definition if M is a stack or a value formula). In this case we write $|M|$ for the interpretation of M.

Example: we can see that $\top$ and $\exists X\, X$ are control stack formulas, because they are closed formulas using no negation.

Proposition 11. *Let $F_1, \ldots, F_n$ be value control formulas and P,Q control stack formulas. If we prove $p : F_1, \ldots, F_n \mid \neg Q \wedge P \vdash$, then for all $\pi \in |P|$ and $e \in |F_1, \ldots, F_n|$, we have $\mathrm{ex}(\langle p/e\rangle, \varphi \cdot \pi) \in |Q|$, with $\varphi = \langle \mathtt{Stop}/()\rangle$.*

Proof. Let $F_1, \ldots, F_n$ be value control formulas and P, Q control stack formulas. We assume $p : F_1, \ldots, F_n \mid \neg Q \wedge P \vdash$. We can choose an interpretation σ such that $|\perp|^\sigma = |Q|$. So we get $\varphi = \langle \mathtt{Stop}/()\rangle \in |\neg Q|$, and we can apply the proposition 9, and we get $\langle p/e\rangle \in |\neg(\neg Q \wedge P)|$ for all $e \in |F_1, \ldots, F_n|$. So we have $\mathrm{ex}(\langle p/e\rangle, \varphi \cdot \pi) \in |\perp|^\sigma = |Q|$ for all $\pi \in |P|$. □

6 Data types.

It is easy to add data types to this system. Let us show how to add the natural numbers. This example is demonstrative enough to show how to deal with any kind of data types.

To add natural numbers, we follow these steps:

* We add a second order value constant of arity one: $\mathbb{N}(\_)$.
* We add the following symbols to the language: 0, s(_), add(_, _), mul(_, _) .... We identify all the elements of the data type with the set of logical terms obtained by its constructors. For natural numbers, this means that the elements of the data type $\mathbb{N}$ are the logical terms of the form $s^n 0$.
* We add to $\mathcal{E}$ some equations to define add(_, _), mul(_, _) ....
* We add all the natural numbers to the set of Values ($\mathcal{V}$). So we can put some natural numbers in the stack or in the environment. We will write $\bar{i}$ for the value associated to an element i of the data type $\mathbb{N}$.
* We add $\texttt{Push}_{\mathbb{N}}[i]$ (for each number i), $\texttt{Rec}_{\mathbb{N}}[p_0][p_s]$ (for each program p_0 and p_s) and $\texttt{Inc}_{\mathbb{N}}$ to the set of instructions $\mathcal{I}$ and we give the following transition tables:

input code output code	input environment output environment	input stack output stack
$\texttt{Push}_{\mathbb{N}}[i];p$ p	e e	π $\bar{i}\cdot\pi$
$\texttt{Inc}_{\mathbb{N}};p$ p	e e	$\bar{i}\cdot\pi$ $\overline{i+1}\cdot\pi$
$\texttt{Rec}_{\mathbb{N}}[p_0][p_s]$ p_0	$(\bar{0})$ $()$	π π
$\texttt{Rec}_{\mathbb{N}}[p_0][p_s]$ p_s	$(\overline{i+1})$ $(\bar{i})$	π $\langle\texttt{Rec}_{\mathbb{N}}[p_0][p_s]/(\bar{i})\rangle\cdot\pi$

* We add the following rules to the type system:

$$\frac{p:\Gamma \mid \mathbb{N}(i)\wedge P \vdash}{\texttt{Push}_{\mathbb{N}}[i];p:\Gamma\mid P\vdash}\,\mathbb{N}_e \qquad \frac{p:\Gamma \mid \mathbb{N}(\mathrm{s}\,i)\wedge P \vdash}{\texttt{Inc}_{\mathbb{N}};p:\Gamma\mid \mathbb{N}(i)\wedge P\vdash}\,\mathbb{N}_s$$

$$\frac{p_0:\ \mid P(0)\vdash \qquad p_s:\mathbb{N}(j)\mid(\neg P(j)\wedge P(\mathrm{s}\,j))\vdash}{\texttt{Rec}_{\mathbb{N}}[p_0][p_s]:\mathbb{N}(i)\mid P(i)\vdash}\,\mathbb{N}_r$$

The first two rules express that we can push any number on the stack (so if we can terminate on any stack of type $\mathbb{N}(i)\wedge P$ we can terminate on any stack of type P) and that we can replace an number i on the top of the stack by its successor.
The recursor rule could be interpreted as follow: if we can terminates on a stack of type $P(0)$ as well as on a stack of type $\neg P(j)\wedge P(\mathrm{s}\,j)$ (this means that we can terminates on a stack of type $P(\mathrm{s}\,j)$ whenever a program terminating

on $P(j)$ is given), then we can terminate on any stack of type $P(i)$, i being any natural numbers. In fact, this is an induction rule to prove $\neg P(i)$. To have a more general rule, we keep a natural number in the environment so we have really an induction rule and not just an iteration[2].

* And finally we extend the notion of interpretation by $|\mathbb{N}|^\sigma(i) = \{\bar{i}\}$ if i is an element of the data type $\mathbb{N}$ (modulo the equations in $\mathcal{E}$) and $|\mathbb{N}|^\sigma(u) = \emptyset$ in all the other cases. With this definition it is not difficult to extend the proof of proposition 9.

As an example, here is a derivation for the addition program, using the usual equation for addition, $\mathrm{add}(0, j) = j$ and $\mathrm{add}(\mathrm{s}\,i, j) = \mathrm{s}\,\mathrm{add}(i, j)$. The proof is given in table 2, and the program extracted from this proof is:

```
Add = Pop3;Push2;Push3;Push1;Pop1;RecN[Pop1;Jump1][Pop2;Push[IncN;Jump2];Jump1]
```

Table 2. Proof for the addition.

To simplify the proof we use this notation:

$$P^j(i) = \neg(\mathbb{N}(\mathrm{add}(i,j)) \wedge Q) \wedge \mathbb{N}(j) \wedge Q$$
$$\Gamma^j(i) = \neg P^j(i), \neg(\mathbb{N}(\mathrm{add}(\mathrm{s}\,i,j)) \wedge Q)$$

$$\frac{\frac{\frac{}{\neg(\mathbb{N}\,\mathrm{add}(0,j)\wedge Q) \mid \mathbb{N}\,\mathrm{add}(0,j)\wedge Q \vdash}\,Ax}{\neg(\mathbb{N}\,\mathrm{add}(0,j)\wedge Q) \mid \mathbb{N}j\wedge Q \vdash}\,Eq}{\mid P^j(0) \vdash}\,\wedge_i$$

$$\frac{\frac{\frac{}{\Gamma^j(k) \mid \mathbb{N}\,\mathrm{add}(\mathrm{s}\,k,j)\wedge Q \vdash}\,Ax}{\Gamma^j(k) \mid \mathbb{N}\,\mathrm{s}\,\mathrm{add}(k,j)\wedge Q \vdash}\,Eq}{\Gamma^j(k) \mid \mathbb{N}\,\mathrm{add}(k,j)\wedge Q \vdash}\,\mathbb{N}_s$$

$$\frac{\frac{\frac{}{\Gamma^j(k) \mid P^j(k) \vdash}\,Ax \qquad \Gamma^j(k) \mid \mathbb{N}\,\mathrm{add}(k,j)\wedge Q \vdash}{\Gamma^j(k) \mid \mathbb{N}j\wedge Q \vdash}\,\wedge_e}{\mathbb{N}k \mid \neg P^j(k) \wedge P^j(\mathrm{s}\,k) \vdash}\,\wedge_i$$

$$\frac{\mid P^j(0) \vdash \qquad \mathbb{N}k \mid \neg P^j(k) \wedge P^j(\mathrm{s}\,k) \vdash}{\mathbb{N}i \mid P^j(i) \vdash}\,\mathbb{N}_r$$

$$\frac{\frac{\frac{\frac{\frac{\mathbb{N}i \mid P^j(i) \vdash}{\mathbb{N}i, \mathbb{N}j, \neg(\mathbb{N}\,\mathrm{add}(i,j)\wedge Q) \mid \mathbb{N}i \wedge P^j(i) \vdash}\,\wedge_i}{\mathbb{N}i, \mathbb{N}j, \neg(\mathbb{N}\,\mathrm{add}(i,j)\wedge Q) \mid P^j(i) \vdash}\,Co}{\mathbb{N}i, \mathbb{N}j, \neg(\mathbb{N}\,\mathrm{add}(i,j)\wedge Q) \mid \mathbb{N}j \wedge Q \vdash}\,Co}{\mathbb{N}i, \mathbb{N}j, \neg(\mathbb{N}\,\mathrm{add}(i,j)\wedge Q) \mid Q \vdash}\,Co}{\mid \mathbb{N}i \wedge \mathbb{N}j \wedge \neg(\mathbb{N}\,\mathrm{add}(i,j)\wedge Q) \wedge Q \vdash}\,\wedge_i$$

This proof and the extracted program could seem complicated, but it's not to far from code produced by real compiler. Moreover, we see that the last four rules of the proof only permute 2 values in the stack. This could be easily optimised by adding a derived rule and a new instruction to perform such a permutation.

Now, we can apply the proposition 11 to the type of natural numbers $\mathbb{N}$, which is a control formula by definition of its interpretation:

[2] It would be better for efficiency to have a more general induction using an environment of arbitrary size.

Proposition 12. *If* $\vdash p :| \exists Q(\neg(\mathbb{N}t \wedge Q) \wedge Q) \vdash$, *using a consistent set of equations* $\mathcal{E}$, *then* $\mathrm{ex}(\langle p/()\rangle, \varphi \cdot \varepsilon) = \overline{n} \cdot \varepsilon$ *with* $\varphi = \langle \mathtt{Stop}/()\rangle$ *and* $\mathcal{E} \vdash t = s^n 0$.

Proof. We substitute $\top$ to Q and apply proposition 11. Thus $\mathrm{ex}(\langle p/()\rangle, \varphi \cdot \varepsilon) = \overline{n} \cdot \varepsilon$ with $\overline{n} \in |\mathbb{N}t|^\sigma$ for all interpretations σ satisfying $|u|^\sigma = |v|^\sigma$ for any terms u and v such that $\mathcal{E} \vdash u = v$ (there exists such an interpretation because $\mathcal{E}$ is consistent). Moreover, we proved that t is a natural number only using equations in $\mathcal{E}$. This means that we can find p such that $\mathcal{E} \vdash t = s^p 0$. Then we have $|t|^\sigma = |s^p 0| = \overline{p} \in |\mathbb{N}t|^\sigma$. Thus we get $n = p$ by definition of the interpretation of $\mathbb{N}$. □

Example: we have

$$\vdash \mathtt{Push}_{\mathbb{N}}[m];\mathtt{Push}_{\mathbb{N}}[n];\mathtt{Add} \; :| \; \exists Q(\neg(\mathbb{N}\, add(n, m) \wedge Q) \wedge Q) \vdash$$

Thus, we have

$$\mathrm{ex}(\langle \mathtt{Push}_{\mathbb{N}}[m];\mathtt{Push}_{\mathbb{N}}[n];\mathtt{Add}/()\rangle, \varphi \cdot \varepsilon) = \overline{n + m} \cdot \varepsilon$$

7 Call by name compilation of system AF_2.

The principle of this compilation is to translate proofs from system AF_2 into MD_{SEC} (You can find the definition of system AF_2 in annex A). The first thing is to remark that we can replace the original implication introduction rule by this multiple introduction:

$$\frac{M_1, \ldots, M_n \vdash_{\mathrm{AF}_2} M}{\Gamma \vdash_{\mathrm{AF}_2} M_1 \to (M_2 \to \ldots (M_n \to M))} \to_i^n$$

The translation of a proof in order to use this rule instead of the original one is in fact the lambda lifting. This first translation is left to the reader. (We need to put a non empty context in the conclusion of the rule because there is no weakening in the system).

Now we translate the formulas of system AF_2:

Definition 13. We define by induction on a formula M of AF_2, a formula $M^0 \in \mathcal{F}^\Pi$, and $\overline{M} \in \mathcal{F}^\Phi$ by

* $\overline{M} = \neg M^0$
* $X(\overline{t})^0 = X(\overline{t})$ where $X \in \mathcal{V}^\Pi$
* $(M \to N)^0 = \overline{M} \wedge N^0$
* $(\forall x\, M)^0 = \exists x\, M^0$
* $(\forall X\, M)^0 = \exists X\, M^0$

Note: All the variables are translated to stack variables, so we identify the set of variables of system AF_2 with the set of stack variables.

Proposition 14. *For all formulas M and N of system* AF_2 *and all variables X of arity n, we have*

$$(M[\lambda x_1 \ldots \lambda x_n N/X])^0 = M^0[\lambda x_1 \ldots \lambda x_n N^0/X]$$

Proof. By induction on the formula M. □

Now it is possible to translate proofs (For any environment $\Gamma = M_1, \ldots, M_n$ we write $\overline{\Gamma}$ for $\overline{M_1}, \ldots, \overline{M_n}$):

Proposition 15. *For all environments Γ and all formulas M of* AF_2,

$$\Gamma \vdash_{\mathrm{AF}_2} M \quad \textit{implies} \quad \overline{\Gamma} \mid M^0 \vdash$$

Proof. We prove this by induction on the proof of $\Gamma \vdash_{\mathrm{AF}_2} M$:

* If the last rule is an axiom: We have $M = M_i$ with $\Gamma = M_1, \ldots, M_n$. Hence, we get the expected result using the *Ax* rule, because $\overline{M_i} = \neg M_i^0$.
* If the last rule is the implication elimination, by induction hypothesis, we get $\Gamma \vdash_{\mathrm{AF}_2} N \to M$ implies $\overline{\Gamma} \mid \neg N^0 \wedge M^0 \vdash$ and $\Gamma \vdash_{\mathrm{AF}_2} N$ implies $\overline{\Gamma} \mid N^0 \vdash$. Hence, we get the expected result using the $\wedge\!\!\neg_e$ rule.
* If the last rule is the multiple implication introduction, we have $M = N_1 \to (N_2 \to \ldots (N_p \to N))$ and we get $N_1, \ldots, N_p \vdash_{\mathrm{AF}_2} N$ implies $\overline{N_1}, \ldots, \overline{N_p} \mid N^0 \vdash$ (induction hypothesis). Hence, we get the expected result using the $\wedge_i$ rule.
* If the last rule is the universal quantifier elimination, we have $M = N[\varphi/\chi]$. By induction hypothesis we get $\Gamma \vdash_{\mathrm{AF}_2} \forall\chi\, N$ implies $\overline{\Gamma} \mid \exists\chi\, N^0 \vdash$. If χ is a first order variable then φ is a term and $M^0 = N^0[\varphi/\chi]$. If χ is a second order variable then we get $M^0 = N^0[\varphi^0/\chi]$ by proposition 14. Hence, we have the expected result using the $\exists_e$ rule.
* If the last rule is the introduction of a universal quantifier, we have $M = \forall\chi\, N$ and by induction hypothesis we get $\Gamma \vdash_{\mathrm{AF}_2} N$ implies $\overline{\Gamma} \mid N^0 \vdash$. Moreover, we know that χ is not free in $\overline{\Gamma}$. Hence, we get the expected result using the $\exists_i$ rule.
* If the last rule is the equational rule, the induction hypothesis and the *Eq* rule give directly the expected result. □

Now, if we compare the term extracted from the proof in natural deduction (with the multiple implication introduction rule) and the code extracted from the translated proof, we obtain the following compilation for the lambda-calculus using super-combinators (we use $\overline{t}$ to denote the code of a term t):

* $x_i \mapsto$ `Jump`$_i$ (axiom rules are translated with the *Ax* rule)
* $\lambda x_1 \ldots \lambda x_n\, t \mapsto$ `Pop`$_n$;$\overline{t}$ (multiple $\to_i$ rules are translated with the $\wedge_i$ rule)
* $(t\ u) \mapsto$ `Push`$[\overline{u}]$;$\overline{t}$ ($\to_e$ rules are translated with the $\wedge\!\!\neg_e$ rule)
* Nothing more, because all other rules of system AF_2 have no algorithmic contents and are translated to non-algorithmic rules of MD_{SEC}.

This is similar to the Krivine's call-by-name compilation (in fact this is exactly Parigot's modification of Krivine's compilation for a machine with environments as arrays). Furthermore, one can easily obtain the usual optimisation. For instance we can translate an implication elimination on an axiom with the Co rule instead of using $\wedge\!\!\neg_e$ and Ax rules. So we get a well known optimisation which gives $(t\ x_i) \mapsto$ Push$_i$;$\bar{t}$ instead of $(tx_i) \mapsto$ Push[Jump$_i$];$\bar{t}$.

Moreover, if we add to system AF_2 the $\perp$ formula with both intuitionist and classical absurdity:

$$\frac{\Gamma \vdash_c t : \perp}{\Gamma \vdash_c (A\,t) : M} \qquad \frac{\Gamma \vdash_c t : (M \to \perp) \to M}{\Gamma \vdash_c (C\,t) : M}$$

We can always translate the proof: we extend the translation of formulas with $\perp^0 = \top$ (we get $((M \to \perp) \to M)^0 = \neg(\neg M^0 \wedge \top) \wedge M^0$. The two previous rules are translated using the $\top_e$ and $\top_c$. This gives the following compilation for the A and C operator: $(A\ t) \mapsto$ Erase;$\bar{t}$ and $(C\ t) \mapsto$ Save;$\bar{t}$. This is a possible compilation for the following reduction rules (in call-by-name) for these operators, which are exactly those proposed by Felleisen [7, 2, 11]:

$$(A\,t\,t_1 \ldots t_n) \rhd t$$
$$(C\,t\,t_1 \ldots t_n) \rhd (t\ \lambda x\ (x\,t_1 \ldots t_n)\,t_1 \ldots t_n)$$

Corollary 16. *We have:* $\Gamma \vdash_{\mathrm{AF}_2} M$ *in system* AF_2 *with the previous rule added if and only if* $\overline{\Gamma} \mid M^0 \vdash$ *in* MD_{SEC}.

Proof. The left-right implication is a consequence of the previous translation. The right-left implication is easy to prove and left to the reader (it's a consequence of the correctness part in proposition 2). □

8 Compilation, correctness and optimisation.

By corollary 16, it might appear MD is isomorphic[3] to AF_2 extended with classical logic, which has already been studied by Krivine [7] and Parigot [13]. But the mapping $M \mapsto M^0$ defined in the previous section is not surjective. Indeed M^0 uses only value formulas which are negations of stack formulas, while in the complete system, value formulas may also be built from value variables or using data types like natural numbers (see section 6). However, we think (though we have no proof) that this mapping can not be extended to be an isomorphism, because it seems impossible to deal in AF_2 with the notion of computed data types that we have in MD (the formula $I\!N(t)$ is the type of a computed numbers, while the formula $\neg\exists Q(\neg(I\!N\bar{t} \wedge Q) \wedge Q)$ is the type of a program computing a number).

[3] We consider two type systems to be isomorphic if there is a translation from one to the other giving bijections between both the extracted programs and the formulas of the systems.

In this section we intend to show that these new features are interesting enough to justify the definition of a new system.

First, we will examine how our approach ensures the correctness of the compilation:

Proposition 17. *We assume that $\Gamma \vdash M \mapsto \overline{\Gamma} \mid M^0 \vdash$ is a translation from* AF$_2$ *sequents with data types (see appendix B) to MD sequents such that we prove the translated sequent (in MD) whenever we prove the original sequent (in* AF$_2$*). Such a translation gives a correct compilation if*

$$\mathbb{N}(t)^0 = \exists Q(\neg(\mathbb{N}t \wedge Q) \wedge Q)$$

Proof. This is true because we are only interested in programs which produce data types (these are the only ones you really execute on a machine). This means that we need to know only the correctness of programs extracted from a proof of $\vdash \mathbb{N}(t)$. Thus we get the correctness of the code from the condition on the translation and proposition 12. □

Corollary 18. *The call-by-name compilation given in the previous section may be extended for data types with $\mathbb{N}(t)^0 = \exists Q(\neg(\mathbb{N}\overline{t} \wedge Q) \wedge Q)$ and thus is correct.*

Proof. We will give only hints for this extension : we just need to translate the new rules dealing with natural numbers. This can be done in call-by-name with a continuation passing style. Indeed, we need to compute an object of type $\mathbb{N}(t)$ only when it's given in argument to the successor or the recursor, and to compute a number we only need to call the associated value of type $\neg\exists Q(\neg(\mathbb{N}t \wedge Q) \wedge Q)$ after pushing the code waiting for this number (of type $\neg(\mathbb{N}t \wedge Q)$) at the top of the stack. □

However, it's clear that call-by-name compilation is not sufficient. The author tried to study call-by-value, but it seems difficult to make call-by-value compatible with classical logic and second order quantification without algorithmic contents. Thus we introduce the *call-by-type* whose purpose is to compute arguments of function whenever they are data. So this reduction strategy looks at the type to perform reduction and needs a non empty algorithmic content for second order quantification.

Definition 19. We give the following translation for the formula of AF$_2$(we assume that there are two bijections $X \mapsto X_p \in \mathcal{V}^{\Pi}$ and $X \mapsto X_v \in \mathcal{V}^{\Phi}$):

* $\mathbb{N}(t)^0 = \exists Q(\neg(\mathbb{N}t \wedge Q) \wedge Q)$
* $\overline{\mathbb{N}(t)} = \mathbb{N}t$
* $(M \to N)^0 = \overline{M} \wedge N^0$
* $\overline{(M \to N)} = \neg(M \to N)^0$
* $X(\overline{t})^0 = X_p(\overline{t})$ where $X_p \in \mathcal{V}^{\Pi}$

* $\overline{X(\overline{t})} = X_v(\overline{t})$ where $X_v \in \mathcal{V}^{\Phi}$
* $E[X] = \neg\exists\overline{x}(X_v(\overline{x}) \wedge X_p(\overline{x}))$
* $F[X] = \neg\exists\overline{x}\exists P(\neg X_p(\overline{x}) \wedge \neg(X_v(\overline{x}) \wedge P) \wedge P)$
* $(\forall X M)^0 = \exists X_v \exists X_p(E[X] \wedge F[X] \wedge M^0)$
* $(\forall x M)^0 = \exists x M^0$
* $\overline{\forall \chi M} = \neg(\forall \chi M)^0$

The difference from the previous translation is that $\overline{\mathbb{N}(t)} \neq \neg\mathbb{N}(t)^0$. With this translation, we can distinguish two kinds of formula: those which type functions ($\overline{M} = \neg M^0$) and those which type data types ($M^0 = \exists Q(\neg(\overline{M} \wedge Q) \wedge Q)$). In both cases we could say that one of the formula is the negation of the other. For predicate variable, we express this condition by keeping two hypotheses on $\overline{X}$ and X^0: $E[X]$ and $F[X]$.

Proposition 20. *If we prove in* AF_2 $M_1, \ldots, M_n \vdash M$ *then we can prove in* MD $\overline{M_1}, \ldots, \overline{M_n}, \Delta \vdash M^0$, *where* $\Delta = E[X_1], F[X_1], \ldots, E[X_n], F[X_n]$ *if* $X_1, \ldots, X_n$ *are all the free predicate variables in* $M_1, \ldots, M_n$ *and* M.

Proof. We just sketch this proof. We prove this result by induction on the deduction. To translate the implication elimination we distinguish three cases:

* The argument's type is an arrow: we translate like in call-by-name
* The argument's type is $\mathbb{N}(t)$: we call the code associated to this number (of type $\neg\exists Q(\neg(\mathbb{N}t \wedge Q) \wedge Q)$) after pushing on the stack the code of the function (of type $\neg(\mathbb{N}t \wedge Q)$).
* The argument's type is $X\overline{t}$: we call the code associated to the hypothesis $F[X]$ after pushing both code for the argument and the function on the stack.

For the axiom, we introduce a similar distinction, using hypothesis $E[X]$ for the last case. There are also some problems with implication and second order introduction rules which need some manipulations to put things in the right order in the environment. For the second order quantifier elimination, we prove $E[X]$ and $F[X]$ after substitution using again the same three cases depending upon the nature of the substituted formula. Finally the other rules (first order quantification and equation) are straightforward. □

This translation can be optimised to produce efficient code: by choosing carefully in which place we put formula in the environment (we just need to preserve the introduction order, but to do so we have to mix formulas corresponding to a quantification introduction ($E[X]$ and $F[X]$) and those corresponding to an implication introduction.

Another optimisation consists in replacing both hypothesis $E[X]$ and $F[X]$ by only one, built using a new binary connector $F \star P$ which is a value formula telling you that either $F = \neg P$ of $P = \exists Q(\neg(F \wedge Q) \wedge Q)$ and whose algorithmic contents is just a boolean. Moreover, for some polymorphic programs the $E[X]$ and $F[X]$ hypotheses are not used, so we can forget them and simplify the extracted program.

We remark that the first and the last optimisation are not uniform: the translation of a sequent inside a proof may depend upon this proof. This implies that we really use some information in the type of the code: namely "Where are data stored in the environment ?" and "Do we need to give some information about the predicate variable to a polymorphic program ?".

Note: at first sight this compilation could seems complicated and inefficient, but it may be compared to Leroy's ZINC machine [10] whose purpose is to compile call-by-value using an environment stored in an array. The call-by-type is an alternative to call-by-value which can also be compiled with environment stored in an array. However, in the ZINC machine one needs to perform a test for each function call, while in our approach the tests are associated with the introduction of polymorphism and so should be less frequent.

9 Conclusion and further outlook.

In this paper we presented a type system to extract code for an abstract machine. We verified that the extracted code is correct by building a semantics for the type system, and we applied this result to prove the correctness of two compilations for second order typed λ-calculus (system AF_2). The first compilation was call-by-name known as the compilation for Krivine's machine, extended for classical logic using Felleisen C operator [2, 11] for call-by-name. This demonstrates a near isomorphism between MD and classical AF_2.

Then in the section 8 we use the ability of MD to manipulate machine representation of data types to study an alternative compilation: call-by-type. We briefly explained how it works, and how the optimisation of this compilation involves using information stored in the type.

The author thinks this shows the interest of this approach: by using a type system for an abstract machine we get a secure system to write a quite complex compilation scheme. However this approach has some limitation: In what sense do we control the evaluation strategy ? The translation of types given for call-by-name does not ensure that any proof will perform only call-by-name function calls. However we could show that call-by-type ensures that we compute the argument for a function of type $\mathbb{N} \to \mathbb{N}$ (function from data-types to data types). Nevertheless, it seems that there will never be a total control over the evaluation order (for instance in the arguments' evaluation order) without giving some restriction on the proof. Another problem is the use of the first order part of the system to get correctness. This two problems imply that these technics can't be use directly to get the correctness of an ML compiler.

Nonetheless, this approach should allow good optimisation of programs extracted from proofs, because the only restriction on the proof translation is the conclusion sequent of the translated proof. In the near future, the author plans an implementation of both MD and AF_2 system to really explores the practical possibility of the system to optimise code.

A Definition of system AF_2.

System AF_2 uses classical second order formulas constructed with first order terms from a language $\mathcal{L}$, atomic formulas, implication, second order and first order universal quantification $(X(t_1, \ldots, t_n) \mid F \to G \mid \forall X\, F \mid \forall x\, F)$.

It uses also a set of equations on first order terms $\mathcal{E}$. Sequents are of the form $x_1 : F_1, \ldots, x_n : F_n \vdash t : F$ where $x_1, \ldots, x_n$ are lambda-variables and where t is a lambda-term (whose free variables are among $x_1, \ldots, x_n$). This sequent may be proved using the following rules:

* Axiom and equational rules:

$$\frac{}{x : F, \Gamma \vdash x : F}\, Ax \qquad \frac{\Gamma \vdash t : F\,[x/u] \qquad E \vdash u = v}{\Gamma \vdash t : F\,[x/v]}\, Eq$$

* Implication rules:

$$\frac{x : F, \Gamma \vdash t : G}{\Gamma \vdash \lambda x\, t : F \to G} \to_i \qquad \frac{\Gamma \vdash t : F \to G \qquad \Gamma \vdash u : F}{\Gamma \vdash (t)u : G} \to_e$$

* First order abstraction rules:

$$\frac{\Gamma \vdash t : F \qquad \chi \notin \Gamma}{\Gamma \vdash t : \forall \chi F}\, \forall_i \qquad \frac{\Gamma \vdash t : \forall \chi F}{\Gamma \vdash t : F[\varphi/\chi]}\, \forall_e$$

The reader could find more information about system AF_2 in [12], [8] and [5].

B Adding constants to AF_2.

It's easy to add λ-calculus constants to AF_2. For instance, to add the natural numbers, we add **zero**, $\succ$ and **rec** to the λ-calculus, with the following reduction rule:

$$(\mathtt{rec}\, a\, f\, \mathtt{zero}) \rhd a \qquad (\mathtt{rec}\, a\, f\, (\mathtt{suc}\, n)) \rhd (f\, n\, (\mathtt{rec}\, a\, f\, n))$$

Then to type these constants, we add 0 and s to the first order language and the following typing rules:

$$\frac{}{\Gamma \vdash \mathtt{zero} : \mathbb{N}(0)}\, \mathbb{N}_0 \qquad \frac{\Gamma \vdash t : \mathbb{N}(x)}{\Gamma \vdash (\mathtt{suc}\, t) : \mathbb{N}(sx)}\, \mathbb{N}_s$$

$$\frac{\Gamma \vdash a : P(0) \qquad \Gamma \vdash f : \forall x(\mathbb{N}(x) \to P(x) \to P(sx))}{\Gamma \vdash (\mathtt{rec}\, a\, f) : \forall x(\mathbb{N}(x) \to P(x) \to P(sx))}\, \mathbb{N}_r$$

References

1. H. P. Barendregt. *The Lambda Calculus: Its Syntax and Semantics.* North-Holland, revised edition, 1984.
2. M. Felleisen and D. Friedman. Control operators, the SECD machine and the λ-calculus. In *Formal Description of Programming Concepts III*, pages 131–141. North-Holland, 1986.
3. J.-Y. Girard. The system F of variable types: fifteen years later. *Theoretical Computer Science*, 45:159–192, 1986.
4. W. Howard. The formulae-as-types notion of construction. *To H.B. Curry: Essays on combinatory logic, λ-calculus and formalism*, pages 479–490, 1980.
5. Jean-Louis Krivine. *Lambda-Calcul : Types et Modèles.* Etudes et Recherches en Informatique. Masson, 1990.
6. Jean-Louis Krivine. Oprateurs de mise en mmoire et traduction de gödel. *Archive for Mathematical Logic*, 30:241–267, 1990.
7. Jean-Louis Krivine. Classical logic, storage operators and second order λ-calculus. to appear in APAL 1994, 1992.
8. Jean-Louis Krivine and Michel Parigot. Programming with proofs. *Inf. Process. Cybern.*, EIK 26(3):149–167, 1990.
9. Daniel Leivant. Typing and computational properties of lambda expressions. *Theoretical Computer Science*, 44:51–68, 1986.
10. Xavier Leroy. The ZINC experiement: an economical implementation of the ML language. Technical report, INRIA, 1990.
11. Chetan R. Murthy. Finding the answers in classical proofs: A unifying framework. In *Logical Environment*, pages 247–272. Cambridge University Press, 1992.
12. Michel Parigot. Programming with proofs: a second order type theory. *Lecture Notes in Computer Science*, 300, 1988. Communication at ESOP 88.
13. Michel Parigot. $\lambda\mu$-calculus an algorithmic interpretation of classical natural deduction. In *Proc of Log. and Automatic Reasoning*, volume 624 of *Lecture Notes in Computer Science*, pages 190–201, St Petersbourg, 1991. Springer Verlag.
14. Michel Parigot. Recursive programming with proofs. *Theoritical Computer Science*, 94:335–356, 1992.
15. Simon L. Peyton J. *The Implementation of Functional Programming Languages.* Prentice-Hall, 1987. Prentice-Hall International Series in Computer Science.

Type Theory and the Informal Language of Mathematics

Aarne Ranta

Department of Philosophy, P.O.Box 24,
00014 University of Helsinki, Finland.

In the first comprehensive formalization of mathematics, the *Begriffsschrift* (1879), Frege gave up the structure of informal language, in order to reveal the structure of mathematical thought itself. Attempts to apply Frege's formalism to informal discourse outside mathematics followed in this century, e.g. by Russell, Carnap, Quine, and Davidson. In this tradition, the application of logical formalism to informal language is an exercise of skill, rather than an algorithmic procedure, precisely because the linguistic structure is different from the logical structure.

It was Chomsky (1957) who started the study of natural language itself as a formal system, inductively defined by the clauses of a generative grammar. But the structure he gave to his fragment of English was quite different from the structure of a logical formalism.

Finally, in the late sixties, Montague unified the enterprises of Frege and Chomsky in an attempt to give a systematic logical formalization to a fragment of English (see the collection Montague 1974). His grammar applies to a piece of informal discourse outside mathematics. But as modern logic, even in the form employed by Montague, stems from Frege, who designed it for mathematics, a grammar like Montague's should be applicable, if at all, to the language of mathematics.

Following roughly the format of Montague grammar, I have been working within the constructive type theory of Martin-Löf. (See Martin-Löf 1984 and Nordström & al. 1990 for type theory, and Ranta 1991 and 1994 for the grammar.) In addition to the constructive way of thinking, this type theory provides an important generalization of the type structure implicit in Frege and explicit in Montague. The latter has, in addition to the basic types of entities and truth values, function types

$$(\alpha)\beta,$$

where α and β are types. These function types come out as a special case of Martin-Löf's function types

$$(x : \alpha)\beta,$$

where α is a type and β is a type dependent on $x : \alpha$. The use of dependent types makes type theory structurally closer to natural language than predicate calculus at least at the following points.

First, type theory makes a distinction between substantival and adjectival terms, e.g. between *number* and *prime*. These are formalized as N : set and

$P : (N)$prop, respectively, whereas in predicate calculus they are both formalized as one-place propositional functions. To define quantifiers in a way that works with this treatment, one must use dependent types:

$$\Pi : (X : \text{set})((X)\text{prop})\text{prop}$$

Second, in virtue of this definition of quantifiers, type theory has quantifier phrases, like the one corresponding to English *every number*, which is obtained by applying the quantifier Π to the set N:

$$\Pi(N) : ((N)\text{prop})\text{prop}.$$

Complex common nouns can be formed by modifying simple ones with predicates, using the operator

$$\Sigma : (X : \text{set})((X)\text{prop})\text{set}.$$

Thus $\Sigma(N, P)$ is the set of prime numbers, and

$$\Pi(\Sigma(N, P)) : ((\Sigma(N, P))\text{prop})\text{prop}$$

corresponds to the complex quantifier phrase *every prime number*. Predicate calculus dissolves quantifier phrases, because it does not have expressions corresponding to them.

Third, type theory has progressive connectives, i.e. a conjunction and an implication of the type

$$(X : \text{prop})((X)\text{prop})\text{prop}.$$

Such connectives are abundant in informal language, in sentences like

if this equation has a root it is negative.

To express this in type theory, first look at the implicans *this equation has a root*. It is an existential proposition, of the form

$$\Sigma(R, E).$$

To form the implicatum, use the propositional function *x is negative* defined for $x : R$, i.e.

$$L : (R)\text{prop}$$

in the context of a proof of the implicans,

$$z : \Sigma(R, E).$$

Left projection gives $p(z) : R$, whence

$$L(p(z)) : \text{prop}$$

by application,

$$(z)L(p(z)) : (\Sigma(R, E))\text{prop}$$

by abstraction, and finally

$$\Pi(\Sigma(R, E), (z)L(p(z))) \ : \ \text{prop}$$

to express the implication. Predicate calculus, which only has connectives of type

$$(\text{prop})(\text{prop})\text{prop},$$

cannot compose the sentence from the implicans and the implicatum, but must use something like

$$(\forall x)(R(x) \& E(x) \supset L(x)),$$

which does not have constituents formalizing the two subclauses of the sentence in question. This lack of compositionality has been first noted in the discussion of so-called donkey sentences, e.g.

if John owns a donkey he beats it

which has the same form as our mathematical example. That such sentences can be formalized in a very natural way in constructive type theory was first noticed in print by Sundholm (1986).

Linguistically, the study of mathematical language rather than everyday language is rewarding because it offers examples that have complicated grammatical structure but are free from ambiguities. We always know exactly what a sentence means, and there is a determinate structure to be revealed. The informal language of mathematics thus provides a kind of grammatical laboratory. Amazingly little use has been made of this laboratory in linguistics; even the material presented below is just an application of results obtained within the standard linguistic fragment containing donkey sentences etc. It is to be expected that a closer study of mathematical language itself will give experience that is useful in general linguistics as well.

In logic and mathematics, the study of linguistic structure is necessary for the design of natural language interfaces to proof systems. Some very penetrating analyses, outside the tradition of linguistics, have been given by de Bruijn, (Cf. de Bruijn 1982, and especially the unpublished series of lectures "Taal en Structuur van de Wiskunde" ("Language and Structure of Mathematics") from 1978.)

1 Formalization and Sugaring

There are two directions of grammatical investigation. One can ask:

> How is this sentence / mode of expression / fragment of discourse represented in the formalism?

Questions put in this way, starting with what is given in the informal language, are questions of *formalization*. But one can also start with what is given in the formalism and ask:

How is this proposition / logical constant / theory expressed in natural language?

These questions will be called questions of *sugaring*.

A special case of formalization is *parsing*: given a string of words belonging to an inductively defined set of such strings, find the grammatical structure. This notion of parsing is of course secondary to the notion of *generation*, the inductive definition of the set of strings. Furthermore, as we can think of generation as the composition of (1) the definition of the formalism and (2) the sugaring of the formalism, we see that parsing is secondary to sugaring in the conceptual order.

2 Basic Expressions of Geometry

In what follows we shall, even if not define a complete sugaring algorithm, look at mathematics expressed in type theory from the sugaring point of view. We shall apply the sugaring principles of Ranta 1991, 1994, originally presented for everyday discourse (like the donkey sentences), to the language of axiomatic geometry such as in Hilbert 1899 and, within type theory, von Plato 1994.

Start with simple set terms,

point : set,
line : set,
plane : set.

The sugaring of simple set expressions into common nouns is simple (in the absence of the singular and plural number of nouns),

point ▷ *point*,
line ▷ *line*,
plane ▷ *plane*.

We use the form $F \;\triangleright\; E$ to express the relation

$$F \text{ can be sugared into } E.$$

Thus it is not an expression for a clause in a deterministic sugaring algorithm.

Then some propositional functions sugared into verbs and adjectives.

lie_PL : (point)(line)prop,
lie_PL(a, b) ▷ *a lies on b*,
lie_PPl : (point)(plane)prop,
lie_PPl(a, b) ▷ *a lies in b*,
lie_LPl : (line)(plane)prop,
lie_LPl(a, b) ▷ *a lies in b*,
parallel : (line)(line)prop,
parallel(a, b) ▷ *a is parallel to b*,
equal : $(A$: set$)(A)(A)$prop,
equal(A, a, b) ▷ *a is equal to b*.

Observe how sugaring overloads the English expressions *lies in* and *equal*. The adjective *equal* is fully polymorphic, the verb *lies in* has two uses. The adjective *parallel* and the verb *lies on* are, in this fragment at least, uniquely typed.

3 Logical Constants

There are quantifier words like

$$\begin{aligned}&\text{every} : (X : \text{set})((X)\text{prop})\text{prop},\\ &\text{Indef} : (X : \text{set})((X)\text{prop})\text{prop},\\ &\text{some} : (X : \text{set})((X)\text{prop})\text{prop}.\end{aligned}$$

A quantified proposition is sugared by replacing the bound variable by a quantifier phrase,

$$\begin{aligned}&\text{every}(A, (x)B) \;\rhd\; B[\textit{every } A/x],\\ &\text{Indef}(A, (x)B) \;\rhd\; B[\text{INDART}(A)\ A/x],\\ &\text{some}(A, (x)B) \;\rhd\; B[\textit{some } A/x].\end{aligned}$$

INDART(A) is the indefinite article corresponding to the sugaring of A, either *a* or *an*. Observe that if the number of occurrences of x in B is other than one, we may get odd results like

$$\begin{aligned}&\text{every}(\text{line}, (x)\text{parallel}(x, x))\\ &\quad\rhd\; \textit{every line is parallel to every line}.\end{aligned}$$

The uniqueness of replacements can be attained e.g. by using pronouns (see Section 6). It is one of the central problems of the logical formalization of natural language, stemming from the apparently quite different modes of expression of quantification in them. Following Frege (1879, § 9), we shall use the word *main argument* for the occurrence of x to be replaced by the quantifier phrase. (See Ranta 1991, Section 5, for a definition of the main argument.)

The rule of substituting quantifier phrases for variables is due to Montague. He avoided the particular problem of multiple substitution by stipulating that pronouns, instead of the quantifier phrase, are used for all occurrences of the variable but the leftmost one. This is relatively complicated as a sugaring procedure, and it does not always give a correct result; for instance, the example above would come out as *every line is parallel to it*. In the present treatment, we shall retain the simple sugaring rule formulated above, and state it as an extra condition that there be exactly one main argument in B.

Another difficulty with the replacement procedure in the sugaring of quantifiers is that the relative scopes of the quantifiers get lost. The rules give e.g.

$$\left.\begin{aligned}&\text{some}(\text{point}, (x)\text{every}(\text{line}, (y)\text{lie\_PL}(x, y)))\\ &\text{every}(\text{line}, (y)\text{some}(\text{point}, (x)\text{lie\_PL}(x, y)))\end{aligned}\right\} \;\rhd\; \textit{some point lies on every line},$$

and such sentences are indeed considered ambiguous in Montague grammar. But it seems that the mathematician would without hesitation interpret the sentence as the first proposition, although it is a plainly false proposition. He would follow the principle according to which the scopes of the quantifiers get narrower from left to right. (On this rule of precedence, as well as some other ones, cf. Ranta 1994, Chapters 3 and 9.)

As for connectives, we introduce two progressive ones and one that is not progressive.

$$\begin{aligned}
&\text{if} : (X : \text{prop})((X)\text{prop})\text{prop},\\
&\text{if}(A,(x)B) \ \rhd\ \textit{if}\, A, B[\emptyset/x],\\
&\text{and} : (X : \text{prop})((X)\text{prop})\text{prop},\\
&\text{and}(A,(x)B) \ \rhd\ A\ \textit{and} B[\emptyset/x],\\
&\text{or} : (\text{prop})(\text{prop})\text{prop},\\
&\text{or}(A,B) \ \rhd\ A\ \textit{or} B,
\end{aligned}$$

where $\emptyset$ is the ellipsis, the empty morph. The number of main arguments may well be zero or more than one, but they must all appear inside anaphoric expressions, so that empty noun phrases are not produced (see Section 6).

Connective and quantifier words are not type-theoretical primitives, but have the definitions

$$\begin{aligned}
&\text{every} = \Pi : (X : \text{set})((X)\text{prop})\text{prop},\\
&\text{Indef} = \Sigma : (X : \text{set})((X)\text{prop})\text{prop},\\
&\text{some} = \Sigma : (X : \text{set})((X)\text{prop})\text{prop},\\
&\text{if} = \Pi : (X : \text{prop})((X)\text{prop})\text{prop},\\
&\text{and} = \Sigma : (X : \text{prop})((X)\text{prop})\text{prop},\\
&\text{or} = + : (\text{prop})(\text{prop})\text{prop}.
\end{aligned}$$

The main difference between quantifiers and progressive connectives is in the sugaring of the first argument: for quantifiers, it is a common noun, and for connectives, a sentence. But there is another difference, which has to do with the expressive capacities of the two modes of expression in English. We noted before that the sugaring of a quantified proposition $Q(A,(x)B)$ requires there to be precisely one main argument occurrence of x in B. For connectives, there is no such restriction. Thus for instance the vacuous quantification

$$\Pi(\text{equal}(N,0,1),(x)\text{equal}(N,1,10000))$$

gives, by the sugaring rule for every, the falsity *one is equal to ten thousand*, and it is the rule for if that gives the right true proposition,

if zero is equal to one, one is equal to ten thousand.

Thus connectives provide a more widely applicable means of expressing propositions than quantifiers.

4 Objects and Expressions

Sugaring is not a function on type-theoretical objects, such as propositions, but on expressions for those objects. For by the extensionality of functions, a proposition would otherwise be sugared in the same way, in whatever way expressed. But we certainly want to sugar every(A, B) differently from if(A, B), although they are both equal to $\Pi(A, B)$. Even more clearly, if we introduce an abbreviatory expression by explicit definition, we want to sugar the definiendum differently from the much longer definiens. Consider, for instance,

$$\text{triangle} = \Sigma(\text{line}, (x)\Sigma(\text{point}, (y)\text{outside\_PEl}(y, \text{extended}(x)))) : \text{set},$$

where outside_PEl(a, b) says that the point a lies outside the extended line b, and extended(a) is the infinite extension of the finite line a.

In general, we want to introduce so many definitional variants of type-theoretical expressions that there is a one-to-one correspondence between English and type-theoretical expressions. We can then define sugaring as a function on the set of expressions, and each expression will have a unique sugaring. But a given proposition can generally be expressed by several English sentences, obtained from the definitionally equal variants of the proposition.

The propositions as types principle is, analogously, assumed for the objects of type theory only. We want the type prop to correspond to sentences, and the type set to common nouns. For type-theoretical objects, we have

$$\text{prop} = \text{set} : \text{type},$$

but, for expressions, this equation is not effective, whereas we assume the transformation

$$\text{there} = (X)X : (\text{set})\text{prop}$$

sugared

$$\text{there}(A) \ \triangleright \ \textit{there is}\ \text{INDART}(A)\ A.$$

It may happen that some expression cannot be sugared, e.g. if it contains a quantifier with no or multiple main arguments. In such a case, the sugaring of the proposition expressed must proceed by finding a definitional variant that can be sugared.

5 Relative Pronouns

To form complex set terms, we can use relative pronouns, e.g.

$$\begin{aligned}
&\text{that} = \Sigma : (X : \text{set})((X)\text{prop})\text{set},\\
&\text{that}(A, (x)B) \ \triangleright \ A\ \textit{that}\ B[\emptyset/x],\\
&\text{such_that} = \Sigma : (X : \text{set})((X)\text{prop})\text{set},\\
&\text{such_that}(A, (x)B) \ \triangleright \ A\ \textit{such that}\ B[\emptyset/x].
\end{aligned}$$

These definitions accord with Martin-Löf's (1984) explanation of *such that* as forming a set of elements of the basic set paired with witnessing information. This treatment is necessary for a compositional formalization of quantifier phrases whose domains are given by using relative clauses, and reference is also made to the witnessing information; cf. Section 7 below. But at the same time, we will have to sugar e.g.

$$\text{every}(\text{that}(A, B), (x)C) \;\triangleright\; C[\text{that}(A, B)/p(x)],$$

i.e. not replace x but $p(x)$. This can be accomplished by the general rule

$$p(x) \;\triangleright\; x.$$

The slight unnaturalness of the solution is, so it seems to me, one instance of the problems we have in formalizing separated subsets by Σ and trying to get rid of the extra information in some cases, while having to keep it in some other cases.

The difference between that and such_that is analogous to the difference between quantifiers and connectives: that requires there to be exactly one main argument in the relative clause, but such_that does not. such_that is thus more widely applicable than that.

6 Anaphoric Expressions

Pronouns are introduced to our fragment of English by the rules

$$\begin{aligned}&\text{Pron} = (X)(x)x : (X : \text{set})(X)X,\\&\text{Pron}(A, a) \;\triangleright\; \text{PRO}(A).\end{aligned}$$

In mathematical language, we do not need *he* or *she*, so PRO(A) is always *it*, and we could as well have

$$\begin{aligned}&\text{it} = (X)(x)x : (X : \text{set})(X)X,\\&\text{it}(A, a) \;\triangleright\; \textit{it}.\end{aligned}$$

Observe that our definition of *it* as the polymorphic identity mapping whose argument is sugared away is very similar to the *it* of ML. The main difference is the *interpretation rule* stating in what situations *it* may replace a singular term. In ML, *it* always refers to the value of the latest value declaration. But this rule is too simple for the informal language of mathematics, where *it* can have different—yet definite—interpretations in one and the same clause, e.g.

if the function f has a maximum, it reaches it at least twice.

Our main rule regulating the use of pronouns (and other anaphoric expressions; see below) is that

> the interpretation of an anaphoric expression is an object of appropriate type given in the context in which the expression is used.

Context here is, in the technical sense of type theory, a list of declarations of variables assumed when the expression is formed. For instance, the proposition B in $\Pi(A,(x)B)$ is formed in the context $x : A$. To these variables we add the constant singular terms used in the same sentence. Moreover, we close the "universe of discourse" based on the context under selector operations (cf. Ranta 1994, Chapter 4, for more details).

An interpretation $a : A$ of a pronoun E in the English expression $--E--$ must thus fulfil the following two conditions.

$\mathrm{Pron}(A, a) \ \triangleright\ E$,
there is a propositional function $B(x) : \mathrm{prop}\ (x : A)$
such that $B(a) \ \triangleright\ --a--$.

As the only pronoun in the mathematical fragment is *it*, the first condition is always satisfied. If there are many objects given in context, it is the second condition that saves the ***uniqueness*** of reference, expressed by the principle that

> the interpretation of an anaphoric expression must be unique in the context in which it is used.

In other languages, like German, the sugaring of $\mathrm{Pron}(A, a)$ may depend on A. Thus

$\mathrm{Pron}(\mathrm{Punkt}, a) \ \triangleright\ $ *er*,
$\mathrm{Pron}(\mathrm{Linie}, a) \ \triangleright\ $ *sie*.

This means that when German is translated into English, a pronoun sometimes loses its unique interpretation and must be replaced by some other expression. And when English is translated into German, it is often impossible to translate pronouns correctly without interpreting them.

There are other anaphoric expressions besides pronouns, more specific in the sense that they do not suppress all information about the object referred to. A definite noun phrase formed by the definite article the preserves the type of the object. A modified definite phrase formed by Mod makes explicit some more information given about the object in the context.

$\mathrm{the} = (X)(x)x : (X : \mathrm{set})(X)X$,
$\mathrm{the}(A, a) \ \triangleright\ $ *theA*.
$\mathrm{Mod} = (X)(Y)(x)(y)x : (X : \mathrm{set})(Y : (X)\mathrm{prop})(x : X)(Y(x))X$,
$\mathrm{Mod}(A, B, a, b) \ \triangleright\ $ *the A that* $B[\emptyset/x]$.

7 Example: the Axiom of Parallels

To see how the sugaring principles work, take as an example the axiom of parallels in the formulation (written in lower level notation for readability)

$$(\Pi z : (\Sigma x : \mathrm{point})(\Sigma y : \mathrm{line})\mathrm{outside\_PL}(x, y))\mathrm{DAP}(p(z), p(q(z))),$$

where

outside_PL(a, b) $\triangleright$ *a lies outside b*,
DAP(a, b) = $(\exists! x : \text{line})(\text{lie\_PL}(a, x)\&\text{parallel}(x, b))$: prop
for a : point, b : line,
DAP(a, b) $\triangleright$ *a determines a parallel to b.*

To find the different possibilities to express the axiom of parallels in English provided by our grammar, recall the definitional variants

every and if for Π,
Indef, some, and, that, and such_that for Σ,
A and there(A) for A : set,
Pron(A,a) and the(A,a) for a : A.

Start sugaring from the outermost form of the proposition. First choose the definitional variant every for Π. Then you must sugar the domain of quantification

$$(\Sigma x : \text{point})(\Sigma y : \text{line})\text{outside\_PL}(x, y)$$

into a set expression. The only choice for the first Σ is a relative pronoun, that or such_that. The domain of this Σ must be sugared into the common noun *point*. The remaining part must be found a sentence-like expression. All ways of sugaring Σ are usable: if you choose the relative pronoun, just apply there. The domain of quantification of the axiom of parallels thus has the following sugarings, among others.

point that lies outside a line,
point that lies outside some line,
point such that there is a line and it lies outside it.

The third sugaring is a little strange, because the interpretation of the two occurrences of *it* seems not to be unique. The language of geometry overloads the verb *lie outside*, so that

$$\left.\begin{array}{l}\text{outside\_PL}(x, y)\\ \text{outside\_LP}(x, y)\end{array}\right\} \triangleright \ \textit{x lies outside y},$$

whence *it lies outside it* has two interpretations that, although equivalent, are distinct propositions. We cannot tell whether the sentence says that the point lies outside the line or that the line lies outside the point. But this explanation of the strangeness already contains the solution, which is to use definite noun phrases instead of pronouns,

point such that there is a line and the point lies outside the line.

To finish the first way of sugaring the axiom of parallels, we replace the first argument in

$$\text{DAP}(p(z), p(q(z)))$$

by the quantifier phrase, as explained in Section 5, and the second argument by a pronoun or a definite phrase of the type line. Applying the sugaring rules for DAP and Pron and choosing the expression for the domain to be the first one cited above, gives *every point that lies outside a line determines a parallel to it*

as an unambiguous statement of the axiom of parallels. The word-to-word formalization of this sentence is the definitional variant

$$\text{every}(\text{that}(\text{point}, (x)\text{Indef}(\text{line}, (y)\text{outside\_PL}(x, y))),\\ (z)\text{DAP}(p(z), \text{Pron}(\text{line}, p(q(z)))))$$

of the original proposition.

The reader can check that the proposition also has the following variants, and find some more of them.

if a point lies outside a line, it determines a parallel to it,
if there is a point such that there is a line such that the point lies outside the line the point determines a parallel to the line.

Observe that the two occurrences of *it* in the first variant are uniquely interpretable, because *determines a parallel to* is not overloaded. An early implementation of sugaring, written in Prolog by Petri Mäenpää, found 1128 variants of a donkey sentence with the same structure as the axiom of parallels.

8 Some Uses of the Plural

In the informal language of mathematics, it is often possible to find clear and unambiguous usages of linguistic structures that appear as hopelessly complex, if an unlimited fragment of natural language is taken under consideration. One such structure is the plural, which has been a persistent problem in logical semantics of Montague style. It has several uses that, when cooccurring, lead to multiple ambiguities. Mathematical texts still make unambiguous use of the plural, e.g. in the sentences

points A and B lie on the line a,
A and B are equal points,
all lines that pass through the center of a circle intersect its circumference.

The first of these sentences shows what von Plato (1994) defines as the term conjunction,

$$C(a.b) = C(a)\&C(b) : \text{prop for } A : \text{set}, C : (A)\text{prop}, a : A, b : A.$$

It is thus propositionally equal to the sentence

the point A lies on the line a and the point B lies on the line a,

in which no plural form occurs. In this case, the plural is just used for finding a more concise expression.

The second sentence does not employ the term conjunction, but it is propositionally equal to the singular sentence

A is equal to B

The difference between the first sentence and this one is an instance of the distinction between what is called distributive and collective plural in linguistics (cf. e.g. Scha 1981). The distributive plural can be analyzed as a conjunction of singular instances, but the collective plural cannot. For this particular sentence, we do have a nonplural equivalent, but I am not sure whether we always do.

The third sentence is propositionally equal to

every line that passes through the center of a circle intersects its circumference.

Here there is no difference between *all lines* and *every line*, except the number agreement of the verb.

We have formulated a sugaring algorithm producing these uses of the plural (Ranta 1994, Chapter 9 and Appendix). In each of these cases, the plural forms of nouns and verbs are only produced in the sugaring process, and there is no type-theoretical operator corresponding to the plural. The rules we have discussed do not yet cover all uses of the plural in the informal language of mathematics. (But as long as we work in the direction of sugaring only, it makes no harm that all uses of an English mode of expression are not produced.) For instance, we do not yet quite understand the collective use of the quantifier word *all* as in

all lines that pass through the center of a circle converge.

Nor do we quite understand the use of the plural pronoun *they*, which is sometimes distributive, paraphrasable by the term conjunction, e.g.

if A and B do not lie outside the line a, they are incident on it,

but sometimes used on the place of the "surface term conjunction", so that it fuses together the arguments of a predicate, e.g.

if a and b do not converge, they are parallel.

9 Problems and Prospects

As indicated in the beginning of this paper, very little linguistic work has been done concerning the informal language of mathematics. To capture the essential structure of mathematical text, a grammatical representation of it should, at least, be able to express the mathematical propositions precisely. This can hardly be expected from all grammars in standard linguistics, but requires a grammatical formalism that comprises logic. Moreover, the formal and the informal language should be tied together by sugaring and parsing algorithms that satisfy the following condition.

> A correct informal proof results, when parsed, in a correct formal derivation, and vice versa.

There are two properties concerning ambiguity that can be stated. First, all expressions of the informal fragment are unambiguous.

But this is maybe too severe a condition. It makes little harm if the English fragment recognized contains ambiguities, if only the parser can detect them and ask the user to disambiguate. Instead, one can pose the weaker condition that

every proposition of the formal theory can be expressed by an unambiguous English sentence.

A sugaring program satisfying this condition can provide a natural language interface to a formal proof system, stating theorems and their proofs in an easily readable form.

When considering mathematical language, instead of the fragment of everyday language familiar to the linguist, one soon realizes both a higher demand of unambiguity and a higher complexity of the propositions. There is still work to be done to find a sugaring algorithm that gives unambiguous expressions for all propositions of a formal theory. One particular problem is that the context in which a proposition is formed can be arbitrarily large, so that there are not enough anaphoric expressions to refer to each object uniquely. A very simple such context is created by the opening

given two lines, ...

formalizable by the quantifier

$$(\Pi z : (\Sigma x : line)line)$$

The anaphoric expressions that can be used for an arbitrary line are *it* and *the line*, but neither of these refers uniquely in this context. One way to solve this problem is to use the expressions *the first line*, *the second line*. Another one, much more idiomatic in mathematical language, is to introduce variables,

given two lines a and b, ...

whereafter reference can be made to *the line a* and to *the line b*. But this opening cannot be formalized as a quantifier, because the variable names are not usable outside the scope of the quantifier. The axiom of parallels in the formulation

if a point A lies outside a line a, A determines a parallel to a.

cannot thus be given the logical form we gave it in Section 7.

A more general defect of our Montague style grammar is that it only concerns propositions and not judgements, of which type theory has several forms that are all needed in the precise formalization of mathematics. What we have done here only suffices for expressing axiomatic theories, in the format familiar from the algebraic thinking prevalent in the logical study of mathematics. Going beyond this format in mathematics, type theory also shows a model for grammar in general, to extend its views from propositions to judgements and other linguistic acts.

Note. The type-theoretical form of a theorem, employed in the ALF system of Gothenburg, is indeed not a proposition but a judgement

```
c : (D1 ; ... ; Dn)A
```

where the variables introduced in the declarations `D1`, ...,`Dn` may occur in the type `A`. After this paper was written, we have experimented, together with Petri Mäenpää, with the sugaring of this form into English and the corresponding parsing of English. It was amazingly easy to give this treatment to the whole of the geometry of von Plato (1994). For instance, the axiom

```
Cos_ln1 : (a,b:Point; c:DiPt(a,b))not(OutsidePL(a,ln(a,b,c)))
```

corresponds to the sentence

```
Cos_ln1. If a and b are points and a is distinct from b,
         then a does not lie outside the line through a and b.
```

This mode of expression is, in a sense, closest to the mathematical structure itself, and quite typical of informal mathematical texts. With the more familiar everyday modes of expression discussed in this paper, it is not so easy to reach the same level of precision. If we just want to build a natural language interface to a proof system, a safe way to start is to use explicit variables and declarations. Quantifiers and pronouns can then be added gradually, to provide alternative ways of expression.

References

N. G. de Bruijn. Formalizing the mathematical vernacular. Technical report, Eindhoven University of Technology, 1982.

Noam Chomsky. *Syntactic Structures*. Mouton, The Hague, 1957.

Gottlob Frege. *Begriffsschrift*. Louis Nebert, Halle A/S, 1879. In English, van Heijenoort 1967.

David Hilbert. *Grundlagen der Geometrie*. Teubner, Leipzig, 2nd edition, 1903. 1st ed. 1899.

Per Martin-Löf. *Intuitionistic Type Theory*. Bibliopolis, Naples, 1984.

Richard Montague. *Formal Philosophy*. Yale University Press, New Haven, 1974. Collected papers edited by Richmond Thomason.

Bengt Nordström, Kent Petersson, and Jan Smith. *Programming in Martin-Löf's Type Theory. An Introduction*. Clarendon Press, Oxford, 1990.

Jan von Plato. The axioms of constructive geometry. Manuscript, University of Helsinki, 1994. To appear.

Aarne Ranta. *Type Theoretical Grammar*. Oxford University Press, Oxford, 1994. To appear.

Aarne Ranta. Intuitionistic categorial grammar. *Linguistics and Philosophy*, 14:203–239, 1991.

Remko Scha. Distributive, collective and cumulative quantification. In J. Groenendijk, T. Janssen, and M. Stokhof, editors, *Formal Methods in the Study of Language, Part 2*, pages 483–517. Mathematisch Centrum, Amsterdam, 1981.

Göran Sundholm. Proof theory and meaning. In D. Gabbay and F. Guenthner, editors, *Handbook of Philosophical Logic, Vol. III*, pages 471–506. D. Reidel, Dordrecht, 1986.

Semantics for Abstract Clauses

D.A. Wolfram

Oxford University Computing Laboratory
Wolfson Building
Parks Road
Oxford OX1 3QD

Abstract. We give declarative and operational semantics for logics that are expressible as finite sets of abstract clauses. The declarative semantics for these sets of generalized Horn clauses uses inductively defined sets and fixed points. It is shown to coincide with the operational semantics for successful and finitely failed derivations. The Abstract Clause Engine (ACE) implements proofs with abstract clauses. The semantics given here provide criteria for ACE's correctness and completeness.

1 Abstract Clauses

The approach here to the semantics of abstract clauses was presented first for two concrete examples: pure first-order logic programming [15], and the logic programming language based on the higher-order logic called The Clausal Theory of Types [17]. The generalized form of this approach which is discussed here is not a direct extrapolation of them. It goes beyond these problems to provide a meta-theory of proofs and logics.

Experiments with the Abstract Clause Engine (ACE) [16], which implements abstract clauses, suggested that apart from logic programming, a generalization could be made which would also encompass simpler combinatorial problems and some relatively elaborate logical frameworks in a uniform way.

The semantics for this generalization relates the theorems of a logic expressed by abstract clauses to proof procedures for such a logic. It does not involve extra models such as those of the first-order predicate calculus, Henkin-Andrews general models [2], or categorical models of the Calculus of Constructions [9]. Soundness and completeness results for logics which are based on such extra models can be combined with the results here, but we do not provide a general means to do so.

Our aim is to provide a meta-theory of logics and proofs which is general enough to express the main features of logical frameworks, logic programming, and classical combinatorial problems. In particular, we give declarative and operational semantics by defining derivation search trees, and show that the latter is sound and complete. These results provide conditions for ensuring that ACE, and other implementations, are sound and complete.

2 Terms and Substitutions

The meta-logic of abstract clauses is based on the monomorphic simply typed λ-calculus. This formalism is sufficiently expressive for encoding calculi with dependent types and polymorphic type theories [12].

To define the meta-logic, we first provide some notations and definitions which are based on those of the simply typed λ-calculus [2, 3, 7]. A variable or constant symbol that occurs in any of these terms has an associated type. The terms that are used with particular abstract clauses is defined in Section 3 below.

We denote the sets of variables, constants, and simply typed λ-terms by $\mathcal{X}$, $\mathcal{C}$, and $\mathcal{T}$, respectively. The type of a term $t \in \mathcal{T}$ is denoted by by $\tau(t)$. The set of free variables of a term $t \in \mathcal{T}$ is denoted by $\mathcal{F}(t)$. The symbols t, u, l, w, and the same symbols with subscripts denote terms in $\mathcal{T}$. The symbols x, y, z, possibly with subscripts, denote variables in $\mathcal{X}$.

Definition 2.1 A *substitution* is a function $\theta : \mathcal{X} \to \mathcal{T}$ which is written in postfix notation, and where $\forall x \in \mathcal{X} : \tau(x) = \tau(x\theta)$.

Notation 2.2 The domain of a substitution θ is written $D(\theta)$.

Notation 2.3 The symbols $\gamma, \mu, \pi, \rho, \sigma, \theta$, possibly with subscripts, denote substitutions. A substitution θ, for example, is represented by a set of the form $\{\langle x, x\theta\rangle \mid x \in D(\theta)\}$.

Definition 2.4 If for all $x \in D(\rho)$, $x\rho$ is a variable which is not x, and for all $x_1, x_2 \in D(\rho)$, $x_1\rho = x_2\rho$ if and only if $x_1 = x_2$ then ρ is a *renaming substitution.*

Definition 2.5 Let V be any set of variables, and θ be any substitution. The *restriction* of θ to V is $\theta\lceil V = \{\langle x, x\theta\rangle \mid x \in D(\theta) \cap V\}$.

As a consequence of the Strong Normalization Theorem and the Church--Rosser Theorem, we can extend the definition of substitution to an endomorphism on $\mathcal{T}$.

Definition 2.6 The *instance* $t\theta$ of a term t by a substitution θ where

$$\theta\lceil\mathcal{F}(t) = \{\langle x_1, t_1\rangle, \ldots, \langle x_m, t_m\rangle\}$$

is the β-normal form of $(\lambda x_1 \cdots x_m.t)(t_1, \ldots, t_m)$.

A *closed instance* $t\theta$ of a term t is one where $\mathcal{F}(t\theta) = \emptyset$.

Definition 2.7 If σ and θ are substitutions then their *composition* $\sigma\theta$ is the substitution $\{\langle x, x\sigma\theta\rangle \mid x \in \mathcal{X}\}$.

3 Clausal Labelling Problems

We call the general form of problem encodable with abstract clauses a *clausal labelling problem.* Abstract clauses encode sequents:

$$\frac{u_1 \quad u_2 \quad \cdots \quad u_n}{l}$$

where the u_i are hypotheses and l is the conclusion. Such a sequent is represented by the abstract clause $l :- u_1, \ldots, u_n$. Similarly, the formula to be proved is a sequent of the form

$$\frac{u_1 \quad u_2 \quad \cdots \quad u_n}{}$$

which is represented by the clause $:- u_1, \ldots, u_n$.

Proofs are built up by composing sequents subject to a consistency test on the compositions. Each composition mainly involves pairing the conclusion of a sequent with an hypothesis of another sequent.

A proof built from clauses is a tree whose root is the sequent to be proved, and whose leaves are pairs of hypotheses and conclusions. The collection of all of the pairs of hypotheses and conclusions in a proof must meet the consistency test of the problem. Building proofs can be seen as searching for conclusions of sequents which enable such a collection to be formed. A solution of a clausal labelling problem is one of its proofs.

We introduce some notations for such pairs before giving more formal definitions.

Definition 3.1 A *constraint* is a pair $\langle u, l \rangle$ where $u, l \in \mathcal{T}$. A *system* is a finite set of constraints.

It follows from Definitions 2.1 and 3.1 above that a substitution is a special form of system.

Definition 3.2 Two systems V and W are *equal up to a renaming of variables* if and only if there is a renaming substitution ρ such that the function $f : V \to W$ where $f\langle u, l \rangle = \langle u\rho, l\rho \rangle$ is a bijection.

Similarly, two sets Θ_1 and Θ_2 of substitutions are *equal up to a renaming of variables* if and only if there is a renaming substitution ρ such that the function $g : \Theta_1 \to \Theta_2$ where $g\theta = \theta\rho$ is a bijection.

Remark 3.3 For simplicity, from now on we shall say that two systems, two substitutions, or two sets substitutions are equal if and only if they are equal up to a renaming of variables.

Definition 3.4 A *positive clause* has the form $l :- u_1, \ldots, u_n$ where $l, u_i \in \mathcal{T}$, and $0 \leq i \leq n$. The term l is called the *head* of the clause, and the finite sequence $u_1, \ldots, u_n$ is called the *body* of the clause. The head and the terms u_i in the body of a positive clause are called the *terms* of the clause. The set of *free variables* of such a clause is the set $\mathcal{F}(l) \cup (\bigcup_{1 \le i \le n} \mathcal{F}(u_i))$. When $n = 0$, the positive clause is written l.

A *negative clause* is a headless positive clause. It has the form $: - \ u_1, \ldots, u_n$. The terms u_i are called the *terms* of the negative clause. The set of *free variables* of such a clause is the set $\bigcup_{1 \le i \le n} \mathcal{F}(u_i)$. When $n = 0$, the negative clause is written $\Box$.

An *abstract clause* or *clause* is either a positive clause or a negative clause.

Using these definitions of clauses, we can now formally define clausal labelling problems and the consistency test.

Definition 3.5 A *clausal labelling problem* is a tuple $(\mathcal{U}, H, P, G_0)$ where

- $\mathcal{U} \subseteq \mathcal{T}$, and for every free variable x which occurs in a term in $\mathcal{U}$ where $\tau(x)$ is a base type, there is a constant symbol c which occurs in a term in $\mathcal{U}$ such that $\tau(x)$ is $\tau(c)$.
- H is a *test* which is a recursive function. Its domain is the set of all systems each of whose constraints is a pair of the form $\langle u, l \rangle$ where $u, l \in \mathcal{U}$. Its range is the set of all countably infinite sets of substitutions each of which is an endomorphism on $\mathcal{U}$. The test H also satisfies the following conditions for every system S in its domain.
  - H is *hereditary*: HS is non-empty if and only if for every subset $R \subseteq S$, HR is non-empty.
  - H is *sound*: for every $\mu \in HS$, $H\{\langle u\mu, l\mu \rangle \mid \langle u, l \rangle \in S\} = \{\emptyset\}$.
  - H is *complete*: for every substitution θ such that
  $$H\{\langle u\theta, l\theta \rangle \mid \langle u, l \rangle \in S\} = \{\emptyset\}$$
  there is $\mu \in HS$ and a substitution α such that $\theta = \mu\alpha$.
  - H respects equivalence: if S and S' are systems in the domain of H and are equal, then HS is equal to HS'.
- P is a *program* which is a finite set of positive clauses which have been totally ordered. The terms of every clause in P are elements of $\mathcal{U}$.
- G_0 is a *goal* which is a negative clause each of whose terms is an element of $\mathcal{U}$.

The semantics of Abstract Clauses uses sets of terms which do not contain free variables. The definition of $\mathcal{U}$ above ensures that such a set always exists. Informally, H tests whether a renamed clause can be used as an inference rule at a leaf of a partially constructed proof tree for its clausal labelling problem. If it can, the test returns a non-empty set of substitutions.

Notation 3.6 We shall sometimes abbreviate a positive clause of the form $l : - \ u_1, \ldots, u_n$ to $l : - \ B$ and possibly add subscripts, where B is syntactically identical to $u_1, \ldots, u_n$ and $n \ge 0$. We shall list clauses in a program P following their ordering where the first clause in the list is the least one in the ordering.

Many combinatorial problems are examples of clausal labelling problems.

Example 3.7 One such problem is the eight queens problem. The goal G_0 is $:-\ u_1, \ldots, u_8$ which represents the eight columns of a chessboard. P is the set $\{1,2,3,4,5,6,7,8\}$ which represents the rows of a chessboard. The test H tests whether the queens do not attack each other. The constraint $\langle i,j \rangle$ where $1 \leq i,j \leq 8$ encodes that there is a queen placed at the intersection of column i and row j of the chessboard.

For example, $H\{\langle u_1,1\rangle, \langle u_2,3\rangle, \langle u_3,5\rangle, \langle u_4,2\rangle, \langle u_5,4\rangle, \langle u_6,6\rangle\} = \emptyset$ because the queens in the first and sixth columns attack each other. However,

$$\{\langle u_1,1\rangle, \langle u_2,3\rangle, \langle u_3,5\rangle, \langle u_4,2\rangle, \langle u_5,4\rangle\} = \{\emptyset\}$$

because no queens attack each other in this case.

Similarly,

$$\{\langle u_1,1\rangle, \langle u_2,7\rangle, \langle u_3,5\rangle, \langle u_4,8\rangle, \langle u_5,2\rangle, \langle u_6,4\rangle, \langle u_7,6\rangle, \langle u_8,3\rangle\} = \{\emptyset\}$$

because this is one of the ninety-two solutions of the problem.

Example 3.8 The distinct representatives problem is the problem of finding all tuples of choices of elements from finite sets so that in any tuple all of its elements are distinct.

For example, given the sets $\{2,8\}, \{3,5\}, \{4,5\}, \{1,3\}, \{6,7\}, \{1,3\}$, a system of distinct representatives for them is $(2,5,4,1,6,3)$.

If we call the sets $u_1, u_2, u_3, u_4, u_5, u_6$, we can see that this is a clausal labelling problem. The goal G_0 is $:-\ u_1, u_2, u_3, u_4, u_5, u_6$. The program P is the set $\{2,8,3,5,4,1,6,7\}$ of the possible representatives.

The test H tests whether the elements selected are distinct. For example, $H\{\langle u_1,2\rangle, \langle u_2,3\rangle, \langle u_3,4\rangle, \langle u_4,3\rangle\} = \emptyset$ because the elements selected from the sets labelled u_3 and u_4 are not distinct. $H\{\langle u_1,2\rangle, \langle u_2,6\rangle\} = \emptyset$ because 6 is not an element of the set labelled u_2. However $H\{\langle u_1,2\rangle, \langle u_2,3\rangle, \langle u_3,4\rangle, \langle u_4,1\rangle\} = \{\emptyset\}$ because $(2,3,4,1)$ is a system of distinct representatives of the sets labelled u_1, u_2, u_3 and u_4.

More generally, logic programming languages and some logical frameworks provide further examples.

Example 3.9 A pure first-order logic program P with a goal clause G_0 is a clausal labelling problem when there is at least one 0-ary constant symbol in the terms of the program or goal.

The set of terms of the set $\mathcal{U}$ which do not contain any variables is the Herbrand Universe [5] for the program and goal, and the test H is first-order unification.

Example 3.10 An object logic with a theorem to be proved which is expressed using the meta-logic of Isabelle [11] is an example of a clausal labelling problem.

The program P is the set of rules of inference for the logic expressed as abstract clauses, and the goal G_0 represents the theorem to be proved. The signature of the logic must contain constant symbols with the same base types as free variables with base types that occur in terms in $\mathcal{U}$. This ensures that ground terms exist in $\mathcal{U}$ whose types are the same as the free variables in P and G_0.

Higher-order unification corresponds to the test H, and higher-order unification procedures usually satisfy the soundness and completeness properties of Definition 3.5, (see Huet [7], for example).

Isabelle's inference rules which have eigenvariable conditions can be similarly treated, but H must also test these conditions.

4 Operational Semantics

We now define derivations of a clausal labelling problem. They involve renamed clauses.

Definition 4.1 A *renamed form* of a clause of the form $l :- u_1, \ldots, u_n$ is the clause $l\rho :- u_1\rho, \ldots, u_n\rho$ where ρ is a renaming substitution. Two clauses c_1 and c_2 are *renamed apart* if and only if $\mathcal{F}(c_1) \cap \mathcal{F}(c_2) = \emptyset$.

Definition 4.2 A *derivation* of a clausal labelling problem $(\mathcal{U}, H, P, G_0)$ is a sequence $(G_0, W_0), (G_1, W_1), \ldots$ of pairs of goals and systems which is defined as follows.

The system W_0 is $\emptyset$.
Suppose that G_k is $:- u_1, \ldots, u_n$ where $k \geq 0$ and $n \geq 0$.

- If $n = 0$, the derivation is a *successful derivation of length* k, and the set of *answer substitutions* is $H(\bigcup_{0 \leq i \leq k} W_k)$.
- If $n > 0$, and there is an *input list* I_k of m_k clauses $l_j :- B_j$ where $1 \leq j \leq m_k \leq n$, which are
  - any m_k clauses of P chosen in strictly ascending lexicographical ordering with respect to the ordering on P, and to which a renaming substitution has been applied to them so that they are renamed apart, and each is renamed apart from G_i and each clause in I_l where $0 \leq i \leq k$ and $1 \leq l < k$, and
  - $H(\cup_{0 \leq i \leq k} W_i \cup \{\langle w_1, l_1 \rangle, \ldots, \langle w_{m_k}, l_{m_k} \rangle\}) \neq \emptyset$ where $w_1, \ldots, w_{m_k}$ are m_k distinct terms in the terms of G_k which are called the *selected terms* of G_k

  then, G_{k+1} is the goal clause formed by replacing w_j by B_j where $1 \leq j \leq m_k$, and W_{k+1} is the system $\{\langle w_1, l_1 \rangle, \ldots, \langle w_{m_k}, l_{m_k} \rangle\}$.
- Otherwise, the derivation is a *failed derivation of length* k.

When $H(\cup_{0 \leq i \leq k} W_i \cup \{\langle w_1, l_1 \rangle, \ldots, \langle w_{m_k}, l_{m_k} \rangle\}) = \emptyset$, one of the clauses in the input list I_l represents a sequent which cannot be used in an inference at this point of the proof. The definition of derivation above has two special cases, and we give examples of them below.

Definition 4.3 A derivation is a concurrent breadth-first or *BF-derivation* when m_k equals the number of terms of G_k where $k \geq 0$. It is a depth-first or *DF-derivation* when $m_k = 1$. A *fair derivation* is either a failed derivation, or one in which every term of a goal is a selected term after a finite number of derivation steps.

Example 4.4 Here is an example of a DF-derivation. The test H is first-order unification, and the program P is the following logic program.

$$\begin{array}{l} rev(nil, nil) \\ app(nil, x, x) \\ rev(cons(x, y), z) :- rev(y, x_1), app(x_1, cons(x, nil), z) \\ app(cons(x, y), z, cons(x, x_1)) :- app(y, z, x_1) \end{array}$$

The goal G_0 is $:- rev(cons(1, cons(2, nil)), x_0)$. The steps of the DF-derivation are as follows.

$$\begin{array}{ll} I_0 &= \{rev(cons(x, y), z) :- rev(y, x_1), app(x_1, cons(x, nil), z)\} \\ G_1 &= :- rev(y, x_1), app(x_1, cons(x, nil), z) \\ W_1 &= \{\langle rev(cons(1, cons(2, nil)), x_0), rev(cons(x, y), z)\rangle\} \end{array}$$

$$\begin{array}{ll} I_1 &= \{rev(cons(x_2, y_2), z_2) :- rev(y_2, x_3), app(x_3, cons(x_2, nil), z_2)\} \\ G_2 &= :- rev(y_2, x_3), app(x_3, cons(x_2, nil), z_2), app(x_1, cons(x, nil), z) \\ W_2 &= \{\langle rev(y, x_1), rev(cons(x_2, y_2), z_2)\rangle\} \end{array}$$

$$\begin{array}{ll} I_2 &= \{rev(nil, nil)\} \\ G_3 &= :- app(x_3, cons(x_2, nil), z_2), app(x_1, cons(x, nil), z) \\ W_3 &= \{\langle rev(y_2, x_3), rev(nil, nil)\rangle\} \end{array}$$

$$\begin{array}{ll} I_3 &= \{app(nil, x_4, x_4)\} \\ G_4 &= :- app(x_1, cons(x, nil), z) \\ W_4 &= \{\langle app(x_3, cons(x_2, nil), z_2), app(nil, x_4, x_4)\rangle\} \end{array}$$

$$\begin{array}{ll} I_4 &= \{app(cons(x_5, y_5), z_5, cons(x_5, x_6)) :- app(y_5, z_5, x_6)\} \\ G_5 &= :- app(y_5, z_5, x_6) \\ W_5 &= \{\langle app(x_1, cons(x, nil), z), app(cons(x_5, y_5), z_5, cons(x_5, x_6))\rangle\} \end{array}$$

$$\begin{array}{ll} I_5 &= \{app(nil, x_7, x_7)\} \\ G_6 &= \Box \\ W_6 &= \{\langle app(y_5, z_5, x_6), app(nil, x_7, x_7)\rangle\} \end{array}$$

The constraint $\langle x_0, cons(2, cons(1, nil))\rangle$ occurs in the answer substitution $\theta \in H(\cup_{0 \leq i \leq 6} W_i)$ of this derivation.

The BF-derivation for this logic program and goal has three steps: $(G'_0, W'_0), \ldots, (G'_3, W'_3)$. Its goals are

$$\begin{aligned} G'_0 &= :-\ rev(cons(1, cons(2, nil)), x_0) \\ G'_1 &= :-\ rev(y, x_1), app(x_1, cons(x, nil), z) \\ G'_2 &= :-\ rev(y_2, x_3), app(x_3, cons(x_2, nil), z_2), app(y_5, z_5, x_6) \\ G'_3 &= \Box \end{aligned}$$

The systems which respectively correspond to these goals in this derivation are the following.

$$\begin{aligned} W'_0 &= W_0 \\ W'_1 &\doteq W_1 \\ W'_2 &= W_2 \cup W_5 \\ W'_3 &= W_3 \cup W_4 \cup W_6 \end{aligned}$$

A derivation tree represents a search space for derivations.

Definition 4.5 A *derivation tree* of a clausal labelling problem $(\mathcal{U}, H, P, G_0)$ is defined as follows. Given a fixed method of selecting terms from goals:

1. The root of the derivation tree is $(G_0, \emptyset)$.
2. If (G_k, W_k) where $k \geq 0$ is a node of the derivation tree then its immediate descendants are all pairs of goal clauses and systems (G_{k+1}, W_{k+1}) which can be derived from (G_k, W_k) in one step from the selected terms of G_k.

In general, there are many methods of selecting terms in a goal G_k, such as always choosing one term at random, or choosing all terms. Consequently, there are many derivation trees for a clausal labelling problem.

Example 4.6 Consider the following propositional logic program P

$$\begin{aligned} &a :-\ b, c \\ &a :-\ d \\ &b \\ &c \\ &d \end{aligned}$$

and the goal $G_0 =:-\ a$. This is part of the clausal labelling problem where $\mathcal{U} = \{a, b, c, d\}$, and H is first-order unification.

Here are the branches of two derivation trees for this problem. The first tree has two branches.

$$\begin{aligned} I_0 &= \{a :-\ b, c\} \\ G_1 &= :-\ b, c \\ W_1 &= \{\langle a, a\rangle\} \end{aligned}$$

$$\begin{aligned} I_1 &= \{b\} \\ G_2 &= :-\ c \\ W_2 &= \{\langle b, b\rangle\} \end{aligned}$$

$$\begin{aligned} I_2 &= \{c\} \\ G_3 &= \Box \\ W_3 &= \{\langle c, c\rangle\} \end{aligned}$$

Its second branch is represented as follows.

$$\begin{aligned} I_0 &= \{a :- d\} \\ G_1 &= :- d \\ W_1 &= \{\langle a, a\rangle\} \end{aligned}$$

$$\begin{aligned} I_1 &= \{d\} \\ G_2 &= \square \\ W_1 &= \{\langle d, d\rangle\} \end{aligned}$$

Here is the representation of the first branch of the second tree.

$$\begin{aligned} I_0 &= \{a :- b, c\} \\ G_1 &= :- b, c \\ W_1 &= \{\langle a, a\rangle\} \end{aligned}$$

$$\begin{aligned} I_1 &= \{b, c\} \\ G_2 &= \square \\ W_1 &= \{\langle b, b\rangle, \langle c, c\rangle\} \end{aligned}$$

Its other branch is the same as the second branch of the first tree above.

Definition 4.7 A *successful branch* or *failed branch* of a derivation tree is a successful or failed derivation, respectively. If every branch of a derivation tree is a failed derivation, then the derivation tree is a *finitely failed derivation tree.*

A derivation tree is a *fair derivation tree* if every branch of it is a fair derivation.

Definition 4.8 A derivation tree is the *BF-tree* if every branch of it is a BF--derivation. A derivation tree is a *DF-tree* if every branch of it is a DF-derivation.

The lexicographical ordering on the selected clauses in Definition 4.2 ensures that trees do not differ because their branches occur in a different order. The BF-tree for a clausal labelling problem is unique because the ordering of its branches is fixed, and all terms are selected in the goals in its nodes. We shall see that BF-derivations are a normal form of derivations, and the BF-tree is a normal form of search trees.

4.1 Derivation Tree Equivalences

We shall show equivalences of derivation trees defined in Definition 4.5.

Let T_1 and T_2 be derivation trees of the same clausal labelling problem. The following algorithm traces a derivation $(G_0, W_0), (G_1, W_1), \ldots$ in T_2 from a given fair non-failed derivation in T_1. These derivations are called *equivalent* derivations.

Tracing Algorithm
Step $i \geq 0$.
Set I to $\emptyset$, and V to $\emptyset$.
For every selected term u in G_i do the following three steps in turn:

- If u appears in G_0 then trace the corresponding term down the given derivation in T_1 until it is a selected term which is replaced by a sequence B of terms and a constraint $\langle u, l \rangle$.
- Otherwise, u is introduced in some goal G_k of T_2 where $k \leq i$ in a body of a clause which replaces a term v. Find the corresponding term v in T_1 (this must have been done already) and trace down the given derivation in T_1 to where u is selected and replaced by a body B of a clause and a constraint $\langle u, l \rangle$.
- Set I to $I \cup \{u :- B\}$ (or $I \cup \{u\}$ if B is the empty sequence), and set V to $V \cup \{\langle u, l \rangle\}$.

(G_{i+1}, W_{i+1}) is the immediate descendant of (G_i, W_i) where each clause in I is a renamed form of a clause in G_i, and V is equal to W_i.

The node (G_{i+1}, W_{i+1}) can be identified by the Tracing Algorithm because at step i, we form a system V and an input list of clauses whose renamed forms agree with Definition 4.2 of a derivation. The immediate descendant node (G_{i+1}, W_{i+1}) must be present by Definition 4.5 of derivation tree, and because H is hereditary by Definition 3.5.

Tracing a term down the derivation in T_1 terminates because it is a fair derivation. If the derivation in T_1 is a successful derivation, then the traced derivation must also be finite. It is easy to verify that in this case, the union of all of the systems of the derivation in T_1, and the union of all of the systems of the traced derivation in T_2 are equal, and that the set of answer substitutions of both derivations are also equal. If the given derivation is an infinite derivation, then so is the traced derivation.

Lemma 4.9 *Let T_1 and T_2 be derivation trees of the same clausal labelling problem.*

- *If T_1 has a successful branch then so does T_2.*
- *If T_1 has an infinite fair branch then T_2 has an infinite branch.*

These equivalences allow us to concentrate on the BF-tree.

Corollary 4.10 *The following statements are equivalent for derivations trees of a clausal labelling problem.*

- *The BF-tree has a successful derivation whose set of answer substitutions is Θ.*
- *There is a derivation tree with a successful derivation whose set of answer substitutions is equal to Θ.*

– *Every derivation tree has a successful derivation whose set of answer substitutions is equal to* Θ.

The equivalence of fair derivation trees with respect to finite failure is shown by the following lemma which is a consequence of Lemma 4.9.

Lemma 4.11 *Let* T_1 *and* T_2 *be derivation trees for a clausal labelling problem. If* T_1 *is finitely failed and* T_2 *is fair, then* T_2 *is finitely failed.*

Proof: Suppose that T_2 has a successful or (fair) infinite branch. As T_2 is fair, T_1 must have a successful or infinite branch by Lemma 4.9. This is a contradiction, and T_2 must be finitely failed. □

Corollary 4.12 *The following statements are equivalent for a given clausal labelling problem.*

– *The BF-tree is finitely failed.*
– *There is a finitely failed derivation tree.*
– *Every fair derivation tree is finitely failed.*

5 Declarative Semantics

The declarative semantics of a clausal labelling problem is characterized by two inductively defined sets, and also by fixed points.

5.1 Inductive Definitions

We shall define the declarative semantics of a clausal labelling problem, and show that this semantics is equivalent to the operational semantics discussed above.

Definition 5.1 A clause is a *closed clause* if and only if its set of free variables is the empty set.

Let $(\mathcal{U}, H, P, G_0)$ be a clausal labelling problem. The set $|P|$ is the set of all closed clauses of the form $l\theta :- u_1\theta, \ldots, u_n\theta$ where $l :- u_1, \ldots, u_n$ is in P and θ is a substitution which is an endomorphism on $\mathcal{U}$.

Definition 5.2 Given a clausal labelling problem $(\mathcal{U}, H, P, G_0)$, its *base*, $b(P)$, is the set of all terms of clauses of $|P|$.

By the first part of Definition 3.5 of clausal labelling problem, such a base is never the empty set. We now define T_P.

Definition 5.3 Let $(\mathcal{U}, H, P, G_0)$ be a clausal labelling problem, and $D \subseteq |P|$. T_P is the function $2^{b(P)} \rightarrow 2^{b(P)}$ such that

$$\begin{aligned} T_P(D) = \{a \mid (l :- u_1, \ldots, u_n \in |P|) \wedge (\mathcal{F}(a) = \emptyset) \wedge \\ H\{\langle a, l\rangle, \langle u_1, l_1\rangle, \ldots, \langle u_n, l_n\rangle\} \neq \emptyset \wedge \\ (l_i \in D) \text{ where } 1 \leq i \leq n\}. \end{aligned}$$

We now relate a clausal labelling problem to an inductive definition.

Definition 5.4 The *success set* is

$$S_P = \cup_{i \geq 0} {T_P}^i \emptyset$$

where ${T_P}^0\emptyset = \emptyset$, and ${T_P}^{k+1}\emptyset = T_P({T_P}^k\emptyset)$ and $0 \leq k < \omega$.

Kernels are the duals of such inductive definitions [1]. Here is the kernel of the preceding definition which defines another set of closed terms.

Definition 5.5 The *finite failure set* is

$$F_P = \cup_{i \geq 0} F_P^i \emptyset$$

where $F_P^0\emptyset = \emptyset$, and $F_P^{k+1}\emptyset = b(P) - T_P(b(P) - (F_P^k\emptyset))$ and $0 \leq k < \omega$.

5.2 Fixed Points

A fixed point characterization of declarative semantics for clausal labelling problems uses classical results of Tarski [14] and Kleene [10] which are based on monotonic functions on complete lattices. It is defined here by using a set of closed positive clauses.

Proposition 5.6 *T_P is a monotonic function on $2^{b(P)}$: if $X \subseteq Y$, then $T_P(X) \subseteq T_P(Y)$ where $X, Y \in 2^{b(P)}$.*

Proposition 5.7 *$(2^{b(P)}, \subseteq)$ is a complete lattice, with $b(P)$ as top element, $\emptyset$ as bottom element, $\cup$ as join, and $\cap$ as meet.*

We shall use the following result [14].

Theorem 5.8 *(Tarski.) Let T be a monotonic function on elements of a complete lattice. Then T has a least fixed point* lfp(T), *and a greatest fixed point* gfp(T).

Corollary 5.9 *The function T_P on the complete lattice $(2^{b(P)}, \subseteq)$ has a least fixed point* lfp(T_P) *and a greatest fixed point* gfp(T_P).

Definition 5.10 Let L be a complete lattice and $T : L \rightarrow L$ be a mapping.

- $T \uparrow 0$ is the bottom element of L.
- $T \uparrow \beta$ is $T(T \uparrow (\beta - 1))$ if $0 < \beta < \omega$.
- $T \uparrow \omega$ is $\text{lub}\{T \uparrow \beta \mid \beta < \omega\}$.
- $T \downarrow 0$ is the top element of L.
- $T \downarrow \beta$ is $T(T \downarrow (\beta - 1))$ if $0 < \beta < \omega$.
- $T \downarrow \omega$ is $\text{glb}\{T \downarrow \beta \mid \beta < \omega\}$.

Definition 5.11 A function T on elements of a complete lattice L is a *continuous function* if $T(\text{lub}(X)) = \text{lub}(T(X))$ for every subset X of L all of whose finite subsets have an upper bound in X under the ordering $\subseteq$.

Proposition 5.12 *T_P is a continuous function on* $(2^{b(P)}, \subseteq)$.

The next theorem is the First Recursion Theorem [10]. It will link the inductive definition of the success set to the fixed point treatment.

Theorem 5.13 *(Kleene.)* $\mathrm{lfp}(T) = T \uparrow \omega$ *where T is a continuous function on elements of a complete lattice.*

As a result, we have:

Corollary 5.14 $\mathrm{lfp}(T_P) = T_P \uparrow \omega$.

The next definition links the finite failure set to the fixed point treatment.

Definition 5.15 $\overline{T_P \downarrow \omega} = b(P) - (T_P \downarrow \omega)$.

5.3 Summary

The following theorem states the equivalence between the inductively defined sets and fixed point constructions which were discussed above to define the declarative semantics of clausal labelling problems.

Theorem 5.16 *These are identities:*

- $S_P = \cup_{i \geq 0} S_P^i = \mathrm{lfp}(T_P) = T_P \uparrow \omega$.
- $F_P = \cup_{i \geq 0} F_P^i = \overline{T_P \downarrow \omega}$.

6 Soundness and Completeness

Definition 5.4 of success set, and Definition 5.5 of finite failure set correspond to successful and finitely failed BF-trees respectively. We shall prove the soundness and completeness of the BF-tree for successful and finitely failed derivations, and so the coincidence of operational and declarative semantics. We restrict attention to finitely failed search trees because the general detection of infinite branches in a search tree is undecidable.

The following lemma is used in proving the completeness of the BF-tree for success, and its soundness for finite failure. Since the production of an element of $T_P^i \emptyset$, and $b(P) - F_P^{i+1} \emptyset$ where $i \geq 0$, is tantamount to a closed BF-derivation, by lifting such a derivation to the form of a BF-derivation, the results can be proved directly.

From now on, the symbols $\mathcal{U}$, H, P, and G_0 refer to an arbitrary but fixed clausal labelling problem $(\mathcal{U}, H, P, G_0)$. We also introduce the following notations.

Notation 6.1 We abbreviate

- $T_P^k \emptyset$ to S_k,
- $F_P^{k+1} \emptyset$ to F_k, and

– Y_k uniformly stands either for S_k, or for $b(P) - F_k$.

Lemma 6.2 *(Lifting Lemma.) Let $(G_0, W_0), \ldots, (G_j, W_j)$ be an initial sequence of a BF-derivation, G_j be the goal clause $:- \ u_1, \cdots, u_n$, and $\mu_i \in HW_{i+1}$ where $0 \leq i < j$. If there is a substitution α_j such that the terms of $G_j\mu_0 \cdots \mu_{j-1}\alpha_j$ are in Y_{k-j} where $k - j > 0$, then there is a BF-derivation step from (G_j, W_j) to (G_{j+1}, W_{j+1}) and a substitution α_{j+1} such that the terms of $G_{j+1}\mu_j\alpha_{j+1}$ are in Y_{k-j-1} and $\alpha_j\rho_j = \mu_j\alpha_{j+1}$.*

Proof: By definition of Y_{k-j}, there are n closed instances of clauses of P, $l_h\gamma_h :- \ B_h\gamma_h$ for $1 \leq h \leq n$, where $l_h :- \ B_h$ is a clause of P and the γ_h are closed substitutions such that $H\{\langle u_1\alpha_0, l_1\gamma_1\rangle, \ldots, \langle u_n\alpha_0, l_n\gamma_n\rangle\} \neq \emptyset$, and when $l > 0$ the terms of $B_h\gamma_h$ are in Y_{k-j-1}.

Let $\rho_j = \gamma_1 \ldots \gamma_n$ and $I = \{l_h :- \ B_h \mid 1 \leq h \leq n\}$. We can assume that the clauses in I are renamed apart, and each of them is renamed apart from all of the goal clauses $G_0, \ldots, G_j$.

This implies that $u_h\alpha_j\rho_j$ is $u_h\alpha_j$, and $l_h\alpha_j\rho_j$ is $l_h\gamma_h$ for every $h : 1 \leq h \leq n$. Therefore, $H\{\langle u_1\alpha_j\rho_j, l_1\alpha_j\rho_j\rangle, \ldots, \langle u_n\alpha_j\rho_j, l_n\alpha_j\rho_j\rangle\} \neq \emptyset$.

By the completeness of H from Definition 3.5 there is is $\mu_j \in HW_{j+1}$ and a substitution α_{j+1} such that $\alpha_j\rho_j = \mu_j\alpha_{j+1}$.

Hence, by Definition 4.3 of BF-derivation, there is a derivation step from (G_j, W_j) to (G_{j+1}, W_{j+1}) with input list $I_0 = I$, and when $k - j > 0$,

$$G_{j+1}\mu_0 \cdots \mu_{j-1}\alpha_j \text{ is } :- \ B_1\mu_0 \cdots \mu_{j-1}\alpha_j, \ldots, B_n\mu_0 \cdots \mu_{j-1}\alpha_j$$

and $\{B_1\mu_0 \cdots \mu_{j-1}\alpha_j, \ldots, B_n\mu_0 \cdots \mu_{j-1}\alpha_j\} \subseteq Y_{k-1}$. □

6.1 Success Set

Suppose that the terms of a closed goal clause G_0 are in S_k. They are produced from elements in S_{k-1} which are in turn produced from elements in S_{k-2} and so on. From the definition of S_P, it is easy to construct a BF-derivation of $(\mathcal{U}, H, P, G_0)$.

The following soundness theorem states that all terms of any closed instance of $G_0\mu$ belong to S_P where μ is an answer substitution for this derivation.

Theorem 6.3 *If $(\mathcal{U}, H, P, G_0)$ has a successful BF-derivation of length k, then the terms of any closed instance $G_0\mu\alpha$ of $G_0\mu$ are in S_k, where μ is any answer substitution of the derivation.*

Proof: Apply $\mu\alpha$ to all the goal clauses of the derivation and apply any substitution so that all terms are closed. By Definition 4.3 of BF-derivation, and Definition 5.4 of S_P, if all terms of the instantiated goal clause G_n are in S_{i-1}, then all terms of G_{n-1} are in S_i.

As G_k is the empty goal clause, its terms are in $\emptyset = S_0$. □

The following theorem states the completeness of the BF-tree.

Theorem 6.4 *If there is a substitution α_0 such that the terms of $G_0\alpha_0$ are in S_k for a least $k > 0$, then $(\mathcal{U}, H, P, G_0)$ has a successful BF-derivation of length k such that $G_0\alpha_0 = G_0\mu\gamma$, for an answer substitution μ and a substitution γ.*

Proof: Since the terms of $G_0\alpha_0 \in S_k$, by the leastness of k, after k repeated applications of the Lifting Lemma (Lemma 6.2), there are k BF-derivation steps from $(G_0, \emptyset)$ to (G_k, W_k) and substitutions α_j such that the terms of $G_j\mu_0 \cdots \mu_{j-1}\alpha_j$ are in S_{k-j} for $0 \leq j \leq k$.

From the Lifting Lemma, we have that $\alpha_i\rho_i = \mu_i\alpha_{i+1}$ where $1 \leq i < k$. Therefore, $\alpha_i\rho_i\rho_{i+1} = \mu_i\alpha_{i+1}\rho_{i+1}$, and $\mu_i\alpha_{i+1}\rho_{i+1} = \mu_i\mu_{i+1}\alpha_{i+2}$. It follows, using the associativity of the composition of substitutions [8], that $G_0\alpha_0 = G_0\alpha_0\rho_0 \cdots \rho_{k-1}$ and $G_0\alpha_0\rho_0 \cdots \rho_{k-1} = G_0\mu_0 \cdots \mu_{k-1}\alpha_k$. The substitution $\mu = \mu_0 \cdots \mu_{k-1}$ is an answer substitution, and $\gamma = \alpha_k$, as required. □

6.2 Finite Failure Set

The following theorem states the soundness of the BF-tree for finite failure.

Theorem 6.5 *If every BF-derivation of $(\mathcal{U}, H, P, G_0)$ is failed by length $\leq k$, then every closed instance of G_0 contains a term in F_k.*

Proof: The proof is by induction on k. If every BF-derivation of $(\mathcal{U}, H, P, G_0)$ is failed by length zero, then by definition of F_0 every closed instance of G_0 contains a term in F_0.

The induction hypothesis is that the theorem is true for all BF-derivations of length $k - 1$. If every BF-derivation for G_0 is failed by length $\leq k$ then, by the induction hypothesis, every closed instance of every G_1 contains a term in F_{k-1}. Suppose there is a substitution α_0 such that the terms of $G_0\alpha_0$ are in $b(P) - F_k$. Then by the Lifting Lemma, there is a BF-derivation step from $(G_0, \emptyset)$ to (G_1, W_1) and a substitution α_1 such that the terms of $G_1\mu_0\alpha_1$ are in $b(P) - F_{k-1}$. This is a contradiction. Therefore every closed instance of G_0 contains a term in F_k. □

The next theorem states that the BF-tree is complete for finite failure.

Theorem 6.6 *If every closed instance of G_0 contains a term in F_k, then every BF-derivation of $(\mathcal{U}, H, P, G_0)$ is failed by length $\leq k$.*

Proof: The proof is by induction on k. If every closed instance of G_0 contains a term in F_0, then every BF-derivation of $(\mathcal{U}, H, P, G_0)$ is failed by length zero. Otherwise, by the definitions of BF-derivation and F_0, a closed instance of G_0 could be found which does not contain a term in F_0.

The induction hypothesis is that the theorem is true for all BF-derivations of length $k - 1$. Let every closed instance of G_0 contain a term in $b(P) - F_k$. If there is a descendant (G_1, W_1) of $(G_0, \emptyset)$ and a substitution β such that the terms of $G_1\mu_0\beta$ are in $b(P) - F_{k-1}$, by the definitions of BF-derivation and F_k, the terms of a closed instance of $G_0\mu_0\beta$ are in $b(P) - F_k$ where $\mu_0 \in HW_1$.

This is a contradiction. Hence every closed instance of every descendant goal clause G_1 contains a term in F_{k-1} and by the induction hypothesis, every BF--derivation of $(\mathcal{U}, H, P, G_0)$ is failed by length $\leq k$. □

6.3 Operational and Declarative Semantics

We now combine Theorem 5.16 for declarative semantics of clausal labelling problems with Theorems 6.3- 6.6 of the soundness and completeness of the BF--tree for successful and finitely failed derivations to show the coincidence of their operational and declarative semantics. This coincidence is extended to derivation trees in general by using Corollaries 4.10 and 4.12.

Theorem 6.7 *The following statements are equivalent.*

- *There is a substitution α such that the terms of $G_0\alpha$ are in S_P.*
- *There is a least $k > 0$ such that the terms of $G_0\alpha$ are in S_k.*
- *The BF-tree of $(\mathcal{U}, H, P, G_0)$ has a successful branch of length k with answer substitution equal to μ, and $G_0\alpha$ is $G_0\mu\beta$ for a substitution β.*
- *There is a derivation tree of $(\mathcal{U}, H, P, G_0)$ which has a successful branch with answer substitution equal to μ, and $G_0\alpha$ is $G_0\mu\beta$ for a substitution β.*
- *Every derivation tree of $(\mathcal{U}, H, P, G_0)$ has a successful branch with answer substitution equal to μ, and $G_0\alpha$ is $G_0\mu\beta$ for a substitution β.*

Theorems 6.5 and 6.6 are now used in a similar way to characterize goals which do not have refutations.

Theorem 6.8 *The following statements are equivalent.*

- *Every closed instance of G_0 contains a term in F_P.*
- *Every closed instance of G_0 contains a term in F_k for a least $k > 0$.*
- *The BF-tree of $(\mathcal{U}, H, P, G_0)$ is finitely failed, and the length of none of its branches exceeds k.*
- *There is a finitely failed derivation tree of $(\mathcal{U}, H, P, G_0)$.*
- *Every fair derivation tree of $(\mathcal{U}, H, P, G_0)$ is finitely failed.*

7 Implementing Abstract Clauses

The main features of the meta-logics of Isabelle [11], and type-theoretic logical frameworks [4, 6, 13] can be expressed with clausal labelling problems. Abstract Clauses provide a uniform meta-theory of logics and proofs; one that also includes classical combinatorial search problems, and first- and higher-order equational logic programming. We have provided declarative and operational semantics and shown their coincidence.

The Abstract Clause Engine (ACE) [16] implements proof searches for clausal labelling problems. It has been used for concrete problems such as combinatorial searches, first-order logic programming, and equational first-order logic programming with equational unification. Adding tacticals would make it more useful for large proofs.

The tree that ACE searches is a DF-tree. In the implementation, the branches are searched sequentially and constructed during the search. For most problems, except some logic programming ones, finite failure does not play a significant role in their solution.

The user of ACE can specify how terms should be selected from goals. Theorems 6.7 and 6.8 provide implementation rules for ensuring that ACE is sound and complete with respect to the set of solutions to a clausal labelling problem, and with respect to the terms which can be shown not to be solutions.

An advantage of working with ACE is that prototype proof procedures can be constructed relatively quickly. One just needs to implement the test, specify the syntax of the object logic, and sometimes to provide parsers and printers. The user can also specify which of ACE's ten generic search methods should be used for a particular problem, as well as the depth of searching in the search tree, and the maximum number of solutions to be found. The number of nodes visited in a search can be recorded and displayed.

ACE can be used to implement any clausal labelling problem. It has good performance on logic programming problems, but of course a dedicated interpreter is faster. The features discussed above should enable relative empirical comparisons of search methods to be made easily for an object logic before such a specific proof system is designed.

Acknowledgements

I thank the referees whose comments led to improvements in the presentation of this work. This research is supported by Esprit Basic Research Action 6453: "Types for Proofs and Programs", Christ Church, Oxford, and Oxford University Computing Laboratory.

References

1. P. Aczel, An introduction to inductive definitions, in: *Handbook of Mathematical Logic*, (J. Barwise, Ed.), North-Holland, Amsterdam, 1977, 739–782.
2. P.B. Andrews, *An Introduction to Mathematical Logic and Type Theory: To Truth Through Proof*, Academic, Orlando, 1986.
3. H.P. Barendregt, *The Lambda-Calculus: Its Syntax and Semantics*, Volume II, Second Edition, North-Holland, Amsterdam, 1984.
4. Th. Coquand and G. Huet, The Calculus of Constructions, *Information and Computation* **76**, 2/3 (1988) 95–120.
5. M.H. van Emden and R.A. Kowalski, The semantics of predicate logic as a programming language, *Journal of the Association for Computing Machinery* **24** (1976) 733–742.
6. R. Harper, F. Honsell, and G. Plotkin, A framework for defining logics, *Journal of the Association for Computing Machinery* **40**, 1 (1983) 143–184.

7. G.P. Huet, A unification algorithm for typed λ-calculus, *Theoretical Computer Science* **1** (1975) 27–57.
8. G.P. Huet, *Résolution d'équations dans des Langages d'Ordre* $1, 2, \ldots, \omega$, Thèse de Doctorat d'Etat, Université Paris VII, Paris, 1976.
9. J.M.E. Hyland and A.M. Pitts, The Theory of Constructions: categorical semantics and topos-theoretic models, *Contemporary Mathematics* **92** (1989) 137–199.
10. S.C. Kleene, *Introduction to Metamathematics*, Van Nostrand, Princeton, 1952.
11. L.C. Paulson, The foundation of a generic theorem prover, *Journal of Automated Reasoning* **5** (1989) 363–397.
12. L.C. Paulson, Isabelle: the next 700 theorem provers, In *Logic and Computer Science*, (P. Oddifreddi, Ed.), Academic, Orlando, 1990, 361–386.
13. F. Pfenning, Logic programming in the LF logical framework, in: *Logical Frameworks*, (G. Huet and G. Plotkin, Eds.), Cambridge, 1991, 149–181.
14. A. Tarski, A lattice-theoretical fixpoint theorem and its applications, *Pacific Journal of Mathematics* **5** (1955) 285–309.
15. D.A. Wolfram, M.J. Maher, and J-L. Lassez, A unified treatment of resolution strategies for logic programs, *Proceedings of the Second International Logic Programming Conference*, Uppsala, 1984, 263–276.
16. D.A. Wolfram, ACE: the abstract clause engine, System Summary, *Proceedings of the Tenth International Conference on Automated Deduction*, Kaiserslautern, Federal Republic of Germany, 23–27 July 1990, Lecture Notes in Artificial Intelligence **449**, Springer, Berlin, 1990, 679–680.
17. D.A. Wolfram, *The Clausal Theory of Types*, Cambridge Tracts in Theoretical Computer Science **21**, Cambridge, 1993.

Springer-Verlag and the Environment

We at Springer-Verlag firmly believe that an international science publisher has a special obligation to the environment, and our corporate policies consistently reflect this conviction.

We also expect our business partners – paper mills, printers, packaging manufacturers, etc. – to commit themselves to using environmentally friendly materials and production processes.

The paper in this book is made from low- or no-chlorine pulp and is acid free, in conformance with international standards for paper permanency.